The Terracotta Army
China's First Emperor and the
Birth of a Nation

John Man

W F HOWES LTD

This large print edition published in 2010 by
W F Howes Ltd
Unit 4, Rearsby Business Park, Gaddesby Lane,
Rearsby, Leicester LE7 4YH

1 3 5 7 9 10 8 6 4 2

First published in the United Kingdom in 2007
by Bantam Press

A CIP catalogue record for this book is available
from the British Library

ISBN 978 1 40745 407 8

Typeset by Palimpsest Book Production Limited,
Grangemouth, Stirlingshire
Printed and bound in Great Britain
by MPG Books Ltd, Bodmin, Cornwall

CONTENTS

A NOTE ON SPELLING

Most Chinese words in this book are names, and all except for the occasional very well-established ones are transliterated using the modern system, pinyin (as opposed to the old one, known as Wade-Giles). In pinyin, most letters and diphthongs are roughly as in English, but some have their own pronunciation. These are the main ones:

Consonants:
c as in ra**ts**
q as in **ch**urch
x is between **s** and **sh**
z as in su**ds**
zh as in fu**dge**

Vowels:
e as in the US pronunciation of **nur**se
ie as in **yeah**
ue as in a contracted form of 'you were' –
    y'were
eng as in s**ung**
ei as in **gay**

Commonly, pinyin omits the tones, which help define the Chinese character. In Mandarin, there are four tones, indicated with accents on the vowel (the first, in diphthongs):

First (high, level) tone: ā ē ī ō ū
Second (rising) tone: á é í ó ú
Third (falling-rising): ǎ ě ǐ ǒ ǔ
Fourth (falling) tone: à è ì ò ù

Even so, pinyin cannot always specify the exact sign, so in cases of doubt or particular significance I add the Chinese signs; not, however, for proper names, which are generally well known to specialists and need neither tones nor signs to identify them.

ACKNOWLEDGEMENTS

Catharina Blänsdorf, Chair of Conservation, Technische Universität, Munich; Pat Cox, former senior tutor, Fire Service College, Moreton-in-Marsh; Anne Cullen, London; Prof. Duan Qingbo, Director of Archaeology, Shaanxi Province; Vince Dunn, fire expert; Hu (Howard) Xiaojun, Intrepid Travel, Xian; Tom Jenen, Pharm; Miu Yee (Polly) Kwong; Joe Lally, fire expert, US Dept of Interior, Bureau of Land Management, Albuquerque, NM; Ningrui (Aileen) Ren; Helen Tang, SOAS; Jin Kai, Terracotta Army Museum; Li Bin, Cultural Affairs Bureau, Xian; Li Junyi, Jerry Wong and Cha Hai Bo (Charlie), Xian Ceramics and Lacquer Factory; Li Naifu, Xian Architecture and Technology University; Stephanie Lin Feng (Manager) and Anthony Lee (my terrific guide), Xian Everbright International Travel Service, Xian; Maggie, Huaqing Aegean International Hot Springs Resort, Lintong; Ma Yu, Restoration Dept, Terracotta Army Museum; Nin Shodo, Grandmother Temple, Mount Li; Niu Xinlong, Stone Armour Archaeology Team, Terracotta Army Museum, Lintong; Jane Portal, British Museum, London; James Quintière, fire

ix

expert and author of *Principles of Fire Behaviour*;
Wang Tao, SOAS; Wang Lianyuan, Qin-Style Eighth
Wonder Reproduction Factory, Beitian; Wang Zhan,
monumental sculptor, Xian; Wang Qinren and Yi
Xiaoqiang, China Youth Press, Beijing; Wang
Zhigao, the best of drivers; Pablo Wendel, perform-
ance artist, Stuttgart; Bob Wyllie, Fire Service
College, Moreton-in-Marsh; Yang Shuanshuan, Xi
Yang village; Yang Zhefa, Terracotta Army Museum;
Yuan Zhongyi, former President, Terracotta Army
Museum, Lintong; Zhang Hui (Roy), Xian; Zhao
Kangmin, Lintong; Zhong Tangyan, Xian Centre,
China Geological Survey. And on the production
of this book: Doug Young, Simon Thorogood and
Sheila Lee at Transworld; Gillian Somerscales, for
superb editing; Malcolm Swanston and Jonathan
Young, Red Lion Mapping; and, as always, Felicity
Bryan and her wonderful staff.

PREFACE: AN ARMY OF THE PAST AND PRESENT

The Terracotta Army attracts clichés as light attracts moths, and none of them do it justice. There is a nobility in the serried ranks of warriors, in the hint of a smile here, the gravity of a glance there, the patience with which they await orders, their Confucian aura of strength and tranquility. Part of the impact made by those ranked figures comes from the gut feeling that they are the guardians of hidden universes – of artistry, organization, religious and historical significance, and raw power.

All these lead back to one man, the First Emperor, the man who turned a China of warring states into the core of today's single nation. It was an astonishing achievement by one of history's towering personalities, a man who combined vision, leadership and utter ruthlessness to force unwilling rivals together. Even more astonishing, it was all done in under ten years (230–221 BC), a decade which many believe to be the most significant in China's 5,000 years of history. The First Emperor took a vague sense that unity was a good idea, and thrashed it into an ideal that has anchored China to this day.

Unity, character, the Army, the vast tomb-mound and the body it contains: these elements are inseparable. Without the First Emperor's skills, there would be no unity; without unity, no organization, no industrial-scale artistry, no tomb-mound, no need for a spirit army at all.

There are many surprising things about the Army. For one thing, the warriors were never intended to be seen, or at least not by human eyes. For another, it is strange that these clay figures – terracotta means nothing more than 'baked earth' – with their shades of greys and blue-greys and browns and oranges were not like this when they were buried, but lurid with bright colours. Our view of them is skewed by events: by the fire that destroyed them, by the passage of time that stripped them of their colours, by the desire to see them arrayed in parade-ground magnificence – a prospect that no one ever had until the opening of Pit No. 1 in 1979.

Perhaps the most surprising thing about the Army is its contemporary significance. It emerged into the light of day only because the First Emperor's character and achievements suited the times, as defined by the inspirational, authoritarian, ruthless, nation-building Mao Zedong. As a result, the Army has escaped its original purpose as defence against malign spirits, and has come to stand for the nation, past and present. Like the Great Wall, it states two grand themes of China's history: geographical unity and continuity.

PART I

ORIGINS

CHAPTER 1

DISCOVERY

Approaching the Terracotta Army from Xian, China's one-time capital, feels like a movement towards something of immense significance: the throne room in a palace, perhaps, or the altar of a great cathedral. First, the expressway eastwards. You will be grateful for it, because you are free at last from Xian's glutinous traffic. Then, if the day is clear of haze, the mountains welcome you, a ridge of greenery swinging in from the right. That's Mount Li in the distance, the Army's backdrop. You can follow the expressway to the warriors' gates if you like the fast, bland approach, but I prefer the other way, through Lintong, where emperors came to bathe in mineral-rich hot springs, and where tourists now do the same. Lintong, once a little place of mud-walled farmers' houses, is today all new building, with its own university and a growing number of plush hotels, proof of the wealth brought by the Army over the last 30 years.

At the town's centre the road divides, and in the split between the two stands a formidable monument to the Army's creator. From several thousand tonnes of granite explode horses and a chariot, driven by the man himself, the First Emperor, who made the armies that unified China and the Army that still guards him in the spirit world. At his shoulder stands his greatest general, Meng Tian, builder of the Great Wall designed to hold back the northern barbarians. The Qin Unification Statue is energy petrified, a modern (1993) declaration of what this man and his achievements mean.

Keep right, past the old Winter Palace and its hot springs, past the cable car which would carry you up Mount Li if you had the time, until you come to a line of factory outlets offering reproductions of the warriors, harbingers of the real things.

On your right rears the tomb itself, a vast, shallow-sided green mound against the mountains, a presence that has brooded over the surrounding orchards and fields for 2,200 years. It is veiled in firs now, but they are new. Historically, it had no veil but its earth, which is deep enough to keep its secrets hidden: the emperor's coffin, his underground palace, and who knows what treasures.

And who or what was there to protect it all? A kilometre more, and you're almost there. A low wall edges the huge estate that surrounds the Terracotta Army Museum. There's a car park, dominated by a towering white statue: the First Emperor, of course, ruling over a parade-ground of concrete, cars and tourists. On the gentle uphill walk, with your destination concealed by the rise and the newly built gauntlet-run of stalls, you sense again that you are approaching something grand.

Once through the turnstiles, standing on the immense concourse, you will feel the urge to enter Pit No. 1, and gaze down at last on the ranks of the clay warriors. Don't rush it. The warriors will wait, and you have a chance to imagine what this place was like before the coming of the tourist-trap shops, the seven halls, the vast plaza, the camera-clicking crowds. Stand in front of the great railway station arch of Pit No. 1 and look to your left. You will see a white-tiled building, rectangular, 1980s utilitarian. It contains a circular film-screen, which shows a docu-drama about the warriors. The film is on a loop, so there's no hurry. Pause in the entrance lobby, where stalls sell books and reproductions of warriors, from full-size down to chessmen.

Over on the left, if you press through the throng, you come to a book counter, behind which sits an old man wearing heavy round glasses. He scribbles his name hastily in books thrust at him by tourists, but he meets no one's eye. He's not happy. Much of the time he covers his head with a paper fan. He is hiding, from attention, and, because his eyesight is poor, from the occasional camera-flash. 'No photo!' pleads a notice on the table in front of him, in English as well as Chinese, but not everyone obeys. His name is Yang Zhefa, and he is one of four surviving brothers (two others have died), all in their eighties, all of whom earn a living signing books here, and at other stalls outside, and at the hot springs resort nearby, because they were the ones who, as your guide will tell you, were the 'discoverers' of the warriors. They are too old, too deaf, too weary of media interest, too battered by attention, to retell their story yet again, and anyway you would be unlikely to hear the details, because there are aspects that do not quite fit the image of discoverers. Look at Mr Yang, present your book for his signature, do not take his picture, and bear in mind that this was a discovery he and his brothers emphatically did not wish to make.

In the spring of 1974, the middle of Shaanxi province was stricken by drought. Normally, the steep flanks of Mount Li, rearing up to the south, kept the rocky ravines flowing with enough water to fill the wells and nourish the orchards of persimmon and pomegranate. Not that year.[1]

One evening in mid-March, the six Yang brothers gathered among the persimmon trees edging the village that bore their family name,

[1] This section is based on Yue Nan, *Xi Bu Mai Fu (Hidden Underground in the West)*, with additions and modifications from my interview with Zhao Kangmin and Wang Lianyuan.

Xiyang (West Yang). Squatting on their haunches and smoking, they worried out loud about the lack of water. All in their forties and fifties, they had spent their whole lives here, in the simple mud-brick houses of their village, venturing down to the road a few hundred metres below to lay out their fruit in late summer, but seldom taking the bus to the ancient capital of Xian, 40 kilometres away. If this kept up, there would not be enough of the fat red fruit to see their families through the following winter. They all agreed that someone had to do something. They needed water, fast. That meant a new well. They should have had help from the boss of their commune; but they and their forefathers had been used to relying on themselves since long before Mao's 1949 revolution.

'OK, let's make a start,' said one.

But where? The most senior of the brothers, Yang Peiyan, looked up at Mount Li, and pointed out a cleft. If there was any water to be had, it would follow that course and feed into the orchards that lay a couple of hundred metres uphill to the south. Nods and grunts of assent: that would be the best spot.

So next morning the brothers carried their spades up through the little trees, some already showing spring shoots, and started to dig, taking turn and turn about to make the beginnings of a hole, a big one, some 4 metres across, because they knew they would be digging deep. Everything went well. By noon they were a metre down when they hit an unexpected layer of red earth, hard as iron it seemed – so hard some of them said they could see sparks fly when they struck it.

'What's this – the top of an old kiln?' one of them wondered. Perhaps, because it was common knowledge that there used to be a lot of kilns for firing pottery here in times past. If it was a kiln, it should be possible to cut through its roof. It was either that or start again somewhere else. So they agreed they had to press on. Taking turns, they began to hack their way into the hard red earth.

It took them the next two days to chip through 30 hard-packed centimetres, at which point they found the going easy once again. As they dug deeper, about half a metre a day, they propped a ladder against the side and tossed the soft earth into a basket, which was hauled to the surface and emptied. They began to turn up small bits of pottery, which was not too surprising if they had just chopped through the top of a kiln. They hadn't, of course. It was earth baked by fire, and they were now inside the burial pit of the Terracotta Army, digging down through the ashes of collapsed roof-timbers and earth that had built up over the intervening 2,000 years. At the end of a week, they had a hole as deep as it was wide.

On 29 March 1974, one of them – Yang Zhefa says it was him, others dispute it – unearthed the first large piece of pottery. Not that anyone paid much attention. What they wanted was water, not useless bits of pottery. On they went, throwing up unidentifiable little pieces, until someone sighed, 'How come there's so much rubbish?'

'Well, it's a kiln. So obviously there's rubbish,' said another. 'Get on with it. We need water.'

A few minutes later, Yang Zhefa, who happened to be digging down in the hole at the time, suddenly stopped and shouted up: 'I've found a jar, a big one!' All his brothers crowded round above him and peered down at what looked like the top of an earthen jar still buried in the soil. This could be useful. If it was intact, they could take it back home and store persimmons and pomegranates in it for the winter.

The find lifted their spirits. With two or three working together in the pit, and the others above hauling dirt up in the basket, they slowly scratched away the soil, until Yang Zhefa gave a sigh of disappointment. It wasn't a jar at all, but part of a torso made of pottery. Completely useless, like all their other finds – and also bad luck, because it came from underneath the ground, where the dead dwelled. He hauled it into the basket and called out, 'Pull it up and throw it away. It's nothing.'

But as he started to dig again, earth fell from the side of the dip made by the torso, and he saw something that made him shout out.

'An earth-god!'

Again everyone crowded round, and there was a collective gasp of horror. Sticking out of the earth was a head: two eyes staring up at them, long hair tied into a bun, and a moustache. Someone touched the head with a spade, and they all heard the dull clunk which told them it was intact, and very solid.

'Yes, an earth-god,' someone said.

'If this is a kiln,' said another, 'how come there's an earth-god here? I think this is a temple.'

'Kiln or temple, what does it matter?' said Yang Zhefa, keen to suppress his fears. 'Stop imagining things. Let's keep digging.'

So they all dusted themselves down, muttered reassurances to each other and told themselves not to mention anything about an earth-god because it would bring bad luck and stop them reaching water.

The head came up, followed by the rest of the torso, arms, legs and other bits, all hauled up in the basket and thrown aside on the field.

Now some local kids who had been playing nearby saw what was happening, and ran across to examine these odd objects. Enemies, said one, let's get them. Some started throwing stones at them. Others took a few bits back to their own orchards and fields. One group put a long pole in the hand of an almost intact torso, wound a cloth round a head and put the two together to make a scarecrow. A few adults came to stare. A 70-year-old lady picked up a head, took it home, washed it, put it on her table, lit incense and prayed to it.

Meanwhile, there were other discoveries back at the well, now down to 5 metres – brickwork, three pieces of bronze which turned out to be crossbow triggers, and many bronze arrowheads. Obviously, these had nothing to do with kilns or temples, and the Yang brothers were delighted. They may not have found water, but what they had was something almost as good. Back in the 1920s, around the tomb of the First Emperor, their fathers had found bricks like these, so they knew they came from Qin times. This had been considered wonderful luck, because wealthy people liked to buy them, and because, if they were used as pillows, they cooled the blood, improved eyesight, brought good luck and lengthened life.

Among those eager to profit from the finds were several who saw possibilities in the bronze arrowheads. Bronze was good scrap metal. One young farmer started the rush, collecting several kilos of arrowheads and taking them through the orchards to Dai Wang village 2.5 kilometres away, where a recycling centre gave cash for scrap.

One who almost followed his example was a six-year-old boy named Wang Lianyuan, now a man of some consequence in the area, because he controls a business making copies of the terracotta warriors. In a sense, that day in early April was the start of his interest. 'I recall one thing clearly,' he told me in the reception room that now stands a few paces from the site of the well. 'One of my friends, he was a few years older, took

11

me to the place and we gathered up some arrow-heads that had been thrown down in a pile. He took them off to the recycling centre and got some pocket money for them. I couldn't go, because I was too small.'

In under two weeks, events seemed to have run their course. The bricks had gone, the arrowheads had been sold, the bits and pieces scattered. The Yang brothers were not eager to talk about how they had found strange and possibly evil things in their field, and went on with their digging.

They had no idea, of course, that their well with its strange contents lay right at the south-east corner of the pit that contains the Terracotta Army. A few paces south or east and they would have missed it entirely. Even so, their find might still have escaped wider notice if their boss, the head of the agricultural cadre, had not decided to check on all the work his team had been doing. He saw the bits and pieces of what looked like the pottery equivalent of a massacre, and decided someone had better be told. The Yang brothers, who had been so determined to ignore the apparitions from the world of the dead, were about to have their lives changed willy-nilly.

The man who engineered that change was working in the small county museum in nearby Lintong, which was then a small place of low brick houses and unpaved backstreets and fields that came right into town. Zhao Kangmin had been running the museum since 1961, when no other county in the province had its own museum. He regarded himself as a lucky man. His job had been farming, but he loved history, and read what he could in his spare time. When the provincial government decided to set up a museum, they needed someone to run it. There was no archaeologist to hand, but they heard of Zhao's interest and offered him the job. Not bad for a 24-year-old. From then on archaeology became his life. He taught himself, delighting in the work because it provided the evidence to support written sources. When the warriors brought fame and fortune to Lintong in the 1980s, he was given another opportunity: to design a new museum. He made it charming, and traditional – three halls of painted columns and criss-cross beams and upturned eaves. He's still there today, retired but living in a basic little grace-and-favour apartment in the museum, a gaunt and frail 71-year-old who put on a trilby hat and brown weatherproof jacket to show me round.

It's not really true to say the warriors were discovered in 1974, he explained. People had always known there were figures hidden underground. When they dug up the warriors, they found five Han graves dating from the first or second century, and 20 Ming tombs from the fifteenth century. The graves were right in among the warriors, some of which were missing, so of course people had known, in one sense. But they

13

didn't *want* to know, because such things were bad luck, as was everything to do with the land of the dead; so the news never spread beyond those who made the burials.

Nor did it spread last century, when other finds emerged. In 1948, farmers (it was always farmers who made these finds) working just outside the outer wall of the First Emperor's tomb unearthed a complete figure: not a warrior, but a demure 'kneeling servant'. They didn't know what it was, so they put it in a temple and prayed to it as if it were a Buddhist deity, an immortal. In 1956 another was found, and soon after that both figures were moved to the museum. No one showed much interest in them, because no one knew what they were or when they had been made. In 1962 Zhao himself dug out three kneeling crossbowmen, in excellent condition, which were later dispersed, one each to the provincial museum in Xian, the Terracotta Army Museum and Beijing's History Museum.

'So it wasn't a huge surprise when the Yangs made their finds?'

'Oh, it was, because one of the kneeling servants had been destroyed in the Cultural Revolution' – that crazy time when teenage Red Guards became Mao's hooligans and set about assaulting anything old – 'and not many people knew about the other one. Anyway, we could not know for sure they were Qin.'

Zhao, the guardian of old things, had found

himself embroiled in this madness. Soon after Mao launched the Cultural Revolution in the summer of 1966, Zhao was summoned to one of those meetings at which crowds of callow revolutionaries threw insults at the victims, forcing them to 'purify' themselves by self-criticism.

'They knew I was involved with old things which had something to do with an emperor,' Zhao said, 'so they accused me of encouraging feudalism. Everyone sat, except for me. I was made to stand. They read out a long article listing my mistakes, and told me to admit them. I refused, because I knew everything I had done had been correct. Later I was told to write a letter of apology. Again, I refused. But just to avoid trouble I joined the revolutionary guards until the fuss died down.'

He was lucky. These were early days. Later the same year, Mao chided the Red Guards for being 'too civilized', and they turned extremely nasty: officials were brutalized and murdered, books burned, historical monuments desecrated (almost 5,000 in Beijing alone) – but only one terracotta statue smashed, thanks to Zhao's zeal.

Not much of this affected the villages scattered around the First Emperor's tomb, but those terrible years burned into Zhao's memory, and were with him still when he heard of the farmers' finds.

'The first I knew was on April the twenty-eighth, a month after the find, when my bureau chief called me: "The cadre chief says some farmers have found pottery heads the size of human ones."

'I thought: This could be an important discovery. "Anything else?" I asked.

'"Bronze arrowheads. You'd better go and check."

'So I got on my bicycle and rode to the field. The Yangs were still at work there, digging their well. I saw seven or eight pieces – bits of legs, arms and two heads – lying near the well, along with some bricks. All the bronze arrowheads had gone.'

He knew at once that these were finds of immense, perhaps national, significance. They had to be bits of Qin figures, because the bricks were Qin – he knew that because he had seen others found near the First Emperor's tomb. They were all alike: hard and smooth, with a particular pattern and the name of the kiln in old-style characters.

So he also knew at once the historical events that had preceded and followed the burial of these objects. His two passions, archaeology and history, made past and present one. The seven Warring States that had kept China bitterly divided for 200 years from the fifth to the third century BC; the rise of Qin; the dictatorship of the man who defeated all six of his rivals, united China in 221 BC and called himself the First Emperor; his ruthlessness, his paranoia, his obsessive desire to rule as effectively in the life to come as in this; the building of the tomb that he, Zhao, had known from childhood; the sudden fall of the dynasty to its successors, the Han. All this was familiar because Zhao had read Sima Qian, the great Han historian whose account, written a century after the First Emperor's death, had brought these events to life for generation after generation for the last 2,000 years.

So Zhao didn't hesitate. He ordered all work on the well to stop, and had the pieces collected – no small matter, because the legs were solid clay – and taken down to the museum. Then he went to the recycling station and bought back as many bronze arrowheads as he could. Finally, that same evening, he started work on restoring the figures – two of them, as it turned out, both of which still stand in his museum, along with the kneeling servant that survived the Cultural Revolution.

It's an odd figure, this kneeling servant. In a simple wraparound costume, he is humble, his hands resting lightly on his thighs, fingers slightly bent, his head slightly cocked, as if listening for instructions. The coat is wrinkled but below the waist there are no mouldings, as if he is on a plinth. But the odd thing is his head: shaved, no beard, no moustache. It is a face that looks almost feminine. There are no women among the terracotta figures, but I wondered if perhaps this very unmilitary figure was a eunuch.

★　★　★

So here we are at the end of April 1974. The finds that will transform the area from poor villages and orchards to China's second most important tourist site after the Great Wall are in the hands of an expert who recognizes them for what they are – life-size clay figures, almost certainly created for the tomb of the First Emperor, a find unmentioned in any source, and totally without precedent. No doubt about it: as his card states in English, 'He is the very first man who discovered, determined, restored and unearthed' the warriors.

'Do you wonder what would have happened if you had not gone to the field that day?' I asked. 'Perhaps the warriors would never have been found?'

'It would have been a disaster. The farmers would have destroyed the figures, because they thought they were unlucky things. They would have abandoned the well, and no one would have told the authorities.'

Yet Zhao hesitated. What if he made his report, and because of it he was summoned again for anti-revolutionary activities? The Red Guards were gone, but Mao was old and who knew what madness might erupt? Better to wait until he was sure of his ground.

So, despite Zhao's awareness and expertise, the warriors still might have remained a secret. How they were revealed is another story. In China, the present echoes the past more intensely than in most other cultures; politics and history are intertwined. To tell the story involves looking at the power struggle gripping the upper reaches of the Communist Party in 1974 – but to understand that, you first have to know about the First Emperor, his empire and the circumstances leading up to his death.

CHAPTER 2

THE GRAND HISTORIAN'S
HIDDEN AGENDA

Why do those clay figures so fascinate China and the world? One reason is because they are ghosts from history's subconscious, capturing in outward and visible form the crucial two decades – the years from 230 to 210 BC – when the First Emperor forced seven states to become one and then imposed on his new nation a series of giant projects. It's not simply that the upright military figures seem to symbolize their times; it's that their faces seem to reflect the character of the man himself: stern, expressionless, implacable.

Power made the First Emperor a terrifying figure. He seems to have been physically unattractive – high pointed nose, slit eyes, pigeon breast, stingy, cringing, graceless. Traditional portraits of him don't conform to this lean and hungry image, showing him as bearded, bulky, and always wearing headgear like a mortarboard with tassels dangling down the front to hide his semi-divine features from mortal gaze. It's all totally inauthentic, of course, since there were no contemporary portraits; but as with Christ, Genghis Khan and alien abductors, there arose an accepted, iconic version of what he was supposed to look like. Certainly he was moody, easily angered, unpredictable: traits that he shared with other dictators (Hitler and Stalin come to mind). Almost from his own day, the First Emperor was seen as a 'brutal tyrant, inhumanely impressing hundreds of thousands of people into forced labour to fulfil his grandiose ambitions'.[1] It has been part of accepted history that he burned books, destroyed the records of his predecessors and buried scholars alive because they opposed him. His ruthlessness has been a fact of life for the past two millennia. National unity was bought with extreme suffering, was it not?

Perhaps. Probably. But before we get to the details, it is worth asking: How do we know what we think we know? For it almost all comes from one man, the historian Sima Qian (Ssu-ma Ch'ien in Wade-Giles) and his monumental *Shi Ji* (*Historical Records*), the usual English title of which is *Records of the Grand Historian*. The book covers the whole history of China down to Sima Qian's own day in 130 chapters. A brilliant synthesis of oral and written sources, it is to China what the histories of Herodotus or Thucydides are to western culture: original in structure, fundamental, judicious – and therefore,

[1] Li Yuning in his Introduction to *The First Emperor of China*.

21

given its virtues, traditionally considered to be totally reliable.

Is it, though? Sima Qian's experiences suggest that his reputation needs revision. He was writing 100 years after the events we are interested in (and centuries after many others he records), using sources that he does not quote. He was active during the Han dynasty,[2] which succeeded the Qin in 202 BC, after four years of civil war, and it was always the habit of new dynasties to rubbish the old. He was writing during the reign of an emperor every bit as ambitious and every bit as ruthless as the First Emperor. Throughout history, politicians and writers wishing to criticize their own bosses have directed their venom at substitute targets whose character and actions resemble those of the real objects of their remarks. And in addition to his historian's perspective, Sima Qian had deeply personal reasons for such criticism: he was the victim of a gross miscarriage of justice that left him with a powerful motive to criticize his own emperor by exaggerating the truth about the First.

Actually, Sima Qian, born around 145 BC, owed his inspiration to his father, who had planned and

---

[2] Confusingly, Han (*Hàn*) the dynasty, which also gives its name to China's dominant ethnic group, is not the same as the state of Han (*Hán*), one of those defeated by Qin, which is sometimes transliterated Hann.

perhaps started the *Records*. When his father died in 110 BC, his 35-year-old son took over the labour. He was appointed Taishi (Grand Historian) at court, and all went well, until disaster struck. To understand how he came to suffer as he did, you need some background.

One of his themes was the threat posed by a tribe known as the Xiongnu, the 'barbarians' who dominated what is now Mongolia and other lands north of the Great Wall. Once, 50 years before, they had almost seized Xian, the Han capital. Now they were kept in check by hand-outs of cash and silk. It's hard to say who was more to blame for the antipathy – the Xiongnu, who wanted to trade their furs and horses for Chinese goods, or the Han, who refused to have anything to do with a people they considered utterly inferior. Whoever was to blame, the result was confrontation. In effect, the Xiongnu did what they could to help themselves by turning to extortion, with the price rising and raids continuing.

It couldn't go on. No emperor of a unified China could claim the Mandate of Heaven and at the same time tolerate as neighbour a 'barbarian' ruler who saw himself as an equal, and who was liable to launch raids whenever he felt like it. The man who grasped this nettle was Sima Qian's emperor, Wu (140–87 BC). Wu was a monarch of genius – autocrat, statesman, strategist, artist – with a court to match his own brilliance, and a reign long enough to allow both to flourish: 53 years, a tenure

23

unmatched for 1,800 years thereafter. His despotic ways mirrored those of the First Emperor, and his achievements – his laws, institutions and conquests – would mark China from then on. His answer to the Xiongnu menace was to set the boundaries of China wider, and to do that he decided to escalate the rumbling rivalry into a full-scale war.

From this decision flowed many consequences – for the Xiongnu, who were eventually broken and scattered; for China, which spread westward, defended by the newly extended Great Wall; and for poor Sima Qian, who incurred the emperor's displeasure and paid a terrible price.

Wu's was a high-risk strategy, with two aims. The first was to control the grasslands of Mongolia, which started just north of the Yellow River and ran eastward. The other was to seize the 26 independent tribal areas which lay westward, along the Gansu Corridor leading to the Central Asian deserts of the Western Regions. The difference between them was this: the steppe, which was in effect infinite and open, could not be conquered and held; the oasis kingdoms of the Western Regions could, because they were small and enclosed. The war aim that Wu adopted, therefore, was to 'cut off the right arm' of the nomads (the west, since the dominant direction for nomads was southward) – i.e. to pick off the tribal kingdoms one by one and garrison them in order to deny them to the Xiongnu. With the Western Regions in Chinese hands, it would be possible to isolate, invade and destroy – if not to hold – Xiongnu lands.

The war was catastrophic for both sides. Repeatedly, the opposing armies thrust into each other's territory. A dozen times – almost every year – the Xiongnu went on the offensive. Sources speak of 20,000 horsemen here, 30,000 there (though as usual the figures are suspiciously round and suspiciously large). Almost every year, too, the Han launched an offensive, with anything from 40,000 horsemen (129 BC) to 100,000 (124 BC). The 124 BC attack probed 350 kilometres northward, snaring 15,000 Xiongnu captives and 'several million' animals; another 19,000 Xiongnu casualties were notched up the following year, 30,000 more in 121 BC. Han, too, suffered appalling losses: tens of thousands of dead, 100,000 horses lost in 124–123 BC alone. But eventually, for the Han Chinese, the risk and the effort paid off, because the great campaign of 121 BC snatched from the Xiongnu most of the strategic Gansu Corridor and compelled the surrender of 40,000 Xiongnu, who were forcibly resettled south of the Great Wall.

Military victory itself, though, was not enough. Something had to fix the frontier, define what was China and what wasn't. That something was, of course, the Wall. So Wu picked up where the First Emperor had left off. In the centre and east, old walls were repaired and sections linked. In the west, new bits of the Wall arose, running over the border of what is now Xinjiang. Soldier-farmers began to arrive by the hundred thousand, supplementing volunteers, conscripts and convicts. Families followed, bringing the total number of settlers to an estimated 1.5–2 million – roughly equal to the whole Xiongnu population – and all were provided with land, animals and seeds. Where there was water, villages and farms arose. Roads would lead to the Wall, canals would be built. Silk began to flow westward in prodigious amounts.

But the results of this immense effort, which drained the Han economy, took some time to emerge. Meanwhile, war continued. In 103 BC a Han force of 20,000, which had advanced 1,000 kilometres across the Gobi, was surrounded and massacred. In 99 BC another campaign ended in total catastrophe. One army, attacking westward, killed 10,000 Xiongnu yet lost 60–70 per cent of its men. A second army, 5,000 men with wagonloads of food and arrows, struck northward under a general named Li Ling, an acquaintance of Sima Qian. 'We never so much as drank a cup of wine together,' wrote the historian. 'But I observed that he was clearly a man of superior ability. He was filial to his parents and trustworthy with his associates, honest in money matters and just in all his giving and taking . . . I believed him to be truly one of the finest men of the nation.' This was the man who was soon to become the focus of his attention, and the unwitting cause of his tragedy.

Li Ling led his troops for a month across the Gobi and the Mongolian heartland, aiming for northern Mongolia, where the Xiongnu had built at least one large city and established a royal necropolis.[3] It was not a big force for so ambitious a project. Perhaps Li Ling was confident that his repeating crossbows, with arrows carried by the hundred thousand in his wagons, would sweep him to victory. But even these terrifyingly effective weapons, the ancient equivalent of machine guns, were no match for 30,000 Xiongnu horsemen, reinforced by another 80,000 from neighbouring tribes.

Li Ling staged a fighting retreat over grasslands and the Gobi's gravel plains to the Gurvan Saikhan (Three Beauties) range. Perhaps he fled into these dark, rocky hills and valleys because he needed water – there is at least one river that flows year-round through a ravine, now known as Vulture's Gorge, so shadowy that its winter ice never melts. Anyway, he and his wagons were trapped. 'The enemy was lodged in the hills, surrounding him on all sides and shooting arrows like drops of rain,' according to the first-century historian Ban Gu, who speaks of half a million arrows being shot in one day. In Sima Qian's

[3] Noyan Uul, 50 km north of the present-day capital, Ulaanbaatar. I give an account of the Xiongnu and Noyan Uul in *Attila: A Barbarian King and the Fall of Rome* (Bantam Press, 2005).

words: 'Li Ling with one cry gave courage to his army, so that every man raised himself up and wept. Washed in blood and choked with tears, they stretched out their empty bows and warded off the bare blades of the foe.'

The surviving Chinese – only half of the number that had set out – fled through a narrow valley, while the Xiongnu tossed rocks down on them, blocking escape until night fell. That night, Li Ling took ten men and galloped clear, only to be hunted down and forced to surrender. Just 400 of his men, armed with clubs made from the spokes of their wagons, made it back home.

Emperor Wu was enraged, first by the defeat and second by the humiliation: he expected his military leaders to die in battle rather than surrender. Naturally, all his officials backed him up – all except Sima Qian.

A subject who will go forth to face ten thousand deaths, giving not the slightest thought for his own life, but hurrying only to the rescue of his lord – such a man is rare indeed! Now he has committed one act that was not right, and the officials who think only of saving themselves . . . vie with each other in magnifying his shortcomings. Truly it makes me sick at heart!

Unfortunately for Sima Qian, Li Ling's superior was the eldest brother of the emperor's favourite concubine. To exculpate the No. 2 would be to blame the No. 1, which was inconceivable, since he was still in office at the behest of the emperor himself. Sima Qian was summoned to explain himself, and spoke again in Li Ling's defence. The general, he pointed out, had always shared hardships with his officers and men, always commanded loyalty, always served his emperor to the best of his abilities. 'But I could not make myself fully understood,' Sima Qian wrote, with outward humility that (I suspect) was bitterly ironic. 'Our enlightened ruler did not wholly perceive my meaning.' He was charged with attempting to deceive the emperor, and was arrested. There was no money to buy his freedom; no one spoke up for him. He was condemned to the ultimate humiliation: castration.

He wrote of his experience to an old friend who was at the time accused of some unspecified offence and was under threat of execution. In his memorial,[4] widely seen as one of the finest and most deeply personal pieces of writing in Chinese literature, he equates himself with the lowest of the low. The least a man can achieve is to bring no shame on his ancestors, or himself. Below such a person, he writes, is one who is bound with ropes, and below him, in a descending sequence of degradation, are the prisoner, the fettered, the beaten, the shaven-headed, the manacled and

[4] Included as an appendix in Burton Watson's fine translation, *Records of the Grand Historian: Qin Dynasty*.

the mutilated. Finally, lowest of all, is the eunuch. 'Alas! Alas! A man like myself – what can he say? What can he say?'

The customary way out of such humiliation would be to commit suicide. As he says, a gentleman would surely settle the affair in accordance with what is right. 'Even if the lowest slave and scullion maid can bear to commit suicide, why shouldn't one like myself be able to do what has to be done?' he asks, and then answers his own question. 'The reason I have . . . continued to live, dwelling in vileness and disgrace without taking leave, is that I grieve that I have things in my heart that I have not been able to express fully, and I am ashamed to think that after I am gone my writings will not be known to posterity.'

In brief, he had a higher purpose: to finish his history, to bear witness to his times. To do this demanded that he tell the truth about his emperor and the imperial excesses – not simply the military campaigns, but the ruthless commandeering of men to build and guard the Great Wall, the burdens of taxation, the overspending on vast palaces, and the obsession with death that led to a lunatic hunt for the 'elixir of immortality' and to decades-long labour to build a tomb that would outdo the First Emperor's.

But, having received his punishment, Sima Qian still held his position as a court official. He could not be direct in his criticism. So he was indirect, attacking the First Emperor instead of Wu. The result was an overblown portrait which, in Burton Watson's words, skilfully juxtaposes 'examples of the grandiose rhetoric employed by the monarch to celebrate his achievements with grim accounts of the cruelty, folly and oppression of the populace for which he has been remembered in later ages'. Sima Qian also had a go at the First Emperor's officials for 'bowing too readily to the will of the ruler, for accommodating themselves too readily to the trend of the times, instead of endeavouring to reform it'.

So, in what follows, bear in mind Burton Watson's caveat: 'No one, it seems to me, would have greater reason than Sima Qian himself to paint a grim picture of the reigns of the First and Second Emperors, and almost no one in succeeding centuries to my knowledge ever accused Sima Qian of being unfair in his treatment of the Qin or attempted to correct the record.'

Until recently: for the First Emperor has acquired even greater significance, and some nuances. In part this was due to Mao, who dismissed his ruthlessness as necessary egg-breaking to complete the omelette of unification (as we shall see in more detail in chapter 12). This, however, was not a revision of the First Emperor's character, but of the way his ruthlessness was to be judged. Bad became good. What Burton Watson is suggesting is that he was not as bad as Sima Qian painted him, and others make the same point.

One of the people I spoke to when researching this book was the man in charge of archaeology for all Shaanxi province, Duan Qingbo. Before he would see me, he sent a message to say I would have to get permission from the local government, so I assumed he would be a bureaucratic type, backing traditional views of the First Emperor. Not a bit of it. He turned out to be a youthful forty-something brimming with enthusiasm, and very much his own man. 'Remember,' he said, 'that some of Sima Qian is a literary fiction. Here was his own emperor spending money on grand projects, building palaces, the Great Wall, a tomb that he started in the second year of his reign, which would last another fifty-three years, wasting money [in a way] that threatened his realm with collapse. Sima Qian could not criticize his emperor directly. So he criticized the First Emperor instead.'

Where does that leave us?

Re-evaluating, that's where. Not taking things at face value. Using archaeology to reassess tradition. Ready to ask whether the First Emperor was less of a tyrant and more of a brilliant and original leader, as befits the man who unified China and left a spirit army that is the admiration of the world.

CHAPTER 3

WARRING STATES,
CONFLICTING IDEAS

From his reputation, you would think that the first Emperor, who 'unified China', invented the very idea of unity. Not so: it was an idea rooted much further back, in a dream-time of scanty records where figures and themes and events drift like ghosts.

It is surprising that such a vast and varied region should have yearned for unity. Geographically, it seems to have none. It is the same size as the United States, but with no shining seas to hem it in. Yet its fertile heartland, as defined by its two great rivers, the Yellow River and the Yangtze,[1] is turned in upon itself by the deserts of Central Asia, the highlands of Tibet and the forests of the south. By about 1800 BC the lower Yellow River,

---

[1] Yangzi in pinyin, but the old spelling is a fixture in English. The name, from an ancient ferry crossing on the lower part of the river, was adopted in English and many other languages for the whole. The modern Chinese name, Chang Jiang ('Long River') is increasingly used internationally.

with its deep and fertile soils, was home to a kingdom named after its people, the Shang. You would hardly equate this with China – it was only the size of England – but it was the core from which China would eventually spring. The Shang confronted a host of rivals and enemies, of whom little is known, but who shared the main elements of Shang culture. On this basis, later rulers came to believe that political unity was an ideal towards which they should strive.

For many centuries, however, unity in China was an ideal in abeyance. In about 1050 BC Shang fell to one of its rivals, Zhou. Over centuries, cultural practices and spiritual beliefs became more complex, more sophisticated. Divination remained popular, becoming dependent on that wonder of simplicity and complexity, the *Book of Changes, Yi Jing* (*I Ching*, in its Wade–Giles transliteration). Kings looked to heaven as the source of their authority and morality. They believed they ruled with the Mandate of Heaven, which could be withdrawn should they not come up to scratch. But as Zhou's cultural influence spread – supposedly destroying 50 statelets in the process – so political unity receded. Zhou rulers appointed family members and local chiefs as lords of estates of all sizes, from provinces down to single cities – 1,763 of them, according to one source. Though bound to the king by feudal ties and providing troops for the king's army, all these princelings had their own courts, armies, administrations and rituals, and

34

asserted their differences from one another with intense pride. All were obsessed with war, and all fought according to arcane rules of chivalry: no attacking a state if it was in mourning; charioteers to take turns shooting at each other in battle. Over five centuries, in what is known as the Spring and Autumn Period (*c*.700–475 BC) and the Warring States Period (*c*.475–221 BC), these states, mini-states and city-states struggling for survival absorbed each other and whittled themselves down to seven.

Under the pressure of constant warfare, social evolution went into overdrive. As bronze gave way to iron, tools improved, agriculture became more productive, trade increased. Qin, for instance, imported white silk from Qi, jade from the Kunlung mountains to the west, dyes from Sichuan, horses from the northern grasslands, drums made of bronze, tin and iguana skins from Jiangxi and Anhui provinces in the south-east, pearls and rhinoceros horn and ivory from even further away.

A principal effect of this mix of rivalry and trade was on warfare itself. Little, temporary armies of upper-class charioteers gave way to large peasant forces. For any ruler, success in war was the prime consideration, marking 'the road either to survival or to ruin'. The words are those of Sun Zi (Sun Tzu in Wade–Giles) in the opening to his classic of war theory, *The Art of War*, which sprang from the heart of his turbulent times, probably in the fourth century BC. It sprang also from the mind of a supreme professional who had studied every aspect of war, beginning with the 'five fundamentals' – politics, weather, terrain, command and management – and continuing down to details like the cost of entertaining envoys and the price of glue. It contains lessons that are valid for most times, if not all: avoid battle except when victory is assured; don't take risks; overawe an enemy with psychological means; plan well; strike hard and fast. 'While we have heard of stupid haste in war . . . there has never been a protracted war which benefited a country.' He was studied by Norman Schwarzkopf, commander of US forces in the first Gulf War of 1991; not studied by President Bush, who in 2002 was warned of trouble ahead in Iraq by Missouri's Democratic representative Ike Skelton, quoting Sun Zi: 'To win victory is easy; to preserve its fruits, difficult.'

But this obsession with war was accompanied by equal and opposite obsessions: with peace, diplomacy, art, philosophy and poetry. Great thinkers struggled with great questions, the greatest being Kong Fuzi, or Confucius to give him his Latinized name. Dismayed by the evils of his sixth-century BC world, he devised a system of ethics and government that promoted the good. He taught that people should see clearly their place in a hierarchical universe, from king to commoner, and fulfil their responsibilities to those above and below, exercising loyalty, piety, filial

36

respect and benevolence. This was the way to divine approval, the way for rulers to deserve and preserve the Mandate of Heaven. At bottom, human beings are part of one big family, governed by family virtues. That is the core of his teaching, as revealed by his Conversations (or Discourses, or Analects), gathered by his followers and revered as a fundamental guide to good behaviour and good government ever since. Some of it is surprisingly close to Christianity as promulgated by medieval reformers such as St Francis and St Benedict, who sought to regenerate the established church by returning to Christ-like basics.

How do we know what the virtues are? How do we practise them? Guidance lay in the hands of scholars and advisers, those learned men who understood rituals, calendars, divinations and record-keeping – men like Confucius's greatest follower Meng Zi, Master Meng or Mencius, who travelled around from state to state in the fourth century BC offering advice to rulers. He had no time for power and profit; the only virtues he recognized were those of goodness. When the king of Liang (c.100 kilometres north-east of Xian) asked about ways to profit his state, Mencius replied, 'Why must Your Majesty use the word "profit"? All I am concerned with are the good and the right.' Those virtues come naturally to us, and will emerge if encouraged. 'Goodness is to human nature what flowing downward is to water.' In brief, the advice to rulers from Confucius and

Mencius was: Rule virtuously and peace will follow.

Peace, though, was not a condition achieved for long amid the incessant squabbling of the Warring States. A school of cynics arose, asking each other and their rulers a tough question: what was the point of cultivating the arts of peace if they did not lead to peace? Their answer was brutally pragmatic: none at all. The only thing that mattered was effectiveness, in war and in peace. In peace, the wise ruler prepared for war; in war, he ensured victory; in victory, he preserved peace by preparing for yet more war. Stability was all, and stability could be guaranteed only under strong leadership. Out went the notion that virtue and wisdom would spread by example. There was no room now for the old families, the old feudal estates, the old rules of chivalry, the old individualism, the old Confucian virtues.

This line of thought, known as Legalism, was given forceful expression by an ambitious young scholar named Shang, Lord Shang (Shang Yang) as he became known. Shang was born in the state of Wei, which dominated the middle Yellow River, probably around 400 BC. As the protégé of the prime minister, he presented his ideas to the king, Hui, who didn't approve of them. The prime minister, Gongshu Cuo, was so awed by Shang's abilities that he feared what might happen if the young man took his ideas to a rival king. Visited on his deathbed by the king, Gongshu advised Hui to keep Shang's loyalty by making him the next prime minister. If not, he said, 'be sure to have him killed. Don't allow him to leave the state!' King Hui, lacking both insight and ruthlessness, dismissed both ideas (Gongshu was very sick, he confided to attendants, 'Quite out of his mind') – and did nothing, thus ensuring that Gongshu's fears were realized.

For Shang turned to the neighbouring state of Qin. Originally Qin had been nothing more than one of Zhou's little fiefdoms. From its capital, Yong (100 kilometres west of Xian), it had carved itself into an independent kingdom dominating the broad and fertile valley of the river Wei, which ran eastward into the Yellow River valley. Now, in the long struggle among the seven Warring States, Qin was emerging supreme. Its base, present-day Shaanxi, now considered the cradle of Chinese civilization, was then a backwater on the southern edge of the semi-desert known today by its Mongol name, Ordos (an old plural of *ordon*, a palace-tent, after the many Mongol chiefs who used to live there). Qin, the most westerly of the seven contending states, was considered by the others almost as barbaric as the nomad tribes who lived to the north and west. As a prince of neighbouring Wei put it to his king over a century later: 'Qin has the same customs as the Rong and Di [barbarians]. It has the heart of a tiger or wolf. It is avaricious, perverse, eager for profit, and without sincerity. It knows nothing about etiquette, proper relationships and virtuous conduct.' By the early fourth century BC, it had 400 self-assertive years of history behind it, and was ambitious for more of the same. It advertised for expert help. Not a place for gentle Confucians, but perfect for an ambitious, ruthless Legalist.

Shang responded to Qin's expressions of interest, moved to its capital Yong, and put his ideas to Qin's ruler, Duke Xiao. The duke liked what he heard, and Shang was given a free hand, so much so that he was able to shift the capital 100 kilometres eastward from Yong to Xianyang, with its better strategic position on the river Wei. Here he 'carried out the construction of the Memorial Gate and of palaces and gardens', the Memorial Gate possibly becoming the core of the palace that would later be the home of the First Emperor.

We know Shang's thinking, for he (or – more likely, in the view of most scholars – one or more of his followers) recorded it in a book that became one of the classics of ancient China. *The Book of Lord Shang* has special significance for our story because it is the programme adopted not just by Duke Xiao, but also 140 years later by his heir, the First Emperor.

Shang's teaching was the mirror image of Confucius's. Intended solely for the ruler, it was the essence of institutionalized ruthlessness. Might is right, power the only virtue. Human beings are idle, greedy, cowardly, treacherous, foolish, shifty; so Confucius's idea that they respond well to good treatment is simply naïve. The only way to rule is to entice, terrify, reward and punish. This treatment is not arbitrary (as has often been the case with dictators), but is to be based on the stern rule of law, applied to everyone without distinction. 'Law', wrote Shang, 'is the basis of government. It is what shapes the people.' The ruler's task is first to devise the law, then to record it, then to ensure that it is applied impartially through officials utterly subservient to the state's institutions.

His programme might be a manual for totalitarian rulers down the ages, with astonishingly strong echoes in organizations and states attempting centralized control in the twentieth century. The Gestapo, East Germany's Stasi, the KGB and the Romanian Securitate were his modern offspring, born of the same urge. In the words of his follower Han Fei: 'Lord Shang taught Duke Xiao of Qin how to organize the people into groups of five or ten families that would spy on each other,' and 'anyone who failed to report criminal activity would be chopped in two at the waist'. Moreover, 'he advised him to burn the *Book of Odes* [i.e. poetry] and *Book of Documents* [i.e. historical records] . . . and to glorify the lot of those who devote themselves to agriculture and warfare.'

Note the book-burning reference, which will return to haunt us later. These books were not the same as our books, because paper would not be invented for another 400 years, and China never used papyrus; instead, 'books' were scrolls of silk or bamboo-strips bound together. Reading and writing were for the very few and the very wealthy. That made the imposition of controls relatively easy. Shang's advice was intended to impose the ultimate control – on records of the past, on memory itself, an aim famously pinpointed by George Orwell in *Nineteen Eighty-Four*: 'Who controls the past controls the future: who controls the present controls the past.'

These grim policies are justified by the tyrant's defence of tyranny down the ages: if you do no wrong (as defined by the state), you have nothing to fear. As Orwell observed, the perfect totalitarian society is one whose citizens are so drilled to conformity that there is no need to kill or torture anyone. Lord Shang foreshadows *Nineteen Eighty-Four*: the aim of Legalism is to create a world in which laws are never broken, and so there is no need for punishment. If light offences are punished heavily, then heavy offences are not committed. 'This is said to be abolishing penalties by means of penalties, and if penalties are abolished, affairs [of state] will succeed.' In such a system, in which officials prove themselves by the rigidity with which they administer the law, the ruler's court will not be a prey to flattery and slander. Intelligence, thoughtfulness, judgement: these qualities are undesirable in an official, for they inspire criticism and opposition.

All of this had one principal end: to ensure the strongest possible army. As Mark Lewis, Professor of Chinese Culture at Stanford University, writes, all social rank and status reflected military performance.[2] Advancement up a hierarchy of 20 ranks depended entirely on the killing of enemies. The whole country was divided into units of military service, administered by the imposition of a grid of paths and roads that ran north-south and east-west, dividing all agricultural land into blocks that could be worked by a single adult male. 'In this way the state could obtain the maximum amount of land in cultivation and the highest possible number of adult males liable for military service and taxes.'

History has no laws, but it does throw up the occasional generalization. Here's one: similar conditions are likely to produce similar reactions. Take Italy in the early sixteenth century, with its proud city-states, its bitter rivalries, its intrigues, its unreliable mercenaries, its brutal little wars, its brilliant artists and its writers. Among them was Niccolò Machiavelli, whose book *The Prince* offers advice remarkably similar in its cold realism and cynicism to Lord Shang's. He too was a keen observer of his world, and what he saw drove him to equally grim conclusions. The state is all, and power the only currency. Theology, metaphysics, idealism – all should be set aside, unless they serve

[2] Lewis, *Sanctioned Violence in Early China*.

the state. The bottom line is self-interest. If the Prince wishes to display idealism, it must only be for show. 'A prudent ruler', he said, 'ought not to keep faith when by doing so it would be against his interest.' Machiavelli's best-known portrait shows a man with a mean and hungry look, just the type, you might think, to propose such cold and uncompromising views. Not at all. He was an astute diplomat, conventionally Catholic, a good poet and the author of a first-rate comedy. He simply believed that his advice sprang inevitably from a world that would self-destruct unless taken firmly in hand.

Machiavelli drew on precedents to argue his case. Shang, several shades more authoritarian, refused to acknowledge any. Ancient customs and other schools of thought were all anathema, for nothing must rival his prince's laws, not even the cries of the people: 'A weak people means a strong state,' he wrote; 'a strong state means a weak people.' Out went Confucianism, with its subtle arguments for private virtue. Out went the old feudal system, with its local lords, their self-serving intrigues and their destructive little wars. In came a triumvirate of powers: a professional army; farm labourers who supplied food; and the Law, applied uniformly and without exception to everyone, high and low, except of course the king himself, for he personified the Law and administered it by whatever means he could, moral or immoral, and was above such distinctions. Shang even persuaded the

44

Qin ruler to punish the crown prince. As you might imagine, he was not popular, nor did he go out of his way to cultivate allies. As his follower Han Fei recorded, 'when he came and went at court, he was guarded by iron spears and heavy shields to prevent sudden attack.' When Duke Xiao died, being succeeded by the very prince whom Shang had punished, Shang didn't last long. He was caught, 'tied to two chariots and torn apart by the men of Qin'.[3]

But his policies worked. Qin grew strong, and expanded. Protected by the Yellow River and mountains to the east, hardened by dealing with even more uncouth barbarians to the north and west, Qin spread southward into Sichuan, then eastward into neighbouring Zhou. War followed war, and death piled on death. The main source (Sima Qian, as always) claims 1.5 million dead in 134 years, probably a wild exaggeration, but one that reflects the emotional impact of extended warfare. Applying Legalism in its most extreme form, Qin toughened itself, turning itself into a Chinese Sparta, the most centralized, the most authoritarian, the hardest of the hard. Its ideologues would have approved of Fascism: virtue and tradition were out, power the only virtue. Every official act had to go towards making the state rich, the bureaucracy efficient, the army

[3] Both quotes from Han Feizi, *Basic Writings*, in Burton Watson's translation.

strong, agriculture productive and expansion rapid.

Yes, totalitarianism can work, for a while at least. It makes trains run on time, it builds armies, it is good for grand projects. In Qin's case, for example, it provided the cash and manpower to confront the problem of meltwaters that every spring devastated the valley of the river Min in Sichuan. One official, Li Bing, came up with a solution. He cut away a mountain to create a spillway and then divided the river with an artificial island. The result: no more floods, and controlled irrigation for the surrounding countryside, turning the Chengdu plain from an annual catastrophe into China's most productive farmland. It still works today. Li Bing is a local hero and his creation, Du Jiang Yan, is a major tourist attraction, a UNESCO World Heritage Site and a national treasure.

Some good works, then; but they are incidental. Shang's advice was not for rulers who wished to be remembered for their good works, but for those interested in power. In addition, it was advice for a leader who was already in power, having inherited his position. There was nothing here about how to win power in the first place, nothing about the wider aspects of leadership: the need for an inspiring vision, the business of winning friends, the need for virtues like loyalty and generosity – all the positive traits that we associate with charismatic leadership, as exemplified by (among others) Alexander, or Napoleon, or Genghis Khan, or Mohammed.

Shang's spirit lived on in Han Fei, a prince of a neighbouring state from which he took his family name. Han the state was smaller and weaker than Qin, and therefore often an unwilling ally, acting like a weakling cowed by a bully. Han Fei's destiny was fixed by three apparently unrelated facts. The first was that he became a student of a famous Confucian philosopher named Xun Zi (Master Xun), under whom he 'learned the methods appropriate to an emperor or king', that is, political science, except that he steadily turned against the teachings of his master as they applied to rulers, and developed instead a deep attachment to Legalist theory. The second was that he had a terrible stutter, with the result that he could never master the eloquence demanded of a court adviser; so he wrote a book to publicize his ideas, setting out the Legalist agenda with brilliant clarity and readability. The third was that one of his fellow students was an ambitious but not quite so brilliant young man named Li Si, who 'considered himself not equal to Han Fei', according to Sima Qian. Despairing of getting a job in his home state – and perhaps eager to escape from Han Fei's shadow – Li Si moved to Qin, saying 'The king of Qin wants to swallow up the world . . . this is the moment for commoners like myself.'

It was Han Fei's book that was the making of

him, and his undoing. It took Shang's teaching to its logical conclusion, proposing an agenda of a cynicism far more Machiavellian than Machiavelli, more Shangian than Shang. Since Han Fei was a great essayist and stylist, with a flair for historical anecdote, he has been admired ever since. You can see aspects of his thinking reflected in many of China's more extreme rulers, down to the present day. Take four pieces of his polished, sharp and extremely scary advice on how rulers should behave:

- 'It is said: "So still he seems to dwell nowhere at all; so empty no one can seek him out." The enlightened ruler reposes in non-action above, and below his ministers tremble with fear.'
- 'This is the way of the enlightened ruler: he causes the wise to bring forth their schemes, and he decides his affairs accordingly; hence his wisdom is never exhausted. He causes the worthy to display their talents, and he employs them accordingly; hence his own worth never comes to an end. Where there are accomplishments, the ruler takes credit for their worth; where there are errors, the ministers are held responsible for the blame; hence the ruler's name never suffers.'
- 'Be empty, still, and idle, and from your place of darkness observe the defects of others. See but do not appear to see; listen but do not seem to listen; know but do not let it be known that you know.'

- And finally: 'This is the way to listen to the words of others: be silent as though in a drunken stupor. Say to yourself: Lips! teeth! Do not be the first to move; lips! teeth! Be thicker, be clumsier than ever! Let others say their piece – I will gain knowledge thereby.'

Other writers have independently come to similar conclusions about the nature of kingship. Take the analysis of the role of the British monarchy by the great Victorian editor and political analyst Walter Bagehot: A monarch 'should not be brought too closely to real measurement. He should be aloof and solitary . . . [Royalty] seems to order, but it never seems to struggle. It is commonly hidden like a mystery, and sometimes paraded like a pageant, but in neither case is it contentious.'

Unfortunately for Han Fei, there is a logical flaw in his advice. If the god-ruler must remain forever on guard, distrusting everyone, he must also distrust the man who offers this advice. This was the catch-22 that, with the malign intervention of his former fellow student Li Si, would lead to Han Fei's sad end.

First, however, he had to meet the man who would welcome his ideas, apply them in this life, and then take them even further, into the next.

CHAPTER 4

FROM PRINCE TO KING

The scene is set for the arrival of the first Emperor: the man who forged a new unified China, sealed it with a Great Wall to protect himself in this life, and made a clay army to fight for him in the next one.

It started, as it always seems to with dictators, in a deep sense of insecurity rooted in his origins.

As Sima Qian tells it, the story opens in the next-door state, Zhou, with a rich and ambitious merchant named Lü Buwei meeting a down-at-heel Qin prince, Zichu, the son of a junior concubine of the heir to the Qin throne.[1] Zichu, it seems, is never going to amount to much. He is not in line for succession – indeed, there is no line, because the crown prince's official wife, of whom he is very fond, is barren. One of 20 sons by various concubines, Zichu has been sent off to the Zhou court as a hostage, a common diplomatic ploy to provide a guarantee of Qin's good behaviour. But being low in the pecking

[1] These anecdotes are from Bodde's translation of Sima Qian, *Statesman, Patriot and General in Ancient China*.

50

order, Zichu lives frugally, without a retinue or carriages, or indeed a future, until Lü spots in him a chance of advancement.

Lü is a novelty in the changing society of the time. Merchants had previously been despised by Confucians as non-productive, undereducated parasites, their low status preserved by legal restrictions. But in these Legalistic times, Confucianism is at a low ebb. Smart, self-serving, unscrupulous, Lü invites the prince into a back room and proposes a scheme to lever him on to the Qin throne. The prince has nothing to lose. If it works, he promises, he will share the state of Qin with his benefactor.

Lü begins to put his plan into action. He gives the prince some cash to hire himself a band of followers, and with a similar sum he buys some 'rare objects, trinkets and toys', which he takes to the Qin capital, Xianyang. He strikes up an acquaintance with an intermediary and has his purchases delivered to the queen, along with a message about how Zichu is distraught at being separated from the queen, whom he adores. Since she has no son, he says, she will have no one to look after her interests when the emperor dies. She had better find a stepson. Then 'as long as your husband lives, you will enjoy honour; and when his hundred years of life are ended, and the one whom you call son becomes king, you need never fear any loss of position'. The one she should choose is, of course, Zichu, whose own mother is out of favour and who is therefore devoted to the queen. So it happens. The emperor agrees, Zichu becomes the crown prince's heir – second in line to the throne – money is sent to Zichu and Lü becomes his tutor.

Now comes an incident which adds to the drama but which seems highly suspicious. Lü has a very beautiful girlfriend. She becomes pregnant. Zichu sees her, falls in love, and asks for her. Lü, whose whole future is now tied to Zichu, swallows his outrage and hands her over. Then, in Bodde's translation, 'The concubine kept to herself the fact that she was pregnant and [in 259 BC] at the expiration of a great period [or 'when her time was up' in Burton Watson] she bore a son,' whose name is Zheng.[2] This is the future First Emperor, unifier of China and maker of the Terracotta Army.

Why be suspicious of this? Because it is a little too convenient, a little too glib. It is just the sort of smear you would expect from a later dynasty, but not from Sima Qian. It's not his style. He would have supported it with something more convincing, not tossed it away in half a dozen lines. In a detailed analysis of this matter in 1940, Derk Bodde pointed out that the story does not appear in Sima Qian's

[2] Two characters are used in the sources for his name, both of which are pronounced *zhèng*.

major source,[3] that his text is corrupted by obvious interpolations – unnecessary repetitions that he would not have made – and that a very similar story from another state appears in another source. He concludes: 'The story of the First Emperor's birth, therefore, is probably the clever invention of some Han Confucian, who has used it to defame the First Emperor by representing him as the bastard son of a shrewd, unscrupulous, uneducated merchant, and a mother who was little better than a prostitute.' Interpolation or not, the slur stuck. For the last 2,000 years Chinese have believed that the First Emperor was a bastard, literally as well as figuratively.

Eventually, after a couple of royal deaths, Zichu becomes king and Lü his prime minister, having been made a marquis controlling 100,000 households around present-day Luoyang, 350 kilometres east of the capital. Four years later [in 247 BC] Zichu dies, leaving twelve-year-old Zheng to succeed, under the control of his mother and his all-powerful patron. Lü sets about increasing Qin's power and influence still further, recruiting 3,000 well-educated retainers. Among them is the ambitious young social scientist Li Si, who has come to Qin because he has heard that its king 'wants

[3] *Zhanguo Ce / Stratagems of the Warring States* (third century BC).

53

to swallow up the world'. Since the old king has just died and the new one is so young, he will have to wait.

Eager for the status that comes with literary fame, Lü commissions from his entourage a book to record what his retainers know of philosophy and metaphysics, and has the results published under his own name as *Lü's Spring and Autumn* [*Annals*]. This is to help realize his ambition to achieve total domination of the state and government before the prince comes of age and can act alone. It is also a piece of supreme vanity, for it was a title of several other regional histories, including one attributed to Confucius himself. Lü is so proud of 'his' work that he has a copy attached to one of the capital's gates, with 1,000 pieces of gold hanging above it, together with a notice that if anyone could improve it by so much as a single character, the cash was theirs. No one dares try. Bodde adds a succinct comment: 'At the present day we are still not unfamiliar with the activities of the crude, uncultivated, self-made man, who becomes a patron of the arts chiefly in order that he may gain the plaudits of the *élite*.'

Meanwhile, Lü and the beautiful queen restart their affair, but Lü, afraid of discovery, hatches another plot so complicated it sounds unworkable, and so lurid it sounds incredible. Some of it probably is. Yet no one has suggested the following paragraph was forged by some Han interpolator. It seems we should accept the story, with its startling details, as Sima Qian's own words. Here it is:

> The queen dowager did not cease her wanton behaviour. Lü Buwei began to fear that, if her conduct were ever brought to light, he himself would become involved with the scandal. He therefore searched about in secret until he found a man named Lao Ai who had an unusually large penis, and made him a servant in his household. Then, when an occasion arose, he had suggestive music performed and, instructing Lao Ai to stick his penis through the centre of a wheel made of paulownia wood, had him walk about with it, making certain that the report of this reached the ears of the queen dowager so as to excite her interest.

Never mind the queen: this extraordinary image would surely excite anyone's interest. It contains just the sort of detail lacking in passages that are possible forgeries. Why paulownia wood, for heaven's sake? I had never heard of it, but Google throws up websites by the score. Paulownias, with their huge dark-green leaves and decorative mauve flowers, have been cultivated in China for over 2,300 years. Also now known as the 'princess' or 'royal' tree, the most popular species (*Paulownia tomentosa*) is fast-growing (almost 3 metres a year,

55

good for reforestation); is easily worked; resists rot well; has a very high ignition point; is good for making the soundboards of stringed musical instruments; and much more. Why a 'wheel' of it should be suitable for showing off the attributes of a stud-in-waiting is not clear; but I believe the scene.

So did the queen, with more astonishing revelations to come. She wanted to see Lao Ai in the flesh. But there was a problem. The palace system did not allow 'real' men into the dowager empress's quarters. So Lü's complicated plot gets its next twist. He arranges for Lao Ai to be falsely accused of a crime for which the punishment is castration. The official in charge of castration is then bribed to pretend to carry out the procedure, plucking out Lao Ai's beard and eyebrows to make him look like a eunuch. 'In this way he eventually came to wait on the queen, who carried on clandestine relations with him and grew to love him greatly.'

I don't think we should take all this at face value. What 'crime' exactly might Lao Ai have been accused of? How would anyone have known? But the outlines carry conviction. Bear in mind this is deceit on a huge scale. The queen has her own palace, staffed by hundreds. Lao Ai himself, now in a position to exert great influence, acquires a retinue of 1,000 retainers, all hoping for advancement.

The affair continues for many years, with the

queen bearing Lao Ai two sons, who thus became half-brothers and possible heirs of the teenaged King Zheng, the future First Emperor; and Zheng is still being advised by his mentor, Lü Buwei, his mother's ex-lover and – according to word on the street – his father. This was a time-bomb ticking towards an explosion.

It would be good to place these dramatic events in their setting, to see something of the Qin capital, Xianyang, and its array of palaces. I'm sorry to say you can't. Qin architecture, like almost all building of its day, was all rammed-earth walls and wooden rafters, which rotted away or were burned. But if you go to the site, not far from today's Xianyang, you can get a feel for what King Zheng faced in his struggle to make Qin China's dominant power.

His ancestors had moved from the west two centuries before on the advice of Lord Shang, who saw that an ambitious, centralized state needed a capital better placed for assault. Both new and old Xianyang lie on the north bank of the river Wei, which flows eastward to the Yellow River, 130 kilo-metres away. What a contrast it makes to drive between the two Xianyangs. If you start with new Xianyang, half an hour by expressway from the later capital, Xian, there is nothing in the surge of new building to suggest an ancient past. For that you have to visit the charming old museum, with its brightly painted beams and upturned tiles and its Qin and Han artefacts, all the broken bits and pieces picked up from sites like the one we were on our way to visit.

The name 'Qin' lives on, but it takes fine-tuning to pick up the faint echoes of Qin culture, and its swaggering machismo. A ten-times-life-size three-legged cauldron in the middle of a roundabout is a modern reminder that power once depended on the ability to cast bronze. Other cultures were proud of their swords; in Qin times, they loved their cooking-pots. Still do, actually, because of what comes from them. It was the first day of spring, and lunchtime, and on sunny sidewalks people addressed themselves to Qin noodles. Unlike the thin, effete, girly, machine-made noodles eaten everywhere else, Qin noodles are rough-cut, hand-made symbols of manliness, solid as leather armour. And the pancakes: none of your wimpy sheets that fall apart at a touch, but bars of dough solid as telephone directories. 'There were no chopsticks then,' said my guide 'Tony' Lee. 'No knives and forks. So we tore our food apart with our hands.'

So, strengthened by Qin cuisine, driver Wang powered his 4×4 eastward out of new Xianyang, heading for the old one, King Zheng's capital. It was a fine day; one of those charming-if-puzzling roadside signs in English reminded us how lucky we were to be alive, if we acted correctly: 'Life does not come twice, so don't run inversely.' Then we were away from Xianyang's dual carriageways, away from any risk of running inversely. As we rolled along back roads, through fields of winter wheat and budding apple orchards that dusted the grey earth with green, Tony – a lanky thirty-something with hair fizzed as if by electric shock – spoke of the traits that define Qin culture.

'They like yodelling.'

'What?'

'I mean yowling. No, yelling. They talk very loud. Listen to Qin opera. Maybe it will scare you because it is so loud and piercing.' He experimented with the radio-tuner, and to my astonishment found a station that broadcast nothing but Qin opera. 'You see? It sounds like shouting or crying. We think this must have been King Zheng's entertainment too.' This struck me as very likely, because it was clearly based on the battle cries of berserk warriors and the screams of tortured criminals. (Later, in a Xian club that specialized in Qin opera, I heard the real thing. It starred both professionals and amateurs, who stepped out of the small audience to belt out the songs through a microphone at a gut-wrenching volume. I felt shaken by sound, like a rat by a terrier; shaken also by my ignorance, for this was a serious subculture, with aficionados as dedicated and expert as Wagner freaks.)

My attention swung outwards again, away from the fortissimo howl of Qin opera. The road was now running past hillock after hillock, the royal tumuli left by the Han dynasty, the Qin's successors. There was not a house in sight.

'Where on earth are we?'

'Today we are in the middle of nowhere,' said Tony, who was rightly proud of his idiomatic English. 'We are in the back of beyond. But two thousand years ago, it was different. There were Zhou tombs here before the Qin came, and Han afterwards. This was a historic place for centuries.'

We turned between two Han burial mounds, along a lane, past a little museum that was closed for repairs, and up a path towards higher ground. A little gnarled old lady working in a field of vines happily and effusively told us we were on the right track. 'How friendly she is,' remarked Tony. 'You ask her one question, she answers ten. And listen.' A tinny noise came faintly through the vines. 'You hear her radio? Qin opera!' She noticed our interest and carried the radio over, so I could appreciate the clashing cymbals and high shrieks. I wonder how many farm workers anywhere in the world listen to opera while they work.

An overgrown brick path led between fir saplings and plantations of palm bushes. Then we were on a plateau, its undulating surface covered with coarse grasses and thorny bushes that grabbed at trouser-legs and shoelaces. A sign said that this had been declared 'a national cultural relics protection spot' in 1988, which must have been when the gardens were made. But in almost 20 years nothing else had been done: there was no sign of any building. The archaeologists had done their work, taking roof-tiles and floortiles and drains off to museums,

60

tracing post-holes, sketching ground plans, leaving nothing but rolling earth and coarse vegetation. Once, there had been the remains of the base of a terrace; if there's anything left now, I missed it. There was no one else around except the little old lady and her radio – not surprisingly, because the place was hard to get to, with no public transport and nothing to see.

Suddenly, though, the attractions of the site for Qin rulers were revealed. We waded clear of bushes, towards a . . .

At this point my attention was snatched away by a very odd sound, a vibrato twanging that rose and fell in volume, but always on the same note. I looked around for some electrical source, a wire vibrating in the wind, perhaps, or some machine. A second later, I saw where the sound came from: a flight of birds swooping and swerving overhead. Obviously they were some local species with a peculiar cry, or a weird evolutionary adaptation of their wing-feathers. I stood spellbound. Such is the idiocy brought on by ignorance. They were pigeons, explained Tony, to whom the sound was so routine he had hardly heard it. Domestic pigeons. Their owners tied whistles to their feet to keep track of them.

A cliff. That was what lay beyond the bushes. A cliff of clay and earth, about 10 metres high, at the base of which was a village of earth-brick houses, and beyond an immense plain leading to the Wei river, invisible in the distance. Perhaps

2,200 years ago, when King Zheng ruled from here, it had been a marshy flood plain. Serenaded by the flying choir, we made our way along the cliff-top. A bluff jutting out a few metres gave a view along the whole site, a 5-kilometre platform of scrub and little mounds, which at last provided a framework for a mind's-eye view of what had once been here.

The centrepiece had been King Zheng's palace. Actually, according to the reconstruction based on archaeological surveys,[4] it was a graceful, low-rise building, more a villa than a palace. In King Zheng's day, as the many repairs and reconstructions revealed, this villa had been there for some time, perhaps ever since Lord Shang created Xianyang as the new Qin capital 200 years earlier. If you get a chance, look at the model in the Xianyang museum; otherwise imagine a gallery of 40 arches stretching for 120 metres, topped by a terrace along which courtiers could stroll. Above, and set back, was a third storey, each wing having three low towers: in effect, three separate houses, the central one of which – the emperor's quarters, perhaps – had another terrace, giving a fine view southward over the plain. Surprisingly for a man dedicated to war, there were no defences. Surprisingly also, considering King Zheng's

[4] The best single account in any language is in Ledderose and Schlombs, *Jenseits der Grossen Mauer*, which contains many Chinese sources.

massive expenditures, it was quite modest. What turned it from a villa into a palace was its depth – 40 metres – and its decorations: ceramic tiles, bronze hinges, wall-paintings. One round tile-end was embossed with a text: 'Only with the approval of Heaven can our dynasty last for over 10,000 years and everything under Heaven thrive and live in peace.'[5] Inside was a warren of rooms and corridors floored by embossed red tiles, all supplied with water and drained through four systems of terracotta pipes, and all decorated with scenes of men, horses and mythological beasts, the oldest Chinese wall-paintings yet discovered.

And that was only the crown jewel of Xianyang's buildings. It was set in a palace complex almost a kilometre long and 500 metres wide, among many more buildings, some probably linked by roofed corridors and bridges. All along the earthen platform were scattered other grand houses, some 270 of them, either side of a gorge, now called the Ox and Goat Creek, that sliced southward through the platform of earth to the Wei. In all, the city was 7.2 kilometres (east-west) by 6.7 kilometres (north-south), though a good deal of the southern section seems to have been washed away when the river Wei changed course. The capital was supplied by seven bronze and iron foundries,

[5] The dating of this piece is uncertain. It may be Han. But the manufacturing technique and the sentiment could just as well be Qin.

proof that Qin was the centre of a rich, self-confident little kingdom long before Zheng took it over. As the ex-president of the Terracotta Army Museum, Yuan Zhongyi, has written,

> Formerly, as a result of the lack of documentation and archaeological finds, it was assumed that Qin had been backward. Now, following a wealth of new discoveries, this judgment has to be thoroughly revised . . . The Qin dynasty reigned over a glorious, flourishing period in the cultural history of old China . . . a treasure worthy of scrupulous research and compilation.[6]

This was the base where King Zheng planned the unification of China and his own elevation to its first emperor. But these ambitions presented him with a new insight, and inspired new ambitions. Xianyang might be a lot better placed than the previous capital, Yong, 100 kilometres further west, but for campaigns to the south and east it was not ideal. The Wei and Yellow rivers were in the way. Armies could be based the other side of both, but to lead them, he himself, and his entourage of officials, needed to cross the Wei. Back then, the Wei spread much more widely at certain times of the year. Was there a bridge?

[6] Quoted in Ledderose and Schlombs, *Jenseits der Grossen Mauer*.

Certainly not a stone one, because China did not as yet have a tradition of building in stone. Possibly a wooden one; probably, for such a broad and variable river, a pontoon bridge. But pontoon bridges were rickety structures, vulnerable to floods. He needed a permanent base south of the Wei. That was where he would plan conquest with his army commanders and his officials. And that was where he would build the tomb from which he would rule his kingdom in the afterlife.

In the ninth year of his reign (238 BC), 'someone reported' to King Zheng the truth about his mother's affair with Lao Ai. Moreover, ran the report, 'He and the queen dowager have agreed that, when the present king passes on, one of [their two] sons shall succeed him.' The king ordered an investigation; then, before hearing the results, he had to travel 100 kilometres westward to the old capital of Yong to perform some essential ritual sacrifices. Lao Ai, afraid his deception was about to be revealed, turned to revolution. 'Using the queen dowager's seal of authority without her permission, [he] called out troops and initiated a revolt.' Action focused on a palace close to where the king was performing his rituals, presumably with the idea of capturing him. Once the news reached Zheng, however, the uprising was quickly crushed. Lao Ai fled, with a reward of one million strings of coins offered for his capture alive, and half that if dead. He was soon taken, though Sima Qian does not record any pay-out.

The investigation was completed, and all the sordid facts revealed. Imagine the young king's reaction. Zheng knows something of his origins – son (perhaps) of a minor prince who had no real right to the throne, which he came to by luck and scheming, and an ex-dancer of ill-repute. His paternity is already in doubt. Now his mother turns out to be not only obsessed by a well-endowed – and treacherous – gigolo, but also conspiring to control the succession, probably with the connivance of the man to whom he owes his throne.

The 22-year-old king, having just 'donned the cap and sword' that symbolized his coming of age, faced his first hard choices as fully fledged ruler. The stakes could hardly be higher. Either he would remain a puppet, or he had to assert himself, crushing his mentor, his mother, her lover and all their armies of retainers. Action would risk civil war; but inaction spelled annihilation. He had Lao Ai killed by the long-established method of being tied to four chariots, which were then driven off in different directions. His associates and relatives were executed. So were the two boys, Zheng's half-brothers and possible future rivals. Lao Ai's 1,000 hangers-on and 4,000 other noble families had their estates confiscated and were sent off to Shu, Qin's southern borderland (today part of Sichuan). His mother he exiled to Yong; 100 kilometres away was not too dire – and anyway she was soon brought back to Xianyang, where she remained until her death ten years later.

What to do with Lü Buwei was not so easily determined. He deserved death, but his past distinctions spoke for him, as did many of his followers. So the king fired him and exiled him to his estates around Luoyang – and, to make extra certain that no similar conspiracy could ever happen again, he announced that he would expel all foreigners from the state of Qin. This was an ill-considered edict, for it would have removed his other chief adviser, Li Si, a native of Chu (before he moved to Han). As Li Si quickly pointed out in a memo, a rejection of foreign things would mean the loss of a good deal of what adorned the palace, including the 'lovely and enchanting women of Zhou, such as blend in with our custom and lend elegance to the scene'. In these matters, His Majesty selected carefully, yet now, when men and talents are at stake, he says: 'He is not a native of Qin, so away with him! Because he is an alien expel him!' Did His Majesty really want to cast away aliens so that they might become an asset to enemy countries? 'This is what is called lending arms to bandits and supplying rations to thieves.' That did it. The king rescinded his order, and Li Si remained in position, to serve his king for another 20 years.

As for Lü Buwei, 350 kilometres turned out not to be far enough. He remained influential with the feudal lords, whose followers and envoys flocked to his palace, so much so that 'carriages were never out of sight of each other on the road'.

To remove the threat still further, the king sent a note of steely politeness: 'Be so good as to take your family and retinue and move your residence to Shu!'

To be sent off to the Qin equivalent of Siberia was one humiliation too many. To refuse to move would be to risk the death penalty, not only for himself but for his family and followers. So Lü committed suicide by drinking poison.

That leaves King Zheng, aged 24, alone, betrayed by his father-figure and his mother, without his closest adviser, surrounded by thousands of clamorous courtiers, any one of whom may turn traitor. What should he do?

Well, he already has the answer, from Li Si, who had been advising him throughout his teenage years: Look at Lord Shang, and the stern Legalist advice that served your forefathers so well. Prince Zheng had listened, and was ahead of his teacher. He had come across chapters by a Legalist author who seemed to wish to remain anonymous, and admired them. The author told charming little stories to state great truths. Take, for instance, his essay entitled 'The Five Vermin':

> There was a farmer of Song who tilled the land, and in his field was a stump. One day a rabbit, racing across the field, bumped into the stump, broke its neck, and died. Thereupon the farmer laid aside his plow

and took up watch beside the stump, hoping he would get another rabbit in the same way. But he got no more rabbits, and instead became the laughing stock of Song. Those who think they can take the ways of ancient kings and use them to govern the people of today all belong in the category of stump-watchers!

The Confucian past was no guide for the present, let alone the future. 'Benevolence and righteousness served for ancient times,' Zheng read in the same essay, 'but no longer serve today . . . Men of today vie to be known for strength and spirit.' In the past, rulers were compared to fathers, people to children, and the rule was one of love. But love cannot prevent children from becoming unruly, so how can it bring the people to order? People will bow only to authority, 'and he who wields authority may easily command men to submit'.

Should a ruler admire Confucius? Of course. He was a great sage, a truly righteous man. Once, rulers aimed to achieve the benevolence and righteousness he advocated. But that was then, and states were destroyed. Should a ruler today follow Confucius, when preserving the state is all-important? Certainly not, because that would be 'to demand that the ruler rise to the level of Confucius', not that of a ruler. The love of parents is not enough to make children learn what is right, 'for people by nature grow proud on love, but they listen to authority'. Even lame sheep may graze up and down a mountain, even the humble abuse easy laws; 'therefore the enlightened ruler makes his laws precipitous and his punishments severe'.

Here, too, King Zheng found advice on how to behave as ruler. If the ruler was the maker of the Law, and above it, how should he act? Obviously, he, as the Son of Heaven, could not be guided by the same principles as his earth-bound officials. Like a Daoist sage, he is above right and wrong, and must withdraw into a world of mystery and transcendence, shunning all contacts that might breed familiarity, concealing his thoughts and motives. He must guard against all impulses towards mercy and affection. Since all – officials, family, even his wife – stand to gain personal freedom by his death, he must trust no one. He must be beyond emotion, doing only that which increases his power, whatever it takes. Self-interest should be his only concern.

The ways to power are these: make the Law; make it simple; never look for men of integrity, because you will not find them; keep your officials on the straight and narrow with rewards and punishments. If people can get rich and eminent without hard work on the land and risking death in battle, they will do so, and the state is weakened; therefore discourage the pursuit of wisdom. 'In the state of the enlightened ruler there are no books . . . there are no sermons . . . there are no fierce feuds of private swordsmen; cutting off the heads of the enemy is the only deed of valour.' Don't think that you can build security by playing at foreign affairs, for no alliance is reliable. 'Neither power nor order can be sought abroad – they are wholly a matter of internal government.'

Remember this: in the past, when Confucians were honoured, states fell; what people praise and the ruler honours are actually policies that lead to the ruin of the state.

These, then, are your enemies, the 'five vermin' of the essay's title: scholars who praise the ways of former kings and speak in elegant phrases; speech-makers who propound false schemes and borrow influence from abroad; swordsmen who gather bands of followers; draft-dodgers who bribe their way out of military service; and merchants and artisans who make articles of no practical use, accrue wealth and exploit farmers. 'These groups are the vermin of the state. If the rulers do not wipe out such vermin . . . Then they should not be surprised . . . to see states perish and ruling houses wane and die.'

On reading this, King Zheng could have felt the contemporary equivalent of an air-punched '*Shi!*' ('Yes!'), but came out with something rather more formal. '"Alas!"' he said to Li Si,' in Sima Qian's account. '"If I could once catch sight of this man and move with him, I would die without regret.'

'Li Si said: "These writings have been made by Han Fei,"' and would surely have explained that this man had once been his fellow student, and had remained in Han, trying, without much success, to secure a position as royal adviser. King Zheng could only bide his time.

Soon after this, in 234 BC, to meet some unspecified 'critical situation', King Zheng planned an attack on his junior ally, Han, the state where Han Fei had been trying to convince his own king of the merits of his uncompromising Legalism. Unexpectedly under threat, the Han king suddenly decided that Han Fei must know what he was talking about, and sent him off to Xianyang as an ambassador to King Zheng, with a persuasive list of reasons for restraint. Han, he argued, had always been as submissive as a straw mat, had supplied Qin with soldiers, and had paid tribute; but, having endured the attacks of others, it had also taken care to build up its defences. It would not be a pushover. An attack might weaken Qin, and offer others a chance. Best, surely, to conserve one's strength for assaults on Qin's real enemies.

Zheng was delighted to see him, until Li Si, in what seems to have been a fit of jealousy, warned the king that Han Fei was, after all, a Han, and that his home state was where his loyalties would always lie. His memo was nothing more than self-serving deception: Although Han is Qin's vassal, there has never been a time when it has not been a disease to Qin. War on other fronts would simply grant Han a chance to attack. Han Fei 'makes dialectical speeches and well-rounded phrases,

72

and utters falsehoods and invents cunning plots . . . while he spies on Your Majesty for Han's benefit'. 'Such is human nature. If now Your Highness . . . returns him after detaining him for a long time, this will bring disaster upon yourself. The best thing would be to punish him for having transgressed the laws.'

It was a spiteful thing to do, to betray a fellow student, a foreign envoy and a thinker with whom he was in full agreement. Zheng concurred, and Han Fei was arrested. To make sure that there would be no comeback by his former colleague, Li Si made it impossible for Han Fei to see the king; then, with his prisoner reduced to despair, he had poison sent into the prison and induced him to commit suicide.[7]

Li Si was on his own, unrivalled, free to advise his young monarch, guiding him to conquest, unification and an empire of this world and the next.

---

[7] Another source (*Zhanguo Ce / Stratagems of the Warring States*) implicates a certain Yao Jia, but Bodde dismisses it as unreliable: 'The motives . . . for Li Si's deed are sufficiently strong, and make the reasons for absolving him unconvincing.'

CHAPTER 5

THE MAKING OF CHINA

Given the speed with which King Zheng conquered all his six rivals – in eleven years, 230–221 BC – you might think that the army possessed some secret weapon. Not so. The same repertoire of equipment – bows, arrows, halberds, swords, armour – was used by all the warring states; even the crossbow, a devastatingly effective weapon because it was far more powerful than an ordinary bow, and could be prepared and held ready like a loaded rifle.

The crossbow is worth a small digression because crossbow triggers were found when the Terracotta Army was first unearthed, which may seem to suggest that Qin had a monopoly on this fearsome weapon. In fact, the days of aristocrats with bows and arrows exchanging shots from chariots were long gone, and the crossbow had been in wide use for over a century, as Sima Qian's account of a famous battle near Maling (in western Shandong, almost on the Henan border) shows.

It took place in 341 BC. A Qi army, advised by Sun Bin, a descendant of *The Art of War*'s author, had invaded Wei, and was being pursued to Maling by Wei troops commanded by Pang Juan. One evening, Sun Bin saw that the Wei army was about to enter a certain defile which was ideal for a night-time ambush:

> He cut down a big tree, whittled off the bark and wrote on the exposed white wood: 'Pang Juan will die under this tree!' Then he got together 10,000 of his best crossbow marksmen, hid them along the narrow road, and ordered: 'Shoot together if you see a fire lit!' Pang Juan came across the place where the tree had been felled. He saw there was something white with writing on it, so he lit a torch. Before he had finished reading what was written on it, the 10,000 crossbows fired together and the Wei forces fell about in disorder. Pang Juan realized that his whole force was lost through his own lack of judgement and so he committed suicide, saying 'So much for my reputation now!'

A decade or so later, it was the state of Han, apparently, that had the best crossbowmen. An ambassador to Han commented on them: they 'have a range of more than 600 paces. Your Han troops use their feet to pull their crossbows and when they shoot, not a shot in one hundred fails in its effect: they pierce the chest of an enemy who is far off.' According to one source,[1] cross-bowmen used bows with a draw-weight of up to 12 *shi*, which is just over 350 kilos.[2]

We are not concerned with the most powerful weapons, because they took time to load, and in the heat of battle there was no time. You can see the remains of a crossbow – actually more like a fossil – preserved in the earth in the Terracotta Army Museum, and it is quite simple, loaded probably by standing on the bow and hauling the string back with both hands until it was caught and held by the trigger.

It was the bronze trigger that was the key to

[1] Quoted in Selby, *Archery Traditions of China* and *Chinese Archery*, which are my major sources here.
[2] This is a murky subject. No one could have loaded a 350 kg bow by hand, even lying down. Pulling a bowstring like this is like performing a 'deadlift' in weightlifting, with the severe handicap of pulling on a string rather than a bar. Today's world record deadlift is about 440 kg, almost 1,000 lb, achieved by super-heavyweights. For the world record in 'flight archery', firing an arrow by muscle power alone (1.8 km in 1971), the American Harry Drake lay on his back, placed his feet on the bow and pulled the bowstring with both hands. His bow's draw-weight was 'only' 300 lb (136 kg). To draw a bow over two and a half times that 'weight' needed a lever or winch (as Europe also discovered some 1,600 years later), though no examples have survived. On the other hand, units of weight varied over time by anything up to threefold, so perhaps we are talking of crossbows with draw-weights of only 120 kg.

the military crossbow, because it held the taut bowstring in place until the moment of release. Triggers were wonderful devices. As Joseph Needham puts it in his monumental *Science and Civilisation in China*, they were 'among the greatest triumphs of ancient metallurgical and engineering practice in any civilisation'.[3] In its most sophisticated form, the crossbow trigger consisted of up to six pieces of bronze, which all fitted together on two shafts in the stock of the bow. It would cock automatically, and may even have had a safety catch. It had to have the precision of a bolt-action rifle. As Lü Buwei (or rather, one of his commissioned authors) put it in his *Spring and Autumn Annals*, 'If the mechanism of a crossbow trigger is out of alignment by no more than the size of a rice-grain, it will not work.' This was what made the crossbow the ancient equivalent of the Kalashnikov: sophisticated but simple, easily made, easily dismantled, easily maintained.

But triggers had been around for 400 years before unification (the first known triggers date from about 650 BC). Possibly there was something special about Qin bronze casting techniques that made their triggers better than anyone else's. Possibly also Qin cross-bowmen had sighting devices that improved accuracy. But it was not

[3] Needham, *Science and Civilisation in China*, vol. 5, sec. 30.

any substantial advantage in weaponry that under-pinned Qin's military successes. What was it, then? Something obviously did, or there would have been no conquests, and no reason to commemor-ate the army full-size in terracotta.

The answer lay in organization, on every level. Qin society was a state-sized fighting machine. At its heart, under King Zheng's iron hand, were three interdependent elements: efficient agricul-ture, based on the rich farmland of the Wei valley, which provided food and excess manpower; a committed bureaucracy which gathered taxes, made lists of recruits, oversaw irrigation and managed the food supply to the army; and the army itself, a large, professional force.

The army was the nation's spearhead: tough, mobile and highly disciplined, the product of years of training for men and commanders alike. They could march 50 kilometres a day in leather armour, carrying crossbows, pikes, swords, and provisions for three days. The main force, which could be divided, was backed up by separate groups of reinforcements, the whole being co-ordinated by messengers in four-horse chariots. And of course the commanders all knew the vital importance of quick and accurate commands on the battlefield, as Sun Zi had recognized over a century earlier: 'Gongs and drums, banners and flags are used to unify the action of the troops. When the troops can be thus united, the brave cannot advance alone, nor can the cowardly withdraw. This is the art of directing large masses of troops.'

No doubt discipline underlay the way crossbowmen fought, for the layout of the Terracotta Army shows them in front of the infantry. Possibly they operated as an eleventh-century source described.[4] A crossbow 'needs to be used so that the men within the formation are loading while the men in the front line of the formation are shooting . . . each in their turn draw their crossbows and come up; then as soon as they have shot bolts they return again into the formation. Thus the sound of the crossbows is incessant and the enemy can hardly even flee. Therefore we have the following drill: shooting rank – advancing rank – loading rank.'

We cannot be sure, because there are no contemporary accounts of the way crossbowmen and infantry interacted, but it seems we should imagine a Qin army engaging their crossbowmen rather as early nineteenth-century European armies used their riflemen, advancing rank by rank, each kneeling, firing and reloading in sequence, except that crossbowmen withdrew after firing, allowing the next rank its turn, instead of advancing before firing.

There was nothing new in any one element. It was the whole coordinated package – the food

[4] Zeng Gongliang, quoted in Needham, *Science and Civilisation in China*, vol. 5, see 30, p. 122.

supply, the recruitment, the vision of conquest and unity, centralized control, communication, training, discipline, weaponry – that set the Qin army apart. Thus, for the first time in Chinese history, an army arose dedicated not simply to victory in battle but to the conquest of territory, from which Qin would gain more food, men, weapons and forward bases, all of which would secure progress and provide the foundation for yet more conquest.

Of the conquests themselves, hardly anything is recorded, except their dates. Han fell in 230, Zhou two years later.

Then there came a three-year hiatus, marked by an incident so famous that it has become a popular subject for film and TV dramatization, most effectively in the epic *The Emperor and the Assassin* (1998),[5] directed by Chen Kaige, one of the 'new wave' or 'fifth generation' of Chinese film-makers, who had won international recognition five years previously with the intimate, restrained *Farewell My Concubine*. *The Emperor and the Assassin* was the opposite – a vast canvas, huge personalities, epic battle sequences. Leaving aside the love interest, provided by the delectable Gong Li, Chen Kaige's main source was Sima Qian, whose

[5] Two others are Quentin Tarantino's martial arts epic *Hero* (2002) and *The Emperor's Shadow* (directed by Zhou Xiaowen, 1996).

account is as vivid as a film synopsis. Here it is, with his words as dialogue:

The back-story:
Prince Dan, the heir apparent of Qin's neighbour once removed, Yan, lives in fear of King Zheng. Two states have already fallen, and his is next in line. Dan and Zheng have known each other as young men. Moreover, Dan was a hostage in the Qin court, where he was so badly treated that he fled. Not long before, a Qin general, Fan Yuqi, defected, and is now under the protection of Prince Dan. The general needs all the protection he can get, for Zheng has offered a reward of a city plus 250 kilos of gold ($5.25 million, at today's rates) for his head.
  We open on Dan's tutor warning him of trouble:

TUTOR:
This will not do! Violent as the King of Qin is, and with the resentment he nurses against Yan because of your escape, it is already enough to make one's heart run cold.

Zhou has just fallen, he says, Qin troops are massing on Yan's border, and the only way to stop Zheng's meteoric rise is by finding an assassin to kill him.

(In Chen Kaige's film, the plot is all carefully orchestrated by the emperor, who wants to inspire an attempted assassination to give him a reason for declaring war on Yan. This is where Gong Li comes in. She is the king's favourite concubine, the love of his life, and it is she who decides to initiate the plot by having her face branded, then pretending to defect to Yan, her branded face giving her an apparent motive for betraying the emperor. It is she who then finds the assassin, with whom, in another twist, she falls in love.)

Back to Sima Qian:

The emperor's death will surely spark revolt from the dispossessed feudal lords, and Zheng's Legalist revolution will be reversed. A young adventurer named Jing Ke is chosen for the task. He is an ice-cool character of high intelligence, who likes 'to read books and practise swordsmanship'. He refuses to quarrel: if offended, he simply walks away.

Jing Ke is too smart to agree at once, but his reluctance is overcome by being made a minister and given a mansion. Knowing he has no chance of getting close to Zheng without a good excuse, he approaches the renegade Qin general, Fan, with an extraordinary suggestion: if only he can have the general's head, he will go to Zheng offering Yan's surrender, with the head as a sign of good faith. He will also have a map of Yan territory. These two items will gain him access. Inside the rolled-up map he plans to conceal a poisoned dagger, with which he will stab Zheng.

The general finds this an excellent plan –

GENERAL FAN:
Day and night I gnash my teeth and eat
out my heart trying to think of some plan.
Now you have shown me the way!

– *and obligingly cuts his own throat.*
Head and map gain Jing Ke and an accomplice
entry into the court, and an audience with the king.
At this moment the accomplice has an attack of
nerves, leaving Jing Ke to go on alone. Watched by
a crowd of courtiers, Jing Ke unrolls his map, seizes
the dagger, grabs the king by the sleeve, and strikes.
The king leaps back, tearing off his sleeve, and Jing
Ke's lunge misses its mark. Zheng flees with the
assassin in pursuit, while the unarmed courtiers
stand back, appalled, watching their lord and master
dodging around a pillar, trying in vain to untangle
his long ceremonial sword from his robes. A doctor
has the presence of mind to hit Jing Ke with his
medicine-bag, which gives the king a moment's
grace.

CROWD:
Push the scabbard around behind you!

Even as Jing Ke comes at him again, the king
manages to untangle his sword, draw it and wound
Jing Ke in the leg. Jing Ke hurls the poisoned dagger,
misses, and falls back as the king strikes at him,
wounding him again. Jing Ke, seeing he has failed,
leans against the pillar, then squats down, alternately

laughing hysterically and cursing the king. The crowd moves in and finishes him off.

This is a terrific story, perhaps Sima Qian's best, and one which he claimed to have from the horse's mouth – friends of the doctor, Xia Wuju, who hit Jing Ke with his bag, thus becoming the only one among the emperor's lily-livered courtiers to do anything, and probably saving the emperor's life. The two friends 'learned from him exactly what happened', writes Sima Qian. 'I have therefore reported everything just as they told me.'

To bridge the intervening century is a stretch, but possible. The assassination attempt was in 227 BC; the (young) doctor might have lived until (say) 180 BC. Imagine him as an old man telling his story to two open-mouthed teenagers, who could have lived until 130 BC. In their old age, the two could have passed on the tale to the future grand historian, who would have been a teenager himself when he heard the story.

An insatiable desire for security in an uncertain world now further fuelled Zheng's drive to national unity. Campaign followed campaign, all justified (as is the way of conquerors) by reference to broken promises and perceived acts of aggression. With attacks, counter-attacks, setbacks and final victories, Wei fell in 225, Chu in 223, Yan – the source of the head, the poisoned dagger and the would-be assassin – in 222, and finally Qi in the far east in 221.

The First Emperor thus came to be lord not only of six other kingdoms and their cities, but of dozens, scores, probably hundreds of tribal peoples, a few of whose names survive in the records: the Sushen of the bleak north-east borderlands; the nomadic Donghu of the northern grasslands; a dozen groups of south-western 'barbarians', both settled and semi-nomadic; the half-dozen tribes of Sichuan, among them the slave-raiding Po and the Zuo, named after the bamboo- and-rope bridges they built to span Sichuan's ravines; the hunting-and-fishing Yue groups of the south-east – the whole patchwork of peoples that foreshadow today's 56 nationalities.

Qin became recognizably the core of today's China, for Chinese and foreigners alike, though under different names. Those in the heartland, roughly the seven rival states united by the First Emperor, had long referred to their lands as the centre, the 'Central Nation' or 'Middle Kingdom' (*zhong guo*). So it has remained. But not to foreigners. Now unified from the borders of Tibet to the Pacific, from the Inner Mongolian escarpment to the South China Sea, this region was gradually equated by outsiders with its dominant power. Thus, as the name passed from language to language across Eurasia, did Qin become China.

CHAPTER 6

A RUTHLESS FRENZY

This was to be a new age, as the first Emperor declared: 'Insignificant person that I am, I have called up troops to punish violence and rebellion. Thanks to the help of the ancestral spirits, these six kings have acknowledged their guilt and the world is in profound order.' Qin had succeeded Zhou as the nation's heart and soul, with consequences far beyond mere military conquest. Now would begin what Germany's Nazi regime called *Gleichschaltung*, the centralizing process that seized total control over all aspects of society.

It started, as Nazism did, with a title. How was the king to be addressed now that he was sole ruler? As everyone agreed, never before had such a huge area been unified; never before had laws proceeded from a single authority. Only the grandest title ever conferred on a king would suit: Greatly (*dà*) August (*huáng*), one of the legendary emperors who had founded Chinese civilization some 2,000 years before. But Zheng, emperor by the grace of Heaven, did not like the idea of a precedent, understandably, because legend spoke of three emperors, or five, or somehow both. The five were known as the Wu Di, the Five Emperors, and they were considered to be the embodiments of wisdom and purity. Di was also a term for the highest supernatural power. Zheng came to the logical conclusion: 'We will drop the Greatly, keep the August and adopt the title used by the emperors of high antiquity': Huang Di, often translated as August Emperor, thus declaring himself imperial ruler, god, sage and ancestor all in one.[1] Moreover he was to be the first, the beginning, the *shi̯*. His heirs would bear the same title with their number added – Second, Third, Fourth – unto the ten thousandth generation of Qin emperors. Many books call him by his full title: Qin Shi Huang Di, The First Qin August Emperor. Some academics would like to call him a 'thearch', on the grounds that he headed a thearchy or theocracy, a god-ruled state, which is unlikely to catch on, partly because it is obscure and partly because it encourages lesser mortals to call him The Arch. For the sake of simplicity, let's go with 'the First Emperor'.

[1] This gets even more complicated, because Huang Di sounds the same as a different *huáng*, meaning yellow, recalling by a pun one of the legendary Five, the Yellow Emperor.

The First Emperor, raised on the fringe of the Chinese heartland, was not noted for his intellect, and he had just achieved something that must have seemed miraculous. Heaven was surely with him. To understand himself, his achievement and his future, he turned to those who claimed to know the ways of Heaven.

According to a popular line of Daoist thought, each historical age was dominated by one of the five elements: earth, wood, metal, fire and water, which overwhelm each other in a fixed cycle, like a cosmic version of the children's game of scissors-rock-paper. Zhou had ruled through the power of fire. Its successor, Qin, would be the age of water, which extinguishes fire. Water had certain attributes, its colour being black, its number six. So flags became black, six the preferred unit of length for measuring almost anything, from the height of hats to the width of chariot-axles.

Then there was a public statement of the emperor's achievement to be made to his own people, and thanks to be given to the spirits of Qin for victory. This involved a royal progress to Qin's western border, 470 kilometres away, and up a sacred mountain, Qitou, an expedition that served as a trial run for tours to more distant parts of the new empire a few years later.

This was all very well as a way of beginning a dynasty. But how was one to avoid its dissolution? Only by ensuring control of the forces that governed the sequence of ages. This did not mean, as is often assumed, living for ever in this life, but ensuring immortality in the next. Daoist mystics, self-proclaimed sages who called themselves True Men, claimed to know how to achieve this by finding and drinking a certain elixir. Sima Qian wrote of one famous mystic called Zou Yan, whose followers practised his arts, but could not understand them: 'Thereupon there arose innumerable persons who were skilled in extraordinary prodigies, in deceiving flatteries, and who knew how to win people over' – in particular, this new and superstitious emperor.

Remember that Sima Qian was aiming his barbs at his own emperor, Wu, who was also prey to quackery and dreams of immortality; so some of this must be taken as deliberate exaggeration. You get a sense of what is unreliable when he becomes vague. But the Grand Historian backed these generalities up with a convincing detail. A team of 'magicians' submitted a memo suggesting a research trip: 'In the middle of the sea [by which they meant the Pacific somewhere between China and Japan] there are three supernatural mountains called Penglai, Fangzhang and Yingzhou. Immortals dwell there. We beg that after we have been purified, we may, together with young boys and girls, go there to seek for them.' At once, the First Emperor dispatched the expedition – other sources speak of 3,000 boys and 3,000 girls, though Sima Qian offers no numbers. Anyway, they were never heard of again. It was rumoured that the expedition ended up in Japan. Undeterred, the First Emperor sent out another equally useless expedition six years later.

The same year the First Emperor ordered a revolution in administration. Out went the old kingdoms and their feudal hierarchies; in came three dozen centrally controlled commanderies, under a chancellor, three deputy chancellors and nine ministers, all mirrored by a parallel military hierarchy. The commanderies were subdivided into several hundred prefectures (about the size of counties), and on down to districts, cantons and hamlets. Each commandery had both a civil and a military administrator, together with tax collectors, judges and officials, all of whom reported directly to the emperor.

Former ruling families – 120,000 of them, according to Sima Qian – were all moved to Xianyang, the Qin capital, where the First Emperor could keep an eye on them. But wait: 120,000 *families*? That's about 600,000 people. But Xianyang was never *that* big. Frankly, it's incredible: another of the extreme 'statistics' that Sima Qian throws into his text to exaggerate the emperor's authoritarian policies. Then come more startling numbers: from all the six defeated states, weapons were collected and melted down to make bells and twelve vast statues of barbarians, each weighing a conveniently round 1,000 piculs (about 30 or 50 or 60 tonnes, for sources vary; again, a figure to be taken with a large pinch of salt).

So much had been confused when China was divided. Each of the seven states had used different measures of area, different widths for cart-axles, different laws, coins, weights, measures, styles of clothing, and scripts. Under the direction of the great Li Si, all were now collated, unified and imposed nation-wide. From now on, for instance, vehicles had a standard gauge, with results that you can see today on the stone floors of many old gateways, like Cloud Terrace beside the Great Wall outside Beijing, worn away in two deep ruts by the passage of countless wagons and their evenly spaced wheels.

The revision of the script and its widespread imposition was perhaps the one change that ensured China's future unity, because governments could issue edicts that everyone everywhere could read, even if their pronunciations varied wildly. Away went the old script variants, with their curly lines, replaced with what came to be called the Small Seal script. It was this script, with its straight-line brush-strokes, that evolved into today's. As a result, as Derk Bodde puts it, 'China has suffered political disunity, but never has there been a time when she has lost her cultural continuity, a fact which explains why, of all the great civilisations of antiquity, hers is the only one to survive today.'

Labour now became available on an unprecedented scale, not only because of the empire's vastly extended population but because hundreds of thousands of soldiers had been freed by the ending of the wars of conquest. Peasants had always been liable to forced service as soldiers and labourers in their own kingdoms. Now they were called up nation-wide. Every male between 15 and 60 was eligible for labour on state projects; so a population of about 20 million could provide a workforce of perhaps one or two million a year (one prime source of labour being criminals), with many older men left to work the fields – without which the economy would collapse. Over the next decade, a national system of paved roads arose, including an 800-kilometre north-south highway of rammed earth across the Ordos – and this at least is backed by evidence, because parts of the road are still visible today, as are the remains of five royal palaces, nine command depots and numerous beacon-hillocks. Other roads fanned out from Xianyang, adding up to a grand total of some 6,750 kilometres.

Supposedly, the grandest of the First Emperor's projects was the Great Wall, the most massive state enterprise since the building of the pyramids, with millions drafted in to build it, and millions dying in the process. I say 'supposedly' because the evidence is scanty, consisting of a few lines in the only source, Sima Qian's *History*.

The project was under the command of Meng Tian, one of the emperor's top generals. In 215

BC, six years after unification, Meng Tian took an army of 300,000, headed north across the Ordos, chased out two barbarian tribes and 'set about constructing the Great Wall, following the contours of the land and utilizing the narrow defiles to set up frontier posts'. When finished, it extended 'for a distance of over ten thousand *li*', about 5,000 kilometres. Reading most non-specialist sources, you get the impression that the First Emperor built the Great Wall as it exists today north of Beijing, but stretching all the way across the empire's northern border. Not so. The *wàn* (10,000) is not an exact distance, but a frequent synonym for 'very large number'; and it is unlikely that any of this wall was of stone. Whatever was built from scratch was of rammed earth, and most of it has now vanished or been incorporated into other, later, walls. There is a stone section labelled 'Qin Great Wall' north of Baotou, but it was probably built by the king of Zhou around 300 BC, some 80 years before Meng Tian hijacked it and made it the Qin frontier. Nor did the First Emperor build a single Great Wall from nothing. What he did was to repair and join up a collection of little walls; a project which, considering its 2,500-kilometre length, was quite enough to keep his million-plus work-force employed between his accession and his death. It seems that the First Emperor's Great Wall, if we are talking about one structure built on his orders, is a figment of later imagination,

93

made to seem solid by confusion with later and earlier walls, and given spurious historical roots in history by Sima Qian's vague words.

Oppression, brutality, excess and barbarism: these were the elements that formed the dynasty's later reputation, confirmed (so later generations believed) by two acts in particular. They are known as the Burning of the Books and the Burial of the Scholars. To destroy the records of the past and to bury alive one's intellectuals would indeed call forth condemnation. But, bad as the First Emperor was, it is possible he was not quite as bad as is generally believed.

The book-burning comes first. The story started at a banquet in the palace in Xianyang in 213 BC. Scholars and officials delivered eulogies to the empire. But one conservative, bolder than the rest, warned of trouble. Previous emperors, he said, had rewarded their sons, younger brothers and meritorious ministers with estates. Not so the First Emperor, who had broken with the past by destroying feudalism. This was bad news, for 'I have never heard of any undertaking that failed to imitate the example of antiquity, and yet was able to endure for long!' He went on to speak of the emperor's 'error', and of the disloyalty of his flattering ministers.

The man must have been out of his mind, for the emperor had come to absolute power by doing the exact opposite. The emperor's leadership training would have told him to make no reaction, to retain his mystery at all costs. So it was his bulldog, Grand Councillor Li Si, the second most powerful man in the empire, who responded, in a furious memo to the emperor:

In the past, the empire was in confusion and fragmented. Why? Because rulers disparaged the present by 'declaiming on antiquity'. They didn't see the need to sweep away the old, as His Majesty has done. His Majesty has unified all under heaven, yet still there are those who criticize and debate, which they can do because they have access to the opinions of others. And they're proud of it! If such behaviour is not prohibited, 'then in upper circles the authority of the ruler will be compromised, and in lower ones cliques will form'. The answer is to ban works of literature and poetry, historical documents and 'the sayings of the hundred schools of philosophy'. They should all be destroyed, Sima Qian has him say in one chapter (87, Li Si's biography), and anyone failing to destroy such books within a month should be branded and subjected to forced labour. In another chapter (6, 'The Basic Annals of the First Emperor'), the punishments are much more dire. Li Si demands that

all persons in the empire daring to store [these books] should go to the administrative and military governors so that these

95

books may be indiscriminately burned. Those who dare to discuss the *Odes* and the *Histories* should be [executed and their bodies] exposed in the market place. Those who use the past to criticize the present should be put to death together with their relatives.

The emperor agreed to this Orwellian attempt at mind control. The books would be destroyed 'for the purpose of making the people ignorant', and so that no one should 'use the past to discredit the present'. So it happened. The poetry books and the historical sources, which were all in the royal archives, 'were all destroyed. How regrettable! How regrettable!' This was the act known as the Burning of the Books, for which the First Emperor has been demonized as the destroyer of China's literary heritage.

But hang on. How bad was it really? Much was to be spared, as were certain people: the records of Qin; books on medicine and pharmacy, divination, arboriculture and agriculture; the 70 officials of the Bureau of Scholars of Wide Learning. True, the poetry and history in the royal archives vanished, but most of the poetry books survived in private hands. 'Destroy' becomes 'burned' from one chapter to another, almost as if Sima Qian were keen to make bad into worse. There is something particularly nasty about burning books: it is a symbolic, public act of reducing information and opinion to nothing, used by other totalitarians, particularly religious zealots, in attempts to destroy a competing religion, or a heresy, or unacceptable behaviour.[2] Sima Qian knew that book-burning was on the Legalist agenda. Remember Han Fei's account of how Lord Shang taught Duke Xiao of Qin about informants, and his advice about burning books of poetry and history? There is no evidence that Xiao actually burned any books, but it was an idea Sima Qian could tap into in order to discredit the First Emperor. Many scholars agree that this was less total destruction than an attempt to impose a state monopoly on certain subjects.

Derk Bodde, my main source for this analysis, even finds a silver lining to this cloud: the fact that books were destroyed made the Chinese inordinately conscious of their heritage. 'The result has been the development of what may almost be called a cult of books in China, and a tremendous reinforcement of the interest, already strong, of the historically-minded Chinese in their historical records ... Thus did Li Si's aim defeat itself!'

Anyway, the destruction was nothing compared

[2] Perhaps the most infamous example was the burning of 20,000 Jewish books by the Nazis in Berlin on 10 May 1933. A Wikipedia article lists 50 other examples, including Muslims burning Salman Rushdie's *Satanic Verses* and three Christian churches in the USA burning Harry Potter books.

to that unleashed when the dynasty fell, or to the gradual loss of material later as century succeeded century: Bodde points out that of 677 works listed in the Han imperial library – the first Chinese bibliography – 524, or 77 per cent, vanished not by wilful destruction but simply through carelessness and decay.

And what of the punishments? Sima Qian does not say; there is no evidence that anyone was actually executed for the possession of banned books. That raises a point about the harshness of Qin law. It was indeed severe in principle, but how was it applied in practice? Until recently, no one could say, because neither the laws themselves nor the sentences were known; all that survived were adverse comments by later writers. But in 1975 workers digging a drainage canal in central Hubei province discovered some graves, one of which was that of a Qin official named Xi who was buried in about 217 BC. It contained 1,155 strips of bamboo – the standard material for writing on in those pre-paper times – half of which recorded Qin laws, court cases and punishments.[3] These show that justice could indeed be harsh, with death sentences that included beheading, being torn apart by carriages, boiling to death in a cauldron and quartering, and lesser sentences like banishment and mutilation (amputations of the

[3] This analysis is based on Hulsewé's *Remnants of Qin Law*.

nose and of one or both feet, removal of kneecaps), which might or might not be combined with hard labour (especially wall-building). In 1973 nine neck-irons were unearthed near the emperor's tomb; these were used to fetter prisoners who had served their gaol terms, during a three-year stint of forced labour on public works.[4] Castration seems to have been reserved for the privileged, which was lucky for the underprivileged.

It sounds grim. But perhaps it was not *that* grim. The actual case records show that in practice Qin law was rather more lenient than its code suggests. Investigations were meticulous. A report on a man found murdered by the roadside describes the exact location, the wounds, the clothing, and the shoes found at some distance from the body. Investigators were told to exercise patience with suspects, and avoid torture, which produced inferior evidence. Those convicted could ask for a retrial. Officials had to consider precedents that modified the written law. A distinction was made between manslaughter (punished by a heavy fine) and murder, for which the killer unsheathed a weapon (long-term forced labour, please note, not execution).

In general, the laws reveal a complexity and sophistication rather at odds with Qin's reputation for barbarism. It was not so much the laws

[4] Ledderose and Schlombs, *Jenseits der Grossen Mauer*, pp. 212–13.

that oppressed as their abuse, as the First Emperor's demands drove the Qin economy into crisis.

Xianyang was now a capital of unprecedented wealth, with grand Qin-style houses for the newly tamed aristocracy and others in the styles of the conquered territories. But it had not been conceived to be this size. And the original palace on its platform overlooking the flood plain of the Wei was not really impressive enough for the emperor of all China. 'In view of the large population of Xianyang,' writes Sima Qian, 'the palace of the former kings of Qin was too small.'

Nor was it in quite the right place. The First Emperor looked south and east, across the Wei, towards present-day Xian. He had good reason to do so. Xian was well supplied with little rivers, but was not hemmed in by large ones; it had a big river (the Wei) to the north and mountains to the south, which meant that from the point of view of geomancy, it had good *feng shui*. In addition, it was within easy reach of the burial grounds of the First Emperor's immediate ancestors. In 212 BC he gave the order to start work on an immense new project, his palace in Epang. Already, as we shall see in more detail in chapter 8, an army of labourers were working on the tomb in Lintong. Together, says Sima Qian, the workforce totalled 700,000, all criminals – 'persons condemned to castration and convict labourers' – a figure that is surely inflated tenfold or more.

Xianyang, Epang, Xian, Lintong: these four places are linked by roads which swoop between them as if traversing the base of a bowl some 70 kilometres across. Given the phenomenal rise in tourism to Xian and the Terracotta Army, and given that airborne visitors land at Xianyang airport, all four will eventually be linked by a light railway. To the First Emperor this would have seemed right and proper.

We will be returning to the tomb and its army many times in the following pages, but first let me take you in the opposite direction: to Epang, the site of the emperor's new palace on the western outskirts of Xian. It's a little hard to find, partly because there is so much disagreement on how to pronounce it. Locals say 'Erpang', but in E-pang the first character may also be pronounced 'ah', and the second one is a rare sign that looks like *fang* (house), so that's what outsiders say and what many maps record. Epang, Er-pang, Ah-fang, even O-pang, if you follow the old Wade–Giles version – it's very confusing, especially as no one seems sure what it means either. Some claim it means 'Next to', i.e. next to Xianyang. I have even been told that the emperor had a concubine called Epang, and this was a palace dedicated to her. Best to avoid speculation: it's the name of the place and the palace, period.

Epang was intended to dwarf the First Emperor's Xianyang palace: some 690 metres long and 115 metres wide, according to Sima Qian.[5] Could this be true? At 79,000 square metres, it would have been larger than the modern world's most extreme expression of megalomania, Nicolae Ceauşescu's Palace of the People. Above a ground floor with 11-metre ceilings, its upper hall was to seat 10,000 people. Apparently, work was started on this immense project. Stone was quarried from the northern hills, timber brought from the south, and 'an elevated walk' built across the river Wei to Xianyang, some 25 kilometres away.

There is a site marked on some maps, so I could check on the First Emperor's ambitions. We – my driver Wang, Tony and I – turned down side-roads in the suburbs of western Xian, and pulled up by something that looked promising: a huge structure of pyramidal stone bases topped by wooden towers with austere roofs in the Qin style, lacking the usual upturned eaves. It called itself the Epang Palace. Well, not exactly. It was built in 1984, and it doesn't face south, as a palace should, because it has to welcome the tourist cars and buses that come along the road to the north. It is guarded by twelve statues recalling the 30- (or 50-, or 60-) tonne ones supposedly made from the weapons

[5] 500 *bu* long (1 *bu* = 1.38 metres) × 50 *zhang* wide (1 *zhang* = 2.31 metres), according to Loewe, *Records of Han Administration*.

of Qin's conquered states, and by two mythical animals that embody fierceness, each with the head of a lion, an eagle's claws, a wolf's body and a tiger's tail. Inside is an amphitheatre, and a giant stairway to a hall where an actor playing the First Emperor is regaled by dancing girls. It is not too surprising to learn that the place was built as a film set, and features in practically every film and docu-drama about the First Emperor, except Chen Kaige's.

Its only claim to authenticity is that it stands opposite the site of the original Epang Palace, which at first glance was far less inviting, being a cross between a rubbish tip and a ploughed field. Still, we could drive in, because the mess was crossed by 200 metres of new road, the first step in some grand new plan yet to be realized.

We knew we were in the right place because, beside a sad collection of bushes that served as a visitors' toilet, a stele – an engraved stone pillar – laid claim to forgotten grandeur: 'This is one of the most famous traditional complexes in China,' it began, 'the location of the first political centre in Chinese history.' Moreover, it continued, archaeological research suggests it was even bigger than Sima Qian claimed: 1,270 metres from east to west and 426 metres from north to south, which means – the stele concluded – that 'the front hall of the Epang Palace was the largest basement to survive in China, if not the world'. You could hardly find a greater contrast between the grandness of the claim and the poverty of the site.

Where the palace itself had stood was unclear at first. It was only the fact that something was being planned here that drew me on, past a dip that was going to be a lake, and an unfinished basketball court. Beyond was a steep bank of earth about 3 metres high, topped by orchards. That was it: it had to be, because, as we climbed the bank, we emerged on to a plateau. This was a platform, which, like old Xianyang, was an ideal base for a palace, with a fine view southward. A glance east and west showed it was at least a kilometre long, as the stele said. Imagination turned the earth platform and fruit trees into a palace under construction: a line of arches below, a great assembly hall above, several hundred thousand workers landscaping and laying foundations.

But that was about as far as things got, because two years later the First Emperor died and work ground to a halt. It was supposedly finished by his heir, and then burned to the ground in the revolution that threw out the Qin. Sima Qian says the flames lasted for three months.

But here's a strange thing: when archaeologists probed the site in the autumn of 2002,[6] they

[6] The team was from the Institute of Archaeology of the Chinese Academy of Social Sciences (CASS), in co-operation with the Xian Municipal Archaeological Research Institute.

found no trace of fire. 'We found burned red soil and traces of ashes during our excavation of the Xianyang Palace, but we've found nothing of the kind at the site of the Epang Palace,' the team leader Li Yufang told the Beijing-based *Guangming Daily*. They didn't find much else, either. 'We found tiles of the Qin Dynasty,' she said, 'but not a single piece of eaves tile, which was the most common part of buildings of the period.' Floor-tiles, no roof-tiles, no ashes, no fire-hardened earth: it all suggests that the palace was started, but never completed.

Tony and I wandered round among the fruit trees. A hundred metres away was a long plastic polytunnel that might have been covering an archaeological dig, but was in fact shielding vegetables. An old farm worker dozed in the shade of a peach tree in a reclining chair, soothed by a radio blaring – I could hardly believe it – Qin opera.

'Did you know that China invented ice-cream?' remarked Tony. 'Actually, it was the First Emperor. When the archaeologists were here, they found a hole that went down very deep and ended in a little room. It must have been an ice-well, which they filled with ice in the winter so the First Emperor could have ice all through the summer.'

It seemed a bit of a leap from hole to ice to ice-cream, but the find supported the general idea that this had been a dream-palace. What we were standing on was the foundation not just of the palace, but of a myth – that the Epang Palace was the hugest ever built, that it was not only the fount of political power but also the expression of unprecedented wealth. It has also been seen as an expression of egomania, a vast waste of national resources, and a symbol of oppression that inspired revolution and the end of a dynasty that was to have lasted 10,000 generations. Some of this was true: referring to the Second Emperor, who restarted work on the palace, Sima Qian quotes Li Si as saying, 'For the making of the Epang Palace, he has exacted taxes throughout the empire . . . without regard for the expenditure.' Plans and taxes never added up to a palace. It was not this unfinished enterprise that became the focus of discontent, but the tomb and its spirit army.

Yet with hindsight the idea of building such a structure with such a workforce suggests that the First Emperor was becoming somewhat divorced from reality – and not without reason. He was emperor by the grace of Heaven, yet he was surrounded by enemies, not just Confucians eager to turn back the clock, but also would-be assassins. The suspicions that must have dogged him ever since the Jing Ke episode were confirmed by an odd incident that had its roots in that affair.

On the conquest of Yan, the First Emperor had initiated a drive to uncover all those who had been part of the plot five years before. One of them, a certain Gao Jianli, went into hiding, changed his name and became a simple labourer. It happened that he was an accomplished lute-player, a talent that came to the attention of his master. Eventually, his fame spread to court, and he was invited to play before the emperor. A mistake. Someone recognized him, and he would have been put to death, had not the emperor admired his talent. So he got off lightly: his eyes were put out, and he was kept on as a court musician. Gao, though, wanted revenge (more than ever, I should imagine, having been blinded), and dreamed up a plot almost as remarkable as that of Jing Ke's: he fixed a piece of lead in his lute, and when next playing close to the emperor, he tried to club him to death. Not surprisingly, he missed. This time there was no reprieve: he was 'summarily executed, and after that the emperor never again permitted any of the former followers of the feudal lords to approach his person'.

Living increasingly in a world of his own, the First Emperor was encouraged by his 'magicians' to give more and more thought to their ideas about how to become an immortal. One of them told him they had looked everywhere for the herbs that would make the Elixir of Immortality, but had so far failed because they were blocked by evil spirits. So the emperor had better take action.

The magic arts teach that the ruler of men should at times move about in secret to avoid evil spirits. If the evil spirits are avoided, one can reach the status of a True Man. If the whereabouts of the ruler of men are known to his ministers, this hinders his spiritual power . . . Do not let others know where you are. Once that is done, I believe the herbs of immortality can be obtained.

'I shall imitate the True Men,' promised the emperor. Then, if Sima Qian is to be believed, he ordered that the roads connecting Xianyang's 270 palaces should all be walled and roofed. He would travel between them in secret, and anyone who divulged his whereabouts would be executed. One day, at a certain palace, he expressed concern at the number of Li Si's carriages and horsemen. Soon afterwards, Li Si cut his entourage. Obviously, said the emperor, someone had passed on his opinion without his permission, which he interpreted as treachery. Of those who had been with him, no one owned up, and in a rage the emperor had them all killed. 'From this time onward, whenever he moved about, no one knew where he was.'

There soon came a time when even his two top 'magicians' could no longer stand the emperor's erratic and despotic behaviour. Telling each other that he had become remote, brutal and surrounded by flatterers, they fled. In a fury, the emperor turned upon his officials, or intellectuals, or 'scholars' as they are usually called, and subjected them to 'investigation'. Accused of violating 'prohibitions', they accused each other, as the accused often do when interrogated by secret police, and 'over 460' of them were . . . what?

There follows a much disputed word, *kēng*, which is sometimes translated as 'executed' but is traditionally rendered as 'buried alive'. That is certainly one meaning in modern dictionaries. Given that the word also means 'a pit', it seems more than possible. But the sign has changed, and possibly the modern meaning merely reflects tradition. There is a vagueness here that plants doubts: '*over 460*' scholars and unnamed 'prohibitions'. And 'burial alive' does not appear as a form of execution on the bamboo strips in Xi's grave; nor are there any other recorded examples. Whatever the fate of the scholars, there was nothing furtive about it. The emperor 'made this act known throughout the empire as a warning'. Would a Legalist emperor, even a furious and unbalanced one, have resorted to such well-publicized brutality? Many modern scholars doubt it. As Burton Watson remarks, 'buried alive' is the translation preferred by 'commentators anxious to emphasise the satanic nature of the First Emperor'.

There remained one vital task to complete the confirmation of the new era. The First Emperor had to assert his rule not simply in Qin (he had done that already) but over the whole empire. This he did between 219 and 211 BC with ritual tours of inspection during which he set his mark on seven sacred mountains – acts that were the political equivalents of a lion marking his territory. The marks were made in a totally original way: by placing on each mountain stone pillars, or stelae, engraved with poetic statements singing his praise.

He seems to have got the idea by combining two traditions. Previous kings had toured their territories, and had commissioned commemorative inscriptions on bronze cauldrons, on 'stone drums', and in a couple of cases on stones. But there had never been anything on this scale. The mountains honoured by the First Emperor include one in the far north near Beijing, three others down the east coast, and a fourth 200 kilometres from the coast in the far south. Nothing could have been more explicit. All emphasize conquest, the foundation of the new empire, the arrival of a new social order.

Previous rulers wishing to make political statements with a spiritual dimension had made sacrifices. These were known as '*feng* and *shan* rituals'. Sima Qian devotes a long chapter to the subject. These hugely significant rites were performed from the earliest times, at least 2,200 BC. Unfortunately, rulers had to qualify to perform them: 'When each dynasty attains the height of its glory, then the *feng* and *shan* are celebrated, but when it reaches a period of decline, they are no longer performed.' So there had been long gaps of hundreds of years, or even 'as many as a thousand', between enactments of these rites, with the result that 'the details of the ancient ceremony have been completely lost'. Confucius himself said he had heard that over 70 rulers had performed the sacrifices, but 'it was impossible to say much about them'. By Qin times no one had a clue. It was as if Christians knew they should be taking communion, but had forgotten about the bread and wine.

Never mind. Something had to be done to mark the momentous nature of the First Emperor's achievement; so when he and his entourage arrived at the most sacred mountain – Mount Tai in Shandong province – he summoned 70 scholars and demanded rituals. (As an aside, note that these were experts in history and ritual, Confucians not Legalists, who had obviously not been buried alive: the First Emperor needed such scholars to help him assert legitimacy. What he didn't need was outright opposition.) They ummed and aahed and argued, until he lost patience, dismissed them all and decided on his own private ritual, namely the placing of engraved stelae, followed by an announcement that he had succeeded in performing the sacrifices. Obviously, he hadn't. But no one was to know that. 'The directions for the ritual were sealed and stored away, being kept strictly secret.'

111

Thus was an ancient tradition revived in theory, if not in practice.

There were other, lesser, sacrifices as well – to mountains, rivers, springs, the Eight Spirits – but the engravings were what mattered. In the words of one scholar, it was the stelae that 'completed his conquest by inscribing the reality of his power, in the newly created imperial script, into the sacred landscape of his new subjects'.[7] The stones themselves have long vanished, but six of the seven inscriptions were recorded by Sima Qian, and all were copied several times in manuscript or rubbings.

This was history as the First Emperor wanted it: Qin history, without the competition, and with him spotlit in glorious perfection. The stelae were the equivalent of posters and newspaper headlines in modern dictatorships, the cult of personality at its most extreme, rivalled only by a select few: Stalin, Mao, Kim Jong-Il. Like them he claimed to bring the blessings of strong rule: wisdom, peace, the rule of law, the elimination of evil, the promotion of virtue, and care for the reverential and obedient common people.

Here is the sort of thing his fawning officials wrote for him, in rhyming lines of four signs each:

They [his officials] record and contemplate
the times of chaos:

[7] Lewis, *Writing and Authority in Early China.*

When they apportioned the land, estab-
    lished discrete states,
And thus unfolded the impetus for struggle.
Attacks and campaigns were daily waged;
How they shed their blood in the open
    countryside.
(Inscription on Mount Yi; trans. Martin Kern)

That was then. How much better things were
now:

In his twenty-sixth year
He first unified All under Heaven –

There was none who was not respectful
    and submissive.
He personally tours to the distant multi-
    tudes,
Ascends this Great Mountain
And all around surveys the eastern
    extremity.
The attending officials meditate upon his
    feats,
Trace the roots and origins of His deeds
    and achievements
And respectfully recite His merits and
    virtuous power.
(Inscription on Mount Tai; trans. Martin Kern)

Seven sacred mountains, seven pillars, seven
grand statements about how wonderful the new

regime was. The last, set in place in 211 BC on Mount Kuaiji, on the coast east of Hangzhou, declared 'His virtuous power and favour is permanent and lasting.'

Had he never heard of tempting Fate?

PART II

BEYOND THE GRAVE

CHAPTER 7

THE WORLD TO COME

Meanwhile, what of Zheng's tomb? It had been a dominant focus of his attention right from the time of his accession at the age of thirteen. That was when work started, so Sima Qian tells us.

Nothing remains of the original conception, for reasons that will soon become clear, but you can get an idea of what it was for by considering the fundamentals – what the teenaged Prince Zheng and the twenty-something King Zheng believed, and how other kings planned their existence beyond death.

Here is a rough, brief guide to 3,000 years of Chinese belief and practice concerning the afterlife:

The dominant ideas in the remote past were that we have souls; that souls live for ever; and that we should make provision for them. But by the time of the First Emperor these ideas had evolved. Now it was believed that we have two souls: the 'spirit soul', which inspired thoughts, virtues and artistic abilities and which flew off to the land of the immortals at the moment of death; and the 'earth

117

soul', which was at that point left behind, in some way attached to the corpse, to be buried with it. Both souls needed care and attention, so that the one could travel freely, and the other find peace rather than roam the earth, lost, restless and hungry.

We don't know much about the afterlife, but we assume a general principle: as below, so above. The spirit world was ruled like a Chinese kingdom, under the direction of the Yellow Emperor, one of the mythical five founder-emperors, with teams of messengers and powers and bureaucrats who kept tabs on the lives and deaths of individuals. In attendance were the spirits of ancestors, who were joined by the newly dead, forming a sort of community of the spirits. It was this belief in a 'spirit community' that injected into China a deep concern with the after-life; a concern, an *obsession*, as powerful and as thoroughly human as that of almost any other culture you care to mention. No one except a few sceptical philosophers doubted that there was a hidden reality, the world of the dead, and that there were deep patterns connecting that world, with its various guides and entities – gods, forces, ancestral spirits – to this one. There was, however, much uncertainty about the nature of that connec-tion, how to make contact with the spirit world, and how best to deal honourably with it or control it. In temples devoted to the ancestors, priests did their best with rituals, sacrifices and offerings, which would draw ancestral spirits down from the sphere of the highest god, Shang Di, as he or it was named. Oracles revealed the spirits' will to the living.

One thing everyone seemed to 'know' from time immemorial – back at least to 3500 BC – was that the dead could use things in the next life that they had used in this. The dead, particularly its senior members, should therefore be properly housed in lavish tombs, protected either by huge mounds of earth or by rock into which the tombs were cut. With them were buried the things they would need in the afterlife. Naturally, the richer and more powerful the person, the more stuff they needed. Graves of the rich contained ceramic cups and vases (later bronze containers for food and wine) – for the dead would need to conduct their own religious ceremonies – as well as bells, objects of jade and gold, parts of chariots, weaponry, and wonderfully weird creatures in bronze which were probably to ward off evil spirits. One fifth-century BC tomb was found to contain some 15,000 artefacts.

Traditionally, also, rulers and other aristocrats were given an entourage of servants, concubines and lesser relatives, who were either killed first or buried alive. Sima Qian mentions a certain Duke Mu who was buried in 621 BC with 177 of his staff; the sixth-century BC tomb of an early Qin duke contained 166 skeletons. In Qin, this grisly practice was largely suppressed in the fourth century BC, though it remained in occasional use for almost another 2,000 years, being formally abolished only in the fifteenth century AD.

All this was necessary, because it was the most realistic way of fulfilling the dead person's needs. It was realism that was the key (or at least had become the key by the time of the First Emperor) – realism, though, not quite in the western sense. Flesh-and-blood was not enough, because it decayed. Nor was function important. Real objects as used in this world were included; but often the objects would be made deliberately non-functional – carriages without their fittings, earthenware made too thin for use. Size was not significant either. What was crucial was a certain sense of detail. So real people – and animals – were replaced by small figures in wood, clay, bronze, stone and jade; and real sacrificial vessels in bronze were increasingly replaced by 'fake' ones in pottery, so-called 'spirit vessels', which did not even have to be baked hard. They were, in a sense, toys. In the words of the German scholar of Chinese art Lothar Ledderose, 'The tomb represents, idealizes and perpetuates the reality of life on earth.'

The toy artefacts, together with a rich array of everyday and ritual objects, provided the elements from which spirits were expected to recreate the living world. As Jessica Rawson, the Warden of Merton College, Oxford, and a noted scholar in Chinese art and archaeology, puts it, 'If an image

120

was convincing, that is, if it had the correct features, then these features gave the image the powers of the thing or person depicted.' In some sense, once in the grave, the image became the thing itself: the statue of a servant was a servant. The aim was to provide the means to recreate life in all its essentials, complete with music, banquets, entertainments, hunting and fighting. If the grave was a place of solemnity, it was also a place for fun. In addition, grave-builders aimed to provide a cosmic setting, with images of the two spirit worlds, above and below; the sun, moon and constellations; and the animals associated with all of them. In brief, as Jessica Rawson says, 'Each tomb was an entire universe centred on its occupant.'

How could one ensure that one's souls did not simply dissipate, and that one could therefore remain in this hidden world? Answer: only by becoming an immortal.

The idea that immortality could be achieved seems to have arisen slowly from the idea of longevity, the commonest term in the most ancient prayers for blessings. Since we age slowly, some more slowly than others, it did not strike Daoist philosophers as impossible that the process could be made slower still, indeed extended indefinitely. In the words of an old saying, 'The sage evolves but undergoes no sudden change.' By the time of the First Emperor, it was widely believed that there were men who had freed themselves from mortality, and would live for ever. How to achieve this was the subject of countless musings. Objects and places 'of Immortality' were commonplace. In the words of Joseph Needham, 'a mountain, a country, a land, a wilderness, a river, a people, a tree, a herb, a drug – all were very attractive, if only one could get there, or find the medicine.' All might enable one to become a *xiān*, an immortal. Poets wrote of the lives of the holy immortals, those who had 'departed from the flux of change and vanished from the sight of men', as one said, before describing how he himself learned to journey through earth and heaven until he merged with the universal spirit. Would-be immortals could aim to join one of two groups: those who remained on earth and those who roamed the heavens, with clouds as their vehicles and rainbows for canopies.

As always when belief combines with wishful thinking, no amount of experience undermined faith. Han Fei tells the story of a certain philosopher who taught the Prince of Yan something of the art of immortality. The prince sent off some men to study with the philosopher, who unfortunately died before they could complete their studies. The prince scolded the students for their slowness, rather than drawing the conclusion that a philosopher who died was hardly qualified to teach deathlessness.

For ordinary people, aiming for immortality required long-term commitment to demanding practices. But emperors had no time for all that. What they wanted was a quick fix: rituals that would persuade the gods and immortals to bestow deathlessness, and/or an elixir of immortality.

The taking of elixirs was a dangerous business, justified only by the supposed rewards. To experiment not only with gold and mercury – the favourites – but also with arsenic, lead, copper and tin was to poison oneself. Here, too, experience was no match for optimism. To quote a sixth-century text that ticks off an array of metal-poisoning symptoms:

> After taking an elixir, if your face and body itch as though insects were crawling over them, if your hands and feet swell dropsically, if you cannot stand the smell of food and bring it up after you have eaten it, if you feel as though you were going to be sick most of the time, if you experience weakness in your four limbs, if you have to go often to the latrine, or if your head or stomach violently ache – do not be alarmed or disturbed. All these effects are merely proofs that the elixir you are taking is successfully dispelling your latent disorders.

The theory behind these practices, wildly eccentric though they sound to outsiders (and sounded back then to Confucians), was mainstream among

Daoists for centuries. The elixirs were supposed to somehow rarefy or aetherialize the body (an idea that may have derived from the trance-inducing 'magic mushroom' potions taken by Siberian shamans and ancient Indian mystics), the purpose being to generate a new self that was immortal though still physical. Adepts took elixirs during life to prevent decay after death. Indeed, arsenic has precisely this effect, presumably because it poisons not only the victim but also the bacteria that cause decay. Death thus becomes a doorway to immortality. The corpse of the successful adept would remain incorruptible, and emerge like a butterfly from a chrysalis to dwell with the immortals. This (it was believed) was hard to achieve, but possible; certainly it was possible to take a few steps in the right direction. Japanese monks of the Shingon sect make themselves into 'self-mummified Buddhas' by avoiding cereals and eating only chestnuts, pine-tree bark or grass roots. Then, after death, as Needham says, incorruptibility can be seen as proof of coming immortality.

Now, a few paragraphs cannot possibly do justice to such ancient and complex beliefs. This was not a coherent system, any more than Christianity is wholly coherent (as anyone knows who has tried to come to grips with the Trinity, the Resurrection or the way communion wine is supposed to turn to blood). Contending philosophies and religions – Confucianism and the various mystical strands of Daoism – made conflicting claims. Sages struggled to make sense of it all by exploring patterns of cyclical change, by linking the seasons with bodily organs, by applying complex astronomical and calendrical systems, by imposing concepts of alternating Yin and Yang forces, and by using divination, notably the *Yi Jing* (*I Ching*). How this world interacted with the next was a matter of much dispute. Some rivers were seen as spirits, and so were some mountains. Here one could get direct access to the spirit world – hence the First Emperor's mountain-climbing tours and the shape of his tomb and those of his immediate ancestors: they were artificial mountains where the spirits would feel at home. Either the dead person's soul would visit spirits in their own realm, or the spirits would visit the tomb, or both.

One thing even a thirteen-year-old would have known: as king, he would need a tomb suitable for his status. It may seem strange that a new young ruler should be so keen on preparing for the world to come, but he would have believed that the very process of building a 'living tomb' conferred longevity. This was to be an ongoing project right up until death dictated its end. Lü Buwei, father-figure and chancellor, would surely have advised His youthful Majesty that, life being uncertain and death certain, it would be best not to delay, especially as it would have been obvious where the tomb should be.

* * *

Back then, before the growth of Xian and the coming of industrial haze, the young Prince Zheng could have stood on his private veranda on the third floor of Xianyang Palace and seen a dim line of hills fringing the southern and eastern horizons. This was Qin's old frontier, beyond which lay mountain barbarians and the hostile kingdom of Chu. One of the mountains, Mount Li, had particular significance, because it was there that Lao Zi, the founder of Daoism, had lived and taught in the sixth century BC. So people say. They also say that he met Confucius here. Maybe it is true, maybe not. Who can tell?

Even after all this time, and even though you will take the cable-car and climb the new cement stairs to the summit, old ways and spirituality linger in the air, inclining you to believe. Li Shan, which means Black Horse Mountain because that's what they say it looks like from a distance, is protected, revered even, as a notice suggests in two quirky, poetic phrases: 'Caress Mt. Li, breath green.'

People had cause to remember the mountain from long before Lao Zi's day. Tony told a story as we climbed the nice new steps through fir trees, part of the Green Great Wall of forests planted all across north China to control the sandstorms that sweep in from the Gobi. It is the local equivalent of 'The Boy Who Cried "Wolf"'.

The Smile That Cost a Kingdom

This happened long, long ago [the eighth century BC, if it happened at all], when Qin was young and threatened by southern barbarians called Quan Rong. For this reason, there was a beacon fire on the top of Mount Li that was lit when the barbarians approached. The king had a beautiful concubine whom he loved very much, but he was unhappy because she always had a long face and never smiled. So he said, 'Anyone who makes her smile will be rewarded with a thousand gold pieces.' A certain official said, 'Your Majesty, you could make her laugh by playing a joke. Light the beacon fire and your feudal lords will come running to defend you. Then you can tell them you fooled them, and send them home.' The king thought this was a great idea. The fire was lit, the lords came running, the king had his joke at their expense, they complained bitterly – and the lady smiled, and the official got his 1,000 gold pieces. But (of course) later there was a real attack, the beacon blazed a warning, and the feudal lords said 'Oh, another joke!' and stayed put. The lady was captured, the king killed and the dynasty fell. Moral: don't let your heart rule your head.

I had been hoping for a view of the First Emperor's tomb, but we were in clouds. Beyond the beacon tower – no, not the original, but a newish one occupied by fire prevention officers – the forested hills rolled away into mist. From the invisible town of Lintong below came the sound of traffic and the distant crackle of fire-works celebrating a wedding. Below I could see, through trees, upturned eaves and a courtyard – a Daoist temple, which, I hoped, would recall the days when Lao Zi walked here.

On the way down, at a bend in the track, an old man in a blue jacket and track shoes sat on a folding stool, looking at me through vast spectacles. He beckoned. 'I can see you are good at solving problems!'

'How do you know that?'

'I am an expert in the *Yi Jing*!'

Once a schoolmaster, he was now a fortune-teller, with the tools of his profession on the ground before him: a sheet of paper, strips of inscribed wood. 'Come, it will only cost ten yuan, but do not pay me yet. You sit here, on my left, because you are male. Now, your left hand.'

He began a long monologue, speaking with absolute conviction for 20 minutes. This is the condensed version: 'Oh, a ring on your middle finger, so you have many ideas . . . this finger is longer than usual, so your brain is a computer, and if this little finger is long' – he measured it with a little plastic ruler – 'oh, yes, it is; so you

128

will live longer than ninety-three years. The second finger is shorter, so you are a little bit obstinate. The thumb is long, so you will be rich. Your ears go backwards, so you have power, and you are pink, so you don't worry. Now I have to give advice.' He became serious, a Chinese Polonius. 'Insist on your principles. Do not lend money, and don't borrow too much either. Buddha will protect you, and you will lack accidents while travelling. There, that is your life. Why do I not ask for payment in advance? Because then I would tell you only good things! I suggest you pay fifteen yuan.'

I gave him 20 (£1.35), because it looked as if I was going to be his only client for many hours.

'Why do you sit up here, when there are more people down below?'

'Up here is better. It is easier to see the truth. The higher you are, the better the view.'

That, I supposed, was why a temple had been built here, 668 steps below the fortune-teller (I know this because Tony and I bet on the number, and I counted). Not this precise temple, which is pristine – a plaque states that rebuilding finished in 2001 – but the original, which supposedly marked the birth-site of the legendary Grandmother who made humans out of mud from Mount Li's yellow soil.

Steps led up to a temple of grey bricks, in which stood three statues of fierce warrior-protectors. Through a soft drift of incense, I wandered out into a paved yard and across into another temple, this one of blue-patterned beams, red pillars and pink tiles. Three goddesses presided inside, wearing expressions of beatific calm. A gentle bell turned my attention to one side, where a woman attending a postcard stand had just struck a bowl with three holes in it. She was dressed in a blue jacket, padded blue trousers, white gaiters and black shoes. 'A nun,' whispered Tony. 'Blue, black, white: the colours of Daoism. Look, here is another.' The two muttered together for a moment, until I approached to speak to them. The first turned away shyly, but the second, a sturdy figure with confident brown eyes and her hair in a chignon, was content to talk. Content was the word. She exuded peace, calm and timeless contentment, perhaps because she was not at all concerned with time. 'I have no age,' she said when I asked. 'We have no concern for age.'

There were about 20 living in the temple at present, she said, but they came and went, for everywhere and anywhere could be their home. Their purpose was to understand the pains of the world through study. No, there was no teacher. They had their books, and studied any time, any place. The only guidance they needed was Buddha.

I asked about the goddesses. 'They are immortals, ancestors of humans, who make our lives happy. We show them respect, for all immortals know our thoughts. If you have evil thoughts, they will know and punish you. We should trust them, for if you really trust, they will help.'

To recreate the earlier mood, I wanted to hear the sound of the bell-bowl again.

'If you wish to hear, you should pay your respects to the Grandmother. She is in charge of longevity.' She nodded to the central figure. 'Go to her, hold your hands in prayer, kneel and bow three times.'

So I did. And, as the bell-bowl softly rang three times, one for each bow, and the incense drifted up around the Grandmother's face, I lost myself in a moment of peace, then returned to the nun and thanked her. I'm not sure why. For a brief glimpse of tranquillity, I suppose.

'You will have a longer life,' she said. 'Because this religion is about longevity. Of all religions, it is this that makes it perhaps the most practical.'

It sounded good. Maybe learning more about Daoism would help me in my work, give me some sense of why the First Emperor chose the site below for his tomb.

'I am very certain he was here, because here was a temple to the Grandmother of all humans. She would have been like his own Grandmother. He must have decided that this, of all places, was the place to ensure safety in the afterlife.'

I asked if she minded if I took her picture, to help me remember her. She waved a finger to say no. 'We have no interest. You must keep these things in your heart.'

I lacked practice in using my heart to remember

things, so outside the temple I turned to take a picture through the doorway, only to find that the camera would not stay switched on. It was old for a digital camera, and had developed some odd little quirks, but I found it strangely coincidental that it had chosen this moment to give up the ghost. So I have no goddesses to print out, no Grandmother, no nuns, only scattered images that drift like incense between heart and mind.

As we walked back down to the cable-car, the mood lightened. Tony recalled Daoism's roots in a combination of mysticism, folklore, extreme physical techniques and alchemical experiments to discover elixirs of immortality. 'Did you know that gunpowder was invented by Daoists trying to find medicines to extend life?'

We agreed that life is full of little ironies. You try to take forbidden pictures and your camera breaks. You try to live longer, and blow yourself up instead. Somewhere below, in the industrial haze that clouded Lintong, an emperor had sought immortality by burial, and was achieving it by un-burial.

So King Zheng needed a tomb, and here was an excellent spot, because that was what his ancestors had thought. Niu Xinlong, a young archaeologist from the Terracotta Army Museum, was eager to show Qin's ancestral burial ground to me, Tony and Tony's boss, Stephanie, who packed a great deal of intelligence, curiosity and dynamism into a very small space.

132

If you drive west out of Lintong, then turn north under the new expressway to the Terracotta Army, after about 5 kilometres a small concrete road leads uphill to the left. This is farm country of deep earth, terraced fields and orchards. The road turns to a track. Where the slope flattens out, the track slices through the top of a hill in a 100-metre cut.

Except, as Mr Niu pointed out, it is not a hill but a Qin tomb. No one knew this until 1986, long after the road had been cut straight through it, and an orchard planted on it, and a house built on its flank.

Did anyone know whose it was?

'We think so. Sima Qian says the First Emperor's ancestors were buried here. That was why we came looking. When we found these two fish-backs, as we call them' – he indicated this tomb-mound and a next-door one I hadn't noticed – 'they didn't look natural. This one has passageways, which give it the shape of *zhong* ['middle'; the sign that is the first element in the Chinese for China, Zhongguo, Middle Kingdom], so we think it belongs to the First Emperor's grandfather.'

It is still unopened and its contents unknown, but by drilling down from the surface and recording how the soil changed, archaeologists have mapped the tomb. It is like an upside-down pyramid with a flat floor and four entrance ramps. Not that outsiders get a hint of this at first glance. To my eyes it looked just like a normal hill, so

133

Mr Niu was at pains to show how, if you get up close to the earth at the side of the cutting, you can tell the difference by the cracks. If it's rammed earth, and therefore artificial, the cracks are horizontal; if ordinary undisturbed earth, then they're vertical. Yes, I could see. The cutting had allowed us to stroll right to the top of the southern edge of the First Emperor's granddaddy's grave.

You can make tombs like this – deep holes, with big mounds – because this rich, reddish earth, typical of the farmland all over northern China, is so deep.

How deep? I was about to learn. For there were other tomb-mounds in the area – a couple of other Qin ones, and several built later under the Han dynasty. Mr Niu directed Wang to drive up a side-track, past a lone house, to a set of handkerchief-sized fields a couple of hundred metres beyond, and pointed to a steep-sided mound.

Our presence attracted a farmer, a fit and voluble 60-year-old in a flat hat and many shirts. It was his house, his land, and we were welcome. The mound? Of course. He would show us. We struggled over an apricot orchard and soft fields of winter wheat, until he could point to a hole at the base of the mound. 'A few years ago someone came and blew this up, thinking they would rob the grave. Then archaeologists came and drilled down seventeen or eighteen metres, and they didn't find anything either, no bottom, no treasure. People started to come almost every year to dig, so we volunteered to protect it.'

As he talked we had climbed the mound, from the top of which there was a good view over orchards to his house. It looked remarkably nice for a farmer's house. Instantly, he invited us to visit, to see how he lived with his family: his burly wife, his thirtyish son and his beautiful three-year-old granddaughter.

But it was not so much the house that attracted attention as what was beside it. The ground rose steeply, and into the slope was cut a square, brick-lined arch, which led into a tunnel, with light at the end. Following the farmer, I found myself in a huge pit, a good 8 metres high, with sheer sides. Into the sides had been cut three semi-circular arches, each with a door and a window. This was where the family had lived before they had the house – a little village of caves dug from the deep, red earth. A pig snuffled at one end of the pit, beside another cave that was both a sty and a barn.

I stood, astonished, by the labour involved, by the novelty (to me) of the sight, and also by its charm. It was like being held in a loving embrace, and an ageless one.

'Even my father could not remember how many generations ago we made this,' he said. 'It was seven or eight at least' – which took its creation back a good 200 years. Proudly, he showed us inside one of the little dwellings. It was like walking into a huge store-cupboard with air-conditioning, its temperature stabilized by the mass of the surrounding earth. The ceiling was carefully smoothed clay. There was a table, a couple of chairs and a sleeping platform, with room for a stove underneath, big enough to keep a whole family snug in cold weather, all lit by a couple of bare electric bulbs. 'It's warm in winter, cool in summer, which is why we still use it. And it has an upstairs, too,' he said, pointing to a back room, with a ladder climbing into darkness.

And, moreover, there was another crater-village immediately next door. Not long ago, this had been a whole community.

'Are there many families who still live like this?'

'Some. But most have moved into houses.'

He seemed to feel some nostalgia for the old days, and I'm not surprised, given the sad story that came out as we went around the new house. Large, with echoing tiled rooms and much unused space, it was built ten years ago, 'the same year Hong Kong came back to China'. In the son's room, Tony and Stephanie saw a woman's photograph. 'Oh, the woman of the house,' said Stephanie, at which our host glanced away, obviously upset. 'That was the past,' he said. 'Don't ask any more.' So it was Mr Niu who revealed to the rest of us what had happened, for it was general knowledge in the area. The young man's wife had come from a distant province to this new house far from the nearest village. Despite her beautiful

136

little girl, she was unhappy. Neither she nor her daughter had friends. One morning, without any warning, without speaking of her loneliness, she killed herself, leaving this close and hospitable family shattered.

Outside, as the wife pressed on us handfuls of small bread rolls, baked as hard as biscuit, Tony pointed to a mirror over the door, too high for anyone to use. It was to ward off Evil, he said later. 'If Evil comes to the house, he will see his face in the mirror, and Evil, who has never seen his own face, will be scared away.'

Well, it hadn't worked. I was left pondering about time and earth. This modern house and its tragedy, the blink of an eye at the end of two centuries of community living beneath and inside the soil; the leap back two millennia to the unplumbed Han tomb; and back a few more centuries to the Qin royal tombs – all succeeding each other on these few acres, thanks to this deep, red earth.

So there could have been no doubt that King Zheng should start preparing his grave somewhere close by present-day Lintong. They made a start where Mount Li's lower slopes level out into ravines and orchards and wheat fields. By comparison with what followed, this was not a huge operation, because at that pre-imperial time the labour force came only from Qin, no doubt including teams of prisoners captured in the incessant cross-border raids.

137

Imagine a few thousand men, summoned by the order of Lü Buwei on behalf of the king, beginning to clear soil from Mount Li's lower slopes, presumably living in a small town built nearby. The spot must have been chosen with care: close to the sacred mountain, high enough to ensure that the water from Mount Li would run off down into the lowlands below, low enough to be on relatively level ground.

As it happens, archaeologists have identified the actual spot of this first excavation. It lies some 700 metres south of the edge of the tomb, higher up the mountainside. Not many people know this, except people like the head of the province's archaeological department, Duan Qingbo, a master of the technical surveys done all around the tomb, who brought a laptop bearing a collection of diagrams along to my hotel to brief me on his research. 'How do we know the original site? We discovered it by soil analysis and gravitational studies. This part had an anomaly in the consistency of the soil. The only possible explanation is that this part had been dug out and refilled. It's not at all like the surrounding soil.'

OK. But what about Sima Qian's words: 'When the Emperor first came to the throne' – that is, in 246 BC – 'he began digging and shaping Mount Li', with the implication that this was the beginning of the massive mound we see today? Well, Sima Qian may have tweaked the truth in order to get at his own boss, Emperor Wu, who notoriously ordered work to begin on his own tomb just two years into his rule – work that continued on and off for the full term of his reign, 53 years. Work may have started in Lintong in 246 BC; but it was not work on the real thing. It was a first attempt, a small-scale excavation, suitable for a boy-king.

And it was in the wrong place.

As Duan Qingbo said, 'It was too close to the mountain, so the soil was not deep enough and they hit rocks.' That would have presented a problem, and a choice: either to dig out a grave in rock – possible, but expensive for a boy-king with an uncertain future – or to put everything on hold until his death or until his rule was more secure.

Probably, then, work was stopped. It was simply left, a hole in the stony ground, with its rocky bottom, until the flow of events told the young king and his chancellor Lü Buwei what to do.

CHAPTER 8

DIGGING THE TOMB

Imagine the sudden change inspired by unification in 221 BC. The lower slopes of
Mount Li would have been a mess – the
beginnings of a hole, a square of earth outlining
the base of a pyramid-shaped mound, piles
of overgrown soil carried off by the army of
labourers ready to cover the tomb when the time
came, the nearby town abandoned. But now,
suddenly, came the need for a new vision, with
the prospect of virtually unlimited manpower.
This presented an opportunity – no, a necessity – to do something far more ambitious than
anything that had been done so far. As ruler by
Heaven's will, the First Emperor had clearly
been given a mandate to do more than follow
old ways; now he must add to them, and improvise new beliefs and practices suitable for his
10,000-generation empire.

There is no blueprint of his plans. But we can
get an idea of what he was aiming at from the
tombs of the Han dynasty, which took over from
the Qin empire, inheriting the Qin belief system
and accepting much of it. Han tombs – some

scholars argue – therefore suggest what the First Emperor had in mind.

The easy, bland approach is to take the expressway due north of Xian for half an hour. The more interesting one is to follow the cliff from Xianyang and the site of the First Emperor's palace, east-wards along the base of the cliff, past the new double-gated houses built with cash sent by the citified young to their farming parents, then steeply uphill to the top of the plateau, where you will find one of China's more staggering pieces of modern architecture. It is Yangling Museum, created from the tomb-mound of the fourth Han emperor, Jing Di (188–141 BC), and it hints, in glistening, space-age terms, at what the First Emperor had been aiming for 70 years previously.

There are in fact two mounds, belonging to the emperor and his wife, a his-and-hers of the after-life surrounded by 200 cemeteries containing 10,000 graves of Han nobles. His has been turned into a wonder, a suitable memorial to an emperor who presided over a time of peace and prosperity. 'Everyone was well-off,' wrote the historian Ban Gu 200 years later, 'all the granaries and barns bursting with grain, government repositories teeming with money.' Opened in 2006 after 16 years of work, the tomb beneath its 31-metre mound is an air-conditioned glory of light and space in which you walk on glass over everything considered necessary to make the afterlife comfortable, in vast quantities – 50,000 objects have been unearthed so far, and estimates for those unfound range up to half a million. The finds include several thousand terracotta attendants, soldiers, even female equestrians, and animals by the hundred – goats, dogs, sheep, horses, oxen, pigs and chickens, all painted appropriate colours. The human figures look a little odd because their clothing has rotted away, along with their wooden arms. But they are impeccably modelled, walking, kneeling, running, many with cheerful expressions – smiling, quizzical, humorous – for the emperor would be in need of good cheer in the afterlife. All are painted, with red skins and black eyebrows. All have small but perfectly formed genitalia – all except the eunuchs, who are also impeccably modelled in their own way. With the figures are thousands of objects in bronze, gold and clay: seals, bells, axes, spears, swords, ovens, pots, chariots, ploughshares, granaries filled with grain, farm implements, agricultural carts, and more, always more.

All of this is extraordinary; but even more so is the fact that the people, the animals and the objects are, on average, one-third life-size. In fact, some are even smaller: a tiny copper crossbow is only 6.7 centimetres long, complete with front sight and trigger, both of which move. We are in a world of dolls. Clearly, accuracy of modelling – realism, if you like – was of more importance than size or consistency of material. The artists might, for instance, have modelled clothing in clay, as the makers of the Terracotta Army did. But instead they chose to cover their figures in silk or hemp, presumably draping it over the wooden arms.

There is one other thing about Jing Di's tomb that suggests something about the First Emperor's, and helps explain the existence of the Terracotta Army. The purpose of the exercise was to provide the deceased emperor with his entire realm, not simply by giving him figures, animals and objects, but by providing the means to organize them: the tomb is surrounded by 81 satellite pits, each one representing a government department.

'How do we know this?' asked my guide (who called himself Sean) rhetorically. 'Every pit we found had a seal,[1] so we know which department is symbolized. Here is the Department to Punish Prisoners' – we were walking slowly along heavy glass, looking down at the remains beneath our feet – 'here the Department for Sacrifices. And here all the figures are eunuchs, so this is the Eunuchs' Department, and this, Number Sixteen, you see the animal bones, the fat animals for eating – this is the Royal Kitchen. And here, the blackened grain shows we are in the Grain Preparation Department.'

---

[1] A slight exaggeration. Only a few seals have been found, but scholars would agree that he makes a fair assumption.

It is fair to assume that Jing Di inherited and developed the idea of recreating this world for the next from the First Emperor. Since the First Emperor now ruled 'all under Heaven', all under Heaven had to be taken into account: the universe, the physical world, the spirit world, together with all spirits, demons and deities and the ways by which they travelled – all had to be modelled in the new tomb.

But no one had done this before. What exactly might it mean? The emperor was spoiled for choice, for the answers were now to be sought all over the new empire and beyond its borders, as we know from the contents of tombs in newly conquered areas. Gold was imported from the lands beyond the western deserts (Iran, Scythia, Siberia) and used to decorate weapons and make small animal motifs. Images of new deities – winged beasts, fighting animals – arrived along these same trade routes. From western Asia too came fashions for lamps, mirrors and lions, which were unknown in China. Somewhere in un-explored lands to the north or north-west lived the Queen Mother of the West, whose legendary cave-palace ought perhaps to be a model for a royal tomb. From the state of Chu came the new tomb tradition, according to which the tomb should have several rooms – for ceremonies, for entertainment, for attendants, for weapons. Chu rulers (notably Marquis Yi of Zeng) had a preference for ordinary household goods, for musical instruments

144

and for attendants of all kinds to create banquets. Life in a Chu tomb would be one long party, if the models were accurate enough. Possibly, the Qin had also come across ancient tombs in Zhejiang on the east coast, in which there were numerous jade discs with holes in them; these both conferred protection and allowed the soul to escape. All these possibilities and more were available to the First Emperor as he contemplated the design of his tomb. In the words of Jessica Rawson, 'It would seem that the unification of the empire had brought within reach of the court a concern with the full sweep of the universe and all that lay within it' – a universe that was no longer foreign, but part of the unified realm that the emperor sought to control.[2]

Following more recent fashions, the First Emperor would have naturally opted for a mound covering several rooms, as if the tomb were a sort of house, like his grandfather's tomb outside Lintong, and like the Han dynasty tombs to come – but grander than anything to date. His tomb was to be a symbolic representation – a reflection, a microcosm – of the physical world, representing an imperial city: outer wall, inner wall, *inner* inner wall, many buildings and a palace, this one being underneath its vast four-sided pyramid, doubling as a tomb.

The first step was to choose exactly the right

[2] Rawson, 'The Eternal Palaces of the Western Han'.

spot for the tomb itself, for on its position depended a multitude of other projects: housing for those who would look after the rites, the many kilometres of walls, the additional buildings, the pits that would contain officials, animals, chariots and eventually the clay warriors that would protect the emperor in the afterlife. This time, there would be no mistake. Planning and scheduling would have been meticulous: designs drawn on wooden boards, lists made on bamboo strips (timing, numbers of workers, food supplies, artisans). There would, I imagine, have been a number of test digs until engineers settled on a site 700 metres further downhill from the first, where the soil was deep enough for the emperor's underground palace.

Sima Qian gives a hint of the preparatory work, saying that the labourers 'dug down to the third layer of underground springs' and put in drains to carry the water clear of the tomb. This sounds a huge operation. How huge, I wonder? Sima Qian, in his casual way, says that 700,000 men were involved from the First Emperor's accession in 246 BC. That's the number that is unthinkingly quoted in almost all accounts. But this vague figure includes the force working on the Epang Palace, and is anyway hugely exaggerated, both in time (as we know from the false start) and in numbers. It would be far larger than the population of any city in the world at the time. Where would such numbers live? How would they be fed?

146

A computer simulation would be welcome, but so far there isn't one. To introduce a sense of realism, we must resort to some back-of-the-envelope calculations.

These suggest a slow start, a long pause, and then – only on the emperor's death – a big push with an army of labourers, large to be sure but still far short of Sima Qian's numbers.

'A slow start' means work on the palace foundations. But at once we are in a much disputed subject-area, for beginning work on the palace foundations means having an idea of the size of the palace, which will have to fit beneath the funeral mound, which means we have to know – right now, in advance – the size of the mound. The base of the mound today measures about 350 × 350 metres, and its height something between 50 and 75 metres, depending on which side the measurement is taken. That gives a volume of 1.8–2 million cubic metres. Many sources quote the official history of the Han dynasty, which says that the original height of the tomb was 'more than 50 *zhang* [115 metres]'. They almost always add that in the subsequent 2,200 years 'erosion' brought it down to its present size. Really? This sounds to me like a pseudo-explanation, because erosion has not affected other mounds anything like that much.

Even more problematic are assumptions made since 1981, when a number of trial drillings struck brick and rammed earth. It seemed, as Yuan

Zhongyi writes in his archaeological survey, that what had been found were walls; and if so then these walls must belong to the underground palace. Joining the dots and extrapolating them beyond the area of the drillings suggested an immense structure of 460 × 390 metres. This is considerably larger than the base of today's mound, and was considered 'proof' that the mound must have been much larger in the past – *much* larger; something like 500 × 500 metres, and 115 metres high. But doubling the height and adding one-third to the length of each side does very peculiar things to the volume: it makes it 8.6 million cubic metres – *five times* the size of today's mound (and almost four times the size of the Great Pyramid).

It makes no sense. If the palace is really larger than the base of today's mound, either its outlines should be visible, which they are not; or the whole thing would have to be beneath ground level, which it isn't, because the probes did not go that deep. Indeed, some 'walls', if that is what they are, lie some 40 metres from the top, which means that the 'walls' are at least 10 and perhaps 18 metres high, depending how far below ground the foundations lie.

The fact is, the only thing everyone agrees on (backed by one other vital piece of evidence that we will get to later) is that something big is under there. No one knows how big. Most likely, as the archaeologist Duan Qingbo insisted to me, the standard assumptions are wrong. 'From our research, it seems the hundred and fifteen metres was just the *planned* height. When the emperor died and they started to pile earth on his tomb, it was almost the end of the dynasty. They did not have time to complete the plan. Probably the tomb we see today was just like it was over two thousand years ago.' His view makes his conclusion persuasive: 'We know there is a burial chamber beneath the tomb measuring about eighty by fifty metres. It is surrounded by a stone wall of about one hundred and forty five by one hundred and twenty five metres.'

It seems slightly odd to place a rectangular building beneath a square mound. Let's assume an upper limit for the palace of half the size of today's mound: 175 × 175 metres, rising about 10 metres above ground level, with foundations that go down perhaps 5–7 metres below ground level. This is about as large as it could be, bearing in mind that the walls and the roof must be covered with earth thickly enough to deter vandals.

Now to return to the starting point: If the pit went (say) 7 metres below the surface, then the workers would have had to shift some 200,000 cubic metres, or 300,000 tonnes, of earth (always working in very round numbers).

In what time? And with what size of workforce? These are questions that Li Si's quantity surveyors would have needed to answer in order to estimate their needs for tools (mainly spades, hoes and two-man, earth-carrying slings-on-poles), food and housing, a schedule and countless other planning details.

Compared to the problems to be faced later, the foundations of the underground palace were a minor challenge. As a first step, assume that the earth must be carried well clear of the site, not with wagons and horses, because they are expensive, but by men with two-man teams, because men, especially criminals, are cheap. A man with a spade takes up (say) 2 square metres, so you could fit a theoretical maximum of 15,000 labourers in the foundations. But with that number nobody could swing a shovel, and there would be no room for the earth-carriers to move between them. Further constraints are imposed by the speed with which the earth is removed and the numbers needed to move it. Today, quantity surveyors work on the assumption that the average digger can remove 1 cubic metre (about 1.5 tonnes of soft earth) in 2.7 hours. But at that rate, especially with slave-labour conditions, you will work your men to a standstill pretty quickly. Assume 5 tonnes per day per digger. Let's pick several other round-number assumptions out of the air: that the two-man earth-carriers carry their earth in three different directions (i.e. not uphill); that every team makes three journeys back and forth to their dump every day; that each dump is 2 kilometres away; and that each two-man sling carries 40 kilos. Imagine three double lines of earth-carriers plodding back and forth on three roads, which gives us 8,000 two-man earth-carrying teams. Digging his 5 tonnes daily, one digger supplies 35 teams.

The slightly surprising conclusion is that the 16,000 earth-carriers will be supplied by just 200 diggers, who will shift 1,000 tonnes a day, digging the underground palace's foundations in 300 days, or ten months. (The burial chamber inside the walls – 80 × 50 metres, according to Duan Qingbo – would require the removal of a mere 42,000 tonnes, which hardly counts as labour at all by comparison.) The real labour will come later, after the emperor's death, when the mound will have to be built and the surrounding walls finished in double-quick time.

It's not quite that simple, though, because the foundation, whatever its size, demands meticulous design. It needs access ramps, probably four of them; not too steep, because earth-carriers must go up and down, come rain or shine, and later processions bearing coffins and grave goods will need to make stately progress. The whole thing will eventually have to be divided into several different compartments, floored with clay tiles (like those on which the Terracotta Army stands) and lined somehow to prevent the walls collapsing. The floor-tiles will number up to 1.2 million, depending on how much of the floor space is taken up with pillars and rammed-earth walls, which will be needed to support a roof of sturdy timbers (more about them in chapter 10).

It is perhaps during the preliminary survey for the excavation that the Qin engineers make an unpleasant discovery. There is a stream, the Sha (still there today), which, after heavy rain, careers down from Mount Li, and will, if it floods, threaten the grave – if not now, when it is nothing but a hole in the ground, then some time in the future, literally undermining the whole project. Perhaps they realized the danger when the first attempt at the grave was made, but the implications were so dramatic that nothing, it seemed, could be done. The answer, in fact, is to build yet another wall, the Wu Ling (Five Hills) Dam, to deflect the water away from the tomb's south-east corner. Some dam: 1.5 kilometres long, 30 metres across and perhaps 10 metres high. I'm guessing the height, because if you go there today, working your way uphill along muddy tracks, past small-holdings, through a couple of villages, you will find that the First Emperor's dam is a fine, raised foundation for what will soon be a new highway running from Lintong to the mausoleum. I can vouch for the dam's width: the smooth earth, scraped flat by bulldozers, was easy to pace. The dam adds another 450,000 cubic metres – 675,000 tonnes – of earth to be moved. This is over twice the volume and weight of the grave's foundations. Yes, a formidable challenge – Where does the earth come from? How does the work dovetail with the grave-digging? – yet, once the logistical problems are solved, our 16,000 labourers, shifting 1,000 tonnes a day, could handle the job in just under two years.

Of course, the labourers will need to be supplemented by additional contingents of families, overseers, engineers and troops to keep control. Li's new township will have a population of perhaps 25,000 – which, so far, is a fraction of the number mentioned by Sima Qian. The notion of construction stretching over 30 years is pure hogwash.

All of this is mere infrastructure, a stage set waiting to be filled with life when the emperor dies. No one knows in advance what lands the emperor will rule, what he will possess, what the governmental departments will be, whether his queen will still be alive, how many concubines he will have, what children, what other nieces and nephews, princes and princesses, high officials, horses, carriages, and treasures of bronze, jade and pottery he will have around him when he dies. But whatever he has will somehow have to be either buried with him or buried in separate pits, even as he is reverently placed to rest and the vast task of sealing the tomb begins. That lies in the future.

Meanwhile, someone has dreamed up the idea of making an army of full-sized warriors, and the emperor likes it. As Lothar Ledderose writes, it was as if the emperor had said: 'Make me a magic army. It must never decay, but protect my residence for eternity. It must look like a real army in all respects. Only then will the magic work!'

153

The warriors will have to be buried, somehow, somewhere; but that can wait, because their pit is only 75 per cent of the underground palace's foundations, and, as our time-and-motion study on those foundations suggests, that pit could be dug in not much over six months.

The statues, however, demand immediate attention. Qin artisans were terrific at bronze casting and making substantial bits of pottery, but no one had made a clay statue on this scale, let alone an army of them. In workshops and kilns far removed from the creation of the tomb, work started on an unprecedented operation.

CHAPTER 9

MAKING THE ETERNAL ARMY

The Terracotta Army was a one-off creation, original in both concept and execution, unmentioned in any source, no sooner buried than destroyed and forgotten. Seen from the viewing platform of Pit No. 1, lined up in their geometrical columns, with their calm expressions, the warriors seem at first sight as enigmatic as a regiment of sphinxes. Why so realistic? Why this many? Why full-size? Why clay? So many questions – and now, after three decades and much specialist attention, some answers.

The initial inspiration was the need to duplicate a new force, of which the main element was infantry, conscripted from the emperor's newly acquired masses of peasants, and protected not with custom-made armour but with scales of leather and simple, standardized weapons. It was the combination of archers, infantry and chariot-eers, this particular balance between officers and men, that had enabled the First Emperor to unify the nation. Since the next life was thought to reflect this one, and since soldiers would anyway be part of life in the tomb, unity would have to

155

be achieved and/or maintained in the afterlife as well. Unification and the army would be honoured together. To reflect the novelty of what had been achieved by the emperor and his army, a new level of realism was called for. How better to achieve this than by giving the spirit army real weapons, which already existed by the ten thousand and which could be topped up by long-established manufacturing techniques? And if the weapons were real, clearly they could not be held by anything but full-size figures.

Then there is the question of the numbers. If realism was the key, then they had to represent a real army. No army could be called an army unless it was a *wan*, 10,000 strong – not, as we have already seen, that a *wan* was an exact number. It was a word that evoked a very large number, as 'zillion' does. The Great Wall was a *wan* of half-kilometres (*li*) long, the Epang Palace could hold a *wan* of people, and no doubt if Sima Qian had recorded the Terracotta Army he would have said it consisted of a *wan* of soldiers. So far, counting all pits discovered to date, archaeologists estimate there are about 8,000, which is close enough to count as a *wan*.

Achievement, status and logic all combine to dictate size and numbers. But what of the material? That too springs from the First Emperor's requirements. Think of the alternatives. The First Emperor might have opted for human sacrifices; certainly, he would not have hesitated if he thought

156

it necessary. But he himself, as a commander, would have instantly seen three major drawbacks: men dispatched into the next world cannot fight in this one; such old-fashioned practices, long since condemned as barbaric, were not suitable for a new, forward-looking dynasty; and bodies rot – this army was to be eternal.

Other considerations were cost and speed of manufacture. No point in an ambition that could not be realized in something like the time it would take to build the tomb – a few years. And no point either in decreeing full-size figures made in bronze, say, or jade, let alone gold. Even in bronze, several thousand full-size figures would stretch the Qin budget beyond breaking point, even if the expert artisans could be gathered. The figures could conceivably have been made of wood. But the labour of carving each figure would have been immense. What was required was a way of mass-producing the figures, fast. That left only one possible medium: clay.

All of China's diverse cultures understood clay. There were and are beds of it all over north China, so it was cheap, widely available and easily worked. Moreover, clay had been used in mass production techniques for well over 1,000 years.

The greatest artefacts of the ancient Chinese, their huge bronze vessels, depended on their skills in making the clay moulds in which the bronzes were cast. This was a process of great sophistication, brought to perfection in the Shang dynasty

157

(eighteenth to twelfth centuries BC). For instance, a four-legged food cauldron, probably made around 1200 BC, weighs 875 kilos – the largest bronze vessel discovered so far – and was cast in six moulds (four sides, top and bottom). Each mould holds the shape to be cast, plus any decorations, in reverse; that is, if the finished vessel is to have a raised pattern – 'in the positive', as it is called – then that shape must be pressed or cut into the mould to create the same pattern 'in the negative'. This could be done directly by the artist; or the artist could make a model of the finished object in clay, raised decorations and all, which could then be used to make a mould. Then the pieces were joined, and molten bronze poured in. Once the metal was cool and the moulds removed, you then used the same moulds to make the next vessel, and the next. You could also change designs by using different decorated blocks to stamp the clay, or attaching additions – an animal here, a handle there, three legs instead of a single stand – that had been cast separately. It took time to refine the process, but by the sixth century BC several great foundries had mastered the factory-line mass production of bronze vessels, with the possibility of personalizing any product by the addition of details.

Henry Ford, who introduced the world's first moving assembly line to produce his Model T cars in 1913, would have understood exactly what a Chinese bronze works was up to in the second

millennium BC. Mass production meant specialized workmen. Some prepared the furnaces, some
the bronze, some the clay, some the basic designs,
some the moulds, each man an expert in his own
field. There must have been constant pressure
from management to lower unit cost and increase
volume. The end result was the same for 1,000
years: high quality; efficient, regular, fast production; and no room for individuality and creativity.
All the foundries lacked was a moving assembly
line.

No one had ever thought of making full-size
figures before, but Li Si would have brushed
objections aside. Every element was to hand –
clay, furnaces, artisans, and labourers ad infinitum.
The challenge was not in the artistry, the techniques or the expense; it was in the scale. As
Adele Schlombs, Director of the Museum of East
Asian Art in Cologne, says, 'The production of
life-size figures in this enormous number set a
new level in terms of practicality and organisation, which was neither foreshadowed nor
matched later.'[1]

Astonishing, therefore, that word of it did not
filter down to Sima Qian. Perhaps it was because
of the routine nature of the work. Perhaps people
got so used to seeing the warriors that no one
commented. Besides, there were so many vast

[1] 'Die Herstellung der Terrakotta-Armee', in Ledderose
and Schlombs, *Jenseits der Grossen Mauer*.

159

projects – the Wall, the palaces, the road-systems, the canals, the tomb itself – that perhaps the true scale of the operation only emerged when the time came to bury them, just when the project was overshadowed by the closure of the tomb and the chaos unleashed by dynastic collapse.

Whether it was low-key, or officially concealed, or simply forgotten, the business of making the figures was a huge operation. How huge? What does it take exactly to produce figures on this scale? There are no historical sources to consult. But it is possible to consult the next best things: the reproductions.

They are around the museum like a halo, the grey ghosts of the real things, haunting every step of your approach. They are present on every scale, from chess-pieces weighing a few grams – 'Hey, mister! One dollar one box!' – to the full-size ones crowding courtyards and roadsides and show-rooms and tourist-traps. Some are so amateurish that you wonder why anyone would bother to set them up. But they exist in such numbers (greater even, surely, than the original army), that I became curious to know more about the business. I thought I would learn only about the local equivalent of tourist tat. Far from it. I was led straight to the heart of an operation that would have been strangely familiar to the First Emperor.

On your way to Lintong, the expressway leading

through Xian's eastern suburbs takes you across the river Ba, a muddy swirl running down from the mountains between a chaos of ruts cut in times of flood. If you turn off left, aim for the tall chimney stacks, and penetrate the haze along Power Plant Road, you come to the Xian Art Ceramics and Lacquer Factory. It makes and sells many things, including silk carpets and reproduction furniture, but what greets you as you go into the first hall is a line of full-size terracotta warriors, perfect except that they have no heads, the heads being made separately. They flank a dozen tables where employees work to produce small-scale warriors in many different sizes.

I had questions, not so much about the small copies, but about the full-size figures, which looked just like the originals. The factory's manager, Li Junyi, took me into his office to brief me, speaking in Chinese through my guide, Tony. In a thick smoker's voice, Li said he had been here since before the discovery in 1974, when this place had been a ceramics factory. The reproductions business had started almost at once. Now they did about eight million dollars' worth of trade annually, half of which was in reproductions. They sold 200,000 of the small statues every year, and about 200 of the full-size figures, at $1,200 a piece, insurance and shipping included. A pretty good deal, I thought, considering they weigh up to 200 kilos each.

'What on earth do people do with them?'

'They put them in their gardens to protect their families. If they have a business connection in China, they use them as advertisements.'

At this point his young, handsome, crew-cut deputy 'Jerry' Wong took over, in very good English, his looks, western name and language skills reflecting the several tens of thousands of foreign tourists who come here every year. He led me round the workshop to see how the copies were made. It's pretty simple, really. You take raw clay from a pile dumped near the entrance (wonderful dark brown stuff, thick and smooth as well-rolled plasticine). You go with it to your desk. You pummel it to get the air-bubbles out; squeeze it into the right size mould or moulds, depending on the size of statue you are making; let it harden for a few days; prise the mould(s) off and make the finishing touches – a few hairs added with a stylus, a stroke or two to smooth an imperfection – and off the statue goes for firing in kilns alongside the factory.

The same principle applied to the full-size statues, some of which were standing around clamped into their moulds (ten for the body, another two for the head). After setting for several days, they would be stripped and taken to a kiln for firing.

'Why are the heads done separately?'

Because when you make a life-size warrior, said Jerry, you have 1.8 metres of clay, so you have to consider how to keep it balanced. It was the same

2,000 years ago. There are three ways. One is to make a base, which is what some of them have. Another way is to make them kneeling, like the kneeling archers. The third way is to make sure the legs are heavy and the rest of the body is light, so you give them solid legs and a hollow chest. That's how most of them are made.

And if the statue has a hollow chest, what happens when you put it in the kiln with the head on?

'The air expands, and it would blow up. So we leave a big hole for the neck and add the head afterwards.' I think perhaps he was joking. All you would have to do is leave a *small* hole or two somewhere. 'And of course there is another reason. The clothes don't vary much, but the heads do, so it makes them seem like individuals.'

The factory did not provide all the answers. For one thing, its seven coal-fired kilns could not be used all the time because in Xian's suburbs there was already too much pollution. So most of the full-size figures on display had been produced in other kilns out in the countryside. In terms of production, this factory was just a sideshow.

Second, copying statues with moulds was not hard. Where did the moulds come from? Were they, perhaps, allowed to make casts from the original figures?

'Er, no.' His tone told me how ludicrous the idea was. The terracotta warriors were untouchable, sacrosanct. 'We have experts. They make an original copy, not with a mould. That is a most important job.'

Indeed it was; absolutely fundamental. His words gave me a sudden insight, making two things clear:

- First, that the techniques for making these copies were almost identical to the original techniques. By studying the reproductions business, I would learn how the originals had been made.
- Second, that *it was actually impossible to make exact copies*. The 'copies' that I saw all around me were not like xeroxes, more like artist's versions of the original.

Who, then, were these experts? Where did they work their magic?

If you like to see patterns in lives, here is one. As a six-year-old boy Wang Lianyuan was playing around the orchards where the warriors were found in 1974. He saw an older friend gather arrowheads for sale at the scrap-metal shop. He saw the heads and torsos lying around in the field before the arrival of the archaeologists. I'm tempted to say he was inspired, because now, three decades later, he is the top man in the four-million-dollar-a-year reproductions business. Dressed in a casual-chic black leather jacket and driving a top-of-the-range 4×4, he was taking me to his main factory a few miles north of Lintong.

In fact, he explained, through a steady flow of cigarette smoke, there was no direct inspiration. It was just luck, a combination of the emergence of the warriors and his own rare mixture of commercial and artistic aptitude. At heart, he is a sculptor, having trained as a teenager in the Xian ceramics factory. By the time he was eighteen, he was a master of his trade, able to copy any statue.

I imagined that it would be possible these days to store images in computers and apply software that would somehow help out with making the copies.

'No, I do it all by eye.' Later, he showed me his old references – battered photographs torn from picture books and a set of detailed measurements scribbled alongside – but he scarcely needs even these aids. 'The images of all the warriors are stored in my brain. I don't need the pictures now. It's like a concert pianist, I don't need the reminders.'

'So you must know them better than anyone.'

'Well, I still come to study them, wondering if there are ways to make my copies closer to the originals.'

'Do you get the impression they are portraits of real men?'

'I think some are. Did you notice that, among the thousand warriors you see in Pit Number One, they all have moustaches – all except one?' (No, I hadn't. I've been trying to find the clean-shaven one in pictures ever since, but so far no luck.)

'What strikes me is the craftsmanship. From the style I can tell that one man was responsible for many of the warriors.'

We crossed the Wei and turned left along a muddy road, into the little town of Bei Tian, ordinary square brick houses backing on to fields of winter wheat and vegetable gardens. Wang turned through rickety iron gates, beneath a sign stating we were entering the Qin-Style Eighth Wonder Reproduction Factory (more about the 'eighth wonder' later), and into a courtyard that was a chaotic cross between a building site and an open-air art gallery. It was the most basic, grubby, hands-on, practical place you could imagine. Standing in random clumps were scores of headless, full-size terracotta warriors. Buildings in various stages of dilapidation edged the yard – tin-roofed sheds with open fronts apparently filled with discarded pottery, two workshops filled with shadowy figures, a house with a veranda where two women were attending to an extremely cheerful baby built like a miniature sumo wrestler, and four smoking kilns dug into a bank of earth.

Wang proudly showed me into the first workroom. The figures I had glimpsed from outside were contingents of warriors newly released from their moulds; one still encased and bound looked like a giant Easter egg on a stand. The figures were all the colour of the original clay, toffee in the shadows, more like caffè latte where the sunlight spilled on to them through the dusty window. Some were still supported by wooden struts to keep the soft clay firm against the pull of gravity. Two men were at work, smoothing armour plating, heightening details. Obviously they were not direct copies, because two of the figures were not soldiers at all, but two versions of the First Emperor himself, his ceremonial sword strapped round his paunch. And at a bench a woman in a red jacket was working on a dozen officers in miniature sizes, which of course had no counterpart in 210 BC.

I still hadn't quite grasped the essence of this operation. All these full-size statues came from moulds, of which there were many, still enclosing statues, or lying about on the floor. But there were several different statue designs: emperors, officers, soldiers, kneeling archers – ten of them in all.

'Where do all the moulds come from?'

'We make them. From the original statues.'

'But who makes *those*?'

'I do.'

With hindsight, I was being incredibly dim. 'Wait a minute. You make the originals, then use those to make moulds, and from the moulds come all these statues?'

'Yes.'

'So where are the originals?' I wanted to see the foundation, the starting point of the process.

'Oh, once I have made the moulds, there's no point in keeping them. Perhaps I have a few left. I will show you.' And he led me out, past a smaller

167

shed where the clay was stored, and into his own workroom, which was as basic as a prison cell. A couple of rough branches stuck up from a stand to act as a frame for the clay. A head stood on a shelf, along with dozens of small moulds. He showed me the tools of his trade: a little poly-styrene box containing three wooden styluses, three small trowels, two loops of wire on handles, a tape measure, a ruler. That was all.

Let me get to the bottom line here rather more quickly than I managed to understand what Wang had created. Around me in the sheds were repro-ductions of 10 different styles of warrior in 10 different sizes, from 6-centimetre miniatures to full-size ones. So Wang had made 100 original statues, copying by eye, his only references being photographs and his own memory. From his ori-ginals moulds had been taken, and from the moulds, with the help of his 20 workers, came the litter of statuary I saw around me – the piles of pottery in the open-fronted sheds at the far end of the yard turned out to be miniature warriors by the thousand – and the scores on display at the museum and the ceramics factory and the other tourist outlets around Xian.

Making the statues was a slow and steady busi-ness. New statues must be left to harden for a few days, carefully protected from the elements in a darkened room, with no windows open. Then the firing takes a week on low temperatures to ensure regular heating, then a couple of days at high temperatures, up to 1,000°C. Several figures could be fired at once, the gaps between them being filled with dozens, scores, hundreds of smaller statues, the numbers depending on the sizes. In this way, Wang's workers produced several hundred full-sized figures – up to 1,000 was possible, he said – and some 10,000 of the smaller figures every year.

I felt I was almost down to bedrock. One more thing: where did the clay come from? For without the clay there would have been no spirit army, none of Wang's artistry, no reproductions business. Most of it came down by the tractor-load from Mount Li, Wang said, where we could not go because spring rains had made the track dangerous, even for a 4×4. But there was another smaller source in a village just outside Xian. Wang had never been to the spot, which for some reason I assumed would be by a river. But after many side-roads and several phone calls we were met by a local farmer who led us along a track leading into the middle of fields green with young wheat. Ahead, down a muddy slope torn up by tractors, was an open-cast pit about 10 metres across which ended in a wall some 4 metres high.

While the others held back, wary of the mess, I started forward, and at once understood why this clay was ideal for sculpting. It was the stickiest stuff imaginable. Every step sucked up more of it, until I was struggling in slow motion, and getting taller as well, like the Qin opera singer I had seen the night before parading on platform shoes. This rich, thick, even-textured, chocolatey gloop was mined by hand, then prepared by a sort of baling machine, which swallowed it and cut it up into brick-sized slabs. That was the only nod to modernity. Otherwise, the clay that clogged my track shoes was the same now as then, and so was the whole manufacturing operation: natural materials worked by nothing but artistry and heat.

That night a thought leaped out of my dreaming mind and punched me awake. I had assumed that every terracotta soldier was an individual creation. Not so: once an original had been created, and once moulds had been taken from it, this was a mass production, factory-based operation which could produce – how many soldiers? In what period of time? What were the constraints, the upper limits? Using Wang's experience as a guide, it should be possible to do a time-and-motion study on the whole Terracotta Army and come to a new understanding of what it was all about.

So Wang agreed to perform a thought experiment, talking in the reception area of the museum. First I wondered what would limit the production of warriors: the amount of clay, perhaps, or the number of kilns available?

No, the clay would not have been a problem. Wang has used about 150 tonnes a year for the last 10 years – 1,500 tonnes – and he foresees no problems in supply for many years to come. The

Terracotta Army needed between 1,200 and 2,000 tonnes.

Kilns? It takes about ten days to build a kiln out of bricks, said Wang. 'But they didn't have kilns like ours. The topography round here is special. We have many places with cliffs of earth. The kilns were dug into cliffs.' Yes, like the cave-houses I had seen not far from Lintong. There is no shortage of hillsides and deep earth. The making of kilns would not impose restraints.

He thought the number of craftsmen would be the biggest problem. After all, he was the only designer and artisan in his factory.

'So how long does it take you to create one full-size figure?'

His reply was instantaneous: 'Twenty days.' (Incidentally, it takes almost as long, fifteen days, to make a smaller figure.) So his ten full-size designs represented a little over six months' work for one man.

Now, Wang does not have to live under the pressure imposed by the First Emperor, who would surely have wanted work completed as quickly as possible, with the greatest possible variety. This could only have been done by making many small moulds for various parts of the body – hands, legs, heads, ears – and thus producing a range of interchangeable parts. An analysis of the warriors reveals some 80 different moulds. Even assuming that all these were as complex as Wang's (they weren't), the original statues and sections of statues from which the whole army was made could have been completed in under five years by one man. In fact, of course, there would have been many. A team of, say, 80 master sculptors – and surely such a team could have been assembled, given that the emperor had the whole of his newly formed empire to choose from – could have had the moulds for the whole army ready in three weeks. OK: master craftsmen do not grow on trees. Let's say they could only find 20. Even so, all the moulds would be ready in three months.

What about the numbers of Qin workers and their output?

There would have been no shortage of clay-workers in Qin times, because armies of potters were used to produce drainpipes, floor-tiles and roof-tiles, not simply for the emperor's new Epang Palace but for all the palaces built in Xianyang after unification. Co-opting a few dozen trained workers, even a few hundred, would make hardly any difference. Bearing in mind that Wang employs 20 people, who could produce 1,000 full-size statues a year, let's put 200 on the job, which boosts production tenfold – to 10,000 full-size statues a year. At that rate, the 8,000 statues needed to fill the main pit and all the others with full-size statues would be ready in under ten months.

I'm guessing, but my guess is pretty much in line with another, very much more expert, estimate by Yuan Zhongyi, one of the Army's top excavators, whom I went to see in his Xian apartment.[2] Yuan points out that it was common for potters to sign their names on their products, as part of quality control, so that over-seers would know whom to blame for shoddy work. The same is true of the warriors. And signatures on some of the tiles from the Xianyang palace match those on some of the warriors, so it is fair to infer that the techniques used to make the warriors were familiar to potters. More: on 1,383 warriors and 132 horses examined by Yuan, there are 477 stamps and incisions, mostly serial numbers, but also the names of 87 foremen, who often identified themselves by their place of work or residence. One, for instance, was Gong Jiang (Jiang of the Palace, the state factory); another, Xianyang Ge (Ge of a local factory in Xianyang). The arguments are highly technical and uncertain, but serial numbers suggest that figures were worked on and counted in multiples of five, which in turn suggests that sculptors worked in teams of ten. Suppose that these foremen also produced most of the other unrestored warriors, but let's add fifteen more for the sake of argument, which gives us a workforce of 1,000. Suppose it takes a ten-man team two weeks to complete their five figures. That means the 1,000 artisans will, in one year, produce 12,500 figures.

[2] His work is also summarized by Lothar Ledderose in *Ten Thousand Things*.

Often, you will read that this operation involved 'hundreds of thousands' of workers, but that is to confuse the tomb as a whole with the Terracotta Army, which was by comparison a small-scale affair with the potential for huge production figures, rather like a modern car factory.

You see where I am going – as Wang did, because he was smiling gently.

The emperor clearly wished to have a spirit army that would represent his real army. But his real army was numbered in the tens of thousands. Why would he be content with the 7,000–8,000 that are buried near his tomb?

'If you are the First Emperor, and you say: "Give me my whole army in terracotta," is anyone going to tell you that you cannot do it for this or that reason?'

Wang's smile grew. 'No. It is possible.'

'What I'm wondering is: why is the Terracotta Army so *small*?'

I went on, improvising. On the basis of Wang's work with reproductions and Yuan's calculations, it seemed that, allowing (say) a year for the fundamentals – the creation of figures to make moulds, the building of kilns – by the time of his death in 210 BC, after a decade of work, the emperor could have had not 8,000 warriors but over 100,000: enough to produce not only an army facing east, but others facing west and north (not south: it's uphill and too rocky).

It seemed to me that Wang's work had opened

up a line of thought that was entirely new. The Army is presented as a pinnacle of achievement, the greatest of the First Emperor's works, only to be matched perhaps by the tomb when it is finally opened. But what if it is not a pinnacle? What if it was only a beginning?

And why had no one else examined this idea? At the time, I strongly suspected it had something to do with a glass wall between academics and artisans. The academics look to archaeologists for their evidence, which lies in the ground and must be dug up with extreme care and skill and reported in journals in the proper way and then turned into a tourist industry through government departments. But Wang's world was utterly different. It was a world of mess, and hands-on artistry, and simple labourers doing simple things, and making money privately. I suspected a barrier between officials and academics on the one hand and workers and artisans on the other. I thought: it's time for the academics to pay Wang a visit, get some mud on their shiny shoes, and learn something about the past by studying the present.

Well, in hindsight, I was being a little hasty, because I had not yet realized the importance of colour. More about that in a moment.

Work on the statues began. Not that it was precisely the same as Wang's in every detail. The Qin sculptors did not use moulds to make the

175

heavy legs, or many of the torsos. These they built up by rolling the clay into long, thin cylinders, coiling these on top of each other and then smoothing out the dents and bumps, the same way as potters make a pot freehand. In some broken figures, the strips of clay are clearly visible. Nor does Wang make horses, which had solid legs, for strength and balance, and bodies that were also made with coils of clay.

Still, the essence of the operation depended on the moulds: ten for heads, four for boots, two for legs, three for shoes. From the modular production process, heads, boots, bodies and legs emerge, still soft from their moulds. Now details must be added; these may be produced from smaller moulds (ears, moustaches, buckles, hairstyles and shoes) or by hand, achieved (as by Wang's workers today) by refining noses, beards and eyes with scrapers, shavers and sharpened bamboo sticks. In this way, realism is heightened. Indeed, when the figures first came to light the realism seemed so astonishing that it was widely claimed – still is, in the more unthinking brochures – that the warriors were actual portraits of every man in the First Emperor's army.[3]

That would be truly astonishing, for the Chinese had never developed a tradition of portraiture to

[3] The definitive statement on this matter is by Eleanor von Erdberg in 'Die Soldaten Shih Huang Ti's'.

match Greek or Indian art. There were animals modelled in clay, carved in stone or cast in metals; there were masks; there were superb bronzes, even the occasional figure. Then, later, artists became adept at portraying movement, hairstyles and clothing. But the figures were heavily symbolic. A figure might represent the essence of kingship, but it never occurred to any ruler or any artist to capture the actual features of the king.

Or of the individual soldier. What the sculptors and production workers had to capture was the essence of military ability, which meant exactly the opposite of individuality. As Eleanor von Erdberg says, 'In these heads there could be no place for any thought other than military discipline and duty. To act as an individual would be gross insubordination.' Of course, the emperor's recruiters would have selected the best, rejecting the super-tall, the undersized, the lame, the diseased, the weak. But even for cannon-fodder, or in this case arrow-fodder, entry standards into the real army would have been lower than perfection. Yet in these warriors there are no deformities, no faces disfigured by smallpox, no pimply teenagers, no earless or one-eyed fighters, no gnarled ancients, not a single wound. The army would surely have recruited from every newly conquered land, incorporating for example the tough little horse-riders of the steppes, yet you would be hard-pressed to find racial differences (which are well represented in the little figures in the Han tombs at Yangling). Impeccable hair, neat eyebrows, trim moustaches, every eyelid delineated: they are all suspiciously good-looking, as idealized as a Michelangelo Christ, with expressions, or rather lack of them, to match – inscrutable, calm, with hardly a frown or a smile to sully those perfect features.

Take their heights: the rank-and-file soldiers range between 1.66 metres and 1.87 metres, with an average of 1.77 metres (5 feet 10½ inches), which may or may not mirror the average height of the emperor's real army. But officers average 1.9 metres (6 feet 3 inches), while a general is an imposing 1.96 metres (6 feet 5½ inches), though he is in boots and on a little tile. In the real world, generals are not necessarily taller than their men, and some are notoriously shorter. The differences are further evidence of idealization.

The intention was to capture a deeper reality. For this army, like all armies, depended on group actions, group loyalties, total obedience. As anyone knows who has watched *An Officer and a Gentleman* or been through an old-fashioned English public school, basic training in the hands of sadistic sergeant-majors and housemasters involves stripping away individuality to create the group. That is what is being idealized here: the group, composed of individuals all made obedient and calmly ready for whatever fate lies in store.

Yet in real life men and boys do not become

indistinguishable one from another, no matter how they are depersonalized. They are *not* like pawns on a chessboard, because differences can never be eradicated. Reality would not have been served by making them identical. In these idealized faces and bodies, there had to be individuality – but only *apparent* individuality. For an artisan to take the next step, to become (in western eyes) an artist, to portray a real individual, would have been unthinkable.

This variety was intended to achieve far more than the appearance of individuality: it also stated differences in rank and speciality. If personal variation is suggested by a dozen different face-shapes, combined with varieties of eyebrow, moustache, beard and lips, difference in status is indicated by distinguishing headgear, collars, belt-buckles, armour and tassels, providing extraordinary insights into Qin military uniforms. Armour, for instance, was all made of leather, either in large pieces or in plates tied together with little straps. Some had sleeve-armour, some didn't. Charioteers wore full armour; cavalry not much, to ensure lightness and speed. Lower ranks had larger leather plates (between 119 and 147 of them, according to the statues), which made their armour less flexible, while officers had up to 229 nice little flexible ones. All officers wore caps. These gradations suggest seven divisions: high-ranking officer (seven so-called 'generals'), middle-ranking officer, armoured soldier, unarmoured soldier, charioteer, cavalryman and archer (kneeling or standing).

Under the armour soldiers wore coats, shirts, vests, trousers, puttees and shin-pads, which the soldiers had to supply themselves. The main item was the long wraparound coat (always closed with the left side over-lapping the right),[4] a relatively new style adopted from the horse-riding Xiongnu the other side of the Great Wall. Evidence that soldiers had to provide their own undergarments comes from a Qin grave unearthed in Shuihudi (near Yunmeng, Hubei). Here archaeologists found a wooden tablet written by a third-century-BC soldier named Hei Fu: 'Mother, would you please check when the silk in Anlu is reasonably priced and then make me a couple of unlined skirts and coats? Send them to me together with the money.' Hei Fu was lucky to be able to ask for light summer wear. Most soldiers had to make do with coarse hemp material. Cavalrymen, though, had tunics with narrow sleeves and a smaller overlap, to give them better freedom of movement, if less warmth – and not much protection: surprisingly, the warriors lack shields. No one knows why. Perhaps because they slowed reactions, or were considered effete, or were simply omitted by the

[4] If you did the opposite, you showed you were in mourning, because it imitated the northern barbarians and meant 'turning your back on life'.

sculptors to assert the macho qualities of their creations.

Qin hairstyles were of particular importance, as revealed by bamboo scrolls found in the Shuihudi grave. Question: How should a man be disciplined for severing another's hair-knot? Answer: 'Forced to build walls,' for four years. Even tearing out another's hair in a brawl was a 'hair-crime'. And what if things get really bad – if, during a fight, the victim's hands are bound and his eyebrows and beard torn out? Not a common crime these days: it implies some sort of ritual way of causing grievous bodily harm combined with an outrageous insult. Anyway, the answer is the same: building walls, for four years. To be condemned for any serious offence meant being shaved – head, beard or both.

Clearly, then, the warriors' hairstyles were of great social, military and aesthetic significance, which is why they were modelled in such detail: hair-knots on the top right side made from one, two or three plaits bound or tied in a dozen styles; flat hair-knots made without plaits or with a single, six-stranded plait; knots that are held with pins, slides, caps or scarves. Most, but not all, infantrymen had the top-knot on the right, a fashion that was conventional in the past, but dropped out of use in later dynasties. Those infantrymen with flat knots presumably wore helmets. Officers, cavalrymen and charioteers favoured flat knots on the back of the head.

The Qin cared equally about their beards and moustaches, which were marks of beauty and status. Beards could be worn as side-whiskers, 'three-drop' beards (with three little tufts), half-shaved, divided, full (one warrior has a beard down to his chest) or residual; moustaches could be upturned crescents, down-turned, arrow-headed or flat, all in large and small versions. Varying the styles and combinations of moustaches and beards offered scores of different possibilities.

And this pseudo-individuality was guaranteed to perfection by the modular process. The operation was a three-dimensional version of the children's book in which pages of heads, bodies and legs can all be turned over separately to make a huge variety of different figures, with underlying similarities further disguised by the fact that similar figures are separated to intensify the impression of endless human variety.

Then there are the colours. Colour turns out to be a matter of much complexity and labour. It was not shortage of clay or kilns or sculptors, I think, that placed a limit on the number of warriors, but the drive to apply colour.

For non-specialists, the fact that the warriors were painted is both strange and disturbing, for it flies in the face of the evidence as you see it today. We have all got used to the terracotta warriors looking like terracotta. But they weren't like that at all when they were made. They were lacquered, and bright with reds and blues and greens and purples – not just the uniforms, but the faces too. You have to imagine one of the most famous figures, the towering 'general', as he is known, with painted patterns on his tunic and armour, green and purple clothing, and bright green shin-protectors. And a pink face, like virtually all the warriors: a gentle pink created by mixing red and white, even gentler for the more senior officers, perhaps because (then as now) a pale skin suggested upper-class status, whereas a weather-beaten skin indicated the hard outdoor life of the common soldier.

Why the colour? I turned to the German conservator Catharina Blänsdorf, who holds the Chair of Conservation in Munich's Technical University and has been masterminding colour conservation at Lintong since 2003. She answered the question by widening it, then turning it on its head.

First, colour was all the rage in the ancient world, in the West as well as the East. The Parthenon, the Elgin Marbles, the Venus de Milo – all were originally a riot of colours. Weather and the passage of time stripped them; and it is to this process that we owe our view that Greek statues should be earth- and clay- and marble-coloured. The Romans avoided colour, as did Renaissance sculptors, so that remained the fashion defined by the art historian Edward

Strange as 'the solemn grandeur of the international Classical style'.[5] It was an attitude strengthened by determined 'restoration'. The Elgin Marbles were robbed of most of their remaining colours when they arrived in London in the early nineteenth century, and subsequent cleanings removed the rest. That is why browns, greys and whites are seen as 'noble', 'tasteful' and therefore 'authentic'.

It's an attitude that will be hard to change. When I was at the reproductions factory in Xian, I asked about the colours. Surely true authenticity ought to mean that the reproductions should be painted? Jerry Wong, who was showing me round, reacted as if I had made an improper suggestion. *Paint* them? Of course not! It would run counter to the expectations of the customers. Everyone knows the warriors are 'really' grey-brown, earth-coloured. That is the way they expect them to be. In fact – I am looking at Wang's miniatures as I write this – reproductions of all sizes have mud rubbed on to them, to suggest that they have just come out of the ground. This is crazy, since the only true originals were full-size figures that were crisp, sparkling, coloured – and totally unmuddy until their roof fell in. I look again at the array of little figures Wang gave me: miniatures,

[5] The 'Lacquer' entry in the *Enyclopaedia Britannica* from 1922 onwards, now incorporated into 'Decorative Arts and Furnishings'.

184

unpainted, artificially dirty – how inauthentic can you get?

An *authentic* warrior was a brightly coloured warrior. As Catharina Blänsdorf says, to ask why is to look at the matter the wrong way round. 'As so many objects of the antique world were painted – in the West as well as the East – and especially the sculptures, the question should rather be: why *not* paint them?'

The fact is that Chinese adored their colours, mainly because they were hard to come by, hard to make, expensive, and therefore symbols of luxury. It would have been inconceivable *not* to paint the statues, never mind that this would add labour, management, time, expense and complexity, and never mind that this was in a sense frivolous. The colours did not reflect reality, for ordinary soldiers would not have invested in colour. If officers did so, it would have been a personal indulgence. As Yuan Zhongyi writes in a long analysis of the warriors' looks: 'Differentiation between various ranks is not possible on the basis of clothing colour alone nor is differentiation between the various military units.'[6] This is art for the sake of art.

Take the lacquer, a remarkable substance which was vital to seal the clay and act as the foundation layer of the paint. Hard and lustrous, lacquer

6 Yuan Zhongyi, 'Hairstyles, Armour and Clothing of the Terracotta Army'.

185

had been known for 3,000 years as a protection against acid, water and mould – 'the most ancient industrial plastic known to man', in the words of Joseph Needham. Though common enough even in the West, it is a mystery to non-specialists, like me before I researched it. Lacquer is the thick, light-grey sap of the lacquer tree (or varnish tree, as it is sometimes known),[7] obtained in egg-cup amounts – 10 grams per tree on average – by cutting through the outer bark and bleeding the sap into a cup, rather like gathering rubber, or maple syrup. Trees have to grow for six years before they are ripe, and they can be tapped only during four months, June to September (carefully, because the sap is toxic and causes a nasty rash if touched and a violent reaction if inhaled). The lacquer, which turns black on exposure to humidity and warmth, has to be stirred, beaten and sieved to make it pure and even. If many coats are needed, each has to 'dry' before the next is applied. The quotes are there because the sap doesn't exactly dry, but reacts chemically with the water in damp air to harden into something like enamel. It can be used on almost anything: it seals wood, bamboo, even cloth, and was used for

[7] Botanical note: *Toxicodendron vernicifluum*, as it is now, after years of dispute about classification. The lacquer tree is related to other toxicodendrons, e.g. poison ivy and poison sumac. Strictly speaking, lacquer goes under paint, varnish over it.

centuries to make wooden dinner services that resisted the heat of cooking as effectively as metal. One hundred coats applied over many months create a surface thick enough to carve. Even lesser-grade lacquer-work – of the kind used to seal the warrior statues – takes weeks, and a lot of lacquer: each statue would have been sealed using the sap from up to 25 trees. In all, the 8,000 warriors would have needed the sap from 150,000–200,000 trees.[8] At a production rate of 1,000 statues a year, that's 20,000 trees annually to be tapped, and the sap processed and stored. Often, tapping the tree kills it, which means that this operation killed whole forests, creating a shortage in the following dynasty noted by Sima Qian.

Catharina Blänsdorf took part in a lacquering experiment, though she did not watch the work closely because, after three severe reactions, she realized she was highly allergic to the lacquer. Two Chinese painters, using slightly diluted raw lacquer, took a day to cover one statue, which took five days to harden. She suggests that an untreated statue would have needed three coats (one to prime, two to seal), over the course of about three weeks, depending on the time of year. We have just added 3,000 to the warriors' work-force and quadrupled the production time to a month per statue.

[8] Cristina Thieme, 'East Asian Lacquer', in Blänsdorf et al., *Qin Shihuang*.

Of the colours used – red, white, green, black, brown, blue, purple – each has a story, the last being the most extraordinary. Known as 'Chinese [or Han] Purple', because it was made only in China, it was an unlikely combination of minerals. No one knew the details until recently because Chinese Purple fell from use over the next few centuries. Experiments in the 1980s revealed the formula: barium, copper, quartz and lead melted together at 900–1,100°C, which (not coincidentally) was the temperature at which the terracotta warriors were fired. The process was so complex that it must have been the result of many experimental trials and errors.

But why perform the experiments? A few years ago, a seven-man team of American physicists undertook a research project to find the answers, and in January 2007 they published their results.[9] The team noted that the process was like that used in glass-making, which developed at the same time, from about 500 BC onwards. Glass production was of great interest to Daoist monks, mainly because they were obsessed with making artificial jade, which they believed to be a vital ingredient in any possible elixir of immortality. During countless experiments over many years, they discovered that adding barium to glass makes it turbid, resembling jade. Lead, which was

[9] Liu et al., 'Influence of Taoism on the Invention of the Purple Pigment Used on the Qin Terracotta Warriors'.

anyway an ingredient of red and white pigments, was routinely added to reduce the melting point of other minerals. Inevitably, over the course of such experiments with these ingredients, someone would eventually, by chance, stumble on 'Chinese Purple'.

(As additional evidence for this idea, the American scientists also note that Chinese Purple fell from use in the following dynasty, the Han, as mystical, alchemical Daoism gave way to down-to-earth Confucianism, 'a striking example of how cultural changes affected scientific developments in ancient China).'

All this should revise the standard view of the production process. First, we have to include the lacquer-men and their back-up army of sap-collectors. Then we also need teams of alchemists, in particular one dedicated to the highly specialized task of brewing up Chinese Purple.

Other colours are almost as demanding. Whatever the original material, it had to be ground to exceptional fineness. The red, for instance, was made with cinnabar, a rare mineral of red crystals which, when processed, produces mercury (of peculiar interest to the First Emperor, as we shall see). A major source was some 200 kilometres south, where an enterprising widow named Qing had made herself rich running a cinnabar mine – a hazardous occupation for the miners, since mercury is poisonous. To produce red pigment for paint, it had to be ground into the finest of powders by hand.

No wonder the First Emperor wanted his figures coloured. In real life, his warriors were dressed in drab materials, so would the emperor not wish something better for his spirit army? Something lavish? Something extremely expensive and difficult to produce? To make the spirits happy with their lot, and even more eager in death than in life to fight for their generous emperor? Of course he would.

Meanwhile, the warriors' own tomb had to be prepared. There is absolutely no mention anywhere in the ancient texts of the Terracotta Army's pit, or indeed any other. This could surely be only because they were all lesser operations compared to the gigantic task of covering the tomb-mound. Lesser, yes; but still vast compared to the work achieved to date. Some department head in the Qin administration must have known how many men it took to dig a pit of such and such a size, and how long it would take them. In the case of the Army pit, they had a size in mind, because they knew what sort of an army would be required – soldiers, officers, chariots, infantrymen, archers – and already had most of them in storage.

Let's see what would have been involved. The pit is 260 metres long, 62 wide and almost 9 deep: 145,000 cubic metres. First, labourers had to shift 217,000 tonnes of soil, which was about two-thirds the amount dug for the main tomb's underground palace. It is also less demanding in design terms. Let's assume 200 diggers (again) and 16,000 earth-carriers shifting the same 1,000 tonnes a day. Could be faster, because there are no surrounding walls to hem in the earth-carriers. Even at this slow rate, they could dig this pit in just over seven months.

With good planning, the two operations – the Army pit and the underground palace's foundation – should be happening simultaneously. In that case some of the earth could have gone into the tomb's walls, the rest being kept to be returned to the Army pit in the form of the rammed earth walls that will bear the rafters and make the 11 corridors in which the soldiers will stand. That's 30,000 cubic metres – 45,000 tonnes – of earth to be rammed into 3 kilometres of walls 5 metres high and 2 metres across.

This had to be done because the Qin, who did not build in stone, did not know about arches and used horizontal beams for all their ceilings. This would have to be a strong ceiling, with each beam supporting 5 tonnes of earth. The beams would be rough-hewn, some 425–450 millimetres across, sawn into 5-metre lengths (saw-marks have been found on several). These are big beams, twice as thick as telegraph poles, weighing 500 kilos – half a tonne – each. There will be 575 beams per aisle, over 6,000 in all – 3,000 tonnes of wood! And that's just Pit No. 1. It needed to be as carefully planned as a military campaign. You would not want to forget the floor, sealed with grey-blue bricks, 256,000 of them. Who makes them? When? Where?

Final question: When would the roof be added? After the warriors were in place? That's risky, because a dropped beam would mean broken statues, let alone the engineering problem of raising a half-tonne beam to enable the broken warriors to be replaced from above – lifting out broken pieces and carefully lowering new ones into position. Or was it the other way around, with the warriors placed after the roof was finished? That would surely be even worse, for they would all have to be carried along dark, narrow corridors (always with the risk of breakage) and placed in very restricted spaces. Once roofed, no corridor could see over into the next. Yet the rows match up pretty well. It seems to me that the Qin surveyors would wait for the emperor's death, and then place the warriors and roof the pit in a joint operation, putting a few warriors in position at a time, then roofing that small section.

Meanwhile, production continues. As the figures emerge from the kilns, the painters get to work on them. Some acquire two layers of soft pink, to give them the glow of healthy skin. Blackened hair shines against red headbands. Eyes with darkened pupils stare with piercing gaze, very different from the blank look of the warriors today. Brightly coloured clothes contrast with the scales of the leather armour, lacquered as they were in life, the connecting fabrics that stitched them together coloured in white, orange, green and ochre.

And as other specialists work on their own creations – bronze-workers producing animals and intricate, perfect models of chariots, stone-workers wiring flakes of stone into dozens of suits of mock-armour, and tens of thousands labouring on the tomb itself – the terracotta figures in their garish colours are placed under wraps or in storehouses to await the day, years in the future, when the emperor's body will release his spirit, and the whole massive enterprise will shift gear to prepare his final resting place.

CHAPTER 10

SUDDEN DEATH

We left the First Emperor up Mount Kuaiji, furthering his own personality cult. It was the end of 211 BC, with winter well advanced. He was approaching 50, and was as keen as ever to maximize security and minimize risk.

There had been bad omens. The previous year a meteorite had fallen on which someone had engraved, 'The First Emperor will die and his land will be divided.' The emperor ordered an investigation that ended without result, except that the locals were all executed and the offending rock destroyed. A stranger had given a royal envoy a jade disc inscribed with the enigmatic words, 'This year the primal dragon will die.' Did he mean the First Emperor? Could be. The emperor had his magi consult the *Yi Jing*. A journey, they concluded, would be propitious, which suited the emperor, because he wanted to make another tour – the fourth – of his new dominions.

Hence this immense journey, with most of his government in tow (for he needed to be as much in control as ever) – nine ministers and unknown numbers of assistants and families, all in scores of four-horse chariots, with who knows how many troops and herds of replacement horses. Besides the emperor himself, this mass of people included the following *dramatis personae*:

- Li Si, chancellor. In office for 37 years and now in his early seventies.
- Huhai, one of the emperor's younger sons (18th of 20). Aged 20. Ineffectual, compliant. He needs to be brought on stage, because it is he, in the end, who will supervise the burial of the Terracotta Army.
- Zhao Gao, the villain. Transport chief, responsible for carriages and communications. He doubled as Huhai's law tutor, and was also the most senior of a small group of eunuch attendants.
- Meng Yi, chief minister. Zhao's enemy. He is the brother of Meng Tian, the great general who is guarding the northern frontier and building the Great Wall.

This was more an official migration than a procession, fraught with all the tensions of government at home. In particular, the villainous eunuch Zhao Gao and Meng Yi loathed each other. Zhao Gao had once been accused of committing some crime, probably corruption of some kind, which is quite possible given that his mother was a long-term prisoner, though with enough freedom to bear Zhao and several other sons. It was chief minister Meng Yi who had had Zhao tried and condemned. Even though Zhao was a senior official, as a good Legalist, Meng Yi argued for the death penalty. But Zhao, as young Huhai's tutor and himself a legal expert, was a slippery lawyer, and persuaded the emperor to pardon him. Zhao never forgave Meng Yi, and nursed a bitter resentment against both brothers.

Almost certainly, given his well-justified paranoia about assassins, the emperor was travelling in any one of several identical carriages. This would have been a basic precaution for many years, and an effective one: a third assassination attempt seven years earlier had failed because the assailant attacked the wrong carriage. Each carriage in this group would have been like the bronze one now on display in the Terracotta Army Museum: topped with a huge round roof that overlapped walls with small sliding grilles for windows, and driven by a single man armed with a crossbow. All were designed to keep warm in winter and cool in summer, all were equally discreet.

The immense retinue, moving sedately at an average of only 15 kilometres a day, worked its way 600 kilometres south-east to the Yangtze, another 500 kilometres downriver in a fleet of boats, then cross-country again for 250 kilometres to the sacred mountain of Kuaiji, near Shaoxing, famous for its wine, where, in the long-ago dream-time of semi-mythical founders, Yu the flood hero had succeeded in controlling China's waters.

Here the emperor claimed to be Yu's heir by sacrificing to him, then left the pillar promoting his own power, purity, beneficence and popularity. 'The officials in his retinue praise his brilliance, begging to inscribe this stone,' concluded the text. 'May its glorious message shine through the ages.'

The emperor might then have turned homeward. But he was drawn to the sea as the route to the islands that were the supposed source of the immortality drugs promised by his entourage of Daoist mystics. He had sent out two expeditions, remember, and nothing had been heard of any results. So instead of going home he headed north along the coast for some 700 kilometres, to two mountains where he had previously erected stelae. First stop was Mount Langya, where he had placed a stele eight years before. He had loved it there, so much that he had 30,000 families resettled nearby.

He must have had high hopes, because it was from near here – today's Jiaonan, a river port a few kilometres inland – that his Daoist adviser Xu Fu had dispatched the last expedition to find the elixir of immortality. On arrival, he questioned Xu Fu. Had he not promised that the elixir existed on islands in the middle of the sea? Had he not spent years searching, at huge cost? Xu Fu replied that indeed the islands could be seen afar off, but unfortunately – the excuse is so ludicrous as to be laughable, except that the emperor had never been to sea and would apparently believe anything – unfortunately 'always there are large fish that cause difficulty,

197

and therefore we are unable to reach the island'. Xu Fu had a solution to hand: what they needed was a skilled archer with a repeating crossbow so that they could shoot any fish they saw.

The emperor's response seems to have been an intense mixture of hope and doubt. He was by now, perhaps, almost (but not completely) in thrall to his paranoias and obsessions. He dreamed that he was wrestling with an ocean-god. When he asked one of his advisers what this meant, he was told that his opponent, though real, could not be seen except in the form of a 'large fish or dragon'. That did it. All doubt vanished. It was him versus the fish. The emperor ordered that his seamen should carry with them nets and lines to seize any huge fish, while 'he himself carried a repeating crossbow and watched for a great fish to appear so that he could shoot it'.

He then proceeded along the Shandong coast and round its peninsula for some 350 kilometres to another of his mountains, Zhifu, near present-day Yantai. On the beach there, so Sima Qian says, he actually saw some large fish and shot one of them. It's an unlikely story, which suggests an image of a deranged emperor urged on by obsequious courtiers and firing all the arrows in his repeating crossbow at a non-existent target out at sea, to be hailed by the watching crowd as a master bowman.

He then continued west, perhaps via Penglai, because this was also the name of one of the fabulous islands where the elixir of immortality was supposedly to be found. It is a place that inspires fantasy, first because there are a number of islands offshore, some close enough to be seen; and second because it is famous for occasional sea-mirages, in which mountains, trees, even people seem to float on the horizon (you can find recent accounts of this mirage by Googling 'Penglai'). He then set off for home, minus any elixirs.

But after some 500 kilometres, suddenly, at a place called Sand Hill on the flat and river-rich expanses of southern Hebei, he fell ill. It was high summer, and Xian locals tell you he went down with heatstroke. That seems unlikely, given his well-shaded and well-aired carriage. No source reveals his disease, which suggests no one knew what it was. In any event, he went downhill fast.

Fearing the end was coming, he dispatched Meng Yi home, with orders to make life-saving sacrifices along the way. Then he turned to the succession, a matter he had been avoiding and no one else had dared mention because he hated the very idea of death. He had exiled his eldest son Fusu to the northern frontier as a punishment for criticizing the execution of the 460 Confucian literati, but Fusu was still his heir. The emperor wrote him a peremptory letter: When mourning is announced, go to Xianyang and arrange the funeral. Few words, yet a huge order – work on the tomb to be resumed, subsidiary pits dug, horses and concubines and officials designated for suicide or execution (for there would be some human sacrifices to be made), the Terracotta Army to be retrieved from storage and buried, countless other artefacts to be gathered, all the correct rituals to be organized.

By implication, this letter confirmed Fusu as the next emperor. And there was another implication: Fusu had been seconded to the great general of the northern frontier, Meng Tian. When he came to take up his inheritance, he would have the empire's toughest army at his back.

Having handed the letter over to his communications chief and senior eunuch, Zhao Gao, the First Emperor died.

At this point, the top officials faced a problem. So far, not many people knew what had happened. The emperor's hold on his new estates was tenuous. That was, after all, why he was making this long journey, to show his restless people that the empire was there for keeps. What might the reaction be when they knew he had died – and died, moreover, far from Xianyang and the mass of his armies? Dreadful prospects loomed, dark imagined futures: uprisings, revolution, an end to the Qin empire, and back to the bad old days of seven states and eternal wars.

This was one of those rare moments when history held her breath. Not even Prince Huhai knew the emperor was dead. The only ones who did were the eunuch chief of carriages, Zhao Gao, the chancellor, Li Si, and a few other trusted eunuchs. To tell or not to tell? The high stakes, the few characters involved, their moral dilemmas, their fears, the rising tension of the next few days – once again, we are in the realm of high drama. As far as I know, there is no film. There should be; there could be, because Sima Qian wrote the script, or at least some powerful dialogue. He's not so good on scene-setting. Where do these intense and secretive exchanges take place? Back and forth between carriages on the move, presumably. These are mere details. More important are the plot, the characters, and the outcome.

But is it history? In his long biography of Li Si, on which this account is based, Sima Qian does not give his sources. Remember his agenda: to discredit his own emperor by discrediting the First. In this case, he is dramatizing treachery in order to condemn it. The empire is about to go to hell, thanks to plotting and the imposition of an illegal heir. This must somehow be explained, and the cause lies in the *éminence grise*, Zhao Gao, who, as a eunuch in charge of eunuchs, was head of a group suspected through all Chinese history of being malign and self-serving. Real events and outcomes provide a sound historical framework, but it is the invented dialogue and characterization that fill it with life.

It was eminent, trustworthy, elderly Li Si who took the first step, perhaps with the best intentions: namely, to gain time to work out the best policy. He secretly had the body placed in the imperial carriage, which no one could enter without the permission of the attendant eunuch. I imagine Li Si, Zhao Gao and Huhai in adjacent carriages, hemming in the emperor's along the narrow mud roads as the great procession moved slowly west-ward. Ministers continued to deliver state papers for the emperor's approval, cooks delivered food. Inside, a second eunuch placed the emperor's seal on the papers, and handed them out. For a couple of days – it could hardly have been more, given what happens to dead bodies in the height of summer – business continued as usual.

Zhao Gao still had not handed the emperor's last letter to a messenger. He had a motive for delay, because he loathed the whole Meng family. If the letter was sent, then Fusu would take over – Fusu the pro-Confucian, the man who had defended the Confucian scholars and criticized his own father. And what then? An outcome almost as bad as revolution and imperial collapse, at least from the Legalist point of view. Out would go the long-standing chancellor Li Si and minister Zhao Gao, their extensive families and all their retainers. If they were lucky, they would be allowed to commit suicide; if not, their deaths would be almost as unpleasant as being buried alive. In would come Fusu and Meng Tian and their Confucians, and all would be set at risk. It was Zhao, therefore, who took the next crucial step.

Zhao had only a few hours to act. Perhaps he told himself that there was no treachery, for the emperor had written to Fusu, 'When mourning is announced . . .' Well, there would be no mourning announced. Zhao Gao seized the moment, strode up or down the line to Huhai's carriage and broke the news, with its stark consequences: The emperor's dead, and there is no will securing the position of any prince, except Fusu; if Fusu becomes emperor, 'you will be without so much as a foot of territory. What will you do?'

Huhai was too young and too distraught to be an instant convert to treachery. It's obvious what I have to do, he said. Nothing. There's nothing I can do, nothing at all.

Not so, said Zhao Gao, and laid out for him the decision before them, in words that make Sima Qian seem to foreshadow Shakespeare. He did not quite have Zhao say 'There is a tide in the affairs of men which, taken at the flood, leads on to fortune,' but that's what he meant: 'At this moment the decision of who shall take control of the empire lies with you, me and the chancellor alone. I beg you to think of this! To make others your subjects or to be a subject of others, to rule men or be ruled by them – how can the two be discussed in the same breath?'

Huhai, still the good son, hesitates. An elder brother betrayed, a father's edict ignored by a man like me, so lacking in ability – it is unrighteous, it is unfilial, the empire would never consent, the altars would not accept my sacrifices . . .

Zhao Gao, still the prince's tutor, seizes his pupil,

203

shakes him, and snarls sense and treachery together in his face. Other princes have done worse, actually killed their fathers, and no one said they lacked virtue! 'Great actions do not wait on petty scruples, abundant virtue does not trouble with niceties! Only dare to be decisive and the gods and spirits will step aside! I beg you to see this through!'

Zhao Gao sees he's on the verge of winning, and changes tack. Look, he says, we have to see the chancellor about this.

But how is that proper, argues querulous Huhai, seeing as how the death is still hidden, the mourning rites not yet performed?

'Now is the time! Now is the time!'

And at last Huhai buckles. Zhao Gao locks him into the plot by giving him the emperor's letter. He then seeks out Li Si and brings him up to date. Now that Huhai has the letter, 'The choice of an heir apparent depends solely on your say, my lord, and mine. What do you intend to do?'

Li Si is shocked to his core. 'How can you speak words that might destroy the nation!'

There follows a series of exchanges in which Zhao Gao convinces the upright Li Si to back his treacherous scheme.

My lord, consider, says Zhao Gao. If Fusu rules, he will be backed by Meng Tian and his border army. Can you compare with Meng Tian in ability, merit, strategic planning, allies, or friendship with the emperor's eldest son?

Li Si admits that on none of these counts can

he match Meng Tian. Why does Zhao Gao want to labour the point? To humiliate him?

Zhao Gao reviews his own 20-year career in the service of the emperor, then adds the clinching argument: never has he heard of a minister who was able to pass on his estates to the next generation. 'All in the end have been condemned and put to death.' So it will happen to Li Si. If Fusu becomes emperor, Meng Tian will be his chancellor, and you, my lord, will be impoverished. Now consider Huhai, his pupil for many years. He is kindhearted, generous, thinks little of wealth but much of his men, reserved, punctilious, respectful – in brief, an ideal emperor. He, not Fusu, should be the heir.

Now it's out in the open. Here's how the debate continues, adapted from two sources, Sima Qian and Derk Bodde:

LI SI (*aloof*):
Please return to your post. I will honour the command of my sovereign and heed the Mandate of Heaven.

ZHAO GAO:
What is secure may become perilous, the perilous can become secure. Choosing between security and peril – that is wisdom.

LI SI (*increasingly distressed*):
I was but a commoner who through imperial favour rose to become chancellor and

marquis. I have been entrusted with the nation's preservation or its ruin. How can I betray that charge? A loyal subject does not reach perfection by shunning death, a filial son does not heed peril. Each man has his own duty. I beg you say no more, for you would force me to do evil.

ZHAO GAO:

And yet I have heard that the sage shifts his course, goes along with changes, follows the times. It is in the nature of things to change. How can there be unchanging rules? When spring waters stir and flow, ten thousand things come to life. How can you be so slow to see this?

(Pause)

At this moment, the fate of the empire hangs on Huhai, and I am able to have my way with him.

LI SI:

There were those who changed heirs, who fought their brothers, who put their kinsmen to death, and the results were turmoil, death, a kingdom turned into a wilderness. Don't talk to me of plots!

ZHAO GAO:

Listen! If you do, you will keep possession

of your fief and title, for generation after generation. But if you permit this chance to slip away, then the disaster that will extend to your sons and grandsons is enough to make the blood run cold. The skilful man turns disaster into blessing. How will you proceed?

LI SI (*casting his eyes to heaven,
    weeping and sighing*):
Alas! That I alone should face such troubled times! Since I must live, what fate can I hope for?

With this, he too came on board.

And the conspiracy that Sima Qian refers to as the Sand Hill Plot moved forward. The three destroyed the original letter and concocted an imperial edict making Huhai heir and a fake letter that was sent to Fusu in the name of the emperor, saying: While I have been touring the empire and making sacrifices, Fusu and Meng Tian have been campaigning with several hundred thousand to no purpose. Moreover, Fusu has criticized and slandered me on many occasions. 'Fusu has not acted as a filial son. I present him with a sword so he may settle the matter for himself.' As for Meng Tian, 'as a subject he has acted disloyally. I present him with the opportunity to take his own life.'

Off went the letter carried by a trusted messenger, presumably not in an official carriage but on horseback for speed, and anyway accompanied by a troop of fast horsemen. It was a 500-kilometre gallop to Meng Tian's HQ, which at 100 kilometres a day would take them the best part of a week.

On the northern frontier, at Meng Tian's dusty head-quarters town in the eastern Ordos (where the Great Wall runs to this day), Fusu wept on reading the fake letter, but accepted it at face value. He was prevented from immediate suicide only by Meng Tian, who pointed out there was perhaps something fishy going on. They had both been appointed to guard the frontier with 300,000 troops; this was a 'weighty responsibility'; yet here comes this letter, delivered by a single messenger, out of the blue. They should at least get confirmation.

Fusu thought this would show an unfilial lack of trust, and committed suicide anyway.

Meng Tian, however, said he needed to know the order was genuine. Of course, the messenger could not possibly allow this – it would delay things by two weeks – so he had the general and his entourage of officers arrested (it is this that implies the 'single messenger' had a substantial body of troops with him). Meng Tian and his officers were taken to a prison some 60 kilometres south-east of the Great Wall fortress of Jingbian (it means 'Warn the Border'). Only now could a message be sent back to the conspirators that all was well: Fusu dead, Meng Tian in gaol.

★　　★　　★

Meanwhile, on the road to Xianyang, the emperor's dead body was becoming a problem. The emperor had now been dead for over a week, and his carriage was beginning to smell, embalming en route apparently being out of the question. From his carriage, therefore, came an odd order: that all official carriages should take on board 30 kilos of dried fish, which gave off enough of a smell to disguise the stench of decay. The imperial procession was still 450 kilometres and one month from home. It was only when news arrived of Fusu's suicide that the conspirators could announce the emperor's death and the fake edict appointing Huhai as his heir.

So at last, in September 210 BC, the great procession arrived back in Xianyang and the business began of installing the Second Emperor and burying the First.

Well-formed plans swing into action. The foundations of the tomb are dug, of course. There are springs beneath the tomb and all around the surrounding area, which means that the base of the tomb needs a dampproof course, a rather expensive one. Now, in Sima Qian's words, 'they poured in bronze to make the outer coffin', and the workforce completes the basics, in a famous passage that has fuelled imaginations ever since. This is Burton Watson's translation:

> [Replicas of] palaces, scenic towers and the 100 officials, as well as rare utensils and wonderful objects, were brought to fill up

the tomb. Craftsmen were ordered to set up crossbows and arrows, rigged so that they would immediately shoot down anyone attempting to break in. Mercury was used to fashion [imitations of] the hundred rivers, the Yellow River and the Yangtze, and the seas, constructed in such a way that they seemed to flow. Above were representations of all the heavenly bodies, below the features of the earth. 'Man-fish' oil was used for lamps, which were calculated to burn for a long time without going out.[1]

This paragraph, often quoted without comment as if it were proven and literal truth, owes a good deal to hype. Sima Qian gives no sources. It is folk memory, much embroidered by the passage of a century. An underground palace, treasures,

[1] The words within square brackets are not in the Chinese, but are implied. Watson's has been the standard version, much quoted. Here is another: 'They filled the grave chamber with models of palaces, towers and the Hundred Offices in addition to valuable vessels and precious stones and wonderful treasures. Crossbows with mechanical automatic releases offered protection from intruders. The country's various waterways, the Yangtze and the Yellow River as well as the ocean itself, were imitated in quicksilver, and a mechanical device produced flowing waves. Above the stars and the firmament were depicted, below a geographically realistic relief of the earth. Lamps filled with whale oil burned permanently.'

cocked crossbows, rivers of mercury, the constellations glittering in the ceiling, lamps glowing: this is Hollywood material, just right for the opening of an Indiana Jones movie.

Much of this work – the completion of the underground palace, the burial within it, the digging of secondary pits – would have gone ahead at speed. No record, however, mentions the funeral itself. The only details given by Sima Qian were the gruesome ones. Huhai, now the 21-year-old Second Emperor, but firmly under the thumb of the dreadful Zhao Gao, ordered that all concubines who had not born a son should 'accompany the dead man', presumably so that they could fulfil their duty in the next life. How many received this strange honour? Sima Qian just says 'many'. We know the emperor had 20 sons, so a dozen or two seems a minimum, assuming that concubinage was not yet the sub-world of thousands it became centuries later.

Now comes the job of roofing the tomb and the Army. The roof would require a forest of timbers – about 18,000 5-metre sections of pine. Felled in the forests of Sichuan, Henan and Hubei 200–300 kilometres to the south, the trees would have been rough-cut with iron axes after the emperor's death had been announced, and hauled northwards on cumbersome ox-wagons. The possible scope of this operation? Four beams to a wagon, 4,500 wagon-loads, the first ones arriving after a month, the rest rolling in over the following six months.

After the underground palace was sealed comes another of Huhai's grim decisions. 'Someone pointed out that the artisans and craftsmen who had built the tomb knew what was buried there' – so, to prevent word leaking out, 'the inner gate was closed off and the outer gate lowered, so that all the artisans and craftsmen were shut in the tomb and were unable to get out.'

This is another of those popular melodramatic details that turn up in every account. But I don't believe it. Horses were buried alive, and possibly a few people condemned for some crime. But teams of artisans and craftsmen, whose only fault was to have knowledge of the tomb's contents and their own work? It sounds more like the legends that arose around several other emperors: Attila the Hun, Genghis Khan, his son Ogedei, indeed any emperor (according to Marco Polo, who claimed that all living things on the route of the imperial funeral cortège were slain). Such assertions do not stand much scrutiny. Even a young maniac like the Second Emperor needed artists, if only to complete work on the unfinished Epang Palace. What would the deaths do to the morale of the survivors? What of the cocked crossbows? Well, we shall not know the truth until the day when the underground palace is opened.

There will be more digging to do – dozens of other pits for sacrificial animals, bronze carriages, suits of stone armour, officials, horses – but they can wait until the mound is either well under way or complete. So now, at last, comes the most formidable task of all: shifting the earth that covers the tomb and building the surrounding walls.

Today, the pyramid is between 50 and 75 metres high, depending on which side is measured. Remember from chapter 8, 'Digging the Tomb', that the official history of the Han dynasty claims the original height was 'more than 50 *zhang* (115 metres)', a figure often justified by reference to 'erosion' that has reduced it to its present dimensions. As far as I know, there is no evidence for such a massive reduction. Earth has gathered in some places at the base of the pyramid, but nothing that would suggest that the mound's height has been cut by 60 per cent or its floor area by a third. Today, you can hardly see its original shape – with a step halfway up – because of the trees, but on a photograph taken in 1914 the treeless, stepped shape is quite clear. If there had been severe erosion, that outline would have long since vanished. On other tombs (such as that of the Han emperor Wu Di), erosion has apparently had little effect. These thoughts make sense of Duan Qingbo's insistence in speaking to me that the standard sources are wrong, that 115 metres was just the *planned* height, that today's tomb probably looks much as it did 2,000 years ago. (This interpretation also makes sense of his belief that the underground palace is 80 × 50 metres, far smaller than the estimate quoted by Yuan Zhongyi).

This means the volume of the tomb is, and always was, about 1.8 million cubic metres. That's about 2.7 million tonnes of earth to be dug up and carried in from outlying areas – perhaps one in particular: a research paper quoted by Yuan Zhongyi states that in mineral content and colour much of the mound's soil matches that found in a pond about 2.5 kilometres away to the north-east, implying that the soil 'came from two sources: one was the earth dug from the original tomb, the other was the nearby reservoir'. Unless the workers are to file through gates, thus limiting their numbers, the tomb must be covered before the walls go up. We can get an idea of the numbers involved, because we know that the tomb was not completed by the time the dynasty died four years later. Indeed, it may have stopped earlier, only one year after the Second Emperor's accession, because by then civil war had spread to Lintong.

Meanwhile, there would be a lot more going on. For a start, the architects had planned for two sets of surrounding walls, with a separate enclosure for the emperor's concubines. The walls would be about 8 metres wide and some 10 metres high. That's 6 kilometres of rammed-earth wall, or almost half a million cubic metres (another 750,000 tonnes, over three times the amount removed from the palace foundations) of earth to dig, and pound, and finish, not forgetting ten gates, each with three storeys. And the guard-towers at each corner of each rectangle. And the tiled roofs that covered the walkways along the top of the walls, for the whole complex would be patrolled by guards who needed to be protected from the rain and sun. To the 2.7 million tonnes of earth for the mound must be added the 750,000 tonnes that form the walls: a total of 3.5 million tonnes to be shifted in four years, maximum.

In round figures, 175 million earth-carrying journeys in 1,500 days comes to 120,000 back-and-forth journeys per day. Assume each man makes three journeys per day. That's 40,000 workers, minimum.

The walls, though, were merely the shells for the real business of the tomb, which would be to honour the emperor's memory with rituals. These would centre on the Room of Rest, or Retiring Hall, a huge complex measuring 57 X 62 metres – gateway, courtyard, tiled hall and a 'holy of holies' – which would be the centre for the cult devoted to the dead emperor. It was to contain the emperor's clothing, headgear and other accoutrements, which would be taken in procession every month to a temple nearby for sacrifices and veneration. Here, probably, the emperor's coffin would be placed, ready for when the time came, and here his body would lie before it was consigned to the coffin and then the tomb. Nearby would be the Side Halls, where members of the imperial family would don their mourning clothes and prepare for the monthly rites. Finally, there would be a building for the preparation of the sacrificial food – a complex of a dozen halls set between the inner and outer walls, which would be used for weighing, measuring, food preparation and cooking. Officials would have planned that these buildings would be used for daily, weekly and monthly ceremonies in the years to come.

All this demanded a second, smaller army of several thousand administrators: engineers, overseers, geomancers, priests and cooks, all of whom would need their own houses, most of whom would probably have their own families. So imagine a line of houses standing on raised platforms between the inner and outer walls: normal single-storey houses, with wooden beams and curly-tiled roofs with round, decorated tile-ends.

The 40,000 labourers have to be housed and fed somewhere among the surrounding villages that wrung a living from the soil. Were they all criminals without families, working in concentration-camp conditions? Did some have families with them (Zhao Gao's mother, remember, had been a criminal, yet had borne several children while imprisoned)? No one knows. Then there were the craftsmen who made the bricks and tiles: they needed their workplaces and their families and their housing – a whole sub-community that lay to the west, outside the outer wall, well removed from the ritual sites. And who took care of security? Long-term criminals had to be supervised, new ones punished, possible mutinies crushed, which meant contingents of soldiers, and a barracks somewhere. And of course, there were many deaths, from disease, overwork, malnutrition, old age, so there had to be cemeteries, also outside the outer wall.

Off to one side, 1.5 kilometres from the heaving mass of labourers building the main tomb and its walls, were the pits of the Terracotta Army – pits in the plural, for there were enough terracotta figures to stretch the original concept. Perhaps Pit No. 1 had been prepared long since. But now it was clear that work would go on for years, there was a chance to heighten the realism of the Army by adding four specialized units to back up the 6,000 warriors of Pit No. 1. In Pit No. 2, there would be 64 wooden chariots and their 256 horses (no grooms), a mixed force of 25 chariots, 100 horses, more cavalry and infantry, 108 more cavalrymen and 332 archers – 1,300 figures in all. There's something odd about the shape of this pit, as if it started as a rectangle but then the designers changed their minds and added an extension. Pit No. 3 was tiny by comparison, with 68 well-spaced figures and a four-horse chariot facing an exit ramp. Archaeologists suggest this was the command centre, the Army's headquarters from which the action would be directed in some battle of spirits, with a chariot standing by to carry a messenger into the field. Pit No. 4 is an enigma, unfinished, awaiting contingents that never came.

Adding the three additional pits to the first

makes another 100,000 cubic metres, or 150,000 tonnes, of earth to be removed. By now the Qin quantity surveyors can take such figures in their stride, for it is less than a twentieth of the earth the workers have been shifting on to the tomb itself. If a quarter of the workforce (10,000) were seconded to the pits, they would finish the job in nine months.

Now we have to factor in another immense operation: the roofing. Recall the 4,500 wagon-loads of half-tonne beams lumbering in at the rate of half a dozen a day. To the beams must be added 3,300 3-metre supports which are to stand against the walls and help take the weight of the beams and the over-burden of earth. That's another 1,000 tonnes of timber, another 250 wagon-loads.

How would the beams be handled? Not with a great deal of respect, for they remained rounded, with their bark removed, but not squared off to fit close. They could have been, for Qin craftsmen used adzes to make planks (as the flooring on one of the small sacrificial pits shows). So quality was not of the essence. Perhaps speed was: better, apparently, to have a quick roof than a pretty one. The next challenge would be to get the beams in position, fast, which could have been done by laying a couple of planks along the top of each wall and rolling the beams into position.

Pit No. 4 was mysteriously left empty, un-finished, unroofed and unfilled. Did they run out of terracotta figures? Or time? Perhaps more figures were on order when revolution forced over-seers to drive the work-force away from the spirit army into the real one, to be scattered by the forces that would soon destroy all their labour.

CHAPTER 11

CONSUMED BY FIRE

For four years the Terracotta Army stood in pitch-black silence, an eternal army ready for imaginary battle, until some time in 206 BC the real world intruded. As I imagine it standing deep within one of the corridors, distant sounds of digging give way to thumps of falling earth and the cries of intruders. Flaming torches send red light dancing between the shadowy statues. People begin to shove their way along the corridors. There's no room, and the intruders are in a hurry. Warriors teeter and crash like falling dominoes. Living hands seize still-bright weapons from clay hands. Someone trips, curses, drops a scattering of sparks.

Some such scene occurred, for there is evidence: an entry shaft, fallen warriors, scattered horses' tails, a fire. But before we get to the details, I should tell you how the intruders came to be here.

It was all the fault of the Second Emperor, the emperor who should never have been. His top adviser was, of course, Zhao Gao, the king-maker, the instigator of the Sand Hill Plot which had brought him to the throne. Huhai's hold on power was weak, and would fail completely if his guilty secret ever came out. How to strengthen it? By doing as his father did – by touring distant parts to show his people who was boss. That's what he did in the spring of 209 BC, visiting the same mountains as his father and adding to all his father's inscriptions. All he added, though, was a statement that the inscriptions were by the First Emperor, in the hope that venerating his father's name would claim his mantle. Not enough, really, as the young emperor whined to Zhao Gao. Life was a misery. 'A person lives in this world no longer than it takes a team of six thoroughbreds to gallop past a crack in a wall. I want to savour all the pleasures of eye and ear.' Besides, 'The chief ministers are unsubmissive, the various officials still have great power, and the other imperial princes are certain to contest my rule. What can I do?'

Zhao Gao proposed a Stalinist solution: unleash a reign of terror. You are surrounded by disloyal subjects, he said, eminent men who are, incidentally, jealous of me and my humble background. Make the laws sterner and penalties more severe! See that persons charged with guilt implicate others! Wipe out the chief ministers and sow dissension among your kin! 'By doing so you can strike terror into the empire as a whole, and at the same time do away with those who disapprove of your actions.

'"Excellent!" said the Second Emperor.'

The most immediate danger came from his own family, from those princes who ranked above him and below the true, but dead, heir, Fusu. Six princes were put to death, and three others, protesting their innocence, chose to fall on their own swords. Was the total nine or twelve? Sima Qian has both. He also mentions ten princesses killed by being torn apart by chariots. This could all be so, because so far 17 graves have been found with possessions showing that those buried there were nobles; 'and from their teeth', Professor Yuan added when he was briefing me, 'we can tell that most of them were in their twenties'. Of one group of seven skeletons, six had been dismembered, and two were women. The numbers do not quite add up yet, but there is surely more evidence still hidden to show that there was a terrible blood-letting as the Second Emperor did away with his rivals and critics. Fear spread from the imperial family to the population at large.

Zhao Gao, now lord high executioner, was free to turn on his old adversaries, the Meng brothers and their families. Meng Yi, accused of opposing Huhai's accession, was asked to commit suicide. He naturally denied the charge, and delivered one of his own in a long memo that ended, 'One who governs by the Way does not put to death the guiltless.' It did him no good. Zhao Gao ordered his execution. Meng Tian, still in prison after his arrest on the northern frontier, was confronted by an envoy also demanding his suicide. He too wrote a memo, which the envoy refused to pass on, saying he had his orders. Meng Tian despaired, and swallowed poison. Sima Qian gives him a tragic and highly imaginative death. 'What crime have I committed before Heaven that I should die an innocent death?' he asks. Then he realizes: in building the Great Wall he 'cut through the arteries of the earth. That must be my crime!' Not so, says Sima Qian, taking a swipe at his own emperor's ministers. He deserved to die for reasons that had nothing to do with the arteries of the earth. His crime was not standing up to the First Emperor – 'He did not strive to bring about the well-being of the mass of the people.'

For his next project, the Second Emperor turned to the Epang Palace, which had hardly been begun when the First Emperor died. To complete it would be to strengthen his claim to his father's mantle. Unknown thousands were set to work. Then, because a show of strength is always of help to an insecure ruler, 50,000 crossbowmen were brought in from all over the empire to reinforce the capital's garrisons. Since they needed food, all farmers within 150 kilometres were forbidden to eat their own products. So cruelty and deprivation built on each other: complaints multiplied, suffering spread.

Later the same year (209 BC) came the first hint of revolt, an uprising with highly eccentric roots. It started some 400–500 kilometres away to the

223

south-east, in the old kingdom of Chu (mostly present-day Henan) defeated by the First Emperor fourteen years before, where 900 conscripts were being transported to their garrison. Heavy rain delayed them, and delay of any kind was an offence. The three commanders would exonerate themselves with excuses, but the two sergeants would be executed for dereliction. The two men, a former farmhand called Chen She and his sidekick Wu Guang, conferred. As things stood, they faced inevitable death, whereas if they revolted, though they would also face death if defeated, they would at least have a chance.[1]

Having consulted a diviner, the two became convinced they needed a way to attract followers. Chen She got some silk, wrote on it in red letters 'Chen She shall be king', and secretly stuffed the banner into the belly of a newly caught fish which was about to become an item in the conscripts' supper. He also persuaded Wu Guang to hide in a clump of trees beside a nearby shrine, and told him what to do. That evening, a soldier duly found the banner and held it up. At the same time, Wu

[1] Sima Qian includes an aside about Chen She dreaming up a cover story. Fusu, the true heir to the throne, was dead, but ordinary people did not know this. The same went for a general who might or might not have perished in the First Emperor's conquests. What if he, Chen She, pretended to be Fusu and his sidekick pretended to be the general? This they do, but the subterfuge leads nowhere, so it becomes a footnote.

Guang, in his hiding place, lit a torch, partially concealed it in a basket and, with this ghostly light jigging about in the bushes, set up a fox-like wail that turned into words: 'Chen She shall be king!'

This rigmarole was enough to set the soldiers talking among themselves. Wu Guang, a popular figure, then stage-managed a fight with his commander, boasting he was going to run away until the commander started to beat him. At this, Wu Guang and Chen She seized swords and killed the commanders. Chen She then inspired the rest of the troops with a rousing speech: Missing the rendezvous means death! Even if you live, most of you will die fighting! 'If you would risk death, then risk it for the sake of fame and glory!'

The fires of revolt spread. Towns and counties fell in behind the growing army, until it had several hundred chariots, 1,000 horsemen and over 20,000 infantry, all united by the urge to restore their old state to independence. All across the region, locals embittered by Qin rule murdered officials and governors. Within weeks, Chen She was sending deputies off to seize cities and districts beyond Chu's borders and having himself declared king of a resurrected Chu. It was a remarkable thing, as the second-century BC Confucian scholar Jia Yi remarked in a famous study known as *The Faults of Qin*:[2]

---

[2] Quoted by Sima Qian at the end of his biography of the First Emperor, in *Records of the Grand Historian*.

Chen She, born in a humble hut with tiny windows and a wattle door, a day labourer in the fields and a garrison conscript, whose abilities could not match even the average . . . led a band of some hundred poor, weary soldiers in revolt against Qin. They cut down trees to make their weapons and raised their flags on garden poles, and the whole world . . . followed after them as shadows follow a form.

Quite quickly, it all went horribly wrong, as revolution bred armies and kings like weeds. One of Chen's commanders, now far away to the east, created a king of Chu, without knowing Chen She had done the same to himself. When he discovered what had happened he slew his own 'king', reported back to Chen She, and was himself executed for his error. Another of Chen's commanders, sent northward to seize what had once been Zhou, set himself up as king, then planned conquests on his own account, inspiring yet another bid for independence. Time went backwards. The empire was torn apart by Warring States – Chu, Wei, Zhao, Pei, Yan, Qi – each with its would-be king; each state was threatened by jumped-up feudal lords, every lord by self-declared generals. Fortunately for everyone, Chen was assassinated by his own charioteer. He had ruled, if you can call it ruling, for six months.

Back in Xianyang, the old state of Qin was also

226

approaching collapse. In the winter of 209 BC an invasion force was approaching from the east, up the Wei valley, through the strategic Hangu Pass. Ban Gu says in his history of the Han dynasty: 'Construction of the Li Mountain grave site was not yet complete when millions of soldiers arrived, led by [rebel general] Zhou Zhang.' What was to be done? One of the Second Emperor's generals told him: 'The robbers have arrived. They are many and they are strong. It is already too late to call soldiers from other districts to help. But there are many forced labourers at the Mount Li grave complex. Grant them amnesty and supply them with arms.' Which is apparently what was done – a move that successfully blocked the rebel army, and also stopped work on the First Emperor's tomb.

The emperor became ever more removed from reality. First, when a messenger told him of the rebellion, he had the messenger executed. Thereafter no one dared tell him the truth: that the rebels were closing in, that his troops had lost a major battle, that a general had been captured, that a second rebel army of 30,000–40,000 men was approaching. Second, Zhao Gao played on his isolation, which became increasingly psychopathic. Always eager to increase his own influence, Zhao Gao advised the young emperor to remain aloof, hidden away in godlike isolation, ostensibly to save him from making youthful errors, while his ministers applied policies of increasing harshness.

Now, in another of his unpleasant intrigues, he turned on the ageing Li Si, whom he had arm-twisted into supporting the Sand Hill Plot to enthrone Huhai. Poor old Li Si was already a husk of his former self, having been refused the chance to remonstrate with the Second Emperor. Zhao Gao turned to guile. He complained to Li Si that rebellion was in the air, but that the emperor's attention was on the Epang Palace, dogs, horses and other useless activities. He suggested that Li Si was surely the one to reprimand the emperor.

Quite right, replied Li Si. But 'the ruler does not sit in the court. He stays deep within the palace, so I have no chance to see him when I wish.'

'Allow me to assist you,' said Zhao smoothly. 'I will see when he is at leisure and let you know.'

So when the emperor was dining, enjoying himself in the company of women, Zhao Gao did just that. Li Si came calling three times, and three times the emperor refused him entry. He never comes at ordinary times, complained the emperor to Zhao Gao; 'then, as soon as I am enjoying myself in private, immediately he appears and wants to talk about affairs of state. Is it because I am so young that he treats me this way, or because he thinks I'm stupid?'

Zhao Gao made his move. Maybe Li Si is not to be trusted, he said. Remember this: he has a son, the governor of Sanchuan, who failed to quell the rebel Chen She, did he not? Surely this reeks of treachery.

Doubts having been planted, the emperor started to investigate Li Si's son. Li Si, still unable to gain access, wrote to the emperor warning him about Zhao Gao, a man of 'evil and unbridled ambitions and dangerous and treasonable ways', who has acquired immense wealth and is 'undermining Your Majesty's authority'.

A bad mistake. The emperor was incensed that Zhao Gao, the man he most relied upon, should be accused. 'Mr Zhao is a man of integrity and diligence. He understands other people's feelings and knows how to please me.'

No, replied Li Si. 'He has no understanding of principles, but is insatiable in his greed and never ceases his quest for gain.'

The emperor, of course, told Zhao Gao of this, who could smugly say: Obviously the old man wants me dead, so *he* can acquire wealth.

Next, Li Si dared join with two other top advisers to state the unacceptable truth: that bandits were arising without end because of the burdens of garrison duty, forced labour and heavy taxation. The emperor ranted at them like a child – I want 'a thousand chariots, to be attended by ten thousand, so I can live up to my name and title!' I've been on the throne two years, and all I get is bandits! It's all your fault! He ordered Zhao Gao to arrest the three of them. Two committed suicide, while Li Si was shackled

229

and carted off to prison to await trial for treason. The old man railed against the injustice of the times: sad work ... an unprincipled ruler ... disorder imminent ... an emperor who destroys his brothers, executes loyal ministers, enlarges palaces, increases taxes ... won't listen ... sleeping his way to insurrection ... I'll live to see wild deer roam the palace.

All true, but all to no avail. All his family were arrested. He – who had devoted almost 40 years to Qin and was now 72 – was accused, and beaten on the soles of his feet 1,000 times until he confessed to plotting treason. He wrote an ironical memo listing his 'crimes' – upholding the law, honouring merit, annexing six states, elevating the Qin ruler to Son of Heaven, driving out barbarians, ensuring the loyalty of ministers, standardizing weights and measures and coinage, building fast roads, winning hearts and minds etc. etc. 'This is the kind of subject I have been, and my crimes have long been deserving of death!'

The emperor never even saw the letter, because Zhao kept it. More questions broke the old man utterly. By now his son had been killed by rebels. Zhao Gao controlled all the evidence, and could 'prove' his guilt. The Second Emperor condemned him to a terrible death by the 'five penalties' – branding on the forehead, amputation of the ears, nose, fingers and feet, flogging to death and exposure of the head and corpse in the market place; although some of the five seem to have been rescinded in Li Si's case, because he actually met his death by being cut in two at the waist.

Zhao Gao, almost supreme, was just one step away from total control, and in taking it he was helped by the emperor's increasing separation from reality. It started with a strange incident. In what seems a cross between a practical joke and a test of his own influence, Zhao Gao presented the emperor with a deer, but insisted it was a horse. Courtiers, totally cowed, backed him up. The emperor began to doubt his sanity. Was he losing his mind because of something he had done? Yes, said Zhao, it's because you are impure. So the emperor went off to a royal park to fast, and here he sank into superstition and psychopathy. He was worried by a dream in which his carriage horses were attacked by a white tiger (a symbol of malevolence from the river Jing, so a diviner said). When a passer-by happened to wander into the park, the emperor shot him. Zhao Gao reprimanded him: 'The Son of Heaven for no reason has wantonly shot an innocent man. Such conduct is forbidden by the Lord on High.' To avoid misfortune, he went on, it was necessary to carry out sacrifices. The emperor accepted, and retired to a palace in Xian, intending to drown four white horses in the malevolent river Jing.

As madness took hold, the end approached. Zhao Gao, fearful that he and his family would be blamed for the rebellions, planned a *coup d'état* with his brother and son-in-law, Yan Yue. Claiming the bandits were upon them, the son-in-law led a force to 'protect' the palace where the emperor was staying. The palace commander, protesting there were no rebels, was cut down, his guards overwhelmed, the emperor trapped. Yan Yue yelled at the emperor that it was his fault the rebels were upon them: 'You are arrogant and wilful and you punish and kill people without reason! The whole empire has turned against you!' There was only one way out: suicide. Desperately, the emperor tried to negotiate. Could he keep one province? Become a marquis? Become an ordinary person, with his wife and children? No, no, no, on all counts. There was nothing for it but to kill himself.

And, hard though it is to believe, he did.

Sima Qian does not record the court's reaction, but an attempt by Zhao Gao to make himself emperor proved underwhelming, so he summoned a compliant grandson of the First Emperor, Zi Ying, who was not much younger than his dead uncle. Fear bred fear, and plots. Suspecting Zhao was planning to kill him, Zi Ying at once feigned sickness, locked himself away in a temple and started a counter-plot.

A few days later, as Zi Ying hoped, Zhao Gao came to demand that the coronation take place. Zi Ying (and his attendants, presumably) stabbed him, and quickly rounded up his family. After far too long, the empire was rid of a monster.

★　　★　　★

As it happened, Zhao Gao had not been far wrong: the rebels were at the gates, amid the birthpangs of a new dynasty. The peasant uprisings had led to the rebirth of the old kingdoms, and several new ones, nineteen in all. In the assault on Qin, two rival leaders had emerged, each with his own forces. One was Liu Bang, of peasant stock, future founder of the Han dynasty. The other was Xiang Yu, of special interest to us because he started off as leader and was responsible for the violence that destroyed Xianyang and the Terracotta Army.

Liu Bang came from Pei towards the coast of central China, where he had been a low-ranking official. According to the historian Ban Gu, he was a charismatic character, with a prominent nose, a beautiful beard and 72 black moles on his left thigh (72 being a number with many mystical connotations). His career as a revolutionary started through bad luck. He was escorting convicts to work on the First Emperor's tomb, but many of them escaped. Since he would be held responsible on arrival, he decided not to arrive. Instead, he freed the remaining prisoners, fled home and went on the run, gathering a gang of 100 or so. As rebellion spread, Pei's local magistrate was ordered to capture Liu and his gang. Liu wrote on a piece of silk a message suggesting an uprising, and shot it over the walls. As a result, the townspeople rose up, killed the magistrate and placed Liu in charge. Having declared himself Lord of Pei, he led his army towards Qin.

Xiang Yu, from further to the south-east, also started off by murdering the local governor, then struck out northward with his army, joining up with Liu Bang before heading west into the Qin heartland. It was Xiang Yu – 'fiery, violent and very destructive', in the opinion of generals quoted by Ban Gu – who proved the more effective leader, but Liu Bang ('habitually generous') who was first into the Qin capital of Xianyang, an act that should by rights have allowed him to claim the succession.

When in late 207 BC the emperor surrendered – in a plain chariot, with his imperial seals packed up and ready for delivery – Liu Bang declared it would be inauspicious to kill him. He ordered a peaceful occupation, securing the treasures and records from harm so they could all be accounted for, and replacing all Qin's laws with two: death for murder and just punishment for robbery and injury. 'All I have come for is to deliver you, Elders, from harm,' he told Qin's surviving officials. He even refused to accept the cattle, sheep, wine and food that were offered, saying 'I do not wish to be a burden upon the people.'

Two months later Xiang Yu arrived, with a rather different agenda, and a reputation for brutality reinforced the previous summer, when he had massacred the whole population of one city. Jealous of Liu Bang's success and suspicious of his designs, he reversed Liu Bang's easy-going regime, killed the ex-emperor, massacred the

234

people of Xianyang and burned the palaces. As Homer Dubs, Oxford Professor of Greek in the 1930s, says in his introduction to his translation of Ban Gu, 'That fire was the real "Burning of the Books," for in the imperial palaces there had been preserved the proscribed literature for the use of the imperial erudites and officials.'

A few months later, Xiang Yu turned the nineteen small states of the former empire into a confederacy, with himself at the top as king-protector. But this lacked legitimacy. Liu Bang had secured the victory; it was he who had taken Xianyang and received the emperor's submission; it was he who was the rightful heir to Qin. There followed a complicated civil war, the details of which we can ignore, except to say that it lasted for four years, with Liu Bang emerging victorious. In late 202 BC Xiang Yu was surrounded, forced his way through Liu Bang's lines, found himself down to 28 followers, and committed suicide. Liu Bang was free to accept the title of Emperor Gaozu, the first of the Han dynasty.

So Han replaced Qin, a dynasty that had shone low for many centuries, then exploded to fill its universe with a brief burst of energy before collapsing into madness and murder.

How did it come to this? Jia Yi in *The Faults of Qin* had no doubts of the answer. 'Because it failed to rule with humanity and righteousness.' The First Emperor had his faults, but the Second Emperor was a disaster, an example of how *not* to rule laid out in a fine passage describing what he should have done:

> If the Second Emperor had acted in the manner of even a mediocre ruler, if he had employed loyal and worthy men and had joined with his officials in single-mindedly caring for the nation's ills, correcting the errors of the former emperor . . . If he had emptied the prisons, pardoned those condemned to execution, abolished slavery and other forms of humiliating punishment, allowed each person to return to his native village; if he had opened the granaries and disbursed funds to succour the orphaned and lonely and those in dire poverty; if he had lightened taxes and [forced] labour to relieve the distress of the common people, simplified the laws, and reduced penalties for the sake of prosperity; if he had allowed the people of the empire to make a new beginning . . . then the empire would have flocked to him.

So it was the appalling Xiang Yu who released the violence that broke the terracotta warriors. Sima Qian mentions the burning of the capital and the palaces. There are only fleeting references to the tomb, only one (doubtful) to the Terracotta Army. For practical purposes, all we have to go on is the evidence as it comes down to us. To reconstruct what happened requires more than good, old-fashioned archaeology. We have several crimes in one: breaking and entering, theft and arson. We think we know who did it. But how? Our particular concern will be the fire. How did it start? How come every beam collapsed, ensuring that, of all the 6,000 statues in Pit No. 1 and the 1,500 or so statues in other pits, not a single one survived intact? To answer these questions demands a forensic approach, drawing on scientific disciplines that would not normally count as part of archaeology.

To review the scanty written evidence:

From Sima Qian and Ban Gu we know that there was fighting in the area and that in 209 BC, the second year of the Second Emperor's reign, the on-site work-force became an army to fight off the rebels. They were successful, but they would surely not have returned to work on the grave because the war continued for another three years. In that case, work may have stopped dead that year, as the Archaeological Team for the Excavation suggest in a throwaway remark in brackets: '[209 BC, construction of the grave complex was interrupted]'. A suggestion only – there is no historical evidence. And then, three years later, according to chronicles quoted by Ban Gu, 'the soldiers entrusted with the grave complex dug it up' and 'the above ground grave complex was destroyed by the pillaging of Xiang Yu, the underground complex was trampled down by the herds grazing above'.[3] It's confusing. Which grave complex was dug up? Were these soldiers part of the original workforce or new arrivals? The 'above ground complex' could mean just the buildings, but in that case does 'below ground' mean the tomb, the Terracotta Army, the subsidiary pits – some or all of them?

Remember that both the historians were writing well after the events they describe, Sima Qian a century and Ban Gu 250 years later. The events themselves occurred during years of war and civil war. They were reporting memories passed down through generations (at best: Ban Gu often relied on Sima Qian). It's not surprising they are a little vague.

Let's imagine. Xiang Yu's people had known of the Terracotta Army since 209 BC, when they had been driven off by its hastily recruited labourers. There would have been prisoners, there would have been talk. So in early 206 BC, with the palaces of Xianyang still blazing, Xiang Yu arrives at Lintong, eager for more booty and more vengeance. He knows about the tomb, and also its dangers and difficulties: the risk of mercury poisoning, the loaded crossbows, the depth of soil. He knows, too, of the Terracotta Army, knows that it contains things that would be very useful: not the clay soldiers, of course, but the many

[3] These quotes are included in the Archaeological Team's survey in Blänsdorf et al., *Qin Shihuang*.

238

thousands of real weapons they hold – the crossbows, bows, swords, lances, dagger-axes, arrows – almost all made of bronze. True, iron would have been better, as several of the Warring States had discovered; but with more fighting to be done, bronze weapons, especially the crossbows with their superb bronze triggers, would be just fine.

In the film tourists see at the museum, it's the vengeance that is dramatized in a scene of pure vandalism. Soldiers break in en masse, as if through a door, and simply torch the place. The beams catch fire instantly. Obviously the whole pit is going to be a wreck in no time, and the inferno is going to be enough to incinerate the ceiling and create the layer of hard-baked earth discovered by the Yang brothers when they broke in through the roof in 1974.

Well, it couldn't have been like that.

Pit No. 1 was well covered, and would take weeks to open up. Xiang Yu did not have weeks. Qin had fallen, new kingdoms had emerged, but no one ruled in Qin and it looked as if there would be a showdown between Xiang Yu and Liu Bang. There was no time to strip off the 3 metres of earth and the thick beams that held it up. The best way in was to dig straight down. Is that what they did? Almost certainly, because that was precisely what was done in Pit No. 2, where a hole like a small mine-shaft seems to be a point of forced entry. It is a professional job, dropping vertically for several metres right at the edge of the pit to bypass the ceiling, then taking a right-angle turn at just the right depth to make an entry on to the floor. It's a metre or so square, big enough to hand out weapons and any other items of treasure. Clearly, no one was interested in the warriors.

So the thieves had good information. If they entered Pit No. 2, it stands to reason they entered the Army pit, even if no traces remain of the hole they dug. It would have taken them a few days (as the work done by the well-digging Yang brothers revealed), working with spades and a sling for co-workers to lift the loose earth clear.

This is not simply conjecture. It is a scenario inspired by the Army's senior archaeologist, Yuan Zhongyi.

'There is no evidence of *organized* destruction,' he said, as we sipped tea in his simple, impeccable apartment: lacquered tea-table, black leather sofa and chair, big cherrywood book cabinet and light-grey tiles. 'I imagine small groups going to different parts of the same area. But the warriors are close-packed, so it was hard to get through. They were in a rush. We found remains of warriors which seem to have fallen in a zig-zag pattern. This suggests they were pushed over as people forced their way through. One horse was standing apart from its tail, which lay a few metres away, as if someone had thrown it. One of the generals had a broken sword – the top bit, which had gold and jade decorations, had gone, leaving the bottom bit of the blade in its scabbard. And in the hole in Pit Number Two, we found the gold decorations for a horse.'

Then, somehow, the fire started.

'All the time, I wonder who committed this crime,' said Yuan. 'When we first saw the warriors in Pit Number One, we asked ourselves: who destroyed them? At first some of us said the fire could have been started by natural causes, by spontaneous combustion, from gas. But we could not find any materials that might cause a fire, like straw. Certainly, it could not have started with the warriors. So our second suggestion was that it was the result of a funeral ceremony, a sort of ritual immolation. The Qin burned everything to do with the emperor, perhaps. So I began checking the history books, and realized it must have been to do with Xiang Yu's uprising. But where would it start? That hole leading down into Pit Two – there are many ashes around the base. Perhaps what happened is that after robbing the place, the intruders started the fire to stop anyone else coming back for more.'

Here's an odd thing: there was no fire in Pit No. 3, the headquarters pit. You would think it would have been a natural target for anyone seeking revenge. Here were the top men conferring, and a chariot ready to take off with messages for the troops. Entry could have been gained by the same method used in the other two pits. But it didn't happen. My guess is that the grave-robbers knew from their informants that there was not enough

241

here worth taking. And no one was interested in more destruction.

Breaking through at one end of Pit No. 1, the first soldier in smells rich earth, and sees—

—absolutely nothing, because it's pitch black. He stands, raises his arms, bumps his hands on hard, cold shapes. Behind him, above a colleague who is busy clearing more earth, a faint light filters down the hole. Pass me a torch, he calls. He doesn't mean a vegetable-oil lamp, but a cloth one steeped in pitch, with a big, bright flame. Its flickering light reveals the front lines of pink-faced archers, in their brightly coloured coats. Behind them, in cavernous corridors, the soldiers range backwards into darkness. And, as their informants had told them, they all hold a weapon or two. It's a treasure trove of militaria.

Others slither down the hole, more torches send shadows dancing away to left and right and down the corridors. But there's hardly room to stand up against the shoulder-to-shoulder statues. The intruders begin to shove their way through, grabbing weapons, passing them over clay shoulders towards the shaft-entrance and up to the open air.

There's chaos, men knocking over statues, trampling on them, grabbing weapons, passing them to each other and up the exit hole. Their work is badly hampered by the need for light. It is hard to grab weapons with one hand while holding a torch, so they improvise, passing torches between each other, maybe jamming a torch into the hollow

242

bits of a broken statue. The destruction and the absence of weapons show that they penetrated only a few corridors, and no more than 40 metres. Most of the weapons were left behind. Something cut the break-in short.

The most likely cause was fire. It is easy to imagine a torch discarded or a piece of smouldering material lying under smashed pottery against a wooden pillar or on the floor of one of the wooden chariots. So two of the three elements for a blaze were present: fuel and a source of ignition. Flames lick up a pillar. Within seconds it is out of control.

To understand what might have happened next, I must introduce you to an extremely small, but growing specialism that links archaeologists and fire protection engineers. Traditionally, archaeologists have accepted the fact of fire in ancient structures without examining the cause, implying that fire is self-explanatory or the result of 'ritual destruction'. As a small group of experts in this arcane field say, 'Formal, ongoing collaborations with fire investigators and archaeologists are recent developments.'[4] So far, the Terracotta Army awaits that sort of collaboration, but as a start I asked for help from Joe Lally, an archaeologist with the US Department of the Interior's Bureau

4 David Icove et al., 'Scientific Investigations and Modeling of Prehistoric Structural Fires at Chevelon Pueblo', paper presented at International Symposium on Fire Investigation Science and Technology, Cincinnati, Jan. 2006.

of Land Management in Albuquerque, New Mexico. He is interested in explaining fires in ancient buildings. He also understands about looters. 'We have a lot of looters here in New Mexico, and from my experience looters are usually better and faster at finding valuable items than professional archaeologists.' He tests scenarios with a computer program called CFAST, into which he fed mine, together with statistics about the Terracotta Army pit: the materials available, the entry-hole which would provide ventilation, the height and length of the corridors. This is his conclusion:

> With ventilation being on floor level and none within the upper portions of the compartment, there would be no exit for heat and smoke, which fill a compartment from the top down, no matter where the fire is burning. Heat would not be a problem. Heat loss to the walls (the heat being absorbed) would be more than ten times greater than heat loss through the looters' shaft. The corridors would fill with smoke at the rate of seven cubic metres a second. A medium growth fire would allow 3.8 minutes for a safe exit from anywhere within the structure. The exit time would be increased by creeping low beneath the upper, smoke-filled portions of the corridors.

It's the smoke that cuts the break-in short. That's why so many weapons remain behind in the pit, and why archaeologists today know so much about them.

The smoke spreads along corridors, and round the ends where the three lines of archers stand. There are yells and the intruders rush for the exit, toppling more warriors and horses. They have only a few minutes, and there is only room for one at a time up the exit shaft. Come to think of it, there could not be all that many down there – 30 or 40, assuming that each one takes ten seconds to enter the shaft – because they all made it out: Yuan and his co-workers found no charred skeletons down there.

But there is something odd about this fire. It takes hold, it flares, it catches a chariot, even the roof. But now it is a big beast, and it needs a flow of oxygen – the third vital element in any fire after fuel and an ignition source – to keep it going. There's not enough in the pit, and not enough coming in from outside to feed the flames. Perhaps some bright character orders the hole to be filled in, thinking to douse the fire and return at some later date.

In any event, the flames go out.

Yet we know fire destroyed the pit. No flames, yet a destructive fire – how is this to be explained?

E-mails back and forth threw up two possibilities. One is the phenomenon known as 'spontaneous combustion', familiar to anyone who has felt the inside of a pile of cut grass. Within hours, the core is warm, in a day or two it smokes, and a few days later, if you open it, you find ash. In nature, spontaneous blazes are quite common. I received this note from the US fire expert Jim Quintière. Having investigated several underground woody landfills, which can ignite spontaneously, he says:

> I believe the earthen-bamboo with moisture-promoting bacterial growth could first produce heat from the bacteria, then chemical heat due to oxidation of the bamboo. This can lead to spontaneous ignition. The nature of the subsequent fire is likely to be smouldering, but can also break out into flames. I have seen this happen. In one fire I know of, the fire moved across the land-fill beneath the ground in days. Later, when the land-fill was covered with asphalt to impede the oxygen flow, temperature soundings still indicated combustion.

A second model is a coal-seam fire, a subject that is worth a brief diversion. Usually these fires start in mines and spread underground along unmined beds of coal, but some are natural, started by bush fires or lightning. The US has hundreds of coal-seam fires, with at least 38 in coal-rich Pennsylvania alone: among them is a notorious fire 100 metres under the once-thriving town of Centralia that has been smouldering for half a century and may go on doing so for 250 years before its fuel is exhausted. China and India, coal-rich and coal-dependent, have thousands of these fires, which contribute about 1 per cent of the earth's carbon emissions. Scientists estimate that Australia's Burning Mountain, the oldest known coal fire, has been smouldering for 6,000 years. Coal-seam fires poison the earth, and the people, and the atmosphere, and there is absolutely nothing anyone can do about most of them.

Of course, the Terracotta Army's roof would hardly be a major seam fire. But it is a prime candidate for smouldering. So the scenario continues like this: the flames are dead, the pit dark again, smoke drifting along the corridors. But the fire has found a home in the roof, where the overlay of matting acts as tinder and the overburden of earth keeps a lid on the fire. Traces of oxygen seep down the shaft and from the surrounding earth, enough to keep the roof smouldering. Over months, the slow fire eats away at the beams. At some point, a few charred timbers fall, breaking a warrior or two. A section of earth from above follows.

And so it goes, for years, the beams being consumed until they fall, the warriors steadily smashed, the chariots and crossbows either burned or (occasionally) protected by fallen earth, the surface subsiding bit by bit, washed by the rains of the passing centuries until not a trace remains of what lies beneath. The foreign troops depart, locals see only the tomb-mound and forget about the warriors. Orchard and field succeed orchard and field, for 2,180 years, until the spades of the Yang brothers break through the shell of fire-baked earth.

PART III

THE EIGHTH WONDER

CHAPTER 12

SIX THOUSAND CHARACTERS
IN SEARCH OF A ROLE

I t all so nearly came to nothing.

We are back in May 1974. The Yang brothers have abandoned their well under pressure from Zhao Kangmin, the local museum assistant, and his boss. Zhao is busy at work restoring the first warrior. Obviously, it's a wonderful find – the broken bits of statuary, the bronze arrowheads, the crossbow trigger, the bricks – and will complement the three kneeling servants which have been found over the years. But no one has a clue that the Yang brothers have actually broken through into the far south-east corner of the greatest archaeological discovery of the century. It could have remained hidden. Zhao, remember, was nervous about reporting the finds, nervous that he might be swept up again by the madness of the Cultural Revolution, whose teenage Red Guards had forced him to criticize himself for being involved with old things and therefore encouraging the revival of feudalism.

In fact, the excesses of the Cultural Revolution were five years in the past. The thuggish gangs of students waving their little red books of Mao's thoughts had had their day. Students by the million were back from 're-education' – hard manual labour – in the countryside. Universities and schools had reopened. The army was stable again, mainly in the face of a challenge being mounted by the Soviet Union along China's far western and north-eastern borders. China had re-engaged with the world.

Still, at the top, tensions multiplied. Mao, 80, was in physical decline, having been diagnosed with a form of motor neurone disease which would gradually make it impossible for him to walk, or even to swallow. He was not told, and was depressed by cataracts that made him almost blind until they were removed the following year. Despite all this, or perhaps because of it, he was ever more jealous of potential rivals. In 1971 his designated heir and main rival Lin Biao, knowing his days were numbered, had fled the country in such haste there was no time to finish fuelling his plane. It crashed in Mongolia, killing him. When Mao learned that Lin's son had plotted his assassination, he again purged the army. The affair, which seemed to discredit any remnants of revolutionary fervour, profoundly disillusioned Mao's supporters. Two main factions emerged. The country was being managed by Premier Zhou Enlai, but Mao's wife Jiang Qing and her three cronies, the Gang of Four as Mao called them, tried to preserve Mao's radicalism, whipping up a campaign to discredit Zhou. In late 1973 Mao allowed the balance to swing back towards Zhou and his protégé, the tiny, energetic future leader Deng Xiaoping, who had been purged and was now back in favour. So the top echelon of government was divided between the Gang of Four on one side and Zhou plus Deng on the other. This unresolved power struggle in Beijing was known to very few, certainly not to a lowly museum official like Zhao Kangmin. Yet that context would prove crucial to the fate of the warrior he was busy restoring, of the undiscovered Army, and of the whole tomb complex.

For the power struggle had an odd historical resonance. In much the same way as Sima Qian criticized his own emperor, Wu, by describing the excesses of the First Emperor, so the two sides of the ideological battle under Mao criticized each other by reference to the ancient dispute between Legalists and Confucians. Suddenly, and bizarrely for foreign observers, the politics of the Qin empire leapt into the present. The Confucians were Zhou Enlai and his supporters, who became targets for the 'Legalist' – and ardently Maoist – Gang of Four. Confucius and his followers were reactionaries and representatives of the slave-owning class; the First Emperor was chief representative of the up-and-coming, progressive landlord class. Traditional views were turned topsy-turvy. Confucius, previously revered for nobility and wisdom, was reviled; the First Emperor, tyrant and mass murderer, became the admired founder of the nation.

In fact the roots of this attitude went deep. Although in his later years Mao became power-obsessed as an individual, in the early days, before his personality became a cult, he was power-obsessed on behalf of the Party. He was a dyed-in-the-wool Legalist, a Machiavellian Prince, a Lord-Shang-style 'sage ruler', who defined the law according to revolutionary needs. He saw himself and his followers as 'truly great men' or 'the truly great man' (for Chinese does not easily distinguish between singular and plural), as he wrote in a famous poem, *Snow*, in 1936:

> This land so rich in beauty
> Has made countless heroes bow in homage.
> But alas! Qin Shihuang and Han Wudi
> Were lacking in literary grace,
> And Tang Taizong and Song Taizu
> Had little poetry in their souls;
> That proud son of Heaven,
> Genghis Khan,
> Knew only shooting eagles, bow outstretched.
> All are past and gone!
> For truly great men [or 'the truly great man']
> Look to this age alone.

He, of course, was one of the great men himself, greater as a poet and as conqueror than all those long-dead rulers, particularly the First Emperor,

Qin Shihuang. Like him, Mao reformed Chinese script, introducing the simplified characters now in use in mainland China. Like him, he was eager to destroy the past in order to control the future. And like him, he was utterly ruthless, even more so. At the Second Plenum of the Eighth Party Congress on 8 May 1958, Mao scoffed:

> The First Emperor – how great was he really? He buried[1] only four hundred and sixty Confucian scholars. We have buried forty-six *thousand* Confucian scholars . . . You democrats scold us for being like the First Emperor. You are wrong. We are a hundred times worse than him. To the charge of being like the First Emperor, of being a dictator, we plead guilty. But we need to add to your accusations – they are not enough![2]

In another of his poems, Mao responded to the eminent scholar Guo Moruo, who had criticized the First Emperor for practising slavery:

> Please don't slander the First Emperor, Sir,
> For the burning of the books should be thought
>   through again.

[1] The problematic word *keng* again, which mixes the old meaning 'buried, killed' with the additional modern one, 'buried alive'. But he is not suggesting 46,000 were buried *alive*. See p. 109.
[2] Trans. Polly Kwong.

Our ancestral dragon, though dead, lives on in
  spirit,
While Confucius, though renowned, was really
  rubbish.

Mao despised Confucian orthodoxy for its wishy-
washy benevolence, the way it worked against the
building of a strong state that would dominate the
Chinese and neighbouring peoples. He would be a
new First Emperor, ruling all China's traditional
domains through the same kind of totalitarian institutions. Marxist ideology provided what he wanted,
for it backed the monopoly of power by an educated
elite (under his direction). It justified suppressing
the self-determination of peoples whose destinies (he
thought) lay in China's hands – Tibetans, Uighurs,
Mongols. Lost territories should be regained, former
tributaries whipped into line. Military success had
freed China; now it would restore the empire, and
extend its reach. That was why he intervened in
Korea, invaded Tibet, bombarded Quemoy,
demanded the return of Taiwan, attacked India over
Tibet, confronted the Soviet Union almost to the
point of war, and aided Vietnam.

The new approach was typified in a popular
biography of the First Emperor by Hung Shih-Ti
(Hong Shidi).[3] Hong emphasizes the Marxist view
that history is controlled not by great men but by
grand historical forces, which some great men just

3 Included in Li Yuning, *The First Emperor of China*.

happen to represent. 'It was not because he had any inborn and extraordinary ability, but mainly because he was the chief representative of the rising landlord class . . . the masses of people had an urgent need for the unification of China.' As Li Yuning, the editor of a book in which Hong's biography is included, writes:

> Now [in 1975] [the First Emperor] is seen as a far-sighted ruler who destroyed the forces which had kept China divided, unified the nation, and established the first central-ized state in Chinese history. In particular he is praised for following the Legalist policy of 'emphasizing the present while slighting the past' [a Maoist slogan] and scorning the Confucians. His achievements in creating a unified centralized government, it is now argued, justified his use of violence, in particular the 'burning of the books and burying Confucian scholars alive'.

Nothing could have put the case more clearly: now equals then, the First Emperor equals Mao, violence is OK if the cause is great, unification equals revolution and excuses all excess.[4]

[4] This simplifies a complex campaign which saw the publication of many articles in which every leading Qin character had a part to play in the present, including the loyal minister Li Si and the treacherous ministers Lü Buwei and Zhao Gao.

All of this explains why Jiang Qing and the other three Gang-members accused Lin Biao and his successor Zhou Enlai of being treacherous Confucians, why they unleashed a campaign known as 'Criticize Lin [Biao], Criticize Confucius', why Lin and his treason were equated with Confucius's alleged attempt to roll back the tide of history by upholding slavery. In brief, as Yue Nan says in a detailed analysis,[5] the First Emperor was seen as 'a vigorous revolutionary, a true tiger', while Confucius and his followers were 'corrupt and clownish anti-revolutionaries'. Anything that could be used to support this view would come in handy.

Into this ideological maelstrom fell a very small stone of information about some pieces of clay discovered in far-off Shaanxi. That the news reached the ears of high-ups in Beijing was pure chance. It happened that a journalist named Lin Anwen, from the official news agency, Xinhua, was in Lintong on holiday and heard of the discovery. He came to see Zhao, who briefed him. On returning to Beijing, he saw the potential appeal of the finds – and, no doubt, the possibility of doing himself some good – and wrote them up, not for general consumption but in *Internal Affairs*, a journal for official eyes only. Its tediously long headline ran: 'A group of pottery

[5] Yue Nan, *Xi Bu Mai Fu* (*Hidden Underground in the West*).

figures unearthed near the First Emperor's mausoleum in Lintong County'. After Lin's report, another writer, Wang Yongan, added a paragraph to underline its political message: 'The discovery of the warriors has a great importance in helping us to evaluate the First Emperor in studying the struggle between Legalism and Confucianism, and the political, economic and military circumstances of the Qin dynasty . . . they are very precious, as they are modelled after Qin Dynasty soldiers and were never recorded in the historical records.' He then continued with, in effect, a call for action:

> Because of the harvest, work has stopped. Some leaders in Lintong County placed their own self-interests first and so never reported the finds. The mausoleum is a national cultural relic, under the protection of the central government, but it has not protected it well. The commune just dug up the mausoleum and the cultivated land around it. Metals (i.e. the bronze arrowheads and crossbow triggers) were just treated as rubbish and the bits of pottery were cast aside.

When the Gang of Four read this, they at once saw its potential. One phone call from Mao's wife, Jiang Qing, to the head of media relations, Yao Wenyuan, was enough to get action. Yao called

259

Vice-Premier Li Xiannian, once purged, now finance minister and deputy prime minister, and a future state president. On 13 June, Vice-Premier Li called the heads of Cultural Affairs and the National Bureau of Cultural Relics: 'Comrade Jiang Qing is very concerned about this discovery! Please consult with the Shaanxi Provincial Government and get them to move as soon as possible!'

In Xian, the provincial leader stuttered – No, he had no idea . . . There had been no news from Lintong . . . The farmers didn't know what they had found – and promised action.

So at last the news was out, and an archaeologist from Beijing went out to check the site with Zhao. He turned out to be quite polite, Zhao recalls. 'He said, "Your county and you made a big contribution to the country."' A few days later, about two months after the Yangs' discovery, five officials, including Zhao, turned up with 20 farmers to plan the work of excavation, which started the following month.

'It took us twenty days just to find out how wide the pit was,' said Zhao. We were sitting in the reception area of the museum he had designed himself, where he is still an honoured presence. 'From the well made by the farmers we dug in all directions. There was nothing to the south, but a wall to the north. So we discovered it was right on the edge in the pit's south-east corner.' (You can still see the place when you go into the pit today). 'We were working slowly, drilling by hand. We were just tracing the walls to find the edges, drilling down as far as we could, to the bricks. We had no idea what to expect. As we opened up squares of the pit, we realized the size of the discovery. We got an idea of the spaces between the warriors, we knew the size of the pit, and so we worked out how many warriors there should be.'

'You realized the warriors were Qin?'

'They had to be, because the bricks were Qin and the soldiers were on the bricks. So they had to be placed there on the order of the First Emperor. I was the first person to call them Qin warriors.' He paused to make sure I got the point. 'I was the first man to give them that name. Because before that there were figures, but no warriors. *Qin warriors.*' He nodded, as if to himself, lost in memory. 'Then [Communist Party Central Committee member] Gu Mu came. He was in charge of the building over Pit No. 1. He also told me I made a big contribution. I said, "It was the farmers." He said, "No, they found them but they didn't know what they found. You were the first who realized."'

Given the Army's international fame today, it seems odd that no one appreciated the scale of this discovery at the time. But bear in mind that this was just a single find, even if a large one. Whatever its size, some sort of protection obviously had to be provided for the site, as fast as

261

possible. The man made responsible for this was a local architect, Li Naifu, now a senior member of the Xian Architecture and Technology University, a collection of concrete-and-glass rectangles hard to separate from the other 45 colleges and universities scattered across this extremely well-educated city. With eyes made heavy by years of teaching and poring over plans, Li recalled the strange assumptions made in those early days.

'In the beginning we thought we would only need a building that would protect the site, the soldiers and the experts. We gave no thought to tourists at all.' Nor to foreign interest either, for Mao was still alive, just, and China was still largely shut away behind a bamboo curtain. 'We didn't think about a reception area, or administrators. We never considered we might need a car park, offices, toilets even. Besides, we hardly had any money. They just gave us four million yuan [£266,000].

'As you know, the pit is sixty metres wide. So we knew we had to build something about seventy metres wide, seventy-two actually. At that time, for that money, all we could think of was a simple arch. This was the simplest, most economic solution. At the time we thought it was quite ambitious, because there were not many arches with a seventy-two-metre span in the country. We didn't have to consider the whole site, because there was nothing but the single pit, and only fields all around. So up it went, just like an enormous greenhouse.' (Though the arch always conjured up a different image in my mind – a Victorian railway station, with the soldiers lining up to catch the spirit train to the battle front.)

It was finished in 1976, after not much more than a year of work. By then, two more pits, Nos 2 and 3, had been discovered, alongside the 'greenhouse'. Excavation work began in Pit No. 1 in May 1978 and went on for the next four years. A team of 50 pressed on with the intricate business of removing the seven layers of earth, sand, gravel and sludge – for water had leaked in even before the roof collapsed. The layers lay in waves over the twelve walls and eleven corridors. Recording every shard of every shattered warrior, often over 200 of them, the teams began rebuilding statues, matching up their bits and sticking them together with special glue that does not dry hard, so that pieces can be unglued when necessary. It helped that all the pieces for any one of the warriors had to be close by, but it still took up to a year for a warrior to be completed.

Work having started at the Yangs' well and continued both northward and westward, decisions had to be made. How far to dig? How many to unearth and restore? After four years, work slowed. With just over one-fifth of the pit opened, the excavators had unearthed just over 1,000 warriors, 8 two-wheeled chariots, 32 horses, several hundred weapons and many thousands of arrowheads. Another section was left partially open, a final one still earthed in.

Excavation work, still under way in Pit No. 1, was started in the second and third pits, and was still going on when the museum opened for business on 1 October 1979 – to total chaos. There was a small car park and a ticket office ('Do you know the price of a ticket? Ten yuan [0.7p]!') but then people had to walk over grass, which soon turned to mud, to a building with no toilets, no entrance lobby for people to wait in, and no café. And from the start 30,000 or more people came every day, rising to 50,000 on main holidays, like May Day. 'There were so many people no one could see anything but people. Thousands just came, because it was all new, saw the crowds, and went away without seeing the soldiers!'

'We had to start again,' Li went on. 'So we applied for more money to do more building. This time we had a little more, 5.81 million yuan [£387,000].' Work started in 1986. 'Of course, now we realized the museum would be a landmark. We needed to do something special. It's easy to design a building, but hard to design a *great* building. We thought of the warriors as gold. To display gold you need a special sort of background, so the idea was to give them a setting that seemed like silk. Good design would emphasize the value, which would attract more people, so we would enhance the value twice over.'

Building went on for eight years in all, with Pit

No. 3 opening in 1989 and the larger one, Pit No. 2, in 1994. This time, Li had the time and backing to plan proper buildings, their blockish look inspired by Qin architecture, with pepper-pot towers and black-tiled roofs – not that the Qin built in stone. This time, there were toilets, fire-proofing, a visitors' area, security for the warriors. 'We still made mistakes, though. We took care of the visitors, but we forgot that excavators would need to keep working when they came. So they have no separate paths to remove the soil. That has caused a great deal of inconvenience.'

There is far more to the site than three buildings over three pits: a Multiple Exhibition Building to show the best of the finds, service halls, restaurants, an information centre, bookstalls, the cinema, reproductions of the warriors, places to sell tourist kitsch: all the boring but vital extras that make a modern museum and excavation site. Along the way, Pit No. 1 acquired a proper entrance area.

At the museum's heart, though, is the great arch of Pit No. 1, in its day a miracle of efficiency, economy and speed, but a construction which, let's face it, becomes year by year more old-fashioned railway station than modern museum. There is no heating and no air-conditioning. Visitors freeze in winter and melt in high summer. And, as the experts know all too well, the warriors suffer, their remaining colours flaking off, their clay surfaces slowly gathering patinas of microscopic moulds.

The site has evolved, like a garden, in response to new and unpredictable needs. Yes, Li agreed, it is a medley of architectural styles, because styles changed.

'So it's like a survey of Chinese architecture in the late twentieth century,' I said.

'Yes, it is,' Li agreed thoughtfully. 'But I feel I have helped to create something for the future, and for the warriors. I'm proud of that.'

There is greatness here, but it does not lie in the buildings. It lies in the totality of the site, starting below, with the car park. There's not much inspiration in a car park, even when dominated by an immense statue of the First Emperor ('That's nothing to do with our team! That was the local government!'). But there is inspiration in the setting, with Mount Li and its neighbouring peaks and ridges rippling along the site's southern edge. There is inspiration, too, in the winding, uphill approach, that feeling of approaching something majestic. Li nodded when I remarked on it: 'Yes, the whole idea was that the approach would be a zigzag to give you a chance to think about what you are about to see.'[6]

[6] Not much inspiration, though, in the laboured English of the huge posters proclaiming the glories of Qin: 'Working together with many international fame design and build team featuring Qin culture.' Who writes this sort of thing? Who passes it as fit to print? Please, guys, forget your dictionaries and have your English checked by native English-speakers.

The real genius lies in something that no one mentions. After your long, slow climb, you walk through a grove of firs – this is going to be wonderful in years to come, because there are 6,000 trees planted across the whole site, one tree per warrior in Pit No. 1, which I guess could stretch to 8,000, a *wan* of trees, as time goes by. Then there is the ticket barrier. And then, at last, the plaza. You are struck, perhaps, by the space, or the well-kept flower-beds, or the buildings. These are details, but the reason you focus on them is because of something you don't notice: they are well framed, not by anything physical, but by the colour. The plaza, the staircase, the buildings are all light grey stonework that has a hint of other colours, like the overtones that lend depth to orchestral strings. It is this that turns an unresolved mix of styles and purposes into a unity.

Li had mentioned security. Like all famous objects, the warriors occasionally draw the wrong sort of attention. Millions of yuan have been spent on them, millions of people come to see them, and it follows, in some minds, that they have a monetary value, and are therefore worth stealing. But the Chinese were honest and respectful of authority. When it was opened in 1979, the museum had no security system, and for a while it didn't matter.

Times change. In 1985, an unemployed 21-year-old named Wang Yengdi was set up by a friend who worked in the museum and his accomplice. The three hatched a plot to make them all wealthy. Wang would steal a head, for which he would receive 70,000 yuan (about £4,500), and which would then be sold in Hong Kong (so the court was told later) for a million yuan. The museum friend briefed him. Wang was to remain behind on the site after it closed, and after dark he was to go to a particular shed being used for restoration work. The door would be open. Inside, he would find the head of a general. Everything went according to plan. The head was instantly missed. Wang's friend was interrogated, and fingered Wang and the fence. In the friend's apartment police found the missing head, *and two other heads that no one knew were missing*. For the first time, the administrators realized that something would have to be done about security. Now comes the nasty bit. The two accomplices received life sentences, but Wang was executed by firing squad.

In went a security system, which proved its worth in a tale of love and idiocy. Once upon a time – in fact, 1993 – there was a poor Tibetan named Huan. He was 21, and desperately in love. His problem was that the girl's parents would only agree to a marriage if he came up with 3,000 yuan (£200). Such a sum was way beyond him. He heard he could get a job in Xian, and while looking for work he took a trip to the Terracotta Army. One of the tour guides, exaggerating the previous story, said, 'These statues are priceless. With ten warriors you could buy the whole United States! A few years ago a young man stole a general's head and could have got a million yuan for it in Hong Kong.' Huan's mind filled with dreams of cash and marriage. On 5 January 1994 he was back in the grounds of the museum, where he managed to undo the catch on a high window in Pit No. 1. He then hid outside in a pile of straw until after dark, when he climbed in, went to the back section of the pit where there were many unfinished statues, picked up a warrior's head, and tried to leave the same way. It is hard to climb while holding a pottery head, and anyway he had not taken any notice of the security cameras. Within three minutes, the doors were sealed and the guards were on him. Since he had not actually stolen the head, he got off lightly with a sentence of life imprisonment.

Since then there have been no serious problems, only an unserious one. In 2006 a 26-year-old German arts student, Pablo Wendel, from Stuttgart's Academy of Art, was on a short scholarship at the National Fine Arts Academy in Hangzhou. He was studying performance art, and had already had half a dozen installations back in Germany. He was low-key, even shy, but committed to original and disturbing acts, actions, occurrences, performances – I'm not sure there is a correct word for what he did (and does). In Hangzhou, he took a mud-bath in a canal and then walked the streets, observing reactions – amazement, amusement, pity, and finally rejection, by a taxi driver, who refused him a ride. On finishing his three months' study, he went travelling. He was drawn to the Terracotta Army, partly because the warriors look like performance artists. Haven't we all seen those 'statues' who intrigue holiday-makers by confusing flesh with stone and metal? He was also fascinated by the idea of armed guards guarding the First Emperor's guards. He conceived a strange tribute to the warriors: he would join them. This was not going to be a stunt. Confronting officialdom in China is no light matter, and he was prepared to end up behind bars.

Preparations took three months. He grew a moustache, dyed a long, stiff shirt, made a *papier mâché* hat, turned bits of a tyre into boots and organized a film crew to record the event. Mixing with crowds in Pit No. 1, he slipped over the side near the back, where a rail and a one-metre drop are the only barriers to a square secondary pit which holds about 50 reserve warriors. He had spotted a gap in the line, and was in place within seconds, frozen. A guard watching the CCTV screens saw a movement, stared, and could see nothing out of place. Many hundreds of people had, of course, and were busy taking pictures. But that was no help to the half-dozen guards, who began to search through the ranks for the intruder. 'I was looking for him, but I couldn't see him, because he was just like the real thing,' the security chief Jiang Bo said later. Wendel himself began suddenly to feel very frightened as the tension rose: the prowling guards, the camera-clicking crowd, his own discreet film crew, himself locked rigid, trying not to blink. After a few minutes, they had him. They asked him politely to leave. No response. Wendel speaks no Chinese, but in the circumstances it hardly mattered. As he told me, 'For the duration of the performance, I was a sculpture, so of course I could not speak or move.' Jiang Bo raised his voice. Still no response. After another few minutes, six guards took Wendel by the elbows and levered him out of line. He remained in character, and toppled over. In the end, six of them carted him off rigid – 'like a fallen tree', in Wendel's words – for questioning, in faltering English. (You can see pictures on the Web.) By now the guards knew he meant no harm – indeed, the opposite – and could scarcely hold back their smiles as they confiscated his clothing. Wendel could hardly believe his luck. He left with as stern a warning as Jiang Bo could muster to a man who was obviously passionate about his art and his subject. Six hours later, he was free, on a train back to Hangzhou, in borrowed clothes, travelling into a storm of publicity that blew his story around the world, and in the process showed Chinese officialdom as surprisingly polite and cheerful. At least on this occasion. To a foreigner.

Passionate interest in China quickly whipped up equal passions overseas. Official backing from Beijing turned the Terracotta Army into big business for foreign tourism and also a must-see destination for visiting dignitaries. There have been dozens, scores, hundreds of such visits, more every year, very few adding much of value to the warriors or saying anything of significance about them. That's not the point. Honoured visitors are led there to show their respect, to pay homage to these symbols of a united and powerful China. There are only two who matter, the first because he's a star on a level with the warriors, the second because he really did add something stellar to the museum.

The first in star quality was not the Queen, or Putin, or Reagan (1984: guides like to tell Americans how Reagan, on his departure, turned back to the Army and said 'Dismiss!'), or even Nixon (1985). Star No. 1 was, and still is, Bill Clinton, who came with Chelsea and Hillary on an extremely rushed viewing during the 1998 state visit. On 25 June the three were granted an experience given to very few except scientists: a chance to get in among the warriors on the pit-floor. It did not make enough of an impression to figure in either of the Clinton memoirs, but it immediately seared itself into the collective memory of the locals, who recall the visit in the form of a completely untrue anecdote:

Clinton is coming. The museum chiefs are

272

quivering with excitement. How to do something original, interesting, significant? Someone has an idea: the President should meet the old farmer, Yang Zhefa, who discovered the warriors (forget the complexities outlined in chapter 1; this is mythology). But they have to say something to each other. It has to be quick and simple, like this:

CLINTON:
Hi.

YANG:
How are you?

CLINTON:
I'm fine.

YANG:
Me too.

They grab Yang and brief him: 'Clinton's coming, with Hillary and Chelsea. He's going to shake your hand. All you have to say is "How are you? Me too." No, not in Chinese, in *English*.' They tell him the words, they make him repeat them, time and again, 'How are you? Me too. How are you? Me too.'

Clinton comes, with Hillary and Chelsea. He is introduced to Yang. The two shake hands.

Clinton says 'Hi.'

Yang, overcome with nerves, tries to say 'How

are you?' and falters. Instead he says, '*Who* are you?'

Clinton, modest as ever, replies, 'I'm Hillary's husband.'

Yang, of course, says, 'Me too.'

It started as a joke. It became a behind-the-scenes anecdote. Now it's told by guides, with my-friend-who-was-Clinton's-interpreter as a source. English-speaking tourists tell other English-speaking tourists with swear-to-God certainty, which is how I heard it. If it goes on like this, it will get into a book, and become a truth.

The other star leader is the former French president Jacques Chirac, who owes his stardom to his knowledge of, and genuine passion for, Asian history. This fed into his presidency as a belief that the Chinese dragon was wide awake and that it was in France's interest to get on well with him. The interest goes back to Chirac's teenage years, when he was a frequent visitor to Paris's Guimet Museum, which has the largest collection of Asian art outside Asia. He is an old friend of one of China's greatest archaeologists, Han Wei, former head of Shaanxi's Institute of Archaeology and thus the Terracotta Army's ex-commander. During his tenure as president Chirac made four trips to China, where he won hearts and minds by revealing an intimate knowledge of the Sui and Tang dynasties.

Anecdotes about his erudition abound. In 2000, when he was the guest of President Jiang Zemin, he asked one of his companions if he knew how many emperors there were in the Sui dynasty. Yes, came the reply, two – Emperors Wen and Yang. 'No,' said Chirac, 'there were three.' It's a historical footnote: the third was a five-year-old named Gong, who was placed on the throne in 617 AD by the incoming Tang dynasty, and removed the following year. To Chinese politicians, this level of interest by a foreign diplomat is even more unlikely than Jiang Zemin being an expert on Joan of Arc. Chirac also revealed an interest in an eighth-century Tang poet, Li Bo ('wanderer . . . great drinker . . . supreme example of irresponsibility', says the *Penguin Book of Chinese Verse*), about whom he wants to make a film after his retirement, hoping to persuade Gong Li to play the role of an imperial concubine. So when he comes out with *bons mots*, official China laps them up. For example: People who haven't visited the pyramids have not really visited Egypt; people who haven't seen the Terracotta Army have not really visited China.

But most of this came later. On his first official visit to China in 1978, he was still Mayor of Paris. In acknowledgement of his expertise and his friendship with Han Wei, he was granted access to the Terracotta Army, even though it had not yet officially opened. It was here, having seen the Army's open pit and its other army of workers, that he commented, 'There are seven wonders in the world, and we may say that the

275

discovery of these terracotta warriors and horses is the eighth.'

The Eighth Wonder. The perfect tag. The Chinese seized on it, and have pumped it out in articles and handouts ever since, encouraging it to float free of its context so that it sounds like an ancient saying or simply a historical fact. The Army 'is recognized as', 'is known as', 'is commonly called' the Eighth Wonder – never mind that two dozen other places, including the Great Wall, also lay claim to the same cliché; and never mind also that of the seven ancient wonders, only one (the Great Pyramids of Giza) survives. That's why Xi-la-ke is a star. That's why his photo has a place of honour at the museum.

Lintong is a city reborn since 1974. Unpaved streets, simple brick houses and orchards have given way to boulevards, high-rises and a university campus. No one is in any doubt about why the wealth flowed in. A street placard proclaims: 'Thank the Communist Party for your changed status, but thank the First Emperor for making us rich!'

In the middle of Lintong is a reminder of this great truth. One of the world's biggest statues cuts apart the eastbound main road. It is the First Emperor on the warpath, driving 5,000 tonnes of pink granite. His horses form the bows of a triangle, bursting from the rock while he towers above them, impassive and remote as a mountaintop. Around him, forming the body of the triangle, are lesser mortals. Meng Tian, the general of the northern frontier and scourge of the barbarians, stares over his left shoulder, while charioteers and outriders surge about below. The statue is as gigantic as the emperor's ego, a monument to him, to his original achievement and to his significance for the town today.

I wanted to know where this immense object, the Unification Statue, came from. The sculptor, Wang Tianren, was out of town, so with Wang (yes, there are many Wangs) and Tony, I went to find out from his son, who follows in his father's massive footsteps. We wove into Xian's south-west suburbs through rain that reduced visibility to a few hundred metres. It was like driving along the bottom of the Yellow River.

'You know,' said Wang the Driver, 'I was at art school with Wang.' Wang Zhan, he meant, the sculptor son of Wang Tianren. I don't know which was the greater surprise, that Wang the Driver had once been an art student, or the coincidence of the two Wangs being fellow students. 'That was before the college moved into town, when it was in caves. Yes, dug into a hillside, like the house of the farmer who lived near the tomb of the First Emperor's grandfather.' As we moved slowly through the murk, he told his story, a lesson in how to get on in today's China. Having trained in design, he joined a Japanese film company in south China, which taught him Japanese and English. The pay was good, but he was far from home, 'and, you know, I was the only child for my parents, so I came back home. It is hard to make a living in art, so I bought this car and became a driver.'

By now we were, in Tony's phrase, in the back of beyond, and would have been lost without mobile phones, with which Wang the Sculptor was summoned to meet Wang the Driver at a round-about. In convoy, we proceeded murkily, past vague apartment blocks, along a canal, through a maze of narrow side-streets, reversing clear of piles of cement and three-wheelers until we came at last to iron gates, and I understood why Wang the Sculptor needed the back of beyond. He wanted the space provided by this ex-farm, its cavernous sheds and its field to carve and cast and display his huge creations – landscape statuary, as he called it, including a twice-life-size bull, two 3-metre hands reaching out of the ground and a 5-metre Lenin look-alike which turned out to be the Canadian surgeon Norman Bethune, who was with Mao during the anti-Japanese war in the 1930s and is a hero in China.

Wang the Sculptor parked and got out, revealing himself to be ideally built for his chosen occupation. Beneath a head shaved into stubble was a small but solid body, with shoulders like a weightlifter, which, as he explained as he led the way inside, was because he used to be a swimmer.

His studio, a converted barn, was a litter of screens, paintings, tables, copies of Han statues, a wagon-wheel, and black leather sofas and chairs. In a screened-off kitchen area, several people were skewering kebabs for a party that evening. Wang the Sculptor sat me down, poured tea from a pot of his own design, had a short, intense conversation with the other Wang about schooldays, vanished briefly to check on the kebabs, then zipped back to tell me about his father's statue. He was a man in a constant hurry. None of my photographs of him are in focus, which is entirely down to the fact that he was always a blur. It was like talking to a ricocheting bullet. His hair-stubble was created not by a razor but by air-friction, such as burns away the heat shield of a space capsule on re-entry.

The idea for the statue came from the Xian and Lintong councils, who wanted something grand to commemorate the First Emperor, something that combined historical significance and grandeur, a landmark that suited its position and a statement for centuries to come. This was in 1990. His father was eminent, a teacher in Shaanxi Art University, president of the Xian Institute of Sculpture and also a representative in the People's Congress, so he was a natural choice.

The first step had been to choose a shape, which depended on the site. The best place, where Lintong's incoming roads split apart, gave him the triangular outline. Then there was the choice of style. The statue was to commemorate Qin, so it had to be a rough-and-ready contrast with the sophistication of later dynasties. Then came the design – he led the way into a corridor to point out a table-top plaster model – then approval, then work. It was as simple to describe and as massive as any of the First Emperor's grand projects. Construction involved ordering 1,000 blocks – 'about a thousand, I never counted' – of granite, each weighing 5 tonnes. Then an army of masons started three years of work to turn the plaster model into an expression of raw power and Qin machismo.

'That's why we left the granite rough,' he said. By now we were moving fast through a studio full of gigantic heads. 'That's why you can see the lines between the blocks.'

'This was a project on an industrial scale!'

He shrugged. He and his father were used to operating like this.

'How many masons?'

'Three hundred, four hundred.'

'Good heavens. From all over China?'

'Not at all. We can find that many masons from just around here.'

And the cost? We were out in the garden now, circling the bull the size of a small house. About three million yuan (£200,000), and . . . Wang's words faded. He was on his way back inside, disappearing in the drizzle like the Cheshire Cat. It seemed to me astonishing value. If any western city wishes to create something like this, it should fly in a planeload of Shaanxi's masons.

The story of how the warriors were brought into the light of day and the eyes of the world poses a deep question: what do the warriors mean? You may say that to ask about meaning is meaningless, that they simply are, full stop; and that once discovered everything else followed as inevitably as night and day.

Not so, as the details of their emergence reveal. They were lost to memory because the times changed. If the Qin dynasty had endured, so would all its rites, which would have been recorded for all time. Though known about in a sense, because so many finds leaked to the surface, they remained lost because no one wanted to know about them. They were found only when the political context was right. Originally, they fulfilled the purposes of a huge ego determined to impose his will on the world; they emerged two millennia later to fulfil precisely the same purpose: to serve another huge ego, equally determined to impose his will on the world.

But there is another meaning, suggested not by history or by the immense and self-seeking characters behind their creation and emergence, but by the warriors themselves, which makes them even more appealing to China today. Thirty years ago they were propaganda justifying oppression. Now they have escaped from their roots – and from the context of their re-emergence – to serve the present (which is what Mao himself intended, ironically) as propaganda for the new, emergent China. It is not the emperor or present-day ruler who matters now, but the warriors themselves. They are seen as an expression of communal talents, a people's army, made and hidden by the masses, to use a Marxist term. They symbolize everything positive that China wishes for itself: a unified state, a creative people, a *compliant* people, and a government that works for the people. In the words of Don Fowler, an anthropologist in the University of Nevada, they are 'visible symbols of the strength and genius of the People throughout three millennia of oppression that ended in 1949' and thus 'serve to convince the governed that those in power rule legitimately'.[7] Whatever the course of China's future, the Army will be there, standing up for whatever the government defines as right.

[7] Fowler, 'Uses of the Past'.

CHAPTER 13

NEW MARVELS IN
BRONZE AND STONE

This is a story to which more chapters are being added year by year, with ever-increasing variety, and no sign yet that the end is in view. Let me give you an idea of the scope of the discoveries, some of which I used as evidence for descriptions of the creation of the tomb:

- Thirty-one skeletons of birds in clay coffins, attended by terracotta wardens, perhaps to recreate the First Emperor's pleasure garden (were they intended to breed spirit children, I wonder?).
- Between three and four hundred pits, 100 of which have been opened, each found to contain the skeleton of a horse, some buried alive, or the figure of a kneeling groom, like the one in Zhao Kangmin's museum, or both.
- A second stables-pit holding some 300 horse skeletons and kneeling terracotta grooms.
- Seventeen tombs that contain, together with objects of gold, silver, jade and lacquer, the

remains of humans – all put to death either because they were victims of the Second Emperor or because they asked to follow their lord and master into the next world. Their limbs had been cut off.

- A graveyard of 100 more skeletons of convict workers who either died or were sentenced to death, buried in a crouching position, with accompanying clay tablets giving names, origins and fates. Of the nineteen inscriptions, which show the dead men came from Shandong, ten bear the phrase 'sentenced to labour'. These are the earliest tomb inscriptions found in China to date, and also proof that convict labour was used on the tomb.

- Remains of ramparts and gates and buildings galore, all producing huge collections of bronze bells, weights, lamps, porcelain bowls and tiles.

- An enormous stone workshop, measuring 1.5 × 0.5 kilometres, from which came iron tools, half-finished stone pipes, and limestone blocks.

- Terracotta figures totally different from any others. Clothed only in short skirts, they are highly individual, one being as slim as a male model while another has the paunch and buttocks of a weightlifter. Several have their arms raised, which suggests their official role – acrobats. All different, they may have been made individually, not with moulds.

- A pit made as a water-garden, complete with

stream, for a collection of bronze birds, on which more in the next chapter.

This is a Pompeii of remains that will take decades to catalogue, let alone analyse. Meanwhile, there are two finds acknowledged to be world-class treasures and at least one Army pit that poses another mystery.

In 1978, even before the museum was opened, some experimental drillings at the western base of the tomb-mound turned up some small metal bits of horse harness, some bronze and one piece of gold. Two years later, after more detailed work probing down through almost 8 metres of soil, archaeologists found an irregular series of four pits, one of which had five 10-metre-long sections. And in the end section, in the remains of a wood-lined container, crushed beneath the fallen earth, lay what have become the crown jewels of the museum: two four-horse, two-wheeled carriages, in bronze, half life-size, complete with their horses and drivers. Over the centuries, the weight of earth had flattened the chariots and the lower limbs of the sturdily built horses like a car-crusher.

Careful excavation uncovered both the brilliance of the work and the extent of the problem. The horses were largely intact, but the carriages, their canopies and reins as thin as tinfoil, had been smashed into fragments, producing a giant, three-dimensional jigsaw of some 3,000 pieces. It would clearly be impossible to restore them while they were down their pit, so a base was slid under the whole 6 × 2 metre block, which was then lifted as a single 8-tonne unit and trucked to a workshop. Horses and carriages were separated, bent bits restored to their original shape; glue was devised to stick the pieces together, resin used to fill in small holes and cracks; plates, pins and metal wire were attached as reinforcement. Not much was lost (though the tassels on the heads of the lead horses, the two on the front right, had to be replaced because the originals were made of bronze wires just one-hundredth of a millimetre thick). After eight years' work by a team of 30, both carriages were restored to full working order. They are on display, beautifully lit, in the Multiple Exhibition Building.

They are breathtaking objects, perfect down to every rein and harness and free-spinning axle-flag, so minutely accurate that when talking about them it is hard to remember they are not the real things but two tonnes of metal. Several metals, in fact. They are mostly bronze (a 50–50 mixture of copper and tin), plus some lead, but different bits of the chariots have varying amounts of lead in them to alter their hardness. There is a thesis to be written simply on the bridles, alternating segments of inlaid gold and silver bosses, 42 of each. Of many intriguing details, here are two. Inside each horse's mouth, and therefore invisible to human eyes, each bit has a sharpened point that can be pulled on to the tongue in case the horse bolts. ('In case it bolts', indeed! You see how easy it is to forget that these are half-size bronzes, not going anywhere.) The second detail addresses this question: in a team of four, with loose leather harnesses that would allow the two outer horses to drift inwards and obstruct the central pair, what keeps them at the right distance? Answer: a sort of goad or spur attached to the outside flank of each horse in the central pair. The two outer horses have to keep their distance to avoid being pricked.

The first chariot, an open one variously known as a 'high', 'war', or 'inspection' chariot, has the driver standing on a platform holding six reins, with the inside reins of the two central horses attached to the chariot. It has a canopy that, rather like a modern beach parasol, has a pointed end for sticking in the ground while at rest, and a lockable joint that allows it to be set in any direction. In real life, the driver could drive or rest protected by his canopy from the rain and sun, and sleep under it at night. He was ready for anything, this driver. He had a long sword on his back and a crossbow beside him, along with a box of 54 arrows and a shield. These look like very special weapons, as much symbolic as practical. The crossbow has a nicely decorated trigger, and the shield (which would be wooden in real life) is beautifully curlicued and painted; the canopy's shaft is inlaid with gold and silver cloud motifs.

The second chariot is the emperor's, and it is an even more brilliant creation. It has a front section for a charioteer – who drives sitting back on his heels, poor chap – and a second, enclosed, section for the emperor. It (or rather the original on which this model is based) is big enough to lie down in. The roof, laid on a network of struts, is a dome of silk or leather waterproofed with grease. It overhangs all around to shelter the driver, shade the sides and carry rain well clear of the wheels. In the windows there is mosquito netting – all this being rendered in bronze, of course – and, on the side windows, a little sliding panel so the emperor can see out, get air in and issue orders without being seen. The walls and the outward-opening back door are decorated with detailed patterns. There is even a case, for personal possessions perhaps, or for bamboo-strip documents.

Clearly, the chariots were waiting for the soul of the emperor to emerge from his tomb and order a tour of inspection, such as he had undertaken four times during his life. Those who buried the chariots were clearly expecting the horses to wait a while before they saw action, because – weirdly – large quantities of hay were buried with them. Once again we see the paradoxical mixture of incompatible beliefs, the assumption that bronze horses would become spirits and need real hay.

The emperor's tours had been to the east. These chariots were facing west and were painted white, the colour of the west. Now, remember that there had been attempts on the emperor's life and he travelled in one of several identical carriages. There are four other sections to this pit, as yet unopened. His officials, if they had really been determined to model an alternative universe as real as his own, would have had another four carriages ready for him to choose from. One day, we shall know if they did their job or not.

Once again, the farmers pointed the way. By 1997, all the locals had known for years that any anomaly – a dip, a bump, a difference of earth – might indicate another pit; so when a farmer planting trees dug into a layer of red earth just outside the remains of the tomb's inner wall, the archaeologists took over. After probing this way and that, they realized they had another huge find: a pit of 100 by 130 metres, divided into thirteen sections by rammed-earth walls. Another 65,000 cubic metres, almost half the size of the Terracotta Army's pit, another 100,000 tonnes of earth to be dug out, another three months' work by the 40,000 labourers. And for what?

At first the assumption was that this was a tomb – the first to be found within the inner and outer walls – perhaps for crowds of concubines off to join their master in the next world. The following year, they had the beginning of a different answer. At a depth of about 5 metres they came upon a layer of little square slivers of stone, as if Qin craftsmen had manufactured a collection of symbolic fish-scales. As the earth was lifted clear grain by grain, however, it became clear that the scales had once been joined together. There was nothing fishy about these scales. They were suits of armour such as no one had ever seen before.

Beyond the mausoleum we turned south, towards the hills, right past an immense sewing-machine factory blaring music, then along what was once the outer wall of the mausoleum complex and was now a rough track. In a maze of paths and fields, the tomb-mound (east) and the mountains (south) were my anchors. The pomegranate orchards, as yet without buds, bore a disturbing crop of tattered plastic bags, obviously random rubbish blown from local tips.

Past the tomb-mound, we turned through low trees and a rickety iron gate, guarded by a black dog barking and straining at his chain, and parked by a line of blue corrugated iron sheds. Beneath us was our destination, the pit of the stone armour, a place for experts only. Our expert, Mr Niu – late thirties, black jacket, round face and hair as flat as a skull-cap: the same Niu Xinlong who took me to the tomb of the First Emperor's grandfather – was expecting us. He led us inside, into the end shed, which was as simple as it looked from outside: an oven in high summer and a fridge in winter. A rough-cut wooden staircase led down into the pit. We followed him down, into shadows, past earth scarred with fire-scorched blotches and boards holding up crumbly bits. It's often surprising, the contrast between utter, down-to-earth basics on the surface and the treasures that lie beneath.

'This was very much like Pit Number One,' said Niu. Having worked here for almost 20 years, since his teens, he was an enthusiast eager to impress me with the significance of the finds. 'They dug this enormous pit, then put in rammed-earth walls, lined them with wood and put a roof over the top.' Easily said, but that meant another kilometre of walls, another 7,500 tonnes of earth, and another 3,000-plus beams to be added to the tomb's construction – and we hadn't got to the purpose yet.

At the bottom was a platform of planks on a beam framework, about 3 metres across and 10 metres long, except that the planks did not go all the way to the end. They were loose, so they could be moved about a few centimetres above what we had come to see: a litter of little stone flakes, which had once formed jackets of armour. Now the jackets were shredded into hundreds of bits scattered over the floor like shells on a tide-washed beach. They are incredibly delicate, having been baked by the fire that destroyed the pit and then partially dissolved by mineral-rich earth. Someone had been doing careful work down here, sticking tiny numbered labels on each flake to ensure they could be re-ordered correctly after being lifted.

291

My imagination does strange things at moments like this. Once, in Ulaanbaatar's university, I was with a Mongolian palaeontologist, Perlee, who had discovered and named a type of little herbivorous dinosaur. He opened a cupboard, took out a cardboard box, lifted out the skull of his precious find and handed it to me. It was delicate as a cobweb, fragile as porcelain, a jewel of a fossil. I thought: What if my brain seizes up and I drop it? And now: What if I slipped, lost my balance, fell in slow motion with flailing arms and crashed down like King Kong across those tiny brittle squares? I squatted for safety, as if suffering from vertigo on a cliff-top, and took a careful picture, to capture the patterns of tiny holes, the way the scales here and there still kept the shape of the armour. Some were still fixed with the copper wire, so delicate after two millennia underground that it would crumble when raised.

'How many of these suits are there, do you think?'

'We believe about two hundred. But we have not yet opened all the other chambers. We think there may be twenty-four chambers altogether.'

'But who wore them?'

'No one. They are too heavy to wear—' 22 kilos, actually '—and no use anyway. They are stone! They break if you hit them. We think they were hung on the walls, like baked meat.'

Back upstairs, two charioteer-warriors, their arms supported by wooden frames, flanked a suit of armour and a helmet on a simple wooden table. The warriors were real, the armour and the helmet copies in resin, to see how the plaques could hang together. The restored suit, though, was not the only style. 'We can identify different ranks,' Mr Niu went on. 'In one style, the pieces are very small, very delicate, like fish scales. We have found only two suits like that, so we guess they are for generals. These suits need one thousand and sixty pieces. The suits of lower officers have about six hundred, and those of ordinary soldiers just over three hundred.'

So the First Emperor's craftsmen had made over 100,000 of these fiddly little scales, and wired them into snugly fitting tops that were utterly impractical and, once in position, would never be seen again by human eyes, until the invaders came down and started the fire that burned the pit.

Unlike the mould-based techniques that produced the warriors, there could have been no short cuts here. Each flake was a work of art, smooth as oil (I felt one later, upstairs), a mere 8 millimetres thick, crafted for a particular spot in its suit, rectangular, square, trapezoid or rounded, with bevelled edges if they overlapped, so that when stitched together the garment moved as easily as the skin of an armoured dinosaur. My Mongolian palaeontologist would have loved them. Sizes varied, so that shoulder flaps descended in size as they followed the upper arm muscle downwards. On the flap below the waist, side flakes were trimmed into diagonals to skirt the hip.

There is one astonishing set of large flakes, not from the pit I was in, averaging 14 × 7 centimetres, notepad-sized plates. The first few were mysteries. Only when many more emerged did it become apparent that they were for a horse, or horses (no one knows yet how many), about 300 plates per horse. This was an amazing discovery, because the earliest horse-armour known up until then dates from about 430 years later (early third century AD, when an infamous warlord named Cao Cao unified north China, but failed to unite the rest). Here was evidence that the First Emperor owed his success to horses armoured in leather, though it has not survived the passage of time any more than the armour of the real soldiers has. Interestingly, it was not modelled in terracotta: none of the Army's horses are protected. Perhaps this was a new invention, reserved for only a few top generals.

In any event, all of this armour is totally impractical, as Mr Niu said. If you wore it, you would hardly dare move. Swing a sword-arm and you would sound like a wind-chime gone haywire – though not for long, because bits would crack and fall. In a fight, it would be as much use as porcelain. So what on earth was it for?

Perhaps knowing where it came from might help. Later, I went to see someone who knows, Yang Zhongtang at Xian's branch of the China

Geological Survey. It would be nice to be able to describe him, but it had been a long day and I had a severe stomach problem. By the time I arrived, I could hardly take in the unremarkable office block or his office, let alone the personal appearance of my host. I remember him saying he had become intrigued by the armour and determined to discover the kind of stone it was made of and where it came from. 'When you feel them, they are so smooth, so perfectly made, so thin.' Other than that my mind is a blur. But I have my tape, his paper,[1] and his conclusions. He and his colleagues took 21 flakes, cut them – yes, you have to torture your subjects to make them reveal their secrets – analysed the mineral content, chose eleven minerals, and compared the results with rocks taken from all over the province. They discovered they were dealing with a rather special form of limestone which comes from northern Shaanxi, from hills outside a village called Manding, near Fuping, about 50 kilometres north of Xian. 'It is a source of very fine limestone,' he concluded, 'made five hundred million years ago by tiny shells deposited on the bottom of a shallow lake. This we think is the quarry that produced the limestone for the stone armour.'

One mystery solved, and another created. On my tape I hear his sigh. 'In this factory, we found

[1] Yang Zhongtang et al., 'Tracing the Source of Material of Stony Armours'.

295

some other limestone which is more thickly textured, unsuitable for the stone armour. What was it used for? We have no idea. For statues, perhaps? We have not found anything yet.'

As Ann Paludan, Britain's leading expert in Chinese sculpture, says, 'stone was a late-comer'. The Qin seemed to have very little interest in working in stone, although there are some intriguing hints to the contrary – that Li Bing quelled water spirits when he built his mighty system of water controls at Du Jiang Yan; that there had been a stone god-figure on a bridge over the Wei. There was a persistent folk tale that the First Emperor had a statue made of one of his guards, a huge man called Wengzhong, to scare the enemy. Events proved this to be effective: unification followed. From then on, statues of commanders on tombs were referred to as *wengzhong*. It is to such a statue that a sixth-century emperor referred when he wrote, 'One can find all the best qualities of scholar and soldier in a general wearing stone armour.' And we know that the following dynasty believed in the protective powers of stone, because one of them was buried in a jade suit every bit as intricate as these limestone ones. No extensive interest in stone *statuary*, perhaps – an interest that arose only a century later, at the beginning of the Han dynasty; but there was something in the air about stone and its supposed powers. Perhaps, like the discovery of horse-armour, there are surprises still to come.

But what was it all *for*? The tentative answer seems to be that the armour had to do with combating demons, believed to cause illness and decay after death. An 11th-century stele has an inscription claiming that 'this hard stone' can suppress ghosts. Other references – bamboo strips found in a 217-BC tomb, a 4th-century Daoist text – advise throwing white stones or burying them beneath house-corners to keep ghosts away.

It may help to look at the elements that the stone armour shares with the warriors. Like them, it is life-size, and hyper-realistic, even better than the 'leather' armour worn by the warriors, because it actually moves, and because you cannot bevel the edges of leather scales to make them glide against each other more easily. And for whom was it intended? Were unarmoured terracotta warriors expected to leap through the earth and don stone armour in some spirit battle against demon foes? Or were the suits talismans, their very existence enough to scare off the enemy, like garlic waved at a vampire? Something like that, probably, because stone was indeed an important guardian – witness the seven stone stelae set up by the First Emperor on his tours.

It hardly seems likely that the First Emperor would invent out of the blue the idea that limestone would make a good talisman, send off experts to find the best source and train sub-armies of stonemasons, all so that he could have stone armour in his mausoleum. More likely, surely, that he grew up with the idea, and developed it.

On that assumption, there is good sense to be made of this. The First Emperor wanted the best for his spirit army. He had warriors, weapons, chariots, all life-size, all realistic. Let us suppose they fight their battles in the spirit world, and need replacement armour. Their own is of leather, which, after all, is not as eternal as it should be. They need something longer-lasting. Nothing lasts longer than stone. What better material for armour than something everlasting? Now the question arises of which stone to choose. You can't make granite or sandstone into fiddly little armour flakes. Jade would have been the obvious choice. Rare, beautiful and one of the hardest of stones, it had been central to art and belief for at least 3,000 years. By the time of the First Emperor it was sacred, its qualities making it a metaphor for virtue and spirituality. Senior officials loved to sport jade pendants. But there is a problem with jade: its hardness makes it extremely difficult to carve. Limestone is the perfect material.

One thing for certain: if this was some superstition held by the emperor, it would have been a lot more than that by the time he died. As Ann Paludan remarks, 'the quarrying, transporting and carving of hundreds of thousands of small panels . . . must not only have mobilized vast numbers of stonemasons and workers, but spread the idea among such people that stone could provide possible protection in the next world'. By then it must have been a universally accepted truth.

Mr Niu led the way across a living room – a couple of iron beds, an iron stove, a stovepipe through the corrugated iron roof – unlocked a door and took us into a dim room with a single window. It was lined with shelves stacked with what looked like the contents of a large garden shed. This was the store-room, where all the stuff dug from the pit was kept before anyone made sense of it: Qin drainpipes, cooking pots, bits of tiling, and bag upon grimy plastic bag of stone armour flakes.

'Look at this one,' said Niu. 'Broken before it was made part of a suit. That's the problem with limestone, it breaks very easily. It's still rough on one side, so it broke while it was being polished. And this one – broken while the maker was drilling the holes, so he threw it away. And this one, it has a slight bend, and is still unpolished.'

'So many different types. How many?'

'So many! They are like snowflakes, all different.'

Here in the store-room and down in the pit and on brilliantly lit display over in the museum was evidence of yet another highly sophisticated industry about which historical records are silent. This too would have remained unknown, its products consigned to near-oblivion by fire. Yet it was the fire that ensured discovery, baking the earth above into a red crust that gave away the pit's presence. How many other troves might await discovery?

Like a bunch of kids wandering home from school, we idled along the tomb's southern inner wall. Mr Niu was leading the way to another pit, in which a group of so-called 'officials' had been found, a pit with its own unique story. It was a warm spring afternoon, with Mount Li and its subsidiary peaks making a hazy barrier to the south and the tomb blocking the view northwards. A well-worn path ran along the remains of the wall, rising at one point to a mound of earth and stones that had once been the inner wall's South Gate. On either side were orchards of gnarled pomegranates fed by ditches that directed rain-water to their roots. Little store-houses dotted the fields. It was very pretty, except for the litter of plastic bags caught in the trees, which looked like the detritus left by a retreating flood.

'No, it is not just rubbish,' explained Tony. 'This is a very dry area. We learn from Israel. The plastic bags keep the fruit warm and preserve moisture, so it will be juicy and sweet, and also saves water for irrigation.'

Not *just* rubbish, so that I guess makes it accept-able.

The path dropped down from the wall and swung a few metres north, to another hut of corru-gated iron, this time painted white. Inside it was not the rough-and-ready, hands-on workplace

I expected – indeed, it was almost completely empty. All the work had been done; all the figures except for one charioteer had been taken for display. As a result, it was antiseptically neat, with boardwalks along the side of the pit, which was made up of a square and three rectangles – two in the pit, one a 45-metre access ramp – like the start of a game of giant dominoes.

Yes, this building was better than the stone-armour ones, said Niu. There was a reason. It was because of President Chirac. 'You know that Xi-la-ke is a big fan of China. When he came back in 2000, he had heard of the new excavations and wanted to dig something up. That's why they made it nicer.'

Chirac was right to be interested. These were phenomenal finds: four charioteers, a chariot (or rather its faint remnants), and eight dignified and very unmilitary men, with their hands tucked up their long sleeves. They were officials, whose job involved taking notes, as revealed by the writing implements hanging from their belts: writing tablet, brush, ink and knife for scraping the tablet clean. Other finds suggested exactly what their job was, and turned the scene into a tableau of life and death.

For at the far end of the pit were found the bones of many horses. We wandered along, staring down into the pit. It was like a fossil bed, all the bones jumbled as if they had been tipped in from a refuse truck. Mr Niu said there had been nine horses, but there may be 20 or more. Sacrificial offerings, I assumed.

'No, they were alive,' said Niu. 'How do we know? Because we found a wooden stick among the bones. It is the sort of stick used to hitch and control horses. So they must have been led down the ramp, tethered and then sealed in. They would have died days later from lack of oxygen.'

This added a new element to the First Emperor's paradoxical belief system. First, the lifelike soldiers. Next, bronze horses and real hay. Then the protective symbolism of the stone armour. Now, not only more terracotta figures, but live horses, despite the fact that they were destined to die. Apparently, this was a hangover from the old idea that the emperor would need real flesh and blood with him in the tomb.

Perhaps it was something to do with the status of the sacrifices, suggested Mr Niu. Who can tell? Perhaps it had something to do with being closer to the tomb, those horses further away beyond the walls of the tomb-city being all terracotta, those inside the walls being sacrificed in the pit. This was becoming a drama, the purpose of which I couldn't see.

'But these are not complete skeletons. They're all mixed up.'

'It seems that after they died, there was a leak, a flood, which washed all the bones together.' An underground stream, perhaps, escaping from beneath the Wu Ling Dam.

It also softened the floor so that the line of officials and charioteers, once standing patiently along one side of the pit, fell flat on their faces in the mud.

'We also found four *yue*, a sort of axe that had developed into a ritual object.' These ceremonial axes, like the axe carried by the Beefeaters' second-in-command in the Tower of London, had been used as status symbols for 1,000 years. 'We know from official records that once the emperor had granted an official a *yue*, that man had the power over life and death. So we guess this must have been a law court.'

As Mr Niu elaborated, a picture began to emerge. 'Qin was a centralized regime, with all important decisions being made in the capital. Then the decisions, the written tablets, would have to be taken to other cities. That's what they needed the horses for – to pull the official chariots.'

It was a vivid tableau, thanks to an odd circumstance. This is the only other pit, besides No. 3, which was not destroyed by fire. If my scenario of how the other fires started is correct – a break-in, a spark, a blaze, a long, slow, smouldering collapse – then in this pit there was no break-in. It sounds to me as if the rebel forces knew enough about the place from their local informants: It's only small, sirs, containing a few officials and some dead horses, and (crucially) no weapons. Definitely not worth the effort.

CHAPTER 14

ON HANDLING TREASURES

Remember Han Fei's advice to the ruler to be still and observe from the place of darkness? Well, the First Emperor hides behind his Army, a spirit behind his spirits, and the closest we can get to him is to pay homage to his spirit Army's outward and visible manifestations. As we approach on our uphill climb, passing through the entry gates only when we have purified ourselves by paying, we become a little awed. Then, as we enter the Army's sanctum, Pit No. 1, we are treated like the Qin populace. We are kept back, on platforms and walkways, not allowed to get close to the emperor's guardians, who exist on a different plane from us. Getting close is a privilege only granted to near-equals of the First Emperor, and to courtiers, who now call themselves experts and officials.

I am stretching a point. This is, after all, a museum, and museums must protect their exhibits. In early 2007 I visited an exhibition of early Chinese bronzes and terracotta statues in Rome, just before the show ended. Here, a few terracotta warriors and various Qin objects were presented as magical things, spotlit like jewels in a shop window, like film stars on opening nights, set apart not only by lighting but by screens of fine netting that protected them from being touched.

One glowing exhibit was a recent discovery. In summer 2000, farmers (of course) identified a possible pit some 3 kilometres north-east of the tomb, close to where the new motorway from Xian runs. By 2003, another treasure trove had been unearthed: 46 life-size bronze water-birds – 20 swans, 20 geese and 6 cranes, one of them on the point of seizing a fish, another swallowing a worm. They had been placed in a water-garden, on the wooden banks of a stream, for the pit floor showed the footprints both of Qin workers and of others who had broken in: nothing of value found, apparently, but much damage done. Nearby were fifteen terracotta statues dressed in caps and heavy coats, in odd positions. Seven of them kneel, one hand raised as if holding something; the others sit with legs stretched out, reaching forward as if to touch their toes, but with their fingers bent, one hand facing up, the other down. They are musicians, plucking long-vanished zither-like instruments, raising mallets to strike bells or drums, perhaps improvising to mirror in sound the movements of the birds.

Displayed in the lobby of the Scuderie del Quirinale was one of the cranes, supported by a Perspex frame, its snaking neck and head poised to strike, its star quality emphasized by the spot-light, the protective netting, a plexiglass box – and a peculiar ban on photography, which was made impossible anyway by the netting and the plastic. It was as if the crane were a totem, its high priests nervous that we commoners and our rude cameras would suck out its power.

The sense of worshipful remoteness is the same in the museum, in the pits, and in the carefully dramatized presentation of selected figures – a crane included – in the Multiple Exhibition Building. Not being Clinton, it never occurred to me to ask if I could get on intimate terms with the warriors or anything else.

So what happened one afternoon was a shock. I wanted to talk with someone actually involved with hands-on restoration, mainly to appreciate the frustrations and joys of piecing the warriors together. I had acquired an army of my own – Tony the guide, Wang the driver, Jin from the museum – all of whom were keen to get behind the scenes. My informant was Ma Yu, who worked in the Conservation Department, in one of the grey concrete blocks at the back of the museum site. You know you are getting on a bit when conservation officers start to look really young. Ma, in a tracksuit and with a shock of Beatles-style black hair, seemed hardly more than a teenager. In fact, he was 36 and had been doing this job for fifteen years, having trained with Italian

306

experts in Rome. He had worked on the stone armour and the warriors, and they no longer awed him. It crossed my mind he had become a little blasé, handling these priceless objects every day, even a little cynical about the fundamental purpose of his daily work. What was restoration, anyway? he wondered, drifting off into philosophy. We dig the warriors out of the ground, add glue and plaster to them, make them look authentic, but it's a pretence. A figure stuck together is not the original. Anyway, they are not repainted, so not properly restored. Was there a better way? I asked. He didn't know. Perhaps it was a mistake to restore them at all. Perhaps it would be better to expose them and leave them half uncovered. Or completely covered, like most of the warriors, where they are quite safe. I wasn't sure this was getting me anywhere, but he suddenly suggested I go and see what he was working on right now, which was saving a wooden pole.

He led us all into his laboratory next door, and showed the first item on view, a wooden halberd-handle, which was being saved by the injection of chemicals. Very interesting, no doubt, if you like that sort of thing. I felt my curiosity draining away.

'Are there perhaps any warriors here?'

Ma pointed over my shoulder. I turned, and—

It was like being electrocuted. There, lying on its back on a table, unprotected by anything, was the body of a kneeling crossbowman, right knee

307

down, left knee raised. Instantly, I denied the evidence of my own senses.

'It's a copy, I suppose?'

'No,' he said. 'It's real.'

Oh. My. God, as my teenage daughter would have said. There are other kneeling archers, of course, all from Pit No. 2, which contains between 112 and 144 (no one knows how many exactly because so little has been excavated).[1] According to the accounts I had seen, seventeen were registered in the museum, and about ten others remained in the pit, half-buried. It is hard to keep track of what was uncovered and recovered when, and which statues were moved when and where, but I had assumed that all those excavated must have been restored by now. Yet here was one in the process of being cleaned, not by Ma as it happened, but by team-members who were working elsewhere.

'Can I touch it?'

He shrugged a why-not. So began an exploration as gentle as a seduction, not as sensuous as it might have been, given that this archer was missing his head. It was my first time with a warrior, so I felt a responsibility to remember every touch of the hard, smooth clay. While the others went a little wild with cameras over this first-ever chance to feel what they had so often seen only from afar,

[1] Blänsdorf et al., *Final Report 2006: Testing and Optimising Conservation Technologies*.

I went over the overlapping leather plates of his armour, feeling the rivets and ties, still with traces of red on them, as if I were learning Braille. The right hand was missing, but the left was perfect, down to the well-trimmed fingernails. Fingers that once held the stock of a crossbow rested on a lump of light grey mud that the archer had been pressing against his waist for 2,213 years, give or take a few months. I counted the stipples across and down the non-slip soles of his boots (they seem to have been made with a little cylindrical tool, and there were about 800 in all). I ran my hand over the robe as it swung up over the remarkably solid left thigh. I spotted the maker's signature etched into one of the armour-plates so that his supervisor could hold him to account if need be: his name was Chao or Zhao and no one had any reason to accuse him of lack of quality. It was a shame the head was missing, but its absence did allow me to feel down inside the neck, where Chao or Zhao's fingers had left their mark as they squeezed the clay into its mould.

For many minutes I was absorbed, finally raising my head to re-engage with the world. I looked across the room, and in the far corner was another sight, another oh-my-god moment, another sharp intake of breath.

It was a bronze crane, its snaking neck and head in a strangely familiar pose, for it was the very same bird I had seen in Rome two months before. There, it had been made remote by netting and plexiglass. Here it was not only close up but touchable. Not only touchable, but liftable, because it was Ma's very own handiwork and now, seeing my response, he was eager to show it off. I felt like a child being offered a present, seething with excitement at what was on offer, and equally anxious that it would be snatched away.

Ma started to explain. 'When we found it, the leg was snapped off and a bit in the middle was missing. The neck was broken as well. So we had to analyse how it looked originally, so we could restore it correctly. We found pictures of cranes so that I could get the correct height and shape.' They were still there, pinned up on a notice board. 'Then I made new legs to fit the broken bits. I tried new bronze, but the old bronze was too weak to attach it. I tried glass, and in the end settled on epoxy.'

All this was down to Ma, who was emerging as a man of awe-inspiring self-assurance. He was a master craftsman, and he knew it. At one point he actually said, 'I am a genius at restoration.' If he didn't – and I only have Tony's translation to go on – he should have done, because it's true.

Originally, the crane had been fixed, standing firm on a bronze plinth, but now, with its epoxy lower limbs, it could not stand on its own; hence the need for the support. 'When I was restoring it, I gave it an iron support. The plastic one is for exhibitions.'

Then, to my surprise, without explanation,

Ma reached out and started to wring the bird's neck, as if he were practising butchery. But the neck was broken already, and had been for over 2,000 years. He pulled, and it came apart in his hands, revealing two sturdy little metal studs sticking out of the stump. They looked dreadfully familiar.

'Oh, they're like the posts my dentist used to fix a new tooth,' I said.

'Yes, the tools I use are dental drills. First you drill a hole in both sections, then you insert the little support posts in the stump. It's a technique I learned when I was in Rome.'

He handed me the head and top part of the neck. Thoughts careered through my brain: Please God, let me not drop it, it's 2,000 years old, it's gorgeous, and oh-oh it's *heavy*. About 5 kilos, I guessed, which meant the whole bird weighed in at about 30 kilos. The surface, once a delicate patina of feathers, was roughened by corrosion, as if it were growing barnacles. Close up, it was a kaleidoscope of rusty greens and earthy browns and sky blues, with little flecks of white.

'Is the neck solid metal, or did you fill it in to make the join?'

'Most of it is solid, but not the head, which has to be lighter so it can be supported. We took an X-ray of the neck, which shows how much is solid. Inside there is a spine made of heavier bronze, to act as a support between the body and the head. It broke at the most vulnerable spot. I could see

311

on the X-ray that if I could make a strong joint, it would support the head again.'

The bird was a fine example of sophisticated bronze casting, he explained as I fitted the neck together again with a satisfying little clunk. The neck and legs were made separately from the body. The neck's spine of denser bronze was made first, then the 'skin' of a different mix cast around it. The body was hollow—

'What – made in two halves like the head of a warrior?'

'No. It was made in a double mould, probably with clay round the outside and wax in the middle.'

'Oh, what we call the lost-wax method?'

'Yes, I think so, with the wax being melted out through a hole after the outer mould was removed. That's what I think. No one has done any work on this, except me. But there are many things we don't know. Look at these feathers. They overlap each other. We suppose they must have been pressed in during casting, and bent out afterwards.' He touched the wafer-thin flanges of bronze sticking out of the back of the body. 'And they are so delicate . . . oh.' The end of one of the feathers moved with his fingers. 'This one got damaged in Rome.'

What sacrilege was this? *The Romans damaged a feather?*

He sighed. 'It's what happens when these things get sent abroad. Many have been damaged. I reglued this, and this, and this.' He ran his fingers along feathers as if over a keyboard.

'You have to glue? Can't you reweld the bronze?'

'This is another theory of restoration. In the West, you reweld, but to do so adds new material, and it is no longer original. That would be re-creation, not restoration. It changes the texture. So I will repair what the Romans damaged with glue.'

'What about the colour?'

'The feathers would have been white, but we don't know if the colour was painted on or done by firing, with heat.'

'Would you ever scrape off the rust and repaint it?'

'Never!'

Of course, silly of me. That would be re-creation, not restoration. 'I'm glad to hear it,' I said. 'It's lovely as it is, the colours, the simple shape.'

'Come. I will show you the X-ray.'

He led me back across the room, with its arrays of desks and lights. By now I was wide awake to the possibility of lurking treasures, so I was drawn towards a desk with a clutter of devices on stands, a big magnifying glass, an arc-light and a vacuum-pump for removing dust. Beneath them lay a large piece of crumpled paper which had been gently pressed over a lump of something. While Ma opened a drawer across the room, I raised the paper.

Staring up at me was the head of the kneeling archer.

313

'Tony, Wang, Mr Jin. Look at this. I've never, I mean, what a.' I was incoherent with astonishment. While showing his piece of wood earlier, Ma had not thought to mention the archer's body. During those intense minutes with the body, he had not mentioned the head or the crane. He was obviously as used to handling treasures as dealers in gold bars or diamonds, and could no longer imagine what it was like coming to them fresh. 'Oh my God' didn't come near.

I set about getting to know this archer with hands, and eyes, and camera. He looked stern, determined, with a slight aggressive frown that dispelled any hint of Zen-like calm. His head was turned a little to the left, with almond eyes looking even further left, the direction in which he would be firing his crossbow. A neat little moustache, divided into two, and an underlip beard made up the 'three-drop' style of facial hair. He still had the mud of centuries on his face, but through rub marks – his skin was as smooth and hard as metal – it seemed he had a blue face, which would have been quite a rarity. All other archers so far had skin-pink faces, except one whose face was green, which Catharina Blänsdorf guesses is 'make-up, maybe some kind of war-paint'. But no, this was the original blue-grey terracotta, all traces of lacquer and paint removed by mud. He had the look of an experienced warrior, about 35, I should think.

When I came to study him further, in photographs,

314

he seemed somehow familiar. I realized why when, in one of the museum's publications, I saw him staring proudly out of a muddy background near the northeast corner of Pit No. 2, his original base. He had been ninth from the front in a corridor of 40 archers. He had not been pushed over, like his immediate neighbour, when the intruders came barging through, and had suffered less than most when the roof fell in. Though cracked across the shoulder, he had not lost his head. After 2,000 years, he was exposed with twelve others, most of them in pieces, by excavation. He had been given an official name, SH002, and an official address: T19G18, that is, Pit No. 2's nineteenth excavation hole, which is in Corridor 18. After 2,000 years underground, he had had quite an exciting life just recently, having been exposed in 1977, lost several colleagues to restorers, re-covered when the building was put up over Pit No. 2, half-uncovered again in 1999 – shortly before the portrait I had seen was taken – then finally lifted out for restoration in 2006. That was when he lost his head. Now one of seventeen registered by the museum as ex-members of the pit, he was due to be ready for display – head on and mudless, if also colourless – at the end of 2007.

'We could get a bed in here for you,' said Ma, breaking in upon my rather intense relationship with SH002. Well, liking him didn't mean sleeping with either his body or his head. It was time for lunch.

CHAPTER 15

TO BE REVEALED

To call the Army 'the Eighth Wonder' suggests a sense of fulfilment, as if the caravan of discovery has reached a plateau. In fact, when you look closer, you might think that it is close to falling off the far side. Work on the Army and the tomb has slowed almost to a standstill. When I was there in early 2007, no one was digging anything out of the ground, or piecing together broken warriors, or probing to find more pits. In Pit No. 1, visitors freeze or sweat, roofs leak, earth walls dry and crack and moulder. Great discoveries are hidden away in cheap sheds. Like the film shown in the circular screen, with its fading colours and overused soundtrack, the site is showing signs of complacency and decay.

Do not be deceived. It is not complacency and decline you are seeing; it is more like a gathering of breath for the next big effort. The labour of the past 30 years has been a warm-up for what is to come. In 2007, work was about to begin on a new park that will take in the whole vast complex of the tomb and its surroundings – 57 square kilometres in all, 25 times the size of the tomb itself.

Three thousand households were on a long-drawn-out move to the old village of Xiyang, much extended by new housing, just east of the museum, leaving as empty shells their old houses in the villages around the tomb. It has been a long, slow process, with many hiccups.

I spoke to one young building contractor who had done well: big-screen TV, minimalist glass table, water-cooler, huge reproduction view of the Yangtze gorges on the wall. 'Usually they offer a hundred thousand yuan [£6,500]. But my house was big so they offered me three hundred thousand yuan [about £20,000], but because I'm in the construction business I got the new one for a hundred and fifty thousand.' A fat profit, then? 'Not really. I lost it all gambling.' But what the hell, he could afford it.

Poorer people tried to profit in other ways. 'When they know there is compensation coming, they quickly build more houses,' as Tony said. But the change was inexorable, as always when dealing with authorities determined to have their way. In July, just as this book was going to press, the process was complete, freeing the archaeologists to begin a detailed survey of the whole area.

It is anyone's guess what will be revealed, beyond the 180 pits and several hundred graves already known. If the Han emperor Jing Di had 81 government departments to serve him in the afterlife, perhaps the First Emperor has as many, not in a tight-knit circle, but scattered randomly, their

317

positions in death dictated by their original positions in the First Emperor's capital, Xianyang.

The problems that persuaded experts to keep the remaining warriors buried are being solved. Only a few years after restoration started, the museum noticed that decay sets in the instant a soldier is released from the earth: it's not a prison, more a protective womb. There is, for instance, a sort of mould that grows on clay when it is exposed to damp air, mixed with the breath of millions, rising ground moisture and thousands of cubic metres of wood-mulch. In fact, as two experts say, between May and September the temperature (averaging 18°C) and humidity (65 per cent) are 'ideal for the growth of micro-organisms'.[1] And it's not just one mould, as it turned out. No fewer than 48 different species of fungi have been found in and around the pits – even, at one place in Pit No. 2 in 1995, mushrooms.

Help was at hand. In 2000, the Belgian anti-fungal experts Janssen Pharmaceutica agreed to set up a laboratory with four Chinese companies to identify and eradicate 'the fungal problem'.[2]

[1] Thomas Warscheid and Curt Rudolph, 'Microbiological examinations . . .' in Blänsdorf et al., *Qin Shihuang*, which also contains many technical articles on lacquer, colour identification and conservation, and is the source for the information in these paragraphs, together with personal communications from Catharina Blänsdorf.
[2] Xian-Janssen Pharmaceutica Ltd, a joint venture with four Chinese companies.

Opened in 2001, the laboratory grew into one of China's most advanced in the field of mycology. In 2006, after much experimentation with fungicides, the partners proclaimed in a press-release headline, 'Terracotta Army Museum now officially declared mould-free'. A new agreement that year extended research for another five years, and also enlarged the lab's remit to include silk, wood, bones – indeed, anything that has been or will be discovered at the site.

Mould-free clay is an essential base for the colours. Already an encyclopaedic amount of work has been done on them and the base layer. At first, of course, with most of the colours gone, no one knew what they were or how they were applied. When the first studies in the 1980s revealed an uncoloured bottom layer, experts guessed it was a sort of glue known as gum arabic. Only in the mid-1990s, after experiments that analysed the atomic structure, did it become clear that the material was lacquer – at which point work could start to solve the problems created by 2,000 years of burial. Much of the lacquer peels off like a child's transfer, taking the colours with it, when the earth is removed. But then comes further trouble: if air humidity is below 84 per cent, which it is for most of the time, lacquer shrinks, rolls itself up and falls off.

There is a dilemma here, with no easy solution: the very attempt to preserve and restore leads to destruction. The preservation of lacquer demands high humidity; the control of moulds, the opposite. That is the prime reason for keeping all the other warriors covered up.

But all is not lost, thanks to the cooperation between the museum and Bavaria's Office for the Protection of Monuments. If a piece of clay is to be unearthed, it can be bagged in plastic, transferred to a humidified container which has built-in gloves, and operated on in isolation. The lacquer can then be fixed with chemicals which work magic by combining with the lacquer, holding it flat and allowing it to dry. One chemical, polyethylene glycol, worked pretty well, but didn't stick the lacquer on to the clay strongly enough. More experiments revealed that a substance known as HEMA (2-hydroxyethylmethacrylate), vital in the making of soft contact lenses, was almost perfect: coated with this chemical, a slab of lacquer-based colour flattens out, sticks and dries. The remaining lacquer and paint would, in brief, pretty much return to its original condition. Simplification of highly technical material inspires an odd thought: a warrior blinded by his re-emergence can have his eyes restored with the chemical equivalent of contact lenses.

More results emerge every year. Until 2006 no one knew what held the paints together, for ground-up minerals cannot be painted on without being suspended in some sort of liquid; and until that could be identified no one would understand how they were made, how to conserve them, how to restore them. Work on eleven minute flecks of paint by a team in Pisa came to a startling one-line conclusion: 'The binding medium used in the polychromes of the Terracotta Army is egg.'[3] So if someone really wants to do a good job on restoring – or perhaps I should say re-creating – a warrior as he was before the roof fell in on him, they will need whole farmyards of eggs. No doubt other details of this conclusion await examination: Chickens' eggs or ducks' eggs? Yolk or white? If both, in what proportions? Will it matter? Experiments will tell.

In years to come, the mausoleum will receive tourists on a scale dreamed of only in the upper echelons of government departments. Lintong, already transformed, will be transformed again, by places like the lavish Aegean Hot Springs Hotel, with its 26 steaming pools, in one of which live 'kissing fish' nibble at your flesh with soft lips ('we call it fish-massage', said Maggie the English-speaking manageress). And by other places, like the Flourishing International Hotel (yes, the name is in English), whose owner has a rags-to-riches story:

In the early 1990s, she was without a job, down and out. She climbed Mount Li and found a fortune-teller who told her, 'Don't worry; you will be a millionaire.'

[3] Ilaria Bonaduce and Maria Perla Colombini, 'The Binding Medium of the Terracotta Army Polychromies', in Blänsdorf, *Final Report 2006*.

321

'How can I be a millionaire?' she said. 'I do not even have enough money to buy food.'

'Have patience.'

So with patience and hope, she and her husband set up a little restaurant to cater to buses bringing tourists to see the Terracotta Army. One thing led to another, and now she has a big hotel – all, she says, thanks to the First Emperor.

The tourists will come, in their millions, because those corrugated iron sheds over the armour, the officials and the 'acrobats' will become museums in their own right. The unpaved cross-country tracks will be access roads and walkways taking in all the outlying areas, the craftsmen's homes and the tile-factory. Perhaps the walls will be restored, with paths to the side-buildings, the food-preparation room and the stables. There are no plans yet, for this is decades down the line, but one day Pit No. 1 will be as ultra-modern as the Han Yangling Museum a few kilometres away. Glass corridors and floors will bring visitors face to face with the warriors in air-conditioned comfort, complete with virtual-reality shows.

And one day, decades hence, the Army will appear complete, if not restored to its full colourful glory, and we shall know if the estimates for the numbers of warriors are correct: whether there really are 6,000 in Pit No. 1, whether the numbers 8 and 64, so significant in Daoist teachings, are reflected in the layout of the pits, whether – as hypothetical reconstructions suggest – there really are 64 soldiers behind every chariot in Pit No. 1, or 64 chariots in Pit No. 2 and 256 (which is 2^8) soldiers in the pit's southern square.

The big one, of course, is the tomb itself. The dangers and mysteries it conceals are the stuff of folklore now, but many years hence they will become the stuff of research and then, perhaps, of direct experience. Jin Kai, one of the Army's guides, echoed the general opinion: 'We believe that one day we will find the treasures inside, and they will be far more wonderful than the treasures outside.'

So they will be, if Sima Qian is anything to go by. We should discount the idea of automatic crossbows still being ready to shoot down intruders after 2,000 years, but drillings have revealed the presence of large-scale structures, even if the actual shape is a matter of dispute. The most intriguing snippet is his suggestion that the tomb contains representations of the constellations and the earth – presumably the empire – with mercury 'used to fashion [imitations of] the hundred rivers . . . and the seas, constructed in such a way that they seem to flow'. It sounds incredible, but often what is apparently folklore and legend turns out to have a basis in fact. In this case, the First Emperor's obsession with immortality suggests that Sima Qian's depiction – or something like it – should be taken seriously.

We can be sure what the First Emperor was

aiming for: to make his physical remains immortal – or at least, to last as long as possible, so that his heavenly soul would then find its way skywards, while his earthly soul took command of the government departments – the officials, the entertainers, the water-garden, and of course his waiting warriors – to continue life as he knew it while alive.

How was this to be achieved? Well, we can be sure it has something to do with mercury. In 1982 researchers undertook a series of 560 drillings into the tomb and its surroundings to test for the presence (or absence) of mercury vapour. They could have saved themselves a lot of work by trusting Sima Qian. All the soundings round the edge of the tomb showed no more than background traces of mercury vapour: less than 70 parts per billion. But actually on the tomb, 120 results (20 per cent), all crowded together around the middle, mainly on the south side, showed double the background reading, with a sharp peak of eight results at four times that level, one of which recorded over five times the background reading. In other words, an irregular patch of about 8,000 square metres is being created on the surface of the mound by something emitting a mild whiff of mercury, with something just to the east of the middle emitting a much stronger dose. Probably it all comes from the same source, since the vapour would diffuse sideways as well as vertically through the overburden of earth.

This sounds dangerous, if and when archaeologists gain entry. What might 350 parts per billion at the surface represent 50 metres below ground? No one knows. It could be 1,000 times stronger than the surface reading, or 10,000. But this is not as nasty as it sounds. Mercury vapour is usually measured in parts per *million*, not per billion. According to the standard guidelines, you could breathe 1ppm – one part per million – of mercury vapour for eight hours a day for your whole life without ill effects. Most of us ingest such minute quantities from our fillings. A few litres of mercury do not produce a lethal gas. Anyway, the chances are that, however high the vapour content inside the chamber, it would dissipate rapidly if the tomb were opened.

Assuming archaeologists proceed with care, what could they expect to find inside the underground palace? No probes or scans can tell us directly, but there is indirect evidence of what the First Emperor could have wished for and of what his aides might well have made. In an astonishing review of 'self-mummification', Joseph Needham poses a question and provides an intriguing answer. In the quest for incorruptibility, could one believe that anything ever really succeeded? Before 1972 the answer would have been no; if researchers had opened the tomb any time until then, they would have entered expecting to find a skeleton. But in that year an unprecedented discovery showed that the ancient Daoists knew how to achieve almost all that the First Emperor dreamed of.

In three tombs excavated in 1972–4 at Mawangdui, near Changsha, Hunan, were buried three members of a noble family: the Marquis of Dai, his wife and (probably) their son. The graves, dating from the early second century BC – only 30 years or so after the First Emperor's death – contained 3,000 objects, which on their own would have made the tombs a treasure trove. One tomb contained three maps drawn on silk, the oldest Chinese maps then known. The greatest surprise, however, was the tomb and body of the marquis's wife. Layers of white clay and charcoal protected an outer container of cypress planks, which held a nest of five lacquered coffins, one inside the other like a Russian doll, at the centre of which lay the marchioness, wrapped in 20 silk garments, and astonishingly well-preserved: her joints still mobile, her organs and surrounding tissues still intact, the skin still flexible. When the skin was pressed, it returned to normal; an injection of preservatives raised swellings that subsided shortly afterwards. She could have been dead a week. She was in such good condition that an autopsy was performed, revealing that she had probably died of a heart attack. She had been preserved not by embalming, or mummification, or freezing, or tanning, but by the extreme circumstances of her burial: in an air-tight and water-tight nest of coffins, at a constant temperature of about

13°C, and partly immersed in a brownish liquid which turned out to be a bath of mercuric sulphide, otherwise known as cinnabar, the ore from which the First Emperor's workers made their red paint.

So now we know, as Needham concludes, that the incorruptibility stories of the Daoists were not all myth. It is fair to assume that the emperor's aides knew of these preservation techniques. He could therefore aim to preserve his body until his two souls were ready, one to rise to the heavens, the other to roam the earth and continue the great work of empire-building in the afterlife. We know the First Emperor used mercury and its products. We know there is something in the tomb producing mercury vapour. Does this mean that it's him in there, preserved in mercury or one of its derivatives?

Well, yes and no. If the emperor is in a nest of coffins, and the mercury is in there with him, how does mercury vapour find its way out and percolate to the surface? The readings on the tomb suggest a strong source outside the coffin. Either he's not the only one pickled in mercury or there is something in Sima Qian's account after all, mercury having been used to preserve not simply the emperor, but his empire, or at least a map of it on silk, like the one found in Mawangdui.

If other royal and aristocratic tombs are anything to go by, there will be a mass of burial goods around the coffin. Assuming that the government departments with their own accoutrements are buried in subsidiary pits, whether already found or awaiting discovery, the tomb-goods are likely to be the First Emperor's personal treasures, the best examples of craftsmanship from Qin and all the conquered regions, a *wan* of things, ten thousand of them: jewel-encrusted weapons, ritual cauldrons, bronze bells, ceramic figures and vessels, gorgeous lacquered plates, odd-shaped coins, handwritten scrolls of silk and bamboo, clothes and armour and masks and tiles and model buildings, and on and on to the limits of the imagination.

Whatever is in there will not be easily won. There was, for instance, a roof, presumably of wood, which must have collapsed long ago. The chances are that the work of excavation will be long and difficult. Experience has shown what happens when hidden treasures are exposed: bones collapse, paint peels, clay grows mould, precious information vanishes, unless everything is well protected while still in an earthy bed.

No one yet has dreamed of building such protection. It could be done, discreetly, with an air-conditioned, air-locked wing over one of the underground palace's entrances. But surely such a site demands a vision to rival that of the First Emperor's. How about a domed roof over the whole site? It's possible, if China wished to build the world's biggest enclosed space, 500 metres across, which is what the tomb's diagonal is – 1.5 times the size of London's Millennium Dome.

What a triumph it would be to celebrate the centenary of the Revolution in 2049 with a tribute to the man who unified the nation 2,270 years before. And what an astonishing outcome for an emperor aiming to live for ever in the spirit world by burying himself and an Army in eternal darkness – to gain immortality of a different sort, in the light of day and the eyes of the world.

APPENDIX 1

DATES AND DYNASTIES

(Many early dates are traditional, and unreliable.)

Period	*Dates*
Ancient times	
Xia (legendary)	2207–1766 BC
Shang	1765–1122 BC
Zhou (western and eastern, including Warring States, 475–221)	c.1100–221 BC
China united (1)	
Qin	221–206 BC
(Interregnum)	206–202
Han (Western or Former Han)	202 BC–AD 6
(Interregnum)	6–25
Han (Eastern or Later Han)	25–220
Middle Ages	
Three Kingdoms	220–65
Western Jin (brief reunification)	265–316
Many kingdoms	317–580
Sui (reunification in 589)	581–618
Tang	618–907

Five Dynasties, Ten Kingdoms	907–60
Song (unified nation)	960–1127

In north:

Liao (Khitans)	907–1125
Jin (Jurchen)	1115–1234
Mongols	1234–

In west:

Xi Xia (Tanguts)	1032–1227

In south:

Southern Song	1127–1279

China united (2)

Yuan (Mongols, unification 1279)	1234–1368
Ming	1368–1644
Qing (Manchus)	1644–1911
Republic	1912–49
People's Republic of China	1949–

APPENDIX 2

QIN AND THE TERRACOTTA ARMY IN CONTEXT

Year BC

441   Qin conquers Shu.

356   Lord Shang initiates Legalist reforms in Qin and moves capital to Xianyang.

316   Qin conquers Ba.

c.300   Li Bing builds Du Jiang Yan irrigation system.

c.261   Lü Buwei befriends Prince Zichu, father of First Emperor.

259   Zheng (future First Emperor) born.

256   Qin deposes ruler of Zhou.

250   Zichu becomes king of Qin with Lü Buwei as his counsellor.

247   Zichu dies. Li Si arrives in Qin.

246   Zheng, aged 13, crowned king of Qin, with Lü Buwei as regent.

238   Lao Ai's rebellion.

237   Lü Buwei exiled. Li Si becomes Zheng's main adviser.

234   Han Fei comes to Qin. Li Si forces him to commit suicide.

230   Qin conquers Han . . .

228 ... and Zhao.

227 Jing Ke attempts assassination of King Zheng.

225 Qin conquers Wei ...

223 ... Chu ...

222 ... Yan ...

221 ... and Qi. Unification of China. King Zheng becomes emperor as Qin Shi Huang Di, the First Emperor. New administration standardizes weights, measures, currency and script. Work starts on imperial tomb on Mount Li, and possibly on Terracotta Army figures.

219 First Emperor makes first imperial tour.

215 Expedition to search for elixir of immortality. General Meng Tian retakes the Ordos.

214 Meng Tian starts building Great Wall.

213 Burning of the Books, under Li Si's advice.

212 'Burial' (alive?) of 460 scholars. Banishment of First Emperor's son and heir, Fusu, to northern frontier. Work begins on Epang Palace.

210 Death of First Emperor. Sand Hill Plot by Zhao Gao and Li Si: forced suicides of Meng Tian and Fusu; accession of Huhai, the Second Emperor. Burial of First Emperor. Work starts on completion of tomb. Terracotta Army pit finished and sealed.

209 Royal family purged. Peasant uprising led by Chen She starts.

208 Zhao Gao seizes power in Qin.

Back from the Brink

Alistair Darling

Atlantic Books

LONDON

First published in Great Britain in hardback and export
and airside trade paperback 2011 by Atlantic Books,
an imprint of Atlantic Books Ltd.

This paperback edition first published in 2012 by Atlantic Books,
an imprint of Atlantic Books Ltd.

1 2 3 4 5 6 7 8 9

A CIP catalogue record for this book is available
from the British Library.

ISBN: 9 780 85789 281 2

Typeset by Richard Marston
Printed in Great Britain by Clays Ltd, St Ives plc

Atlantic Books
Ormond House
26–27 Boswell Street
London
WC1N 3JZ

www.atlantic-books.co.uk

For Calum and Anna

Contents

List of Illustrations

1. Customers wait in line to remove their savings from a branch of the Northern Rock bank in Kingston upon Thames, September 2007. (Photo by Peter Macdiarmid/Getty Images)

2. Official Cabinet photo, 1997. (UPPA/Photoshot)

3. Official Cabinet photo, 2007. (PA/PA Archive/Press Association Images)

4. Press conference following a G20 preparatory meeting in Berlin, February 2009. (Action Press/Rex Features)

5. Alistair Darling with finance ministers and President George W. Bush in the Rose Garden of the White House, October 2008. (Official Whitehouse photograph by Eric Draper/Collection of Margaret and Alistair Darling)

6. Sir Fred Goodwin, former Chief Executive of the Royal Bank of Scotland and Sir Tom McKillop, former Chairman of the Royal Bank of Scotland leave Parliament on 10 February 2009. (Photo by Peter Macdiarmid/Getty Images)

7. Alistair Darling, with wife Margaret, holds Gladstone's budget box outside 11 Downing Street. (Reuters/Toby Melville)

8. Alistair and Margaret Darling greeting President Obama and First Lady Michelle Obama, April 2009. (Collection of Margaret and Alistair Darling)

9. David Miliband, Hillary Clinton, Gordon Brown, Barak Obama, Tim Geithner and Alistair Darling in the Downing Street Cabinet Room, April 2009. (Jeremy Selwyn/Evening Standard/Rex Features)

10. Prime Minister Tony Blair and Alistair Darling (then Secretary of State for Trade and Industry) visit a wind farm near Whitstable, July 2006. (David Bebber/AFP/Getty Images)

11. Alistair Darling in his boat, off Lewis, summer 2008. (Murdo Macleod)

12. *Queen K*, Oleg Deripaska's megayacht. (UPPA/Photoshot)

13. A worker carries a box out of the US investment bank Lehman Brothers' offices in Canary Wharf, 15 September 2008. (Davos/Finance Reuters/Andrew Winning)

14. Annual Labour Party Conference, Brighton, 28 September 2009. (Rex Features)

15. Alistair Darling on Lewis, summer 2008. (Murdo Macleod)

Acknowledgements

I am grateful to everyone who helped me write this book. It's my account and any errors are mine, for which I accept full responsibility. I would like to thank, in particular, Nick Macpherson, who was Permanent Secretary at the Treasury throughout my time as Chancellor, and through him I want to thank all the officials with whom I worked through three turbulent years. I also want to pay tribute to the high standards and professionalism of all the civil servants with whom I have worked in five Whitehall departments. Their dedication to public service is something that all of us should acknowledge.

I would also like to thank my Principal Private Secretary at the Treasury, Dan Rosenfield, and all my private office staff there for their hard work and good humour against all the odds. I have been very fortunate that in every Cabinet post I held all my private secretaries have been extremely loyal, dedicated and tolerant; for this I am very grateful.

Equally important to me has been the support of my colleagues in Parliament. Ann Coffey, MP, and before her David Hanson, MP, were my parliamentary private secretaries. Ann's friendship and tolerance proved indispensable. So too was the support of many others, including Charlie Falconer, who provided a safe house on one particularly dark evening.

I particularly want to acknowledge the friendship and support of my special adviser Catherine Macleod and her husband George. Their unceasing loyalty, kindness and hospitality will never be forgotten.

I would also like to thank and acknowledge the help of my special advisers, Geoffrey Spence, who offered helpful advice on early drafts of this manuscript, and also Sam White and Torsten Henricson Bell, who were with me until the end. Special advisers are an essential part of the ministerial team. I'd like to thank all of those who worked with me through my time in government.

I couldn't have discharged my ministerial duties without a strong team in my constituency in Edinburgh, so I would like to thank Isobel Forrester, Carol Wright and my agent Andrew Burns for their unstinting support.

I am also grateful to David Bradshaw, Steve Field, Lewis Neal, Faisal Islam and Anthony Measures for their help, advice and prompting in the writing of this book.

I would like to thank Toby Mundy, Margaret Stead and Orlando Whitfield at Atlantic Books for their encouragement and advice. Thanks also to my literary agents, Maggie McKernan and Georgina Capel, for their support.

Karl Burke, who drove me around the country for more than ten years and remained unfailingly cheerful, is owed another debt of gratitude. I would also like to acknowledge the support of my police protection team, who of course can't be named but who were always there and always supportive.

The camaraderie and kindness shown to us by staff in Downing Street in difficult times will not be forgotten. For providing us with respite at Dorneywood, thank you to Charlotte, Graham and Gemma.

I owe an immense debt of gratitude to all of our friends and family who gave us so much support when we needed it most. They know who they are. Thank you.

Finally, I want to acknowledge the one who has continued to provide me with everything I could ever ask for – Margaret, my wife. She helped keep the show on the road and I was hugely fortunate that she chose to come and live with me in Downing Street for those three years. Without her I wouldn't have lasted the course. I want also to thank my children, Calum and Anna, who, for so much of their growing up, I was an absent presence. This book is for them.

Edinburgh, July 2011

Preface

Walking up Downing Street on a wintry evening in December 2011 it seemed as if little had changed. Yet everything had changed. In the eighteen months since we left, the political and economic climate had seen seismic shifts. I was returning for a farewell reception for the retiring Cabinet Secretary. The scene and many of the faces were familiar. But the overwhelming feeling was of how the mood had altered over the intervening months. The downturn had indeed proved to be more profound and long-lasting than many people had believed back in 2008. It is still being played out and its consequences will be felt for generations.

Evelyn Waugh, in his novel *Unconditional Surrender*, describing war-torn Europe, wrote of a 'malevolent suspension of normality'. Rather like the Second World War, this economic crisis has changed the landscape for ever. If there is to be a new normality, it will be very different from the one we have known for the past three decades.

The coalition government that took office in 2010 was adamant that it had the answers: cut public spending; increase taxes. The private sector would step in to take the place of the public sector. The structural deficit (the amount of borrowing beyond the usual business cycle) would be gone by 2015. All fine – except that it has not worked.

A couple of weeks before my return visit to Downing Street, the government had had to downgrade its growth forecasts for the fourth time since its first budget in the summer of 2010. Worse, the Chancellor was borrowing over £150 billion more than he had predicted. The structural deficit, and with it the austerity measures, will continue into the next parliament.

With the publication of more recent official estimates, we now know that the British economy started to grow at the end of 2009 and continued to do so over the next twelve months. This was, to a large extent, due to the measures we took to stabilize the banking system and to restore confidence, as well as the stimulus the Labour government put into the economy in 2008. This was coupled with the efforts of other countries, from communist China to the United States and across Europe. To varying degrees, they all did the same thing. Governments can make a difference if they have the will to do so.

Unfortunately, much of this was undone during 2010 as a more traditional right-wing orthodoxy took hold. We saw a ramping up of the rhetoric of austerity. Expectations were lowered and fears raised. Confidence collapsed and as a result growth slowed. Added to which, there was a complete paralysis of governance in the eurozone and confidence there spiralled downwards. In the UK, in 2011 there was hardly any growth at all.

In a world where jobs are being lost and unemployment is rising steeply, particularly among the young, and where prospects for growth are being reduced by the week and there is a real fear of countries being unable to pay their debts, it is not surprising that people are rapidly losing confidence that they will see an end to all this. It is hardly surprising that businesses are not rushing to invest or to take on more staff, and that those who can save are doing just that. They are afraid to spend.

Understandably, people fear what the future holds. They are worried about their jobs and that no one seems to be getting a grip. They are confronted with austerity, yet they see their leaders offering little but a weary resignation to years of stagnation. It is hardly surprising that protests, despite their inchoate and disparate demands, attract so much attention. There is not much else on offer.

I couldn't help reflecting that night in Downing Street that this need not have been the case. The solutions may be difficult, but they are not impossible to achieve. We started the job but we never got to finish it, for the reasons outlined in this book.

Globalization, we know, can bring immense benefits. But at times like this the downside is all too evident. Governments struggle to impose order in this new world, where there is no overarching global governance. How frustrating it was, then, in 2011 to see that where there is some semblance of structure – in Europe, for example – it was not being used to the full. The leaders of the world's twenty largest economies, the G20, who met in Cannes in the autumn of that year cut a sorry spectacle. They were reduced to apparent hand-wringing impotence.

The G20 is far from perfect, but it can work. Starting in November 2008 in Washington, and then in April 2009 in London, world leaders agreed on a common policy to stop recession sliding into depression. It gave markets confidence and showed that governments need not be powerless in the face of global events. It worked because ministers were scared stiff of what failure would mean. Sadly, despite all that was achieved, by the summer of 2010 it was thought that the risk of recession had receded, and the mood changed. Advocates of deep austerity came into the ascendant and the chance to address the bigger questions of imbalances between China and the US, as well as within the eurozone, was lost. The G20 was no longer operating effectively because of lack of leadership.

There has also been a re-emergence of the ideological debate, last fought out in similar circumstances in the 1930s, about how to deal with an economic crisis. There are those – many of whom are now in government – who are ideologically opposed to a Keynesian approach to repairing the economy. They believe that it is sufficient to purge the debts and then recovery will automatically follow. No one doubts that borrowing has to be controlled and debt reduced. However, as I set out in this book, it is necessary, when private-sector spending dries up, to maintain public-sector support for the economy until recovery is under way. Borrowing can then be reduced, but it is important to do it in a way that does not wreck the recovery and, crucially, that maintains confidence. That is what is going wrong today: the new government is having to borrow more because the economy is not growing. Fewer people in work means less taxes paid: higher unemployment comes with a huge social and economic cost.

The philosophical battle of ideas continues, just as it has done ever since the Great Depression of the 1930s. The argument rages between followers of the great British economist John Maynard Keynes and those of Friedrich Hayek, the leader of the so-called Austrian economic school. Keynes believed that in order to stave off prolonged recession governments have to stimulate their economies. In fact, he said there is no possibility of balancing the budget except by increasing national income. In other words, it is vital to generate growth so as to bring in the income the government needs in order to cut its borrowing. Hayek, in contrast, deplored such intervention. He believed that government action makes things worse. Only markets, he said, can resolve economic disruptions.

In 2008 it seemed that the Keynesian approach would prevail. But no: in Europe there followed a reaction, both political and economic, that owed much more to Hayek than to Keynes. Predictions are always dangerous, but my guess – and certainly my hope – is that governments will eventually come to see that they cannot simply stand back and hope for the best.

Keynes did not for one moment suggest that borrowing does not need to be dealt with. But he made the obvious point that borrowing will never come down without the means to generate income. Growth will only return with the return of confidence. While no country can do this on its own, governments have a responsibility to do what they can to generate that growth, so this is precisely the time to replenish this country's infrastructure, its roads and railways and energy supply, as well as to maintain its commitment to science, education and training for example.

In the US, where President Obama has maintained policies to support the economy, in the face of stout Republican opposition, there is evidence of recovery, albeit weak. A US recovery would give a huge boost to confidence in the rest of the world. In Europe, though, at the beginning of 2012 the position could not be more dismal. So what has gone wrong?

Let me start with Greece. In this book I explain what happened when European finance ministers first tried to resolve that country's problems, culminating in a meeting in May 2010. It was the last meeting of finance ministers I attended, in the days between the general election and the formation of the new coalition government. After several hours we agreed a package of support and the immediate crisis was averted. But nearly two years later, it has not been resolved. The rescue fund promised in 2010 never really materialized. A further attempt to establish a larger fund in 2011 failed to convince anyone. It had little ready cash and was heavily dependent on what is known in the jargon as 'leveraging': in other words, a bit of public money backed by private investment. The Greek government fell at the end of 2011. By the end of that year there were growing doubts that a plan that would leave Greece with a debt that was 120 per cent of its national income could ever work.

The problems around Greece and some of the other countries that have got into trouble, such as Italy and Portugal, illustrate a wider difficulty with the single currency. The euro will work only if there is much closer economic and political cooperation on tax and spending, if not full union. In the context of the debate about to take place as to whether Scotland should remain a part of the UK, this is a serious consideration. One country can, of course, use another country's currency, but the central bank will take no account of the second country's needs when issuing the currency or fixing interest rates. The alternative is to have a common currency as in the euro area, but that means that there must be common rules and restrictions on taxation, spending and borrowing. It is hardly independence.

As I say in this book, I was sceptical about joining the euro when it was debated in the UK a decade ago. What happened in 2011 has made me even more sceptical. At the end of that year, rather than accepting that a single currency meant that the richer countries had to help the poorer areas to make the changes needed, the eurozone members agreed to sign a treaty which, I believe, not only fails to deal with the problems the poorer countries face but is likely to make the situation much worse. The crisis in the eurozone is largely the result of imbalances between strong countries, such as Germany, which have thrived in the euro and have robust exports and surpluses, and much weaker countries. The eurozone members have decided that, in the current climate, austerity, or fiscal discipline, will eventually generate growth. They require countries to run budgets that are balanced or in surplus.

The draft treaty will not solve the problem, indeed it will make it worse. It doesn't deal with the imbalances and the lack of competitiveness of the peripheral economies. Rather it imposes a straightjacket which will suppress demand.

Worse, countries have to submit their budgets to the unelected European Commission in Brussels, which can impose sanctions on those that break the rules. This means that countries facing recession could be compelled to keep cutting spending or raising taxes in a desperate attempt to balance the books. This harks back to what happened in Europe in the early 1930s. It is not surprising, then, that just a few weeks after the treaty was proposed efforts were already being made to water down its provisions. It looks like another failed attempt to resolve the eurozone problem.

In January 2012 an American credit-rating agency downgraded the status of France and Austria and other countries. They made the point that austerity alone will not work. Where was the plan for growth?

The failure to reach agreement highlights not just philosophical differences but also the practical problems of trying to run an organization which has twenty-seven members, seventeen of them with a common currency. The longer this continues without being resolved, the greater the risk that the euro will fail. That would have profound implications, not only for Europe but for the rest of the world. Until there is a credible plan in Europe, it is difficult to see how confidence can be restored. The longer the uncertainty continues, the longer it will be before any sense of normality returns.

Unless governments can show that there is some hope of a better life beyond the crisis, people will have every reason to lose faith. My generation grew up believing that we would be better off than our parents. We hoped, too, that our children would see a better life for themselves. This crisis has badly shaken that belief. Aspiration and hope are a critical part of any country's development. Yet those two ideals have become the victims of a lack of leadership and the absence of a credible approach to get the global economy back into growth. If we lose those ideals, we lose the motivation needed to get on and succeed. For those of us in the West, that motivation will be essential as the world's economic power accelerates its move to the East and South. Even with a credible plan for recovery, millions in the West on low and middle incomes will find that the squeeze on their living standards will become more painful.

So, what of the banks? Has normality been suspended there? Up to a point. Some bankers continue to expect to be paid extraordinary sums even when it is clear that they have not done anything at all extraordinary. Others have come to realize that the days when there was money to be made by taking on ever more risk are now over. There is also a realization that important institutions such as banks, which, if they fail, can bring down countries, need to be regulated far more closely. Good progress has been made on the supervision of globally significant banks. But there has been less progress in cleaning up banks in continental Europe, which remain very exposed to countries such as Greece. No wonder many European banks seemed reluctant to lend to each other. Had the European Central Bank not intervened at the end of 2011 there would have been every chance we would have had a repeat of the freeze in inter-bank lending that we saw in the US and UK in 2008. We cleaned up our banks then, but too many in Europe did not.

The Financial Services Authority's report into the collapse of Royal Bank of Scotland, produced at the end of 2011, bears close reading. RBS overreached itself, taking risks it did not understand. That reckless-ness was not confined to RBS or the UK. Other banks got into trouble and collapsed or were severely damaged. The costs to taxpayers and to countries as a whole have been immense. RBS, like many other banks, had far too little capital to fall back on when things began to go badly wrong. Its board failed to ask key questions when it took over the Dutch bank ABN AMRO, which proved catastrophic. The FSA said that it failed to supervise RBS properly. Sir Fred Goodwin, the former chief execu-tive, once told me that the FSA did not understand his business. It was not alone in that.

The real problem the FSA report exposes is that here, as in the US and many other countries, the political climate encouraged what was called 'light-touch regulation' to flourish. All political parties went along with it. Some of the most ardent deregulators are now in government. Scotland's first minister, Alex Salmond, personally endorsed the takeover of ABN AMRO by RBS.

Here in the UK, the independent report on banking recommended that banks' investment and retail activities should be separated. The proposals, including those to increase the amount of capital banks must hold, are welcome. But it would be a mistake to believe that only the investment side of a bank is risky. HBOS – the former Bank of Scotland – and the Irish banks proved that it was possible to lose billions on old-fashioned bad lending decisions. As we discovered at a time of crisis, even a small bank, such as Northern Rock, might have to be saved by government in order to avoid panic contaminating the entire system.

Supervision must be tighter, more capital has to be held, and that will mean less, and possibly more expensive, credit. But it will also mean safer lending. We cannot afford to do otherwise. Banking is inherently risky and increasingly global. It will present a serious problem to supervise it effectively because it operates across borders. But it has to be done. It was the banks that took us to the brink.

This book covers the time I spent as Chancellor, which proved to be some of the most difficult days I could ever have imagined. When I started, I thought I was writing what would be a historical account of the crisis. But the story is still being played out and the finale is some way off. I have altered very little of the original text, save to make some corrections and to update a few figures that have changed since summer 2011. Any remaining errors are entirely mine.

January 2012

Prologue

I don't believe in panicking before it's absolutely necessary but I came close to considering it on the morning of 7 October 2008. I left Downing Street in the dark at a quarter to five on a cold, wet morning, for a routine meeting of finance ministers in Luxembourg. It was going to be a bad day, I knew that. The night before, I had met with Britain's top bankers in the Treasury. They had brought with them into the room an air of desperation. An account of that meeting, only partly true, had been leaked to the BBC and the *Financial Times*. It was reported that Britain's largest banks desperately needed money to stay afloat. Some of them needed capital which they could no longer raise from their shareholders. Crucially, it was reported, that the banks were desperate. The bankers' briefing had the whiff of panic. The result was that bank shares plummeted.

We took off from RAF Northolt on a small chartered jet. A sunrise never felt so bleak. I knew the London markets were about to open and that they would react badly to the leaked news, however wrong it was. Iceland and its banking system were close to collapse and one of its banks would probably fail that day. In Ireland the day before they had, without warning, underwritten all the savings in their banks, causing disarray for everyone else in Europe. Three weeks earlier, in the United States, the collapse of Lehman Brothers, one of the country's oldest banks, had pushed the rest of Wall Street to the edge. We were looking over the precipice. It would not take much to tip the world's banking system and its economies over the edge. The fate of Royal Bank of Scotland – or RBS, as it preferred to be known – one of the world's largest banks, was critical.

By the time I landed in Luxembourg, RBS was worth 40 per cent less than before take-off. Dealings in its shares had been suspended twice on the London Stock Exchange. My private secretary Dan Rosenfield and my special adviser Geoffrey Spence called me out of the meeting with fellow finance ministers to say that Sir Tom McKillop, the RBS chairman, needed to speak to me urgently. We cleared a room so that I could take the call. When I put down the phone, Geoffrey asked, what did he say?

'He told me that his bank is going to go bust this afternoon. And he asked me what we were going to do.'

For more than a year a firestorm had been gathering over the financial system in the United States and Europe. We had been singed by the warning flames a year previously, but that was a minor conflagration compared to this.

I gave my first interview as Chancellor of the Exchequer to a newspaper editor about a week after I was appointed in June 2007. His opening remark was to note that I usually was sent to departments that were in trouble in the hope that I could keep them out of the news. 'This must be the first department you've turned up in that's actually not a mess,' he said.

I replied that the same thought had struck me. 'This is the complete opposite. It's in good nick, both the department and also the economy, which is strong and stable after ten years' growth.' What complacency! I tempted fate by adding: 'Of course, there will be challenges to come.' This, at least, proved to be an accurate forecast. Looking back on that interview, neither I nor the editor mentioned banks, or anything approaching the subject. Yet just over two months later, savers would be queuing up outside Northern Rock, desperate to withdraw their money – the first obvious signs in the UK of a global crisis that would bring the world banking system, and our economies, to the brink of collapse.

We were not alone in our complacency. The collapse of banks across the globe was not on people's minds. There were those – some academics, a few economists – who worried about some of the stresses and strains building up within the financial system, much as people worry about earthquakes or tsunamis, but it is fair to say that no one foresaw the crisis that lay just ahead.

Since then many people have claimed to have predicted what was to happen. Most of them failed to mention it at the time. This book covers what happened from the summer of 2007, when I became Chancellor of the Exchequer, through to what proved to be the end of the Labour government which had first been elected ten years before. It was a period of almost one thousand days, none of them easy. There have been, and will be, many accounts written about these momentous events. This is mine.

The story is in the main about the banking crisis: how close we came to the collapse of one of the world's largest banks, a collapse that would have brought down the global banking system within hours. This is not simply a story about banks and bankers, however. The banking crisis precipitated an economic crisis, the worst for more than a hundred years, and one that, even three years later, is far from resolved. These events also took place at a crucial point in history, at a time when the world is still coming to terms with the rapid globalization of our economies. We are witnessing a power shift – certainly economic, and increasingly political – that will not be reversed and which we in the developed economies have yet fully to appreciate, or even fully understand.

Politics above all is about people and relationships. I cannot tell this story without dealing with the often fraught and increasingly difficult relationship with the prime minister, Gordon Brown. The three years I served as Chancellor were also, sadly, a period of decline in the political fortunes of the Labour Party, which I believe could have been avoided had we played our hand differently. As the cliché has it, in every crisis there is an opportunity: in this case, to show that we could deal with the financial meltdown, come through it, and chart a way forward. I believe that we did deal with the crisis and guided the economy through the storm, but we failed to navigate a political course for the future that would convince the public.

For me, this period also marks something of a transformation in my public profile. As that newspaper editor observed, my political reputation had been built on my ability to 'troubleshoot'. The epithet 'a safe pair of hands' will no doubt feature in my obituary. My ability to get trouble out of the headlines and put things back on the right track served me well in my various ministerial roles. Along with Gordon Brown and Jack Straw, I sat in the Cabinet for thirteen years. We were to be the only survivors of the long march of the Labour Party from its resurrection as New Labour, through its triumph at the polls in 1997, to its defeat in May 2010.

After that victory in 1997, I was appointed as the Chancellor's number two, Chief Secretary to the Treasury. Those were heady days. Labour had won a spectacular victory at the general election. The country wanted change and it seemed we could do no wrong. The day after the election I flew with my wife Margaret and my children, Calum and Anna, from our home in Edinburgh to London. They were there, in the crowd outside the gates, to watch me take part in the British ritual of walking up Downing Street in front of the world's press to enter the door of No. 10, to be asked formally to serve by the new Prime Minister, Tony Blair.

On the flight down, the pilot, seeing that I and my colleague, George Robertson, about to be made Defence Secretary, were on board, told our fellow passengers we were on our way to Downing Street. There was a resounding cheer – something rarely heard again. We made the most of it.

I knew I was going to be Chief Secretary because Gordon had asked me a couple of days before the election if I would serve in the job. It was no great surprise, then, when Tony repeated the offer in the Cabinet Room. I felt a bit overawed walking into that room for the first time. I was about to take a chair when Tony said: 'There's no need to sit. You know where you're going.' Just to make sure I did, I said: 'The Treasury, I presume.'

From No. 10, ministers go in their shiny new cars to their departments. As I left the Cabinet Room, I was handed a folder by the Cabinet Secretary. It was empty. He told me that ministers cannot be seen to leave Downing Street empty-handed. I accepted the prop.

I was keen to get to work. Gordon had been at his desk since his appointment as Chancellor the evening before. Ten minutes later I walked into the Treasury. I had never seen inside the building. In those days it was a gloomy place, a cross between a cathedral and a Victorian asylum, with endlessly looping long corridors. The civil servants worked enclosed in cell-like rooms with their own internal corridors. It struck me that while the building was grim, its civil servants were bright, young and enthusiastic. Until a few days before, they had served a Conservative government. For eighteen years the Treasury had been a creature of the Tories. Now, here they were, advising us on how to implement our plan to make the Bank of England independent. Of course, they will tell you why any decision is difficult, or whether there might be a better way; but once it was clear we were determined on our course of action, they worked flat out over the weekend to make it happen on Monday morning.

I remember, a week or two after arriving, one of my Cabinet colleagues, David Blunkett, who is blind, came to see me in a vain attempt to get more money for his department. As I walked him out, halfway along one of those corridors, he stopped and said: 'Tell me, is this a gloomy place?'

I told him it was, in every sense – and not just because he was getting no more money. I spent fifteen months working in that dreary building, in an office next to the room from which Winston Churchill walked out on to the balcony to lead the cheers at the end of the Second World War. Gloomy it might be, but there was a palpable sense of history, as there is in so much of Whitehall. You are conscious of passing through the pages of history, sometimes influencing it, sometimes not. I enjoyed my time as Chief Secretary. From the vantage point of the Treasury, you get to know about every government department.

By the time I returned as Chancellor a decade later, on 27 June 2007, the Treasury had been reincarnated and completely refurnished. It had moved from the front of the building to facing on to Whitehall to the rear. Now it was above the old Cabinet war rooms, overlooking St James's Park, airy and open-plan. The endless loop of corridors remained but the fusty atmosphere was gone. Strangely, there was none of the excitement or anticipation I had felt when I was appointed to previous Cabinet jobs. This was one of the most important roles in government. It was a job I had long wanted, and I knew I could do it. I should have felt elated, but I didn't. There was a sense of foreboding. I was worried about my relationship with the new Prime Minister, Gordon Brown.

My arrival at the Treasury was delayed by a small demonstration outside the building by a group of half-dressed women – protesting about what, we never learned. My colleagues arrived at their departments to stand on the steps and set out a bold vision for the future. I couldn't do that. Perhaps, in retrospect, that's just as well. I eventually got there, to be greeted by Nick Macpherson, the engaging, and somewhat idiosyncratic, Permanent Secretary. As we walked through the doors, Nick said that most of the people working in the building were young and most had never worked for any Chancellor but Gordon. What's more, he observed in his droll style, there were only about three who had ever experienced a recession. That was soon put right.

My arrival as Chancellor heralded something of a culture change in the Treasury, especially for the senior officials. During his ten-year tenure, Gordon had tended to deal with them through his special advisers, principally Ed Balls and Ed Miliband. He worked on the strategy; his advisers made sure the detail fitted that strategy. Unlike other departments I'd worked in, where officials were used to working with the Secretary of State directly, many senior Treasury officials had never actually sat down with the Chancellor himself.

It took me some time to convince them that, although I was intent on, and perfectly capable of, making up my own mind, I did value their advice. There was another consequence, too, of this *modus operandi* – for my relations with Gordon, now that he was Prime Minister. He was persuaded that the Treasury – the majority of whom had in fact taken pride in working for him – had now turned against him. Also, as I began increasingly to take a different view from him, he would accuse me of having been taken prisoner by his erstwhile civil servants. At first it was exasperating, but in time it became a source of anger. Worse still, it eventually led to dysfunction at the top of the government.

On that first day as Chancellor, as I sat down in Gordon's old room, which must have been the most uncomfortable in the Treasury with its battered chairs and floral prints on the walls, there was no hint of what was to come. The landscape seemed extraordinarily tranquil. Britain had seen more than ten years of continuous economic growth, something that had not been experienced for more than two centuries. While other countries had experienced recessions, particularly after the Asian crisis of the late 1990s and the collapse of the dot.com bubble, we had not. Our debt levels had fallen from being the second highest of the world's seven largest economies to the second lowest, behind Canada.

Reading through the briefing papers prepared for the new Chancellor, I remarked to Nick Macpherson, almost in passing, that we seemed very dependent on taxes coming in from the financial services industry. About 25 per cent of our corporate taxes came from that sector. I wish I could claim knowledge of what was to come, but that wasn't the case. And the much-criticized bankers' bonuses and sometimes inflated salaries made a big contribution to income tax receipts.

Living standards were rising for most people, but not for all. People on middle to low incomes, especially those with no children or whose children had left home, were beginning to feel the squeeze well before the crash of 2007. The 'squeezed middle' is neither a new or peculiarly British political problem. It has been a growing feature of most developed countries for more than two decades. But generally, most people felt better off. In addition to the annual holiday, there would be a second break, weekends away. Low-cost airlines thrived as more and more people acquired the means to take breaks abroad. A lot of this was fuelled by increased borrowing and the running up of credit-card bills. People did this on the back of the security that comes when you see the value of your home increase each year and you do not fear losing your job.

On the broader front, China, finding itself with huge savings to invest, was happy to place them in the West, particularly the United States, fuelling even more borrowing and spending. In the eurozone, abnormally low interest rates – appropriate, perhaps, for Germany, but not for countries such as Ireland, where the interest rate brakes should have been applied – caused property prices to soar in what was to prove an unsustainable boom. Icelandic banks, eager to get into the global banking scene, came to London and expanded in a way that would not have been possible had they confined their activities to the streets of Reykjavik. Foreign banks happily lent into Britain, against property in particular.

It is true that rising private debt and the huge imbalance between some Asian economies and the developed world were subjects of concern in some quarters, but it was muted. There were also very few worries expressed about the stability of the world's banking systems, which not only lent a great deal of this money but increasingly found more and more imaginative ways of investing it – without, it would appear, pausing to ask the essential question: what happens if this all goes wrong?

Britain was no exception, and none of us, particularly those responsible for making policy, can remain blameless. London has always been a major financial centre, but from the 1980s onwards, encouraged first by the Conservatives and then by our own government, it seemingly went from strength to strength. It employed ever more people and paid considerable – on occasion, fantastic – rewards for ever greater risk-taking. This success, and the rewards for the country, blinded us to the defects. Naturally, there were two things corporate entities within the financial sector did not like: paying taxes; and what was seen as the heavy hand of government interference, in the shape of regulation. Indeed, for ten years the cry from the City and from politicians of every party was for less rather than more regulation. If ever the claim that we were all in this together were true, it was here. Why, even Vince Cable, in his 2006 address to a luncheon of the Association of Foreign Banks, in which he praised the City's achievements, warned of the dangers of 'the current clamour for regulation of financial products'. On City regulation, like everyone else he favoured a 'light touch'. The problem was that this concept of 'light-touch' regulation came to influence the whole climate in which these institutions operated. If there was money to be made, they did not hold back. There was a general assumption that the global economic boom would continue, that the good times would continue to roll.

Nick Macpherson, in his informal, laconic way, did voice concerns that we were very dependent on tax receipts from the financial sector continuing to flow forever. Nick, unstuffy – about as unlike someone out of C. P. Snow's *Corridors of Power* as could be imagined – is intellectually self-confident. He always had an opinion which I valued but he was intensely relaxed when I didn't follow his advice, as came to happen. Treasury officials expressed no concern about the banking system in the course of the early briefings I was given as a new minister. I don't blame the Treasury for this view. It was widely shared. Subsequently I discovered that, deep within the Treasury and in the Financial Services Authority (the FSA), the UK's financial regulator, questions had arisen about what might happen were a bank to fail. There had been an exercise carried out in 2006 in which they had asked themselves the question *what if?* A lack of adequate legislation was identified at the beginning of 2007, partly as a result of this experiment. But, at that time, putting legislation in place that would allow government to seize control of a failing bank would have been impossible to justify and might well have caused panic in the markets.

This *laissez-faire* approach to regulation was not unique to the UK. There was not a regulatory system, central bank or, indeed, government that saw what lay ahead and how exposed the global economy had become to systemic failure. So the industry was feted for its success, the razzle of new and shiny buildings seen as evidence of riches achieved. The dazzle was blinding and few questions were asked.

That the know-how to deal with a firestorm was not there in the Treasury was both a tribute to the relative economic tranquillity of the previous decade and a sign of a collective failure to ask *what if*? The Treasury did rise to the occasion when the Northern Rock crisis hit. And when, in the autumn of 2008, we were faced with the imminent collapse of the banking system, the experience gained in dealing with Northern Rock meant we were able to act decisively because we knew what would happen if we didn't.

Although it did not seem like it at the time, Northern Rock, it turned out, was to be a well-disguised blessing, the canary down the mineshaft. Without that experience we would have struggled to deal with the far bigger crisis to come. By the time the big crash did threaten, we had learned that we had to act both quickly and boldly.

In the summer of 2007, my first as Chancellor, there was no reason to suppose that our government was about to enter its last three years. The Conservative opposition had yet to find its feet. Gordon had enjoyed a bounce in the polls when he took over. I don't believe that it is axiomatic that if a government enters an economic downturn, or is faced by a catastrophic banking crisis, then it will fall. After all, governments show their real mettle at times of crisis. Throughout those three years there were occasions when our support grew, when our ability to deal with the crisis – by nationalizing Northern Rock, for example – won us approval.

Ultimately, I believe that we failed to win the 2010 election because the public did not think we had dealt with the resultant economic crisis as well as we should have done. The reason is that we were too often divided among ourselves as to what our response should be. In the end, the debate within government, such as it was, came down to a single question: cuts versus no cuts. The tragedy was that the breakdown of our relationships and the lack of collective discussion in private led to a very public falling-out. The result was that we opened the door for the return of a Tory government. But even then, they failed to get a majority when they should have romped home.

It is simplistic to say that Gordon Brown's leadership cost Labour the election. The truth is that we had lost our way some time before he moved into No. 10. We were elected in 1997 with a landslide, and much of the credit for that victory goes to Tony Blair. Here was a leader who captured the mood of the times, a mood of change, optimism and hope. Very few politicians impact on the public in a big way. He did. He was able to get into people's sitting rooms when they saw him on television and they felt at ease with him. It was to change, of course, especially over Iraq. I often wonder how our government would have fared if Tony had not become so absorbed in foreign conflicts, Iraq especially. He became distracted from domestic affairs at just the time when we still had a mandate to carry through the reforms needed to improve public services. By the time he returned to address domestic issues, following a historic third election victory in 2005, it was too late. Everyone in government knew that he was going, and the political centre of gravity swung towards Gordon. In the two years between the election and Tony standing down in June 2007, the business of government was paralysed as the clamour grew for him to go sooner rather than later. Yet when Gordon took over, despite years of anticipation, he was unable to convince the public that he could reinvigorate the government and create something new and fresh.

There is a paradox for me at the heart of this story. Were it not for the banking crisis and its economic and political fallout, I would, most likely, have ended my career as a footnote in political history. The irony is that the pinnacle of my time in government coincided with the end of our time in power. That was the hand I was dealt and I learned, often the hard way, to be bold in playing it. In 2007 we agonized over spending £6 billion to sort out the political crisis caused by the abolition of the 10p tax band. A year later I was signing off a £50 billion rescue package for the UK banks.

I hope that in this book I give a fair account of what happened during those three turbulent years. I had to change from a supporting character to being one of the main actors on the political stage, something I was never really comfortable with. We had to make some enormous decisions. Had we got them wrong, which could easily have happened, the results would have been catastrophic.

The biggest decision of them all would have to be made on a wet Tuesday morning, on 7 October 2008, when I took a call from Sir Tom McKillop, chairman of RBS, whose headquarters is in the city in which I live. He told me his bank would collapse within hours. What was I going to do about it?

1   The Wreck of Northern Rock

The prelude to that chilling call from Sir Tom McKillop had been played out thirteen months before when we were caught out with a run on a small British bank, Northern Rock. That day, 14 September 2007, is seared in my memory. I had been Chancellor of the Exchequer for seventy-nine days. The echoing venue, then, was a grand Moorish hall in the Palacio da Bolso in Porto where European finance ministers and central bank governors had gathered for a meeting of the European Union's economic and financial affairs council, Ecofin. The palatial surroundings made rather less of an impression on me than the scene displayed on a giant TV screen in the hall. What it showed was long, snaking queues of people waiting to make the first run on a British bank in more than a century.

As we gazed at this horrifying spectacle playing out in the Friday sunshine half a continent away, my companion leant over: 'They're behaving perfectly rationally, you know.' It was not what I wanted to hear, even if it was Mervyn King, the Governor of the Bank of England, who was telling me. I watched an elderly lady emerge from a branch of Northern Rock with her savings. She was, she said, off to deposit them down the road at the Halifax. Not such a good idea, I thought.

A banking calamity that had begun with losses on risky loans to US home buyers now threatened catastrophe in Britain. The talks that day in Portugal were intended to find ways to improve crisis management and to guarantee financial stability within the European Union. A management consultant was trying to explain to the assembled ministers and governors how to work more efficiently – useful advice perhaps, but the irony was not lost on me. I left them to it and set off back to London.

What I had witnessed on television that day was potentially disastrous for Northern Rock, for other banks, and for the economy. As the pictures flashed around the world, the damage to our reputation would be immense. Politically, it was potentially fatal. People may have been panicking in a very British way – there was no shouting or hammering on windows – but they wanted their money out. No matter how much the bank staff tried to reassure them that there was no problem, that they could get every last penny, they wanted their savings and they wanted them now. It was going to take a Herculean effort to turn things around.

Safe as the Bank of England? We were all brought up to believe it. Yet, far from reassuring people, the announcement that the Bank was effectively standing behind every last penny simply caused a stampede to the doors of Northern Rock. I had flown out to Porto that morning, despite the fact that the run had started. I knew full well that if I did not turn up for the meeting it would simply reinforce the sense of crisis. But now I had to get home. We had chartered a small jet to allow us to make a fast escape. Jammed together in the back seats, Mervyn King and I had time to get to know each other better. There was ample time, too, for me to reflect on how we had got to where we were.

I had known Mervyn King for some years. We met first when I was a Treasury minister in the early days of the Labour government. He was one of the first people I spoke to after becoming Chancellor. Softly spoken, bookish and an academic economist, I liked his quietly considered, slightly impish style. He could also be incredibly stubborn. There are times when this is an ideal quality for a Governor of the Bank of England, but equally it could be exasperating. He and I were to work closely together over the coming three years. We had our disagreements, but, at the height of the crisis a year later, when it was clear that drastic action was needed to recapitalize the banks, he did what was needed.

In the back of the plane, the Governor and I talked about the unfolding crisis, interspersed with his explanation of how he had come to be an avid Aston Villa supporter when he was growing up in the West Midlands. As we descended through the clouds, the thought came to me: I was damned if our reputation was going to be destroyed over the failure of a small, reckless bank. We had to stop this run and regain control of events, no matter what it took.

When I arrived at the Treasury as Chancellor in June 2007, I was reminded of a perfectly calm sea on a summer morning – not a cloud in the sky, hardly a ripple on the water. On days like that, on my small boat in the Outer Hebrides, you look out for subtle changes in wind and wave: they are the harbingers. They were there in the Treasury too, not too far below the surface. Beneath the calm there was concern about what was happening in the US housing market, although it was thought to be containable. It had barely touched the public or political consciousness. Cheap mortgages had been sold to people on low incomes for properties that would be difficult, if not impossible, to sell when the economic waters turned choppy. Worse, these loans had been parcelled up by banks and sold on to other banks and financial institutions, in an attempt to spread the risks of people defaulting on loans they could not afford. They were certified by the credit-rating agencies as being top-quality, but they came to be known, notoriously, as 'sub-prime' loans.

Normally, if you make a loan to someone it makes sense to insure yourself against the risk of the borrower defaulting. But what happened in many cases was that one part of a bank sold off the loans and, unwittingly, another part of the same bank bought them back. In other words, the risk was simply wheeled down the corridor. Yet despite these indicators of turbulence, it was still thought on both sides of the

Atlantic that this was little more than a temporary squeeze and, even at the beginning of August 2007, the Treasury believed there were no serious implications for UK banks. The view was that this was an American problem which could be contained. Many of the loans, however, had been insured by big companies like AIG – best known in the UK at the time as sponsors of Manchester United Football Club – and that British banks, RBS among them, were very exposed to these insurers. If the insurance companies collapsed, British banks would be badly hit.

There was an additional problem. The Treasury and the regulators tended to focus on the financial health of each individual bank, rather than on how much the banks depended on each other and the extent to which, if something were to go wrong with one of them, it would infect the others. The British authorities were not alone in that. To my mind, this was one of the biggest failures in the global financial system. Most banks borrow very large sums from each other over a short time period in order to fund risks that are very long-term. If they can't roll over this funding, which they often need to do every ten or twenty days, then they are in real trouble. If banks cannot lend to each other, they cannot lend to other people. The banking system grinds to a halt. When, later in 2007, the banks finally woke up to the full horror of what was happening, they did stop lending to each other. Money seized up – giving rise to the so-called 'credit crunch' – and that precipitated the banking crisis.

But at the beginning of August 2007, two months into the new job, as I left the Treasury for a week's holiday, there were few signs of the storm that was about to break. Our family flew out to Majorca, where, aside from the daily call to the private office, we relaxed with friends for a few days. On the morning of 8 August I walked down to the local supermarket to buy the morning rolls. Passing the newspaper kiosk I picked up a copy of the *Financial Times* – as you do when you are Chancellor. Sitting by the pool side, I noticed an item reporting that the French bank BNP Paribas had frozen withdrawals from two of its funds. It could no longer value their assets. The paper also reported problems with WestLB, Germany's third-largest state lender. Lending between banks had begun to freeze, as banks began to fear that what they thought were good quality investments were rapidly losing their value. In response, the European Central Bank had pumped 95 million euros into the European banking system. In the US, it was reported, the Federal Reserve was putting $12 billion into the system.

I had read enough to know this looked bad. London was the world's major banking centre. It was inconceivable that banks there were not also affected. I telephoned my private office at the Treasury to find out what had prompted the European Central Bank to take this action. This being August and the height of the holiday season, it took several hours to find someone with any idea of what was going on. It was infuriating. Why hadn't I been phoned? It was one of those cases when the civil servants dealing with the matter were so close to the problem that they did not see it for the crisis it was about to become. Ministers are not always told everything that the department is concerned about, but the judgement as to when to impart information is a critical one, and I made sure that such a situation should never arise again.

I wanted to know which of our banks could be in trouble and how we were going to deal with it. I asked that the Bank of England and the FSA, which is responsible for the supervision of banks and building societies, work along with the Treasury to identify potential problems. A few days later, back home in Edinburgh, I was told the FSA was worried about Northern Rock. Northern Rock's business model was heavily reliant on raising funds from financial institutions, mainly in the US, rather than from individual savers, and the cost of its borrowing was rising sharply. They feared it was going to find it extremely difficult to raise funds. If that happened, the outlook was grim.

There were also concerns about two more banks. The first was Alliance & Leicester, a medium-sized former building society. Alliance & Leicester had not got into trouble itself, but the FSA feared that once it became known that Northern Rock was in difficulties then Alliance

& Leicester would be seen as the next in line. In the course of the crisis every building society that had given up mutual ownership to become a public company during the 1980s either failed or was taken over. The second bank singled out for concern by the FSA was HBOS, formed by the merger of the Halifax Building Society and Bank of Scotland. HBOS was medium-sized in world terms but was one of the bigger British banks, in a different league from Northern Rock. Its headquarters were in Edinburgh, where I was an MP. There was a growing sense that the party that had been enjoyed by the banks for so long was about to come to an abrupt end. To make matters worse, I wasn't sure than anyone knew how deep these problems were, or what was their exact nature.

It was Northern Rock we had to tackle first, and straight away. A former well-run, small building society based in Newcastle, it was popular locally and had converted from mutual ownership to become a bank. Despite its size, it quickly became one of the major UK mortgage lenders, lending more money to some of its borrowers than their properties were worth, relying on ever-increasing house prices to make up the difference. In fact, a couple of years before the crisis, my wife Margaret had been looking for a mortgage so that we could buy a flat for me to stay in while Parliament was sitting. It had become cheaper to pay off a home loan than to rent. They asked for no evidence that we could pay; everything was done online, by the click of a mouse. Millions of people had been happy to take advantage of this easy credit, and buy-to-let mortgages had made landlords out of savers across the country, confident of good returns on their investments in the property market. It was a far cry from the 1970s, when, as a young lawyer, I advised clients that they would have to save with a building society for at least two years before they would be able to get a mortgage, and even then there might be a waiting list of as much as six months.

What was really worrying, though, was Northern Rock's increasing dependence on the wholesale market – that is to say, borrowing money from other banks – to provide funds for mortgages. In fact, this was the case with mortgage lenders across the board. In the past, as many as 90 per cent of mortgages provided by banks and buildings societies would be funded from deposits lodged by their savers; by 2007 less than a third of mortgages were funded in that way. The upside was that more mortgages were being made available to the public, and more cheaply. The downside was that the whole interlinked system was entirely dependent on the banks' ability to borrow from each other.

My worries about Northern Rock were compounded when it became apparent that the company itself seemed strangely detached from the looming disaster. The management appeared to resent the growing list of questions surrounding their business. In fact, they, as well as the FSA, had been aware of the risk they were exposed to since February 2007. More should have been done to deal with the problems then. They were too dependent on being able to raise money, mainly in the US, to keep their business going. If confidence in them dried up, it would be the end of the road. That is precisely what happened to them six months later, in September 2007.

At the same time, I was increasingly concerned about the relationship between the FSA and the Bank of England. Before 1997, the Bank had regulated most of the business conducted by banks. But some of the banks' activities, such as the sale of insurance, were overseen by a series of independent self-regulating bodies. There was a great deal of confusion as to who was responsible for what. It used to be said that when the Governor of the Bank of England raised his eyebrows the banks would take notice. That was fine when you were dealing with perhaps half a dozen banks, run by the old-boy network typical of the English establishment. By the mid-1990s, however, there was hardly a bank in the world that did not have some presence in London. The system needed to be modernized. So, in 1998, we brought all the regulation of financial services under the control of the FSA.

The responsibility for the architecture was largely mine. When we were in opposition in the early 1990s, Gordon had asked me to take responsibility for the City. I realized quickly that getting the right supervision and regulatory regime was essential and set about planning for the change in regulatory control which we implemented once we were in power. However, the system depended on a strong working relationship between the FSA and the Bank of England. Now, in 2007, it was clear to me that the relationship between the Bank and the FSA was not good. They had not worked as closely as they should have done over the previous decade, each blaming the other for this state of affairs. The FSA was chaired by Callum McCarthy, who had served in a number of City posts after starting his career as a civil servant in the Department of Trade and Industry. A quietly spoken, thoughtful man, he had an incisive mind and I respected his judgement. After we first met when I became Chancellor, both of us assumed we would encounter one another only occasionally. As it turned out, I spoke to him almost every other day until he retired in September 2008.

The relationship between Callum McCarthy and Mervyn King was often strained, at times prickly. As we shall see, in those days I tended to side more often with Callum in his diagnosis of the escalating crisis. There is no doubt in my mind that their difficult relationship contributed to the fact that our response to the crisis was not as sharp and decisive as it might have been. But the real problem was this: for ten years there had been no financial crisis. The regulatory system had only ever operated in good times. The Bank had concentrated on its monetary policy duties, primarily the regulation of interest rates. Although it had had responsibility for financial stability since becoming independent in 1997, it did not have a sufficiently deep understanding of what was going on in the individual banks – or, indeed, of the critical relationships within the banking system. The FSA, in turn, had spent a great deal of time since its inception concentrating on consumer issues, rather than examining the systemic risks that were to bring the entire system to the brink of collapse twelve months later. And the Treasury had not seen financial regulation as a priority. That is not to say that there wasn't a great deal of work being done. It had just not been seen as urgent.

In some ways all this was understandable, given the mood of the times. It was felt that judgements were for the markets. If a bank got it wrong, the shareholders would have to bear the consequences. The trouble was that when the crisis came the shareholders were hit – but so too was everyone else. The strains and stresses that had been there all along, but had not been evident, suddenly became very apparent. The whole system depended on the chairman of the FSA, the Governor of the Bank and the Chancellor seeing things in exactly the same way. The problem was that, in September 2007, we simply did not see things in the same way.

Fundamentally, the big issue on which we were divided time and again that autumn was whether to put money into the banking system as a whole, as the European Central Bank and the US Federal Reserve had done, or to concentrate our fire in the traditional way, helping each failing institution as the need arose. Callum McCarthy and I took the former view. The Governor took the latter. Unfortunately, that internal division of opinion became more and more apparent to the public as the weeks wore on.

At the beginning of September 2007, I returned to London and met with Mervyn King and Callum McCarthy in my office at the Treasury. It was to be the first of many meetings throughout the crisis. It was obvious that the banks were finding it difficult to borrow money, and the longer that problem went on the bigger would be the risk to Northern Rock. One way or another, its business model had failed. The only question was whether it should be wound down or sold – if anyone would buy it. We were agreed that in the meantime we would have to provide it with financial support. The longer that went on, the greater would be the risk that we would end up owning the bank, and that people would panic when they found out just how critical the position was. Banks are not like other companies, which can usually be allowed to fail. The risk with banks is that, rather like dominoes, if one fails it will take others with it. And it was proving very difficult to convince Northern Rock that the party was over.

At the time, we did not have the legal powers to step in and resolve the situation by forcing a sale or by simply taking over the bank. Had we had those powers, once it became clear that Northern Rock could not carry on, we could have resolved the situation over a weekend. That is precisely what we did a year later in the case of Bradford & Bingley, another small former building society that had overreached itself. But although the need for this legislation had been identified in a Treasury planning exercise twelve months earlier, it had not been worked up, which was a great pity. This lack of legal powers caused us huge problems in trying to deal with Northern Rock's business over the next few months.

At the beginning of September, it seemed that the best solution from the government's point of view would be to achieve a sale to another bank. That way, they could provide the capital and funding needed, as well as resolving the bank's problems. Not surprisingly, there was limited interest from the private sector. Lloyds Bank approached Treasury officials and expressed an interest in buying Northern Rock on condition that the Bank of England would continue to support it for two years. There was never any direct discussion at a senior level. It was an informal approach about the potential acquisition. It seemed that Lloyds had a general interest in expanding their mortgage business and that Northern Rock was a possibility, no more than that. At no point did they ever put anything remotely resembling a proposal on the table. I felt they were merely sniffing around for a bargain, knowing Northern Rock was in trouble. And that trouble was growing.

The three of us held a telephone conference call on 9 September. Mervyn King was at a monthly meeting of bank governors in Basel. Callum McCarthy was in London. I was in Edinburgh. My concern that the situation was becoming more acute was mounting. Banks were asking for more money in the system. If we could sell Northern Rock, that would be desirable; but most urgent was the need to get money into the banking system to keep it afloat and to prevent further imminent collapse. I wanted general support as well as whatever was needed to deal with Northern Rock.

Mervyn, not unreasonably, wanted first to deal with how we could establish the value of the assets that the banks owned. That way, we could establish what capital they needed. Callum and I did not dispute the need to find out the value of these assets. However, we were more concerned with ensuring that there was enough money in the system – 'liquidity', in the jargon – and that it did not seize up. The two positions were not inconsistent; it was just that I thought liquidity was increasingly the more urgent concern, and only the Bank could provide it. The Governor, however, thought that that would introduce 'moral hazard', and that a penalty interest rate must apply to any help given by the Bank.

Moral hazard, broadly, is where people become indifferent to the consequences of their actions because they do not have to meet the costs. Charging more for borrowing from the Bank of England is therefore a sensible check to ensure that banks only do so as a last resort. Both of these things hold true in normal times. But these were not normal times. During the conference call, I became increasingly frustrated at Mervyn's insistence that normal judgements could still apply in what were obviously deeply abnormal circumstances. Mervyn and the Bank believed the correct response was to provide, if necessary, support through its role as 'lender of last resort'. This is the fundamental job of any central bank. It used to be the ultimate safeguard, providing complete assurance that, through the Bank of England, the government would support a financial institution in trouble.

My frustration was that I could not in practice order the Bank to do what I wanted. Only the Bank of England can put the necessary funds into the banking system; indeed, that is one of the core purposes of a central bank. The Bank was independent and the Governor knew it. We did not agree on what to do. I put down the phone knowing I had to get back to London. I asked Treasury officials if there was a way of forcing the Governor's hand. The fact that we had given the Bank independence had a downside as well as an upside.

Throughout the next few days the situation continued to deteriorate.

The banking system was beginning to seize up, with banks becoming reluctant to lend to each other. The rate of interest at which banks lend to each other – the LIBOR rate – continued to rise, adding to the cost of lending.

Northern Rock's need for money kept on increasing. The bank was finding it more and more difficult to raise money on the markets. Bluntly, it looked as if it was going to fail. No one was going to lend it any more money. The Bank of England did announce that it was injecting an extra £4 billion into the system, but Northern Rock needed more specific help. By the second week in September it had become evident that asking for support from the Bank as lender of last resort was unavoidable. Our original plan had been to announce this on Monday, 17 September, giving us the weekend to plan not just the operation but also a message designed to reassure the markets. It then became clear that Northern Rock could not last that long. An announcement would have to be made on Friday, 14 September, when Mervyn and I were due to attend the Ecofin gathering in Porto. We knew we had to put in an appearance at the Ecofin gathering in order to quell speculation, even though both of us knew we were much needed at home.

The rescue plan was in place, ready to be announced before the markets opened on Friday. Then, with just hours to go, it all went wrong. The BBC was tipped off and announced exactly what we intended to do. I don't know who told the BBC's business editor what was going to happen. It could have been Northern Rock or its advisers. It might have been someone within the Bank or the FSA, or someone in government. Regardless of the source of the leak, it set in train a course of events that was disastrous for confidence in the government's ability to manage the growing crisis. I cannot be sure that, if the announcement had been made the following morning as planned, people would have accepted it without concern. What I do know is that when we made other, similar announcements over the next eighteen months we did not see a repetition of the queues that quickly formed outside branches of Northern Rock in 2007. The problem was that the BBC's report came against a background of growing concern, and although in the cold light of day the broadcast could be said to have been balanced – though it seemed sensational at the time – it is not too difficult to see why people decided they wanted their money out.

There was another factor too. Northern Rock had only seventy-six branches, of which just four were in London. They were mostly small and had few members of staff. They were used to dealing with customers in ones and twos, not several hundred at a time, all clamouring for their money. It was inevitable that when customers, many of them elderly, arrived at the branches, the staff would try to reassure them. This took time, and as a result the queues began to grow. Twenty years ago this would have been reported on the 9 o'clock news or in the newspapers the following morning, with a natural break between the events as they were reported. But now, rolling 24-hour news coverage meant that images of people queuing outside branches appeared on television in a never-ending loop. Each report fed off another, ratcheting up the tension. Unsurprisingly, more and more people felt they should join the queues to take out their money, just in case. To cap it all, it was a lovely sunny autumn day, so the weather was no deterrent. It was striking how relaxed and yet determined everyone was.

By contrast, a few months later, when there was a mini-run on one Northern Rock branch, the staff had been instructed to pay out to anyone who wanted their money, without question, argument or reassurance. Managers were told that customers were to be brought inside the branch, not left out in the street. It was also pouring a cold November rain. There were no queues and no panic.

But that September weekend, the queues formed on Friday and lengthened on Saturday. I'd raced back from Portugal and then had to fly to Edinburgh for a constituency event. I arrived home to the phone ringing. It was Gordon, asking me to come back. He said, you must reassure people that their money is safe. I said I was not so sure they would believe that: there was something happening here that was all too reminiscent of the fuel crisis of 2000. At that time, because of a strike at oil refineries, people believed that the fuel pumps were about to run dry and huge queues formed. Then word spread that supermarkets might run out of food. We saw panic-buying, supermarket shelves stripped, as people came to believe that if they did not buy now they might starve. For a few days the government seemed to have lost control. We were not yet at that stage with Northern Rock, but there was a mood in those queues that I recognized. It was going to take time to work this through before people would go home, certain that their money was safe.

Gordon was right, though, that I needed to be in London to begin the process of reassurance if the following week was not to end in chaos. That evening I recorded rounds of interviews for all the television channels from the study at No. 11 Downing Street, with all the author-ity that address implies. It did not reassure. What's more, it was clear that the run on the bank would carry on into the Monday if we did not do something more drastic than offer words of comfort.

That Saturday evening marked a turning point for me and for the Treasury. It was clear that we had to up our game. The more I looked at it, the more I felt we had drifted into a situation in which we appeared to have lost control of events. If Gordon and I did not get a grip, Northern Rock would be finished and so would we.

Part of the problem lay with the Treasury, which was simply not tooled up to deal with the job. There were not enough people with the necessary experience. I talked to Nick Macpherson, the Permanent Secretary, about this and we agreed we would have to take the bright-est and the best away from whatever they were doing and put them on to sorting out Northern Rock. There was the additional problem of the usual hectic business of the Treasury: we were preparing for the gov-ernment spending review and the pre-Budget report, both of which I had to present when Parliament returned in less than a month.

Governments right across the world frequently boast about cut-ting civil service numbers. The Treasury had lost many of its staff over the preceding ten years, and the strains were now evident. So, that Saturday night, after the television interviews, I sat down with some of the best people in the Treasury to decide what we should do with a bust bank. For it was abundantly clear that that was what Northern Rock now was.

The first question we had to answer was, how to stop the queues. You cannot resolve a problem until you quell the sense of crisis. You need time to work out the best solution in a calm atmosphere. I had learned this first when I was Secretary of State for Transport, dealing with huge problems on the railways. Now we had to get these queues off the streets, and the only way to do that was to find a way of assuring savers not only that their money was safe but that we had a convincing resolution to the story, ideally one that involved selling Northern Rock to someone else.

At our meeting, downstairs in the study of No. 11, we agreed that we had to try to find a buyer for Northern Rock. Before that, we had to provide a guarantee that every penny of savers' money was safe. That meant a government guarantee, with no qualification. This was a huge step and I was reluctant to use the government's credit in this way, guaranteeing a bank whose own reckless behaviour had brought it to its knees. I was also very conscious that it might not stop with Northern Rock; that we might end up guaranteeing every bank in Britain, which I did not want to do. That is exactly what happened in Ireland a year later, when its banks' debts became Ireland's debts and eventually the country had to go to the International Monetary Fund (IMF).

Although Northern Rock was manageable, others would be less so if we had to repeat the exercise. RBS, for example, had a value at that time of a little less than our total national income. And there was an extra problem. A guarantee on its own might stem the immediate panic, but people would soon be asking what was the government's plan for fixing this broken bank? The plan had to be credible and it had to represent a resolution to the problem.

The next day, Sunday, Lloyds renewed their interest, but they still wanted a guarantee of Bank of England support for two years. The Bank baulked at this. It would be guaranteeing funds for Lloyds, then a healthy bank. I could see the problem with this, but I wanted the Bank to consider what it could do. I had concluded that we would have to offer a guarantee to savers in Northern Rock, but if we could link it to a purchase by Lloyds, thus providing a solution to Northern Rock's problems, that might do the trick. I was reluctant to provide an open-ended guarantee to depositors without being able to say that the bank had been purchased and thus ending the immediate crisis.

Monday morning saw the queues resume, with Northern Rock haemorrhaging money every hour. By now I was sceptical that Lloyds would see anything through. Nick Macpherson had also sounded out the other big banks about the possibility of their jointly buying Northern Rock. Their attitude was illuminating. They didn't at that stage see Northern Rock as being part of a larger problem. They did not want to help. They didn't want us to nationalize it, but neither were they ready to come up with a private sector solution.

That Monday, Gordon and I met two or three times at No. 10. We agreed that the guarantee linked to a sale might work. Like myself, he was reluctant to pledge the government's money, but there was no alternative. One billion pounds had been withdrawn by customers the previous Friday. By Saturday the figure had risen to £1.5 billion.

I had decided that it would be better to make the announcement of the guarantee at close of business on the Monday afternoon, to allow people to see it on the television news that evening. That would provide a natural break, for the risk of making such an announcement in the middle of the day was that it would simply become lost among endless pictures of people forming queues and telling reporters they did not believe anyone and just wanted their money out.

Gordon and I were due to meet the US Treasury Secretary, Hank Paulson, who had unfortunately chosen that day to pay us a courtesy visit. Gordon and Hank were close, having worked together when Gordon was Chancellor, and I was keen to meet him, but we could not have picked a worse day for it. During the afternoon, Lloyds, predictably, pulled out. There would be no sale. I went round to No. 10 as I had to get Gordon to agree to a guarantee with no sale. What's more, during the afternoon, I had concluded that guaranteeing savers' money would not be enough. We would also have to guarantee the money deposited with Northern Rock by local councils and commercial bodies, since if those entities thought that it was only individual savers who were safe, they would pull their money out immediately. This was a huge commitment, although, since the money was there in the bank, I wasn't too worried about it – if only we could stop the panic.

As was to happen time and again over the next few months, I found myself having to make a statement at short notice. I had to reassure the public in a way that would stop the panic escalating further. It was a critical moment and I knew we had only one chance. If it failed, the panic might spread to other banks. I did think that this explicit guarantee would work, but it was very much in the balance. More embarrassingly, I had to announce it at a joint news conference with the US Treasury Secretary.

I warmed to Hank, a bluff, amiable man, who was open and direct. He had worked in a junior role for the Republicans in the Nixon administration, then spent most of his career with Goldman Sachs, the US investment bank. He had reluctantly agreed to serve George W. Bush as Treasury Secretary just over a year earlier. His great strength was that he understood how the markets worked. The two of us remained in close touch over the next two fraught years until he left office.

A good working relationship at this level was essential. Even during what were difficult times for both of us at the height of the crisis in 2008, we respected each other's positions and were able to work closely. Fortunately, Hank has a sense of humour. The news conference after our meeting in the sitting room at No. 10 was meant to report on our discussions. The talks had largely centred on the Americans' perception that the Bank of England was not taking the unfolding drama seriously enough. As Hank said: 'Your guy Mervyn has a high pain threshold. I hope you have too.'

The news conference had been arranged so that the media could speak to both Hank and myself. By the time we faced the press in Downing Street, however, we knew that the British press would only be interested in one question: Northern Rock. Hank duly read out his statement and then had to watch me for the next twenty minutes. The questioning was rough but justified; yet to my American visitor the journalists appeared hostile. Three years later he told me how bad he had felt at not being able to share some of the pain. Certainly, in my experience, the American media is much more deferential.

So I announced the guarantee and, to my immense relief, it worked. The next day the queues, with few exceptions, had vanished. We now had a bit of breathing space, but we had to continue looking for a buyer or we would end up owning Northern Rock ourselves. That was not a prospect that Gordon or I relished. We had stopped the queues but there is no doubt that we had been severely battered. Images of the first run on a bank in more than a century had flashed around the world. Northern Rock was now internationally a byword for disaster – 'Northern Crock', it was nicknamed. As Chancellor, I had to take responsibility. The only good thing to be said about the entire episode was that it was valuable preparation for what was to come a year later. I was determined that the mistakes made in August and September 2007 would not be repeated.

2 The Election that Never Was

In September 2007 Margaret and I caught an early morning train down to Bournemouth. British political parties traditionally choose to hold their annual conferences at seaside resorts. This year, it was the turn of that sedate south-coast town. I was due to give my first conference speech as Chancellor that afternoon. The previous two days had been spent writing it. These speeches take an enormous amount of work and are usually forgotten the day after they are delivered. I knew that the only thing that anyone would be interested in was what I said about Northern Rock, and so it proved.

We and our fellow passengers heading to the conference were in good spirits: despite Northern Rock, Labour was ahead in the polls and Gordon Brown had made a good start as prime minister. Four days into his premiership a blazing Jeep had been driven into Glasgow airport and the UK was braced for a fresh wave of terrorist attacks. It was the most dangerous situation facing the UK since the attacks in London of 2005. With Jacqui Smith, Britain's first woman Home Secretary, Gordon had handled the aftermath with gravity and poise, summoning intelligence chiefs and ministers to a Cobra committee meeting in Whitehall and raising the threat level to the highest degree.

He had also handled the re-emergence of foot-and-mouth disease – which had cost beleaguered farmers dear as their livestock had to be slaughtered – extremely well. We were mindful in government of the loss of confidence and public support during the earlier outbreak in 2001. Gordon had responded effectively, too, to the unusually bad flooding in England that summer. The Conservative opposition had found it difficult to make headway. They had said little about the Northern Rock crisis, and when they did it was frequently contradictory and confused.

On the surface, things were moving our way, so inevitably there was an argument for us seeking a new mandate from the country under a new prime minister, thereby strengthening his personal authority. Whether to call a general election is one of the biggest decisions a prime minister can make. It is his or hers alone. Get it right and you're a hero; get it wrong and you're out. I had recently discovered that the arguments for and against calling an election had been raging all summer among Gordon's key people. Ed Balls and Ed Miliband had been his special advisers when he was at the Treasury and were now ministers themselves, Ed Balls as Education Secretary and Ed Miliband in the Cabinet Office. Gordon was heavily dependent on the economic know-how of Ed Balls, who had been with him at the Treasury for fifteen years. Douglas Alexander was another trusted confidant, now responsible for international development; and Spencer Livermore, the Prime Minister's Director of Strategy, also played a crucial role in these discussions.

I wasn't part of the discussions until late on, in early September. Even then, my involvement was fairly casual and would only occur if I happened to be with Gordon when one or another of his team would wander in and begin rehearsing the arguments for or against. It felt uncomfortable at times, as if I were eavesdropping, since I hadn't been invited to take part; it was just the geography of Downing Street that made me an accidental participant.

Nos. 10 and 11 Downing Street are really one big rambling house, with myriad corridors and rooms running into each other. It is not always clear what is private space and what is not. If I wanted to talk to Gordon, we could arrange to do it through the civil service machine, or, certainly in the early months, when relations between us were still good, we would meet informally since it was easy enough to seek one another out in a downstairs room.

That my involvement in the discussions around a possible general election was so peripheral was a portent of what was to come. I knew that Gordon took advice from a wide range of people; he has always done so and there is nothing wrong in it. The trouble was that only on very few occasions did these people all come together in a meeting, Cabinet or otherwise, so that the arguments on a particular issue could be thrashed out and a decision reached. All too often I would come out of a meeting with Gordon believing that a decision had been reached, only for it to transpire that he had spoken to someone else with a different opinion and changed his mind. That is the way Gordon worked. He liked to canvass a wide range of opinion before making up his mind about what to do – often at the last moment. Far too often, individuals consulted on an issue did not know that he was speaking to others and weren't aware of the competing arguments. A meeting with Gordon involved many elephants in the room.

Gordon always had the ability to gather people with good minds around him. He also attracted – and expected – fierce loyalty. His style of operating was like an old-fashioned court: he was the centre around which trusted courtiers moved. He had worked like this throughout his career, since his earliest years as a student politician at Edinburgh University. Losing his most trusted confidants – Balls, Miliband and Alexander – when he entered No. 10 left him, I think, slightly bereft.

Now, on the eve of conference, I was aware that something else had changed since the summer. This was my relationship with Gordon's inner circle. I had known most of them since they started working for Gordon in opposition in the early 1990s. We had a good working relationship, which carried on into government during my first year as Chief Secretary to the Treasury. Ed Balls and Ed Miliband were always helpful at that time and I valued their thoughts. Douglas Alexander, then in charge of election planning, I had known for many years as a young politician with acuity and strong values. I often called in to see Gordon at the Treasury in his time there and took part in discussions on policy. I was never one of the magic circle; I was one of the many whom Gordon would consult from time to time. We respected and trusted each other. But something changed after he became Prime Minister and suddenly I was definitely outside the tent.

Here I was at the heart of government, appointed by Gordon to a key post, and yet I wasn't privy to thinking or discussion on policy issues within his close team. In a way, it was not personal. I had seen it happen with Gordon time and again over the years. People would be welcomed into his confidence but then find themselves shut out, for reasons that were difficult to fathom.

Opinion among Gordon's advisers was divided over whether to go to the country early. I put in my tuppence worth when I was asked my view. I said that I was against calling an election. Ed Balls and Douglas Alexander had a strong argument for going to the country now, in order to seek a mandate for Gordon. Ed Miliband was more ambivalent. The problem for me was, what would Gordon say to the country that actually required a new mandate? In what way would he seek to differentiate himself from Tony Blair? What did he want a mandate to do that was different? That was not clear. You only seek a new mandate if you are making a break from the past, or if you want to set out the new challenges you wish to confront and your proposed response to them. There has to be a strong reason to go to the country outside the normal four- or five-year electoral cycle. And to be blunt, you have to be confident that you are going to win. Such a strategy, involving a clear set of policy initiatives, should have been worked up over the summer if it was to have any chance of success in the autumn. As far as I could see, that never happened. Gordon seemed to me to be deeply uncertain about an early election: after all, it was entirely possible that our majority would be cut, or that we would lose and he would be the shortest-serving prime minister ever. And if that was his view, he should have halted the speculation before it ran out of control.

It was obvious to me even at this early stage of his premiership that there was no sign of clarity or direction. It was all about tactics rather than strategy. No one seemed to be asking the obvious question: what was it that Gordon wanted to do during his premiership? That is something he struggled with for the next three years. The party, and many in the country, myself included, had keenly anticipated his becoming prime minister. Now we needed a clear understanding of what he planned to do. Instead, what we were presented with looked rather like cold political tactics. Then there were the political facts to consider: the polling evidence was sobering. To win a British election you need to win marginal seats, particularly in the south-east of England, where the polls showed the Tories as being ahead. Inheritance tax was identified as a key issue, part of the Tories' push on property taxes.

Although Cabinet members were never formally consulted, they soon let it be known what they thought, speaking to Gordon individually. Jack Straw in particular shared my view that you shouldn't go to the country if you don't have to, especially if the polls are against you. Jack, a canny operator, who had been an MP for almost thirty years, had a good sense of what would and would not work in politics. He was dead against an early election. So too was Geoff Hoon, the party's Chief Whip. Geoff and I have known each other for a long time and our children are of a similar age. We first met when he was an MEP and we were both on a committee considering the case for electoral reform, which met for what felt like years on end. We both agreed that an early election could be folly.

If we were to have an election that autumn, as Chancellor I needed to know as soon as possible. Budgets, by their very nature, are highly political. A Budget produced in mid-term would inevitably be different from one presented on the eve of a poll. I was somewhat put out to find that I was just an accidental spectator at what was potentially a critical point. It was an issue that would come up again and again: either Gordon and I trusted one other, or we didn't. There was no room for ambivalence. Nos. 10 and 11 have to be in tune. What could be discerned now was more of a discordant hum.

One morning, just as things seemed to be moving towards an early election, I remember looking into the shaving mirror at the Downing Street flat and thinking, if we get this wrong it will be George Osborne who'll be seeing his reflection here soon. If an early election were to be called, it should have been announced almost immediately after Tony Blair stood down. It looked opportunistic to be thinking about calling one several months later, in the dark days of autumn.

When we arrived in Bournemouth, it was clear that the pro-election faction in the Brown circle was in the ascendancy. The atmosphere was febrile. By the Wednesday of the conference journalists were being briefed, anonymously of course, that there would be an election. Then there were angry and rebarbative denials. Having spoken to Gordon, I didn't think that there would be an election. The problem was that the spin machine was allowed to run out of control and fed the story.

Confusion and acrimony seeped into coverage of the week's conference events. Was there going to be an election? Journalists were, not surprisingly, pressing the question. Yes, no, maybe, possibly – it was a mess, and the sense of drift was increasing. The raging arguments between the yes and no camps, the briefings and counter-briefings to the media, made us look shambolic. Thankfully, my visit to conference had to be short and I left Bournemouth the day after Gordon's speech. In August, he had asked me whether or not I could pull the spending review announcement and the pre-Budget report forward to October, to give us the option of an early election. That presented significant logistical problems in that, on top of Northern Rock, I was having to finalize government spending plans for the next three years at the same time as making a major economic statement.

The Tories, who had had a bad summer trailing us in the polls, pulled off a theatrical coup at their conference the week after ours. George Osborne announced an inheritance tax break that in any other circumstances would have been seen as unaffordable, as was shown by the watered-down version they came up with following the 2010 election. We should never have allowed one conference speech from the opposition to destabilize us so badly. Gordon went to Afghanistan the day after Osborne's speech, and this was not well received by the media, who accused him of using the visit to detract attention from the Tory Party conference. There is no convention that says you shouldn't do anything political while another party is having a conference, it just tends not to happen. In any event, it made us look clunky and opportunistic.

So, when it finally came, the announcement that there would be no election was a disaster. We had made the fatal mistake of letting events control us. The announcement itself came out in a disorganized, haphazard way, on a Saturday afternoon, accompanied by briefings from the bowels of No. 10, heaping blame on the supposed author of this misfortune, Douglas Alexander. Who told Damian McBride to do this remains opaque. It was extremely hurtful for Douglas, who was a loyal supporter of Gordon and had always been highly regarded by both camps as someone who could see the bigger picture. He did take it very badly when he was dumped on, since it was clear that the briefing was at least tacitly condoned, and certainly wasn't stopped.

The election-that-never-was was a massive political misjudgement, from which we never really recovered. The public's trust was shaken, if not destroyed. We lost any political capital built up over the previous three months. People stopped believing what we had to say. Faced with mounting problems, with the banking crisis fast escalating into an economic crisis, this was to prove fatal. And once trust is lost, it takes years to recover. Gordon found himself in a position in which he had not only to announce that there would be no election, but also to answer the obvious question: why not? He said it was because he wanted time to establish himself. But voters are not daft; the public knew that the reason the election was called off was because we were not sure we would win.

I was more immediately concerned that I would have to present the pre-Budget report the following week, in the worst possible circumstances. The report had been prepared on the basis that there was to be an election, so it had to include measures dealing with inheritance tax. The election had been called off, but by this stage we were committed to spending a lot of money trying to fix the political problem, at what, in Budget terms, was the very last minute. That meant raising money elsewhere. The politics were awful.

The Budget statement, which should be a major economic event, is usually presented in March or April. However, since we took power in 1997, there had also been the pre-Budget report to contend with. It was originally designed to report on progress since the Budget and to trail measures that might need to be consulted on prior to the next Budget. In practice, the two events were barely distinguishable. There is much more pomp and ceremony around the Budget, but increasingly the major announcements on tax and spending were now being made at the pre-Budget report stage. This meant that during my time as Chancellor I had to deliver what were effectively six Budgets.

Most of Gordon's budgets during his time as Chancellor had not changed the underlying public finances dramatically. What he spent he was able to balance by raising money elsewhere. His macroeconomic policy was concentrated on creating stable economic growth and his balanced budgets earned him the moniker 'Prudence'. Tax revenues were generated through economic growth and getting a high proportion of people into work. New Labour's economic policy was built on discounting the old left's 'tax and spend' approach, whereby the country borrows beyond what it can afford in order to finance spending on public services.

A Budget, or indeed a pre-Budget report, takes months of intense work and planning. You have to decide first what is your forecast for the economy and the level of public finances. Then you have to decide what you want to do in general terms, what in the jargon is called the 'fiscal stance'. Finally, detailed policies have to be worked up. Over the three years I was Chancellor, Gordon and I spent a lot of time arguing over the first two points, which meant rarely getting to the third. The closer you get to making the announcement, the more difficult it is to change the structure both of the Budget and of the message you want to give. It is a wearing process, especially if there are significant changes in strategy at the last minute. Complex figures have to be presented on the day and last-minute changes may, if you are not careful, result in the published figures being wrong. This reflects badly on the Treasury and can create serious difficulties for those affected by the changes.

In the late summer, the planned centrepiece of the pre-Budget report was to be the conclusion of the spending review. We had decided in 1997 when we came to power that government spending on public services, such as schools and hospitals, would be fixed for a three-year period to allow for more sensible planning and decision-making. This then became the norm: plans for each successive three-year period would be fixed at the end of the second year of the spending period. This was much better than the previous system, in which spending was fixed from year to year. In stable times, the new system had worked well. Now, however, in 2007, the timing of the spending review could not have been worse.

In the autumn of that year, the signs of the looming worldwide recession were far from clear. In 2007, it was by no means certain that we were about to enter a steep economic downturn. But by 2008, it was obvious that the assumption that the economy would continue to grow uninterrupted could no longer hold. Had we known what was about to happen, I would almost certainly have fixed spending for the following year, making plans for a further review the year after.

As it was, I had decided to cut the rate of growth of public spending by half. After ten years of almost uninterrupted increase in public spending, we could afford to do so. There are many who have said subsequently that we spent too much in the previous decade. Back in 1997, however, there was a near-consensus that investment in neglected public services, such as an underfunded NHS and decrepit school buildings, was of paramount importance. There were many reasons for the decay of our clapped-out public services. Crudely put, the main factors began with the UK's performance as 'the sick man of Europe' in the post-war years, with two decades of poor economic performance meaning that we had not received the tax revenues from a healthy economy that would have enabled spending on the public services and infrastructure essential to any modern economy. Then what followed was free-market fundamentalism – Thatcherism – which enshrined the market as the dominant force in our lives; the role of the state was reduced for ideological reasons. In 1997 we had to address the costs of that ideology. Unlike the wealth that never did trickle down, as had been projected, the social costs cascaded down through successive generations. The physical degeneration was real and plain to see: hospitals and schools that had been built by the Victorians, who would never have envisaged them still being in use as we entered the twenty-first century. My own children started school in Edinburgh in a building with outside toilets and one teacher to thirty-four infants, with no classroom assistants.

There was something of a political consensus, with the Conservatives supporting our spending plans until right up until the end of 2008. The Liberal Democrats gave the impression that they did too, until very shortly after the 2010 general election. Looking at the Treasury books when I arrived in 2007, the structural deficit – that is, the difference between what you spend and what you receive back in tax, which is not merely the result of economic ups and downs – was comparatively small. And the country entered the financial crisis with less public debt than that of most other developed countries – not my words but those of Vince Cable, the Liberal Democrat Shadow Chancellor, writing in 2009. From a broadly Keynesian perspective, he said, it would be damaging to seek to curb the deficit in recession conditions, since that would be likely to deepen the recession. He added that comfort could also be drawn from the fact that developed countries like Japan and Italy operate at far higher levels of government debt than Britain has, or is likely ever to have. Neither of those countries are in good shape economically, but neither has defaulted on debt or resorted to inflation to 'burn off' debt. That was in 2006. How he has changed his tune.

On 3 September 2007 George Osborne committed a Conservative government to matching our public spending totals for the following three years. He pledged two years of 2 per cent increases. The Shadow Chancellor said government spending under the Conservatives would rise from £615 billion in 2008 to £674 billion in 2010/11. The move would create 'headroom' for cutting taxes because the economy was expected to grow faster than public spending. What's more, he added: 'The result of adopting these spending totals is that under a Conservative government there will be real increases in spending on public services, year after year.' After the 2010 election, the Tories and the Liberal Democrats spent some considerable time, to good political effect, claiming that the deficit was entirely the fault of Labour profligacy, glossing over their own record of supporting what we were doing.

Yet, back in October 2007, as I worked on the spending review, I thought that it was time to apply the brakes on the amount we were spending. I am naturally cautious and so I determined that now was the time to rein in the rate of growth in public spending. That would be easily manageable on the back of a much higher level of spending than we had inherited ten years earlier, and would still allow us to continue to improve public services. That was to be the centrepiece of my spending review.

There was also the vexed issue of inheritance tax. Inheritance tax in this country is paid by very few people. The thresholds are high and it is legally avoidable by those sufficiently affluent to be able to give their estates away, provided they do so seven years before they die. Only the unlucky, or bad planners, are saddled with inheritance tax. Despite this, many people who will never have to pay inheritance tax believe they will have to do so. It is a deeply unpopular tax, except among a minority who believe that the state should redistribute wealth to a far greater extent than it does.

I had discussed doing something about it with Gordon in the

summer before the conference. He showed me proposals that he had considered, but had not pursued, for his last Budget as Chancellor. But following the Tory conference, inheritance tax suddenly assumed a far greater political importance from Gordon's perspective. I understood that we had to do more than we had originally intended and so I proposed a reform that would have taken more people out of the tax. The Conservatives proposed to pay for their plans by taxing people from abroad who live here but are domiciled for tax purposes elsewhere: the 'non-doms'. At first sight, it seemed a brilliant wheeze. What better than to tax non-doms who do not have a vote here and whom the public associates with rich bankers. The problem is that non-doms also include a large number of people who come to this country to work, not just in banks but in hospitals, universities and restaurants, usually for a period of no more than two or three years.

The issue became the subject of my first major clash with Gordon. We were in exactly the same place on Northern Rock, but on the economy we were far too often divided. I did not see how we could tax anyone who set foot in the country, no matter for how short a period, as the Tories had proposed. It was also doubtful if it would raise the money we needed. As I correctly predicted, there would be howls of outrage from the better-off, who could well afford to pay but who had easy access to the media, and some of whom even claimed to be Labour supporters. Quite why we were now going to tax the non-doms, having failed to do so for the previous ten years, wouldn't be clear. It looked like – and it was – a last-minute fix.

The new government of 2010 never did implement the policy the Tories set out three years earlier, probably for the same reasons I didn't. My compromise was that the tax would be imposed only on those who had chosen to make Britain their home, by staying here for more than seven years. This allowed for the research scientist, the chef, the doctor, who came to work here for a few years but for whom Britain was not home. After seven years their position would be different; it suggested they were settling here and ought to pay tax. But the inheritance tax plans still had to be paid for, and I did not want to add to our level of borrowing. So I proposed to pay for it by increasing capital gains tax, on things like second homes or paintings, from 10 to 18 per cent.

At that time we had rules, 'fiscal rules' in the jargon, which put limits on how much we could borrow and how much debt we could carry forward. They were an excellent discipline imposed by Gordon in his first Budget in 1997, in order to underline New Labour's determination to put the health of the economy first. Every British government follows fiscal rules, which change from time to time in accordance with economic conditions. They are there to guide policy. In the 1980s the Tory government was concerned with soaring inflation more than anything else. In 1997 we were concerned with achieving longer-term stability in public finances and economic growth. From 2008, our strategy was essentially to support the economy through the recession and then to cut the deficit once growth was established. The current government, elected in 2010, has implemented what it calls a 'fiscal mandate', directed at cutting borrowing.

These rules are not contained in an Act of Parliament, although ours were referred to in legislation, in a Finance Act. They are there as a yardstick, so that commentators and analysts can judge fiscal measures against the government's stated objectives. Ours were quite simple: they were principally designed to prevent borrowing to fund day-to-day government spending, and to bear down on debt. We had stuck to them over the ten years since we were elected in 1997 and official figures showed that they had been met during that long economic cycle. I later abandoned them as the economic crisis deepened, because to stick to them would have been perverse in the face of the worst downturn of recent times. However, in the autumn of 2007 the rules stood, and they meant that if we were going to give away money by taking people out of inheritance tax, then money would have to be raised elsewhere, or spending cut.

Both issues of contention – the non-dom tax and the increase in capital gains tax – took up days of increasingly fraught discussion between

Nos. 10 and 11. There was much plodding between the Treasury and No. 10, lots of sabre-rattling. The worn carpet in the corridor leading to the PM's office became ever more threadbare as groups of advisers trooped in to give their advice, before stomping back out again. There was a considerable amount of squaring up between officials on the two sides of the negotiations.

Even after the announcement, several months were spent trying to get the policies right. In tax matters, the devil is in the detail, and you cannot safely make big changes in a hurry without thinking through the consequences for taxpayers at every level. The controversy over capital gains tax may have been largely confined to the business pages, but there was another tax problem that would cause us acute problems over the next year.

In his final Budget as Chancellor, Gordon had abolished the 10p rate of income tax, leaving the UK with just two rates of tax: a higher rate of 40p, and the lower rate of 20p. In his ten years as Chancellor, I think Gordon had discussed with me most aspects of his Budgets and pre-Budget reports. We talked more easily in those years. I remember discussing his plan to cut out the 10p rate at the end of 2006. I could see the attraction of a simplified tax system but, I said, we had introduced it back in 1998 to get the lowest earners in the country out of tax and there would surely be many losers from its abolition. His reply was that when we introduced the 10p rate, tax credits were not yet in place. In addition to that, taxpayers at the top of the scale also benefited from some of their income being taxed at the 10p rate. He was right, in that tax credits had provided a huge boost to the incomes of families with children on low and, in many cases, middle incomes. Although the tax credit system has been criticized as being overly complicated, it was part of a move, which I strongly supported, to make work pay. It took some years to try and resolve the complexities inherent in a system that has to take account of ever-changing incomes, but the tax credit policy itself is sound and has survived the transition to a new government.

The problem was that while many qualified for tax credits, many did not. It was not so easy to see how the losers could be compensated for the tax increase that would result from more of their income being taxed at a higher rate. Our conversations concluded with Gordon saying that more work was needed to deal with those who faced losing out from the abolition of the 10p rate.

When it was abolished in the 2007 Budget, Gordon announced measures that compensated many taxpayers, mostly those with children. But a few months later, when I sat in his old seat in the Treasury, looking over the books, I saw advice that painted an extremely bleak picture. While 80 per cent of households would see no effect on their incomes or would even benefit from the change, about five million households stood to lose out. The losers ranged from those on pretty low incomes through to households where there was one earner who could be earning more than £100,000 but with a partner who had lost out. Alarm bells had rung when I received a letter from an elderly constituent just after Gordon's final Budget. She was aged over sixty and had calculated to the last penny how much she was going to lose. What was surprising was that so few others had picked up on the problem until the following spring, just as it was due to come into effect.

As it was, in the autumn of 2007, I was told that it would cost about £6.5 billion to ensure that there would be no losers. It seemed an enormous amount of money. A year later, it would seem small beer compared with the £50 billion cheque I had to write to forestall a global banking collapse. In my pre-Budget report, however, knowing that our financial room for manoeuvre was so limited, I did not try to find another £6.5 billion in the short time available. I would have to return to it later on.

All political statements, especially Budgets, are framed by the environment in which they are made. By the time I stood up in the House of Commons on Wednesday, 13 October 2007, the Tories were ahead in the polls and had very good reason to be cheerful. After ten years in the doldrums, they were now out in front. The commentators were faced with a government that had been battered by Northern Rock and had then clobbered itself over the election-that-never-was. The pre-Budget report failed to do what it should have done. It was cobbled together and did not set out a compelling story on the economy or the banking crisis; far from our regaining the political initiative, it slipped even further away. Why did I agree to include the inheritance tax measure at all? In political terms, the answer is that if we were to fight an election we had to have something to say about the tax, since all the polling evidence showed that it was a problem for us. When the election was called off, we were too far down the track to remove the measure. It would have meant recasting the pre-Budget report, with all its complex interlinked financial implications. But there is another factor. My instinct was to support the Prime Minister, as I had done for the best part of fifteen years. That loyalty was to be severely tested over the next three years.

That pre-Budget report was a low point in my time as Chancellor. It was going to take some time to recover my position, and unfortunately there was a lot more bad news to come. While we had been preparing the report, there were signs emerging that Northern Rock's problems were beginning to spread. We were worried about Alliance and Leicester, whose directors still believed they could sit it out. There was also concern about Bradford and Bingley, which was very exposed to the buy-to-let market, and whose reliance on borrowers correctly certifying their own earnings, with minimal checks, was alarming.

Then there was HBOS, the result of a classic marriage on the rebound in the late 1990s, when the Bank of Scotland had mounted an audacious bid to take control of one of Britain's biggest banks, NatWest. Seeing what they were up to, their Edinburgh neighbours and rivals, RBS, made a counter-bid, and won. Bank of Scotland, which was a douce, medium-sized, well-run bank, felt it had no alternative but to do a deal with the Halifax, then Britain's biggest mortgage lender. HBOS was never a happy union. It was clear that the Halifax was the dominant partner, sometimes referred to by Bank of Scotland staff as 'The Haliban'. By 2007 it was becoming clear that HBOS was losing money, not through involvement in complicated financial dealings, but through bad judgement on commercial loans.

It was little comfort to know that other countries were facing the same problems, and that other banks overseas were in deep trouble. On 4 November, Chuck Prince resigned as chief executive of Citigroup. It was revealed that Citigroup faced an $11 billion loss on mortgage-related securities. Prince was the man who had famously said: 'As long as the music is playing we will keep on dancing.' Clearly the ball was ending all over the world. Then, seemingly out of the blue, I had to deal with an unexpected home-grown drama.

In early September, we had moved into the flat above No. 10 which, until Tony Blair's time, was where prime ministers lodged. Tony, and then Gordon, lived in the larger, more secure flat attached to No. 11 – although, confusingly, it is actually part of No. 12. This made sense because both had young children and needed the space. There is no real separation between the three buildings: there are spiral staircases, corridors and rooms attaching each space to the next.

For the first few months as prime minister, Gordon operated out of Tony Blair's old study next to the Cabinet Room in No. 10. There was a winding staircase down to the outer office from our flat. He then moved his office to a big open-plan space, formerly the Chief Whip's office, in No. 12. Between Nos. 10 and 12 is, of course, No. 11, which the Treasury has jealously guarded against predatory claims for extra space from the Prime Minister's office. The corridor between No. 10 and the new office chosen by the Prime Minister as his nerve centre runs straight through No. 11. Over the next three years it provided me with an unexpected spectator's view of traffic into the Prime Minister's office. Gordon, in turn, had to be fielded through the crush of visitors to receptions in No. 11, negotiating his way past young people dressed as elves and fairies at festive charity parties, or, on one occasion, bumping into a goat belonging to a Welsh guardsman who was leading children from a hospice out to the garden. Privacy was at a premium.

No. 11 is a small Georgian house, built by an early property developer, George Downing, as a speculative sideline to his day job as a spy. Now a bit tattered and faded, it was decided before we moved in that the public entrance needed a fresh coat of paint, as it hadn't been done since the early 1960s. A cheap job was not, apparently, an option. It is a historic space and had to be properly conserved. The paint colour they chose made us laugh: it was called 'Drab', and so it was. The entrance hall had portraits of two of Britain's most famous Chancellors, Gladstone and Disraeli, glowering darkly in the light of 20 watt bulbs. Living at No. 11 is something I never took for granted, especially when I used to see the extent to which people from all walks of life, prime ministers and presidents, schoolchildren and statesmen, excited family and friends, valued the chance to walk through that famous door. We were always careful to warn them not to trip over the carpet patched with sticky tape.

After another week in Downing Street we decided to escape this febrile atmosphere and head home to Edinburgh for the weekend of Saturday, 10 November. It was a rare visit, for we ended up living 'above the shop' in Downing Street far more than we had anticipated, as a result of crisis heaped on crisis. The original plan had been that Margaret would be wherever she was most needed, at home in Edinburgh or at the flat in Downing Street. It was the first time she and I had lived together full-time since we were married. Before I entered Parliament in 1987 she had worked as a journalist in Scotland. On the *Glasgow Herald* she was frequently on the night desk. I was an Advocate at the Scottish bar and frequently away from home. After being elected, we chose to live in Edinburgh, and I was routinely in London from Monday until late Thursday or Friday morning. Margaret's work was in Scotland and we wanted to bring up our children close to family and friends. By the late summer of 2007, however, it was clear that it would be easier to live in Downing Street. The cost of making our London flat secure would be difficult to justify. Our son, Calum, was away at university; our daughter, Anna, had finished her exams and was delighted that we should leave her room to party. But I did look forward to visits home to Edinburgh and to tending our much-neglected garden. And, of course, I had my duties as a sitting MP, holding constituency surgeries, but too often it was just a flying visit.

That weekend was the first in a long time that was relatively free from crisis. It was not to last long. We were eating bacon rolls and reading the papers when my duty private secretary rang. The chairman of Her Majesty's Revenue and Customs (HMRC) was on the line, and it was urgent. HMRC is responsible for collecting taxes in the UK. It is independent from the Treasury; rightly, ministers are kept well away from the affairs of individual taxpayers. Unfortunately for me, though, the Chancellor is still accountable to Parliament for whatever HMRC does. To be phoned on a Saturday morning could only be bad. What followed would have been the stuff of a Whitehall farce had it not been so serious.

HMRC is responsible for paying Child Benefit to everyone with children in the UK. Like any other government department, it is audited by the National Audit Office (NAO), again entirely independent of the government. Earlier in the year, a hapless voice explained, an official within HMRC was asked to send NAO a full copy of all data held by them relating to Child Benefit. For some unaccountable reason, the request was repeated in October. All the data held on families receiving Child Benefit was posted from HMRC's office in the north-east of England to the NAO office in London. The package, containing two discs, was not recorded or registered. It never arrived in London.

I swallowed hard and asked what, exactly, was on these discs? There was a silence. It was like pulling teeth. I was told again that it contained records of parents who received Child Benefit. How many? The answer: 25 million. What was worse, the information included the names and addresses of parents and children, Child Benefit reference numbers, National Insurance numbers – like gold dust to fraudsters – and worse, much worse, bank or building society details. It could scarcely have been more dreadful.

Perhaps because I had just been told about this, I reacted differently from those who worked with this data day in and day out. Here we were, talking in calm tones about the British government having lost intimate and sensitive details of half the population. It was all contained on two CDs which had been popped in the post? No one had a clue where it might end up? My response was terse, perhaps understandably so. Worse still, the discs had gone missing some three weeks earlier. Senior management had been informed two days ago, and I, who would have to answer for this, was only being told now. I flew back to London, but not before going into the garden for an hour. There was not a weed left standing.

By chance, on that Saturday morning Gordon rang me about something else. I told him of the latest blow. You'll have to get the police in, he said. We both knew that that would reinforce the view that the government was not in control. I knew, of course, that the public would have to be informed. It was my job to tell them. This is the sort of announcement that cannot be made without first taking a deep breath and confirming the details. I had to be sure we were absolutely certain the information was lost. Also, the banks and building societies would have to be told what had happened. After all, they would have to protect their customers, especially after the information became public. This would take time. The police and the FSA were both anxious to avoid a premature public announcement. The banks wanted to flag accounts so that they could detect any fraudulent withdrawals, and the police did not want to advertise to the criminal world that this valuable information might be available.

Finally, I spoke to the Information Commissioner, who agreed with my view that we had to tell the public what had happened but that we needed to take enough time to ensure the banks had revised their security procedures and were ready to deal with potentially millions of enquiries. I instructed Paul Gray, chairman of HMRC, to order an immediate search of the Child Benefit office and of the NAO. In the days that followed, both buildings were scoured from top to bottom. The officials involved were questioned. On the Monday afternoon I was told they were almost certain they had found the missing discs. It proved to be a false hope. On the Wednesday we had no option but to call in the Metropolitan Police.

I was far from happy that I was being told all that was going on at HMRC. The senior management did not seem to me to grasp the seriousness of what had happened. More than that, I was told places had been searched which then turned out not to be the case. As part of the fallout I ordered an independent inquiry into what was going on within the organization. It revealed a management structure that was opaque, so that it was very difficult to see who was responsible for what.

I accepted the resignation of Paul Gray. I was sorry about that, as I had worked with him both in the Treasury and at the Department of Social Security, but he quite properly accepted responsibility for these serious failings at HMRC. The banks moved quickly to put in place security measures on all the accounts, while I got ready to tell the House of Commons what had happened. The banks wanted time to complete their security work, and the police wanted to get as far as they could without alerting anyone who might have got hold of the discs. In a situation like this there is always a conflict between doing what is needed to protect the public and at the same time being open about what has happened. I decided to make a statement the following Monday.

Unfortunately, I first had to attend the meeting of the G20 group of finance ministers in South Africa. I had planned to combine what was my first of such meetings with a visit to see some of the development work they were doing in Ghana. This was to be a joint visit with Hank Paulson who, perhaps unusually for a US Treasury Secretary, had a huge interest in development in Africa.

But there was no question of that now. For the second time in two months, I had to show my face at a meeting I did not want to attend, this time 6,000 miles away. I had to go because it had been agreed that the UK would take on the presidency of the G20 in 2009. As it turned out, that proved to be a momentous decision. Not to have gone would have caused offence, and someone was bound to ask what had kept me in London. I flew down to Cape Town on the Friday night, arriving as a spectacular dawn broke over South Africa. I attended a meeting where we discussed the developing economic crisis, and my fellow finance ministers were consoling over Northern Rock. Little did they know that awaiting me at home was another calamity, this time affecting 25 million people.

I was very conscious that the story could be leaked at any time. So many people had to know what had happened. Desperately anxious to get home, eight hours after my arrival in Cape Town I was back on the overnight flight to London. It was a long way to go for lunch.

Scanning the Sunday papers, I discovered that there was still no news on the story. Given the leaky nature of government, that was in many ways amazing. It was a huge relief to me, because I thought the only way we could get through this was if I told the House of Commons first. Over the years, as a minister in various departments, I have attached huge importance to telling MPs what has happened when there's a problem, and to being as straightforward as I can. I have never understood the reluctance of some ministers to go to the House of Commons, or, especially in our early days, to attempt to bypass it when we had something to say. The House is one of the most well-established, well-known public platforms in the world. We should use it, out of respect to our fellow MPs, who represent the people of this country. Even government ministers are MPs, which is not the case in many other countries. And twenty years in politics has taught me that when ministers lose the respect of Parliament, their days are numbered.

I was due to make the statement at the normal allotted time of 3.30 p.m. As I was about to leave my office in the Treasury for the short drive to the Commons, I passed a television screen tuned to Sky News. There they were, the crucial details, being systematically leaked. I was furious. How had this happened? Earlier that day I had briefed George Osborne for the Conservatives and Vince Cable for the Liberal Democrats, on a confidential basis. I expected them to maintain that confidence and remain silent until after my statement to the House. Equally, it could have come from within government. It was a political story and had to have come from a political source.

In the event, the mood in the House of Commons was pretty understanding, although the media was not. The *Daily Mail* discovered that the discs had been compiled in a building I had opened seven years earlier, as Secretary of State for Social Security. The plaque commemorating the happy event was still prominently displayed at the front door. But the real problem was that in people's minds the episode called into question the government's competence. Stories started to appear about the loss of sensitive data all over government: laptops left on trains; papers left in pubs; mobile phones found in toilets; data dispatched from one office never to arrive at another.

The discs never were found. The organization within HMRC meant that it was far from clear who was responsible. There remains to this day no evidence that the information fell into the wrong hands. My guess is that the discs were destroyed once it was clear that the hunt was on, possibly within days.

All of this, though, further darkened the public mood. Nor did it help that the banking crisis was getting worse and the wider economy was bound to start feeling the pain. Our immediate problem was what to do with Northern Rock. It was having to borrow more and more money from the Bank of England every day in order to survive. Its borrowing eventually peaked at more than £25 billion. I sleep easily at night, but this escalating figure was the stuff of nightmares.

Although the borrowing was steadily reduced over the following three years, it was far from clear then that we would ever get it back. There was an additional problem too. Northern Rock was still owned by its shareholders, many of them people of modest means living in the north-east of England who had acquired shares when it gave up mutual status to become a public company. There was also a more unpleasant group of shareholders who had bought in after the bail-out in the hope of making a killing out of the British government. This meant that we had to watch our legal position. These people did eventually sue, after we had nationalized the bank, despite the fact that they had bought in in full knowledge of the trouble the bank was in. They were speculators who deservedly got burned.

At the time, we felt that we would have to continue to seek a buyer for Northern Rock. People understandably ask why we did not nationalize the bank then and there; why did we wait until February of the following year? The answer is twofold. Firstly, we were concerned about legal action by shareholders. They still owned the bank. Secondly, we were worried about the whole issue of nationalization. Then it was a highly controversial proposition. The Labour Party had in the past held the belief that the state should own key sectors of the economy. In the 1970s, for example, there had been a political dogfight between the Conservatives and Labour over whether shipbuilding should continue to be run as a state industry.

New Labour was very much built on the proposition that in a modern economy there is a limit to what the state needs to own. We certainly believed that there were some things the state could and should do, which markets could not. Owning the banks, however, once the battle-cry of the left, was anathema to New Labour. Put simply, I did not want to nationalize a bank if it could be avoided. Nationalization had to be an option for us, but, as I told the House of Commons throughout that autumn, only one of last resort. In fact, plans and draft legislation to enable us to nationalize Northern Rock were being drawn up from October 2007. The main focus, though, was still on trying to sell the bank. The obvious solution would have been to persuade a group of banks to form a consortium to buy up Northern Rock. I spoke to Stephen Green, then chairman of HSBC, whose advice and judgement I valued. He said he would ask his colleagues, but he was not optimistic. It simply was not in their commercial interest, he said.

I reminded him that his colleagues had repeatedly told me that nationalization was an abomination to them, that some had said it was a return to communism. I said that in France there always seemed to be a willingness to act *pour la France* when the call came. The problem in the UK was that the big banks might have their brass plates here in London, but their souls, if banks have such things, and certainly their shareholders, were elsewhere. Stephen was one of Britain's more enlightened bank bosses and immensely helpful over the next couple of years. What he was telling me was a simple truth. In the old days the big banks saw themselves as British banks, albeit with huge operations overseas. Essentially, they were British and could be persuaded to do things that might be said to be in the national interest. But now they were not going to help me with a small rotten bank. How ironic that twelve months later they would view the British government in a very different light, when they came to us cap in hand.

There were three prospective buyers in the mix at that stage. Two were private equity funds. The third was Virgin Money. I had met Richard Branson many times when I was Transport Secretary, since he operates Britain's west-coast railways and an airline. Charismatic, ceaselessly energetic, and understandably very jealous of his brand, he was keen to get into banking and thought he could make a go of it. For our part, transferring Northern Rock to a brand that was publicly known might have helped restore confidence. But the taxpayer would only have seen a share of the private sector's return if the value of the business had reached at least £2.7 billion. The big problem was that all three bids meant we would have to put in a lot of public money upfront. If there were losses, we would have to take them. If there were profits, we wouldn't see them. I could not justify it. The process took weeks to work through, but just before Christmas I reached the conclusion that we would probably have to nationalize the bank in order to protect public money.

The situation was deteriorating. Before the House of Commons rose in December, we had to draw up contingency plans for a recall between Christmas and New Year if there were to be another run on a bank. I thought it unlikely, but we had to be prepared. My preference was to get agreement from Gordon over the Christmas break and, on the assumption the bids would come to nothing, to nationalize Northern Rock in January.

In the meantime, it was becoming clearer by the day that this was no ordinary credit crunch. The fundamental problem was that the banks had woken up to the fact that they were sitting on billions of pounds of what they had thought were valuable assets but were, in fact, worth considerably less than what they had paid for them – if, indeed, they were worth anything at all. There was a growing realization that most banks owned this toxic stuff, but they did not know how much was owned by each individual bank. Only a handful of people understood what was happening, and that did not seem to include the senior executives of the banks. This was not just a British problem: it was a huge problem in the US, as we were to discover over the next twelve months, and in Europe, where many believe the problem still remains three years later.

In autumn 2007 it was believed that once the banks presented their annual results, in the first few months of the new year, everything would become clear. Even if there were some inevitable losses and write-downs, confidence would be restored. However, in a rapidly deteriorating economy, an asset that was worth something one day might be worth nothing just a few months later. Trying to put a value even on something you could see, like a commercial office block, was becoming increasingly difficult. Trying to value a complex financial instrument that few people understood was virtually impossible, especially when no one wanted to buy it. The result of all this uncertainty was that the banks were finding it harder to lend to each other. Worse, this meant they were less able to lend to ordinary people.

I was convinced that we needed to get more money into the economy to free up lending, because without it the system would freeze. The obvious way to do this was through the Bank of England. I had many discussions with the Governor about this, but he seemed to be reluctant to do what I thought was needed. He had some perfectly reasonable arguments: how do you make sure the money ends up where it's needed? He was also worried about inflation. Frankly, at that time, with a recession looming, domestically generated inflation was simply not a problem.

Mervyn's analysis was that the underlying problem was that banks did not hold enough capital. In that he was right. But he did not accept that there was a second problem, a much more immediate one, which was lack of liquidity – that is, the banks' reluctance to lend to one another. That was what had happened with Northern Rock and I did not want it to happen to another bank, let alone to the banking system as a whole.

Mervyn argued that, because the problem was lack of capital, if we were to intervene we would be letting them off the hook. This was the doctrine of moral hazard. He had very strong and fixed views about the role of a central bank. So, while the European Central Bank (ECB) and the US Federal Reserve saw their role as being to boost liquidity in markets when needed, Mervyn favoured a far narrower approach, focused on setting interest rates and funding routine market operations – where the Bank of England makes available relatively small amounts of money, secured against a bank's assets. These operations rarely attract public attention. In August 2007, just before the collapse of Northern Rock, it was reported that Barclays had borrowed overnight from the Bank. They had done this to cover one day's trading and to square off the books – a routine operation. This was seized on as part of a growing frenzy, when in fact it was an entirely normal and prudent step to take.

I agreed with the Governor that capital was a problem. But I could see that unless we got money into the system we ran the risk of further bank failures. The Bank was slow to recognize the nature of the crisis. The underlying problem may have been lack of capital, but the immediate cause was lack of liquidity. Moreover if a liquidity problem remains untreated, it has a tendency to make a problem with solvency worse. It was not a choice of which one to deal with: we had to deal with both. I was so desperate that I asked the Treasury to advise me as to whether or not we could order the Bank to take action. The answer was that it might be legally possible, but that there would be wider implications of such an action. We had set great store by making the Bank independent and a public row between myself and Mervyn would have been disastrous, particularly at this time.

Shortly before Christmas, Mervyn and I met at No. 11 to review the past few months. He told me that he now recognized that a number of banks had a real problem with lack of liquidity, that it wasn't just the lack of capital that was the problem and that one way or another more money needed to be put into the system. He regretted not having confronted these issues before. In the end, as a result of a US initiative, the ECB, the Swiss and the Japanese, together with the Bank of England, did put more money into their economies – in the UK to the tune of about £10 billion.

There was a further development at the end of the year which confirmed in my mind that if 2007 had been bad, the new year would be worse. On a Saturday morning, just before Christmas, I answered the door at home in Edinburgh. There on the doorstep was Sir Fred Goodwin, chief executive of RBS, holding a gift-wrapped panettone.

3 A Home Visit from the Bank Manager

Edinburgh is my home. I have lived most of my life in the city which has been home to banks, insurance companies and other financial institutions since the Scottish Enlightenment. Political economy was born here, in the visionary works of Adam Smith and when thinkers such as David Hume were exploring theories of morality. It has been a long debate.

As the newly elected Labour MP for Edinburgh Central in 1987, I was already well aware of how important the financial services industry was to the city's well-being. Bank of Scotland (now HBOS) and RBS had their headquarters in the city. Scottish Widows and Standard Life, Europe's biggest mutual insurer, are based here. My grandfather started his working life as a clerk in 1908 earning £10 a year, before moving on to Standard Life.

The skyline of the city centre is dominated by the castle on its rock and the grand central dome of the old Bank of Scotland. It looks down from the Mound, a man-made hill created with earth dug from the city's Georgian New Town development and vast tips of rubbish dumped by residents of the medieval Old Town. Founded in 1695, Bank of Scotland predates RBS, which was set up in 1727. The rivalry between the two banks was always been less than friendly and they spent the next hundred years or so trying to bankrupt each other.

RBS's original head office, a splendid Palladian mansion on St Andrew Square, was built at a time when Edinburgh was a centre of government, law, commerce and culture. The founders did not stint on rich ornamentation. A great banking hall, the Telling Room, features a domed roof studded with gold, star-shaped windows. Three centuries on, at the height of its dominance in the world banking sector, the autocratic Sir Fred Goodwin and his fellow executives decided they had outgrown the historic centre. The new RBS headquarters, ironically, is built on the site of a former asylum, at Gogarburn on the edge of the city. It is a splendid contemporary building, designed for a bank with global ambitions, built around a mock high street with all the modern conveniences – coffee shops, chemists, florists, a hair stylist. At the western end are large offices with dramatic views over the Pentland Hills surrounding the city. The management suite, featuring the most palatial offices of all, was out of bounds to more junior staff. When it opened this £350 million campus, RBS bestrode the international banking scene. The expansion of commercial and retail banks into investment banking was the fashion, and it was a leader. Yet by February 2009, it would post a loss of £24 billion, the biggest loss in UK corporate history. It is a shame that its headquarters – a virtual city – now seems like a monument to its hubris, a testament to all that was wrong at this once modest and careful Scottish bank. When the crisis threatened, I was acutely conscious of what it would mean to the city and its people. The banks employ thousands of people, and many others, in the professions, in the service sector of shops and restaurants and the taxi trade, depend on them.

By international standards, Edinburgh is a small city and large numbers of its citizens continue to live in its heart, part of its living history. It tends to be socially stratified. I would often meet the city's bankers in the airport lounge on my weekly commute to Westminster more often than I ever would socially. Now I was about to entertain one of the key figures of the banking world, in my home, on a Saturday morning.

Sir Fred Goodwin then lived about a mile away from me, in the south side of the city. He was an awkward person, clearly very driven, but always warily on edge. At the official ceremony, when the Queen opened the new RBS headquarters at Gogarburn, he was in his element. But, like most senior bankers, who recognize that schmoozing goes with the job, he generally remained aloof on social occasions. It was as if he was there because he had to be. He was not going to enjoy it; it was a matter of duty under duress.

I also remembered attending a meeting of the directors of RBS a few years earlier to hear an economic presentation when I was Scottish Secretary. What struck me was not so much Fred, who as ever wasn't giving much away, but that this was a remarkably Edinburgh-centric board for an organization that was rapidly on the way to becoming one of the world's largest banks. Where was the American? Or an expert on the Far East?

Fred Goodwin's office had contacted me a few days earlier and said he'd like to meet up. Although it would mean not having my private secretary with me, I felt entirely relaxed about seeing him alone, at home. I was also intrigued. I had seen other CEOs of the banks alone in the past – none of this was abnormal – but I knew that his asking to see me in private could only mean that he was worried about something.

I could see that he was exceedingly tense. Fred doesn't do small talk and so we sat down and got straight to the point. I could see him becoming increasingly anxious, although this wasn't new – I'd noted that the more I spoke to bankers around this time, the more anxious they became. His message for me was clear: unless the Bank of England put more liquidity into the system, quickly, it would seize up, inevitably leading to another bank failure. By now, the Federal Reserve and the ECB had been flooding their systems with cash. I knew that there had been a meeting between the CEOs of the banks and Mervyn King earlier that month, at which they'd asked him to take the same action. They felt that they'd received in return a lecture on moral hazard – one with which I was by that time all too familiar. Fred emphasized that by this point they were beyond considerations of moral hazard. Mervyn was continuing to insist that it wasn't the job of the central bank to assist banks in their continued profligacy, but that merely underlined the fact that he didn't recognize the scale of the problem. The collective view of the banks was that whatever the Bank was doing, it simply wasn't enough. I wondered whether the timing of Fred's visit had something to do with the fact that the banks' annual reporting in February and March would reveal the extent of their exposure to toxic assets.

I had a great deal of sympathy with what Fred Goodwin was saying, but I asked the question: why were the markets singling out RBS for particular concern? His answer was that they felt that RBS didn't have sufficient capital. I asked whether he was comfortable that RBS did have sufficient capital, and his response was that he felt that it did. And yet I was worried. It occurred to me that Sir Fred had not come just as a shop steward for his colleagues. He would not admit it, but I sensed that RBS, which until that time had seemed invincible, its directors and senior staff exuding confidence verging on arrogance, was in more trouble than we had thought.

Our conversation was further evidence to me of just how poor was the relationship between the Bank of England and Britain's largest banks. Part of the problem was that in the ten years since we had given the Bank its independence, the Governor's contacts with the chief executives and chairmen of the London banks had become less frequent and somewhat distant. The essential day-to-day contact, to feel the pulse and sense the ever-changing mood of these unwieldy corporate entities, was just not there. It is an essential part of the Governor's role to understand what is going on, but it is not something that can be written into legislation, and I suspect that the Bank considered it to be the job of the FSA. In particular, by the autumn of 2007, I was being told time and again by bank chief executives that the Bank simply did not understand the nature of the problem they were facing, which was lack of liquidity.

Things had been different in the days when Sir Eddie George was Governor of the Bank. He was a man who knew the markets intimately. When I first met him, in the late 1980s, he was sitting at a desk surrounded by screens showing every blip of global share movements, which you could just about make out through a fug of cigarette smoke. I liked Eddie. We worked closely in the summer of 1997, drawing up the legislation to give the Bank operational independence. Relations between Eddie and Gordon had become somewhat strained when Eddie discovered that the Bank was no longer to have responsibility for day-to-day supervision of the banks, which would fall within the remit of the FSA. It suited both of them to let me deal with the mass of detail to get the new legislation on to the statute book. I last saw Eddie at a City dinner about a year before he died. Since then, I have often wondered how he would have handled the banking crisis had he still been Governor. Relationships matter in all walks of life, and the lack of relationship between Mervyn King and the bankers had become a real problem. I guessed that was what had brought Sir Fred to my door.

Seven years earlier, when RBS acquired its much larger rival, NatWest, this latest and largest of mergers reduced the number of British super-banks to four. There was much celebration within RBS, since not only had it seen off its rival, Bank of Scotland, but it had acquired a giant of the British banking scene. RBS, dazzled by its new prestige and power in the banking world, moved in for the next big acquisition. It was this that was to prove fatal. The deal to buy the Dutch bank ABN AMRO had been closed earlier in 2007. Initially, Barclays had gone after it. Just as they had done seven years earlier, when Bank of Scotland went after NatWest, RBS then joined the chase. Barclays pulled out after several weeks of intense bidding and counter-bidding and RBS, along with a consortium of foreign banks, bought large parts of the Dutch bank.

Now, as we sat talking, I asked Sir Fred why RBS had continued to pursue ABN AMRO when the general sentiment had been that it was not worth anything like what they had paid for it. He outlined what he believed to be the advantages to RBS of having an even greater global reach. He accepted that in any takeover there would be bad as well as good once you opened the books. I remember thinking that it was rather like a car-boot sale. You see a box with some goodies at the top and you accept that beneath them there will be some absolute junk. As it turned out, ABN AMRO was stuffed full of junk. There had been no opportunity to carry out a thorough examination of its assets, good or bad. It is quite common when you get a contested takeover with two or more bidders that there is an element of blind bidding. But once Barclays had withdrawn and RBS was the only bidder left there had still seemed to have been no full examination of the books.

I asked Sir Fred again why the markets were so unhappy. Once more, he stressed that they did not believe RBS had enough capital. He went on to repeat that he did not believe this to be the case. But I wondered: markets can be irrational, but they can also be right. At that stage, none of the authorities believed that RBS was in a precarious position. It seemed that they were simply experiencing the same turbulence as everyone else. I was concerned, however. This was no casual conversation. After Sir Fred had set off back into the cold winter air, I rang my private secretary and told him that we should start worrying seriously about RBS and the other big banks. I had no specific inside information but the conversation had left me feeling deeply uneasy. If RBS, the largest bank in the world, could be in trouble, what about the others?

In early January, when I got back to Downing Street on a Sunday night, I went round to Gordon's flat to discuss what we should do about Northern Rock. We were concerned about the urgent need to regain the political initiative that had been so badly lost in the autumn. Neither Gordon nor I wanted to end up owning the bank. It was not just the political difficulty of a Labour government nationalizing a bank, there was also a practical problem. Public ownership would mean that we, the owners of the bank, would be held responsible for everything it did. A decision to refuse a loan could all too easily become a minis-terial decision. We had already spent a great deal of public money on Northern Rock and we were anxious to get it back as soon as we could. We were also conscious that Northern Rock shareholders would be ready to cry foul if we nationalized the bank without having estab-lished beyond doubt that there was no market solution.

All the prospective purchasers wanted the government to take too much of the risk if things went wrong. Lloyds, back on the scene, want-ed the government to nationalize Northern Rock and then sell it on to them on the same day. That would have left the government with all the liabilities, and the risk of litigation from shareholders, while Lloyds received the value of the asset. Ironically, Bradford and Bingley, which was to collapse nine months later, looked the most promising bidder. But the FSA ruled it out because there were worries – correctly, as it turned out – that they did not have enough capital. HBOS wanted to buy the deposits but it did not want the branches. It wanted the cash because it was increasingly desperate – it too would soon be on the ropes. But if we had allowed that to happen we would have had to make thousands of people redundant at Northern Rock. There was also an idea the Treasury came up with: to provide, effectively, backstop insur-ance to a prospective buyer so that if conditions deteriorated further they would have some cover. In short, we had continued to look careful-ly at every possibility while still leaving nationalization on the table.

When I went across to see Gordon in the flat that evening, I told him that nationalization was looking increasingly likely. The other options were fraught with difficulties which I thought would be impossible to resolve. We were committed to exploring them, but I was not optimis-tic. Gordon said he could see the force of the argument but, like me, could also see the political watershed we faced. It would hark back to the wilderness years, when Labour appeared unelectable. Often now overlooked, in the narrow vision of instant history, is the fact that it was Gordon, alongside Tony, who in the early 1990s devised the fresh economic policies for a new political age. Would it be seen as the death of New Labour? We were both in a very bleak frame of mind, that early January. Although at that stage there was no sign of recession, it was clear that the economy was slowing very rapidly and all the problems that would bring were on the horizon.

We had several more meetings that month. We wanted to get a private sector solution if we could, but I was anxious that we should have a plan in place if we could not. It was increasingly clear that the price demanded by the private sector would be too high. Their attitude was hardly surprising: in January 2008, buying a bank without any subsidy or indemnity looked increasingly like an act of madness, and by the end of the month it was evident that there would be no bid that did not leave the taxpayer with all the downside risks and precious little on the upside. I was in no doubt about just how difficult the politics of nationalization would be; it would be only too easy for the Tories to say that this was evidence of the fact that we hadn't changed from the days of Clause 4 of the Labour Party constitution which committed us to public ownership of key sectors of the economy. Gordon was probably more reluctant than I was to call it a day. But he could see that the private sector solution did not stack up. Nationalization was the only answer.

This time we were careful to put in place a proper plan and it was two weeks before we could sign it off. Once it was signed off, for legal reasons it had to be done very quickly and announced to the public. This was, after all, a public company with traded shares. We decided that we would announce the nationalization on Sunday, 13 February. We chose a Sunday because we wanted the news to sink in when the markets were closed and the branch doors shut. Staff would have to be told that they should turn up for work the next day, and that they would be paid. We did not want scare stories on television which might lead to queues forming again. It also helped that we had put together over the previous few weeks a first-class management team, led by Ron Sandler, who had successfully turned around Lloyds of London, one of the oldest and most famous names in the insurance world, when it was in turmoil in the 1980s. All of this planning meant that we could stress that it would be business as usual on Monday morning.

I spent all of Saturday in the Treasury, drafting a statement for the following day's news conference. Preparing such statements takes hours, as each word and sentence is analysed again and again. Detail matters: how I looked at the news conference, my demeanour, what the backdrop should be – irritating maybe, but appearance is key. The Treasury still has pictures of Norman Lamont doing a hastily arranged press conference at the end of Black Wednesday in 1992. He was standing beside two very large dustbins.

The news conference went well, all things considered. Perhaps it was helped by the calming background set, in which I stood bathed in soothing, soft, lavender light. The market reaction the next morning was far more positive than we could have dared to hope. My statement to the House of Commons on the Monday afternoon was also well received. Making a statement to the House remains a vital part of our political process. The detailed preparation involves mastering every minor detail and takes a lot of time. Only a fool would wing it. It's true to say that during my time as Chancellor I had to make more than my fair share of Commons statements.

After the pre-Budget report of the previous autumn, my statement on the missing tax discs, and numerous emergency statements on Northern Rock, I felt that this time we were on the front foot. It worked because we were decisive and in control. For me, it was a turning point. For the first time since the financial crisis had erupted, I felt confident and in command of events. It also seemed to mark a turning point in the party's political fortunes, though sadly that was short-lived.

Hindsight is a wonderful thing and looking back we should perhaps have made the decision earlier, before Christmas; but we were operating in uncharted waters. We had shareholders to deal with who were ready to sue if we got anything wrong. And when we did finally announce the nationalization, far from confidence collapsing there was a palpable sense of relief. If we had done it in the autumn of 2007, it would have been hugely controversial with the public in general and in the City; now only the Conservative Party remained against it. Their response was ludicrous: 'We will vote against nationalization but will not use every procedural parliamentary device to obstruct it,' George Osborne declared at an emergency news conference with David Cameron. He went on to complain that we were planning to take powers that would allow ministers to nationalize any financial institution at any time. It is just as well we did. Without those powers we would never have been able to deal with Bradford and Bingley later that year. Nor with the Dunfermline Building Society the year after.

The legislation had to be rushed through Parliament over the next three days. Our MPs were in good spirits despite the late-night sittings. So too were our members in the House of Lords. I was grabbing a bite to eat in the Commons dining room late one night when a very elderly Labour lord came over to the table. He had been an MP when Clement Attlee was Prime Minister in 1945, and he said I had just made his day. He had waited all his life to nationalize a bank and now he was doing it.

Northern Rock was about to embark on a long, slow process of recovery. Two years later, in the spring of 2009, I visited its headquarters in Newcastle. Talking to the staff at all levels, I was struck by the pride they still felt in the bank. Talk to anyone in the north-east of England and there is a sense that Northern Rock is their bank. It is a region where the private sector is hugely under-represented, and I believe that saving Northern Rock made a positive contribution to the north-east's economy. Three years later, it is now being prepared for sale. At the time, our critics said we might be stuck with it for years. The nationalization worked.

There was another big decision to be made early in 2008. Mervyn King's first term as Governor of the Bank of England was due to expire in June. Governors can serve two five-year terms. The thinking is that this gives them long enough to make decisions independent of government interference, but avoids the problem that occurred in the 1920s and 1930s when Governors seemed to go on and on, to the chagrin of Chancellors of whatever political hue. Not to appoint a Governor to a second term would be seen as remarkable, since the assumption is that he or she will serve two terms. I wanted to avoid leaving the decision to the last minute, as that would reflect badly on us as a government and would undermine the Governor as speculation grew. Normally, there would have been no doubt in my mind. But the strains between myself and Mervyn over Northern Rock and over how we should deal with the difficulties in the banking system worried me deeply. Once a Governor has been appointed for a second and final term he or she is in a much stronger position, more or less untouchable. Above all, I was still concerned that Mervyn had no relationship with the people he needed most to talk to: the bankers.

Mervyn's track record on the monetary side of the Bank was thought to be good, bringing intellectual rigour to the Monetary Policy Committee, although some believed it had been too slow to raise interest rates as the economy began to overheat, and too slow to cut them in 2007 when the downturn came. For me, the test was straightforward. Was there a better candidate? The short answer: no, there wasn't. Despite our ups and downs, I felt I could work with Mervyn, although there were times over the next couple of years when he could see that the political sands were shifting and felt able to make pronouncements that I thought came far too close to criticizing government policy and appearing to side with the Tories. This became a real problem in the run-up to the general election of 2010 and, indeed, in the months that followed.

I told Gordon my view, that Mervyn should stay, and with some reluctance he acquiesced. I don't think that he and Mervyn ever got on. Certainly the next two and a half years saw a growing antipathy between them. This really came to a head during the Treasury select committee hearings in 2009, when Mervyn appeared unilaterally to announce that there was no more money available for fiscal stimulus. Gordon quite rightly felt that this was crossing a line, that he was addressing fiscal policy, which was the remit of government. Certainly Mervyn would have been furious if Gordon or I had expressed an opinion on what the Bank ought to be doing over monetary policy. Gordon was very angry and tried to phone me during the committee session, which I was watching from the Treasury. He asked me what I was going to do about it and suggested I should go in and stop him there and then. It was tempting, but not practical.

Mervyn and I met and I told him that we proposed to reappoint him, but I emphasized the need for us to understand better what was going on in the banking system. It wasn't that the bankers were right, far from it. It was that we needed a far tighter grip on what they were up to. He agreed that there was a need to do this, and that perhaps he had neglected that area in the past. There were some good people in the Bank – Paul Tucker, for instance, who subsequently became a Deputy Governor – and I felt that they should be given their head more often. The core problem with the Bank is the way it is run as an autocratic fiefdom of the Governor, which is anachronistic. This was a problem I would return to time and again, as we developed proposals to reform Bank governance and accommodate a far wider range of views in the decision-making process. Was reappointing Mervyn King the right decision? Yes. I would have needed a lot of convincing that he should be denied a second term.

Meanwhile, I had somehow to shave off time in my diary to work on the 2008 Budget: not an easy feat, because it was crammed full of meetings, briefings and events from breakfast through to bedtime. Although all my senses told me things were getting worse, the Treasury figures were still better than I expected. There was a tremendous fear of a downturn, but it was not yet manifest. Preparing a Budget is a laborious process stretching over several months. Trying to do it against a deteriorating economic background makes it all the more fraught. After the mess that was the pre-Budget report, I wanted my first Budget to reflect more of my nature and judgement. That didn't quite happen.

This was not a time for announcing new spending initiatives. However, a Budget is also a political event. It is the big occasion when the Chancellor can set out a political direction, something Gordon had done to good effect for most of the ten years he held the post. In the years since 2008, a myth has been perpetuated that the economy was bust before the financial crisis, and not because of it. In fact, in 2007, the year before the crash, our economy grew by 3 per cent, which was the fastest growth of any major economy. Borrowing averaged 3.4 per cent of national income between 1979 and 1997. Between 1997 and 2007 it averaged just 1.2 per cent. Debt, which was 43.3 per cent of national income in 1997, had fallen to 36.6 per cent ten years later. In addition to this, unemployment was at a lower level than in Germany, France or Italy. So the picture was far better than the Conservative and Liberal Democrat doomsayers claimed after the general election of 2010. The problem was that it had been assumed that tax receipts would continue to flow in from the financial sector.

Looking at the preparations for my first Budget in 2008, borrowing was £1.4 billion lower than I had forecast in the pre-Budget report the previous October. The structural deficit was small by international standards, at 2.3 per cent of growth, 0.4 per cent of current spending. The basis on which I made my Budget forecasts was therefore not at all unreasonable. Moreover, I told the House of Commons in my Budget speech that our economy would continue to grow, a view supported by the Bank of England, the IMF and the Organisation for Economic Co-operation and Development (OECD). What this shows, of course, is that at the time no one realized just how far economic conditions would decline during the course of that year – me included. It was only following the collapse of the American bank Bear Stearns, immediately after the Budget, that the economic outlook darkened significantly.

So the background to this Budget was that we had a strong economy. It was the only major economy not to have seen any break in growth in the previous decade. There was still a lot of uncertainty, however, and I expected growth to be lower than forecast in the pre-Budget report of the year before.

Most people pay scant attention to growth forecasts in the good times. In a downturn, they are scrutinized not only because they give some clue as to what the Treasury thinks will happen; they also determine the assumptions the government makes about how much money it will get in through taxes. The gap between what the government gets in and what it spends determines how much it will need to borrow, and what that will mean for the country's overall level of debt. Especially at a time when trust in politicians is in short supply, the growth forecast must be credible. That said, forecasting is a best estimate, not an exact science; rather like forecasting the weather, it will probably be only approximately right but almost certainly precisely wrong. The Bank of England publishes its forecasts in the shape of a fan with a range of possibilities. That way, the forecast is almost certainly going to be right over some part of the range. The Bank leaves itself the kind of room for manoeuvre that the government does not have.

Trying to calculate what is 'structural' in the deficit and what is temporary can take years to work out. This is because the independent Office for National Statistics continually revises its figures as more information becomes available. Its judgement about what actually happened in the economy over a particular period is subject to change. For example, when Britain came out of the recession at the end of 2009, the first estimate by the ONS showed very modest growth, of 0.1 per cent. By 2011, two years and a general election later, the ONS had revised the figure upwards to 0.5 per cent – not massive, but very significant in economic and political terms.

Because the growth figures decide how much can be spent on things like schools and hospitals, it really does matter what judgement you reach, and it has to be based on your best guess as to what is happening in the economy. Put simply, if you are too cautious you can crash the economy by taking too much out in the way of taxes or spending cuts. Travel too far in the other direction and you will end up with increased borrowing, which in turn translates into higher levels of debt, all of which has to be paid for.

The forecast figures were to be a point of contention between myself and Gordon at every Budget and pre-Budget report until the end of 2009. He thought I was being far too pessimistic. Certainly during 2008, he was far more optimistic that we were about to see a recovery. In fact, throughout my time as Chancellor, Gordon felt that the Treasury was too pessimistic and was stymying our ability to manoeuvre. The Treasury is financially conservative, that's their job, but it's important to remember that Gordon had been Chancellor during ten years of fair weather – although, even during the good times he felt they were too conservative.

It is true that, left to its own devices, the Treasury will always err on the side of pessimism and caution. It is equally true that you cannot publish forecasts that fit with a story you want to tell, taking account of policies yet to be introduced. My judgement was that it was better to be cautious and to be able to announce that things had improved at a later Budget, rather than announce something that was clearly far too optimistic, only to have to downgrade the forecast at a later date.

You can't wash your hands of the need to make a judgement. I supported the setting up in 2010 by the new government of the new Office for Budget Responsibility (OBR), which is independent of the Chancellor of the day. I had considered such a move in the autumn of 2008, when it was clear that our economic forecasts were going to be very wrong, mainly because of the banking crisis. I was looking for ways to get some independent credibility into our forecasting. But as if to demonstrate how difficult forecasting is, the new OBR had to downgrade its own growth forecasts twice during its first ten months of operation. The Bank of England too has had to downgrade its forecasts for 2012. So too have the IMF and the OECD. This does not mean that they got it wrong, just that forecasting is a difficult task, especially at times of economic stress.

That said, my own forecasts for 2008 turned out to be too optimistic. During the late spring and summer of that year, I became more worried about our prospects. All the indicators were that the economy was slowing down fast. Every economist I spoke to outside the Treasury painted a gloomy picture. However, my view was not shared by Gordon. It was at this stage that it became increasingly apparent to me that he did not trust my judgement. He thought that I had become the prisoner of the doom merchants within the Treasury. I would gladly have listened to a more optimistic assessment, but I couldn't find one.

Gordon continually depended on the advice of those he had worked with for the past fifteen years, particularly Ed Balls. Ed had gone to work for Gordon when he was Shadow Chancellor. Ironically, I persuaded Ed not to leave Gordon very early on, when they hadn't been together long, and there had been a huge row over something now long forgotten. As we walked along Millbank, I encouraged him to stay on. He is a powerful intellectual force, though not always easy to work with. Gordon came to depend upon him for fiscal advice, and then increasingly for all things political. From 2006, Ed was in charge of the planning committee for the handover to Gordon, in the run-up to Tony's departure.

I had no problems with Ed until I became Chancellor; before that he was never hostile and usually very helpful. I know that he wanted to be Chancellor, but in the end Gordon made the call and picked me and that must have been difficult for Ed. He was hugely influential in developing our modern economic policy. At one point I was asked whether I would accept Ed as Chief Secretary to the Treasury while Gordon would retain him as a sort of chief of staff. I refused. That was clearly unworkable and it was obvious that Gordon would try to make him *de facto* Chancellor. Our relationship over the three years I was Chancellor was strained. Notes leaked to the *Daily Telegraph* in 2011 have shown me on a list, apparently prepared by Ed, of people who needed 'handling'. This suggests that, wherever I was slated for in 2006 as Gordon and Ed prepared for Gordon's premiership, it wasn't No. 11.

I did not mind competing views; in fact, I would have welcomed the opportunity to discuss matters. It would have been much better if we could have all sat down in the same room and discussed our differences. Life in government would have been less frenetic and more productive. But the opportunity rarely arose; Gordon would have one conversation with me, and then presumably another with Ed and his other key advisers. Another huge problem was that the people from whom Gordon was taking advice didn't have access to the data the Treasury had – once you're out of a department you lose the institutional knowledge within months – and Gordon himself didn't have details from the Treasury. The main point is that Gordon and I were reading the situation differently. He didn't agree that things were as bad as they seemed.

Increasingly, I found myself in what appeared to be a negotiation with people who were not in the room. The views of other Cabinet members were never sought, which was a mistake. Again, this was a legacy from our years in opposition and the process by which by 1997 our economic thinking had developed into a coherent and compelling policy. Prior to Gordon becoming Shadow Chancellor, economic policy had been developed by committee – hence the unaffordable spending pledges made during the 1992 election campaign, which compelled John Smith to make a manifesto commitment to increase National Insurance. Once in government, both Tony Blair and Gordon Brown were reluctant to consult with – or, indeed, to trust – their colleagues on key issues. Iraq, identity cards, tuition fees, the economy – all would have benefited from proper collective discussion. The Chancellor has to be responsible for economic affairs and the preparation of the Budget, but throughout 2008 and 2009 it would have been beneficial to have canvassed the opinions of Cabinet colleagues, at least as to general strategy. As it was, discussions about the Budget, its forecasts and its measures, were largely conducted between the two of us, with the decisions delayed while Gordon consulted elsewhere. It was often frustrating, sometimes infuriating.

Preparing the 2008 Budget became increasingly fraught. Rather than sitting down two months beforehand and deciding on the strategy we would follow, the whole thing was up in the air until days before it was delivered. This was the pattern we would return to over preparation for the following year's Budget, when the issues were by then much more acute and the tension between us strained to breaking point. In 2008 I decided I needed to raise more money. I did this by increasing alcohol and 'green' taxes. This enabled us to increase Child Benefit to £20 a week, a year earlier than planned, and also to increase the Child Tax Credit for families on low and middle incomes. That was to help the following year when recession began to bite. My view was that our economy and tax revenues had been propelled by a cheap and plentiful flow of credit, which was now drying up. To what extent this would hit the economy was not yet clear. I was in no doubt that the effect would be significant. I did not want to exacerbate the situation by taking action that might overcompensate.

At the time, we believed that the downturn might be short-lived. It was not until the summer of 2008 that I began to believe that the situation was far worse than even the most pessimistic commentators had thought earlier in the year. I wanted a low-key Budget, built around the need to provide some stability. In any Budget there are countless details that must be right, endless meetings with officials, and, of course, ministerial colleagues who want more money and, when they are rebuffed by the Chancellor, make the short trip next door to the Prime Minister. Spending money is always much easier than saving it.

The Budget was earlier than usual, on 12 March 2008, because Easter was early that year. The Budget is followed by a debate in the House of Commons, and sufficient parliamentary time has to be allowed between the Budget statement and the Easter recess. Had it been slightly later, it would have followed rather than preceded the collapse of Bear Stearns in the US on 14 March, which was to have a profound effect on confidence all over the world. Although not quite as bad as the pre-Budget report of October 2007, this Budget did not feel right to me. Again, it had been cobbled together in too much of a hurry, and it was badly received in the House of Commons. Looking back now, too much of it was a repetition of what had been announced before.

Budget Day in Britain has its own peculiar rituals. In the days leading up to it, the speech, which is about an hour long, has to be prepared. It takes longer to write than people might imagine. Every word matters, and every word has to be pored over. It is watched by millions, with a surprisingly large audience overseas. This time, because of the tense negotiations with No. 10, it was only finished the evening before it was delivered, and I was still working on it when it was time to attend another important tradition in the Budget timetable, my audience with Her Majesty the Queen.

This audience, which lasts about an hour, takes place in Buckingham Palace. Only the Queen and the Chancellor are present in her private sitting room. The Chancellor is there to present the Budget, but in practice the conversation ranges far wider. I remember reflecting on the fact that the Queen has seen out eighteen Chancellors since she ascended the throne in 1952. Her first was R.A.B. 'Rab' Butler. I wondered how many times she had listened to her Chancellor setting out how he proposed to recover from a difficult set of circumstances. Conversations with the Queen remain confidential. However, I have always been struck by how remarkably well informed she is on every subject that could conceivably be discussed. If only every minister were as diligent in dealing with their red boxes. Taking my leave, I walked out of the sitting-room door to be met by a long line of corgis waiting in the corridor for their evening audience.

Back at Downing Street, we worked on until midnight, when I went to bed. I left my special adviser, Catherine MacLeod, hunched over the computer in the back bedroom, still working on the Budget broadcast which was due to be filmed some five hours later. This ten-minute presentation by the Chancellor is broadcast on all channels on Budget Day.

If it goes well, very few will notice it. One mistake and everyone will know about it. It has to be recorded early in the morning because there is no time to do it later in the day. I got up at 5 a.m. to read over the broadcast speech. It could not fairly be called a rehearsal. I was still marking it up as I went downstairs in the lift to record it in the No. 11 study. The unfortunate television crew knew what to expect, being more experienced at Budget preparations than I was, when they turned up at No. 11 at the crack of dawn. Because they then know what is to be in the Budget, they have to be locked in the sitting room in No. 11 until after it has been delivered in the House that afternoon. They came armed with books and iPods and packets of sandwiches and, in one case, a pair of slippers.

After filming the obligatory television pictures for the lunchtime news, we had the traditional Cabinet meeting which is the first occasion on which colleagues would hear my assessment of the state of the economy, prospects for growth, and the Budget measures. The formality was somewhat undone by a visit from Sybil, our cat, who sauntered in and settled herself under the Cabinet table as I was about to speak. My colleagues listened politely for what would affect their departments, although in reality there had been discussions with them beforehand to prepare the ground. As we left the Cabinet Room, most wished me well, in the jolly, keep-up-your-spirits manner that I imagine people might adopt before someone is trundled off for life-or-death surgery.

I went back next door to No. 11 to prepare for the departure from behind the famous front door. Tradition dictates that the Chancellor should emerge holding up the red box in which ministers receive their homework papers at the end of the day. Gordon had, when he was Chancellor, used a box made by apprentices in his constituency. To me, that was his box. I opted to return to the old battered box first made for and used by Gladstone in the nineteenth century. It's shabby and the key has long been lost, but it is part of our history. It was disinterred from the old Cabinet War Rooms where it had been stored, along with a pair of white gloves with which it is supposed to be handled, but which I decided to forego.

It was only when an attendant opened the door and I walked out at precisely the appointed time to face the world's media that the reality kicked in. I suddenly thought, here I am on the way to present my first Budget – me, in a scene I had witnessed down the years since my childhood. Those few moments on the doorstep holding up the Budget box for the cameras felt interminable. The occasion felt all the more poignant because my mother had come down to watch me present the Budget. As we stood in the hall behind the door, she said: 'Your father would have loved to see this.' So he would.

Perhaps the most daunting part of it all was presenting the Budget in an hour-long speech to a packed House of Commons. I had spoken in the House on countless occasions and had never had a particularly bad time in the chamber. But I wasn't happy with the speech, and as I addressed the House I knew it could have been better, both in content and style. At one point, during a particularly tedious passage on the environment, I looked up at the visitors' gallery and saw Margaret with Calum and my mother, who appeared to be sleeping.

Returning to the Treasury, I did the traditional round of calls to newspaper and political editors. It is important to try to explain to them what you are attempting to do. I was in no doubt that they would focus on one thing: the growth figures. So it proved.

There was a sort of parallel universe in No. 11, an antidote to the world of bankers, big business and international grandees. Margaret does not stand on formality. When we moved in, she said she wanted to open the doors to people who might never think of visiting Downing Street. She was notoriously keen on scooping up groups of children visiting the street to have their photo taken and offering them impromptu tours. Once the No. 10 security staff had stopped being taken aback they were happily supportive. The grand No. 11 State Room, up a dingy staircase lined with drawings and cartoons of previous Chancellors, became the stately province of small charities, voluntary and community groups invited to hold receptions. They would find a sponsor to pay for refreshments, then invite their own guests, to raise their profile or celebrate their work.

There was only one member of the Treasury staff working in No. 11, as events organizer. The only rule was that guests had to include normal people, not just the great and the good. The only people Margaret does not much like are those with a sense of entitlement. My role was to put in an appearance and say hello. The receptions are organized a long time ahead, so the traffic of visitors carried on even at the height of the financial crisis, with two or three evening receptions a week as well as daily visits. The night before the bank rescue, a happy stream of Red Cross volunteers was leaving as I walked into the sitting room downstairs. Off once again to meet the bankers, the thought that an experienced first-aider might come in useful did cross my mind.

A bemused Egyptian finance minister and his entourage, who had swept in for a courtesy meeting, once watched the sitting-room door swing open and Margaret pass through with a wave and a line of young visitors in her wake, on their way to see the historic Soane Dining Room and to sit in the Chancellor's swivel chair in the study. Then, a week after the bank rescue, I was grilled in the downstairs sitting room by a young man from Scotland, called Alastair, who would have been studying economics but for the brain tumour that would take his life. He had raised thousands of pounds for the Teenage Cancer Trust and was interested in how best to invest it. I had to admit I couldn't help him there. No. 11 was a place to keep you grounded.

What was public space and what was private was never quite determined. The flat upstairs was more an oasis than a haven. It was hard to get home to Edinburgh because most weekends I needed to be in the Treasury. Instead, friends and family came to us. Their presence was a reminder that we had a life outside. They, in turn, enjoyed seeing the bedroom in which Winston Churchill had dictated his speeches to a typist sitting at the end of his bed, and the bath where Margaret Thatcher did her late-night thinking. The decor had not changed much. No, we would assure them, there is no butler and, yes, we do cook for ourselves. I don't know what kind of life people imagined we were leading, but being invited to stack the dishwasher after supper probably helped some of them feel more at home.

The weekend of the Northern Rock nationalization, ten friends, who had been close neighbours when our children were small, came down to London for the weekend on a long-arranged visit. We had supper in the flat on the Saturday evening, unwinding and catching up with news. There was a lot of laughter and I could hardly break up the party by explaining that, actually, I was a very, very important Chancellor with matters of state to attend to. They were, admittedly, surprised to see me make the public announcement the next day.

We did miss our children very much. Calum was a student at Aberdeen, an eight-hour train ride away, and Anna was on her gap year, travelling and working with street children in South Africa, before starting university in Glasgow. They did enjoy their visits to Downing Street, though. There was always something happening. One July afternoon, during the recess of 2008, a production team arrived to film scenes for *In the Loop*, a spin-off film from Armando Iannucci's inspired slant on government spin, *The Thick of It*, of which Calum and I are big fans. I arrived back in the flat to find 'Malcolm Tucker' sitting on the sofa, having a cup of tea with Calum and Margaret. I don't know who was more taken aback. Peter Capaldi, who plays the demented spin doctor, was also the star of one of my favourite films, *Local Hero*, but I managed not to ask for his autograph.

The Chancellor's Christmas party for children was a big event in the No. 11 social calendar. Each year different charities would bring in children who deserved a treat. A kind man, more used to organizing parties for celebrities and royalty, generously offered to give the place a festive facelift for the event. When I left in the morning, No. 11 was its usual drab self. By the time I came home, it was Santa's grotto; there was a full-sized sleigh with reindeer in the sitting room and a machine blowing fake snow in the hall. Peregrine Armstrong-Jones and his team had achieved the miracle of making No. 11 look cheerful. Officials coming to meetings didn't seem to mind sitting in between a row of jolly snowmen.

Margaret said that Calum and Anna and her friends could come but only if they were to be Santa's helpers. That meant Anna dressing up as an elf, and Calum not: he came as a Christmas tree instead. His embarrassment was nothing compared with mine when I went up to the flat to find a pantomime dame's outfit, complete with wig, laid out on our bed. David Walliams, of *Little Britain*, had kindly offered to come along to the party and brought his costume dresser with him. He was solicitous with the children, and very funny, but did not entirely convince one young guest who was peering closely at him: 'You're not a lady,' he announced.

'Who says?' David growled.

The photographers were delighted to catch the Chancellor chatting to a pantomime dame. 'Are you two married?' a small boy asked.

'Thinking about it,' David said.

'No, not even engaged,' I added quickly.

The pace of life as Chancellor was punctuated by these reminders that there is world away from the Treasury. Meeting people whose lives were not always easy, and for whom a visit to No. 11 was a chance to feel valued, was a good antidote to the daily crises. When there was time, we held gatherings in the Soane Dining Room with its beautiful vaulted ceiling and wooden walls. This was a chance for me to hear directly from people from across the economic spectrum and to find out what was happening. We tried to keep such meetings informal, so that guests could relax and I could hear directly from them what was happening to them.

There were some memorable evenings upstairs in the flat too, including an impromptu bagpipe performance in the kitchen for my private office staff just before my last Budget. They watched rapt

– or perhaps stunned – as the piper, a guest borrowed from a charity reception, marched around the flat playing a Hebridean lament. How appropriate. The neighbours did not complain, despite the unintended provocation.

4 'The Worst Downturn in 60 Years'

In March 2008, less than a month before its introduction, few people appeared to have turned their attention to the withdrawal of the 10p rate of tax. I had looked at the problem again, but couldn't see how I could deal with it then. It would have meant breaking the fiscal rules because we would have been borrowing too much. A couple of weeks later, though, on the eve of the House rising for Easter, it was clear that this was the next storm about to blow in.

The British parliamentary system means that ministers are answerable to Parliament, either in the House of Commons or, if the minister is a peer, the House of Lords. The relationship between ministers and their fellow MPs, those sitting on the back benches, is vital. And of particular importance is the relationship between ministers and their own party colleagues; if they lose their confidence, life becomes difficult, if not impossible.

Contact between ministers and their back-bench colleagues can happen in a number of ways. Formal meetings are comparatively rare. What is more common is that, because all MPs vote, usually on a nightly basis, in the Commons lobbies, this provides an opportunity for ministers to bump into colleagues, exchange a few words, either on something in particular or on general policy issues. It allows ministers to sense the mood of the party. I attached particular importance to visiting the members' tea room, a place where only MPs can go and where, during informal chats, a minister can be buttonholed by a back-bench MP. This is an important part of parliamentary life.

For some weeks in the run-up to the withdrawal of the 10p tax rate, MPs would approach me to flag up their concern about the change. The clamour began to rise as we approached the Easter recess. The closer we got to the start of the 2008 financial year, when the change would take effect, the louder the clamour became.

The Parliamentary Labour Party (PLP) meets every week. It is a chance for backbenchers to question ministers, and at the end of each term the Prime Minister attends to rally the troops. This time, the troops were extremely restive. Ever since Gordon had called off the election the previous October, my parliamentary colleagues had become increasingly unhappy with his leadership. Every political party becomes restless when it falls behind in the opinion polls, and especially so if they can't detect any strategy to get back on the front foot. Now, many of them were being besieged by complaints from constituents. One of the things that really upsets backbenchers is their own government taking action that brings irate voters to their surgeries. This is exactly what the imminent removal of the 10p tax rate was starting to do: MPs were returning to Westminster each week having found their surgeries and their constituency postbags full of angry complaints. Even worse, many of those who were about to lose out from the change were traditional Labour supporters. A number of colleagues had approached me in the division lobbies and in the corridors of the House to ask what was happening about the 10p rate. I acknowledged that there was a problem but that it would take some time to fix it. We simply didn't have the money to do so right now.

So there was not much to cheer them when they trooped into the PLP meeting to be addressed by their prime minister. The committee room in which this meeting takes place is like most in the House: dimly lit and gloomy at the best of times. It almost mimics the House itself, with two rows of benches facing one another. There aren't enough seats and so on important occasions it's very crowded. MPs crushed in and some were sitting on the floor. The mood was very tense. MP after MP – loyalists who would normally follow the government line – stood up to argue against the plan. I could see that Gordon was becoming increasingly agitated. He kept insisting that the MPs questioning him were wrong: no one would be worse off when the 10p rate was withdrawn. I do not know why he said this. He remained calm, but became more and more terse. Had he acknowledged the problem and promised to try and sort it out, it is possible that we might have avoided a crisis that severely damaged him and our government. As it was, for the first time I can remember, the party was in a position where it did not believe what it was being told by its Prime Minister. Under questioning, Gordon doggedly maintained that no one would lose out and that most people would gain. The low rumble of disbelieving voices began to swell. He told MPs to send him the letters of complaint from constituents. He would show them that they would not lose out.

Tony Lloyd, the chairman of the PLP, and I spoke afterwards to a number of colleagues who were astounded at Gordon's continued denial, because they'd seen the figures. Subsequently, some of our most loyal MPs tabled a motion for debate in the Commons, criticizing the move and calling for its reversal. I knew that this was a major political problem. Perhaps I should have bitten the bullet and spent another few billion pounds on fixing it. But, because we were still bound by the fiscal rules, there was no immediate room for manoeuvre.

Gordon's instinct was to try to hold the political line, and that there should be no damaging climb-down. It wasn't helped by the fact that the charge was being led by his old bête noire, Frank Field. They had a strong dislike for each other, which to a large extent stemmed from Frank's year as minister for welfare reform when we came into government in 1997. Gordon felt that Frank's reforms were unworkable and too expensive. Frank felt that he was stymied by Gordon at every turn. The problem for us now was that it was not just Frank rubbing Gordon up the wrong way, but most of the PLP and, increasingly, members of the Cabinet.

I spoke to my parliamentary private secretary, Ann Coffey, and asked what was the mood on the back-benches? Ann said it was a disaster; it could not be any worse. Gordon appeared to be denying that anyone would lose a single penny. Most backbenchers were openly saying that he did not understand the consequences of his own policy and was not willing to listen to them. If we could at least have persuaded MPs that we were listening, that we understood the difficulty and were prepared to find a solution, the political pressure would have eased. As it was, a growing number believed the door was firmly closed and were openly talking about voting against their own government on the Finance Bill.

We escaped London for the Easter break and went north to my mother's house on the Isle of Lewis. Normally this is the place where I relax and recharge. From the front door I can look out across a sea loch and a landscape that has not changed in thousands of years. There is nothing between the end of the house and Canada. It is a place where the colours of the sky and the shape of the sea change incessantly. The house was built by my great-grandfather on his croft more than 150 years ago. This Easter, though, it felt less than peaceful. Every news bulletin brought more reports of rebellion over the abolition of the 10p rate.

From the supermarket car park in Stornoway, I listened to Ed Miliband, then the Cabinet Office minister, bravely repeating the lines I had given him: we would keep this matter under review and if necessary bring forward measures to plug the gap in the autumn. He did a good job in the circumstances. It was not the performance that mattered, though, it was the message, and I knew it would not stick. It was inevitable that we would be defeated by our own side if it came to a vote in the House. Presumably the Tories, who had not said a word about it, would join in, as would the Liberal Democrats.

When we got back to London, I appeared on the Sunday morning political show hosted by Andrew Marr. He pressed me on the 10p problem. I held the line that we would return to it in the autumn. I said that there were losers and that I would see what I could do to compensate them. It was clear to me there was now a full-scale revolt, so I made it clear that whatever we did would involve backdated compensation to the beginning of the financial year. I did not want to have to present a mini-Budget to fix it if that could be avoided. It would be reminiscent of the problems faced by the Wilson government in the 1970s. Mini-Budgets suggest that good, orderly government is breaking down. Unfortunately it was.

It was not only the PLP who were in revolt. There was growing unrest within the Cabinet, not just about this issue but about the government's lack of direction and about Gordon's leadership. At the first Cabinet meeting after the Easter recess, Jack Straw passed me a note. Jack is a great survivor and sniffs the political wind. He represents Blackburn in Lancashire, where many people would lose out from the removal of the 10p rate. His note simply said: 'I think you need to sort this out.'

Gordon too was having second thoughts. The question was, what did we need to do? I felt it was important to give a message to the backbenchers. I was trying to walk a tightrope: I knew we would have to do something, but I did not want the political fallout from what would be portrayed as another climb-down. The damage caused by the election-that-never-was the previous autumn was very much on my mind. The more I talked to my colleagues, both inside and outside government, the more I realized that the option of holding out until the next big fiscal event, the pre-Budget report in the autumn, would not work. The Finance Bill had to be got through by the end of July. The important thing was to get across the message that we were listening and would make changes. Practically, it would have been difficult to do this in one-to-one meetings, and I wanted to avoid the formality of addressing the PLP as a whole. Instead, I convened a regular meeting of the back-bench Treasury committee, to which around seventy of my colleagues turned up. That in itself was a signal. Normally such meetings are attended by about a dozen MPs. It was a very civilized exchange, but I was left in no doubt about the strength of feeling. My Cabinet colleagues Harriet Harman, Geoff Hoon, James Purnell and David Miliband were shaking their heads in disbelief, increasingly despairing at the mess and at the level of Gordon's denial.

The chaotic atmosphere in No. 10 worsened. Gordon sent Jeremy Heywood, his Principal Private Secretary, to negotiate directly with Frank Field. I did not think this would achieve anything, since the enmity between Frank and Gordon was so great. What was needed was something that would remove the political sting and solve the real problem for those losing out. This would not be achieved by negotiating with someone who had his views certainly, but was hardly a shop steward for the back-benches. Gordon and I had frequent conversations about how to resolve the problem. In the first two weeks of May, we had a series of meetings, which also included Yvette Cooper, who was then Chief Secretary to the Treasury and had a good grasp of the detail. Looking at my notes, I see these meetings as symptomatic of the problem: instead of coming up with a solution, we covered the same ground over and over again.

Gordon wanted me to find a way to determine to what extent individuals had indeed lost out. This had a superficial attraction, since that way only those who really had lost out would be compensated. The obvious disadvantage was that we would have to means-test hundreds of thousands of people. My experience with the Department of Social Security told me this would be hopelessly impractical, taking months, if not years, to put in place, and even longer to pay out compensation. I believed we had to announce a general measure that would help most of those who had lost out. When we met on 7 May, we discussed providing some relief straight away, but Gordon wanted it to be for one year only and to be presented as an anti-recessionary measure. He too was concerned about spending money we didn't have. He argued that we should indicate that we would be prepared to spend, say, £500 to £600 million pounds in the autumn. I thought it would cost much more than that to fix the problem, and that we needed to act immediately.

Whether or not the compensation would last for more than one year was an issue I was prepared to leave open.

In the end, I concluded that the only way to help most of those who would lose out was to lift the amount of income that was tax-free, by increasing personal allowances for basic-rate taxpayers. It was a broad-brush stroke, but it would be simple and quick. I would tell the House of Commons that we would say how we intended to pay for it at the pre-Budget report. We eventually agreed to this plan, and we announced it on 13 May. It gave everyone earning less than about £40,000 a tax rebate of £120 from the beginning of the financial year.

The result was that 80 per cent of households who had lost out were fully compensated, with the remaining 20 per cent compensated by at least a half. In addition, 600,000 people on low incomes were taken out of tax altogether. It cost another £3.5 billion, being introduced half-way through the financial year. But by this time, because the economy was slowing, I judged it would be no bad thing to give people more spending power. It was just that the political consequences were awful. Not only was it a mess – and perhaps I should have faced up to the inevitable in the Budget – but it also created a profound dilemma: here was a Labour government taking money away from the lowest paid, the very people we were supposed to be protecting. It contributed, along with everything else that was going wrong, to a very bad by-election defeat at Crewe in June 2008, when the Tories gained their first by-election victory for almost thirty years.

In the meantime, the economy was slowing down both here in the UK and in just about every other part of world. The first quarter of 2008 was as bad as I had feared it would be. After the Budget, it was almost a welcome relief to fly to Washington for the annual meetings of the IMF and the G7. The G7 is the group of what used to be the seven largest economies in the world: the United States, Japan, Germany, France, Italy, Canada and ourselves. Russia attends for part of the meeting only. I used to feel sorry for Alexei Kudrin, my Russian counterpart, who was more easy-going than most of his fellow ministers. He had to sit outside the room while we discussed matters thought not fit for Russian ears. Self-evidently, the G7 is an anachronism. China is not there, and China is the second biggest economy in the world. The G7 is representative of the post-1945 order and its legitimacy is questionable. I think that is one of the reasons why the G20, a bigger and more representative group, worked so much better later that year, and again in 2009, in dealing with what by that time was a full-blown international crisis.

The small size of the G7 group does mean that it is possible to have proper conversations with fellow finance ministers. Most finance ministers and central bank governors speak English, so the conversation is free-flowing. Having attended countless international meetings, to be able to conduct something approaching a normal conversation is a real boon. The G7 chair rotates among its members and there are four meetings a year, two in the home country of the chair and two in Washington. This year Japan held the chair and so we travelled to Tokyo in February 2008. The meeting was remarkable. Although everyone was concerned about the downturn, no one had any inkling of how bad it would become in the next six months. Hank Paulson was perhaps the most concerned about the difficulties the US banks were facing. But all of us thought that when the banks reported on their losses, things would calm down. As it turned out, that was far from the case.

The only other thing that sticks in my mind from that trip is the first experience I had of an earthquake, albeit a very small one. I was staying in the residence at the British embassy, next to the Imperial Palace, home to Japanese emperors. Remarkably, these were among the few buildings to have survived the American bombing of Tokyo at the end of the Second World War. As I went to bed, I was shown a helmet and torch under the bed to be used in case of an earthquake. I thought no more of it. Lying in bed early next morning, drinking a cup of tea, suddenly the bed and the room began to move. It was disorientating and a bit frightening. It lasted only a few seconds, but the ambassador did say to me that it was believed it was only a matter of time before Japan would be hit by a large earthquake.

When the G7 met in Washington two months later the mood had changed, although there was still no sense of impending catastrophe. The G7 meetings in April are always held in the old Cash Room of the US Treasury. In its austere cavernous hall, we talked through our worries about the state of our banks, before the customary evening dinner. The ever-affable Hank Paulson had arranged that the guests for the meal should include a number of US and European bankers. By the time we met a year later, very few of them had survived. Bankers the world over are pretty contemptuous of politicians; American bankers especially don't like governments. Yet, during the course of the evening, banker after banker told me that there was a looming problem and that they would be looking to the government to resolve it. In short, it was a one-way deal: when times are good, get off our backs; when they are bad, you have to help us.

The following day, the IMF held its annual meeting at its offices in downtown Washington, next door to the World Bank. At least in the G7 there is always the possibility of getting something done, because it's such a small gathering. The IMF meeting in full session is a sight for despairing eyes. Hundreds of people attend, mostly officials from member states. Not every country is there; many are grouped into constituencies and appoint one of their number to appear on their behalf. But the table around which we sat was so large that it was difficult to make out who was at the far end. The exchanges at these meetings are very formal and formulaic. As ever, the real work is done behind the scenes. Much of the credit for what the IMF did during the crisis and in its aftermath goes to its managing director, Dominique Strauss-Kahn, who was appointed in late 2007. He had the authority of having been a French finance minister and he knew an extraordinary number of people around the world. Crucially, he recognized that the IMF had to come up with realistic programmes for help and reconstruction, as some smaller countries struggled to get through the crisis. Looking back at those two days, there was a great sense of marking time, waiting to see what would turn up. There was no sense of urgency. That was not to come until the next set of meetings, six months later.

From Washington, I flew to Beijing to attend an annual meeting between China and the UK, mainly to discuss trade. Like many people, I love displacement activity. When things are hard or difficult, there is nothing like a few hours off, where the phones don't ring, when you have time to think, when you can be blissful in your ignorance of what's going on back home. I enjoy flying and this flight took me over the North Pole. Looking down on the top of the world was an incredible experience, especially as I had managed to find Pink Floyd's *Dark Side of the Moon* on the aircraft's decrepit sound system.

This was my second visit to China. The Chinese are very formal, but ministers tend to speak more freely on a second or third meeting. I had a meeting in Beijing's Forbidden City with the Chinese vice president responsible for financial affairs and noted that he asked very pertinent questions about the state of the West's banks – not, I thought, without some degree of satisfaction. He was particularly interested in Northern Rock. It brought home to me the global reach of that bank's collapse. Here we were, sitting in the Forbidden City, discussing the misfortunes of a small bank which until recently few people outside of Newcastle had heard of. He was justifying China's caution on trade. I said that in the short term things were very difficult, but I was worried about the medium-term prospects too. He replied that he was also concerned about the medium term: the next hundred years, he said, could be very difficult. I wondered how many general elections there would be at home between now and then.

Catherine MacLeod, my special adviser, was with me on the trip, along with a couple of Treasury officials. After two days in Beijing we travelled to Chongqing. I wanted to see something of rural China, although the city itself has a population of somewhere close to 5 million. I also took the opportunity to promote the cause of Standard Chartered Bank, which was launching a new service for businesses there. After I had spoken to a group of assorted business people and officials, Catherine pointed out that there did not appear to be a grey hair in the audience. Rachel Lomax, a Deputy Governor of the Bank of England, joined us and made the same observation, before a charming Chinese guest sidled up to me: did I, he wondered, dye my eyebrows?

While I was away on the other side of the world, I was in constant touch with the Treasury and with Gordon. We had, up until my departure, been working closely with Mervyn and his colleagues at the Bank of England to address the problem that banks were having in obtaining enough funds to keep going. The result was the implementation of the 'special liquidity scheme'. This allowed banks to lodge securities with the Bank of England, for a fee, and receive cash in return. The Bank always lent less to the banks than the value of the securities they lodged with it, meaning that there would be no risk in the event of default by a particular bank. It was an extraordinary moment: before my departure I had approved a four-line letter sent by my Principal Private Secretary, Dan Rosenfield, to his opposite number in the Bank, effectively conferring a government guarantee of Bank lending up to £186 billion. I reflected that, unlike many of my international counterparts, I had the authority to do so, even if the Bank of England was reluctant, without having first to seek parliamentary authority. I did, of course, report on it to the Commons.

I had worked on this for several months and put a great deal of effort into persuading the Bank to agree to it – technical though it may be, it was one of the most successful things we did. Had we had it in place during the autumn of 2007, it would have been of huge benefit to the banks. It was a very good scheme and I was proud of it. That it was announced when I was on the other side of the world was a bit odd.

What the special liquidity scheme could not do, however, was to address the underlying problem, which was that too many banks were sitting on assets that were fast becoming worthless. In other words, it was the problems caused by the lack of capital that needed to be addressed. Unfortunately, strains between the Treasury and the Bank threatened to rupture our working relationship.

There are in the Chancellor's calendar three annual fixtures: the pre-Budget report; the Budget; and then, usually in June, the annual speech at the Lord Mayor of London's banquet at the Mansion House in the City of London. This black-tie dinner is held in the splendour of the banqueting hall, with lots of flummery. The Chancellor and the Governor of the Bank of England, who also speaks, process to their places to the accompaniment of a ritual slow handclap from the hundreds of guests. It is offputting until you realize they are actually welcoming you. The audience is largely drawn from the City. Bank chief executives are rarely seen, but their chairmen and board members and other City grandees are in attendance. This is not a natural Labour audience, but it was a good platform for me to set out plans for reforms to the Bank of England, including the novel proposition that in future the posts of Governor and Deputy Governors should be advertised. I wanted also to confirm our commitment to the London Crossrail link, which is important for the future of the City of London, linking it to Heathrow airport. And I was anxious to emphasize that Mervyn King and I were working closely together, whatever our differences.

In the days preceding the speech there had been a lot of discussion about who should fill the vacancy left by the retirement of Rachel Lomax. She had been Permanent Secretary at both the Department of Social Security and the Department of Transport during the periods when I was Secretary of State. We had worked well together, and I was sorry when she decided to leave. Her fellow Deputy Governor, Sir John Gieve, was also standing down. At his request, however, this was not to be made public for a few days. I had given John, whom I knew and liked from my days as Chief Secretary, my word about that.

Mervyn and I were to deliver our speeches before the main course was served, in order to allow for coverage on the 10 o'clock television news. After I had spoken, and as Mervyn was addressing the room, I became aware of a commotion at one of the tables across the room. I watched, transfixed, as a man began crawling towards us, weaving under tables and around people's legs. Further down the main table, there was another commotion going on around John Gieve. The man on his hands and knees was a *Daily Telegraph* journalist. He had reached his target and was tugging at Catherine MacLeod's long skirt from under the table. John's departure had been leaked, and they wanted a reaction from me. I was livid. Very few people had known, and it was unforgivable in its hurtfulness to John. In the middle of the dinner I had to take him behind a screen at the back of the main table and apologize, but the damage was done.

I cannot pretend to understand the motive behind the leak. It certainly ensured that the message of my speech, and that of the Governor, was lost. The evening had reflected badly on the government, where most of the mud tends to stick. As we left the dinner, Mervyn was seething and told me in no uncertain terms that he blamed No. 10. Looking over his shoulder, I could see a BBC television crew advancing, happily unaware of what the Governor was saying to me. I kept trying to hush him, to no avail, but managed to escape into an adjoining private room where I found Rachel Lomax. We shared a drink and mulled over the sometimes dysfunctional operation of government and Bank alike.

As the 2008 summer recess approached, it seemed to me that any hope had faded away that the economic downturn of the past year might have been temporary. No matter who I spoke to – economists, business leaders, commentators – everyone felt that the economy was heading in the wrong direction. And the political outlook was just as bad. We were about to lose one of the party's safest seats in Glasgow East.

I did some telephone canvassing. Long experience has taught me that when you ask someone if they will support you and they reply along the lines of 'I haven't made my mind up yet' or 'I'm just having my tea', it means they are going to vote for someone else, or not at all. That is precisely what I was hearing in call after call. It was so bad that voters were reluctant even to tell me what they did not like about us. The loss of the seat to the SNP was a severe blow to Gordon's authority and sapped his morale further. There was now open talk of a challenge to his leadership, although there was no specific candidate around whom people were gathering. There was a measure of desperation, but no one ready to throw their hat into the ring. It was the worst possible type of revolt, a lot of damaging talk but no action. I still believed we could recover and I did not see that a leadership battle would help. I was accordingly careful about what I said. I did not want there to be any suggestion that there were differences between the two of us, although our working relationship was to come under severe strain by the end of the summer. In my view, we were constantly behind events, mopping up as we were dragged along. I felt that we needed to prepare people, to tell them that the next few months, and probably the next few years, were going to be very difficult. We would lose all credibility if we didn't.

I convened a meeting with my ministerial colleagues and the Treasury's top officials to discuss the general outlook and prepare for the autumn. We met, far from the madding crowd, at Dorneywood. Set in idyllic gardens, and under the Heathrow flight path, Dorneywood is the former country home of Lord Courtauld-Thomson, a businessman and philanthropist, who gifted it to the nation in 1943 for use by the prime minister or senior Cabinet ministers. Born in Edinburgh, Lord Courtauld-Thomson was the son of Robert Thomson, the man who reputedly invented the pneumatic tyre. Churchill was entertained at Dorneywood, where he played bagatelle with his host. The board on which they played is still there, along with an oil painting by Churchill and a note from his wife, Clementine, passing on his instruction that his name be entered in the Golden Book where the highest bagatelle scores were recorded. He needed to win, even at games.

Although Gordon was given the use of Dorneywood when he was Chancellor, I don't think he ever visited it. Instead, John Prescott was a regular visitor throughout his ten years as Deputy Prime Minister. When Gordon became Prime Minister he allocated Dorneywood to me, although in the nine months since becoming Chancellor we had visited perhaps four times – not because we didn't want to go more often, but there had simply not been time. The Dorneywood Trust, a bequest from the founder, pays for the upkeep of the property and the Chancellor or other minister is billed for food and drink and other costs, so there is no expense to the taxpayer. When we first visited, the red-brick Queen Anne-style house was dreary and forbidding and sadly run-down. It was a place lost in time, set up for country-house week-ends, with a butler and a cook and under-cook, and no guests. It seemed to exist to service itself. It would have been no surprise to find Charles Dickens's Miss Havisham at the dinner table.

Shortly after becoming Chancellor I had held a Treasury summit at Dorneywood, so that ministers and officials could engage more infor-mally and openly. We arrived and got out of the car to be greeted, if not welcomed, by the man in charge. There was precious little grace and even less favour. A sodden pile of bags and briefcases was being rained on outside the front door. No bags, I was told, were to be left in the hall because of the danger of damage to a mural by Rex Whistler – which might have been fair enough, but there were twenty other rooms in which the bags could have been stacked. The sorry heap was eventual-ly taken in and left to steam in the outer hall, while Whistler's bucolic mural remained safe.

By July 2008, however, the old regime had moved on and the house had been dusted down, the bomb-curtains binned, and three cheerful-ly enthusiastic members of staff recruited. Dorneywood was a retreat from the frenetic pace of the Treasury where we could pause and reflect and consider where we were going. Late in arriving, I hurried in to start the meeting. To my horror, I saw assorted Treasury officials and minis-ters enjoying an evening drink on the lawn. There was nothing wrong with that, but this was no ordinary lawn. It was the notorious spot where John Prescott had been photographed playing croquet in the middle of a weekday afternoon. He had been there with his officials, as was I, to discuss his department's policy. They had taken a break, unfor-tunately oblivious to a photographer concealed in a hedge. On our first visit to Dorneywood, Calum and I took a wander around the estate and found the spot where the photographer had hidden. It was a clever place to have chosen, but not one that he could have chanced upon. I suspect someone must have told him where and when to be there. The story was grossly unfair on John: he worked tirelessly throughout his political career. When we first met in the mid-1980s I think he probably regarded me as another one of those middle-class boys who were taking over his party. But, contrary to the impression he sometimes gives, John is a modernizer. Above all, through his own experiences as a seaman, he knows how government can make a difference to people's life chances. And throughout his ten years as deputy leader he worked ceaselessly to bridge the growing gulf between Tony and Gordon. John and I came to respect and like each other.

Ministers and officials were encouraged, rather briskly, to come back inside. We sat down to discuss where we thought we were. Yvette Cooper and Treasury ministers Angela Eagle, Jane Kennedy and Kitty Ussher contributed their thoughts to the discussions, along with Dave Ramsden, the Treasury's chief economist, and Mark Bowman, who was in charge of bringing the Budget together. It was clear that there was a looming risk of recession, probably by the beginning of 2009. The credit crunch had intensified and the picture was unremittingly bleak right around the world. We did think, though, even then, that if we did what was needed to support the economy, we could still see a return to growth at the end of 2009. But the next twelve months were going to be very difficult, with everything pointing to a far sharper downturn than most people were predicting. It was that meeting that set the tone for two important newspaper interviews I gave that summer, warning of a deep and lengthy economic storm.

Following the Budget in March 2008, very few were predicting a recession. In April, the Bank of England said in its financial stability report that the worst was over and that it expected confidence would return. The IMF report was optimistic and commended the UK on its actions so far. It concluded that there would be a 'global rebound' in 2009. The highly respected National Institute for Economic Research said in July that we in the UK would escape recession. Even a few weeks later, Mervyn King, presenting the Bank's inflation report in August, said that output would be broadly flat over the next year. Dave Ramsden thought that there would be a shallow recession, starting at the end of the year. What was not foreseen was how quickly the economy would slow down before starting to shrink as the recession deepened. Equally worrying was the discussion we had on public sector finances at Dorneywood. A quarter of our corporate taxes came from the financial services sector. The size of our housing market meant that any downturn would reduce stamp duty receipts. A slowdown in spending would mean less VAT, and rising unemployment would cut income tax receipts.

I remember Nick Macpherson musing that if things were bad, borrowing could top £100 billion in a year or so. That brought gasps of incredulity from some around the table. As it turned out, it was something of an underestimate. The problem was that it had been assumed that taxes coming in from the financial sector would go on and on. After all, they had done so since the beginning of the decade. Far from being decried, huge bank profits and massive bonuses meant an increasingly large tax take. The real problem was that the economy had become too dependent on one sector. When the crisis hit, the UK was hit very hard.

As our discussions wore on that evening and into the next day, I was sufficiently alarmed to take Nick Macpherson and Dave Ramsden into a corner. I asked them to get a team working on what we would need to do if the banking crisis did develop further and recession hit more deeply than we feared. This was looking like a downturn that would be profound and long-lasting. Even when the economy started to grow again, it would be a long haul. I was particularly concerned at the increased borrowing and greater debt that I would have to announce in the pre-Budget report in November. Over that weekend, we sketched out our approach. First, it would be necessary to maintain public spending in order to keep momentum in the economy. Secondly, it would be necessary to provide an additional stimulus – that is, more spending to prevent recession from sliding into depression. But the third leg was equally important. We would also have to come up with a plan to cut borrowing and reduce debt as we moved out of recession, in 2009 or 2010.

At this stage, there was no disagreement between myself and Gordon on our strategy. That emerged later. He was, though, far more focused on the need for stimulus than on the deficit. It is worth noting that our fear at that time was that unemployment would rise much higher than it did. Outside commentators, including David 'Danny' Blanchflower, the respected labour market economist on the Bank of England's Monetary Policy Committee, believed unemployment might hit 4 million. In fact, unemployment remained far lower than forecast, which, in my view, is the direct result of the action we took later that autumn.

What was not apparent at Dorneywood that July was that we had already moved into recession. There is always a lag in receiving the official statistics that show whether or not an economy is growing or shrinking. The Office for National Statistics usually revises its initial estimates of what is happening several times, over a number of years. So it would take more than a year for the official statistics to show that we were in recession that summer.

This then was the background to the interview I gave to Rachel Sylvester and Alice Thomson of *The Times* to set the right tone for the summer and autumn. Reading the article now, under the heading 'Prophet of Economic Gloom', I see that I gave a pretty blunt view of what was to come. I was actually in quite a cheerful mood that day. My friend Ann Coffey had surprised me with two tickets to attend what proved to be the first of a number of Leonard Cohen farewell concerts. I was taking Calum and was looking forward to an uplifting performance by the master of gloom at London's O_2 Arena. It was a tremendous show.

I told *The Times* that the downturn would last far longer and go much deeper than I had expected earlier in the year. I went on to say that I thought it could continue for years rather than months. I said that growth was likely to be slower than predicted, and that the problems in the banking system were deep-seated. And I said that while public services were the cornerstone of the welfare state, they had to be paid for. I added that I sensed that people were very conscious of their own financial position, and that now they felt squeezed.

In fact, I had said much the same thing first in an interview on the economy with the *New Statesman* a month earlier, in June 2008, in which I told political editor Martin Bright: 'If you ask fundamentally what's changed … self-evidently it's the credit crunch … The IMF has said that it is the biggest shock to the world's economic systems since the 1930s.' In the No. 11 study, we talked through the year past and I added: 'If you look at the overarching event of the past twelve months, it is a slowdown in the economy and everything that comes with it and that hasn't just affected the economic matters – it's had a huge bearing on politics too. It's the old adage "it's the economy, stupid" and the economy drives politics.' No mention of the interview was ever made to me by either Gordon or his team. That was the pattern. Clearly, each interview was carefully noted. My view of what was happening in the economy was diverging from theirs. They viewed that as disloyalty, but I was determined to set out the truth as I saw it. If the knives weren't yet out for me, they were certainly being sharpened.

It was the middle of August before I could escape London for the Hebrides. For the fortnight before that, in Gordon's absence, allegedly on holiday, I stayed in Downing Street, deputizing for him in 'running the country'. Actually, I did nothing of the sort. Gordon and his court had decamped to Southwold, in Suffolk, where he was still very much not on holiday. Shriti Vadera, his economic adviser, was there, and Ed Balls and his press secretary, Damian McBride, visited. It was almost like the summer camp of the king in days of old.

As far as I could see, my duties were confined to meeting those of his entourage not invited to Southwold. Among them was Stephen Carter, who had been brought in as chief strategist a few months before to restore order to No. 10. He was the former Chief Executive of the media watchdog Ofcom, following a successful career in advertising. Unflappable and efficient, Stephen was still in post but out of favour, as was so often the case. His aura of calm that week was a welcome contrast to the usual chaotic operation in No. 10. He was one of many decent people who looked increasingly burdened and battered by the events of the past year. The most significant decision I had to make during that fortnight was to insist that my colleague, Foreign Office minister Jim Murphy abandon his family holiday to return to head up our response to the crisis caused by the Russian invasion of Georgia.

I had one more task to perform before starting our family holiday. Catherine MacLeod had agreed on my behalf to a *Guardian* request for an interview for their Saturday magazine. It was to be a profile, intended to run the weekend before the party conference in September, which was just weeks away. I had appointed Catherine, whom I've known for twenty years, the previous autumn. She was a former political editor of the *Glasgow Herald* and we knew each other well and trusted one another. I needed someone to speak for me. The Treasury has excellent press officers, but quite properly they cannot deal with the more political side of things, so I needed someone to advise on media and political coverage and to speak to journalists. For most of my parliamentary career I've avoided giving personal interviews, because they open a door which can't then be closed. I don't like talking about myself, but the risk is that other people will then define you and create a picture that might not be true. Catherine encouraged me to put my head above the parapet, to let people know how I ticked. She organized informal meetings for me with political and economic commentators, and handled the political end of media enquiries. Her great strength was that she was deeply respected in the

Westminster lobby, by political editors, reporters and commentators, as well as MPs.

The *Guardian* was explicit. They wanted a 'colour piece', as it's described in the trade, to appear on the eve of the party conference. They didn't want an office interview. They first suggested doing it in Edinburgh, but that would have meant losing another two days of our holiday. I did not want to delay the trip to Lewis any longer. Hoping that the paper was on a tight budget and that I could head the whole thing off, I said: 'Tell them they'll have to come to the Western Isles.' The offer was accepted with alacrity. The result was that feature writer Decca Aitkenhead and photographer Murdo Macleod, a Lewis man himself, whom I knew from Edinburgh, duly presented themselves at the croft house on a beautiful sunny August afternoon, with a pair of golden eagles hanging in the sky above us.

In the fallout from the interview, I was accused of many things, including having been foolish to allow a reporter to visit the croft and join us for supper before doing the interview the next day. All I will say is that we are generally hospitable, and since she had come all the way from London to our remote refuge, it seemed the natural and polite thing to do. Murdo had rung Catherine to say it was such a beautiful day, it might be best to do the portraits a day ahead of the planned interview while the sun was shining. He knows that the weather there is unpredictable. Murdo arrived after a recce to find a few places for the kind of moody island portraits at which he excels, capturing the light and the skies and the swell of the sea. He and I, with Decca and Catherine, set off to do the photographs, around Dalbeg and among the Callanish standing stones. He also wanted pictures of me on my small Orkney spinner boat. Then we went back for a meal of lamb and Stornoway black pudding around the kitchen table. We couldn't offer either Catherine or Decca a bed, there wasn't room, so after supper Murdo left to stay with his mother in Shawbost, while Decca and Catherine headed off for the hour-long drive to Uig, where they were both booked into the Baile Na Cille guest house for the night. On the drive back their hire car had a puncture and they had to be rescued by a passing crofter.

Next morning, Catherine and Decca arrived back for the interview. It was expansive, and ranged over the personal as well as the political. At one point, when we were discussing the economy, I said: 'Arguably, this is the worst downturn there has been in sixty years. And I think it is going to be more profound and long-lasting than people thought.' My prognosis was exactly what I had set out in *The Times* a month earlier and in my *New Statesman* interview. Decca left with Catherine in the afternoon to catch a plane home. We got on with our holiday.

Two weeks later, on the ferry heading from Stornoway to Ullapool on our way home, Catherine rang – to discuss, I thought, another interview, for the *Stornoway Gazette*, in which I had given the same message. The *Guardian*, she told me, was carrying the interview the next day, three weeks earlier than we had thought. That was when alarm bells began to ring. As we were sitting down to a meal with the children in a restaurant at the end of our street in Edinburgh, Catherine rang again to say that the *Guardian* had run my predictions on its front page: 'Economy at sixty-year low, says Darling.' The article had been picked up next door at No. 10 the night before it appeared. Their reaction, fed back to me, was one I'd heard before: I was clearly a prisoner of the Treasury, unable to think for myself. The fact that what I said might be true did not seem to enter their minds. No one wanted to acknowledge that we were heading for an extremely serious downturn.

Early the next morning, Catherine told me she had taken part in a conference call with Damian McBride, Mike Ellam, the Prime Minister's official spokesman, and Joe Irvine, a political aide. It was clear that they were raging. Joe had warned Catherine before the call that the interview was being described as a disaster. The conversation was difficult: they wanted to know how I was planning to respond, and they were asking for me to go out and do interviews. I wanted to do so. What the *Guardian* headline had done was to suggest that this was a British problem, rather than a global one. I was happy to give an interview that spelled out that the problem was global. The front-page article, written by Nick Watt and drawing on Decca Aitkenhead's interview, cleverly spotted a political story and made the most of it. In substance, though, I had said no more than had been reported in *The Times* and *New Statesman*. The real problem was that what I was saying and what Gordon was saying were very different.

The *Guardian* front-page story was uncannily accompanied by the same story splashed in the *Daily Telegraph*. Quite where the BBC got the story to run on the 10 o'clock news the night before it appeared I don't know. The reporter told viewers that she had not seen the article in the next day's *Guardian* but had been told about it, and that it had set alarm bells ringing in No. 10. All of this leaking and briefing whipped up a media frenzy. Catherine spent Saturday fielding calls from journalists, who repeatedly told her how furious the Prime Minister was with me. That was odd, because on the Saturday morning I had spoken to Gordon and he was civil, if terse, and gave no sign of anger. He said that the people he was speaking to were telling him the recession would be over in six months. I replied that that was not what I was hearing. I was as anxious as he was to do a television interview to make it clear that, while we faced a bad downturn, so too did most other countries. The press was briefed that I had been 'ordered' by a furious prime minister to make a public apology, which was simply not true.

The media reaction was extraordinary. It was as if my words had been a bolt from the blue and that I was personally responsible for crashing the economy. Politicians are regularly criticized for appearing to be economical with the truth. I was condemned for having said no more than was true. The Tories, understandably, piled in. They were unsure at first whether to agree with my analysis or to condemn me for having said what I had. So they did both.

It was the briefing machine at No. 10 and Gordon's attack dogs, who fed the story and kept it running. I later described it as like 'the forces of hell' being unleashed on me. That's what it felt like. Damian

McBride was no fan of mine – he clearly disapproved of Gordon's decision to appoint me as Chancellor. He used to look at me like the butler who resented the fact that his master had married someone he didn't approve of. I'm not sure that he ever spoke to me. He would give me a curt nod, nothing more. He had a group of journalists whom he briefed regularly, and when Catherine McLeod finally managed to meet with him, after repeated requests, he told her which journalists she should talk to and which not. Catherine believes that she was largely disregarded at first because no one expected me to be Chancellor for long. McBride was very tense, like a coiled spring. Unlike *The Thick of It*, all of his briefings took place behind the scenes. By contrast, Charlie Whelan enjoyed his reputation as a political bruiser. He was special adviser to Gordon in opposition and then for the first two years in government, when he took up a job at Unite. He started reappearing in an unofficial capacity once Gordon became prime minister, but later, when Peter Mandelson returned to government, Peter discouraged him from taking part in the planning for the election.

The attack dogs set about another colleague that summer. At the beginning of the summer recess, after the loss of the Glasgow East seat, David Miliband, then Foreign Secretary, had written an article for the *Guardian* in which he set out the need for a coherent political strategy to recover lost ground. It was a thoughtful piece, but it was interpreted by the inner circle as an attack on Gordon and a signal that David might launch a leadership attempt. Gordon was told by his team left behind at No. 10 that he should be relaxed about it. They were right. The article would have died a death had a cack-handed press operation not been mounted to trash David.

Exactly the same thing happened at the end of the summer with me. For days after the *Guardian* piece ran, journalists told us they were being told repeatedly that I had made a hash of it. Well-sourced speculation that I was about to be reshuffled began to appear in the media. Perhaps they were using the interview as an opportunity to get rid of me once and for all. At the time, what I didn't know was that on his flight home in late August from the Olympic Games closing ceremony in Beijing, Gordon had told journalists that we would see an economic recovery within six months. Understandably, this open divergence of views between Prime Minister and Chancellor provided fertile ground in which to plant seeds of doubt about the Chancellor's competence.

Those were dark days. It was a defining moment, too, in my relationship with Gordon. It would never be the same again. Subsequently, I learned that when he was at Southwold, Gordon had decided on an economic strategy that was built around the proposition that the economy would recover over the next six months. I had sensed something was up, since while he was there Gordon had repeatedly been in contact with the Treasury, asking for growth figures and other information. When these hadn't been immediately forthcoming, he'd rung me to ask whether I was blocking their dissemination – which, of course, I wasn't. If I had known that Gordon believed that economic recovery lay around the corner – if he'd told me, his Chancellor, this – then we could have had a discussion about it. The problem was that clearly he did not trust my advice, and now he appeared indifferent to what I thought.

I spoke to Gordon and told him that we knew where the anonymous briefings were coming from. It had to stop. It was damaging the credibility not just of me but of the whole government. He said he was not responsible for it; it was nothing to do with him. Politicians have to be pretty thick-skinned. Criticism from political opponents, either upfront or through anonymous sources, is the stuff of politics the world over. But systematic anonymous briefing from people you have known for years, and who are supposed to be on your side, is deeply unpleasant. Living next door to it – literally – made it all the harder. I was reminded of the words Henry II uttered about Thomas à Becket: 'Will no one rid me of this turbulent priest?' He didn't order his knights to go and kill Becket, but they believed they had his blessing to do so.

I won't deny that this episode was deeply hurtful and that it shaped a difficult relationship for the rest of our term in office. But I do have just the faintest sense of gratitude. My fairly accurate prediction of what was to come economically might have been long forgotten but for the inept briefing machine at No. 10. For that I owe them thanks, which is something I am sure they never anticipated.

5   Crisis: the Collapse of Lehman Brothers

I returned to London at the beginning of September 2008 rather less than refreshed. Not only had the fallout from the interview undone any good that the Hebridean break might have done me, but our holiday had been interrupted on a daily basis with calls from my private office, which in turn was being bombarded with demands for action from every part of No. 10. I knew only too well that the economy was slowing down fast and was probably heading for recession. I did not need to be convinced of that. What I wanted, though, was to make a coherent announcement, probably in an early pre-Budget report in the autumn. A single big announcement will always have a far bigger impact than a series of small initiatives announced one day and forgotten the next.

The fallout from the interview continued with a flow of articles by commentators saying that things were not as bad as I had said. Just a few weeks later, however, it was clear that, far from being pessimistic, the picture I had painted was not bleak enough. In that *Guardian* piece I had also said that people were 'pissed off' with us, and that reshuffles of Cabinet positions rarely change anything. In that respect, my prediction was not quite right. People were fed up with us, but in September Gordon decided to reshuffle his Cabinet, this time to good effect. Ed Miliband took charge of a new department of energy and climate change, something I had long believed was needed when I was in charge of energy policy within the large and unwieldy Department of

Trade and Industry. Ed was a long-standing protégé of Gordon's, who had joined him in his early twenties when Gordon became Shadow Chancellor. He was the most personable of Brown's inner circle, and I found him helpful and straightforward. He worked really hard in this new department and did his level best to make the Copenhagen climate change talks work.

The big change was the return to government of Peter Mandelson. This was seen as something of a coup. It was totally unexpected and it also suggested a rapprochement between Gordon and the Blair wing of the Labour Party. I was part of a minority who thought that Peter, who at times could be his own worst enemy, was a tremendous asset to the party. He had identified the need to modernize in the 1980s and he had spotted the potential of Gordon and Tony at that time. His influence, and particularly his presentational skills, were instrumental in the transformation of the Labour Party from a creature nostalgic for the past and wary of the future into a body that was confident, optimistic and sure of what it stood for. More importantly, in 2008 I had high hopes that Peter might bring some order and direction into No. 10. We were not close, although we had worked together, particularly when I was at the Department of Trade and Industry. I knew I could work with him, and I desperately needed an ally to argue my case with Gordon. It was also helpful that Peter was in the Department for Business, so that there was now someone involved in managing the economy who shared my outlook. Peter remains something of an enigma, and probably he likes it that way, but politically he is highly sensitive and astute, and he understands the British press. The crucial advantage from my point of view was that after 2008 he was the one person in Cabinet, other than Ed Balls, to whom Gordon would listen. It was to prove to be a good appointment, and we worked well together until the election. I was sorry that Gordon could not persuade Alastair Campbell to return too. I knew that he had approached Alastair, but he felt it would not work. He did return as part of the general election team, but by that time the die was cast.

Although I was not consulted – nor, in the circumstances, would I have expected to have been, such were the difficulties between us – I was optimistic that these changes would help get us back on our feet. The only appointment on which I was consulted was whether or not I would take Shriti Vadera into the Treasury. Shriti had been a special adviser to Gordon since the late 1990s. She had come to him from an investment bank, to advise him on development in Africa in particular, and was a huge contributor to the debt-relief initiative. When Gordon moved into No. 10, he needed an economic adviser full-time, a position that had previously been occupied by Ed Balls and, to a certain extent, Ed Miliband. I didn't want her to come into the Treasury, not only because she had a difficult working relationship with civil servants there, but more importantly I wasn't having a spy in the cab, which is what Gordon wanted her there for. That would've provided even greater dysfunction and I wasn't having that in the Treasury. So I told Gordon that I wouldn't have her. Instead, I happily took Paul Myners. Gordon's response was to put Shriti into the Department for Business; but she constantly sought to be a presence at the Treasury, undoubtedly at Gordon's behest. I was happy to let her be around, but only on my own terms.

The reshuffle was well received, but already the whole developed world was on a slope that would take the banking system to the brink. The debacle of the summer was about to be overshadowed by the worst banking crisis – not in sixty or a hundred years, but in history. A foretaste of what was to come had been seen in the US, the day after my Budget the previous March. Bear Stearns was one of the oldest and most well-established investment banks in the US. Burdened with a huge amount of securities based on sub-prime mortgages, the bank had collapsed. The US government rightly believed that they could not let it fail, so they engineered, and largely financed, its takeover by another stalwart of Wall Street, JPMorgan Chase. On that occasion, as a result of the prompt action by the US authorities, a crisis was averted.

Any hope that banks could put an accurate valuation on their potential losses had come to nothing. Worse, the whole thing became self-fulfilling: as each bank disclosed its losses, the markets, and other banks, further downgraded the value of the assets they held. In the US, the Federal Reserve had made $200 billion available to the banks a few days before the collapse of Bear Stearns, but its attempt to stave off collapse by providing emergency lending to the bank had failed.

The housing market in the US was in desperate straits. Millions of Americans on low incomes – and in some cases no income – had been persuaded to buy houses on the back of historically low interest rates. Many had been sold mortgages that had incredibly low rates of interest and no repayments for the first few years – so-called 'tasters' – which then reverted to a much higher rate thereafter. All this was predicated on house prices continuing to soar, so that the value of the homes would quickly outstrip the size of the loans made against them. Then house prices began to plateau and to fall; and on top of that, when interest rates went up, millions of people found they could not meet the repayments on their loans. The sale of mortgages in the US was largely unregulated which meant that the very people whom the state should have protected, by insisting that they be told precisely what they had let themselves in for, found themselves completely exposed. Interestingly, in the UK, the Tories had proposed similar deregulation the previous autumn, just before the crash.

All of this had two effects that proved disastrous for the US. First, defaulting loans turned into securities and held by American banks changed from assets into massive liabilities. Secondly, in the US, unlike the UK, a property owner can simply hand back the keys to their house and walk away. That meant that the US housing market crashed, leaving empty and half-completed homes dotted across the country. Some people had made money exploiting the needs of the poorest and most vulnerable of their fellow Americans, and now the whole country would have to pay for it.

In the UK, private sector house-building had virtually stopped and new mortgage approvals were at their lowest level since records began.

I was always less worried about Britain's housing market. I knew it would fall, that was inevitable, but in the long run Britain's problem is that the demand for housing exceeds supply. There are many people chasing too few houses and, until the country's planning laws change, houses are likely to rise in price over time. Ironically, the spectacular failure of successive British governments to deliver increased house-building proved to be a blessing for the housing market, which did not fall by anywhere near as much as people feared, although in parts of the country the falls that did occur will take some time to recover.

However, confidence in the banking system was slowly seeping away. In April, RBS had announced a plan to raise the money it desperately needed from its shareholders through a £12 billion rights issue, the biggest in UK corporate history. In May, the Swiss bank UBS launched a £16 billion rights issue to cover some of its losses on assets tied up in US mortgage debt. In June, Barclays said it was planning to raise £4.5 billion in the Gulf and from its shareholder the China Development Bank.

At the beginning of July, a big US mortgage lender known as IndyMac collapsed, and the government was forced to shore up the country's two largest mortgage finance companies, known as Freddie Mac and Fannie Mae. Freddie and Fannie own or guarantee almost half of all US home loans. This makes mortgages cheaper to obtain, but now it resulted in the US government effectively backing more than $5 trillion of debt. Belatedly, the American authorities had woken up to the fact that what was happening in the housing market amounted to criminal behaviour in some quarters. The FBI had arrested 406 people, including brokers and housing developers, in a crackdown on alleged mortgage fraud worth $1 billion. The guarantee for Freddie Mac and Fannie Mae was welcomed when it was announced. Hank Paulson called the G7 finance ministers to keep us informed, and for a time it seemed as if the rescue measures would work. But that was the summer. By the autumn it had proved to be a false dawn.

It was in July that alarm bells really began to ring around HBOS.

The bank had first appeared on the Treasury watch list when the problems with Northern Rock surfaced. The FSA was concerned about its exposure to the housing market. It too had sold mortgages aggressively, offering amazing deals, to the point that it was not making any money out of them. Although this wasn't so obvious at the time, the bank had tried to compensate for that by making commercial loans, especially on property, which were to result in colossal losses. HBOS was becoming increasingly desperate and needed to raise capital, which it started to do that summer through a rights issue. But it experienced real difficulty in raising money by issuing these new shares, for it was evident that investors – rightly – took the view that the bank was in deep trouble. At the end of July, HBOS profits had halved. Bad debts, as more customers failed to repay loans, were up by a third. There was a whiff of death surrounding the whole operation. Two once solid institutions, the Halifax Building Society and the Bank of Scotland, were heading for the rocks.

We were also concerned about the condition of Bradford and Bingley. Now a bank, it had been a well-run building society based in Yorkshire. However, fuelled by what seemed an endless supply of cheap credit, it had got into the buy-to-let market. People who had previously never thought of buying property in order to let it saw this as a new way to boost the value of their savings. Buying to let is risky, however. Added to that, Bradford and Bingley seemed to have a large number of customers who 'self-certified' their circumstances. The result was that as property values began to fall, borrowers began to default. Its share price was falling as investors decided that Bradford and Bingley had gone bad.

The only good news was that, after months of agonizing, the directors of Alliance and Leicester, another former building society, had decided to sell the company to Abbey, which was itself a subsidiary of the Spanish bank Santander. We had been worried about Alliance and Leicester – not because it had done anything wrong, but after the collapse of Northern Rock there was a general suspicion that, if all these former building societies were in trouble, why should Alliance and Leicester be any different? They had no alternative but to sell if they were to avoid the fate of the others. For us, it was one less bank to worry about.

Throughout that summer, as the dismal picture developed, we at the Treasury were reflecting on what to do. It was obvious that far too many banks were short of capital to fall back on as their losses began to mount. Whereas in the first half of the year we had been worried about liquidity, or cash flow, by midsummer another problem was apparent: the banks needed more capital behind them. They needed more funds to fall back on, because it now seemed inevitable that they would face growing losses as borrowers got into difficulties.

The position in the UK was nothing like that in the US, but because of the size of the housing market here, some of our banks were very exposed. Home ownership in the UK is much wider than it is in Europe. That means that whatever happens in the housing market not only affects the banking system but also the wider economy, including the business sector, since if house prices fall home owners spend less money.

In the Treasury we drew up a list of banks that we thought needed close monitoring. Reports were given to me on a daily basis. They became known as the 'animal and planet reports'. Such was their sensitivity that a well-meaning official devised code names for each of the banks. My private secretary would give me a note telling me how Jupiter was faring, that Lapwing was failing, or that Badger was in a bad way. It got frustrating trying to remember which was which. An apprentice spy might not have had much trouble breaking the code. When bankers came to meetings, the minutes discreetly recorded them by their code names: 'Elvis left the room.' A cursory glance at a report would show that 'Elvis' had headquarters in Newcastle and sponsored Newcastle United FC.

At that stage there was no worked-up rescue plan. That came later. We were dealing with a moving target. It still was not clear how deep the problem was, and because of that it was difficult to know how to treat it. The only thing that was clear was that the situation was getting steadily worse. Looking back at my engagements for early September that year, I see that when I addressed the TUC (the first and only occasion on which I did so) I spoke on the risk of inflation, rather than on the situation relating to the banks. I was concerned about the return of inflation, but it turned out to be the least of our worries that autumn.

The US government's attempt to shore up Freddie Mac and Fannie Mae was short-lived. Their financial position was far worse than had been thought. So, on 7 September 2008, the US government decided it would nationalize the two insurance entities. Hank Paulson arranged a teleconference for the G7 finance ministers and explained the decision to us. The private sector was not going to help with a rescue, and they saw no alternative way to maintain confidence. It was not called 'nationalization' but rather 'conservatorship'. Presumably that was designed to go down better with Republican politicians.

Whatever it was called, $5 trillion of American housing debt now belonged to US taxpayers. Despite that, it was well received both in the US and especially in Europe. This was interesting: in a country where the state – or big government as it's often called – is viewed with suspicion not just on the right but even in some Democratic quarters, the US government action was seen as positive. As in the case of Bear Stearns the previous March, the US had used the power of government to stabilize the situation and avoid panic. Hank Paulson, having worked in financial markets all his life, knew what needed to be done, although, as he has subsequently admitted, he found the politics much more difficult to understand. It was, however, a watershed for a Republican administration.

Paulson was also working on a more ambitious scheme to deal with what he had correctly identified as the core of the problem in the US. He wanted to use taxpayers' money to buy the bad assets that banks held and that were effectively crippling their ability to borrow and lend. The idea was that these 'assets' would be sold off at distressed prices to anyone who would buy them. The plan was known as the Troubled Assets Relief Programme, or TARP. From the time of its announcement, it was the subject of a rising chorus of criticism inside Congress and from leading economists. The main objection was that the US taxpayer was taking on the bad assets, while the banks, whose recklessness had caused the problem in the first place, would keep the good bits. The real problem, as many commentators saw it, was that American banks needed more capital. From this side of the Atlantic, we watched the TARP proposal with foreboding. I could see the attraction of the principle, but I could not understand why any private sector body would buy these toxic assets. If their original owners could not sell them, how would the new buyers?

The Republicans did not like TARP, and neither did the Democrats. The politics were compounded by the fact that the US was at the end of the lame-duck presidency of George W. Bush and the election campaign was in its most critical phase. This was a problem not just for the US, but for us as well. If the scheme failed to get through Congress, the blow to confidence on both sides of the Atlantic would be immense. We watched with dismay as the first version of the scheme was voted down. I could see all of its drawbacks, but I could not understand how these US representatives couldn't see that, like lemmings, they were rushing headlong towards the cliff. I was also struck by the fact that the US president, although frequently described as the most powerful man in the world, cannot automatically get what he wants at home. He has to horse-trade. In contrast, when I effectively wrote a cheque to buy £50 billion of bank shares in the UK, I did not even have to get specific parliamentary authority to do so. We could act overnight. Watching the Americans, I learned another lesson too. It was evident that when the TARP scheme was launched it had not been fully thought through. The original legislative proposal was just three pages long. It was clear to me that whatever happened, we shouldn't announce a plan until we were absolutely sure how it would work.

Throughout this time, Hank kept in close touch with me and my fellow European finance ministers. Every time I spoke to him I could sense that his fear of meltdown was growing. His frustration with the system within which he had to operate was mounting. I felt that a period of acute watchfulness was coming to an end and it was time for action. The call to arms meant alerting the Treasury to work up contingency plans to halt the collapse of our financial system, with the terrible collateral damage that it would do to our economy. From being an interested spectator, the Treasury had to become a department that delivered. This was to be the Treasury's war. The social and economic costs of failure were incalculable.

We were still closely monitoring our banks. On 17 September, HBOS reported much higher levels of withdrawals than usual. There were no queues, but customers were fretting and telephone banking was under pressure as people tried to get their money out. A day later, their shares slumped by another 19 per cent. On 25 September, I took a call from my erstwhile visitor, Sir Fred Goodwin of RBS, or 'Phoenix' by another name. He said conditions were very bad. The bank had been considering whether or not to stop lending to its customers. What would it take to try to resolve the situation? I asked. What he needed more than anything else, he told me, was long-term funding.

A few days later I had to authorize the Bank of England to provide exceptional funds to keep HBOS going. I told John McFall, chairman of the Treasury select committee, but otherwise the facility was to be kept secret in case it created another wave of panic. RBS also needed exceptional funding, to the tune of around £14 billion, which I had to authorize. The Bank had to agree a swap facility to provide short-term financing of up to £30 billion. And we were coming to the view that, unless they could find a buyer, Bradford and Bingley would fail. I saw that a spokesman for the bank had said: 'Our funding foundations are solid and we are well capitalized.' I was reminded of the late Tommy Docherty, who had been manager at many different football clubs. He famously observed: 'When your chairman gives you a vote of confidence, it's time to start looking for another job.'

When the dam did burst, though, it happened much more quickly than anyone had predicted, when one of the US's oldest, and hitherto most respected, banks, Lehman Brothers, got into difficulties. Lehmans' was very much bigger and more complex than Bear Stearns. Around 50 per cent of its trade came through its London subsidiary, so I was alarmed to hear that the US government was indicating that it might not bail it out were it to fail. Not only did Lehmans' employ thousands of people in the UK, but the failure of a bank of that size would be bound to have knock-on effects in London.

I was due to fly to Nice on 12 September for another meeting of Ecofin. We were to discuss how the European Union should respond to the looming crisis. Nice is where the English aristocracy used to winter as late as the 1930s, and I was staying, appropriately enough, in a hotel in the rue des Anglais. I reflected on the fact that in those days British Cabinet ministers would retreat to the south of France for weeks on end and no one at home seemed to notice. I wondered how they would have coped with the demands of 24-hour news coverage.

On the Friday evening we were entertained by Christine Lagarde, the French finance minister (now heading the IMF), at an open-air dinner in the gardens of a splendid chateau looking out over a moonlit Mediterranean. It was a brief respite, if not entirely relaxing, as we talked over the international turmoil and my mind was very much on what was happening on the other side of the Atlantic. Christine Lagarde is charming and formidably intelligent, a former partner in an American law firm. She can bridge the intellectual gap in financial thinking between the Europeans and Americans in a way that few other European ministers can. She sought to build consensus, although at the end of the day, like all good French ministers, she always remembered that she spoke for La France. I have often been struck by how, at critical times, the French establishment, right and left, government and business, comes together in the French interest.

I knew the FSA was already drawing up contingency plans to deal with the fallout from a Lehman Brothers collapse, but they could not

1. In September 2007, panic levels rose as savers queued to get their money out of Northern Rock, in the first run on a UK bank in over a century.

2. Tony Blair's first cabinet in 1997. Top row, from left: Nick Brown, me, David Clark, Clare Short, Mo Mowlam, Chris Smith, Frank Dobson, Ann Taylor, Harriet Harman, Ron Davies, Lord Ivor Richard, Gavin Strang, Sir Robin Butler. Bottom row, from left: Donald Dewar, Margaret Beckett, Jack Straw, Robin Cook, John Prescott, Tony Blair, Gordon Brown, Lord Irvine, David Blunkett, Jack Cunningham, George Robertson. By the end, there were only three of us who'd been there all the way through: Jack Straw, Gordon and me.

3. Gordon's first cabinet in 2007: Top row, from left: Beverley Hughes, Yvette Cooper, Lord Grocott, John Denham, Baroness Ashton, James Purnell, Ed Balls, Hazel Blears, Geoff Hoon, Ed Miliband, Shaun Woodward, Andy Burnham, Tessa Jowell, Baroness Scotland, Sir Mark Malloch-Brown, Sir Gus O'Donnell. Bottom row, from left: Peter Hain, John Hutton, Hilary Benn, Des Browne, Jack Straw, me, Gordon Brown, David Miliband, Jacqui Smith, Alan Johnson, Douglas Alexander, Harriet Harman, Ruth Kelly. Just before the banking storm hit.

4. At the G20 meeting in Berlin, February 2009. From left: Mervyn King (Governor of the Bank of England), me, Angela Merkel (Chancellor of Germany) and Gordon.

5. In Washington, October 2008: with my fellow finance ministers in the Rose Garden of the White House.

6. Above: Sir Tom McKillop, former Chairman of RBS and Sir Fred Goodwin, former Chief Executive of RBS, leaving parliament, February 2009.

7. Below: On the Downing Street doorstep with Margaret, on the day of my final budget, March 2010. The red box I'm holding was made originally for William Gladstone in the 1860s.

produce a comprehensive plan until we knew what the Americans were doing. Before dinner, I had spoken to Hank Paulson. He was about to board a flight to New York from Washington and he was anxious both to let me know what was happening and to hear my thoughts. He told me there were three options: a wind-down; purchase by an industry consortium; or a straightforward takeover. His preferred option was for Lehmans to be bought by an industry consortium. This is where we came in. I said that I knew one of the prospective players was a UK bank, Barclays. I made it clear that I was not against a takeover or investment by a British bank in principle, but I would need to be certain that Barclays was not taking on more risk than it could manage. I did not want the British taxpayer to end up standing behind an American bank that was on the verge of collapse. As with all our conversations, it was calm, businesslike, and to the point. Hank accepted this and said that the US government might be prepared to offer some help in the shape of guarantees, if needed. However, at this stage they were not in a position to do so, and we agreed to keep in touch over the weekend.

An hour later I spoke to Hector Sants, the chief executive of the FSA and someone whose judgement I trust. He and the chairman, Callum McCarthy, had been talking to Barclays; but they too wanted to know what support would be offered by the US Treasury. Both Callum and Hector wanted to be reassured that the deal was sufficiently watertight to cope with any worst-case scenario, including Lehmans' assets turning out to be worse than expected – as, in the end, they turned out to be. All of this was being done in what seemed to me to be undue haste.

Throughout the following day, Saturday, I was kept informed of what was going on. There were two prospective buyers: Bank of America and Barclays. The consortium idea never got off the ground, primarily because the other banks were in an increasingly precarious position themselves. Also, it was not clear why they would want to bail out one of their competitors. The alternative was a wind-down or, to put it bluntly, bankruptcy. What was worrying was that it was becoming more evident that the US Treasury was reluctant to provide the financial support to make the deal work. I was not entirely surprised, having watched Hank Paulson struggle with his TARP scheme. I didn't think he had enough political capital to persuade the Republicans to nationalize another bank. I could not see how Barclays could buy Lehmans without financial help from the US government; but, on the other hand, US legislators might well baulk at subsidising a British bank. On the Saturday evening I flew back to Edinburgh, where I was rung up to be told that Bank of America, whom we had assumed were the front-runners, might be pulling out. That was when I felt that my doubts about the deal were justified. The Americans would not pull out of a good deal and allow the Brits to get it instead. If Bank of America was walking away, something was wrong. What we did not know at the time, but learned shortly afterwards, was that Bank of America had decided to buy Merrill Lynch instead.

My private secretary told me that Callum McCarthy could not get the information he needed from the US side. He wanted to speak to Tim Geithner, who at that time was President of the New York Fed, which, with its responsibility for Wall Street, is second only to the US Treasury in terms of influence. Any bail-out for Lehmans or help with a takeover had to come from them. Callum was unable to reach him, however. Tim, who later became President Obama's Treasury Secretary, was, like Hank Paulson, open and upfront. We saw eye to eye on most of the big issues we had to confront. Here, though, he was doing his job for the United States. He did eventually speak to Callum McCarthy, who made it very clear that we simply did not know enough about what was being proposed. It looked as if the sale to Barclays had been cobbled together too quickly and that our regulators simply did not have full sight of what was being proposed.

On Sunday afternoon, my private secretary told me that the Americans felt we were being obstructive. One of the key issues that had arisen was whether or not the British government would be prepared to waive a legal requirement for Barclays shareholders to approve any deal before it went through. This, for me, illustrated the fundamental weakness in the proposed sale. Not only would we have to stand behind Barclays, as increasingly we were doing for the rest of the banking system, but we would be overriding the rights of millions of shareholders who might get cleaned out. Midway through the afternoon, John Varley, chief executive of Barclays, asked to speak to me. I came to value John's advice over the next few difficult weeks. He was candid and wanted to know if the British government would give its blessing to this deal. I pointed out that no deal as such had been put to us. It was all very vague, but, since he asked, I said I did not see how we could be asked to stand behind something that was so risky. Hank Paulson had talked about US financial help, but nothing was on the table. I got the impression that the Barclays board itself was divided over whether to buy Lehmans, given the risks involved and the lack of US government support. John Varley said he would understand if we decided not to support the deal and, if that was the case, Barclays would not proceed. The negotiations were being conducted on Barclays' behalf by Bob Diamond, head of their investment bank, who was in New York. I told John that we would keep in touch, but I was relieved that there did not seem to me to be any great determination on Barclays' part to acquire Lehmans that day.

I then spoke to Hank Paulson. He was exasperated. He had spoken to Callum McCarthy, who had, in Hank's view, hit the final nail into the coffin of the deal. Hank said Callum had raised some twenty objections but had not unequivocally said no. I told Hank that Callum had raised legitimate objections, because we still did not know what was being proposed. I said that I had also spoken to John Varley at Barclays and explained to him that we could not stand behind any deal until we knew precisely what were the risks. In any case, I added, as far as we could see, there was no deal on the table. In any event, we could not stand behind a US bank that was clearly in trouble.

Throughout that weekend we got a real sense that the US administration was in a state of panic. And perhaps because of that, no one in New York appeared to have thought about telling their UK counterparts what they were trying to do. Nor did they explain why Bank of America had suddenly pulled out of a deal to buy Lehmans, buying Merrill Lynch instead. We were deeply suspicious: why were the Americans prepared to hand over what they claimed was a good deal to the Brits?

Hank acknowledged that everyone had to do what they thought right. He believed we might have got round some of the concerns raised by Callum if he had raised them sooner. Callum was later adamant that they had been raised a considerable time before. My conversation with Hank was brief and to the point, and there was no rancour at its conclusion. We were both doing our jobs. He was trying to fix a big broken bank. I was determined that UK taxpayers would not end up having to bail out a US bank. I asked him if the only option now was administration. He said he needed to discuss that with others, but both of us knew that was where they were heading. He said, 'You'll be the first person I call.' Two hours later, at 11 p.m. our time, he kept his word. His chief of staff spoke to my private secretary, Dan Rosenfield. He confirmed that Lehmans was going into administration and forwarded the draft of Hank's statement which would be released before the markets opened in Asia that morning.

Throughout the weekend, I had kept Gordon in touch. We were agreed that there was no way our government could effectively bankroll an American bank that was in trouble, when the US authorities wouldn't and when other US banks were running a mile. For me, this was one of the most profound decisions made during the course of the entire banking crisis. Lehmans collapsed that night.

It was not the cause of the virtual collapse of the world's banking system a month later, but did precipitate it. The problem was that the US had sent a clear signal: it would not step in to save a failed bank. The markets therefore assumed that if Lehmans was allowed to collapse, the same could happen to other banks. My guess is that if the US authorities were to have their time over again, they would act to prevent the near-chaos that ensued less than a month later. Saving

Lehmans, or at least salvaging something of it, would not have stopped the collapse of confidence, but I have no doubt it would have been far easier to manage.

Even at this late stage, there was no sense that America and Europe would ever work to a single plan. There was not, as yet, the widespread sense of panic that would eventually force more progress in five days than had been achieved in the previous five months. On Monday, 16 September, the world watched police cordon off Lehman Brothers' headquarters in New York as staff carried their working lives out of the building in cardboard boxes. The bank, 158 years old, had filed for bank-ruptcy. Lehman mementoes turned up for sale on eBay.

Lehmans' collapse, and the sale of Merrill Lynch to Bank of America a few days earlier, meant that there were now only two big independent firms left on Wall Street, Goldman Sachs and Morgan Stanley. Even they had to raise huge amounts of capital – Morgan Stanley from Mitsubishi, Goldman Sachs from Warren Buffett. They even had to change their status, from being investment banks to taking some deposits as well, so that they became retail banks, which come under US government protection and regulation, and can borrow money from the Federal Reserve. The face of Wall Street had changed.

When Lehmans went down, it was believed that it held around $60 billion in toxic debts. It was an investment bank and its clients were institutions, not individuals. Its collapse exposed the vulnerabili-ty of the entire international banking sector. A small number of people in the UK held shares, and their investments were now worthless. For most people, though, the effects of the collapse would be felt indirectly. It meant that other banks would be reluctant to lend not only to each other, but also to individuals.

In London, on the Monday morning, five thousand Lehmans staff cleared their desks, amid extraordinary scenes. It was the country's big-gest single loss of jobs since the collapse of Rover in 2005. I had known it was coming all weekend, but to see people carrying their boxes out of the building at Canary Wharf like refugees was a startling sight. It was almost like the grainy black and white footage from the Wall Street Crash of 1929. What terrified me was the obvious question: how many more banks were heading this way? Would there soon be people pouring out of British banks? The FTSE 100 Index tumbled over 200 points that day. Investors were panicky. There was no frenzy in the Treasury, however. Teams were calmly working around the clock to devise a plan not just to deal with the fallout from Lehmans but, more pressingly, to decide what to do about Bradford and Bingley. At the same time, we were working on the pre-Budget report, and I met Gordon for breakfast early on the Monday morning to discuss it. The conversation was dominated by the fallout from Lehmans and, in particular, by the plight of HBOS, which was beginning to crack.

As Hank Paulson had said a year earlier, I do have a high pain threshold, but I was reaching its outer limits. Lehman's collapse was to prove catastrophic. British bankruptcy rules meant that the administrator here in the UK froze Lehman Brothers' assets. He did so with good reason, because he suspected that $6 billion had been taken out of the London office on the Friday evening and had not come back. This demonstrates just how interlinked the banks are, and how quickly money can be moved from one jurisdiction to another. Because of the administrator's vigilance, the US banks became fearful that they would not get their money out of the US arm of Lehman Brothers. They, in turn, refused to settle with other banks. Although these problems were later resolved, it was another jolt to the system. Stock prices plunged in Europe, the US and across Asia. Ironically, that meant Barclays were able to pick up the American end of Lehmans at a bargain-basement price. Had they had bought it on the Sunday, they would have paid a huge amount more. I wondered why they hadn't just waited, as any sensible vulture would.

Commentators and Wall Street were in a frenzy of speculation, some of it well founded, some prompted by panic. Throughout that week I met with Callum McCarthy and Mervyn King, who were monitoring events in the US, where household names like Morgan Stanley and

Goldman Sachs were under severe pressure. The Federal Reserve tried to calm the markets by announcing plans to loosen its lending restrictions to the banks. A hastily convened consortium of banks agreed a $70 billion fund for financial firms that might need it. The ECB said it would pump 42 billion euros into the money markets. The Bank of England offered nearly £9 billion in a three-day auction.

On the Monday the fire-fighters in the US had rolled out the president. He made a public statement to say he was confident the financial markets were resilient enough to deal with the blows raining down. He was bluffing, of course, part of a concerted effort to shore up confidence. His Democratic rival, Barack Obama, pronounced it 'the most serious financial crisis since the Great Depression'. Folk memories of the Great Crash swam into focus.

By Tuesday, 16 September, it was clear to me that the global fallout from the Lehman Brothers collapse was accelerating. HBOS was the biggest loser. Its business model was not so very different from Northern Rock's. It needed to raise a lot of funds in the US, which it had managed to do earlier in the year, but was now struggling. In size, though, HBOS was in a different league. Now, the UK's biggest mortgage lender saw 33 per cent of its value wiped out in one day. The hawk-like eyes of the financial analysts were watching, and there were strong suggestions that short-selling of its shares was driving the price down. This also appeared to be happening to banks across Europe and in the US. Short-selling is basically when someone sells stock they don't own on the assumption that when they do acquire it in order to fulfil their obligation, they will pay a lot less for it than the selling price. We ran the risk that this would rapidly become a panic, so Callum McCarthy and the FSA placed a temporary ban on short-selling, which was followed up in Europe and America. This kind of interference in what is standard market practice in ordinary times had never happened before, and it exposed the extent of the concern that was being felt across the world. It was a month since I had warned that the UK faced its worst economic crisis for sixty years.

Back in London, I was also preparing my speech at the Labour Party conference in Manchester the coming weekend. Because of every-thing that had happened it had to be a good speech, and it was taking up a lot of time. I had also to deliver the annual Mais Lecture at the Cass Business School in London at the beginning of October. Most Chancellors will get to give this prestigious lecture once. It was a major piece of work, and I wanted to use it to explain why the fiscal rules that we had followed for the past ten years were redundant given the economic conditions we now faced. We were currently in the parliamentary recess, usually an ideal time to work on speeches and the like. However, the week was rapidly being taken over by the global banking crisis.

HBOS had the look of Northern Rock about it. There was a grave risk that we would end up having to take on another, much larger and more complex, wreck of a bank. I was increasingly concerned that if we ended up acquiring bank after bank without any grand plan, people would lose confidence in us. It was more and more evident that banks needed capital, but we were not ready yet to execute a plan, let alone reconcile ourselves to the costs we would face. Had HBOS been able to hold on for another few weeks we might have dealt with it differently, as we did with RBS. This would have meant even more public money being needed, possibly to acquire not just a majority shareholding but the whole of HBOS. RBS's balance sheet was almost the same size as Britain's gross domestic product. To have taken over HBOS would have added an even greater burden to our national finances. And there was no guarantee we could have kept it going.

As it was, Lloyds TSB, a fairly conservative but solid bank, had been talking to HBOS about a possible takeover. The Lloyds chief executive, an American called Eric Daniels, thought he saw an opportunity for his bank – which, I must say, was not obvious to me. Lloyds had considered a takeover before but knew that it would fall foul of the competition rules in the UK, because the two banks' combined share of the mort-gage market would be too great. Nevertheless, it looked as if they would now be ready to take over HBOS, thereby providing the bank with the much-needed capital to stay afloat. I discussed the takeover with Eric Daniels on 17 September. I told him that Lloyds would have to be satisfied that it knew what it was taking on. For our part, we would be prepared to consider amending the competition rules in these exceptional circumstances. Until very late in the day, we had two draft announcements ready: one dealing with a Lloyds takeover, the other with nationalization.

I talked about this with Gordon, who was as keen as I was to achieve a private sector solution, if it would work. After all, if we were stuck with HBOS we would have to wind it down, and competition in the mortgage market would be reduced anyway. The announcement of the takeover was made the following morning, 18 September. I did the inevitable media round, this time from the Treasury's remote studio, along from my office. There was concern about competition, but generally the reception was better than expected. In Scotland and in Halifax, though, the announcement was met with considerable trepidation. Job losses were inevitable. All that could be said was that if the bank had collapsed, even more would have gone.

On the Friday, a photograph of Gordon and Sir Victor Blank, the Labour-supporting chairman of Lloyds TSB, appeared in the *Financial Times*. They had been at a cocktail party the day before the announcement and had been seen in close conversation. Someone thought it would be a good idea to brief that this was where the takeover had been conceived and urged on Lloyds by the government. The story was seized on by the Tories, who claimed that, rather than being a commercial decision reached by the two banks, it was a political deal. Anyone who had given this suggestion a moment's thought would have realized that you cannot arrange a takeover of this magnitude over a glass of warm white wine and then announce it next day. The story backfired. It had taken weeks for the two sets of shareholders eventually to agree to the takeover; if they hadn't approved of the deal, they could have voted it down.

6 Keep Calm and Carry On

On Saturday morning we set off for Manchester and the party conference. I had my speech, but I did not like it – which was a pity because many people had put a lot of work into it. I didn't think it would meet the demands not just of the party faithful but of the world at large, which was now focusing on what I would have to say. Nonetheless, we were in better spirits than might have been expected.

There was a sense of crisis, but whereas the previous year with Northern Rock it had looked as if this was a British problem, now people knew it was a problem for every other major country in the world too. I think also that there was a belief that we were getting a grip. Gordon, Yvette Cooper, the Chief Secretary to the Treasury, and I did a question and answer session on the Saturday afternoon. It went down well. Gordon was in good form. The weekend was spent going from event to event, bumping into colleagues and friends.

What I had said to the *Guardian* was very much in the front of people's minds. In a crowded hotel foyer I met an economic commentator whom I greatly respect, who had written an excoriating piece about my interview at the time. He bought me a cup of tea and said he was sorry. He now thought the situation was far worse than I had suggested. It was good of him. It is not an experience I've encountered often.

I duly delivered my speech on the Monday, just before lunch. It was a much better speech than the one I had arrived with, having been substantially rewritten the day before with the help of David Bradshaw, who had worked with Tony Blair. I am not a natural conference speaker, but when I was called to the rostrum, I was astonished at the warmth of my reception. It was my first – and, I expected, last – standing ovation. It helped me personally because the reaction of the conference was carefully noted by others in the hall who might not have had my best interests at heart. Once off the stage, I rushed off to another telephone conference with Hank Paulson and G7 finance ministers. Hank outlined the slow progress he was making with the TARP scheme, which he was struggling to get through Congress.

I went back to London two days later for a series of meetings on the banks and forthcoming legislation to toughen up their supervision, and to discuss the continuing turmoil in financial markets. We also had a meeting with the Bank of England, followed by a call with Christine Lagarde to talk about the deteriorating situation. She was very apprehensive. Like me, she thought the banks were in denial.

The high point of the day was a surprise birthday party for my wife, organized by my private office at No. 11. For a couple of hours we shared a cake and the kind of black humour that sustained us all through the worst of times. I have always been lucky with the staff in the private offices where I've worked, but at the Treasury they probably saw rather more of me than they ever bargained for. It was little consolation, but we did try to keep them fed and watered around our kitchen table, which became an annexe to the Treasury. We were immensely touched that, even though they had been working flat out, around the clock, they had still taken the trouble to set up this small party.

The next boil ready for lancing was Bradford and Bingley. In the past year Bradford and Bingley's shares had plunged by around 90 per cent. Investors believed the bank was in deep trouble. We had been watching it carefully as its share price dropped. By September it was nearing the end of the road. There was a Reuters screen outside my office in the

Treasury and a Chancellor needs to know everything on it. Watching the Bradford and Bingley share price reminded me of the flat-lining heart monitor of a dying patient.

At this point there was a change at the FSA when chairman Callum McCarthy retired. He had previously told me that he wanted to leave his post at the end of his term of office in September 2008. I was sorry, as his calm and considered advice had been immensely helpful over the year we had worked together. His judgements were usually right, but to press him to stay would have been unfair, especially at this time. I could hardly hold out the prospect of the crisis ending a few weeks later. In his place I appointed Adair Turner. He had been Director General of the CBI, a director of a bank, and had done a great deal of work for the government, including carrying out a review of pensions policy where, inevitably, he clashed with Gordon. He was also chairman of the new Committee on Climate Change which we had set up to implement our commitment to cut carbon emissions. I wanted a strong, level-headed chairman to provide leadership within the FSA, but one who could also deal with the day-to-day tensions between the FSA and the Bank of England. He was a good choice. Although he wasn't due to start the job until 1 October, he very sensibly decided to get his feet under the table before that. His first outing was Bradford and Bingley.

The three of us, Mervyn King, Adair Turner and I, were all agreed that the bank was finished and that we would either have to organize a sale or nationalize it. We had to be careful. Its shares were still trading and we had to tread carefully and be mindful of the shareholders' interests. Legally, you can't just take over a company, depriving shareholders of their property. What was different here, though, was that this particular investment was fast running out of money and its shares would soon be worthless. The risk was that if Bradford and Bingley simply collapsed, panic might spread to other small banks, and I wanted to avoid at all costs the spectacle of another run on a bank.

By now, Bradford and Bingley had drawn more than £3 billion from the Bank of England emergency fund. Mervyn King quite rightly said they could not borrow much more, because they could never repay it. The question in our minds was not 'if' but 'when' it would reach the stage at which the FSA would have to say it could no longer meet its financial obligations. This time we had legislation to allow us to deal with a failing bank, to protect savers and maintain financial stability. I had insisted when we nationalized Northern Rock in February that we took powers to enable us either to transfer a failing bank to another one or to nationalize it, which meant that once a bank had failed we could now resolve within hours all the issues that might have taken months under the old regime. This was the measure so bitterly opposed by the Tories when it was approved by the House of Commons six months earlier.

By 26 September 2008 everyone could see the game was up. The Bradford and Bingley management were not surprised when the FSA told them it would have to withdraw their licence to take new deposits, the death knell for any bank. In fact, I sensed they were almost relieved. Now we had forty-eight hours in which to find a solution, before the markets opened on Monday morning.

On Saturday morning, about 10 o'clock, I met Gordon downstairs in his office in No. 10. We were agreed about what needed to be done. He was relatively relaxed about Bradford and Bingley because we were in control of events. He was far from relaxed about what was happening more generally. He felt that world leaders had not grasped the enormity of what was happening. President Sarkozy, ever keen to grab a headline, was planning a meeting with Gordon, the German chancellor, Angela Merkel, and Italy's Silvio Berlusconi to discuss the crisis at the end of the following week. Gordon said, quite rightly, that they couldn't have a meeting without a plan to announce at the end of it. That would be worse than not meeting at all. So it transpired.

I went back to the Treasury. There were three options for Bradford and Bingley. If we did nothing, the bank would go into administration. That would still leave us with the risk of a run, and administration could go on for months, if not longer; and we would have to provide some funding for the administrator, over whom we would have little control. The second option was sale to another bank or building society, but I could not think who would want to buy it. We thought that the most likely scenario would be the sale of the branches, with the deposits in them, and possibly some of the sound mortgages. The other mortgages, where repayment might be harder, would have to be held in a separate entity, a so-called 'bad bank'. The third option was to nationalize it, in part or as a whole. In the long term, this sort of situation can be managed. Most borrowers will manage to repay some or all of what they owe, and in time, provided the economy recovers, so will the price of their property.

Although I had no great expectation of being able to sell Bradford and Bingley as a whole, I wanted to try one last shot if only to remove any doubt that nationalization really was the only option. We might still persuade one of the major banks to buy it, perhaps backed by a consortium of the others. The advantage would be that we would not have to deal with the 'bad bank' element for years to come. The banks had always told us that they were concerned about nationalization: here was a chance for them to step up to the plate and help their own industry and the country. I was not optimistic, but it was worth a try.

Weekends are the only time when Treasury officials can do things that, were they to leak, might cause havoc on the stock market, especially at a time like this when the slightest hint that something was afoot could cause massive gyrations in share prices. So, effectively we had from 5 o'clock on Friday night until 7 o'clock on Monday morning to do what was needed. On Friday night we asked the chief executives of the big banks to come to the Treasury the next morning. We did not tell them why, although no doubt they could guess. We told them to come in by the back door, in case there were any lurking photographers with a nose for when something was up. On Saturday morning, just after 11 o'clock, they gathered in a meeting room down the corridor from my office. I told them that the lead option was to use the emergency legislation to nationalize Bradford and Bingley, but that we wanted to give them the alternative of taking it over in some sort of rescue plan.

Our advisers from Morgan Stanley took them through the numbers. We had to engage advisers from time to time; there was so much pressure on the Treasury that we simply did not have the capacity to do all the number crunching that was needed. We offered the option of one bank purchasing Bradford and Bingley for nothing, with the other banks standing behind them. They were not enthusiastic. Some doubted if they could get it past their shareholders. I left them to talk it over among themselves. It was a short discussion, though. No one wanted anything to do with it. They recognized that nationalization was the only way out, and perhaps it was a sign of the times that they were entirely happy with that. They were gone by lunchtime – but they would soon be back.

Most of Saturday, 27 September, was then spent trying to work out what we should do. The most likely option seemed to be that Santander would buy the more attractive parts of Bradford and Bingley. Santander wanted to expand; they already owned Abbey, and had bought Alliance and Leicester in July. It turned out they were also interested in buying the good parts of Northern Rock. That seemed to me to add another layer of complexity. There was another bidder, though, again for the good parts of Bradford and Bingley. This was HBOS. They desperately needed cash. The branches, with their deposits, were tempting. But we were far from sure that HBOS was in any financial condition to take it on.

Most of the Treasury team had worked flat out since Friday night, grabbing a couple of hours' sleep here and there. It was wearing, going over proposals and counter-proposals, line by line, number by number, but it is something that most officials thrive on. The Treasury is a place with many frustrations, but the scale and importance of the work, especially at times like this, can't be matched. The officials looked worn out but were incredibly cheerful. The atmosphere was frenetic.

Meeting rooms filled with lawyers and bankers brought in to handle some of the most detailed and complex negotiations. In other rooms were lawyers acting for Bradford and Bingley. It would have been easy to muddle them up. I spent the weekend between the Treasury and Downing Street, working on different versions of what I would say on Monday, depending on the outcome.

As I always did when stuck in the Treasury and No. 11 at the weekend, I took walks around the garden behind Downing Street. It was a place of solace, with a small but dedicated team of gardeners with whom I would discuss pruning or their latest design plans. Margaret thought I looked like the prisoner of Spandau, pacing the lawns behind high walls laced with barbed wire and watched by security cameras covering every centimetre of the garden.

On Sunday afternoon, after hours of negotiation and much discussion between the Treasury, the FSA and the Bank, not to mention meetings with Gordon, Santander agreed to buy Bradford and Bingley. By early on Monday, 29 September 2008, we were able to announce that we had saved as much of Bradford and Bingley as we could. The bank was open for business on Monday morning. Sadly, jobs did go, particularly in Yorkshire. But had the bank collapsed, many more would have been lost.

I did the now familiar round of media interviews as soon as the markets opened, and was back at my desk in the Treasury in time for the next crisis. There was a torrent of bad news all day. A financial geyser was bursting in Iceland as the government there had to bail out one of its banks, Glitnir. Its largest shareholder, Stodir, had been due to buy a huge stake in the House of Fraser and Hamley's owner, Baugur. The deal was halted at the eleventh hour as Stodir went into administration. At this stage, Iceland's other two banks, Kaupthing and Landsbanki, were still open for business, but it looked to be only a matter of time.

Iceland's population is about the same as that of the English midland city of Wolverhampton. Yet by 2008 the country boasted no less than three banks that had grown way beyond the wildest dreams of their founders. Much of their activity centred on the UK, and London in particular. They bankrolled a lot of property development, high-street investments, and the English football premiership. They offered attractive rates of interest and attracted billions of pounds of savers' money. The largest, Landsbanki, although based in Reykjavik, had branches in London, trading under the name Icesave.

This was a disaster waiting to happen. In a nutshell, all the action was in London but the regulation and detailed supervision of what was going on was supposed to be carried out over a thousand miles away in Iceland. The problem was that Landsbanki had come to London to attract volumes of money it could simply never have got from a population of 340,000 people back in Iceland. Over the years it funded a range of investments, many of which are, in 2011, being investigated by the criminal authorities. Along the way, quite a few Icelandic citizens seemed to get very rich. Some were even able to make handsome donations to the British Conservative Party. By 2008 it was clear, too, that Iceland itself was rapidly becoming insolvent. Earlier in the year Gordon had spoken to the Icelandic prime minister, who had formerly been their finance minister, and urged him to go to the IMF. He was reluctant to do so, preferring to seek out Russian loans to tide the country over.

Although the FSA had been concerned about Icelandic banks, it was only in early September that it was brought to my attention. I was told that there was a delegation from Iceland, headed by their trade minister, who wanted to see me as a matter of urgency. The FSA was anxious that I should meet with them because they were making no headway in trying to persuade Landsbanki to put more money into its activities in the UK. But if the FSA thought the Icelandic delegation had come to show some contrition and eagerness to respond to the British regulators, it was in for a rude shock.

I was struck, as the minister and his colleagues entered the Treasury, at what seemed an unusually large delegation. The minister, his private secretary, Icelandic Treasury civil servants, representatives from their regulators and assorted others all trooped into my room. The minister spoke at some length, complaining about the attitude of the FSA. He seemed to believe that Iceland was being picked on. The Icelandic regulator spoke volubly, again at considerable length, about the strength of the bank and how we were being unreasonable. I was told that considerable national pride was invested in Landsbanki. It occurred to me that if they did not realize just how bad a state Landsbanki was in, they did not know what they were doing. Alternatively, they did know.

They were not helping matters by trying to pretend to us that everything was well. This meeting coloured my subsequent dealings with Icelandic ministers. I have been involved in talks with many ministers from different countries. You expect them to stick up for their country when their interests and ours diverge. However, you do expect their dealings to be straightforward – and this simply was not the case, as we were soon to find out. Two years later, a different Icelandic government established a 'truth commission'. It examined the relationship between politicians, bankers and business people. Its report makes grim reading.

Icelandic banks were a relatively small part of the problems I had to deal with, but they illustrate the bigger problem when banks become too big for their home countries to manage or ultimately to finance. Iceland, along with Ireland, was part of what Scotland's nationalist first minister, Alex Salmond, liked to refer to as an 'arc of prosperity', to which he yearned to attach Scotland. It was now an arc of insolvency.

Ireland has three banks, all of which got into trouble. Eventually, Irish bank debt effectively became Ireland's own debt, forcing the country to seek an international bail-out. No one visiting Dublin in the ten years before the crash could have failed to notice the extraordinary number of tower cranes above office blocks which had yet to find tenants. The Irish banks had got into property lending like there was no tomorrow, along with HBOS and RBS, which had a great deal at risk, mainly through its Ulsterbank. The Irish banks had lent heavily into the British property market too and got badly burned. I was most concerned about the healthiest of the three Irish banks, the Bank of Ireland. I wondered just how many people knew that the Post Office Bank in the UK is in fact the Bank of Ireland. The closeness of the Irish banking system to the UK was to cause huge problems for us just two weeks later. In the good times, this profusion of banks is good for an economy, but that is only so if the banks are built on firm foundations. There is potentially a huge problem for any country when foreign banks have a significant presence but their regulation is carried out overseas and largely out of sight.

Both Iceland and subsequently Ireland were brought down by their banks. Meanwhile, Belgian-Dutch bank Fortis was bailed out by Holland, Belgium and Luxembourg. The German commercial property lender Hypo Real Estate Holding AG had to be rescued, and shares in the Franco-Belgian bank Dexia plummeted. It was obvious that across Europe they were hitting the same problems as we were. Twelve months before, during the collapse of Northern Rock, I had sensed more than a little *Schadenfreude* when I went to that first Ecofin meeting. I did say to them then that I suspected they had the same problem, if they cared to look.

The problem of toxic loans had spread like wildfire through the banking system. It did not recognize national borders. It was inflamed by the fact that far too many people at senior levels in the banking industry were happy to look the other way when the going seemed good. In the US the fires were still raging, with frantic talks in Washington to agree a $700 billion rescue package for the country's beleaguered financial institutions. The only positive thing was that the Republicans were now giving support to the bill in Congress, as Wachovia, the country's fourth-largest retail bank, was on the verge of collapse.

It was apparent to us in the Treasury that, unless we put some sort of firebreak in place, we would see one bank after another collapse in the UK. Mervyn King and Adair Turner had met and reached the same conclusion. We were now deep in uncharted waters. There was the smell of fear in the air. Those who believed they were still all right, mainly because their business was in the Far East, were afraid of becoming contaminated, as investors and traders dumped the institution they thought weakest and most likely to collapse next.

For much of the previous year, the banks' problem had been lack of liquidity. The introduction of the special liquidity scheme in April had eased the pressure, but the problem now was lack of capital. On 26 September, Mervyn King asked to see me and Adair Turner privately at the end of one of our formal meetings. He said that unless the banking system as a whole was recapitalized, further failures were inevitable. Adair Turner agreed. The only realistic source for that capital was unfortunately the government. My concern was not about the principle of recapitalizing, but the practicalities of undertaking it. The Governor said that the key was to require banks to raise capital. He wanted it to be a compulsory scheme, with the banks obliged to take taxpayers' money and to meet the conditions that came with it. They should be given no option if the FSA were to allow them to continue to operate.

The key was to get capital into the banks that needed it – primarily RBS and HBOS, which was now part of the Lloyds group – but at the same time to persuade a bank like HSBC, which had no obvious need for more capital, to join in the scheme. This was necessary because unless we could show that action was being taken across the board, the risk was that the markets, satisfied that, say, RBS was adequately capitalized, would turn their attention to, say, Barclays, if it had not raised more capital. If they did not stand together, they would be picked off one by one. In other words, we had to show that we had dealt with the systemic problem across all our major banks. We had to convince the still solvent banks to come into the scheme, something they would be very wary of doing.

We were also concerned about the legal and financial implications of overruling shareholders and forcing banks to take government money, not to mention explaining to the public what we were doing. On the other hand, a voluntary scheme had the obvious drawback that it would not be seen as a complete solution and would stigmatize the participating banks. The key might be to persuade those banks who could do so to raise the required capital themselves. It was important, in the interest of stability and confidence, to get those banks that did not need capital signed up to the scheme without fuss.

We would be providing billions of pounds – money the government would have to raise in the financial markets by selling government bonds – to banks that, until now, had been owned entirely by their shareholders. In return, the government would acquire shares in the banks, which would subsequently be resold. Depending on how bad the situation was, we could end up owning all the banks in Britain. Perhaps not surprisingly, the Treasury was very reluctant, and in some quarters downright hostile, to what we were proposing. Nevertheless, I told officials to work up an emergency plan to inject new capital into the banks. They were to work closely with the Bank of England and the FSA. But failure to head off the crisis was not an option. The first piece of written advice that I received from Treasury officials was, in effect, perhaps we should wait and see because the crisis wasn't here just yet. That advice was consigned to where it belonged, and once the initial scepticism was overcome Treasury officials worked day and night to come up with a plan. There were continual meetings at No. 10 too, but they focused on the actual delivery of the package, not the principle.

We were fast reaching a situation where a big British bank could go down. HBOS was having to borrow £16 billion overnight to keep going. Normally, banks can borrow for long periods, six months or a year or even longer. Here we were with the biggest banks in the world in a position where no one was prepared to risk lending them money they could not count on getting back the next day, never mind next week.

So why not let the banks fail?

In normal times, provided it is handled carefully, a bank can fail. It happened with Barings in the 1990s and BCCI in 1992, and there had been smaller bank failures in the 1970s. In the US, bank failures are commonplace. Provided savers' money can be guaranteed, and provided investors can be reconciled to losing money, then it is all manageable. But I was in no doubt that these were not normal times. The risk of one bank collapsing and taking all the others with it was acute. I suppose it could have been tried, but I would not have wanted to be responsible for the economic and social catastrophe that might follow. Banks and their boards had made catastrophic errors of judgement and in some cases they did not even know what they were doing. The regulators had not understood the pressures building up, and neither had central banks nor governments. There were lessons that needed to be learned, but they were for later. What was vital now was to prevent a complete collapse of the financial system.

In the aftermath of this crisis there have been many who have claimed authorship of what proved to be a highly successful plan. Gordon and I had earlier discussed the idea of forcing banks to raise capital, and of us providing it if necessary. He was immediately open to the idea and he did tell me, when I outlined it to him, that he and his advisers had been thinking along similar lines. It really doesn't matter who thought of the scheme first. What matters is that it worked. What I know for certain is that the Treasury, the Bank and the FSA started this work on 26 September, under my instruction.

At 4 o'clock on the Monday afternoon I met with Gordon in Downing Street to take stock. I was about to head back to the Treasury when I got a text from Anna, our daughter, who was travelling in South America with a friend. It opened with the perennially hair-raising line: 'Hey, Dad, no worries but ...' They were stranded on the border between Bolivia and Peru. Her friend Catriona's passport, money and credit cards had been stolen. Less worrying, I suppose, than the previous week's text in which she had described watching a gunfight outside her hostel in Bolivia. The border guard wanted a bribe to let them into Peru to reach the nearest British embassy and was that OK? No, it wasn't; but I was thousands of miles away. Just because you're Chancellor doesn't mean you're not still a father.

At 6 o'clock on Tuesday, 30 September, I awoke to the news on the BBC *Today* programme that the Irish government had decided to guarantee all savers' money held in Irish banks. This was the first we had heard of it. It meant the Irish government was effectively underwriting its banks in a way that no other country in the world had done. We had guaranteed savings in the special circumstances of Northern Rock, but I had been careful not to do the same elsewhere. I knew full well that if the Irish government's bluff was called they would be bankrupt. It was a promise on which they could never deliver. My immediate thought was that in the current climate savers in British banks would shift their money into branches of Irish banks in the UK. As it turned out, that is exactly what was crossing the minds of finance ministers around Europe. We were all hearing this for the first time on the BBC news. Despite frequent undertakings that everyone would keep everyone else informed before taking action, this had been a unilateral declaration. It was the last thing we needed.

I did know that for some weeks there had been disagreements within the Irish government and between the prime minister and his finance minister, Brian Lenihan, about what to do. Their central bank was becoming increasingly frustrated. I spoke to Brian Lenihan shortly after 9 o'clock that morning. We knew each other well and had a good working relationship. I knew sometime after that that Brian had been diagnosed with cancer, to which he succumbed three years later. He worked tirelessly for his country in difficult circumstances. Then, when we spoke, I said that what he had announced put us in an impossible position. The implication for savers was that if they put their money in an Irish bank, it was safe. If it was in a British bank, with no such guarantee, it wasn't. I didn't say that it might occur to some savers that if the guarantees were called, Ireland would be in no position to honour them. I told him in no uncertain terms that the FSA would have to take action if it became clear that funds were flowing from Britain to Irish banks. Brian apologized. He said the decision had been taken very late at night and that there had been no opportunity to tell us, or anybody else, about it. I did later find out that it had been taken at something like 2 a.m., which smacks of panic rather than a plan, although I understood Brian's predicament.

I spent the rest of the morning on the phone: to Neelie Kroes, the European commissioner for competition, to Christine Lagarde, and to Wouter Bos, the Dutch finance minister. We were all deeply concerned at the implications of the Irish announcement. A day later, we heard reports that Germany had announced that they would guarantee all their bank deposits. This was extraordinary from a government that kept telling the world that they saw no need to intervene in the German banking system. It was even more surprising because the Germans set much store on announcements being made by Europe as a whole, rather than by individual member states. Unfortunately, it took some considerable time to find out that Chancellor Merkel had made a general statement that no depositors would lose out, in the context of a bail-out of one of their banks, rather than promising to guarantee all bank deposits.

Sadly, whereas I had a good working relationship with Christine Lagarde, the same could not be said of my German counterpart, Peer Steinbrück. He refused to return my calls that day, and eventually I had to ask David Miliband, the Foreign Secretary, to call his German counterpart to find out what was happening. I would like to think that Peer's problem was that he didn't know what was going on either. These things can happen in a coalition government.

Throughout the day, the FSA monitored the flow of savings between banks. There was some movement, but it was not as bad as it might have been. Our Northern Rock explicit guarantee that no saver would lose money had translated into an implicit guarantee for the rest of the banking system. Confidence is a very fragile thing and in those days any shiver could make it collapse. I knew that if collapse did come, it would happen very quickly.

I had met the main bank chief executives individually and sometimes as a group, as over Bradford and Bingley, to discuss specific problems. Fred Goodwin had been in touch a few days earlier to say that the banks were increasingly worried about both liquidity and capital. They wanted to know what we were thinking. I thought it best to try to meet them all in the same room once more. In my experience, it is very easy when you talk to one chief executive for the conversation soon to move to everyone else's problems. It is a classic defensive position and a bit of displacement activity. We needed to get the banks to work with us, but these were commercial companies, always ready to stand on their dignity, and culturally resentful of any suggestion that they might need to ask the government for help, let alone that government might actually tell them what to do. I was also conscious that relationships between the banks and the Bank of England had not improved since the previous autumn; if anything they had got worse. There was a general feeling that the Governor had not acted quickly enough to put more money into the system.

On the Tuesday evening, 30 September, I held the first of what was to become a series of crisis meetings with the biggest banks' chief executives. My reluctance to do this before now had been due to the fact that even the news that such a meeting had been convened could have provoked further panic, such was the febrile environment. As a politician I am well aware that, very often, once you have a meeting with more than one other person present, you might just as well call a news conference. Even hustling the chief executives in through the back door was problematic, since most of them use the kind of cars that would catch the attention of any nearby reporter.

We assembled in my room at the Treasury shortly after 6 o'clock in the evening. Present were the Mervyn King and Adair Turner. With me was Paul Myners, my Treasury minister. Paul had considerable experience as a banker and in the City but he was not the usual suspect: he took no prisoners and was not in thrall to the bankers. Nick Macpherson and John Kingman and other Treasury officials were there, along with one of my special advisers, Geoffrey Spence. Geoffrey was no orthodox special adviser, he was a specialist, with years of banking knowledge, and had also worked in the Treasury some years previously. Even better, he was resolutely calm in the face of the bankers' finger-waving.

On the other side of the table sat Britain's top bankers. Sir Fred Goodwin, who appeared to be leading the delegation that day, sat in the middle. At that time, hanging on the wall in my room was a huge canvas painted by the Scottish artist John Bellany. Its title was *Death's Head* and its deathly centrepiece was right above the middle seat at the conference table. I am sure it was simply coincidence that Sir Fred chose to sit there. Over the next seven days, other chief executives and their chairmen would take it in turns to sit on that seat, entirely by chance, I'm sure. Curiously, not one of them survived the crisis.

Next to Sir Fred was John Varley of Barclays, who was one of comparatively few bankers who could see the bigger picture. He was measured, and invariably helpful. Also present was Eric Daniels of Lloyds TSB and HBOS, who had presumably by now had the opportunity to open the books to the horrors of what he had bought. António Horta Osório, then of Santander, was there too, always helpful but taking care to sit well away from the centre of the table. Santander, he knew, was not in the firing line. Dyfrig John was there for HSBC, and Peter Sands from Standard Chartered. These last two banks had substantial business in the Far East and comparatively limited activities here and so were not affected in quite the same way as some of the others; but HSBC in particular, under the chairmanship of Stephen Green, knew that it had a definite interest in the health of the banking system. Last but not least was Graham Beale from the Nationwide building society. The Nationwide is, in effect, the lender of last resort for all of Britain's building societies because of its sheer size and influence. Graham was thoughtful and helpful throughout.

The Irish announcement earlier that morning had clearly spooked the banks; it caused particular consternation for RBS and HBOS, which both had branches there. I told them there had been no warning, but that seemed to add to their view that governments were not working together. I reinforced the fact that we were working flat out on a series of plans, but, I said, I did not want to announce them until they were complete, pointing to the confusion in the US where a less than fully worked-out plan had fallen apart. I explained that I was not attracted to the US proposal because it was my belief that it would not work in Britain.

Sir Fred said what we already knew: the banks were dependent on being able to raise money overnight to keep going. They needed to know that the facilities would be there. Despite Mervyn King's protestations that there was money available if they needed it, he and his colleagues wanted the Bank of England to do more. The Governor made the point that a breakdown in lending between banks was part of the problem, but that there was an urgent need for capital against the losses that were mounting up. The arguments were circular. Some, like António Horta Osório, wanted more guarantees to boost confidence. Others wanted more international action.

What became clear was that, even at this stage, there was nothing close to a consensus that more capital was needed. Each bank wanted something different. We would have to put a plan to them. Fortunately, our preparations for that were well advanced, but I was determined not to put a plan forward until it was fully thought through. There was also frustration on the banks' side in that they thought we were not doing enough, even if they weren't sure exactly what they wanted us to do. As they trooped out of the room, my thought was that this had been a less than satisfactory meeting. The meeting that Tuesday night lasted just over an hour. After they had left, it took about fifteen minutes for the first calls to come in from the press.

Meanwhile, the situation in Iceland was deteriorating. The FSA told me that undertakings given by the Icelandic authorities that sufficient money would be put into Landsbanki had not been honoured. It had been agreed that Gordon would speak to the prime minister, Geir Haarde, but he had to go to Paris to meet President Sarkozy, Chancellor Merkel and Silvio Berlusconi, so I was deputized to make the call instead. The Treasury and the FSA had already concluded that it would not be

long before Landsbanki and Kaupthing failed. We were ready, if necessary, to use the new powers we had acquired at the time of Northern
Rock to transfer their UK undertakings to another bank.

Kaupthing marketed a product called Edge, an internet bank with
150,000 depositors and nearly £3 billion in savings. Landsbanki marketed itself as Icesave and had 300,000 accounts with deposits of over
£4 billion. Although these were foreign banks, I decided, against the
advice of Nick Macpherson, that we would have to guarantee savers'
money if the banks failed. So far, we had been able to say that no saver
had lost money. I believed that reassurance was essential.

I told the Icelandic prime minister that it appeared that large sums
of money had been taken out of the UK from the Kaupthing branches,
which was a serious breach of FSA regulations. The FSA had to find out
by the end of the afternoon whether or not that breach had taken place.
If it had, they would close the bank. He asked whether the money was
needed today and how much it was. I said it was about £600 million,
small beer for us but a huge amount for him. It was urgent, I said, that
he look into it immediately. His response rang alarm bells. He asked if
there was any chance that the amount could be negotiated down. I said
there was no chance and that the money had to be returned before the
end of the weekend. I suspected we would end up having to close the
banks the following week.

On Friday night I flew to Edinburgh, hoping to go to a music festi-
val in my constituency the following day. I had promised to go months
before and didn't want to disappoint them. Parliament was due to
return after its long summer recess the following week. The Sunday
political programmes were cranking up, and I agreed to do an interview with Andrew Marr's Sunday show on the BBC, which frequently
set the agenda for the following day's news bulletins. Normally, I like
to do these set-piece interviews in the studio in London. When it was
arranged, because I was determined to fulfil my promises in Edinburgh,
I said I could be filmed live from my home. I had to fly back to London
on Sunday afternoon, but at least this way I would get Saturday night

in my own bed. The producers arranged to interview George Osborne for the Conservatives and Vince Cable for the Liberal Democrats. They were to be together in the studio just before my interview. My intention was to try to reassure people that we were on the case and to prepare the way for a major intervention. The emergency rescue package was close to completion, but I did not want to announce it from my sitting room in Edinburgh.

I listened to the interview with George Osborne with growing incredulity. He referred to a discussion on banking legislation that he'd had with me the previous week, and a subsequent meeting that I'd authorized with Treasury civil servants on banking reforms. He then went on to refer to a discussion he'd had with the Governor, and the possibility of recapitalizing banks. I was dismayed. There was enough there to point people in the right direction. Two thoughts went through my mind. The first was that he had said enough to suggest that he knew of our plans. The second was that if he did know, he must have known he was playing with fire. Clearly his objective, as it had been for the past year, was to claim that he had a cunning plan, so that when we announced ours it would seem as if we were following him. He was letting political advantage override the need not to spook the markets.

When it came to my interview, I was determined not to reveal our thinking. On the other hand, I was not going to let Osborne play the game he had embarked on without a challenge. I could not entirely ignore the politics. I said that we were looking at options and the question of whether there was sufficient capital in banks had to be addressed. There was enough there to point the media in the right direction. We managed to contain the story for at least the next twenty-four hours. What finally burst the dam, came, I believe, from the banks themselves.

I flew to London that Sunday afternoon and was back in the Treasury by 4 o'clock. I still had several hours' work to do on a statement for the Commons the next day as Parliament returned from its summer recess. I was always anxious to keep the Commons informed. The trouble was that there was now a feeding frenzy, an expectation that something big would be announced, which was not going to happen. I simply reported back, broadly, on the summer's work. I did not expect plaudits, but the following day's damning criticisms were hard to take. There was now great expectation that we could not fullfill. Had we been able to, the rescue plan, almost complete, could have been announced in calmer conditions. It was designed to restore confidence in the banking system and to stave off collapse. As it was, we had to make the announcement later that week in the teeth of a raging storm. Who leaked the plan to him, I don't know. I do know that he had been briefed, entirely properly, by Mervyn King the previous Friday. The Governor meets the Shadow Chancellor from time to time. I was told of that meeting in the normal way, but not of what exactly was said. A discussion of government policy is not allowed, but the Governor can of course muse on his own thoughts. I can see what might have happened, but to play politics at that particular time, when the world was teetering on the brink of financial disaster, was not just foolish but dangerous.

On Monday evening, 6 October, I held another meeting with the banking chiefs, who wanted me to give them full details of our specific rescue proposals. I was determined not to do so until they were finalized because, as I rightly predicted, whatever I said at this meeting would be fed to the press. The men in front of me, for the most part, I trusted to keep the talks confidential. But I knew that once back in the office people would talk, and there was now an armada of journalists anxious to break a story regardless of the consequences.

There were other issues in addition to capital. We discussed the difficulty of banks having sufficient confidence in each other to settle the numerous trades they made each day. It was that stark: the banks didn't trust one another any more. They wanted some form of credit guarantee. I said nothing about that, because it was one of the issues we were actively working on. We talked about what more the Bank of England could do on liquidity. I said that when I announced the rescue plan it would be a once-and-for-all solution. If they had other issues, they had better raise them now. Above all, I said, I wanted to keep lines of communication with them open, but that required absolute confidentiality. I added that we would meet again very shortly.

As the bankers left that Monday night, I told my officials that we had to be ready to go in the next thirty-six hours. I knew there was an enormous amount of work still to be done, but we could not delay. In an ideal world, with no politics and no banking crisis and no rolling 24-hour news, we might have taken our time to devise an excellent solution. We did not have that luxury, but the solution still had to be excellent. There would be no second chance. I got back to the flat in Downing Street in time for the 10 o'clock news. Sure enough, someone had given the BBC an incomplete account of our meeting earlier that evening, which was bound to cause panic.

It was already clear that some banks needed more capital. Inevitably, many people had reached the conclusion that this could only now come from the government, and it followed that any bank needing substantial capital would have to take a big government shareholding. Not surprisingly, investors in banks in the firing line knew that the value of their shareholdings would plummet. So, when the markets opened the next morning, first in the Far East and then in London, RBS shares collapsed. Little wonder vulnerable banks were tempted to claim that all the banks represented around the table had asked for more money. That wasn't the case.

A week earlier, as we began working up the rescue plans, I had asked Nick Macpherson to go round the bank chief executives and chairmen and sound them out about various propositions, including the government taking shareholdings in return for desperately needed capital. The chairman of one of the banks had actually said that to make banks take capital from the state would amount to what he called 'expropriation', and would be nothing less than a return to the 1970s – or worse, the 1940s. This, just a week before we announced the bank rescue package. There had been two banks at the table in the Treasury that night that knew the game was up for them: RBS and HBOS.

Sitting in the kitchen of the flat later, going through my homework in the red box, reading up on submissions from Treasury officials, I knew that tomorrow would not be a good day. The last place I wanted to be was in Luxembourg at yet another meeting of European finance ministers. Getting to Luxembourg is a nightmare at the best of times. There are few scheduled flights and none that get you there in time for the traditional working breakfast – a misnomer if ever there was one. There is no food, just coffee, and for some years ministers met in a building that resembles a warehouse on an industrial estate well outside the picturesque capital city.

I needed to be in London to manage the inevitable crisis that day. The dilemma was that my absence would alert the world to the fact that something was very, very wrong with our banks. Normally, unlike our counterparts, British ministers are scrupulous about taking scheduled flights to and from meetings abroad. I was often struck by the ranks of private jets sitting at the airports at international gatherings and I noted that the smaller the country, the bigger the jet. On this particular day I decided that chartering a flight was justified, since a hasty exit was on the cards. As we touched down, Geoffrey Spence, my special adviser, pointed out two Icelandic jumbo jets parked on the runway. We taxíed alongside them in our Spitfire-sized plane.

My intention was to sit through the meeting, which was to be dominated that day by yet another discussion of the solvency requirements of the insurance industry. Arcane it may sound, but given the UK's global importance in the sector, I had to be there. As I left Downing Street before dawn, arrangements were being made not only to monitor what happened when the markets opened but to keep a close eye on what was going on in Iceland. We knew we were not being told the whole story there and it was inevitable that difficult decisions, which might wrongly be interpreted as hostile acts by the Icelandic government, would have to be taken in the next day or so.

I took my seat in the session minutes after the London stock exchange opened. We agreed I would watch for a signal from Geoffrey if there was news. I did not want a huddle of officials causing a commotion around me, surrounded as we were by ministers from other countries. Within minutes, he signalled me out of the chamber. The RBS share price had collapsed. Never a man for overstatement, he said it looked bad. He was monitoring the figures on a screen upstairs. I went back to my seat, hoping to appear normal. I had hardly been in the chamber ten minutes when Christine Lagarde came over and asked, 'What's wrong?' I said nothing, really, and ducked back out of the meeting as Geoffrey was waving from the doorway. Not only had the RBS share price collapsed but dealing in the shares had been suspended, not once but twice.

'That's it. It's over,' Geoffrey said. We went up to the delegation room and he went in ahead, saying, 'Clear the room.' Kim Darroch, the UK's senior diplomat at the EU, slowly closed his laptop, stood up and walked out.

When dealings in bank shares are suspended it is all over. I knew the bank was finished, in the most spectacular way possible. The game was up. If the markets could give up on RBS, one of the largest banks in the world, all bets on Britain's and the world's financial system were off.

Back at the Treasury, my officials were in frantic discussion with the Bank of England. There was panic in RBS itself. To maintain a calm face, I had to take my place at the conference table once more, along with my European colleagues. All looked at me intently, no doubt having been told of what was happening across the Channel. Britain was in the dock again, and they knew it.

Christine Lagarde, ever solicitous and sharp as a tack, appeared at my shoulder, 'It looks bad, doesn't it. What are you going to do?'

I said, simply, 'We will deal with it. You won't mind if we leave early?'

I kept leaving the meeting to be updated. An hour later, I came out to take a call from the RBS chairman, Tom McKillop. He sounded shellshocked. I asked him how long the bank could keep going. His answer was chilling: 'A couple of hours, maybe.'

At the end of the brief call, I put down the phone and told my officials: 'It's going bust this afternoon.' I felt a deep chill in my stomach. If we didn't act immediately, the bank's doors would close, cash machines would be switched off, cheques would not be honoured, people would not be paid. I remember thinking that this was once the small, conservative Scottish bank where I had opened my first bank account in Edinburgh forty years earlier. It was now on its knees.

My initial reaction must have been a bit like that of the captain of the *Titanic* when he was told by the ship's architect that it would sink in a couple of hours. There were not enough lifeboats for all the passengers. Sir Tom had concluded by saying that we had to do something, and what were we going to do? Like a reassuring parent, I had said we would do whatever was needed to keep the bank afloat until the end of the day, when we would be in a position to announce the emergency rescue plan, not just for RBS but for all the banks. I rang Nick Macpherson at the Treasury and told him his hour had come. He was to tell Mervyn King to put as much money into RBS as was necessary to keep it afloat that day. We would stand behind the Bank, even if it meant using every last penny we had. If RBS closed its doors, the banking system would freeze, not just in the UK but around the globe.

I had seen what happened when a comparatively small bank like Northern Rock failed. I had seen what happened when Lehman Brothers collapsed. This was our biggest test. There was no alternative but to keep the bank going and then to do what was needed to stop the firestorm. I spoke to Gordon back in No. 10. There was no disagreement. I thought I should just check that he knew we had bet the Bank on our ability to stop much worse. I was desperate now to get out of Luxembourg, but had to take a call first from a minister in Iceland. I wanted an assurance that they would compensate British investors in Icelandic banks. He said, yes, they would. I came off the call and told my officials, 'They won't stand behind it.'

I returned to the conference hall to discuss the finer points of the insurance directive for a few interminable minutes before making our exit in a way that we hoped did not look entirely unplanned. Inevitably, we were spotted by a passing film crew from Brussels, providing footage for the lunchtime news bulletins. I was muttering under my breath that old British refrain: Keep calm and carry on.

7   Back from the Brink

I got back to the Treasury at about 3 o'clock on Tuesday, 7 October. Officials had been working flat out on the emergency rescue plan for the past ten days, overseen by newly appointed minister Paul Myners, whose expertise and experience were invaluable. The news was not encouraging. Most bank shares were in free fall; RBS shares had plummeted by a third. We had to have a convincing plan ready by the time the markets opened the next morning. Mervyn King had ensured that RBS was kept going during the day by providing funding. The main problem by mid-afternoon was to ensure it had enough US dollars. However, we thought it might make it until the end of the day in the US too.

There were to be three elements to our plan. First, there had to be sufficient funding, or liquidity, to get the banks through the next few months. This had been the main problem we faced earlier in the year and it remained an important element of what we needed to do. So we were going to increase the availability of funding under the special liquidity scheme – in effect, a loan – to about £200 billion. Secondly, we needed to address the problem caused by the fact that the banks no longer trusted one another to repay their borrowing. The only way we could do this was for the government to guarantee that borrowing through a 'credit guarantee scheme'. This was important because, unless banks lent to each other, it would cut down the amount of lending available for businesses and for mortgages. Again, it was a massive liability, amounting to another £250 billion if the guarantees needed to be called in. Finally, in many ways the most important element was to provide capital to those banks that needed it. We thought at this stage that this would amount to a further £50 to £75 billion.

On any view, these were eye-watering sums of money, but if we were to stop the panic and loss of confidence, to avert what even the least excitable commentators were calling economic Armageddon, we had to do whatever it took. The alternative would have been a financial and economic meltdown, not just in the UK but right across the world. I had learned from my experience with Northern Rock a year before. If we got this wrong, the livelihoods of millions of people would be at stake. We had crossed a Rubicon with Northern Rock by not only pledging our credit to stop the bank collapsing but also nationalizing it. Those images of queues of panicked people waiting to get their money out of a small provincial bank were seared in my memory. It would be merely a rehearsal for the panic if RBS were to close its doors and the run spread to every other bank.

What's more, I knew that if the plan worked, the guarantees would not be called in, the liquidity provided would be paid back, and one day the bank shares owned by the government would be sold, perhaps at a profit. Three years on, I was right about the first two points and I see no reason why the shares won't be sold at a profit. However, none of this was obvious that afternoon.

I knew we had to announce our plan the following morning, but there was no way we would be able to spell out how the measures would be applied to each individual bank. That would take days to work up. So the plan would have to be announced in two stages: the first outlining the general level of support; the second, the following week, spelling out exactly how much money each bank had to raise. But the most important thing was to get tomorrow's announcement precisely right: it would make or break us.

At 5 o'clock, Mervyn King and Adair Turner arrived at the Treasury to talk through the plan. Staff at the Bank, the FSA and the Treasury had collaborated closely. Whatever the differences in our approaches in the past, we were at one on this. At about 6 o'clock I went over to Downing Street and met Gordon in the Cabinet Room to discuss the plan. He was aware of the high stakes but had no doubt that if the plan was to work we needed to throw everything at it. He was also keen to alert world leaders to what we were doing. We needed other countries to do the same as we were proposing. It wouldn't be enough to shore up the banking system in one country alone. This was therefore an important step, and Gordon's long international experience and contacts were to prove invaluable. We agreed he should make the calls the following morning, as soon as we had made the announcement public.

There was a long night ahead of us. We would have to meet the bank chiefs again. I also knew we would have to deal with the Icelandic banks the next day. They were likely to go into liquidation and there were many worried savers in the UK, to say nothing of local councils, many of which had a lot of public money deposited in Icelandic banks. A large number of charities also had money in Icelandic accounts, likewise attracted by the high returns. There was another Commons statement to prepare, and one small matter of housekeeping: I was due to deliver my Mais Lecture the following evening. If we were to forewarn them that it would be cancelled, they would know there was a big announcement coming, so I asked my office to call at 7 a.m. the following morning. As it was to be given at the Cass Business School, they would understand the situation.

Back at the Treasury there were teams of officials working all round the building, so we would be ready to tell the banks what we planned to do. This time there was no need to conceal the fact we were meeting the eight chief executives; the whole world knew they were coming. Shortly after 7.30 p.m. they came back into my room on the second floor of the Treasury. As I sat down, I thought, just for a moment, that they might be grateful to the British government for being ready to step in and save them all from ruin. But, even at this late stage there was a reluctance to accept that the problem was now fundamentally a lack of capital.

They did have a lot of questions and they wanted to understand the fine detail. It was obvious that they wanted the government guarantee to underpin their lending and to expand the special liquidity scheme, but they were less keen on raising capital. I said that they could not have the one without the other. I said, we proposed to make available £50 billion. The FSA would decide how much each bank needed to raise. They would then have a choice: they could raise it themselves on the markets, or, if they couldn't, we would provide it in return for a shareholding. I told them that to meet their concern about lack of day-to-day funds the Bank would extend the special liquidity scheme from £100 billion to £200 billion. We would also provide credit guarantees to the larger banks to ensure they had sufficient confidence in each other.

To my lawyer's rational mind, I thought they might say thank you very much for saving us from ourselves – let's work on the detail. And the politician in me told me that they had no alternative. The people who had enjoyed telling us what to do over the past decade had now reached the end of the road. It was a genuine case of take it or leave it. Nevertheless, I was taken aback by their reaction. When we had met two days earlier, they had seemed to be seized by the urgency of the situation. Tonight, they were approaching the whole thing as if they had weeks to seal the deal. True, we had not previously discussed taking shareholdings, but the news that capital had to be raised was hardly new to them. The other measures to make credit more readily available were more or less what they had asked for.

Fred Goodwin again insisted that he was facing a funding problem rather than one of lack of capital. If we announced that the banks needed £50 billion, people would think that the situation was far worse than it was, he said. He did not need anything like that much. There was more quibbling about the credit guarantees and nitpicking over details and just about every possible difficulty was raised. Time was marching on. For the first time, I began to feel worried. It crossed my mind not only that the banks had failed to appreciate that there could be no negotiation, but also that they might be daft enough to take up the option of suicide – and I simply couldn't afford a row of dead banks in the morning. As we broke up to allow further discussions to take place between our officials and the chief executives, one of the bankers – I can't recall which – asked me what would happen if we couldn't reach an agreement. I said, 'We either do something or we don't. If we don't, and I have nothing else, then God help all of us.' With that, the big beast of the financial services industry got up and left the room. Sir Fred, ever cool, strolled out as if he were off for a game of golf. John Varley, the smooth, urbane spokesman for the upper end of the bankers' market, always good at focusing on what was needed, was the only one in shirtsleeves. Andy Hornby of HBOS, on the other hand, wore his heart on his sleeve: he looked as if he might explode. The slight air of disdain I had come to recognize in the bearing of some senior bankers followed them out.

Every nook and cranny of the Treasury was filled with huddles of my officials, bankers, lawyers, advisers, fighting and arguing over every last detail, gathered around desks, sitting in corners, on the floor, in open-plan offices. People paced up and down the corridors, mobiles welded to their ears, weaving around each other, like rush hour in the City. It was an extraordinary sight. I retreated to my office with my private team. I was not going to engage in the hand-to-hand fighting that was happening all over the building. My only interest was in the outcome. The chief executives congregated gloomily a few doors away, in the small office of Paul Myners. Paul and Shriti Vadera kept them company in their gloom. Both did excellent hard work persuading the bankers that while we could debate the detail, the main deal was not open to negotiation.

The atmosphere in my room was quite relaxed. At the end of the day, or at least of a very long night, I thought they would have to cave in. My concern was that some might be so stupid that they would bring everyone down with them. I hadn't eaten since the night before, so, fed up with the traditional Treasury crisis diet of pizza, we sent out for a takeaway. We agreed we should order it from Gandhi's in Kennington, a curry house close to my old flat. Their kitchen rose magnificently to the emergency. Soon the table at the end of the private office was piled high with chapattis and foil containers filled with curries. It was later called the night of the 'balti bail-out', but that was only partly true. I tucked into my usual chicken tandoori, and a stream of civil servants trooped in to sustain themselves for the long night ahead. The bank chiefs and their advisers were invited to help themselves but declined. One came into the room, looked at the table and turned away, as if to say, has it come to this? Perhaps he had just lost his appetite. Whenever the bankers came for breakfast meetings they ate little. We were never sure whether this was due to nervousness or if they had already eaten at a pre-meeting.

The night wore on with the grind of hard negotiations going on all over the building. The streams of advisers pacing the corridors with phones to their ears swelled. We wondered if they were talking to journalists, and someone suggested telling them their calls were being monitored by GCHQ. We didn't, because it wasn't true, but it was tempting.

The negotiators for the banks, I was told, were looking increasingly frantic. The bankers themselves were not. The civil servants remained calm because they had a better overall picture. Most of the negotiators for the individual banks knew only what was happening on their own patch. Panic was setting in as they felt they could not get a deal they could live with. At about 11 o'clock it was apparent that some of the chief executives were putting up a last-stand fight. I called them back into my room and said that of course we could talk about the detail, but tonight they had to accept the key proposals. I realized that as long as I was there they would think we were open to negotiation, so I said I was going to bed at 1 o'clock and wasn't going to be called before 5 a.m.

– and then only if it was to approve the announcement. Leaving the Treasury building to head back to No. 11, I told my private secretaries they would probably give in once I had gone, and said goodnight.

In the years since this rescue it has become fashionable, and perhaps understandable, to bash bankers. For the record, the support of Stephen Green, John Varley, Peter Sands and António Horta Osório was invaluable. They did not need to be at the table, but they could see that everything depended on their being an active part of the plan. But I am not sure their boards or all of their senior colleagues did.

I spoke to Gordon to make sure that he was up to date with all the latest developments. This had been probably the best period of our working together while I was Chancellor. We were of the same mind and in complete agreement. We met frequently and his support, self-confidence and persistence were very helpful. Back in the Downing Street flat, I felt tired but not exhausted. The next day would be the most difficult of my political life. Sleep always restores me, and I did sleep soundly. The phone rang at 5 a.m. It was my private secretary, Dan Rosenfield, who had been up all night. There remained one big stumbling block, he said. He told me that the chief executives had for the most part gone home just after I did. It was clear then that the deal was done. The one remaining problem was whether announcing that the banks needed £50 billion would destabilize the sounder banks. There was a way through, though: it might be better to promise £25 billion now, with a further £25 billion readily available. I was prepared to agree to this presentational compromise so long as all the banks signed up.

I pulled on trousers and a shirt and went down in the lift to meet my Treasury officials in the sitting room of No. 11. It was not yet daybreak. There was a thirty-page submission to scrutinize, details to be read and digested, by the dim light of a table lamp. I asked someone to wake Gordon so he could agree to the final plan, with this one minor change. I was sure he would, but he needed to know. The stakes were high for him. It was a huge political gamble, as well as a financial one. A few minutes later, he came downstairs, to be greeted by a group of ghostly faces, perched on worn-out chairs and sofas in the half-light of dawn.

Gordon was attracted, as was Mervyn King, to the bigger package, but he could see the presentational argument. He could also see the overwhelming need to announce this in an hour and a half's time. Finally, at 5.28 a.m. on Wednesday, 8 October, we signed off the deal which was to be split – £25 billion now, with the balance of £25 billion to be available if needed.

Downing Street never sleeps, and the custodians of the front door bade us a cheerful good morning as the Treasury team headed back to the office to sort out the final paperwork. I went back upstairs to wash and shave and to get ready for what was to be another very long day. Just after 6 a.m. I was back at the Treasury. I had a statement on the rescue to prepare for the House of Commons, to be delivered at lunchtime. Lawyers were still quibbling over final details and there were sheaves of papers to be read through and approved. The devil really is in the detail.

Because of the momentous nature of the announcement, I was keen, if at all possible, to try and carry the opposition parties with us. Unusually, I phoned George Osborne and Vince Cable and took them through the plan. Both were supportive, although I was sure by the time I made my statement in the House later in the day, they would have had time to find a few political quips. The announcement of the rescue package had to be ready for the markets opening at 7 o'clock. As the minutes ticked by, I was told that the lawyers were still quibbling over the official market notice which had to be published on the stock exchange before I could go out and make the announcement. Because it would have a profound impact on shares all over the world, I had to observe this formality. By 7 o'clock it had still not arrived. I knew my failure to appear on the airwaves would lead to damaging speculation that something had gone wrong. What a farce it would be if our carefully designed plans were derailed by lawyers quarrelling over the dots and commas of the statement.

It finally appeared, a few minutes after seven. When it was published, the world could see for the first time what a huge step the British government had just taken. I drove off to the inevitable round of interviews for television and radio and newspapers. I was as sure as I could be that the policy was right. My trepidation was whether this enormous step would be enough to quell panic and avert catastrophe.

I got a call to say Gordon wanted to do a news conference in No. 10. I was not particularly keen. Everything that needed to be said had been covered, I thought, in my press interviews. However, as I knew the detail I agreed to join him. By 9 a.m. I was back in the flat. There was just time to grab a round of bacon rolls from the basement cafeteria and cast a quick eye over the morning newspapers, which were by now well behind the news curve. As the world's media began to assemble two floors down in No. 10, I took a call from my office in the Treasury. As I had suspected, the Icelandic government would not be compensating the losers in its failed banks. We would have to move quickly to protect UK savers' money. My focus had to be on making sure UK deposits did not disappear into a black hole in Iceland.

Connie, who looked after the flat, arriving through the door as I was rushing out, gave me a wide smile and a quick up-and-down glance. She took great pride in making sure I was well turned out. Downstairs, the atmosphere in the lofty state dining room, packed with journalists and television cameras, was, I thought, muted. I sensed the assembled journalists were a bit taken aback by the sheer scale of the rescue package. There had been a lot of speculation about our plans, but the enormity of the measures had not, perhaps, been anticipated. Gordon hailed the plan as innovative, comprehensive and ground-breaking. I agreed it was huge and, yes, historic and a response to extraordinary times. As we took questions, I was itching to get back to the Treasury. There was a lot to do.

Back at my desk, Kevin kindly brought me a cup of his remarkable coffee. He has served Chancellors as far back as Nigel Lawson and by some strange anomaly gets paid for every cup of tea or coffee he makes. I checked on arrangements with Marilyne, my diary secretary, for a planned trip to Washington the next day, Friday, 10 October, for meetings of the G7 finance ministers and then of the IMF, before sitting down to work on my statement to Parliament in a couple of hours' time. Statements to the House involve a lot of time and preparation; it is like doing an exam. When Paul Myners first went to the House of Lords he was astonished at the depth of detail a statement demanded. It was not like being in business, he said, where you do not always need to know what is going on right down on the shop floor. In Parliament you must master your brief.

My statement coincided with the news that at 12 noon, the Bank of England, in a coordinated move with other leading central banks, had cut interest rates by a half of one per cent. The disruption in financial markets around the world had intensified, but we were ready to bring stability to the banking system. The rescue package would protect depositors, safeguard taxpayers, and play an important part in the international response to the crisis. It was designed to help families and businesses, as well as to support our economy. Essentially, the package involved £50 billion to get more capital into UK banks, which they could borrow from the government, and £100 billion of extra money available in short-term loans from the Bank of England, on top of the existing loan facility of £100 billion. To free up the banking system, up to £250 billion in loan guarantees would be available at commercial rates to encourage the banks to start lending to each other again.

There was grudging acceptance of the scheme by the Conservatives. The Liberal Democrats' soothsayer, Vincent Cable, did as he always used to do and supported us. Back at the Treasury in the afternoon, I looked at the trading screens on Dan's desk. The markets around the world remained uncertain. Concerted and coordinated action was needed now to calm the storm and restore confidence. It would be vital that governments did not just talk about what had to be done but got on and did it. The meetings would have to conclude with more than a diplomatic fudge this time. The IMF launched a facility to speed up the approval of loans to countries in need of financial support, ahead of the weekend talks in Washington. While I was there, Gordon would spend the weekend talking to other world leaders from the UK. His knowledge and wide range of contacts proved invaluable, as did his single-minded concentration on what needed to be done.

Before heading for Washington on the Friday, there was one more difficulty to deal with: Iceland. I had spoken to the prime minister on the previous Thursday morning to tell him a letter outlining our plans to save UK depositors' money was on its way. We would need to work together, I told him, and I offered to send a Treasury team to Iceland to see if matters could be resolved and something salvaged from the wreckage. He would issue a statement, he said, putting on record his appreciation of the help the UK government was giving depositors – as well he might.

His gratitude had been short-lived. Landsbanki, with its UK subsidiary, and Kaupthing, would be put into liquidation later in the day. We were going to use the Northern Rock legislation to transfer Kaupthing's UK subsidiary operations to the Dutch bank ING. But I saw no alternative to freezing the assets of Landsbanki, or Icesave as it was known here. Frankly, I no longer believed anything I was being told by the Icelandic authorities, who seemed to be in complete denial. Freezing another country's assets is a major step, and I had sought advice from lawyers and Treasury officials to see how we could do it. Fortunately, it turned out that I did have power to freeze the assets if I believed the action taken by Landsbanki and the Icelandic authorities was likely to be to the detriment of the UK economy. I did think that the Icelandic action, which could mean a loss of £4.5 billion for British savers, was indeed detrimental. Unfortunately, this legislation was contained in an anti-terrorism measure passed in 2001. Because of that, our action was open to the mistaken impression that we regarded Landsbanki – or, even worse, Iceland – as a terrorist organization.

Not surprisingly, a new Icelandic government decided to conduct a root and branch inquiry into how their country had been brought to its knees by such reckless gambling on the part of their banks, their businesses and some of their politicians. The special investigation committee reported in the middle of Britain's general election campaign in 2010. It found significant evidence of negligence and of behaviour that pointed towards possible criminality. They left no stone unturned and found both the former prime minister and the governor of the central bank to have been negligent. Proceedings have been brought against the former prime minister. Criminal investigations are still ongoing in 2011.

We caught the Virgin Atlantic flight to Washington on Friday morning. Newspapers were reporting that the world was 'stunned' by the rescue scheme's boldness, which was good. What wasn't so good was that traders in the UK were panic-selling everything but their shirts, offloading shares at such a rate that it would lead to the biggest one-day fall in the FTSE 100 index for more than twenty years. I was looking forward to the flight. It would give me eight hours in which to take stock of the last few days and to prepare for the G7 meeting that afternoon, as well as to go over the plans we needed to have in place for the coming Monday morning when the detail of how much capital each bank would need to raise would be announced. On top of that, I had the inevitable backlog of papers that is the stuff of ministerial red boxes. The past few days had meant that I had not been able to deal with my nightly homework. Ministers can, if they want, see an extraordinary amount of the paperwork that passes through any government department. The trick is to decide what is important and what is not. It is very often the piece of paper at the bottom of the box, which does not seem important at the time, that can come back to haunt you. In my experience, it is worth ministers reading everything that is put in front of them. Of course, it is the job of a decent private secretary to decide what the minister needs to see. The relationship between a minister and his private secretaries is critical: I was never let down.

I also wanted to think about how we should deal with the G7 meeting. This could not be a routine meeting followed by the ritual communiqué.

I spoke to Hank Paulson on arriving at the US Treasury. We were both determined, along with Christine Lagarde, that it would be far better to concentrate on five or six key decisions, and that the communiqué should not run to more than one page of A4. That would concentrate people's minds. By this time there was unanimity that banks needed more capital. I spoke to many finance ministers from around the world that day, both in the G7 and those gathering in Washington to attend the IMF meeting on the Saturday. All had come to the view that taking shareholdings in the banks, together with the other measures, would provide the confidence that the banking system needed. There seemed to be an extraordinary amount of interest in what we were trying to do in the UK, and a sense that at last something had broken the logjam.

The G7 meeting was short and to the point. Here was an example where a dozen people could talk about what needed to be done, in relation to their banks and their economies, and agree to do it. Just three days later, both the US and Europe were able to announce a bank bailout along the same lines as our own. I managed to have a private word with Hank Paulson on the Saturday morning before the meetings began. He was exhausted after two weeks' wrangling with congressional leaders. He had followed what we were doing in great detail and believed that it would work. Now he wanted to do something similar in the US.

Throughout the day, my thoughts were never far away from what was happening more than three thousand miles away, back in the Treasury. My officials were again working around the clock to convert the general plan I had announced on Wednesday into quite specific and detailed plans for each bank, ready to be announced at 7 a.m. on Monday morning. Not for the first time, though, the fractious relationship between Nos. 10 and 11 took an inordinate amount of time to resolve. Midway through the IMF meeting I was called out, yet again, to talk to Yvette Cooper, the Chief Secretary, who was hard at work in the Treasury to ensure that what we wanted was delivered. She is intelligent and hardworking, and was focused on the fact that we had less than thirty-six hours to sort out numerous apparently intractable difficulties. But she was on the phone for another reason. Shriti Vadera was demanding to be let in to a meeting Yvette was holding to take stock of where we were. I have to confess this was my fault. Increasingly irritated at the querulous calls from No. 10 staff to my office, all of which hinted that we were not up to the job, I had said that Shriti was to be kept informed, but not to be let in to meetings, which she tended to take over. Like many investment bankers I have met, she appears to believe that unless there is blood on the carpet, preferably that of her own colleagues, then she has not done her job. For the sake of peace, I told Yvette to allow her into the meeting. The last thing we needed was another battle between Nos. 10 and 11.

An already strained relationship between Gordon and myself was, I think, often exacerbated by the behaviour of the people around him, who believed they were doing the right thing by him, and often vying to prove their own importance within his court. It did not help that he was constantly encouraged to believe that the Treasury, and consequently myself, was his enemy. The Treasury has always had a high self-regard. It sees itself as the big beast of Whitehall, patrolling the corridors of governments of whatever political hue, fiercely guarding the economic stability of the country. Historically, down the centuries, this has created tensions, and power play, between the inhabitants of Nos. 10 and 11. My own experience was that, under clear and direct control, the Treasury became a crucial tool for government, not a weapon intent on destroying it.

I was intrigued to find that Tony and Gordon, who are both strong-willed and determined men, became unbelievably insecure in Downing Street. It is not hard to see how a bunker mentality can develop. Unlike most countries, the British Prime Minister has a very small staff. The Cabinet Office, despite its name, is there to service Whitehall rather than the prime minister. In my experience, it is a mixed bag, an amalgam of various functions that can't be fitted into other government departments. The Prime Minister therefore depends heavily on individual special advisers. Their value to him depends, in turn, on what they know – or what they think they know. It also lies in their being able to get on sufficiently well with the department they cover to get the information they need, and then having the intellect to challenge what they are being told.

For government to work effectively, the Secretary of State of a particular department and the Prime Minister have to be able to work as close colleagues, sorting out differences and then issuing clear instructions to the civil service about what they have agreed. Once this relationship becomes dysfunctional, the whole system breaks down. By the end of that long Saturday in Washington, I had heard enough from London to know that the constant jarring was going to lead to another difficult day when I got back. Perhaps it was my fault, perhaps I should have been more accommodating, but by this stage I was certain that unless I stamped my authority on what was happening we would never reach an agreement. After the debacle of the pre-Budget report in 2007, and the less than satisfactory Budget earlier in 2008, I wanted to be completely happy with Monday's announcement on the rescue. I had managed to run three major Whitehall departments and I was confident that I could run this one. The difference here, of course, was that this was the first time that my predecessor was now the Prime Minister.

I arrived back in London early on Sunday morning, tired and in need of a good sleep. Unfortunately for me, the pilot had found a quick route back across the Atlantic. There was nothing I could usefully do in the Treasury until the lawyers had finished their work, so I went to bed for a few hours. Another long night loomed. When I got to the Treasury, shortly after lunchtime, I found the place unusually cheerful. The tantrums of the day before appeared to have been forgotten and good progress was being made. I spent the next few hours working on my statement for the Commons the next day and mastering all the detail I would need for the media round in the morning. We also had to manage as best we could the expectations of journalists writing for the papers. You can't tell them everything, but if you don't point them in the right direction and they write something that is wrong you soon find out it is your fault, not theirs.

Throughout the day I held frequent meetings to take stock of where we were, but largely we were on track. The banks had, in the main, accepted what we were doing. The big problem was, of course, RBS, which needed about £15 billion of public money to put it on a stable footing, meaning that the British taxpayer would own more than 70 per cent of its shares. The government would be the bank's major shareholder and with that would come a whole raft of difficult decisions. First, there was no question that the top management, the chairman and chief executive, had to go. I regarded the departure of Fred Goodwin and Tom McKillop as not negotiable, so there was no point in discussing it with them. I had made it clear to John Kingman, who was more than capable of dealing with such matters, that both had to go, and to go immediately. John, an urbane, laid-back Treasury official, became the point man during the banking crisis. He had been brought back to this part of the Treasury because of his ability to find solutions to problems and to motivate what was proving to be a highly skilled and dedicated core of staff. He was of immense support to me and I was sorry when, a year later, he returned to the private sector.

Sir Fred Goodwin accepted his fate, but his chairman, Sir Tom McKillop, saw no reason to go until the next year's annual general meeting. The bank's board appeared to be behind him. They seemed to have no sense of responsibility for what had happened to RBS and were more concerned about saving face. We would not budge. In the end, Sir Tom went and the others followed him a few weeks later. We had lined up Stephen Hester, who had recently left British Land and had considerable banking experience, to replace Sir Fred. Finding a chairman would be more difficult, because the pool is a lot smaller than people might think. In the end, we secured Philip Hampton, who was chairman of Sainsbury's and who had a lot of City experience. He and Stephen subsequently did a great deal to salvage what was a wreck of a bank.

Throughout this period I was intent on stopping the banking system from collapsing, and less focused on the politics. Gordon, however, understood the need to extract something from the banks in return for bailing them out. Subsequent to the bail-out, many have argued that we should have extracted legally binding undertakings on lending and bonuses. As subsequent events proved, trying to get an agreement on levels of bank lending that will stick is well-nigh impossible. It is simply not possible to force a bank to lend to a particular borrower. Then there was the question of pay. Whatever we decided to pay Stephen Hester, people would regard it as too much. Like it or not, bankers are paid a great deal of money, and if we were to salvage anything from RBS, I needed to get the best possible candidate and to pay him what was needed to do so. As it happens, I think he was the right choice.

More problematic was what to do about Fred Goodwin's departure. Paul Myners had done much of the hand-to-hand fighting and negotiating with all the banks, RBS included. Now he was trying to persuade Sir Fred that he had to follow HBOS chief executive Andy Hornby in not taking a redundancy payment. I too spoke to Sir Fred about forgoing his redundancy. It was a terse conversation, and neither of us wanted to prolong it. His pension was another matter. Initially, we were told that his pension was £400,000 per year. It subsequently emerged that it was double that. It proved extraordinarily difficult to find out how on earth he could have acquired such a massive entitlement, but the deal was apparently reached when he was recruited by the then RBS top management, who, of course, were nowhere to be seen when it became public. Not surprisingly, it was a major political problem for us. I cannot understand why Fred Goodwin did not settle for £400,000 a year. Most people could struggle by on that. To insist on even more cost him dearly. He could have walked away and spared himself and, more importantly, his family months, years, of trauma. He could have withdrawn from public life and re-emerged somewhere else later on. That's what most of the RBS directors did. It was not until the following June that Sir Fred saw some sense and accepted that the price of insisting on his full contractual rights was not worth paying. It was too late by then. His taciturn stubbornness ensured that he became the pariah of British bankers and the focus of huge public anger. To the end, he just did not get it.

By late Sunday evening, 12 October 2008, we had the deals we needed. HSBC showed a united front by putting a small amount of extra capital into their British subsidiary despite the fact they did not need it. Barclays, which did need more money, was determined not to take anything from the taxpayer. The board could see all too clearly that the political spotlight would turn on their arrangements for pay – or 'compensation', as bankers prefer to call it – and on their lending. They were, I think, philosophically opposed to any government shareholding. Paul spent some hours persuading them to let us announce that they were making their own arrangements, lest complete silence might signal that they were not out of trouble.

Lloyds and HBOS, now on the way to becoming one bank, needed £17 billion, which meant that the UK taxpayer acquired about 43 per cent of their shareholding. This was difficult. Lloyds on its own would probably not have needed so much capital. It was a conservative, well-run bank. HBOS, on the other hand, was neither of those things. It was apparent, after its desperate attempt to raise money in the summer, that it would need a substantial injection of capital.

Gordon had been invited by President Sarkozy of France to explain our thinking to eurozone leaders on the Sunday evening. It was the first time a British prime minister had ever attended this group. This was one of the occasions on which Gordon's force of personality and determination helped make things happen immediately.

There were no late-night dramas this time. I was in the Treasury before 6 a.m. on the Monday morning. As I sat in my room, waiting for the market press notices to be finalized, as yet again the lawyers demonstrated their uncanny ability to discover problems previously unthought of,

I sat down to sign the documentation that effectively transferred the world's largest bank into public ownership. There was page after page of it, which Gordon and I signed, as Her Majesty's Lords of the Treasury. This was a dramatic moment.

Sitting there, in the silence of my room, looking out over St James's Park before dawn broke, I reflected on how much some of my Labour predecessors would have loved to have done this. The last thing I wanted was to nationalize this bank, bringing with it all the problems that it entailed. As it was, we were bringing to an end a conflagration that threatened to bring down the world's banking system. The media round, a couple of hours later, was largely successful; there seemed now to be a grudging acceptance that we had pulled it off. There should have been a sense of achievement and relief, but there wasn't. The economy was in jeopardy. I knew it. And the rest of the world was about to wake up to how bad things were.

8 Knocking at the White House Door

The world's banking crisis was taking its toll on economies around the world. In America, in Europe, in Japan, no one was spared. As a result, government revenues fell and as they all maintained – and in many cases increased – their spending, deficits rose inexorably. Why did governments carry on spending when their incomes started to fall? Margaret Thatcher cleverly but deceptively made the comparison between government and household debt. The analogy took hold, but it is disingenuous. A household experiencing a fall in income that's likely to last will cut back on what it spends in order to remain solvent. Stay in rather than eat out, shop at Lidl rather than Sainsbury's, cancel a holiday, sell things on eBay. The impact of that family's savings on the economy is negligible. But magnify the actions of that household by tens of millions and the knock-on effects are enormous. Shops and businesses start to lose customers and income. They cut back, make people redundant, the people they trade with find their incomes falling and have less to spend, they lay off people, and so it goes on. If, on top of that, the government starts to reduce what it spends, it propels the downward spiral. If the government cuts back the number of people employed in public services, it has to spend more on unemployment benefit and receives nothing back in tax from those who've lost their jobs. In turn, those who have lost their jobs spend less because their income has been cut. That hits shops and businesses. Fewer people have jobs, and there is less tax coming into the coffers. Cutting spending in one area leads to increased spending in another: more people out of work means more money spent on benefits. A major rise in unemployment cascades job losses down the line and more businesses fail, throwing even more people out of work.

You are unlikely to solve a crisis in the household budget by throwing your granny out on the street in order to make a quick saving on the food bill. So why would a government throw millions of people out of work to cut a deficit that could be managed down at a steady pace over time? Demand for goods and services generates jobs. Lower demand brings in lower tax revenues. The choices a government makes have a massive and profound impact on the economy, most crucially in times of crisis. When households and companies spend less, and governments cut public spending, recession risks turning into depression. Now we were facing the deepest recession in living history. Granny was going nowhere.

The argument for maintaining public spending is therefore quite straightforward: it takes the strain as business activity reduces and people spend less. In many countries, particularly in Europe, public spending automatically increases during an economic downturn. This is because when someone loses their job they are usually entitled to unemployment benefit. Benefit spending goes up and that has the effect of maintaining spending power in the economy, because people on benefits invariably spend rather than save. In economic terms, this is known as an 'automatic stabilizer'. The effect is less pronounced in the US, where the payment of unemployment benefit is more limited. Here in the UK, despite everything that was said after the election in 2010, both the Conservatives and Liberal Democrats supported the operation of this automatic stabilizer. Certainly, to start cutting public spending midway through 2008 would have jeopardized millions of jobs.

None of this was new. After the Wall Street Crash of 1929, as a result of falling government revenues, conventional wisdom meant that the

US government cut its spending. Money dried up, unemployment soared, businesses crashed and recession turned into the misery of the Great Depression. Exactly the same wisdom, or lack of it, led the Labour Chancellor, Philip Snowden, in 1931 to propose cutting benefits, which led to the fall of the government. It would take the advent of the Second World War and its associated spending on rearmament to bring about a full economic recovery.

Fortunately, wiser voices, and most notably that of the British economist John Maynard Keynes, one of the most influential thinkers of the twentieth century, were there to point out that it is better for governments to employ people to work, thus providing them with an income which they will then spend. This will, in turn, boost the income of the people they spend money with, who will spend in turn, and so on. Although Keynes's seminal work, *The General Theory of Employment, Interest and Money*, did not appear until 1936, his thinking was hugely influential on governments struggling to find a way out of recession and the terrible human and economic costs of the Great Depression.

It was the backlash against Keynes's ideas that drove government economic policy in the recession of the 1980s. We were still paying the social costs of this policy a generation later. In late 2008, I was influenced hugely by Keynes's thinking – as, indeed, were most other governments dealing with the fallout from the crisis. I could see that if we did not maintain our spending levels, we ran the severe risk of an inevitable recession turning into a deep depression which might last for years. More than that, I felt the government would have to do something extra to stimulate economic growth. Nor was this just our thinking; it was replicated in most countries. In the US, the Republican president, George W. Bush, increased spending. At the same time Communist China was pumping money into its economy.

Here in the UK, though for completely different reasons, the Conservatives and Liberal Democrats both supported the current level of government spending. There was a consensus that public services lacked the necessary level of investment, and certainly in the case of the Liberal Democrats, they sought not to be outdone by calling for more spending rather than less. On many occasions, so too did the Tories. The Conservatives changed their minds at the end of 2008, sensing, no doubt, where the political advantage would lie at the time of an election two years later. They counted, successfully as it turned out, on a two-year lag which might allow people to forget how close to the brink we were. Curiously, they changed their tune at precisely the wrong time. At the end of 2008 there were very few people in the world who thought that was a good time to cut back public spending. Having supported our public spending levels for years, in October 2008 George Osborne went into fast reverse: 'Even a modest dose of Keynsian spending is a cruise missile aimed at the heart of recovery,' he said.

He might count himself fortunate that he wasn't Chancellor at the time. Much of the growth seen in the UK economy during the summer and autumn of 2010 was due to the measures we took two years earlier, which he fiercely opposed. At that stage, the Liberal Democrats were supportive. Even as late as April 2010, a month before going into coalition with the Conservatives, their leader, Nick Clegg, said: 'Do I think that these big cuts are merited or justified at a time when the economy is struggling to get to its feet? Clearly not.' A month later he was singing a different song.

The situation we faced in the summer and autumn of 2008 was a classic case where the government could make a genuine difference. Millions of people, and tens of thousands of businesses, were facing the possibility of a deep economic slump. It is precisely at this time that they look to government to take action in a way that they cannot do as individuals. That, for me, is one of the core purposes of government. Although the general strategy I wanted to pursue was straightforward, the politics and the economics were more complicated. If spending is to be maintained, borrowing needs to rise, and borrowing adds to the national debt, which is the accumulation of each year's borrowing. A balance must be achieved: how much can safely be spent to support the economy, and how much can be borrowed before the country's ability to repay it is called into question? That is a matter of judgement. But it is a judgement I believe we got right. If we had not stopped the banking system from collapse, there would have been immediate economic meltdown.

In late October 2008, immediately following the announcement on the bank rescue, I sat down to work out what we needed to include in the pre-Budget report. This would be no ordinary report. It would be, in effect if not in name, a Budget. It would need a lot of thought and a lot of work. The first part of the preparation was to confirm what most commentators already suspected, that there was no hope whatsoever of us complying with our fiscal rules. The rules said two things: one, that we should only borrow to invest and not to fund day-to-day spending; and two, that debt must be kept at a sustainable level, which was set at 40 per cent of our national income. That might seem a lot, but most countries maintain debt levels considerably higher than that. In Japan, for example, it is approaching 200 per cent. No British government has ever defaulted on its obligations; indeed, unlike most governments, which borrow over a short period of about seven years, most of our debt is borrowed over a longer period, on average over thirteen years. That is one of the reasons why we were never at any time at risk of being unable to raise the money we needed. The political scare stories that we might default and go the way of Greece were just that, a ludicrous exaggeration.

I had, however, to prepare the way for breaking these rules. As I had planned to do earlier, I used my postponed Mais Lecture in late October to argue the case that our fiscal rules were there to fit the prevailing current economic circumstances. My argument was that, in the extraordinary times we faced in the autumn of 2008, we had to change our approach to meet them. This was a fairly refined argument, which, although widely covered in the greatly respected *Financial Times*, was not explored much elsewhere.

Within the Treasury there was, and will always be, a theological debate about fiscal rules, what they should be and what they do. It was clear that the original rules we had adopted were now irrelevant. The argument was whether we should impose new ceilings on spending and borrowing, or whether they should instead reflect a more general aspiration. I did not want to be placed in a straitjacket, especially one that I would have to discard if things got much worse. This is not an academic discussion. If we set rules, especially in a time of crisis, and then broke them, the markets would turn against us, which would mean that the cost of our borrowing would rocket. Rules would require us to do such things as cut public spending or increase taxes, so they do have a direct impact on people.

The only time I lost my temper at a Treasury meeting was during one such discussion with senior officials, which reached such a theoretical, pointy-headed level, so divorced from life out there on the street, that I suggested to officials that Pol Pot had been right: they needed to go back to the countryside and rediscover their roots. I am normally fairly easy-going and they were, I think, taken aback when I sent them packing. A few minutes later I went out to find them huddled in groups, asking each other what had gone wrong.

We came up with a temporary set of rules, which was provided for in the small print of the rules established in 1997. However, even devising temporary rules inevitably caused problems with the author of the original rules, who was now the Prime Minister. There was no question that the original rules were effectively redundant, but Gordon was concerned about anything that might box us in. I agreed, but felt that we needed something to show that, notwithstanding the times, there was some discipline in our approach. We had to maintain the confidence of the markets.

I thought our approach at Dorneywood in July was right. We had sketched out our approach as to how we should deal with the looming recession. First, it would be necessary to maintain public spending momentum in the economy. Secondly, we would also need to provide an additional stimulus. But the third leg was equally important. We would have to show a plan to cut borrowing and reduce debt as we moved out of recession. We thought this would be in 2009 or 2010. I was in a relatively confident mood as I prepared for the pre-Budget report. The bank rescue had worked. The Mais Lecture was written over three months and it was, I thought, logical and coherent. The press remained bad, unremittingly so, but I suppose it might have been worse.

Firstly, I had to pay for the cost of restoring the damage caused by the abolition of the 10p tax rate. I had also promised to do more to try to reduce the number of losers who had not been compensated in the summer. This was a constantly moving target, as people's circumstances keep changing, and it was to prove impossible to ensure that not a single person lost out. When I announced the measure in May, we were sure the extra spending power, when the money got into people's pockets in September, would help the economy. I wanted to keep the measure as one part of my plan to boost the economy. Measures on tax would also be part of the stimulus. On top of that, I wanted to do more to encourage spending and help shops and businesses.

That is where cutting the rate of VAT came in, an idea we had first discussed at Dorneywood back in July, as the storm clouds gathered. The idea behind a temporary cut in VAT is that it not only increases spending, but also brings spending forward, as people seek to take advantage of the temporary reduction. For this to work, it has to be announced that VAT will go back up on a specified date. What to do with VAT was to dominate the tensions between me and my next-door neighbour right up until the general election. He was initially sceptical about a reduction and was worried what the reaction would be when the rate went back up a year later.

I wanted to put extra money into the hands of consumers as quickly as possible, in the hope that they would go out and spend it and so support businesses. There are two ways in which this can be done. The first, which would have been my preference, was to increase everyone's personal tax allowance, as I had done earlier in the year to compensate for the abolition of the 10p tax rate. This had cost £3.5 billion and it put another £120 per year into the pocket of every basic rate taxpayer. The problem was that, because of HMRC's creaking computer systems, it would take nearly six months from the time of the announcement for the benefit to be felt. It would be early summer of 2009 before anyone would see any money, which was far too late.

That left me with the second option, of cutting VAT by as much as was permitted under European Union rules, to 15 per cent. A VAT cut could come in immediately, certainly in time for Christmas. I settled on the VAT cut. The question then was how to pay for it. I judged that the markets would accept increased spending so long as they could see that we were also putting in place longer-term plans to get the money back once the crisis was over. It was also necessary, in my view, to begin to signal measures that would bring down our borrowing once we thought the recovery was established, which we knew would not be until 2010 or 2011. I therefore proposed that after the temporary cut in VAT we would gradually increase VAT in stages. It would return to the 17.5 per cent rate in January 2010 and would then rise each year by 1 per cent until it reached 20 per cent. This gradual rise was important. I didn't want to put up VAT in one go because I thought that would be a shock to the economy and to consumers, and, because it would increase prices, it would push up inflation.

Because a tax on the cost of goods and services has a greater impact on people on lower incomes, I would also need to do something to help them elsewhere in the tax system. In the jargon, VAT is mildly regressive – that is, it has a greater effect on people on lower incomes, unless you do something to counter it. However, it is not as regressive as some people believe. It is not levied on food and children's clothes, for example.

At this stage I had not turned my mind to the finer details. Before that, I would need to get Gordon's agreement in general terms, and that is where the problems began. The pre-Budget report in 2007 and the Budget in March 2008 had to a large extent been discussed only between myself and Gordon. Apart from talks on individual spending items, we were the only two Cabinet ministers who sat down together.

The pre-Budget report set for the coming November was different in that Peter Mandelson, who had returned to the government in October, sat in from time to time. I think he was preoccupied with trying to bring order to the No. 10 operation. He was also acutely aware that he and Gordon had renewed their relationship after years of acrimony. He wanted to bolster him and maintain harmony. For these reasons, it would have taken a lot to get Peter to side with me against Gordon.

The Budget has to be the Chancellor's. It can't be cobbled together by committee. However, the general principles underpinning the Chancellor's approach can easily be the subject of wider political discussion, certainly among senior ministers. Unfortunately, right from the inception of New Labour, and throughout our time in government, such an approach had never been adopted. The result was that senior ministers who were needed to go out and bat for the government at critical times were not involved in the decision-making process, as they should have been. As it was, throughout my Chancellorship, I often felt that I was having to engage in a pitched battle with Gordon. He had one ally, Ed Balls. I had no one, because no one else was engaged in the discussions. It was not until the following summer, of 2009, when the growing crescendo of concern among members of the Cabinet became impossible to drown out, that they started to be listened to.

Before that, Cabinet members had to content themselves with voicing their concerns to one another and to me. Most of the Budget discussions, from mid-October, were conducted between Gordon and myself, occasionally with officials present, more often not. Gordon did as he always does and took advice elsewhere, not surprisingly from Ed Balls. I had no difficulty with that. But we needed to reach agreement one way or another, and it would have been far easier had we all been in the same room. This was especially so on the discussions over VAT, which is a totemic issue for some of my colleagues. I knew Yvette Cooper was against an increase beyond 17.5 per cent, because she told me so. I knew Ed Balls was against it, because I had heard him say so many times in the past. It was not clear to me precisely what Gordon thought. He did not actually say no to my proposal, but neither did he say yes. Over the next few weeks, we had numerous meetings in which he would sit and listen to what I had to say, ask for more information, and say we needed to meet again. It happened time and again, and all the while the clock was ticking towards that date upon which I had to deliver the pre-Budget report.

It was exasperating, because until the Budget strategy was decided I could not possibly work out the detail, and it is the detail that matters as much as the general approach. I kept asking: 'Why don't we sit down together, everyone with their different views, and at least come to a decision?' That didn't happen until the very last minute, when Ed joined us for one meeting, to reinforce Gordon's view that we couldn't increase VAT in the way that I wanted. So I found myself outnumbered. Gordon, Ed and Yvette were opposed, with Peter unwilling, I thought, to cross Gordon on this.

The real problem, so far as I could discern it, was that to some of the Prime Minister's closest advisers VAT had a special political significance for us. From 1992, Gordon had masterminded a highly successful campaign against John Major's Conservative government, largely based on their attempt to put the full rate of VAT on gas and electricity. The weekly taunts of the 'twenty-two Tory tax rises' imposed after Black Wednesday, when the Tories had earlier promised not to increase taxes, was highly effective. Alliteration required there always to be twenty-two tax rises. When they came up with another tax rise, we would drop a corresponding one off the list to make sure there were only twenty-two. I think it was because of this that Gordon had come to the view that for us to put up VAT, even in a completely different world, would be lethal. He dispatched one of his pollsters to test the water. As was to happen subsequently when he was asked to test something Gordon did not like, this particular pollster declared the policy to be deeply unpopular. That wasn't surprising. I have yet to come across a tax that is popular with the person who pays it. The only taxes that are popular are those perceived to be paid by someone else.

The whole process dragged on until a few days before the pre-Budget report, which was now fixed for 24 November. Unfortunately for me, the same opinion polling had apparently discovered that a tax on income, including National Insurance, was more acceptable. I was doubtful that this was the case. What worried me about a rise in National Insurance was that it would immediately be branded a 'tax on jobs' – and this is what came to pass during the 2010 general election. At a time when our defining purpose was to protect jobs in the teeth of a recession, this didn't seem right, even if it were not due to come into force until 2011. Never mind the economics, in my view the politics were wrong and we would pay a heavy price for it. It finally became clear that Gordon was never going to agree to a VAT increase. Reluctantly, I had no option but to announce a 0.5 pence increase in National Insurance contributions, paid by both employees and employers. To compensate, I made permanent the emergency rise in personal allowances that had followed the abolition of the 10p rate. The effect was to give all basic rate taxpayers a further £145 to help balance the National Insurance increase.

I had another difficult decision to make. It was one that had a profound impact, far wider than the Budget arithmetic, and it concerned the higher rate of income tax. To raise it would be to cross the political Rubicon for New Labour. Since the early 1990s, Gordon and Tony had worked tirelessly to re-establish our reputation not only as being economically competent but also as understanding the modern world. We wanted to ensure that we anchored ourselves in the middle ground of British politics; that we recognized the need to be fair, but also that we wanted people to get on. We needed to embrace not just equality but also aspiration.

That is largely why the Labour Party, in opposition and in government, was determined not to increase either the basic rate or the top rate of income tax. We had made that specific promise in every election since the birth of New Labour. For ten years we defended a top rate of 40 per cent. We were also conscious of the fact that increasingly there was likely to be tax competition. I don't believe that if you raise the top rate for a short time people will pack up and leave the country, but in the longer term tax rates do influence some people's decisions as to whether or not they will stay here. And the evidence shows that the higher the tax rate, the greater the risk of tax avoidance.

There is also a more general political point. No one likes taxes, but increasing taxes on income will always be unpopular. People know that they have to pay taxes to fund the things they use every day, like schools and hospitals. But raising income tax rates is, in the political jargon, toxic. This is particularly so, I believe, for people on low incomes without families, who have no access to tax credits. Those were the voters who deserted us, alienated by the idea that we were doing nothing for them, in 2010 and in the Scottish and local elections of 2011.

However, there is no doubt that raising the top rate does bring in valuable additional resources. For me, the decision to raise the top rate of tax was a difficult one. For ten years, like everyone else, I had defended the top rate of 40p. What's more, even though the increased rate was not going to come in until the end of the Parliament, it would be breaking the spirit of what we had promised in our manifesto in 2005. I was worried, too, about our doing anything that would move us from the centre ground of British politics, a place where Labour must stay if it is to be re-elected. But against all that was the pressing need for revenue to get our borrowing down once we were through the crisis. If we were to do that, it was not unreasonable that those who had done pretty well over the previous ten years should make a contribution. Reluctantly, then, I decided to increase the rate paid by people earning more than £150,000 to 45 per cent. Since we were asking everyone to shoulder an increased burden, fairness dictated that those at the top should make a larger contribution.

There was some argument about whether we should state that this was to be a temporary increase. I could just imagine the laughs in the House of Commons. Income tax, when it was introduced in 1798 by

William Pitt the Younger to pay for the Napoleonic Wars, was intended to be temporary. However, both Gordon and I subsequently made it clear that this was something we had had to do because of the critical circumstances we were in. It was not a change in our political view concerning the top rate of tax. It would be reduced when circumstances allowed. That was my view then, and it remains my view today. Every tax system must be fair and be seen to be so, but it must also encourage aspiration and enterprise. We were in an extremely difficult position, and, as events were to prove, the 45p rate was not enough.

I was to come back to the question of VAT during the preparation of both the Budget in 2009 and the pre-Budget report later that same year. In the meantime, just days before this 2008 pre-Budget report, I had to get on with what we had. Its centrepiece was a £20 billion boost to the economy, largely paid for by increases in income tax at the top end and a smaller increase from the 0.5 pence rise in National Insurance. This was, if you like, an old-fashioned redistributive Budget. It represented the largest change in tax and spending since 1997; I think it amounted to more redistribution than all of Gordon's budgets put together. But it was necessary, and it worked. In addition to the new top rate of tax, I also restricted the allowances available to people earning more than £100,000, and began to remove the tax relief that top-rate earners could claim for pension contributions. I was also careful to ensure that, despite the National Insurance increase, no one earning under £20,000 would pay more.

I also had to deal with the vexed question of public spending. The spending review that I had announced twelve months earlier had only come into effect in April. I did not want to revise it after such a short time when so much was so uncertain. Anyway, I was not enthusiastic about looking at specific cuts in spending at that stage. Things were so uncertain that we would probably end up making decisions that would have to be changed in a few months' time. I had already cut the rate of growth in public spending during the previous year. In the March 2008 Budget, after much discussion, I had planned for annual growth in spending of 1.8 per cent, after the current spending period ended in early 2010. Now I cut it again, to 1.2 per cent growth. This was very tight but, in my view, manageable.

There were two further measures I introduced. The first was to give taxpayers who were facing difficulties more time to pay their tax bills. This prevented a lot of bankruptcies; it proved to be an extremely popular measure and it endures to this day. It also meant that the Revenue collected more than it would have done, since by pressing for a repayment it had pushed firms into bankruptcy. I also increased the state pension by £4.55 per week and brought forward the increase in Child Benefit from April to January.

It was a good package overall, but because Gordon and I did not reach agreement until close to the end, it was impossible to develop a political strategy for handling the media coverage. Attention focused on the forecasts, particularly that I expected us to enter recession for the first time in fifteen years, and that borrowing would peak at £118 billion in 2009. What's more, I forecast that debt would rise to 57 per cent of national income by 2013/14.

On top of that, nearly every single item in the pre-Budget report was systematically leaked in the days preceding its announcement. In fact, there was virtually nothing new to announce on the day except the National Insurance increase. The centrepiece of the pre-Budget report was meant to be the VAT reduction. Its leak to a Sunday newspaper allowed everyone who was against it to denounce it before it was formally announced. In any event, what I believed to be an excellent measure was trashed before it got off the ground. It is almost impossible to find out who is responsible for leaking information. I have never known a leak inquiry that found the source. There is no point in speculating: it could have been a Tory mole, I always suspected that they had one. Looking back, most people now agree that the VAT reduction was a success, even some of the shopkeepers who argued that it would be far too difficult for them. Along with other measures, such as bringing forward some building and engineering works, it helped carry the economy through 2009 and back into recovery at the end of the year.

There was one more event that autumn that was to prove critically important to us, and to many other countries, and it was to be made possible by an unlikely ally in the economic battle. For some time, Gordon and I had been considering how we could harness the efforts of the world's largest economies to try to avert the looming catastrophe. The banking crisis was most acute in the US and Europe, including the UK, but the downturn had spread much further, hitting both Asian and developing economies, including China, India and those in South America. The sub-prime crisis had shown how a problem in one part of the world could infect the entire system within months or even weeks, not years as in the past. The IMF was forecasting that world growth would stall for the first time since the war. We believed that collective action could put a brake on a momentum that might tip the world into deep recession.

The previous November, when I was in South Africa, we had agreed to take on chairing the meeting of G20 finance ministers and central bank governors. Our term of office was to start in January 2009. Until that time, the G20 had been a low-key gathering of finance ministers, which did not include heads of government. It had not even been a regular fixture in Gordon's calendar when he was Chancellor. The G20 had been set up by the Canadians in 1999 to try to engage the large developing economies which were excluded from the more elite G7 group. It had no democratic legitimacy, and was a fairly ad hoc arrangement. Spain, going by the size of its economy, should have been in the group, but it wasn't because there were thought to be too many Europeans. South Africa was the only African country, and the representation from Asian countries was low.

However, what we saw in the G20 was the possibility of a platform for action across the world's economies. Gordon, in particular, with ten years' experience of finance ministers' meetings, could see the opportunities. If the world economy was to recover, no one country could do it alone. On the other hand, if every major economy did the same thing, that might provide the jolt that was needed. However, nothing would happen unless heads of government, prime ministers and presidents, were involved. Many finance ministers are primarily technocrats, advisers to their leaders rather than politicians. I was once at a dinner of finance ministers and it became apparent that I was the only one who was an elected Member of Parliament. One of my colleagues asked me: 'How can you take the big decisions if you have to think of the voters?' My reply was: 'How can you take the big decisions if you don't?'

Gordon had a good working relationship with President George W. Bush, which he'd worked hard at since becoming prime minister. He convinced the president to convene such a meeting in Washington. Gordon reckoned, rightly, that an invitation from the president of the US would be difficult to turn down, and so it proved. It is to President Bush's credit that, even in the dying days of his administration, he was prepared to engage in a lot of heavy lifting to get this gathering under way. It was just two weeks after President Obama had been elected, although he was not yet in office. We hoped he might be there, but understandably he was of the view that there could only be one president at a time.

The meeting was fixed for Saturday, 15 November, in Washington, only ten days before I was due to present the pre-Budget report. The flight out allowed me time to finalize the countless minor decisions that go into these reports and to begin work on my speech. After six hours of mulling over endless numbers, I searched in vain for a film to watch to fill the last couple of hours before landing. The sound system was an ancient one, and the choice was very limited. For thirty years I have managed to resist the temptations of Abba but it was either *Mamma Mia!* or back to the pre-Budget report. Now I succumbed and chose Abba. It did help me decide on one of my Christmas presents for Margaret who, like me, loved it.

On the Friday evening, President Bush held a reception at the White House. The leaders were in one room, finance ministers in another. The idea was that much of the legwork needed to reach the right decisions could be done that evening over dinner, before the more formal meeting next morning. Gordon had flown out a couple of days earlier, but we met briefly at the splendid British embassy on Massachusetts Avenue. This Edwin Lutyens house is one of a number of embassies that proclaim Britain's stature abroad, even though at home the Treasury periodically embarks on a vain attempt to sell them off.

We set off in a cavalcade from the embassy. Because Gordon was the prime minister, he and his security entourage were looked after. Why there were so many cars I don't know, but Gordon's retinue filled them up rapidly. I eventually found a car at the end of the procession. We got to the White House drive and Gordon's car stopped outside the front door, so he could walk up the red carpet and be photographed by the world's media. The White House and its drive are much smaller than people might think. My car, at the end of the queue, was still out in the street. I had to argue my way past a heavily armed police officer, walk up the drive, weaving between cars, and through the crush of photographers, to get to the door. By the time I arrived at the front door, it was closed. They were not expecting anyone else from the British delegation. I had to knock on the door of the White House to be allowed in. There was no sign of Gordon, but there was President Bush ready to welcome the next guest. 'Hello there, Alistair, how are you doing?' he said. I was amazed at the man's memory. I'd had one conversation with him before that, in the summer, at a formal dinner in Downing Street. Bush has an easy charm. His politics are not mine, but those who characterize him as a bit of a dolt underestimate him. He had an astute reading of the situation we were in, especially of the politics of the next twenty-four hours, if not, perhaps, a grasp of the finer points of detail. A few weeks earlier the finance ministers had been invited to meet him in the White House, early in the morning. He congratulated everyone on our work and assured us: 'You folks don't need to worry. Hank's got a handle on this. He's going to freeze that liquidity.'

The mood among the finance ministers at dinner that evening was grim. A lot of the anxiety had to do with confidence, or the lack of it. That is why we thought that a successful outcome to this meeting was psychologically so important. Our evening meal at the US Treasury was not a success. There were far too many people and it was a bit of a mêlée. Hank was very tired. He told me he was counting the days until he left office. In any event, he felt that the ball was now in the leaders' court; any agreement would have to be reached at their dinner at the White House.

We finance ministers were pretty much united at that stage. We agreed on the need to support our economies now and that we had to reform the financial system. So we retired to bed, leaving our officials to work all night on a draft agreement and call to arms. I did take the opportunity for a long talk with Alexei Kudrin, the quietly spoken Russian finance minister. He is a very competent technocrat, rather than a politician, and did not come up through the ranks of the KGB. I always found him more thoughtful than many other Russian ministers I have dealt with. Although it was not central to what we were discussing, I was anxious that we try to rebuild relations between our two countries, which were under severe strain after the murder of the Russian dissident Alexander Litvinenko in London a year earlier. We have a great deal of trade with Russia and I was anxious to get across to Alexei that we needed to work together to give investors more confidence in investing in Russia.

The G20 meeting the next day was held in the National Building Museum, which in just a few weeks' time would host an inaugural ball for the new president. Work was already under way as we met. Gordon and I arrived, this time together, and were formally greeted again by President Bush. There was a hiatus before the arrival of the next delegation so we chatted informally for some time about Barack Obama's recent victory. President Bush was complimentary about the

Obama campaign. He was equally very irritated by the Republicans' decision to trash and disown his record. He said the election of the first black president was a very good thing for America and reflected a maturity on the part of the electorate that would not have existed even a decade before. Politics, I thought, is the same the world over.

It was the first time I had attended a meeting where around the table were the heads of government and finance ministers of twenty of the world's most powerful economies. There was a strong sense of common purpose. President Bush opened by saying that he would not be around for much longer, but he wanted to make sure that we agreed to act in the face of a mounting problem. There was a powerful intervention from Australia's new Prime Minister Kevin Rudd and his Finance Minister Wayne Swan. It was a real call to arms and a warning of what would befall economies across the world if we let depression take hold. Right around the table, from the Saudis to India, there was agreement that we needed to act together to reverse the economic slump. Equally, there was a commitment to boost growth and to seek reform of global financial markets. There were, though, far too many Europeans. President Sarkozy had, for domestic reasons, used his considerable guile to get the Spanish and Dutch under his wing, with the result that European ministers spoke one after another for more than an hour. This was not lost on the others, and my guess is that if the G20 is to continue as an effective organization its representation needs to be rebalanced.

I have been to many international meetings and very few of them can truly be said to be of any great significance. This G20 meeting, though, was crucial, not so much because of its specific conclusions but because it demonstrated that countries were prepared to act together. President Bush and Hank Paulson deserve a great deal of credit for that. So too does Gordon. It was his dogged pursuit that made that meeting happen. It was his determination that we should keep the presidency of the G20, and not cede it to Japan which desperately wanted it, that resulted in the highly successful meetings held the following year.

Rather than let the pre-Budget report stand, Gordon now wanted to make fresh announcements seemingly on a weekly basis, to show we were taking action to deal with the crisis. To the outside world, far from offering reassurance that we were on the case, it looked as if we were panicky, not in control. I remember one occasion when, as we were about to do a series of media interviews, Yvette Cooper and I found that we could not remember all of the things the government had announced, there were so many of them.

As part of his reshuffle in October, Gordon had established what was called a 'national economic council'. He wanted to convey a sense of purpose, and the title was designed to make it sound more important than yet another Cabinet committee. Most of the Cabinet were on it, together with a large number of junior ministers, about thirty in total, making it unwieldy. On top of that, for some reason it met in the Cobra room, deep in a Whitehall basement. This windowless room is reserved for times of national emergency and civil unrest, and was presumably chosen to give the newly invented council some aura of urgency. In practice, it meant that we could not get so much as a cup of coffee, which was especially hard given Gordon's preference for early morning meetings. Food and drink are, for some reason, banned from the bunker.

It was fine for me, I didn't have far to walk to work; but there was no reason not to meet in the Cabinet Room upstairs: what we were discussing was hardly top secret. The council couldn't tell the Treasury what to do, but Gordon used it to drive through various policy initiatives, such as help for home owners. I didn't object to it when he first raised the idea when we met at my home in Edinburgh in August. I wanted to keep the peace. At the end of the day, the Treasury can always say no – no economic council or Cabinet committee can change that. I put up with it, although Gordon would never have agreed to it when he was

Chancellor. No Cabinet sub-committee can tell the Chancellor what to do, but this was an attempt to bypass the Treasury and do just that. On the other hand, he never sought to undermine me in this committee, but he remained frustrated with the Treasury.

The pre-Budget report measures, despite the predictable response from the Conservative media, was necessary, and stopped far deeper damage being done to the economy. However, the deficit, then estimated at £118 billion, was becoming a huge problem, both economically and politically. Although we had entered the recession with a deficit of 3 per cent of our national income, which was not high by international standards, it had now risen to 8 per cent, the highest since records began in 1970. Even so, it was manageable. But it looked to some as though we were simply spending more money that we didn't have. This gave the Tories the space they needed finally to abandon support for our spending plans, which they had maintained up until that point.

By the end of 2008 we had achieved more on the international stage than I would ever have thought possible. At home, the year closed in much the same way as it had opened. Our political stock was still low, and the increasingly fraught relationship between Nos. 10 and 11 was becoming ever more evident, not just in government but to the wider world. What could have been hailed as a great success in pulling the banking system back from the brink was being drowned out by the dissonance. We should have been able to capitalize on our deft response, to move on with the same clear purpose to deal with the economic consequences of the crash. After all, the Tories were all over the place. But in our disarray, with pointless political feuding and half-baked announcements, we allowed them the space to regroup, to leave us to it, and then to present themselves as something new two years later.

9 Global Success, Domestic Failure

We returned to London on the first Sunday of 2009. Christmas with our family and the annual Hogmanay supper with close friends had revived our spirits. It was a wrench to board the plane to London. The first few months of the year would be difficult. At a dinner with the Edinburgh Chamber of Commerce just before Christmas, everyone I spoke to had said the same thing: they were holding on, but business was slowing and bank lending was drying up.

The first Cabinet meeting of the year was held in Liverpool. This tradition of meeting in different parts of the country was started by Gordon and proved very popular with the regional press – predictably less so with the national media. The night before we met, I had dinner with a group of businessmen and women in a restaurant at the top of a block of newly built luxury flats. The man who built them told me they were proving difficult to sell. And the bank, he complained, was being unaccountably difficult about lending him money to build more flats. Although I didn't say so, I could rather see the bank's point. When he told me his lender was one of the Irish banks, I could see in a nutshell why they had got into such difficulties with commercial loans.

Wherever I went, whether it was businesses in Edinburgh, in Liverpool or in London, the story was the same. Lending, or rather the lack of it, was the big problem. We would have to do more to improve lending to businesses and potential home owners. What's more, the economic conditions had deteriorated sharply since the pre-Budget report in November. Then, we were talking about a short recession. Now, it was more ferocious, sharper and deeper. The massive uncertainties about what would happen to other countries and to the banks had increased. We were now talking about a recovery at the beginning of 2010. Ominously, Dave Ramsden, the Treasury's chief economist, said that when the recovery came it would not feel like one. It would be long and slow. Worse still, he thought at this stage that there had been a loss of 4 to 5 per cent of our economic capacity – that is, the amount of income we are able to produce, particularly in the financial services sector – which would be permanent. Forecasting in this climate was incredibly difficult, and it was of no comfort that most forecasters were wrong. The IMF, which in October 2008 was forecasting world growth of 3 per cent for 2009, was now forecasting growth of close to zero. And in the last three months of 2008 the world economy had shrunk for the first time since 1945, with Japan, America, Germany and most of Europe, including the UK, now in recession.

The outlook was bleak, but there was one bright spot on the horizon. The election of Barack Obama would, we all hoped, give a new impetus to international action to help solve the economic crisis. Obama, like us, believed that governments can make a difference. Gordon and his team were in constant touch with the incoming Obama administration. His frustration was that Obama was not prepared to start taking decisions until his inauguration at the end of January. That fits with the American Constitution but was frustrating for us on this side of the Atlantic. We needed the Americans to be big players and their number one player was not going to take the stage for four weeks.

For my part, I didn't get to meet Tim Geithner, the new Treasury Secretary, until the middle of February, at a meeting of G7 finance ministers in Rome. I had, of course, spoken to him several times on the telephone since his appointment in January. When we did meet, I was struck by how paralysed a new US administration is. In the UK, when the government loses power, it is usual for the new government to take office the day after. The civil service remains in post, moving seamlessly from supporting one government to the next. When I met Tim in his hotel room in Rome, he asked me if I would like a cup of coffee, which he proceeded to make himself. He explained that the last coffee maker had been a Republican and the replacement had yet to be confirmed by Congress: he was making a point – so many government appointments in the US are political. My relationship with Tim Geithner was as good as it had been with Hank Paulson. He was unpretentious and easy-going, and having run the New York Fed and been involved in the bail-outs the previous autumn, he knew exactly the landscape we faced. He also knew most of the finance ministers. His quiet style, self-deprecating and relaxed, belied a steely determination. He was a good colleague.

Meanwhile, the mood in Downing Street darkened by the day. It was evident that we needed to do something more to make the bank rescue stick. This was not because it hadn't worked in the first instance, but because the situation in the wider economy, and within RBS and HBOS, had deteriorated very sharply. What action to take, and when to announce it, was a source of further tension between Nos. 10 and 11. It was not that we disagreed on what needed to be done on the economy, and in particular in relation to the growing problems with bank lending. It was more that I began to realize the extent of Gordon's lack of confidence in my judgement, and that of the Treasury, and the Treasury's ability to deliver what was required. Worse, as he became convinced that we weren't seized with the urgency of the situation, endless meetings were called in those early days of January, frequently to cover the same ground. If Gordon and I had been in business, I suspect we would have agreed at this point that it was best to part company and to do it immediately; but it's not that simple in government.

The recapitalization of the banks the previous October had been successful in stopping a meltdown. But the more the new management at RBS and Lloyds looked into what they had taken over, the worse the picture became. RBS was a particular problem. The acquisition by RBS of ABN AMRO was a major part of the trouble. It held a huge number of assets and shares that were worthless and would take years to recover their value – if they ever did. Some of their holdings seemed fantastic. They appeared to own a golf course in Florida that was seventy miles from the nearest road. They owned a cemetery in the Deep South, the value of which was questionable. They seemed to have taken over an incredible number of US trailer parks which were at the heart of the sub-prime crisis. The question was what to do about all this. Left alone, these liabilities would bring down RBS unless they could somehow be split off into a 'bad bank' and run down over many years. The alternative was for the government to insure or guarantee these assets, leaving the bank to run them down as best it could, again over many years. Whatever we did, it was increasingly apparent that RBS would need yet more capital to prop it up. It would have been impossible to discover all this over the frenetic weekend of the bank bail-out in October 2008. Even if we had known exactly what the bank owned, it would still have involved more capital than we put in at that time. Added to that, economic conditions were continuing to deteriorate, with the result that more good assets were rapidly turning bad as their value fell.

The problem faced by Lloyds over their acquisition of HBOS, which was finally voted through by Lloyds shareholders in January, was different. HBOS had made a large number of loans for commercial and residential property which were going to lose them billions of pounds. It was old-fashioned bad judgement calls made in Edinburgh. It had even carried on lending, particularly on commercial property, as its losses continued to mount. It had offered mortgage deals that made no sense. A bank that had once been a symbol of Scottish prudence had been brought to its knees.

Back in Edinburgh in late 2008 there had been a campaign to try and undo the takeover by Lloyds. It was fronted up by two prominent Scottish bankers. George Mathewson had been chief executive and then chairman of RBS. He had brought in Sir Fred Goodwin but had then left before disaster struck. Peter Burt had been chief executive, then chairman, of Bank of Scotland and had masterminded the merger with the Halifax building society. The Bank had tried to sell part of its American operation to a company run by TV evangelist Pat Robertson. That deal fell through, perhaps because it transpired that Mr Robertson believed that Scotland was 'a dark land' where 'homosexuals ruled the roost'. I knew both Burt and Mathewson, and I could understand why they might want to salvage HBOS. I would have agreed with them but for the fact that I knew the bank was bust. Although there was a great deal of noise in the Scottish media in support of their campaign, no offer – or, indeed, solution – was ever put to the Treasury, despite repeated requests that they do so. What it boiled down to was that they would move in, take a look at the books and, if they needed more money, the government would have to provide it. The merger, or, more accurately, the takeover, by Lloyds did at least mean that there was money coming from the private sector, and I couldn't see any justification for taking on another bank entirely at the state's risk. In the event they did not pursue their plan.

The whole picture was further complicated by the fact that all of the banks were rapidly reassessing who they would lend to. A good prospect two years before might look decidedly bad in January 2009. Further action was needed not just to shore up the banks but to try and get lending going again in every sector of the market. This involved an extraordinary amount of work. Gordon was understandably frustrated about bank lending. The bad publicity associated with continuing bonus payments was eroding support for what we had done just before Christmas. I was frustrated too, but I did not want to make an announcement that was not thought through and which might unravel. We needed time to get this right. My hesitation was, I think, seen as evidence, not of a recognition of the need for detailed planning, but rather of a reluctance to act.

Of course, the Treasury is institutionally against spending money if it can avoid it. But, along with the Bank of England and the FSA, we had been working up a complex scheme over the Christmas period. I was

8. Margaret and me meeting the Obamas on their first official visit to London, April 2009.

9. Assembling in Downing Street, in April 2009, on the eve of the crucial G20 summit in London, with our American counterparts. From left: David Miliband (Foreign Secretary, 2007–2010), Hillary Clinton (Secretary of State, 2009–), Gordon, President Obama, Tim Geithner (US Treasury Secretary, 2009–) and me.

10. In calmer waters: inspecting a wind farm at Whitstable with Tony Blair in July 2006.

11. The haves…   12. …And the have yachts.

Me, on my Orkney spinner in Lewis, summer of 2008, while my opposite number, George Osborne, was on Oleg Deripaska's megayacht – an altogether different vessel – in the Mediterranean.

13. Above: A Lehman Brothers employee leaving the London headquarters in Canary Wharf, on 15 September 2008, the day it was announced that the bank had filed for bankruptcy.

14. Left: Addressing the Labour Party Conference, 28 September 2009.

15. On the Isle of Lewis in 2008 at the time of my interview with the *Guardian*, just before the forces of hell were unleashed.

frustrated at the general reluctance and slow rate of progress within the Treasury and I expressed this to Nick Macpherson. I felt I was fighting on two fronts: one in the Treasury, to speed up the scheme; the other with an angry prime minister, whose lack of control over the Treasury made him suspicious that they were an instrument of opposition to his will. It was a view that some of his advisers in No. 10 seemed only too happy to foment.

Worse than that, I was aware that some of his advisers had opened up a separate channel to the banks with which we were negotiating. I could never prove who was behind this, but it was clear that some of the senior bankers had a direct line to No. 10. They seemed remarkably well informed of Treasury plans and thinking. The banks tried to get better terms for themselves. At times some in No. 10 appeared to be arguing the banks' case with the Treasury. As we worked up proposals to stabilize the banks, we had to consider how the risks could be shared between the government and individual banks. There were billions of pounds at stake, and I needed to drive as hard a bargain as I could. That would be difficult if the banks knew our thinking in advance. Any attempt to talk to Gordon about this parallel operation was met with brusque dismissal: it wasn't happening.

In early January, Bank of America needed support and had to be rescued. Citigroup, one of the world's largest banks, was effectively broken up. The Irish government nationalized Anglo Irish Bank. Commerzbank had to be rescued in Germany. It was decided that I would make a statement to the Commons, setting out what we were doing. I had to show that we were dealing with the problem now confronting us. I couldn't have chosen a worse day to do it on, 19 January 2008, when RBS had to announce write-offs that, far from amounting to £2 billion as the markets were expecting, came to £7 billion. I went to the House with a series of measures to boost lending and secure the two banks in which we had major shareholdings, RBS and the newly formed Lloyds HBOS. To try to maintain some capacity in the mortgage market, I decided that Northern Rock would no longer pursue a policy of rapidly reducing its mortgage book. For RBS, I announced an increase in lending of £6 billion over the following twelve months. I also announced that we would insure bank assets, for a commercial fee, against losses on the banks' existing loans. The idea behind this was to provide sufficient protection to allow the expansion of lending. I also extended the credit guarantee scheme I had set up in October. By that time over £100 billion of these guarantees had been taken up, with the result that the interest rate at which banks lent to each other had fallen from 6 per cent to 2.5 per cent. This falling rate indicated that banks were beginning to trust one another's ability to repay loans once more, in turn making it more likely that lending to the wider economy would resume. These were worthwhile measures, but they were drowned out by the RBS losses.

I went back to my office in the Treasury in a black mood. The position at RBS was far worse than anyone had imagined. The insurance scheme set up for the banks in general was likely to end up being used only by RBS. The other banks were not so badly affected, and in time they were able to raise money commercially and did not need further capital from the government. That evening I asked my officials to draw up contingency plans in case RBS were to fail. For the first time, we had to consider full nationalization. The implications were considerable. The remaining shareholders would be wiped out, and it would have a huge impact on confidence in the UK. There was a further problem. Our gross domestic product (GDP) at that time amounted to about £1.5 trillion. RBS liabilities were thought to be £1.9 trillion. What would happen if not only did we have to take on RBS but things got worse and we were required to nationalize Lloyds HBOS, or even Barclays? Fortunately, that didn't happen.

In February I announced details of the 'asset protection scheme', as the insurance scheme was called. It was the largest insurance policy ever written, insuring £325 billion of assets. Most of these were mortgages and business loans, which were hard to value. Although I was far from certain what would happen at the time, this guarantee has worked. RBS is managing the wind-down of those bad loans and the bank is recovering. In return for this insurance, RBS had to pay a fee amounting to £6.5 billion, which came back to the Treasury. It was the culmination of the work that had started over Christmas and was now in place. Although in theory the scheme was open to other banks, none of them needed to take it up. We also increased our shareholding in RBS so that we now effectively owned nearly 84 per cent of the bank. I saw no reason to acquire the rest of the shares. Indeed, the fact that RBS remains a quoted company means it will be easier to sell the shares and allow the government to recover what, on any view, was a massive investment in the bank. This was the final step we had to take to complete the rescue of RBS from its folly. Other countries had looked at splitting banks into 'good' and 'bad' entities, with the bad one taking the worthless assets in the hope of selling them on when their value improved in years to come. That's what we had done with Northern Rock. In the case of RBS, I thought it better to provide a guarantee but to leave the bad assets within the bank. As it turned out, this was the right approach.

Another measure, which I had announced on 19 January, was barely noticed at the time, but was part of a series of measures designed to reassure the markets and to stabilize the economy. It was intended in part to help larger companies that were struggling to raise funds. The Bank of England was to spend £50 billion to buy assets from banks, financial institutions and financial markets, as well as companies. These were good quality assets, which will eventually be sold on, but the cash received by the firms would, at least in theory, be available for investment. Mervyn had agreed that the Bank would run the scheme, provided the government was prepared to underwrite it.

However, this was not just a scheme to help large companies. It was designed to go much further than that. I said in the House of Commons: 'In future the monetary policy committee will keep under review whether this facility could be used as an additional way for meeting the inflation target, in line with similar operations at the US Federal Reserve.' This was barely reported, which goes to show that if you want to keep something quiet, announce it on the floor of the House of Commons. It was, in fact, the beginning of a major new policy which came to be known as 'quantitative easing'.

Interest rates were now down to 0.5 per cent, making bank credit as cheap as it could be. Of course, what customers pay their banks will always be more than the official bank rate, because they are covering other costs, as well as contributing to the bank's profits. But the bank rate is the Bank of England's way of controlling how much it costs to borrow, and so influencing the rate of inflation in the economy. When inflation starts to rise, the interest rate goes up, and when it falls, the rate comes down. When an economy goes into a downturn, the central bank will almost always cut interest rates. But we had reached the stage where the bank rate could not be cut any further. In discussions both with the Bank and with No. 10, we agreed that we were anxious to avoid the problems Japan had experienced ten years earlier. Then, their interest rate had fallen to near zero, but the economy had continued to stagnate. They had left it too late before doing more. What we needed now was the ability of the Bank of England to increase the quantity of money circulating in the economy, hence 'quantitative easing', which was to be implemented by purchasing financial assets in return for cash. It would be necessary for the Treasury to indemnify the Bank for any losses that might arise from the way it did this. This was the first time that quantitative easing had been implemented in the UK, although the US Federal Reserve had used the same tactic in 2008, so it wasn't entirely unchartered territory. The Bank and the Treasury had been working on the scheme for weeks. They called it 'unconventional monetary policy', which to me sounded somewhat sinister. 'Quantitive easing' isn't much better: it sounds like an unpleasant medical prescription rather than an economic one. The key thing, though, is that it worked. Eventually, £200 billion was put into the economy and it was one of the measures that helped restore confidence.

When we announced the measure, Gordon and I were keen that the Bank of England should take the lead since, although we underwrote the operation, we were anxious that it should be seen as part of the Bank's armoury and not as a political ploy. The announcement was made on 5 March, immediately following a meeting of the Bank's Monetary Policy Committee. I believed I had an agreement with Mervyn King that he would hit the airwaves immediately after the meeting. The policy needed careful explaining in an authoritative way. On the day, there was absolute silence from the Bank until halfway through the afternoon, clear evidence that the Bank moves in a completely different way to the rest of us. In a world of 24-hour news, a three-hour gap before an explanation could have been disastrous. It allowed our opponents to characterize the measure as just a way of printing money. Vince Cable claimed we were leading Britain 'down the road to Harare'. However, and not for the first or last time, he was to change his mind subsequently and see the merits of what we were doing. George Osborne's judgement was no better. He said: 'Printing money is the last resort of desperate governments.' How strange, then, that when he became Chancellor he said he would look favourably on any requests by the Bank for more quantitative easing. Two years later there is still discussion about whether more quantitative easing is needed, so maybe it wasn't such a bad idea after all. For my part, if it were to be done again, banks should be compelled to lend out a good deal of the money rather than keep it in their vaults. It may have shored up the banking system, but lending remained constrained.

There was one other banking failure to deal with at the end of March. One of Scotland's oldest building societies, the Dunfermline, had got itself into difficulties. It was a small society with just thirty-four branches and 300,000 members. Its problems stemmed from a range of factors. They had got into commercial property lending in excess of £650 million, much of it in 2005 and 2006 when prices were at their highest. They were now losing money on many of these loans. They had also bought more than £150 million of high-risk, self-certified mortgages from two American firms, including a subsidiary of Lehman Brothers. In addition, they had to write off a substantial sum for the purchase of an IT system. They couldn't raise the capital they needed. It was decided that the society would be transferred to the Nationwide building society, which had already absorbed a number of other societies on a voluntary basis.

It was a sad end for an old-established society. I wasn't surprised, though. A few weeks earlier I had gone into a branch with the children to withdraw a small sum from their accounts, on which I was still a joint signatory. The unfortunate teller took almost an hour to put the transaction through the computer system. He kept apologizing, and I was almost at the point of telling him to close both accounts. I realized, however, that as I knew the society was already in trouble, and the staff knew full well who I was, that closing my children's accounts might be misconstrued. We left the money where it was.

In the meantime, the recession was biting and the differences between Gordon and myself were becoming more visible. In early March I had to go to Reading for a meeting of yet another newly created council. This one brought together regional development agencies with local government and some others. Peter Mandelson and I chaired it. To be blunt, I doubt it ever achieved anything beyond receiving endless reports calling for various degrees of action. While I was there, I took the chance to visit the high street. This is always a risky business, especially when you are accompanied by television cameras and reporters. Sure enough, I wasn't disappointed. As we walked along, a shopkeeper emerged from his jeweller's shop to tell me that the VAT cut had made no difference for him. I decided that it would be better to engage him in conversation than to cut and run, and walked into his shop. I assumed that a shop like his, selling luxury goods, would be feeling the pinch. Not a bit of it, he said, he had had a good weekend. Why, I asked? Because the economy had been out of the newspapers for the last few days. He was making an interesting point. Reading the newspapers day after day, or watching the news bulletins, the picture was bleak indeed. No wonder people stayed at home hoarding their money. But offered a few days respite, they would come out to buy.

I had also arranged to do an interview with Mary Riddell of the *Daily Telegraph* around this time. Inevitably, like so many of my interviews, it did not take her long to probe the differences between me and Gordon. She began with the question of Sir Fred Goodwin's pension. We discussed this for a while, and then it was put to me that the story about his pension had been leaked by No. 10. I had heard the rumour too, although I couldn't see why on earth they would do it since it was bound to backfire. Then I was asked if I minded the fact that Ed Balls gave frequent counsel to Mr Brown. I said I wasn't bothered – because I wasn't. But the very fact that these questions were being asked demonstrated how undermining such tensions can be.

This theme continued. I was asked whether or not the government was to blame for the failures in the banking system. I said the key thing was that a culture had been allowed to develop over the past fifteen years, in which the relationship between what people did and what they got paid for it had gone way out of alignment. If there was a fault, and clearly there was, then that was our collective responsibility. The model of us telling the regulators 'You tell us it's OK and we'll go along with it' had failed. Now we had to regulate according to risk. However, my public acceptance that mistakes had been made was seen as evidence of weakness by No. 10. I thought it far better to admit what had gone wrong and then to try to put it right. No one will listen to a word you say unless you are prepared to show some humility and honesty. Nor did I believe that the political damage would be that great. After all, no other country in the world had foreseen the scale of the calamity; no other regulatory system had picked it up. The real problem was that the political mood of the time had allowed a culture of complacency to grow, with disastrous consequences.

Two years later, both Gordon and Ed Balls acknowledged that bank regulation had failed. I believe that had we all said so at the time I did, people would not have thought any less of us. Rather, they might have been prepared to accept that mistakes had been made and to listen to what we proposed to do to rescue the situation.

While we increasingly disagreed over what to do in the Budget, and relations became more fraught over the banks, Gordon and I were at least as one about what we wanted to get from the G20 summit, now fixed for 2 April. The UK had plunged into a sharp recession in the first three months of 2009. Germany had suffered an even greater plunge, although that was barely reported here. Because of their relatively stronger manufacturing position, they bounced back more quickly than we did. Most European countries were in recession. So was the US. In Japan, growth continued to stagnate. Even the emerging Asian economies had seen a sharp reduction in their growth figures. In short, there was a growing appetite among countries all over the world to act together to try to get themselves out of what looked like a steep decline in their fortunes.

At that stage, travelling around Britain, it did not feel like we were experiencing a recession. In many parts of the country, in Edinburgh and London in particular, restaurants and shops were still full, people were still going out. It was not like the early 1980s or early 1990s, when the terrible effects of recession stared you in the face wherever you looked. It wasn't until two years later that the full effect of the downturn would begin to be felt, its effects exacerbated by the deliberate actions of the new Tory-led coalition government. This was always going to be a long, slow recovery.

The first tangible evidence I had that countries might sign up at the G20 for something more than the ritual communiqué came when Gordon played host to the Chinese premier Wen Jiabao, who came to Downing Street in early February. From my experience of meeting with Chinese ministers, it is apparent that they tend to think on a different timescale. There is also something of a paradox. China was aware that it was the third largest economy in the world (and is now the second largest). They wanted to be at the top table and to influence events. But when it comes to international agreements, and particularly those that might prove onerous – on measures to prevent climate change, for example – they are inclined to say that they are merely a developing country battling with a legacy not of their own making. They are acutely aware of issues like climate change and security of energy supply, and they are intensely political in the way they make decisions. But they move at a different speed: they take time to analyse what is happening and are hesitant in reaching conclusions, particularly those that might commit them to something long-term. I suppose that is what comes of not having to face an electorate.

At this meeting, though, the mood was very different. The premier and his fellow ministers were very focused on the need to do something about what seemed to be an impending disaster. After all, if the Americans were in no position to buy Chinese goods, they themselves would have a real problem. Part of the Chinese government's deal with its people is that they provide employment and rising standards of living. For as long as they do that, the people will put up with living under an authoritarian regime. As Gordon pressed his opposite number on the crucial point, the need to rebalance a world where China exported and America imported, Premier Wen showed that he was open to talking about it, rather than giving the customary response, which was politely to ignore the question. There was a recognition that China needed to do more to boost domestic demand and encourage their people to spend more. Perhaps it was China's worry about the political consequences of a downturn that led them to use their banks to flood the country with money. We may have struggled to make lending agreements with the banks work; the Chinese had no such difficulties.

A further indication of how far some countries had travelled came later in February, at a meeting of heads of government and finance ministers of Germany, France, Italy, Spain and ourselves, held in Berlin on a bitingly cold and snowy Sunday. Germany maintained a rhetoric of opposing spending to stop recession. The previous autumn I had been described by Peer Steinbrück, my German opposite number, as practising 'crass Keynesianism'. Although a member of the SPD, Labour's sister party in Germany, he attacked us in a way that was extremely hostile, and ignored the fact that Germany had spent about the same as us on boosting its economy through various measures, including giving subsidies to its car industry. Just before Peer left office, following his party's defeat that autumn, I asked him why he had made those remarks. He explained that to German politicians, of right and left, debt is anathema because of the connotations it has with what happened to Germany in the 1920s and the political consequences that followed. Germany did spend to boost its economy.

It had been agreed that I would hold a meeting of the G20 finance ministers two weeks before the emergency summit to be held in London in April. This was to get a lot of the donkey work done, and actually nearly all the conclusions reached by the heads of government had been agreed at this earlier meeting, which was held at a country hotel in West Sussex. There was a genuine sense of purpose at that meeting, which, besides the finance ministers, was attended by the governors of the central banks. In addition, the European Commission and the ECB, together with Dominique Strauss-Kahn from the IMF and Bob Zoellick of the World Bank, were there. The IMF was now coming into its own. The brainchild of John Maynard Keynes, it was set up following the Bretton Woods conference of 1944. Keynes had devoted the previous two years to trying to establish an international body that could act as the world's banker of last resort. It became regarded as an organization that rescued countries that got into economic trouble, providing funds in return for their introducing usually stringent economic policies as part of a recovery programme. Inevitably there was some stigma; it was seen as a failure on the part of a government to have to call in the IMF. One of our objectives at this conference in Sussex was to recast the role of the IMF so that it could play a greater role in shaping the direction of countries facing difficulties. In the same way as an individual or a company might go to their bank for a loan to tide them over while they rearranged their affairs, so too could a country use the IMF, and without stigma. We haven't got there yet.

Finance ministers tend to be a cautious breed, particularly the more technical types, and central bankers by their nature lean towards extreme caution. Mervyn King did an excellent job with his colleagues, winning them round to taking whatever action was needed to support their economies. He was very engaged. Some were already convinced, others were more reluctant. Looking back at the notes of the contributions made by ministers, it is striking how worried everyone was. The previous year, when we met in Japan, the problem was seen very much as a Western one. Now, speaker after speaker was seized with the necessity of putting money into their economies, and regulating an unwieldy and often opaque global banking system. There was a genuine sense of fear. Even the Asian countries could see that what was happening in the West would affect them. The weekend involved a series of one-to-one meetings as well as more formal sessions, including a working dinner which stretched into the night. Much of the discussion concentrated on the difficult question of financial regulation. There was still a sense that the UK–American model had been the cause of such a spectacular series of disasters in the banking world.

However, most models of financial regulation had failed. They had failed simply because no one, at whatever level, had been asking the right questions with sufficient determination. And calls for more regulation don't necessarily deal with that problem either. There is much talk about whether institutions are too big to fail, or even too big to save, but there is another category too: too big to know what's going on. We agreed that all systemically important financial institutions and markets needed an appropriate degree of regulation and oversight. Gordon had called for something like this nine years earlier, and a lot of preparatory work had been carried out by Mario Draghi, governor of the Italian central bank. He had helped establish the Financial Stability Forum (now the Financial Stability Board), which was designing the architecture we needed. We also agreed on the need to contain credit in the good times so as to be able to dampen, rather than amplify, the economic cycle. Some of this has borne fruit: for example, on cross-border regulation covering multinational banks. Other areas still require attention, such as the need to regulate credit-rating agencies which contributed to the crisis by certifying sub-prime loans as AAA.

Crucially, there was unanimous agreement about the need to boost demand until growth was restored. We also agreed that the IMF should assess what effect these policies were having and make recommendations on what else might need to be done. Finally, there was an agreement to help developing countries through the World Bank, as well as the now traditional call to resist protectionism and to do more to establish free and fair global trade. This agreement laid the foundation for the major G20 summit in London three weeks later. What was needed now was for world leaders to sign up to what was, on any view, an ambitious and demanding agreement. The problem, as ever, was that a commitment to see it through had to be maintained over the longer term.

On the political front, too, we gained a great deal. Ever since the dramatic rescue of the banks in October, countries had taken a fresh look at us. We had come a long way since the dark days of Northern Rock, when an uncertain response had hardly boosted confidence. I think there was a feeling that the British government could make a success of the emergency summit in two weeks' time. Gordon certainly invested a great deal of effort in building support. He chartered a plane and flew around Europe and South America, as well as visiting the US, where he was the first European leader to meet President Obama in the White House. No effort was spared. Heads of government were met as they arrived in the UK, to make them feel welcome. I was dispatched to meet President Obama and the First Lady as they came down the steps of Air Force One at Stansted airport. As we waited at the foot of the steps for the door of the presidential plane to open, my eye was caught by a huge, and evidently very recently erected, sign on the other side of the airport. It was situated in a direct line between the world's press photographers and the place where the plane would come to a halt, so that as Air Force One was photographed, the name Ryanair would appear prominently in the picture. I was told the airline's chief executive, Michael O'Leary, had visited the site a week earlier and hit on this free advertising ploy.

On this, Obama's first visit to Britain, there was a celebratory air surrounding him, and unsurprisingly he and Michelle captured much of the public attention in the coverage of the summit. As we walked across the tarmac, he said he would do 'whatever it took' to make the summit a success. He knew Gordon had done a lot of work and was determined to help him succeed. Margaret was relieved to find the Obamas as open and warm as she had hoped. 'What if, after all this, they aren't for real?' she had wondered as the plane doors opened.

We met again the following morning when the president sat across the Cabinet table from Gordon Brown. Two things struck me. One was his direct gaze. The other was his clarity about what America would and would not do. As Gordon went through his proposals, it was clear the new president knew the details as well as he did. Some things he would sign up to, some things he wouldn't. Normally, leaders go out of their way not to disagree with each other across the table. It is left to the briefers later to spell out their differences. Obama's approach was refreshingly direct and very welcome.

He was very engaged and, whether it was those of us who met him privately in Downing Street or the harder-bitten journalists who questioned him later, people were impressed. He did embody a sense of hope, something that we all desperately needed. The night before the summit, the Queen hosted a reception for leaders and finance ministers at Buckingham Palace. I lost count of the number of staunchly republican ministers from around the world who asked if they might be introduced to the Queen. For some, this was the high point of the summit.

There were three dinners arranged for that evening. Two were in Downing Street, and mine, with the finance ministers, was in the

Tate Modern. That meeting was workmanlike. It is a shame high security demanded that the spectacular views from the Tate across to St Paul's and the City had to be blanked out by closed blinds. Perhaps, as one of my colleagues remarked, they didn't want us to look at the City of London, haunt of the bankers who were causing us such difficulties. The harder work was done at Gordon's dinner in the state dining room, one floor up in Downing Street. His single-minded resolve to get the conclusion he wants can be offputting to some. But he was determined to make it work. No agreement was reached that evening and it was clear that a lot of heavy lifting would be needed the next day.

The third dinner was probably the one most people would have chosen to attend. Sarah Brown had borrowed the state room in No. 11 to host the leaders' partners and a gathering of invited women. Margaret, greeting guests as they arrived in the downstairs sitting room, was happily surprised to find Michelle Obama among the first to join the gathering. Two young members of staff from my private office were helping out. They were moved beyond words to be greeted by a spontaneous hug from the First Lady.

On the day of the summit we had to be at the massive ExCeL exhibition centre, near Canary Wharf, at the crack of dawn, or so I was told. Moving so many security targets around must have been a logistical nightmare. Protocol demanded that the ministers should arrive at four-minute intervals for the ritual handshake and photograph. It was a long, long wait.

Part of the art of summitry is knowing when to cut short the formal exchanges. Every country wants to set out its stall. The hard bit is getting an agreement. We were sitting around a massive circular table. Opera glasses would have been useful in order to see who was sitting on the opposite side. It didn't make for an informal discussion. The breakthrough did not come until after lunch, when Gordon insisted the leaders meet by themselves, without advisers or finance ministers to raise irritating questions. He locked the doors and told them they were not going until they had reached agreement, which they did two hours later. The sticking point was over tax havens, with President Sarkozy and the Chinese president, Hu Jintao, at loggerheads. Sarkozy wanted to 'endorse' a blacklist. President Hu did not like that word. It took the combined efforts of Gordon and President Obama to come up with a form of words both could live with. It was one word, actually: they agreed to 'note' the blacklist.

Potentially, the greatest achievement was to give the IMF more money, some $750 billion, as well as extra funds to support trade and aid. Looking back, the significance of the summit was perhaps not so much what it agreed as the signal it sent, that countries were ready to act together. This was a time when many were despairing that anything could be done to retrieve the economic situation. I made a statement to the House, reporting on the agreement reached. What was striking was how well it was received on both sides. There was, I think, a genuine sense of hope. There is no doubt too that the aura surrounding so many world leaders in London, especially the new president of the United States, had had a remarkable effect.

I met Gordon in his flat in Downing Street later that evening. He and Sarah were entertaining the Australian premier, Kevin Rudd, and his wife, Thérèse Rein, and asked Margaret and myself to join them. Far from being exuberant, Gordon was surprisingly low. He should have been in his element – big international occasions suit his temperament – but he was already worrying about the next problem around the corner. Being Scottish, Gordon and I find it difficult to compliment one another; it doesn't come naturally. I did say to him that he could look at this summit with a real sense of achievement. Kevin, being Australian, was far more effusive in his enthusiasm.

It was a high point – although, to be realistic, international achievements do not always score points at home. But an achievement it was. The summit helped us begin to claw back political support in the polls. We both knew we had to capitalize on it. Although the momentum was maintained later in the year in Pittsburgh, it was lost when we were defeated in the general election. There was simply no one to do the heavy lifting like Gordon and he deserves immense credit for it. If he had not been there, it wouldn't have happened.

I now had to turn my attention to the Budget. Gordon had intended that the G20 would give us scope to do more in the way of stimulating the economy than would otherwise have been possible. If everyone else was doing it, this would provide us with political cover. I wasn't so sure. And anyway, I thought we had reached the limit of how much we could spend. Our borrowing was set to reach £178 billion – that's 12 per cent of our national income.

As we prepared to go up to Edinburgh for a short Easter break, I knew that this would be the most difficult Budget yet, and that an impending clash with Gordon could not be far off. As it happened, our break was disturbed not by Budget preparations but by an all too predictable political catastrophe in No. 10, this time involving one of Gordon's spin doctors. Throughout his time in government, Gordon had relied heavily on these attack dogs, first Charlie Whelan, then Damian McBride. McBride had been caught out briefing against deputy leader Harriet Harman at party conference in October 2008 – by Harriet herself, who had overheard him. Rightly, she threatened to report him to the Cabinet Secretary unless Gordon did something about him. He promised to move McBride to where he could cause less trouble. It was to no avail. McBride's briefings against me to senior journalists and political editors were faithfully reported back. Gordon refused all entreaties by Cabinet colleagues to let him go and tethered him instead in an office in No. 10. It was another flawed fix, and he continued to roam.

Things finally came to a head when emails were published showing that McBride was involved in a shabby exercise to damage opposition figures and, in one case, the wife of a shadow minister. This time he had to go. Unfortunately, the disgrace did not leave with him. The repercussions for Gordon were disastrous. People had daily questioned our competence and our ability to control events. Now they had confirmation of what they suspected: we were a nasty party too. The perception was that our moral compass had irremediably lost its bearings. The McBride affair further destabilized the whole No. 10 operation.

It also made the Budget preparation even more difficult for me than in the previous two years. Once again, at its heart, lay a dispute about the Budget forecasts. The assumptions we made on these would drive how much we were likely to raise through taxes, how much borrowing would be, and what we had to raise in tax or cut in spending. It wasn't an academic exercise. I wanted our growth projections to be, above all, realistic. If they weren't, no one would believe anything else we had to say. As always, Gordon thought I was being too pessimistic. He kept saying that he understood the Treasury, the inference being that I did not. I just took the view that coming out of recession would be a long haul.

Both Gordon and I had been distracted, understandably, for much of March by preparations for the G20. I had been working on Budget proposals throughout that time, but the details could only be worked up once I had the overall picture in my mind. It wasn't really until the Easter weekend that Gordon and I spoke about it on the phone, and then he was preoccupied by the McBride affair. The same old dispute between us was very much to the fore. At its heart was a political argument rather than an economic one. Gordon wanted to paint the Tories as 'cutters', with us as 'investors'. The 'investment versus cuts' story had worked in 2001 and, to a more limited extent, in the general election of 2005. A hapless Tory shadow minister, subsequently a member of the Tory Cabinet, had played into our hands in 2001 by suggesting that the Tories really wanted to cut £20 billion from public spending. He went into hiding. The whole election campaign was dominated by the media search for this man. Oliver Letwin was finally tracked down at a garden party, dressed in a Roman toga. We could not have paid for such a boost to our campaign.

A more sober assessment of the outcome of the 2005 election, however, was that the Tories' leader at the time, Michael Howard, who was still heavily associated with the Thatcher years, was as much an ally to us as were their spending plans. For most of the New Labour years, the story of Labour investing in public services, and the belief that the public sector and the private sector should complement each other, dominated the British political scene.

The banking crisis changed all that. It changed it in a fundamental way. We could, and did, still argue that government spending was making the difference between recession and depression. Indeed, three years later, it was public spending in the shape of a still substantial deficit that was supporting the economy in the absence of a return of private sector confidence. This was, I believe, a powerful argument. What had changed, though, was that the old battle lines were now hopelessly out of date. We had to show that while we would do whatever was necessary to support the country, we would have to tackle the deficit in order to get borrowing down. It was one of many preconditions for a return to growth.

The argument, therefore, had to be more subtle. It had to strike a chord with voters. Unless what you have to say has a strong ring of truth, people will stop listening. That is precisely what happened to us. It seemed to me, in April 2009, that after showing what we had done in the financial crisis at home and abroad, we had a good platform from which to move to the next stage. I wanted to do a bit more in the Budget to help recovery, but I did not want to spend a lot more money that we did not have. Once again, Gordon disagreed. He felt that we needed to spend rather more in order to ensure our recovery. Gordon believed we had the political cover from what had been agreed at the G20, and didn't want to go into the election offering to spend less than we had done in previous campaigns. I wasn't so sure. I thought the political terms of trade had changed and that our approach had to be far more nuanced.

Our story was this: true, mistakes had been made on supervision of the banks, as had happened everywhere else. But we had stopped the system from meltdown. We took action to support the economy last autumn and would continue to do so. Once the recovery was under way we would cut our borrowing but do it in a way that allowed us to protect essential public services. More than that, we were beginning to develop a good story on the role of modern government in promoting growth. As Business Secretary, Peter Mandelson had done a great deal to re-establish the idea that government could intervene: for example, to good purpose in scientific development or investment in low-carbon technologies, where the market could not or would not function.

Our competing approaches could easily have been the subject of wider discussion. All of us would have been strengthened by that. As it was, most of the Cabinet was excluded from the debate until it was far too late. I found the personal support offered by senior colleagues like Jack Straw, Harriet Harman and Tessa Jowell immensely reassuring. Younger colleagues too – David Miliband, to whom I spoke often, and James Purnell and Douglas Alexander – all expressed their deep concern that summer. They were worried about Gordon's refusal to listen to them and our direction or, rather, lack of it, which would almost certainly culminate in disaster at the polls. The Budget should have been a fresh starting point, building on the G20 and providing a run-in to the election the following year. It didn't happen.

I sat at the Cabinet table for thirteen years. That should be the forum at which government policy is hammered out, where differences of opinion are debated and resolved. Of course, the implementation of policy, getting the detail right, can be left to Cabinet sub-committees. When I first attended Cabinet in 1997, I expected to receive papers from my colleagues outlining their policies, so that we could debate their merits. Instead, I was surprised to find that the Cabinet seemed at times simply to be going through the motions. We would sit down, hear the business in Parliament for the next fortnight or so, and then be told about a policy announcement that was going to be made sometime that day. The prime minister controls the Cabinet agenda and decides what will and won't be discussed. He has to use his judgement as to when he needs to bring colleagues with him – when discussions need to be conducted around the table, as opposed to a minister being squared off at a private meeting in the No. 10 study.

Both Tony and Gordon were reluctant to have open discussions if there was any possibility of controversy. There were other policies too that would have benefited from a far earlier and thorough debate. Iraq is perhaps the prime example. Or Afghanistan, when there was a discussion but only as a prelude to the announcement by John Reid, the Defence Secretary, that we were deploying troops there. Too often, the discussion was simply around the reporting back of the latest development, rather than providing an opportunity to stand back and ask where we were going.

For most of Gordon's time as Chancellor, he would tell us what he was doing on the economy; but because things seemed to be going so well, there was rarely any debate. It was only in the case of the euro that there was extensive discussion involving every member of the Cabinet. But it was a virtual Cabinet discussion, with members having one-to-one meetings with Tony and Gordon to avoid the semblance of a 'row' around the Cabinet table. This fear of 'rows', which stemmed from Labour's turbulent past in opposition and in the Labour Cabinets of the 1960s and 1970s, lived on through our thirteen years in government. 'Rows' are part and parcel of political life, and I think that our government would have been stronger if there had been more discussions around the Cabinet table.

I can remember only one discussion, in the summer of 2009, on 'investment versus cuts'. Yvette raised the matter because she felt that there should be a debate around this issue which was dividing the Cabinet – and, indeed, lay at the heart of the disagreements between Gordon and myself. She wasn't confrontational in the meeting; she simply made it clear that we needed to have the conversation. James Purnell spoke up in agreement; he too felt that there should be a debate.

Gordon listened to what was said, but what exercised him was the fact that it was increasingly apparent that what he and I were saying was at odds, and the discussion was cut short. My guess is that Yvette was more on Ed's side of the debate than was James Purnell, but this was an instance where people on both sides of the political spectrum felt that the situation was becoming intolerable. I spoke to both James and Yvette later that day. Gordon had seen both of them privately after the meeting. Yvette was upset at the way he had spoken to her. This episode did a lot to persuade James Purnell that he no longer wanted to be part of the government.

This tendency to make policy in this isolated way was not confined to us. It's happened many times before, under successive governments of different political hues. It has already happened with the new Tory-led coalition government over health service reforms, an obvious example where a bit of collective thinking might have avoided the need for a very public retreat.

The decision-making process that characterized the Labour governments of both Tony and Gordon is something we slipped into almost by accident. Tony set the pattern in the early days of his government, when the Cabinet purported to discuss whether to continue with the Millennium Dome in 1997. Tony said what he thought, that we should support it, and then told us he had another engagement and promptly left. Although a number of Cabinet colleagues, myself included, raised reservations about the whole thing, John Prescott simply said that Tony wanted it, so we had to go with it. It became a running sore for the next five years.

To understand why this style of government happened, it has to be remembered that in its long wilderness years in opposition in the 1980s the Labour Party had become almost ungovernable. The situation was only retrieved by the determination of Neil Kinnock to impose order where there was none and to do so in a necessarily ruthless way. He ensured that decisions were taken from the top, not through interminable committee discussions or, worse, public spats. By the time Tony and Gordon were establishing themselves as future leaders under John Smith, and after our third consecutive election defeat, the party was ready to accept governance by diktat. It worked, for the first few years. Tony, with his fresh eye and beholden to no one, junked much of the baggage we had grown up with after the defeat of 1979. Gordon, to his immense credit, rewrote our economic policy after 1992. This was fine in opposition. Parties are unwieldy beasts; but, with a few exceptions, they do like leadership. Put another way, for all the criticism a leader gets for appearing presidential and intolerant of dissent, people prefer that to a situation where there is no firm leadership or control. But in government, it is not just about implementing policies that may have been developed over a long time; it is equally about applying those policies in detail and reacting to day-to-day events, which may require a different approach. We did not have effective Cabinet government for the thirteen years we were in power. It is a mistake we should not repeat.

This lesson is not peculiar to the Labour Party, or even to British politics. The prime minister has to remember he is only 'first amongst equals'. True, British politics has evolved. It is hard to envisage Clem Attlee kicking a football around a field for the cameras, or Gladstone hugging a Spice Girl, at least in public. Harold Wilson famously spent much of his time managing competing Cabinet conflicts. In her first term, Margaret Thatcher found it difficult to do what she wanted in the face of Cabinet opposition, and she lost the confidence of her colleagues in the poll tax debacle. If ever there was a policy that should have been road-tested before being implemented, that was it. John Major's administration was paralysed in part by a cabal working against him. Tony Blair's problem was different. His internal conflict was with one man, Gordon Brown. This was not a conflict over policy. It was personal.

The point is that Cabinet government is a critical part of our constitution and it is being neglected. The position of the Chancellor in all this is complex. No Chancellor can produce a Budget as a result of committee deliberation. The Chancellor has to form a view of what must be done from the best evidence available, and then produce a Budget. The first time that the rest of his Cabinet colleagues will hear what's in the Budget is a couple of hours before it is presented. But I think that some of the general principles, and certainly the general approach, can, and should, be discussed. The decisions will be better for it. For example, one of Gordon's major changes to the tax and benefit system was the introduction of tax credits. Its implementation was complicated, but the principle of providing more help for those who need it most is a good one. It is redistributive and it is fair, but it is easy to criticize it when you look at the sometimes complex calculations. Here is an example where the principle could easily have been discussed and debated and that would have provided a greater sense of ownership of the policy, so that, when things became difficult, the Cabinet would still feel this was 'their' policy, not just Gordon's.

This, then, is the background against which, that Easter Sunday morning, I had a telephone conversation with Gordon about the proposed Budget – me in Edinburgh, he across the Firth of Forth in North Queensferry, still grappling with the fallout from the debacle over his errant adviser. Our conversation was perfectly friendly; it was just that we did not agree. The planning for this Budget was, as Peter Mandelson observed, to be a negotiation rather than a discussion. It was also to be the prelude to the complete breakdown of our political relationship.

10 Breaking Point

The Budget is usually the most important political statement of the year. What was needed this time round, in the spring of 2009, was a clear sense of direction, both political and economic. We desperately needed to work together as team, and we needed sufficient time to prepare the ground in order to gain maximum impact. None of this happened. Instead, the Budget strategy, and in particular the forecasts on which it depended, were not agreed until a few days before its presentation.

In retrospect, this Budget was dead in the water weeks before its presentation. It also marked the moment when my friendship with Gordon, which had lasted more than twenty years, was driven to breaking point. Richard Crossman in his diaries observes that political friendships should be cool and detached. I am afraid he is probably right. By now, ours was lacking in both qualities.

We faced three sets of problems in the run-up to the Budget. First, the political landscape simply couldn't have been worse for us in the wake of the McBride affair. Second, the chaotic decision-making process, and all those problems that had surfaced during the preparation of the pre-Budget report, manifested themselves again. Finally, there was the fact that Gordon and I were unable to agree about growth forecasts and strategy; our disagreement can be boiled down to investment in the economy versus the need to cut borrowing. There was little disagreement on specific measures, but they could only be decided once the big issues were resolved.

On the Saturday before the Budget was due to be delivered, I met Philip Gould in my office in the Treasury. Philip had done a lot of polling for us and had been part of Tony Blair's team since the inception of New Labour. Because of this, he was viewed with suspicion by the Brown camp. Rather like Peter Mandelson, Philip (along with Alastair Campbell) was gradually persuaded to come back for the sake of the party. We were on our knees, and the general election was not too far ahead. He told me that the voters were in an ugly and depressed state of mind. They were angry about the recession and the threat to their jobs, and they couldn't readily comprehend how increased borrowing or spending would make things better. Our only chance of improving our standing with them would be if we could explain clearly what we were planning to do and why – that we wanted to take measures to restart growth, for example, through investment in the economy. We were paying the price for our failure to deliver a message. Now we desperately needed a story to tell, and one on which we were all agreed. Time was short to get that right.

The process by which we drew up the Budget was tortuous. Preparing a Budget should not be like a wage negotiation in a trade dispute, with each side waiting until the other blinks. As a former Chancellor, Gordon knew full well the amount of work that had to be done, even after the fundamentals are signed off. A speech has to be written. Expectations have to be set. This was no way to run a raffle, never mind a Budget. Meetings scheduled to thrash out our position were cancelled, often at the last minute, and new ones hastily arranged, all too often early in the morning or late in the day. This was how it was with all the meetings at which we were to discuss big issues, not just economic ones.

Managing the prime minister's time is one of the key factors that will determine his or her success. Deciding what is important and what is not is critical. The management of Gordon's time by No. 10 was, from my perspective, hopeless. There was a permanent air of chaos and crisis.

Perhaps I am too managerial, a charge that has been levelled against me. But I find that a world where meetings start and finish when they are supposed to, and where decisions are reached, even if they are not always the ones I want, makes for better governance. It may be boring; the alternative is totally debilitating.

Our discussions rarely, if ever, reached a conclusion. Sometimes there would be just the two of us, meaning that the wider party machine did not know what, if anything, had been agreed. Towards the end of these negotiations, Peter began to attend, but studiously avoided taking sides. Ed Balls, and sometimes Yvette Cooper, who was still Chief Secretary, were there on a few occasions. Often Dan Rosenfield and Jeremy Heywood – who has been, on and off, private secretary to Tony, Gordon, and now David Cameron – would be present. Jeremy was a Treasury man who knew his stuff. He had also been private secretary to Norman Lamont during his Chancellorship.

Occasionally I would try to include Treasury officials, but since Gordon viewed them with suspicion, and sometimes open disdain, it quickly became counterproductive for them to join us. This I found hard to understand, since there was virtually no one in the Treasury at a senior level who had not been appointed when Gordon was Chancellor. No one could have got a senior post without his say-so. However, the message the Treasury conveyed on the economic outlook was consistently rejected by Gordon as being too conservative. He became convinced that they were determined to thwart him. Gus O'Donnell relayed Gordon's unexpurgated view of Nick and the Treasury in general. Gordon objected to the advice we were providing and the pace at which we worked. The bank interventions were complex, and had to be got right, and Gordon's wish that they be announced before Obama's inauguration increased the risk that we wouldn't. Nick discussed this with me a day or two later, saying he felt he was being threatened: either he gave Gordon the advice he wanted, or he'd be sidelined or even removed. I had sensed Gordon's mood and was keen that the Treasury should work quickly, but also I needed their best advice. Nick did needle

Gordon, though. He would extract his Swiss army knife and languid-ly peel an apple while telling Gordon that he had overestimated the amount of money that was coming into the Treasury, particularly from the financial services sector, and that this was why the structural deficit had increased.

It is the Permanent Secretary's job to make sure that ministers and key officials work together. They are pretty good at picking up who has the minister's ear and who hasn't. That doesn't mean that ministers are pushed around by the civil service. Any ministers with a clear idea of what they want to do will get the machine to work for them. Officials like that, even if they disagree with the policy. For a minister to set himself or herself up in a pointless battle with civil servants – or worse, to blame them for their own shortcomings – is a recipe for failure. Civil servants are there to advise, and the minister is there to decide.

So, the latest in a series of fretful Budget negotiations would be ter-minated when someone would stick their head around the door and say there was another meeting waiting, and another inconclusive con-clave would end with a flurry of papers and a fast exit. I sometimes got the impression that Gordon was genuinely torn between our compet-ing views. He knew that borrowing was an issue and that we could not ignore it. However, he and, I think, Ed felt that to run two arguments at once – the need to invest and the need to cut borrowing – was com-plicated. I knew that to some extent it was, but I also strongly believed that it was a necessary consequence of where we were.

So, the process of discussion was very unsatisfactory and, more importantly, there was still a fundamental difference between Gordon and myself over the forecasts, both for growth and consequently for borrowing and debt. In the three weeks running up to the Budget, we kept coming back to these growth forecasts. Over the last hundred years, the British economy has grown by about 2.5 per cent per year on average – what economists call the 'trend rate of growth'. However, after a downturn, like the ones we had in the 1980s and 1990s, growth tends to bounce back, sometimes hitting as much as 4 per cent, as people get back to work, produce more goods and sell more services. Unemployment starts to fall before growth steadies. In other words, it is not uncommon to get higher growth numbers after a series of lower growth figures. Exactly the same shape can be seen in UK forecasts prepared by independent forecasters. Their estimates frequently change, and the commercial ones tend to forecast one year ahead, rather than five years as the government does. Nor was our forecasting any less problematic than that of the coalition government that took over in 2010. By the time George Osborne presented his second Budget in March 2011, his growth forecasts had been downgraded no less than twice in ten months. He was still forecasting sunny uplands to come in years three, four and five – something he used to criticize both Gordon and me for doing.

I do have to emphasize again that forecasts are just that and that they can be wrong. But I was adamant that our growth forecasts had to be believable. My forecast for growth in 2010 of between 1 and 1.5 per cent, although widely derided at the time, proved to be correct. Gordon was more concerned about the forecasts for the years ahead. I thought that we needed to downgrade the forecasts, because although it was difficult to be sure what would happen in two or three years' time, it would seem incredible if we assumed that nothing would change. He pointed out that in the past the economy had bounced back, in the 1980s and the 1990s, with growth spiking before returning to trend. That was true, but the recovery after this recession looked likely to be slower. This argument went on and on. The outcome was that the forecasts were just about in line with some other forecasters' predictions, like those of the Bank of England. But the predictions from 2011 were optimistic. Of course, by that year there had also been intervening factors, not least decisions made by the new government, as well as much slower growth in Europe.

To compensate for that and ensure that we retained credibility as possible, the Budget figures I prepared assumed a 5 per cent drop in our economic capacity, which would be permanent. It wasn't picked up by commentators at the time, but the people who buy our government bonds certainly noticed, and it did help our credibility in their eyes. Unfortunately, if the capacity of the economy is assumed to have gone down, the structural deficit gets larger. There was one further measure that we took and that was to make provision for losing up to £50 billion following the bank bail-out. In the event, we didn't need to call on any of it and it came out of our calculations the following year. However, it did help reassure investors and the credit-rating agencies that we were being cautious, even if the headline growth figure in the later years of the forecast was optimistic.

Then there was the question of borrowing. I proposed to announce that we would halve the deficit over a four-year period. It would be tough, but we would be able to protect the health service, schools and policing. For me, this provided a credible plan which would allow us to cut borrowing without damaging the economy and would stimulate growth. Although I didn't think carrying out a complete spending review now, when things were so uncertain, would be a good idea, I did want some examples of things we were prepared to cut. I could see, though, that there was no appetite for this in No. 10. I would have to return to this argument in the run-up to the pre-Budget report later in the year.

Clearly, we could not say that we would invest and the Tories would cut. What I wanted was a realistic position that capitalized on what we had done so far, but charted a clear way back to recovery. By accepting the need for cuts in spending, we were only doing what everyone knew we would have to do. I thought the argument that, in the teeth of Tory criticism, we had prevented the banking collapse, stopped the economy sliding from recession into depression, and now had a credible plan to bring down the deficit at a sensible pace, was one we could run with. We knew the Tory position would be to use the cover of high borrowing to make significant and rapid cuts in public spending for ideological reasons.

However, the discussions with No. 10 focused increasingly on the question of tax. I tried to run my idea of increasing VAT with compensating measures for people on low incomes, again without success. I was extremely worried about putting up income tax again so soon after I had announced a new top rate of 45 per cent for people earning over £150,000. But we needed to raise more money, so I would have to increase that rate to 50p and bring it in a year earlier than proposed. And, because I couldn't put up VAT, I would have to raise National Insurance by a full penny, not the 0.5 pence announced the previous autumn. It would still look like a tax on jobs. The increase to a 50p tax rate for top earners, and the big increase in National Insurance, changed the dynamics of the political debate. This was on top of other measures, including restricting the personal allowance available to top rate taxpayers. It was a major change in approach from the past ten years, a big rise on taxes on income. I was prepared to justify it, but was in no doubt about the flak we would receive.

There were times when I thought Gordon was willing to entertain the VAT alternative, but he was persuaded by his advisers that National Insurance was a better tax. It would not, I was told, be seen as a 'tax on jobs'. My concern was not only that it would be seen as just that, but that the messages we were sending would mean the loss of a crucial constituency that had helped put us into power in 1997 – that is, business. We had demonstrated that we could achieve one of the longest periods of growth this country had seen. We had made the right calls in the banking crisis when the Tories were at sixes and sevens. We were now running the risk of losing all that confidence and support. The negative message we were sending out on aspiration contradicted everything we had argued for over the past fifteen years. We needed to be not only consistent but confident in our arguments.

Although Peter Mandelson was to be hugely supportive later in the year, at this stage he sided with the argument against raising VAT. As Business Secretary he was more focused on a growth package, and for political reasons he remained reluctant to side openly with me against Gordon. Quite simply, no minister, even the Chancellor, can insist on a controversial move if his senior colleagues are dead against it. Peter, in his memoirs, published shortly after the general election of 2010, says he regrets the position he took. So do I.

Once these crucial issues had been thrashed out, we easily agreed on measures to help with the recession, particularly the scrappage scheme aimed at boosting car manufacturing and sales, which allowed people to receive cash for trading in an old car in return for a new one. This proved to be successful out of all proportion to its cost, which was minimal. I extended the stamp duty holiday; and there was also assistance for mortgage payers and, critically, a programme to create jobs for eighteen- to twenty-one-year-olds, which Yvette was especially keen on. Youth unemployment is one of the most destructive of forces, as we had seen in the 1980s. It is vital that a young man or woman should not find that their first experience in the grown-up world is unemployment. The terrible legacy endures down generations.

Forty-eight hours before its presentation, we had no Budget. It's a tribute to the Treasury team that they worked through the night to get the thing done. It wasn't new to them. Gordon had always worked like this: someone had told him early on in his time as Chancellor that he didn't have to print it three days in advance, and he'd taken this as carte blanche to take his time. The tension levels are extraordinary, and this Budget was the worst of my time as Chancellor. I can't overstate how important a Budget is, and we were rewriting it literally until the last minute. Most of the staff were in the Treasury, rather than at No. 11, so it was simplest to work there. I'd be called time and again to No. 10 for a meeting, and we'd all know that this meant further changes. There was nothing for it but to be stoical. I vividly remember a speech Gordon made while we were in opposition, the famous 'neoclassical endogenous growth theory' speech. He started speaking as the second half was still being written. Halfway through, a hand appeared from behind a curtain and handed him the rest of the speech. This exemplifies Gordon's approach to working on such matters.

The evening before the Budget was to be presented, No. 10 staff began bombarding me with endless suggestions for rewriting the speech, which I ignored because none of them seemed to improve an already difficult presentation. As for the growth forecasts, they finally emerged as being not much different from the ones I had originally proposed. If they were wrong – and those for the later years were – the fault was mine, not Gordon's. In the end, the Budget was only really signed off when I left for the House of Commons, because no one could change it after I had got into the car with Karl Burke, my driver.

The tax rises and the borrowing forecasts were to dominate the headlines after the Budget was finally presented on 22 April 2009. The coverage could not have been worse. The government was on the ropes. I was forecasting that the economy would shrink by 3.5 per cent in 2009. Because of that, borrowing would rise to £175 billion in 2009, some 12.4 per cent of GDP. The fact that it was expected that the US deficit would be 13 per cent of GDP provided no comfort. Nor did my forecast that borrowing would fall thereafter. Debt, which included the costs of stabilizing the banking system, was then thought to be rising to 79 per cent of GDP in 2013/14. If the government had been on a surer footing, and if we'd had time to prepare the ground, it is possible that we might have had a slightly better reception. Our backbenchers were lukewarm. On the Tory side there was much to cheer. They saw their opportunity and they seized it. Their central allegation was that we were not telling the truth.

Next morning I sat in the departure lounge at Heathrow waiting to fly out to the annual IMF meeting in Washington, reading headlines that were as bad as they could be. The combination of massive borrowing, growth forecasts that were not believed, and a lack of a clear plan to get borrowing down was a lethal combination. What's more, just before take-off I received the latest estimate for growth for the first three months of 2009, published by the Office for National Statistics (ONS). The ONS publishes the statistics on a rigid quarterly cycle. Because the Budget was late this year, due to the G20 and the parliamentary recess, it came just ahead of the next round of ONS data. The trouble was that the ONS estimate was much worse than we had expected. It was only their first estimate. Usually the Treasury has a fairly accurate idea of what the ONS will say, but this time it was lower than we thought. In the end my estimates turned out to be right, because in fact the economy grew more strongly in the fourth quarter than anyone had expected, but this was far from clear in April 2009 and our opponents had a field day. It immediately cast doubt on my forecast of growth for the next year.

Earlier that day I had done the usual media round and made what I felt was an aggressive defence of what we were doing. We still needed to support the economy. Indeed, the decisions I took in the pre-Budget report in 2008 and in the Budget of 2009 were largely the reason why the economy grew more strongly than anyone expected in the summer of 2010, why borrowing came down faster than I had predicted. The problem is that we had lost the high ground. And I still believed that changes in VAT, with measures to compensate the low-paid and a plan to protect key public services, such as health and schools, but with a signal that we would do something about spending elsewhere, would have been a stronger and more compelling argument. Above all, it would have been believable. Credibility has to be central to any economic and political strategy.

An escape to Washington was welcome. This year's IMF meeting did not have the same urgency or tension that had characterized the previous year's gathering. Nor was I troubled this time by calls from No. 10. Tim Geithner and I were focused on how to bring the promises made at the G20 summit in London to fruition. On a gloriously hot spring afternoon, London felt a long way away. The pressure-cooker lid lifted a little. I took time to explore a bit of Washington, climbing the hill at Arlington Cemetery to visit the grave of John F. Kennedy, something I had never managed to do on previous visits.

Kennedy took office in 1960, at a time of what he described as 'national peril', in the wake of a recession, seven years of diminished economic growth, when business bankruptcies had reached their highest level since the Great Depression. The candid words of his first State of the Union address, on 30 January 1961, still resonate. To state the facts frankly, he said, is not to despair of the future nor to indict the past. The prudent heir takes careful inventory of his legacies and gives a faithful accounting to those to whom he owes an obligation of trust. The job of elected officials is to face all problems frankly and meet all dangers free from panic or fear. His words reinforced my resolve. Back in London early on the Sunday morning, I was glad I'd taken time out for a history lesson. In view of the panning it had received, the Budget was hardly the backdrop we wanted for the elections to the European Parliament in a month's time.

Britain's standing in terms of being able to pay its way was never in doubt, but there was always the possibility that one of the credit-rating agencies would change its assessment of our ability to repay. There are three credit-rating agencies – Standard & Poor's, Moody's and Fitch – which have assumed a far greater importance than they deserve. These bodies were, after all, happy to rate sub-prime mortgages as AAA, the top classification. Some of them had a clear financial interest in doing so. They were paid to certify the products by the very banks they had to rate.

Every government borrows money from the markets, which in this context means entities such as pension funds, which need to invest in government stocks to provide them with a stable income. Many others will be people with money to invest, who do it as a commercial proposition. They invest in companies, other financial institutions and government bonds. Everyone is looking to make a turn on the money they have. What a government pays on its borrowing depends not just on the going rate of interest, but also on the risk of default calculated by investors. One of the guides investors look at in making this decision is what classification has been given by the credit-rating agencies. In some ways this is nonsense. A pension fund should have a pretty good idea of the difference between the US government and that of some dodgy dictatorship. But it's a fact of life: people look to the rating agencies.

Treasury officials routinely talk to them, as they do to the people who buy government bonds. It is often a difficult conversation, and they have to be taken through all the Treasury's calculations, including a realistic assessment of our loss of productive capacity and provision for any banking losses. I was very conscious that these investors and the credit-rating agencies follow what senior ministers say very closely. Any suggestion that we weren't committed to getting borrowing down after the recession could be fatal.

In the early evening of Wednesday, 20 May, Dan, my private secretary, came into the study in Downing Street to tell me that one of the credit-rating agencies, Standard & Poor's, had decided to put us on 'negative watch'. This is not a downgrade, but rather a warning. I was determined that, come what may, Britain's credit rating would not be downgraded while I was Chancellor. It would have been a political disaster, along the lines of going cap in hand to the IMF in 1976, or Britain's humiliating expulsion from the exchange rate mechanism in 1992.

I walked through to Gordon's office and told his staff I had to see him urgently on a private matter. I knew he was hard at work on his speech to the Confederation of British Industry that evening, but this couldn't wait. He too could see how serious this was, and we agreed that in his speech to the CBI he would emphasize that we would do nothing to jeopardize Britain's position and that getting borrowing down was our absolute priority. Some weeks earlier I had said, when giving evidence to the Treasury select committee at the traditional post-Budget hearings, that not only was I committed to getting borrowing down but, if things proved better than we expected, we could move even faster. That had helped. The rates that we had to pay to raise money had fallen on the back of it.

We now ran into political difficulty which further undermined us. At one of the weekly sessions of Prime Minister's Questions after the Budget, Gordon began to run his argument of 'investment against cuts'. It was the first time I had heard his argument mounted in public and it was virtually impossible to run it now, when a look at the official

Budget publication, known as the Red Book, showed that we were committed to quite substantial cuts in public spending.

This exchange was repeated the following week, by which time David Cameron actually had the Red Book in his hand. The Budget was based on protecting some departments, but making cuts in others. It allowed the Tories to portray the argument not as 'investment against cuts' but honesty against dishonesty. For the first time, Gordon and I had some very angry exchanges. He told me I was undermining him and it had to stop. I certainly was not, I said. Why would I do that? Didn't he understand that I was trying, desperately, to give him, the government, a realistic platform on which to go forwards? I told him we could not continue to argue a case that did not stand up. The evidence was there for all to see.

A growing number of Cabinet colleagues told me that they could not understand how we had got ourselves into this position. Most of them were by now arguing for the more pragmatic approach that I took. Whether the 'investment versus cuts' argument was or was not a good idea, it should have been discussed. As it was, it became very apparent that most of the Cabinet did not believe in it.

It was at this time that the whole of Westminster became engulfed in the expenses scandal, when the *Daily Telegraph* published over a million pieces of paper containing minute details of every item of expenditure claimed by MPs for the previous five years. MPs are reimbursed for travel costs to and from their constituencies, for the cost of maintaining a second home, either in their constituency or in London, and for the costs of running an office, including staff salaries. The problem was that many of the rules were wide open to interpretation, and in some cases flagrant abuse. The system of requiring receipts was lax and the House of Commons' administration of the scheme left much to be desired.

One of the constitutional highpoints of the Labour government was said to be the introduction of the Freedom of Information Act. Now it came back to bite MPs with a vengeance. After years of trying to prevent publication of detailed claims, it was eventually ruled that they had to be made public. Had everyone's expenses been published at the same time, there would certainly have been a public outcry and justifiable anger. The fact that only one newspaper got hold of the information and was able to drip-feed it, day by day, week by week, meant the impact was devastating.

For some weeks before publication, talk in the corridors of Westminster was dominated by foreboding about what might be revealed. This was one of those occasions on which the fear underestimated the reality. The *Telegraph* began by looking at the Cabinet and then it went on to more junior ministers. It did not get to the opposition front bench for four days and in that time, although it was a political problem for every party, it came to be seen very much as a government problem. Governments always take the blame when things go wrong – and this was no exception.

For weeks on end, expense after expense was detailed. Day after day, the effect was to traumatize not just the government but every MP, who awaited a call from the *Telegraph* or their local newspaper over some aspect of their expenses. Virtually no one was spared. Anyone in politics has to get used to answering difficult or awkward questions about policy. The close questions we were now being asked went to the heart of our personal integrity. It is this that made it so unpleasant and uncomfortable.

This was hardly the ideal background to the upcoming European election campaign. The public now had good reason to hold politicians in contempt. This added to the general uncertainty, and any lack of sure-footedness on our part in dealing with either the expenses problem or the other big issues of the day would spell disaster at the polls.

I spent the spring recess in Edinburgh, doing the odd bit of campaigning for the European elections. Every day now was dominated by fresh disclosures about expenses claimed by MPs. The *Telegraph* had moved on to a more forensic examination of claims, including mine. The paper questioned my reclaiming the cost of accountancy fees for preparing my tax returns in respect of my office costs. Secondly, they correctly spotted a mistake I had made when we moved from our flat in Kennington into Downing Street. I should have seen that some payments made for the flat went beyond the time when we moved out. As Chancellor, I could not afford damaging allegations of impropriety. I decided to do an interview with all the major news channels and deal with anything they wanted to put to me. It was unpleasant but necessary. As I did so, I knew it would add fuel to the fires being lit beneath me for other reasons.

Gordon, correctly expecting terrible election results, had decided to reshuffle his Cabinet, probably the day after the results were announced, on Sunday, 7 June. By now our relationship had broken down. Gordon wanted Ed Balls as Chancellor, and I had to be moved.

To understand what happened in the five days before the Cabinet reshuffle, which Gordon had to bring forward as events moved out of his control, it is necessary to look back at our relationship over the previous twenty years. Although we both come from Scotland, we were never close in the early days. Our political outlook is very similar, but Gordon is a bit older than I am, and certainly of a different generation in the Labour Party. He was already engaged on the national scene long before I even thought of becoming an MP. But he, like Tony Blair, took a keen interest in what I and other newly elected MPs were doing when we came into the Commons in 1987. Gordon was always destined for a career in politics. I wasn't. I was elected almost by accident. Robin Cook had been the MP for the Edinburgh Central seat from 1974 until a slight boundary change handed it to the Tories in 1983. Robin decamped to nearby Livingston New Town, where he remained as MP until his tragically early death in 2005.

I had been elected to what was then Lothian Regional Council, which covered Edinburgh and the Lothians, in 1982. I was beginning to make a name, principally because of my campaign against a plan to extend an urban motorway from the outskirts of the city right into its historic heart. This ridiculous plan, proposed ironically by Edinburgh's first and last Conservative–Liberal Democrat coalition, ran into huge local opposition. We eventually tore up the contract to build it when we won back control of the council in 1986.

With the next general election on the horizon, I was asked by my friends and colleagues if I would stand in the Edinburgh Central seat, which, although Tory, looked increasingly winnable. The tide of change was sweeping through Scotland ten years before it would do so in England. My father, Sandy Darling, was an elder in the Church of Scotland, and he and my mother, Anna, voted Conservative. When Margaret Thatcher gave what came notoriously to be called her 'Sermon on the Mound', at the Kirk's annual general assembly in Edinburgh, my father came home horrified. She didn't quite say 'there is no such thing as society', but that's what is remembered. They never voted Tory again.

I was genuinely in two minds about whether to stand. The Sunday newspaper Margaret was working for had folded in 1982. We invested her redundancy money in the cost of my training as an Advocate – a Scottish barrister – and I was called to the Scottish bar in 1984, having started life as an Edinburgh solicitor in the late 1970s. My career was in its infancy, but I was beginning to enjoy it.

In the late summer of 1985, Margaret, who was now working for the *Glasgow Herald*, and I flew to Liguria in northern Italy for a holiday. There we made two momentous decisions. The first was that I would stand for Parliament. The second, made the day after, was that we would get married. These decisions were almost certainly made the wrong way round. Sitting on the balcony of an apartment in Tellaro, fighting off the mosquitoes and listening to the nightly call of the neighbour summoning her cat, we talked about the approaches that had been made to me to stand for Westminster. The prospects, although better than they were in 1983, were not ideal. Mrs Thatcher still held sway and Edinburgh was a very conservative city. I had joined the Labour Party in 1977. It held values that I shared: a belief in social justice, that life chances should not be stunted by accident of birth, that opportunity should be available to all, and that fairness meant just reward for hard work. We talked on in the dusk, weighing up the arguments. A mosquito was attacking my ear. It was time to go out to eat. Margaret said: 'If you don't stand, you will probably regret it for the rest of your life.' So the decision was made. We went down to the restaurant in the town square, along a route called Via Gramsci.

The decision to get married was altogether easier. Visiting the Cinque Terre, five villages hewn from a hillside, we shared a bottle of wine in the sunshine and thought we would formalize our life together.

When the general election campaign was called, my clerk had booked me into a six-week trial starting in Inverness on the Monday after the election, such was my confidence of winning the seat. In fact, the Tories were on a slope that would eventually lead to a wipe-out of their representation in Scotland in 1997, something they have never recovered from – unless you count one MP as a recovery.

I was elected in 1987, along with a number of my contemporaries, like Brian Wilson, a radical journalist, and Sam Galbraith, a renowned neurosurgeon, winning what would be called 'middle Scotland' seats. We proved that we could win seats that were hitherto seen as Tory if we based our appeal on the centre ground and the common sense of the electorate. The Conservatives, who had effectively run Edinburgh for nearly eight hundred years, saw their representation drop to one seat. Even Edinburgh South, until then a very safe Tory seat, which had been held by my great-uncle in the Tory cause in the 1945 election, was won by Labour.

The grim reality to which we woke up the morning after the campaign celebration was that, while we had won in Scotland, we had done badly in England. I vividly remember entering the chamber of the House of Commons for the first time. Very few people who have done so can have failed to feel the awe, the sense of occasion, on first taking a seat on the green benches. My maiden speech, written on the plane down to London, was no more than adequate. As was customary, I spoke about my constituency and the dreadful effects that unemployment was still having four years after the last recession ended. I was surprised and naturally delighted to receive letters of congratulation next morning from three people who were not in the chamber at the time but who claimed to have read Hansard, the official report of parliamentary proceedings, the following morning. One was the Speaker, the late Bernard Weatherill, who was always kind and solicitous; the other two were Tony Blair and Gordon Brown.

A year after I was elected, Roy Hattersley, then Labour's deputy leader, whom I didn't know at all, asked me to join his shadow home affairs team. Thus began my twenty-two years on the front bench. I remember saying to Roy how grateful I was for his appointing me. He replied: 'You'd better remember that in politics there is no such thing as gratitude.' It was a good lesson to learn.

I enjoyed working with Roy. He is good company, convivial and thoughtful. He allowed me to cover areas I had no expertise in, including immigration, but also broadcasting, sitting on the committee that recast the ITV network in 1990. I was also able to do some work on the constitution, particularly House of Lords reform. We proposed replacing it with a senate representing the regions and nations of the UK. For what seemed like an eternity, I sat on a Labour Party commission, chaired by Lord Raymond Plant, a distinguished academic, that was to advise on whether to support electoral reform. I spent so much time looking at it that I resolved never to touch the subject again. Constitutional reform was, understandably, thought to be of secondary importance to the electors, who were more interested in whether we had a sensible economic policy. Unfortunately they concluded that we did not.

It was good experience, although I doubt if my contribution made any impact on the body politic. After the general election of 1992, John Smith became leader. When John died in 1994, the sense of shock was extraordinary. It was as though MPs had lost a family member. I'd seen him speak at a fund-raising dinner the night before and had been struck by how tired he looked and how falteringly he spoke. When I left at 10 p.m., he was settling down, glass in hand. In the morning, I heard that he'd had a heart attack. He was a good man but he lived hard.

I was lucky enough to be offered three jobs following the Shadow Cabinet elections under John's brief tenure as leader. First, Tony asked me to join him in the home affairs team. I said I would love to help him but I had worked on home affairs for four years and, with broadcasting now under a different department, a lot of what he was going to do was peculiarly English, since most of the Home Office writ does not run north of the border. He sounded disappointed and two years later, when he became leader, I wondered if I had made a mistake in turning him down.

Next was John Smith himself, who asked me if I would shadow universities. Worthy though this was, I couldn't see it going anywhere. In politics you are judged by how you perform in the chamber and in the media, and there's not much chance to make a splash in the Commons on a subject that, at that time, did not feature on the floor of the House. Finally, Gordon offered me the job I really wanted, to look at City affairs in the Treasury team. I told John that was the job I wanted and, as he could see that it had been agreed by Gordon, who was his new Shadow Chancellor, that was it.

For the next five years I worked closely with Gordon. He allowed me a great deal of latitude and in particular let me develop our plans to end the system whereby financial institutions in Britain were largely self-regulated. This had led to scandals like the mis-selling of insurance schemes, with which we were able to attack the Conservatives very effectively.

It was also a logical development for me as an MP representing much of Edinburgh's financial centre, which remains the fourth largest in Europe. I was genuinely interested in the subject. Most of my constituents who work in the private sector depend on the financial services industry in one way or another. Throughout my five years on the City job, I must have met with most of the big financial institutions. It was difficult because in the early years they did not want to know us. They did not believe they would ever have to deal with us as a government.

In the year before the general election of 1997, I became Shadow Chief Secretary to the Treasury. The call came as Margaret and I and the children were setting off for a fortnight's holiday in France. We were driving and had stayed overnight with our friends, Catherine MacLeod and George Mackie, on their farm in Essex. I took the call from Tony and suddenly didn't much want to go to France any more. I was now in the Shadow Cabinet, an exciting prospect. Margaret pretended not to notice my sudden wish to stay and we set off from the farm the next morning. It was to the farm we were to return the night we left Downing Street for the last time, at the sad end of the Labour government. It was a pleasing, if unintentional, piece of political symmetry.

I hugely enjoyed my spell as Chief Secretary, both in opposition and for the first year in government. Because so much of government involves spending, I got to know everything about every policy. In the run-up to what was to be a momentous general election, it was a fantastic job, and Gordon, back then, trusted my judgement completely. I was delighted to accept his invitation to join him in the Treasury when we got into government. It was also a measure of his generosity. Following John Smith's death, he might well have assumed that I would support him for the leadership. It never came to a contest, because Gordon did not stand. But although he never asked me outright, he knew from our discussions that I thought Tony was the right man for the job at the time.

Like many of my generation, and certainly given my background, both personal and political, I very much supported the New Labour approach: broad-based, firmly anchored in the centre ground of politics, recognizing that government can make a real difference to people's life chances and opportunities. This is where I felt we should be. Tony

Blair's style and manner had got through to the British public. They felt at ease with him. His ability to communicate is formidable. He could appear on people's television sets and appeal to them. We would have won in 1997 but nothing like as well as we did had Tony not been leader. As Tony said in his memoir, for 'most normal people', politics is 'a distant, occasionally irritating fog'. As a result, in the absence of strong and readily understood policies, personality is the thing that will cut through the fog. He caught the mood of the time. Equally, however, New Labour could not have been brought into being without Gordon's drive and intellect, which is something Tony acknowledges. It was Gordon who changed our policies on tax and spend, and welfare to work. Those changes were made in the face of internal Labour Party opposition, but they chimed with the electorate, a necessary requirement for winning a general election.

It is true that Gordon found yielding to Tony after John Smith's death difficult. And that was something that never went away. He recognized that a fight to the death would have ruined the project that both he and Tony had spent the previous two years building. He also knew that he did not have enough support to win the leadership contest, certainly among MPs. Unfortunately, the conflict was to fester for years, until by 2005 it had come to dominate much of the day-to-day life of government. It was debilitating and the deep animus drove divisions right across the party. The deteriorating relationship and the stridency of their disagreements destabilized our government and did our reputation great harm. It also created a career path for the disaffected. An act of overt hostility to the 'other side' was seen as a badge of loyalty.

After I left the Treasury to take over as Secretary of State at social security, a job that Gordon was keen I should take (as was Tony), I continued to work closely with him. Both of us wanted to integrate the tax and benefit system, of which the tax credit system is part. We were both keen to introduce the 10p tax rate, as it helped so many people living on low incomes. We did not see so much of each other when I was Transport Secretary. Transport was not Gordon's thing; nor was it Tony's. I took over the department at a time of political crisis, following the resignation of Stephen Byers. The night before Byers went, I was asked to visit No. 10, via the back rather than the front entrance. This was puzzling – it is usually the path of the condemned man. I wondered whether this was the end, but Tony explained that Byers was going to resign and asked whether I'd take over at Transport. I responded enthusiastically and said yes, certainly. He looked startled. 'Really? Why on earth do you want to do it?'

Again, my good relations with Gordon helped in the job. The Treasury's instinct is to oppose any large transport project, as one senior official explained to me at his retirement party. With Gordon's help, however, I was able to get £8 billion out of the Treasury to do up the west coast mainline between London and Glasgow. The Treasury wanted to pull down the spectacular St Pancras Station, now the Eurostar terminal; I thought it important to preserve some of our railway heritage. And the Treasury would almost certainly have blocked the high-speed rail link to the Channel Tunnel when it ran out of money in 1998, had it not been for the persistence of John Prescott and Gordon's and my influence at the Treasury.

When people asked me subsequently why I never joined in the plots to remove Gordon when he was prime minister, the answer I gave is that I had, and still have, a residual loyalty to him which I found impossible to overcome. At a personal level, we saw a lot of each other over the years, as did our families. We live a few miles apart, separated by the Forth Bridges. We were good colleagues. Our political outlook was similar, but I am not tribal and did not subscribe to the grievance and grudge view of Tony held by Gordon's political intimates. I sensed sometimes that socializing with me was, for Gordon, a bit effortful.

Ironically, if it had not been for the banking crisis and the dramatic downturn in the economy, I might have gone much earlier. Although my becoming Chancellor when Gordon became Prime Minister had been widely trailed in the media, almost throughout our term of government from 1997 Gordon, rightly, had never promised me anything.

Nor would I have expected him to. Who knew what might happen during those years?

We first discussed what I might do under his premiership in April 2007. I was out campaigning in the elections for the Scottish Parliament in central Scotland. It had been raining and was about to start raining again, and the prospect of spending the afternoon dripping on doorsteps was not attractive. Gordon phoned me and asked me to come over to his home in North Queensferry to help him write a speech setting out the reasons behind our reform to pensions in the late 1990s. After we had done about four hours of work, I was slightly surprised when he raised the subject. He asked me what job I would like, making it clear he meant one of the top jobs: the Treasury, the Home Office or the Foreign Office. I said that the Home Office was largely English and I thought that would be a problem. I did not have much of a track record on foreign affairs; in fact, I didn't think I had once been to a Foreign Office question time. As he knew, I would like the Treasury, but only, I said, if I had his confidence. I asked the obvious question: why not Ed Balls, who had worked with him so closely for so many years as a special adviser? He had obviously pondered that himself, but he thought that it would be better for Ed to do something else first, as he was still a relatively new MP, elected in 2005.

Nothing was agreed between us that evening. I saw it as a preliminary informal chat. Inevitably, in the period before Gordon was formally elected, there was a lot of speculation, in which I was named as a future Chancellor. It might have been flattering to hear, but it made subsequently accepting another job a more difficult option. The first time that I suspected he was thinking again was at the party after his election as leader in Manchester, when he said he needed to speak to me. I could tell by his manner that he was having second thoughts. The conversation eventually took place late at night on Monday, 25 June, just two days before Tony was officially due to stand down. I went to the Treasury, which was a hive of activity with Gordon's team preparing for the move to Downing Street.

I met Gordon, not in his room but in a specially constructed glass office which looked like a cage and was used to house his special advisers. He asked me if I would consider the Foreign or Home Office. For the third time in my career, I turned down the Home Office. Nothing personal, it is just that I did not want to go there. I repeated what I'd said in the spring: that I would prefer the Treasury but that he had to be happy with his team. I had to have his confidence. There was no point in me taking the job if that was not the case. Gordon disappeared at this stage, presumably to consult. When he came back, he said: 'OK, you can do it, but maybe for just a year or so. I may want to make some changes then.'

No Cabinet job is permanent and so, based, I suppose, on a political lifetime of working with him, I accepted. Perhaps I should not have done so on that basis; not because I was entitled to a long-term contract, but because he was torn about appointing me. If he had decided instead to appoint Ed, of course I would have been disappointed, but I would not have felt betrayed. I had no sense of entitlement, nor was there any understanding between us. Ed Balls was his protégé, and he probably thought that after giving him experience in a spending department he could install him at the first reshuffle. It didn't work out that way.

I offer a full explanation of what happened with Gordon at the time of my appointment because it explains so much of our often troubled relationship when I was Chancellor. I am grateful that he appointed me, but I was clearly a stopgap appointment in his view and, not surprisingly, that of his close circle. So, when we met on 2 June 2009, I was not surprised that he wanted me to move. Indeed, a part of me wanted to go. Fighting economic and financial fires was the easy bit of the job. I was tired of the atmosphere of feuding and the perpetual sniping. Our friendship had been strained beyond breaking point. In many ways I wanted out; I'd had enough. And yet, another part of me – the larger part – did not want to be forced out at this stage and in this way.

11 Discord in Downing Street

Speculation about the reshuffle and my future was well trailed and well informed. The disarray and fractious atmosphere spilled out of the Cabinet Room and on to the front pages. I had never known my Labour colleagues so low. It would have been a relief to go, but also an abdication. I didn't need to take soundings from people I trusted. At a weekly Prime Minister's Questions, when challenged to back me by David Cameron, Gordon conspicuously failed to do so. All of us expected that the European and local election results on Thursday, 4 June 2009, would be bad. The murmurings of discontent with Gordon's premiership among Cabinet members had grown to a crescendo. McBride, the Budget, the fallout from the expenses scandal, and now an impending electoral disaster: it was hardly surprising that the troops were restive. All MPs keenly follow the speculation that precedes reshuffles. Politics is a brutal trade, but I was encouraged by the number of my colleagues in the Commons who expressed support for me.

Ann Coffey, my parliamentary private secretary, whose political antennae are good, said it would be a disaster for me to walk away. There were personal costs too to think about. Margaret had spent two years in Downing Street and was intent on maintaining relationships. But, she said, to be forced out and made the scapegoat for all that had gone wrong was ridiculous. Catherine MacLeod reinforced their views. For you, she said, it would be the ultimate humiliation, which you don't deserve.

I had two meetings with Gordon, the first on Tuesday, 2 June, the next on polling day, Thursday. It was just the two of us and the mood was oddly amicable. I was relaxed and almost glad to see an end to this terrible episode. We had known each other a long time. At the first, he reminded me that when he initially appointed me he had said that he would reconsider my position after a year or so. He said he wanted to make changes in the government and that he wanted to move me. He made it clear that he wanted me to stay in the government. I told him that, in many ways, he would be better with a Chancellor he could get on with and who was in the same place as him in policy terms. If he chose someone else, at least there would be an end to this continual conflict.

But, I said, the only place I am going is out. I had been thinking about this for several weeks, knowing this moment would come. For me to accept another job would be to cling on to office for the sake of it, and I was not prepared to do that. Gordon insisted that people would understand if I moved. I said our argument was now so public that if I clung on it would do neither of us any good. It would be better for me to go altogether. We spoke for about half an hour, going over and over the same ground. As with so many of our difficult meetings, we agreed to meet again.

This we did, at about 7 o'clock on the evening of Thursday, 4 June. That afternoon, Peter had come to see me in my office at the Treasury. We discussed the woeful state we were in. Earlier in the week Hazel Blears, the Communities Secretary, had suddenly resigned. Her frustration with Gordon had boiled over. They had a very public falling-out over the direction, or lack of it, of the party. She felt especially aggrieved about the way in which he had treated her over her parliamentary expenses. Gordon had singled her out for special criticism and she was hurt by it. I had spoken to her afterwards and she was at a loss to understand why he had done it. It was little comfort to her when I said that

I did not think he had intended to. He had been asked about her at a press conference and had gone further in his condemnation than he had meant to. Unfortunately, her resignation came on the eve of the European elections, which was damaging. On top of that, on the day of her departure, Hazel was filmed sporting a brooch bearing the legend 'Rock the Boat'. That had not gone down well with No. 10.

The situation was bleak, Peter and I agreed. He was sometimes frustrated by my Eeyore-like predictions, I know, but there was no denying the state we were in. As I suspected, he had not called in to chew the fat. He wanted to know whether I would stay in the government if Gordon asked me to move. Peter said that if I left the government it could fatally damage Gordon. I said that might well be the case, but I was not going to cling on to office for the sake of it. If I was going anywhere it was to the back benches. I told Peter that Gordon would do far better to make Ed Balls, with whom at least he could work, his Chancellor. I knew he would pass this message on. Peter, I think, was more concerned that the reshuffle should produce a team that could work together. That was understandable. So when I went to see Gordon again that evening, he could hardly have been surprised when I repeated my position.

Again, the meeting was friendly enough. He ended up offering me just about every job that was going – including the Foreign Office – except the one that I held. I said no. If he didn't want me as Chancellor, which I entirely understood, I would go. As was now the habit, it was agreed that we would meet again the following day.

As I went upstairs to the flat, I thought it was probably all over. Frankly, it was a relief. I would be going on my own terms. With Catherine and Ann, we enjoyed what we took to be a Last Supper takeaway from Gandhi's. We sat around the table in the kitchen, and although there was sorrow at the position our government was in, there was also, for me at least, a sense of release. I had done all I could as Chancellor and I could return to the back benches with a clear conscience. Appropriately enough, we listened to the Killers CD that Calum had given me for my birthday. The previous year it had been Leonard Cohen who distracted me from my woes. This year it was time for stronger stuff. Just before 10 o'clock, Catherine left the flat to go home. As she walked down Downing Street, she bumped into her former lobby colleagues rushing through the gates to do live interviews in front of the No. 10 door. She was told that James Purnell, Social Security Secretary, had resigned from the government. It was a totally unexpected turn of events.

James was thoughtful and one of the brightest of his generation of MPs. Earlier in the year he had spoken at my constituency party's annual Burns Night supper and his easy and open style had impressed. He allowed himself to think the unthinkable and he was a loss to government. I had known that James was unhappy. He was one of the younger Cabinet members increasingly dismayed at Gordon's insistence on the line of 'investment versus cuts' who had spoken to me of their frustration. I understood why he walked out. He could no longer pretend; he'd had enough of trying to hold a government line in which he did not believe.

In the political ferment that followed his resignation, there was speculation that it was all a plot, that James was the first of the skittles and that others would follow. It didn't happen. There was no plot. There can't have been any collusion with Hazel Blears or another colleague, Caroline Flint, who resigned after the reshuffle when she was not promoted and made a personal attack on Gordon. Nor, indeed, with Jacqui Smith, the Home Secretary, who had decided to leave the government a few weeks earlier. Had they all resigned on the same day, the consequences would have been very different. As it was, I knew that James's decision had one significant consequence for me: I was not going anywhere. I knew that as soon as I saw the news headlines.

After the 10 o'clock news had run the story of James's resignation, the phones in the flat began to ring. We ignored them and went to bed. Just before 7 o'clock next morning, the No. 10 switchboard called to say the Prime Minister wanted to see me right away. I said I would come as soon as I had washed and shaved. When I went downstairs, Gordon was sitting in Tony Blair's old study, just off the Cabinet Room, its darkened corners matching the mood. There was no one else there. All he said was: 'OK, you can stay.'

That was it. I made no demands of him. We didn't talk on. He was weary and so was I. There will be those who think that if I had said, 'I've had enough, I'm off', it would have brought him down. It might have done. But I was not prepared to do that. I had supported his leadership. If I left the government it would be to sit on the back-benches, not to foment his overthrow. Also, I feel deep loyalty to the Labour Party. I did not want to damage it any further. There was already a sense of calamity; we were in no fit shape to fight an election. To walk away would have been to absolve myself of collective responsibility for the government.

With the general election now less than a year away, I knew that I was there until the end. Still, I hoped that we might salvage something, perhaps attempt a fresh start. That Friday, still in post, I was far from elated. I spent the day working from the flat, taking calls from colleagues including Geoff Hoon, now out of the Cabinet, who felt frustrated and badly treated by Gordon. Geoff had been a strong supporter of Tony but had moved on to work for Gordon when he became Prime Minister, first as Chief Whip, a role for which he was not best suited temperamentally, then as Transport Secretary. He felt that his loyalty had been abused. Geoff wanted to go to the European Commission; he is very much a Europhile. Gordon would not promise him that and he felt let down.

We had taken a pounding in the English local elections. Our share of the vote had plunged to 23 per cent, the lowest in the post-war era. In the European elections we had suffered our worst result, beaten into third place by UKIP. The BNP gained its first seat in Brussels. Our share of the vote was just 15.3 per cent – worse than we had dared imagine. The Tories won with 28.6 per cent, failing to increase significantly their total share. Health Secretary Andy Burnham's analysis was acute: 'The BNP is like the ultimate protest vote. It is how to deliver the establishment a two-fingered salute. I think largely it is a comment on Westminster politics.'

Gordon was not able to make the changes he wanted. He was stuck with me and with David Miliband as Foreign Secretary. He did promote Alan Johnson, a good appointment, as Home Secretary, replacing Jacqui Smith. Alan's easy-going manner, combined with an ability to get people to work with him, had helped us make up lost ground when he was Health Secretary. Peter Mandelson acquired even more titles, including that of First Secretary of State. John Hutton stood down, which was a pity, and was replaced by Bob Ainsworth as Defence Secretary. I had known all along that Gordon would want at some stage to install Ed Balls as Chancellor. That was his prerogative. But I was not prepared to be trashed and sacrificed in the process. Nor was I prepared to change my view of what needed to be done to build a credible economic and political path out of this economic crisis. I knew the next months would not be easy. Gordon still believed that my approach was wrong and that the Treasury was out of control.

There was a procession of comings and goings downstairs in No. 10 on Friday. I kept well out of it. In the reshuffle, Yvette moved to the Department for Work and Pensions, and Liam Byrne moved from the Cabinet Office to take her job as Chief Secretary. I assumed at first that this was the latest No. 10 attempt to keep an eye on me. I was wrong. Very quickly, Liam became a staunch supporter of my argument against the simplistic 'investment versus cuts' narrative. He worked hard to build a credible plan to cut the deficit.

I have set out the events surrounding this reshuffle in greater detail than I might have done because there has been so much erroneous speculation about what happened. Although I was tempted to go, there was no 'Et tu, Brute' moment. I thought it more important to try to restore and rebuild the fortunes of the government that I had spent twelve years supporting, and many more years before that trying to get into power.

There was an unhappy sequel to that unhappy day. At the news conference on the reshuffle in Downing Street, Gordon acknowledged the painful scale of the defeats in the European and local elections and vowed to fight on with a fresh team. He was asked about his attempt to remove his Chancellor. It was a pity that he chose to deny it. Everybody knew he had tried to get rid of me as Chancellor, because they had been told so in private briefings for days before. The Treasury had even been alerted and had begun arrangements for a handover to Ed. The denial further damaged Gordon's relationship with the political correspondents. They no longer believed him.

The next ten days were devoted to preparing for my second Mansion House speech on 17 June. This time, what I had to say was derailed not by the government's wrongdoing but by the Governor of the Bank of England. Mervyn and I were, and indeed remain, on good terms. I had asked a number of times to see a copy of the speech that he was to deliver immediately after I sat down at the Mansion House. Only two days before we were due to speak, I was told that he had not finished it. This I found curious. Mervyn does not deliver many speeches, but when he does they are usually well argued and thoroughly prepared, as you would expect. He's not inclined to deliver a few words knocked up the night before. When I eventually saw his speech, a couple of hours before its delivery, it was obvious that it would be seen as evidence of a deep division between him and me. It was a blatant bid for the Bank to take over the regulation of banks – and what seemed to me to be a rewriting of recent history.

The Bank of England has had responsibility for the stability of the financial system since 1997. However, that responsibility only became a statutory one under the Banking Act of 2009, which I introduced after the Northern Rock debacle. The Governor, using the elegant and well-constructed metaphor of a minister who could preach to his congregation but did not have the power to do what he wanted, called for greater powers to be given to the Bank of England. Everyone knew what he was getting at. It was a naked attempt to wrest powers from the FSA. As such – and all those present knew it – it was a direct challenge to government policy, and therefore to me. The media duly reported it in this way. But whether Mervyn liked it or not, the design of the regulatory system, and the primacy of the Bank or the FSA, are matters for the government, not the Bank.

The speech should have been discussed with me well in advance of its delivery. Mervyn knew I had doubts that the Bank should be the lead regulator, especially as it had been slow off the mark in the banking crisis of 2007. He also knew that I doubted his argument that if the banking system were broken up it would be safer. This was another occasion on which I felt that Mervyn had decided that, because of the government's weakness, he had licence to roam in a way he would never have done if he had thought he would still have to deal with us after the next election. This is dangerous territory for any Bank Governor, and it followed his public suggestion that the government had not done enough to set out a credible plan to reduce borrowing. The problem was that both the break-up the banks and the handing over of the FSA's job to the Bank of England were Conservative Party policy. The Governor's position on borrowing could also be fairly characterized in the same way. Mervyn was careful to cover his pronouncements with caveats, which usually went unreported, but even so he was coming perilously close to crossing a line between legitimate comment and entering the political fray. Given the general political problems we had, the Governor's speech was seized upon by every commentator as well as the opposition. It was another stick with which to beat us.

Immediately after the reshuffle, I went home to Edinburgh for a constituency event on international development with my Cabinet colleague Douglas Alexander. I was surprised by people's reactions to us as we met in a church just off Princes Street. Reading the newspapers, secluded in Downing Street and the Treasury, I truly expected that a lynch mob might be waiting for us. Yet most of the people I met that weekend were extremely warm. Throughout my ministerial career, I had often applied what I call the 'Tesco test'. I make a point of watching how people react when I go shopping. If they look away, you are in trouble. If they engage with you, either through eye contact or, even better, conversation, then you are in with a chance.

At the time of the Northern Rock collapse, our pollster had told me that no one understood that its causes lay in the US mortgage market. However, I rather thought the argument was getting through. One weekend at the end of 2007, I was pushing my trolley around the local Tesco. Two elderly ladies spotted me, and started to talk to each other about Northern Rock. One of the things you get used to as a politician is that people frequently talk about you as if you are not there. While scanning the fruit and veg, I heard one confide to her friend: 'It's the sub-prime mortgages, you know.'

Towards the middle of June we realized we would not get home for Calum's twenty-first birthday. His sister was returning from her gap-year travels around the same date, so we decided to invite close friends and family for a celebration at Dorneywood. It was a very happy weekend. The political weather may have been poor, but we spent a gloriously sunny couple of days. I sat with my Red Box, doing the weekend's homework on the terrace looking out over the summer gardens, thinking of Harold Wilson's dictum of a week being a long time in politics. It was the first time in a long time that we had been able properly to relax.

That summer, when I was able to get back to Edinburgh more often than at any time over the previous two years, I picked up two important points. The first was that people were fast losing faith in us, but that they had not given up on us altogether. The second was that they really did not warm to the Tories. I had picked up exactly the same things in London. The situation was not yet lost, but we would have to work desperately hard if we were to claw back our position.

Our summer holiday of 2009 was less eventful than the previous year. We enjoyed a peaceful two weeks in the Hebrides. The weather was glorious and for days on end we were treated to the sight of a pair of golden eagles with their offspring, floating so close above the house that we could see their eyes looking down at us. It is good to see that these beautiful birds are now returning, when only a few years ago there was the fear of their becoming extinct in parts of Scotland. We even managed to catch a few lobsters. Stocks had been depleted for years but are now recovering.

I hoped to avoid deputizing for the Prime Minister, as I had done for two weeks the year before. This year it was decided that Jack, Harriet and I would each do a week. When I arrived back in London, the breaking news was the decision of the Scottish justice minister to release Abdelbaset al-Megrahi, the Libyan convicted of the murder of 270 people when Pan Am Flight 103 was blown up over Lockerbie in December 1988, on compassionate grounds. Now he was supposedly dying of prostate cancer, and his release obviously provoked very strong feelings, not only in the UK but particularly in the US. The majority of the passengers had been American citizens going home for Christmas. Tony was at that time trying to bring Colonel Gaddafi in from the cold, and al-Megrahi was a stumbling block to the improvement of relations between Libya and the UK and US. The British government was therefore not unhappy about the Scottish government's decision to release him, but there was no collusion. I suspect that the Scottish government was motivated by a desire to be seen to be playing on the international stage; certainly the Justice Secretary had gone to visit the prisoner in his cell, a privilege not accorded to other inmates seeking compassionate release. But what this all suggests to me is a coincidence of interests, rather than collusion, between the British and the Scottish governments.

By the time I met with the No. 10 staff to take stock of what was going on, the story had been running for some days. The line that had been decided upon was that the matter was one for the Scottish government rather than Downing Street. In an age when the prime minister is expected to have a view on everything from *Coronation Street* to football, having no view on the release of a man who had been convicted of a heinous terrorist crime was never going to wash. Catherine MacLeod told the meeting that she thought silence would not work. The response of Gordon's advisers was that it was a Scottish story. She said they were wrong: it was a story that would reverberate around the world. She was slapped down by his team and told that Gordon had closed down the issue. Far from it: the story dragged on for weeks. Catherine's judgement was proved correct once again – and far from being at death's door, al-Megrahi was still alive two years later.

That autumn there was to be a series of international meetings involving the same people and covering a lot of the same ground. Ironically, our carbon footprint would be formidable. My attention turned to the international efforts to maintain the recovery, which had been so invigorated by the G20 summit in London in April. The G20 was due to reconvene in Pittsburgh in September, this time with President Obama in the chair. It had been decided that the finance ministers would convene in London in early September to prepare the way. Two meetings would be time-consuming enough; but there would also be the autumn meeting of the IMF in October, which this year was being held in Istanbul. This was my first visit to Istanbul, and sailing down the Bosphorus, almost able to reach out and touch the shores of the two continents of Europe and Asia, visiting spectacular churches and mosques, feeling the fusion of east and west meeting in one city, I knew I would return. We finance ministers began to think that we saw each other more than we saw our families.

In addition, it had been agreed earlier in the year that the same finance ministers would meet in St Andrews in November. Finally, leaders and environment ministers were due to meet in Copenhagen in December to try to get an agreement on climate change to succeed the 1997 Kyoto protocol. St Andrews offered an ideal location with a secure venue. I knew too that because it boasts world-famous golf courses there would be no difficulty persuading ministers to attend. I hoped that I might be able to get an agreement on climate change in the run-up to Copenhagen. Far too many finance ministers regard climate change as something for others, for their colleagues who are responsible for the environment or energy. But measures to halt the damage being done to the environment do have a major financial impact. Equally, failure to act has great costs.

At that time, hopes for a deal in Copenhagen were high. It was at our London meeting in September that the differences of opinion that would kill off any chance of agreement in December were exposed. It became clear that many countries, India and China in particular, were not willing to sign up to anything meaningful on climate change. Canada too had reservations. At one point, increasingly irritated at the apparent refusal of the Chinese to sign up to anything at all, I said to them that if they persisted with this line I would have to explain who it was that was blocking the agreement. They moved slightly at that point. The trouble was, though, that the Chinese representatives did not have authority from Beijing to agree to much more than a few warm words.

Ministers were, by and large, happy with the agreements on the economy and on regulation, as these were largely work in progress. In the news conference afterwards, attention focused on differences between ourselves and the French over what to do about bankers' bonuses. That, to some extent, disguised the fact that we had been unable to agree anything concrete on climate change. The difficulty was to resurface again at the final meeting of the G20 finance ministers in St Andrews in November.

We met on the sunny, windswept Fife coast in a hotel purpose-built for golfers, just outside the ancient town, for what would be the last meeting under our presidency of the G20. To welcome guests from across the world, students from our children's old school, James Gillespie's High School in Edinburgh, played the *clàrsach*, the Gaelic harp. The music was beautiful and Margaret and I were proud of the students, who had come a long way by bus to be met with the kind of desultory response that is normal on these occasions. Margaret had arranged for the atrium of the hotel to be a showcase for the finest of

Scottish produce, brands such as Harris Tweed, Hebrides and Anta fabrics, as well as an exhibition by the Glasgow galleries of the work of Charles Rennie Mackintosh and Jessie M. King.

On the Saturday morning, we met a long queue of very small schoolchildren lugging very big musical instruments into the hotel theatre. The sound of an orchestral performance by youngsters from Big Noise, a pioneering social project in Raploch, in Stirlingshire, provided the background to the first of many wearying meetings. Mervyn King and his wife Barbara, who joined us for the concert, were immensely moved by the performance.

Try as I might, I could not get China and India to sign up to anything. Eventually we cocooned them in a small room. I asked Tim Geithner and Christine Lagarde to join us. There were also Guido Mantega from Brazil and Anders Borg, the Swedish finance minister, representing Ecofin. But we could not budge them, even towards a minimal commitment; they were not prepared to sign up to anything they thought might constrain their economic development. Watching them at close quarters, the Indian and Chinese ministers played off each other, each relying on the other to be more obstructive. The Chinese civil servant seemed to be more vehemently opposed to our proposed text than did his minister. The shots were being called thousands of miles away. Here were two countries that, on any view, were going to be among the largest economies in the world. They should be at the top table of decision-making. But when it came down to it, they were not willing to accept the burdens that tackling climate change would bring. Their main argument, put simply, was 'we didn't cause the damage, it's your fault, you fix it'. Their second, frequently stated, position was that the developed West was trying to hold back two developing countries that were desperately trying to catch up. In the event, they did agree to something bland, but it was a portent of the failure there would be to make any real progress at Copenhagen, despite the valiant role played by Ed Miliband. He put enormous effort into trying to get a deal, and so too did Gordon.

At the beginning of the year, I had been encouraged by the extent to which countries were prepared to come in from the cold and work together to try to resolve problems through international cooperation. None of this was going to be achieved at one summit. It was a process. At Pittsburgh, with President Obama in the chair and the Americans fully engaged, there had still been a determination to get things done. But by the time of the St Andrews gathering it was clear that somehow we had lost the momentum. It was not just one or two errant finance ministers playing hardball: these were clearly decisions taken at the highest level. International cooperation will only go so far unless ministers feel, as they did over the banking crisis, that they are on the brink and have no choice but to act together. The complete failure of the latest round of world trade talks, started in 2001, is an eloquent reminder of what happens when one or two countries don't feel they have to play.

There is a postscript to the St Andrews meeting. Gordon was in Scotland, campaigning in the Glenrothes by-election, which Labour won emphatically, giving a welcome fillip to flagging spirits and hope of a recovery in our political fortunes. He told me that he wanted to say a few words to the gathering. The 'few words' turned out to be a speech calling for a tax on financial transactions. It would mean that every time money was transferred, a fraction of its value would be paid in tax, potentially raising billions of pounds. The finance ministers responded very badly to his initiative. They were given no warning. However, they weren't entirely surprised: many had worked with Gordon for years while he was Chancellor. He had a long history of using such gatherings as a backdrop for a press release; quite often they'd already read what they were going to hear in the *Financial Times*. It was bound to unravel.

Tim Geithner told me he understood the politics, but that there was no way that he could agree to it. Of course, he was asked point-blank what he thought at his press conference that afternoon, and it was evident that the US government would not agree to this step. Jim Flaherty of Canada was equally emphatic. At my own press conference, I had to square a circle. Back in London, Downing Street was briefing that the case for the tax had been well received by the finance ministers, when in fact they had taken a very different view. I see little prospect of such a tax being implemented unless, at the very least, countries with major financial sectors become convinced of its merits. In theory, it would be a good way of getting a fairer contribution from the financial system. In practice, it would be impossible to make it work unless there was near-universal agreement, and there is no sign of that yet.

After the trauma of the summer reshuffle, we settled back into an uneasy truce in our working relationship. Gordon held his views and I held mine. The more he repeated the 'investment versus cuts' argument, the greater our political problems. The government settled into a period of what seemed like weary resignation. The reshuffle had not provided a fresh start. They rarely do; they are big in Westminster, but seldom cut through to the outside world. It was simply a messy end to a messy episode.

Despite that, when the Cabinet met for the last time before the summer recess, in Cardiff, on a warm bright day, we were in remarkably good spirits. We were, all of us, determined to do everything possible to put up a strong fight at the looming general election. At that meeting we discussed transport. Andrew Adonis, the new Transport Secretary, had brought his intellectual rigour to bear on the future of our railways. He also brought into Cabinet with him a map prepared by the old Ministry of Transport in the 1950s, showing what Britain's motorway system would one day look like. It was remarkably prescient in its size and shape. Andrew wanted to do the same with the railways, with a new generation of high-speed trains. I was extremely interested, and somewhat surprised, given the Department for Transport's long-standing scepticism about the value of high-speed rail. Andrew and I had discussed his plans over the previous month or so. Whether or not a high-speed train will ever get north of the English Midlands – if, indeed, it is built at all – I don't know. Maintaining the present network is tough enough and it needs major investment. Added to that, it's no substitute for measures needed to increase capacity at Heathrow. But Andrew's boyish exuberance and serious intent rekindled the fire that any government needs – particularly one like ours.

The row at the heart of government rumbled on, however. The repeated attempts to run the argument that Labour wanted to invest and the Tories to cut was not working. It wasn't that people did not believe that the Tories would cut. Of course they would. That's what they do. But people knew we would have to cut spending too. A growing number of Cabinet colleagues and fellow MPs were expressing despair at this impossible argument. I discussed it with Peter Mandelson, who, since his recall to the Cabinet the previous autumn, had been an increasingly stabilizing force in No. 10. It was good to have him as an ally. I wasn't going to make any headway with Gordon, but unless we changed course now the pre-Budget report was going to be a disaster. Peter decided to use a speech to the Westminster parliamentary lobby to start the process in the summer. Later in September, both he and I would make further speeches setting out the narrative that would, we hoped, take us to the pre-Budget report and then to the election. In essence, we would prioritize economic recovery, and then get the deficit down. There would be spending reductions, of course. But we had to protect key public services. We also pointed out that all this was being done on the back of increases in public spending over the previous ten years.

My speech, delivered as the James Callaghan Memorial Lecture in Cardiff in September, not only made these arguments but also explored larger themes, about the role of government. I made the point, as James Callaghan had done, that government had the means of changing people's lives for the better. There was a case, I said, for a government actively engaged in doing that, principally through education. But government could also shape the economic weather, as well as making a key difference to the business environment. However, unless Gordon were to change his tone, none of this would work. He was finally persuaded – not by me but by Peter – to the use the word 'cuts' in his speech to the TUC that same month. It was an odd choice; he used the word seven or eight times, but we knew he just didn't believe it.

I did speak to Ed Balls about this issue from time to time and sensed that he was ready to accept a more nuanced argument. Certainly, he told me so on more than one occasion. What he said to Gordon I do not know. Gordon kept telling me he did not want to be labelled 'another Philip Snowden'. Nor, I assured him, did I. Ironically, though I didn't tell him so, I had said the same thing to the 'Taliban wing', as I dubbed the hard-line orthodox economists in the Treasury, on numerous occasions. My officials knew the strength of my views. Snowden, or at least his ghost, was not even in the room.

Gordon was wedded to a dividing line that had been successful in the past, and all attempts to shift him seemed to be in vain. Instead, with increasing regularity, I picked up that the No. 10 entourage believed not only that I was in thrall to Treasury orthodoxy, but that praise from Tory columnists had gone to my head. No doubt my unexpected *Spectator* award as 'Survivor of the Year' confirmed my critics' worst suspicions. I saw it as a bit of fun. As I told the audience at the ceremony, I'd only ever won one national award before, that of 'Most Boring Politician of the Year'. That coveted award, which I had won twice on the trot, was made by a trucking magazine when I was Secretary of State for Transport. I made one final attempt to make a decisive break from where we were. The pre-Budget report was to be presented in December because the Budget had only been presented very late in April. To my mind, it would be the last chance we would have if we, and not events, were to make the weather in the run-up to the general election. The economic background was showing signs of improving. However, we were by no means out of the woods. The banking sector had stabilized, but, as the IMF had said, it was too soon for governments to reduce spending without threatening recovery. Everyone expected that coming out of the recession that followed the banking crisis would be difficult. Britain is the second biggest exporter of services and the sixth largest exporter of goods in the world. Our trade had been hit hard. Our economy had contracted by 4.9 per cent in 2009. The US had seen a contraction of just over 3 per cent, but in Germany it was 5.6 per cent, and 7.7 per cent in Japan. We were not alone. Nevertheless, there were signs that, although the damage had been substantial, recovery would still come by the end of 2009.

When the first figures were revealed at the end of January 2010, it was thought that the British economy had just struggled over the line with growth of 0.1 per cent. It was just enough to see the end of the recession. It wasn't until more than a year later, in 2011, that the ONS finally confirmed that the figure was 0.5 per cent – small, but much better. It vindicated everything we had done to get us through the recession.

In 2009, though, the prospects still looked very uncertain. The political landscape had not changed. We still trailed the Tories, flat-lining in the polls well below 30 per cent. I wasn't involved in the day-to-day general election planning; but, in a welcome development Gordon, at the insistence of Harriet Harman, had set up an inner group of senior Cabinet members to contribute to the election strategy. Harriet, over many years, has devoted herself to the Labour Party. Her enthusiasm is remarkable. Like Jack Straw, she had served on the long march of eighteen years in opposition, and was determined that we should put up a realistic fight.

Douglas Alexander, who was the general election coordinator, Ed Miliband and Ed Balls were there, as were David Miliband and Alan Johnson. Alan's grounded approach and feel for the ordinary person were invaluable. Peter, as often as not, presided in Gordon's absence. I noticed that he took copious notes. This was the first time that such a group had been set up, and serious thought was finally being given to how we might recover so much lost ground. There was much talk about how to win back a whole generation of people who had voted for us in

1997 but who felt we had nothing to say to them now. This group was represented to a large extent by the 10p tax rate losers.

David Miliband said that attacking the Tories was all very well, but we also had to set out our own vision. What struck me then was that unless we did something radical at the pre-Budget report we would never break through. At one meeting, I said that we had to ask ourselves why people were not listening to us any more. I said: 'We have to make the weather. We have to make ourselves the story. We have to take risks. We have nothing more to lose.'

Most of my colleagues agreed, although Gordon and Ed Balls wanted the focus to be on the threat of what the Tories would do if they got in. Slowly but surely, the argument came back to the need to go for growth, not cuts. It was, though, a useful first stab at a return to collective discussion in a small group. I started engaging Gordon on the pre-Budget report at the end of October, when I sent him a long note going through the main arguments. The forecasts would show a deeper recession than anyone had expected at the beginning of 2009, which meant that growth for the year would be lower than we had thought. But I told him that we still expected growth to recover at the end of 2009. I also expected borrowing to be higher than forecast. The big question was what to do about public spending. The measures announced in the pre-Budget report of 2008 and the Budget of 2009 included plans for a reduction in borrowing of £56 billion, a quarter of which would come from increased tax – mainly from the 50p top rate and from reform of pension contribution relief. The other three quarters would come from spending cuts.

I did stress to Gordon that the implication of our spending plans – which were to protect the health service and schools by giving them an inflation-only increase, to maintain police officer numbers, and to maintain our commitment to overseas development – amounted to protecting 60 per cent of everything we spent in government departments. It did mean that other government departments might see cuts of around 15 per cent; the exact figure would depend on what we decided at the end of the day. I went on to say that while we would not carry out a spending review, we had to identify some of the areas where we would stop or postpone spending, or otherwise reduce costs. Finally, I outlined a number of measures to boost growth. As on previous occasions, our first meetings were inconclusive. However, it was apparent that Gordon believed that I was taking the wrong approach.

The government had been preparing papers setting out where we wanted to go on education, health and law and order, as well as measures to get people back to work. Logically, these should have followed the pre-Budget report, which would have set the spending parameters. Instead, Gordon sent me a note saying that we should publish the spending papers first. I remember saying to him: 'When you were Chancellor you would never have agreed to such a proposal.' Fortunately, he took it no further, although it illustrated the continuing gulf between us.

There was also a difference between us on the vexed question of efficiency savings. Every government, in every part of the world, knows it can do things more efficiently. Efficiency savings also have the superficial attraction of being apparently pain-free. This is not true in most cases: the biggest costs are labour costs, so there are implications for jobs or wages. But, of course, improved technology can make government more efficient and less costly, although this is not entirely straightforward and neither can it be done quickly. I was happy to embrace efficiency savings wherever they could be found. But what was also needed was some evidence of other ways in which we were going to spend less.

There was one further prelude to this year's negotiations. In the early autumn Gordon told me he accepted that we had to show we were mindful of the deficit. He therefore proposed a Fiscal Responsibility Act which would commit us to reducing the deficit by half over a five-year period. In my opinion, such a move was wide open to the argument that you didn't need a law to ensure that you act as you should. In the circumstances, though, I seized on it because it did at least provide me with the equivalent of a fiscal rule, providing a ceiling on what we could borrow and spend. The Act was eventually introduced in early 2010, to almost universal derision. Legislation is no substitute for sound judgement.

This time, officials on both sides of the divide made strenuous efforts towards a more satisfactory process of working through the pre-Budget details. It was arranged that we would have a series of breakfasts which, because of the attraction of food, did at least mean we would all be there at the appointed time in the small dining room at No. 10. We did not meet every day, but Gordon, Peter and I met often, essentially to discuss the same fundamental issues that had dogged our relations for the past year. As we approached the day itself, there were more fraught meetings downstairs in Gordon's study. Ed Balls occasionally attended, and was most preoccupied with spending on education. This posed a problem because Ed was in charge of a big spending department. For some of my colleagues, like Jack Straw at Justice, who voluntarily agreed to make some painful cuts in his departmental spending, this seemed unfair: Jack was prepared to do his bit, but expected others to do the same.

The process, then, was much better than in previous years. The outcome, however, was no different. There were long and protracted discussions about the Budget forecasts, both on growth and on borrowing. There was no disputing that the growth figures for 2009 would be bad, and I wanted to hold the growth forecasts for 2010 at more or less the same place, 1.25 per cent. The figures for the years following were more optimistic, but just about within the range of what the Bank of England was forecasting. With the borrowing figures we erred on the side of caution. Two years later, when the ONS gave their latest revision of those figures, it was clear that we had actually borrowed £21 billion less. The reason was that we had stimulated the economy, tax revenues were higher and we had to spend less on the cost of unemployment. The figure was still high, but it again demonstrates that our support for the economy resulted in less borrowing being necessary.

I returned for the final time to the question of VAT. I had discussed what I wanted to do with Peter in the hope of getting his support. Without it, I knew I would be outnumbered again. I had said to him that the only chance we had of extracting ourselves from the mire was to do something that would surprise our critics. I wanted to maintain the stimulus throughout the financial year and I would announce that we were protecting budgets in three key areas: the health service, schools and police. I could only do that if we accepted the need for cuts elsewhere, announcing specific symbolic cuts in order to show that we were serious about making long-term reductions in borrowing.

If I could increase gradually the rate of VAT to 19 or even 20 per cent, I could scrap the National Insurance increase. I could compensate low-earners with a package of measures to negate the impact of the VAT increase. On top of that, I could surprise people by cutting both the basic rate of income tax and corporation tax in order to boost growth. I tried this out with Gordon, but was met with an emphatic no. I talked to both Peter and Ed Balls, trying to convince them that we needed something big if we were to come out of this with any momentum at all. While Peter this time had an open mind, Gordon and Ed remained implacably opposed to the VAT increase. There was nothing more I could do, so we stuck with the tax measures previously announced.

We then turned to discuss spending, something that was not resolved until a few hours before I presented the pre-Budget report. I had no difficulty in seeking to protect front-line services in key areas. But it was clear that Ed wanted more, fearing that he would go into the election campaign being outbid by the Tories. Andy Burnham, the Health Secretary, proved unwilling to accept protection for the NHS only. He was concerned about other areas of health spending as well. Only Alan Johnson, who was always thoughtfully accommodating, said that he would be happy to go into the election protecting police numbers. He recognized that cuts would have to be made somewhere and there was no point in pretending they wouldn't.

I also ran into fierce resistance from Yvette Cooper, now in charge of the biggest spending department of them all, at Work and Pensions. I wanted to delay some pension reforms because of the upfront cost. She didn't. In the end we reached a compromise, but again only at the last minute. The wrangling on spending went to the wire. On the night before the pre-Budget report, I went to bed at 11 o'clock and told my office that no more changes could be made. Next morning, Dan Rosenfield told me that one of my colleagues had been demanding to speak to me at 1.30 a.m., trying to reopen the settlement. I'll spare their blushes. That is no way to run anything.

The coalition government now has to run all its proposals past the independent Office for Budget Responsibility. That means that the Budget has to be signed off some time in advance. That to me is a major attraction.

There were in that pre-Budget report worthy measures announced to help industry and the environment. On the latter, Ed Miliband pressed hard, but recognized the constraints we were working under. We were able to take more children out of poverty and to announce a number of measures that would help people during the recession. It is worth remembering that unemployment had risen by far less than independent forecasters had expected. If we had seen the same rate of job losses relative to GDP as were seen in the early 1990s, four times as many people would have been out of work. We had, too, a guarantee to stop school-leavers going straight on to the dole. House repossessions were running at half the rate of the recession of the early 1990s, and the rate of business failures was likewise down by half against those years. And we had been able to help many families. The tax credit system may be complex, but nearly 400,000 families whose incomes fell because of the recession received on average £37 more per week as the system automatically topped up their wages.

None of this helped us. The pre-Budget report simply lacked credibility. It was trashed in the press. Even if I had been wrong in my argument, any coherent argument is better than none. We simply didn't have one.

There was one tax, however, that did strike a chord and was to prove extremely popular with the public, but deeply unpopular with the people who had – amazingly, given the expenses scandal – managed to snatch the title of 'most hated people in Britain' from the politicians: the bankers. The subject of bank pay had been highly contentious since it emerged that the people who ran Northern Rock had been paid exorbitant sums without any apparent relationship to what they actually did. Throughout the entire banking crisis, huge bonuses continued to be paid. The banks' defence was that everybody else paid out salaries and bonuses. If they didn't, then they couldn't attract the best people. Rather like premiership football players, if you want the best, you have to pay for it. The problem is that, rather like the premiership, it becomes apparent from time to time that very large sums are being paid for very little in the way of results. Even in the football industry there is a growing realization that clubs can't carry on paying stratospheric wages without getting deeper into debt. This is not the case in the banking industry, where, as far as I can see, there is not even an acceptance that there needs to be a better relationship between performance and reward.

A bonus should be just that: a payment for doing something particularly well. Instead, it has come to be paid as a matter of course. We need to get this into some degree of perspective. Most people who work for banks, the people you meet in your local branch, the backroom staff, are not paid over the odds; yet it is the bank staff in the high street who frequently had to endure the most abuse from angry customers. On top of that, many of my constituents employed by RBS and HBOS had given up pay rises and instead taken shares in the bank, which by 2008 were next to worthless. They had done the right thing, but were cleaned out. Some of them have every right to be very angry. As one of my constituents, an RBS middle manager, said to me: 'We thought these people, Fred Goodwin and the like, knew what they were doing and that's why they got paid so much.' Bonuses are used to benchmark the relative standing of bank employees. It is about status. Just after

I introduced a tax on bonuses in my pre-Budget report, I was accosted by a very senior bank executive. I knew him quite well and was rather taken aback at his anger. His bonus amounted to around £1 million. I asked him to look at this through the eyes of ordinary people. 'What does your next-door neighbour say when you tell them you've got £1 million by way of a bonus?' I asked.

He told me, 'He doesn't mind.'

'What does he do?' I asked.

'He's a banker as well, and he earns more than me,' was the reply.

The actual amount really does not matter any more to these high-rollers. It is all about their relative status. In many conversations with bankers who were trying to rehabilitate themselves in the eyes of the public, I made the same point over and over again. Unless you start to show some restraint, some understanding, no one will listen to a word you say. If people continue to believe you are simply raising two fingers to them, you will get nowhere. I do understand the need to hire the very best staff. After all, I agreed to get the best people into RBS so that we could turn the bank around and get our money back.

I did consider a windfall tax. But as some banks had been losing billions of pounds it would have looked like an empty gesture. On top of that, governments have to be very careful about changing the rules of the game. A windfall tax might have won a headline or two, but I was sure that the press would be only too happy to paint a lurid picture of banks moving overseas. Far better, I thought, to deal with the thing causing so much anger: bonuses.

So I decided to announce, without warning – since this is an industry filled with experts at cunning tax avoidance schemes – a 50 per cent tax on all bonuses over £25,000. It eventually brought in over £3 billion. I said in my statement to the Commons that I would rather the banks practised restraint, but if they wouldn't do so, bonuses would be taxed at 50 per cent. The outcry was predictable. The right-wing press that Gordon's camp believed I was courting ran lurid stories of bankers planning to flee the country and decamp to Switzerland.

I did not believe it. As one banker said: 'Have you ever been to Geneva?' And he was Swiss.

Over the following days, I started to receive frantic calls from No. 10 officials who were clearly being lobbied by senior bankers, all of whom seemed to be speaking from the same script, urging me to reconsider. Crucially, the calls were not from Gordon. He was as adamant as I was that we would not give in on this. There was, though, in the run-up to Christmas, a crescendo of complaints. The most voluble came from Jamie Dimon, chief executive of JPMorgan Chase. Like many American bankers, he comes from humble origins and has worked his way to the top. He speaks bluntly. He asked for a telephone call with me, which I took in the sitting room of the No. 10 flat. Normally I would regard any conversation with someone like Mr Dimon as confidential. However, since a fairly accurate account of it appeared in a newspaper a few days later, and it didn't come from me, I think I am entitled to recount it.

Mr Dimon was angry, very angry. He pointed out that his bank had not been the cause of this crisis. That was true, but, I said, in 2008 his bank, like every other bank, had depended heavily on both ourselves and the US government in order to stay in business. He said that his bank bought a lot of UK debt and he wondered if that was now such a good idea. I pointed out that they bought our debt because it was a good business deal for them. He went on to say that they were thinking of building a new office in London but they had to reconsider that now. I knew full well that they were considering consolidating their offices in London and I guessed correctly that to teach us a lesson they would postpone their decision until after the general election. That they did.

Mr Dimon then went on to say that I was punishing the many Veterans he employed in his office doing fairly humdrum jobs. I said I doubted that. The Veterans were working in the US and were beyond the reach of UK taxes, although I did say I was pleasantly surprised that he paid humble employees such high salaries that they would be affected by the bonus tax aimed at top earners.

I met Jamie Dimon in London some weeks later and he was charm itself. By that time the Obama administration had unveiled plans (never really implemented) that made the bonus tax a mere distraction. When they were first announced, it looked as if the Americans were going to restrict the size of their banks and the range of their operations. Here, the Tories leapt on to that passing bandwagon, only to jump off it a few days later when it became apparent that the idea wasn't going to fly.

In early 2010, I attended the annual jamboree of top industrialists and financiers up a mountain, in the ski resort of Davos in Switzerland. This is a relatively informal gathering, the only virtue of which is the opportunity to meet dozens of people on a casual basis for the few minutes necessary to exchange views without having to make an appointment. What might otherwise take months can be done over a weekend simply by bumping into people.

I was concerned that the continuing anger about bonuses was deflecting attention from the need to get the right regulatory regime in place. I was also concerned that, notwithstanding the excesses shown by some of the well-paid bankers, we should not lose sight of the fact that this industry employs more than a million people in the UK. The only way we were going to have a constructive discussion about this was if the banks showed restraint. It was worth a try. I sat down with a group of about ten of the top bankers in Europe and America. I said to them that the stand-off would do irreparable harm to an industry that was exceptionally important. There would be no winners. Politicians may rail against bank pay, but, as I and my successors have found, it is hard to do much about it when half the world's financial centres don't regard it as a problem.

The pre-Budget report had not helped us politically, and the grumbling against Gordon among my Cabinet colleagues began to grow louder. I intended to speak to him to try and resolve these problems before I left to go to Edinburgh for Christmas. But the last straw was the briefings that followed the pre-Budget report, proclaiming that it had been a triumph for those who had advocated increased spending, particularly on education. It meant that what had been a serious attempt at dealing with our public finances was being presented by No. 10 as another go at tax and spend. Ironically, this is the very impression that Gordon Brown and Tony Blair had dispelled so successfully fifteen years earlier.

12 Leaving

This was to be election year, 2010. I never look forward with unalloyed joy to general election campaigns, even those that I think we will win. I've been involved in every election since 1979 and have been a candidate in every general election since 1987. Luckily, I have never had to endure the ignominy of making the losing speech at the count.

It still feels to me like intruding when I knock on a door or accost someone whose innocent purpose in walking along the street is to do a bit of shopping, not to be molested by canvassers and candidates. I do enjoy the debate, such as it is, and making the argument that is an essential part of any campaign. Since 1997 I've spent most campaigns in or around the party headquarters in London, doing interviews in between visiting marginal constituencies. I had a strong sense that we could still win the election, or at least make it a very close-run thing, right up until the end. I had been tracking George Osborne's pronouncements very closely and so often what they were offering didn't add up or wasn't budgeted for. We did this in all of the general elections from 2001 onwards and were very good at it: recording their pronouncements and then responding to them.

Over Christmas 2009 we had been working on a line-by-line costing of Conservative Party promises. Because of our weakened political position, the Tories had been allowed to get away with murder, and it was time to strike back. We had planned a press conference for 4 January, although in truth I was reluctant to leave a snowbound Edinburgh so early in the year. I asked Peter Mandelson whether he thought that our attack on the Conservatives would have any traction. He, like me, thought that at best it would provide grit in the wheels. In fact, it was far better than that, and within an hour or so the Tories were on the back foot, particularly over what they intended to do about the married couple's tax allowance. David Cameron fumbled the ball badly. First he said the allowance was an aspiration; then, presumably after a hasty conversation with the *Daily Mail*, it became a commitment again. Their promise to enter the new year with 'a policy per day', when they were unable to answer some basic questions on what they had already promised, made them look weak. We had the momentum. I enjoyed that press conference. It was like the old days, when we continually had the Tories on the ropes. Push these people and they wobbled. Press them further and they began to panic. Perhaps we could claw back their poll lead and make a fight of it.

The following day, at the first Prime Minister's Questions of the new year, Gordon had a good outing, easily besting Cameron. Then, halfway through this parliamentary joust, news came of another attempt to force a leadership election. A letter had been jointly signed by Patricia Hewitt and Geoff Hoon, calling for a leadership contest. Geoff had been unhappy for a long time. He had called me over Christmas. 'Don't do anything until I've come down and we've spoken,' I told him. No letter was mentioned but I did dissuade him from writing a newspaper article. Since before Christmas Ann Coffey had been telling me that there was increasing despair among backbenchers and ministers at the thought of going into the election with Gordon as leader. I too was a recipient of almost daily tales of woe and dire predictions. My Cabinet colleagues felt alienated. Perhaps I should have warned Gordon, but I was still angry about the briefings after the pre-Budget report and decided that it would be better for us to keep our distance.

Now, we were faced with the second serious attempt to replace Gordon with someone else. The fact that the replacement was to be 'someone else' was precisely the problem. When Mrs Thatcher was overthrown in 1990, Michael Heseltine was seen as heir apparent, even though in the event he did not win. Here, there was no declared challenger. Most coups do at least have someone who says they are ready to assume power. Ever since the publication of his newspaper article in the summer of 2008, David Miliband had been consistently mentioned as a possible challenger. Had Gordon stood down, he almost certainly would have been. But he wasn't behind this coup. He, like I, thought it was never going to get off the ground.

The first time I really had a conversation about this with David Miliband was in June of 2009, when James Purnell had just resigned. David and I met at Catherine MacLeod's farm, with our families. We had agreed that we needed to talk because, although we'd had snatched conversations, he'd been Foreign Secretary and I'd been tied up with the banks and we'd never sat down and talked through what should happen regarding the leadership of the party. We knew we needed to speak away from Downing Street for privacy's sake. We had reflected on what an appalling week it had been. I told David that Gordon had offered me his job as foreign secretary but that I'd refused it. We wanted to discuss whether there was a way the government could avoid a Conservative landslide – the question at that time wasn't whether we'd lose, but how badly – and whether there was any way of getting rid of Gordon. I said that I knew him well and that there was no way he would go voluntarily. Anyone who had lived through the Labour Party during the 1980s was terrified at the thought of another bloodbath along those lines. We were really conscious that once we were out it would be terribly hard to get back in – hence David Cameron being so willing to get into bed with the Lib Dems in 2010. Earlier, I'd had similar conversations with Jack Straw and Douglas Alexander – not so much about the leadership as about the fact that we were facing a landslide defeat.

We were also painfully aware of the Heseltine factor – that he who wields the knife never wears the crown. Unlike under Thatcher, there was no one who was actually willing to put in the knife, partly out of tribal loyalty. For myself, I'd worked with Gordon for twenty years, many of them happy. I would have found it very difficult to take part in a coup. But I had always seen eye to eye with David and we had a high regard for one another. I made it clear that I would back him were he one day to make a run as leader. That afternoon, as we strolled around Catherine's garden, we came to a pretty unsatisfactory political conclusion: that Gordon wouldn't leave; that there was no alternative leader in prospect; and that there was an inevitability that we must just soldier on.

There is no doubt that on that January afternoon that the delay in front-line ministers coming to stand by the Prime Minister's side demonstrated the degree of unhappiness within the Cabinet. Most chose to stay at their desks rather than embark on a tour of the television studios. Gordon asked to see me. I met him later that afternoon, shortly after 4 o'clock. He was in a dark mood, unsurprisingly, but there was no way that he was going. He was convinced that he had to stay on and see it through. We had a long talk about the need for him to engage with his colleagues. I explained that members of the Cabinet for the most part felt disengaged at precisely the time when they needed to be working together. I also said that the tension between us, and the constant disagreements on policy, could not continue. He agreed that we had to work together and pursue a common line. In particular, we had to talk about making cuts to reduce the deficit.

There was never any question of me extracting concessions or demanding that Ed Balls or anyone else be excluded from our discussions. All I wanted was a working relationship, which was essential in the run-up to the general election. By the time I left the room, I was satisfied that we had a mutual understanding of what we needed to do together. Sitting in his study that January evening, I remembered the energetic, focused, driven Gordon Brown I had known, the one I had supported and worked with down the years. Both of us were low. The policy row had been long and debilitating. We both knew we were close to the end of our working relationship, whatever the outcome of the election. There was a weary resignation on both our parts. We both knew that this latest leadership challenge would derail the progress we had made in our attack on the Tories. The momentum was lost once again.

Although I was hard at work preparing the Budget, I was looking forward to the next meeting of the G7 finance ministers, which was to be held in February up on the Arctic Circle in northern Canada. It was so remote we could only get there by small plane. Because of that there was only a handful of journalists and the ministerial entourages were kept to a minimum. The meeting was held over a Friday and Saturday in what looked in every respect like a frontier town. It was bitingly cold. There was said to be a polar bear padding around the frozen harbour, though I didn't see it myself. We were all issued with huge goose-feather coats so as to avoid frostbite. There was an opportunity to go dog-sledding, but the politician in me knew that while being propped up on the back of a sledge, surrounded by seal skin, might have been good fun, the solitary photographer who attended the event was not there to take pictures of the magnificent polar landscape. Mervyn King found himself on the front page of the *Financial Times* sitting on a sled shrouded in furs and skins. I just didn't think it would make a great pre-election picture.

Ministers met without anyone else present, in front of a roaring log fire in a local hotel. With the exception of the Japanese minister, who had just been appointed, we all knew each other, and it was a chance to have a proper discussion about where we thought the world economies were going. It was off the record, no notes were kept, but it was the sort of occasion on which you could actually hear what people honestly thought, as opposed to a statement of more formal positions.

We left early, thus avoiding having to eat seal at the concluding dinner. Eating seal is controversial in Europe, but the Inuit make the point that hunting is what they've done for thousands of years; just as we eat cattle and sheep, they eat seals. The trip back was memorable too. After telling the pilot that on no account was he to fly into Icelandic airspace, we flew through the aurora borealis above the Arctic Circle. I had seen the Northern Lights from the ground in Lewis many times, but to fly through millions of green crystals for more than two hours as they glittered on the polar icecap was truly spectacular.

Despite the attempted coup, we managed to emerge in slightly better shape than might have been expected. We were behind in the polls, but the country was not ready for the Tories. Indeed, they looked more shaky over the next two months than they had for the last year.

This year's Budget, then, was driven by the election. Most of the spring was dominated by its preparation. It was to be presented on 24 March 2010, just before the expected dissolution of Parliament. I had presented what was in effect a Budget at the time of the pre-Budget report in December. Now, I was required to present another one, just three months later. I was, to a large extent, left to get on with it this time. Of course, Gordon and I had discussions, but the whole process was much easier. I decided to downgrade the growth forecasts, not for the coming year but for future years. Gordon demurred. There was some pressure to spend more; the introduction of free school meals for under fives was an example. But the additional spending wasn't being seen as a further economic stimulus, more as a dividing line with the Tories. I fully understand the politics of spending, in which a party makes an offer that its opponents can't, or won't, match. But I was acutely aware of what would result from another Budget that could be characterized as being out of tune with the times. I did not want to give the markets any excuse to turn against us at such a critical time.

This Budget was still intensely political. It was written as a clear statement, setting out what we had done and why. We had decided to intervene to stop economic collapse, and it was becoming apparent that

that intervention was working. Unemployment had not risen as much as had been feared. Borrowing was lower than I had forecast a year earlier. However, I made the point that the recovery was in its infancy, and that the choice before us was how to maintain the recovery while at the same time bringing down borrowing in a way that did not damage it or the services on which people depended; hence the decision to maintain our aim of lowering the deficit by half over a four-year period. That was the essential difference – the dividing line, if you like – between us and the Conservatives, and it still is in 2011.

Growth had returned at the turn of the year, as I had forecast. But in Europe the position was still grim. At that time, Germany had seen no growth, although it was to recover later in the year. Ireland had seen its economy shrink by more than 10 per cent. Ireland and Greece were heading inexorably into deeper trouble. Spain was in recession. All of this was important to us because we have a great deal of trade with these countries. That's why, during the course of 2010, both we and our successors knew full well that it was in our interests to contribute towards their rescue, through the IMF, the European support package, and, in the case of Ireland, a direct loan made at the end of the year.

The banks here were more stable and the recovery plans were beginning to bear fruit. They had paid the government more than £8 billion in fees and charges for the financial support they had received. The bankers' bonus tax was already bringing in more than we had expected. That said, it was now clear that our economy had shrunk by about 6 per cent over the recession, compared with 8 per cent in Japan, 7 per cent in Germany, and 4 per cent in the US.

Although things were beginning to get better, to reduce public spending now at a faster rate than I had proposed in the pre-Budget report would have run the risk of derailing the recovery, which would mean that, far from reducing borrowing, it would increase. That is exactly what George Osborne had to report in his second Budget, in March 2011. Because of lower growth forecasts, he had to borrow £40 billion more than he had anticipated.

I also decided to maintain the help for home owners and people who had lost their jobs. Because of our actions, tax receipts were better than expected. VAT receipts were bringing in £3 billion more; corporation tax receipts were increasing; and, because more people were able to stay in work, income tax revenues were stronger. Because of this, borrowing in 2010 was forecast to be £11 billion lower. The structural deficit, which takes into account the economic cycle, was now expected to fall from 8.4 per cent of gross domestic product to 2.5 per cent in 2014/15. The bulk of it would therefore be removed and would disappear thereafter. Moreover, our approach of ensuring that the recovery was self-sustaining before cuts in public spending were made chimed with the view of many other governments, the IMF, the World Bank and the OECD. Twelve months later, as the political mood swung towards fiscal austerity, the IMF and the OECD changed their tune.

Had it not been for the open disagreements in government about our economic approach, I think we could have made a far greater virtue of the three strands of our argument: support to avoid recession becoming depression; then, as recovery took hold, halving our borrowing over a reasonable period to avoid damaging the recovery; and finally, protecting vital services that take years to build up and where deep cuts can set back progress for decades. We also had a good story to tell on growth, including a new green investment bank controlling £2 billion of equity. The new government were to announce this as their own policy a few months later.

I was much happier with this Budget. I felt confident with it. A great deal of my speech was devoted to the need to improve our country's infrastructure, including energy and transport. The case for government investment in infrastructure remains a strong one. These are areas in which, without government support, both financial and over important matters such as planning laws, we will fall further behind other countries. This speech was better received by our side, not least because it had a few good lines in it aimed at tax avoidance by large-scale Tory donors. But it was also a clear statement of Labour values and the difference a Labour government had made.

As I knew this would be my last Budget, I wanted to give Gladstone's ancient red box its last outing. It was deteriorating and the National Archives, who kept it in the old Cabinet war rooms, did not want it taken out again; but they relented for what they said was the last time, although subsequently they appeared to relent just once more for the new Tory Chancellor in his first Budget. The box has finally been retired, but will, I hope, remain on permanent public display.

There was one poignant coda for me. After I had delivered the Budget in the House, Margaret had friends and family in for afternoon tea, and I called in to say hello. Margaret took me aside to tell me that my uncle, my father's brother, had died. It was a shock. He had been a constant pillar in my life. She had been telephoned as we were preparing to leave the No. 11 front door to face the world's press gathered in Downing Street. I had known there was something up then, from the way she looked, but I had put it down to the occasion. She did the right thing by delaying the news. I was very fond of my uncle and spent most of my childhood holidays with him on his farm. It was probably better that I didn't know as I delivered what is one of the most difficult speeches anyone has to deliver in the House of Commons.

The Budget over, the general election campaign was shortly to get under way. First, though, a novelty for me: the first televised UK election debate. For much of the previous year, there had been a campaign to get the party leaders to agree to take part in a series of televised debates to be run during the general election campaign. From a sitting Prime Minister's point of view, there is no advantage in this whatsoever, provided he is ahead in the polls. He is well known, can be on television whenever he wants, and all he will be doing is giving an equal platform to the leaders of the main opposition parties. For that very reason, Tony had refused to take part when debates had been suggested in previous elections, despite the fact that he would certainly have come out on top.

Now things were different, and Gordon concluded that it would be seen as weakness on his part if he declined to debate with his opponents. He is a good debater in the Commons chamber, although television demands different skills. Demeanour and appearance dwarf the need to be acquainted with the facts. It was agreed, then, that ITV, Sky and the BBC would each screen a debate over the three weeks before polling day. Channel 4 lost out and therefore asked whether there could be a Chancellors' debate. Neither George Osborne nor I was especially keen. Neither of us knew what Vince Cable thought, but we kept in touch through our special advisers; each agreeing not to do anything without consulting the other. It was one of those occasions when the fear was that you could only lose. If you do well, no one remembers; put a foot wrong and it is a disaster. However, we eventually decided to take part. Our staff set stringent rules on timing and conduct down to the point where the possibility of spontaneity was entirely eliminated. At this point I realized that I couldn't just turn up on the night. Instead, I had to put in some hours practising at the podium, under the tutelage of an American who had been brought across to advise Gordon on his debate preparations.

On my first practice run, Alastair Campbell acted the part of George Osborne, a role he relished. I forget who played Vince Cable. I was pleased that Alastair had agreed to come back to help us with the campaign. Although demonized by large sections of the media by the time he left No. 10 eight years earlier, he was an extremely effective operator. In fact, the more ferocious the attacks from his right-wing critics became, the more it was evident how effective he was. He has many strengths. He understands the British media in a way that few others do. And, like me, he enjoys gallows humour.

On the night, looking at my two colleagues, I could see that we had all been to the same acting class. I'd been thoroughly schooled on what to do, to lean into the podium, not back, to be seen to make the occasional note, as if paying careful attention to what my opponent was saying. Critically, none of us was going to take a chance. We almost played for a draw, and that is more or less what the audience thought. We did another one for the BBC for a daytime audience, half-way through the campaign. It was much better, not least because Vince Cable's inconsistencies were exposed in a pincer movement. He was caught flip-flopping on the issue of whether running a deficit during the recession was a good thing or not. His lofty dismissal of his opponents' 'schoolboy economics' was at odds with his nervous failure to explain his own complex tax redistribution plans. Even George Osborne's ill-guided opposition to nearly all of our economic recovery plans sounded logical by comparison. He was further trounced when reminded by the host that he had compared Britain to Zimbabwe when when we introduced Quantitive Easing, only to back the plan now that it was working.

Sadly, few people watched it. Those who did were mostly viewers sitting in the parties' headquarters. In the event, I enjoyed the debates. In the days that followed I was struck by how much people commented on the style and demeanour of the three candidates. When I would gently ask what they thought of what we had said, very little had got through. That, I think, was a big problem with the leaders' debates too.

Those debates dominated the entire election campaign, to the exclusion of just about everything else, including close scrutiny of policies. As Douglas Alexander had accurately foreseen, the first week was spent looking forward to the first debate. The second week, or at least the first part of it, was spent discussing how the candidates had fared. This was especially so because Nick Clegg for the Liberals had done surprisingly well. I very much hope he savoured the moment. Speculation then moved on to who would win the second debate, after which opinion was more evenly divided. Then discussion moved on to the final debate. Having three people in the debates made it very difficult to have the sort of spontaneous exchanges that have from time to time proved so devastating in US presidential debates.

The focus on the leadership debates meant that all three parties got by without ever having to spell out in any detail what they would do in government. The gladiatorial style masked the essential policy questions. Given that whoever was going to be elected would have to take some of the most difficult decisions faced by any post-war government, this was a pity. Traditionally, parties will devote a day to their economic policy, then a day to education or transport. In that way, issues are explored and details drawn out. Very little of that happened during the general election campaign of 2010. Next time around we will need to think long and hard about what we do. There's no closing the door, there will be televised debates now – although just how a coalition is to be represented against a single opposition party remains to be seen. But in a democracy there needs to be some scrutiny of what the parties promise, it can't all be wrapped up in the dazzle of television.

This campaign, for me, was different from the previous three general elections. In 1997 I spent six weeks in our headquarters in Millbank Tower, making sure that we made no unfunded promises, scrutinizing every item we put out, and doing numerous interviews to feed the 24-hour news channels. I got out occasionally to campaign in my own seat in Edinburgh, and it was a welcome relief to meet normal people. In 2001 I performed a similar role for the first part of the campaign, but as it was clear that we were going to win by another landslide I spent the second half visiting marginal constituencies, something I enjoyed.

In 2005, as I was Secretary of State for Scotland as well as transport secretary, I ran the Scottish campaign. I enjoyed that, especially as I was fighting a slightly different constituency in Edinburgh. My old Edinburgh Central seat had disappeared as a result of boundary changes and I was now seeking to represent Edinburgh South West. It was a new seat which took in a great deal of the old Pentland constituency which Sir Malcolm Rifkind, a former Tory foreign secretary, had held on to through thick and thin until he finally succumbed in the landslide of 1997. So it suited me to be in Scotland. I made one trip to London that election, to arrive in the midst of yet another spat between the Brown and Blair camps. I was happy to leave to return north.

In 2010 my role was less clear. Unlike the previous campaigns, which had largely been run with military precision, this one was not. The problem was that Gordon was increasingly absorbed with preparation for the televised debates. That meant he was out of London for days at a time, which resulted in his being detached from the day-to-day campaign. We had good people running it: Peter, Alastair and Douglas all knew their stuff. And, as ever, we had many dedicated staff and volunteers who were happy to work around the clock, doing all that was asked of them and more.

In previous campaigns, the day would begin with a news conference to set out the themes we would be campaigning on, as well as to attack or respond to the opposition parties. There is a sort of rhythm, and it does mean that many more issues are covered. This time there were many fewer such news conferences. The whole campaign was overshadowed by the leaders' debates. However, the early days were dominated, all too predictably, by our plans to raise National Insurance – the so-called 'tax on jobs'. Day after day, the Tories plugged the story, with a succession of business people coming out to support them. I remember being asked by a naive soul at party headquarters to get some business support for the National Insurance rise. Maybe they are still looking.

Of course, I defended our position, and made the point in an interview with George Osborne that if he wasn't going to put up National Insurance he would have to put up VAT. He said he didn't have to. Yet I know that that is precisely what they always planned to do. This focus on National Insurance was bad for us. First, it reminded the voters that they would be paying more; secondly, for the first time in years, we had lost the support of the business constituency; and thirdly, there was no appetite on the part of commentators to ask the Tories how they were going to find the money they would lose by cancelling the increase. It was obvious to me, and I said so, that they would have to put up VAT; but they got away with it. Although I attended many strategy meetings, somehow we just had no clear sense of momentum. I was happy, then, to spend an increasing amount of time on the road. There was one final spat before I set off. Ed Balls and Gordon wanted to make a virtue of us not increasing VAT by ruling it out for the whole of the next parliament. They then wanted to challenge the Tories to do the same. Nice electoral politics, but economic madness, was my view. No Chancellor can tie his hands on tax.

Leaving special advisers Sam White and Torsten Henricson-Bell to look after my interests at party headquarters, Catherine MacLeod and I set out on the road or, more precisely, on a train. We visited every part of the country during the campaign. We even managed to get the last flight to Plymouth before most of Europe's air transport was grounded by the cloud of volcanic ash blowing in from Iceland. To get to my next stop, Edinburgh, I had a ten-hour rail journey through England's highways and byways. Iceland finally got its revenge on me.

We visited marginal seats in the south-east, where the reports were not good; in South Wales, where the picture was worryingly mixed; and in the north-west, where it was bad. Only in London and in Scotland were things better than expected. In Hammersmith, in west London, a real bellwether seat which the Tories had to win to get a majority, I was pleasantly surprised at the warm reception we received on a walkabout in the high street. In my own constituency, I thought my majority would be down but I was fairly sure we would hold on.

I did not see much of Gordon during the campaign, although we did have one stage-managed joint visit to the East Midlands and Yorkshire. I was told that Gordon wanted to discuss things with me and for us to be seen together. The discussion on the train journey north turned out to be a list of instructions, but the visits were illuminating. These were precisely the areas in Derby and south Nottinghamshire where we should have been able to capitalize on what we had done, but time and again I met people who felt that, while others had done all right, they hadn't. It was the same story everywhere. People had worked hard, struggled at times to bring up their families, their sons and daughters had been the first generation to go to university, and yet they felt badly done by.

In the middle of this visit, Gordon and I attended a coffee morning with our candidate. This format is imported from the US – where else? – and is meant to show politicians listening to the people. The people, as far as I could see, were either related to, or friends of, our candidate. Not surprisingly, they were all enthusiastic – as the media invited to view the spectacle soon clocked. I escaped early. I was to talk to the press entourage, who were being taken by coach to the next stop. As I left the scene of the coffee morning, in a cul-de-sac with well-tended gardens, I passed a crowd of weary hacks waiting for Gordon to come out of the house. Up and down the street were many people who had come to their gates to see what was going on. Halfway along, I saw a lady emerge from her house with an all-too-purposeful stride.

The lady accosted me and demanded to know what Labour had ever done for people like her. She was angry and felt let down. Behind her were three teenage children, crimson-faced, staring at the ground with oh-no-mum expressions on their faces. Seasoned campaigners know that you have to decide early on in an encounter like this whether or not you will make any headway by having a discussion, or whether the whole thing will escalate out of control. If that is to happen, it's better to break it off. A row in public can be very damaging; but appearing to run away can look worse. As these thoughts crossed my mind, Catherine drew my attention to the hacks, who had sprung to life and, sensing prey, were running up the street, cameras and microphones at the ready.

So I decided to stay, and said to her, 'You must have lived around here when this area was devastated after the miners' strike in the 1980s.' She agreed that those had been tough times for her generation. I asked what she hoped for for her children. She was hugely ambitious for them, as you would expect. By the time the press corps had caught up with us we were chatting away amiably, and the journalists trudged away in search of better quarry. I knew, though, when I parted company with the lady, from the expressions on the faces and the brief conversations I had had on the way up the street, that we would lose this marginal seat – and, as it turned out, seats like that, right across areas of England that should have provided our bedrock support. We had failed the 'Tesco test'.

A reception in Sheffield, on the other hand, was warm indeed. Parting company with Gordon, we headed off to visit one of the many Morrison's supermarkets I was to visit in every corner of the land. They were most accommodating, I think, to all parties. I can tell you where exactly to find the fish, how the meat is displayed and the bread cooked, in any branch of the chain. It was the same in every store we visited. This one, just outside Leeds, again confirmed my fears: this was a marginal seat and we were not going to win it.

There was one vignette which, although comical, illustrates the problems we had. I think it was next to the bread and cake aisle that a lady came up to me with the familiar I'm-never-going-to-vote-Labour-again look. She said, 'You have let all these foreigners take over our country. You should keep them out.' There was no point in an argument amidst the biscuits at a busy teatime. Seeking to terminate the discussion, I asked her if she lived locally. 'Oh no, I'm just visiting my mum. I live in France,' she said. She saw no irony. But what she said illustrated another weakness for us: immigration is an issue, and for too long we refused to talk about it.

I did make one speech on the economy, which was a repeat of the themes I had covered in the Budget, as well as an attack on the Tories. It was fairly strong, I thought, delivered on the top floor of an Edinburgh hotel, with splendid views across the city's dramatic skyline to the River Forth. Just as I began to take questions, disaster struck. Catherine took me aside to tell me that she had only the sketchiest of details, but that something had gone very wrong on a walkabout in Rochdale on which Gordon had apparently fallen out with a voter, Gillian Duffy. Happily, the press contingent 300 miles further north hadn't heard this yet. We got good television coverage, for about twenty-five minutes. From then on it was clear that my message on the economy was sunk.

We stood grouped around the television. It was as bad as it could be. I could see exactly what had happened, having been in similar situations myself. Someone will come up to you, mount a robust attack, then it becomes apparent that they are actually on your side and feel entitled to have their say. Gordon dealt with the confrontation itself quite well. The damage was done by the failure to remove his lapel microphone when he got back into his car. The effect of his comments about Mrs Duffy, his blaming of his closest aides, and above all his evident discomfiture on television in the aftermath, was devastating. Amazingly, we held the seat.

Throughout the campaign I managed to get back to Edinburgh more than I had expected. The reception was polite, even warm. One thing was clear: even in this traditionally conservative city, they did not want the Tories. Many former Labour voters who had voted Liberal Democrat in protest at the Iraq war came back to us. I thought we would hold the seat, although with a reduced majority. I met up with Gordon in the last few days of the campaign, when the Cabinet assembled for an eve-of-poll photo-call in Birmingham. It became, literally, a car crash. We were arranged in a semicircle, where Gordon, Harriet and myself were to say a few well-chosen words before dispersing to different parts of the country. Facing us was a bank of journalists and party workers. As Gordon was saying his piece, I caught sight of a council refuse lorry driving past with its crew leaning out of the windows, shouting at us.

'That lorry's going to crash,' I thought, with a sinking feeling. Sure enough, it did. It appeared to hit a passing car with an almighty crash. Naturally, many of the party workers, with photographers close behind, ran off to see if anyone had been hurt. Our photo-call continued.

A few minutes later, I'd said my piece and Gordon whispered out of the side of his mouth, 'Is it bad? Do you think we should stop?'

'No, if we stop now you'll give them the headlines they want,' I muttered.

We stood where we were for the remaining few minutes of the photo-call before we were told that the driver of the car was badly shaken, but unhurt. Needless to say, our juxtaposition with a car crash was just what the media wanted before polling day. I returned to London, to what I thought would be my last day in No. 11.

I then set off on a tour of marginal seats in the north-west of England, including a visit to Burnley, a seat we were to lose for the first time in eighty years. These were traditional Labour voters who had become completely disengaged from us. Nevertheless, having travelled the length and breadth of the country, on the eve of election day I sensed that we would lose but that it was not going to be anything like as bad as we had feared a year earlier, when the polls were predicting a Tory majority of perhaps a hundred.

I spent polling day, as candidates do, going round the many polling stations in the constituency. I have an excellent constituency team, run by Andrew Burns, my agent. They make few demands of me and turn out to work in droves. The enthusiasm to help was moving: this year we ran out of leaflets to distribute the weekend before polling day. As usual, I asked Andrew to phone me from the count once it was clear what my result would be, so that I could enter the hall wearing a suitable expression. Knowing that the Edinburgh count always takes longer than most to declare, for some inexplicable reason, the family settled down to watch the results on television. It was clear it would be a bad night for us. Our majorities were down and seats lost in our heartland areas of the north-east of England and South Yorkshire. The results in the south of England outside London were terrible. Yet, overall, the picture was mixed.

The Tories were not winning where they should be. The Liberal Democrats, despite Nick Clegg's ephemeral success in the television debates, were starting to lose seats. By 2 o'clock in the morning I was concerned that Andrew hadn't phoned. I was determined not to ring and sound worried. Both of us expected the majority to be down, but surely I couldn't have lost the seat or be facing a recount? Eventually I could bear it no longer. It turned out the results in Edinburgh were very good for us. 'You've increased your majority. There's no problem,' Andrew told me.

On entering the city's Meadowbank Stadium, where the election count takes place, I bumped into Ian Murray, who was standing in the now highly marginal next-door seat of Edinburgh South. He looked stunned. He had been selected as the candidate only a few weeks earlier and was defending a majority of just over four hundred. His two rivals, the Tories and Liberals, had spent three years and a small fortune between them trying to win back the seat. Ian told me there was a recount and I immediately commiserated, saying, 'Never mind, you did your best.'

'No,' he said. 'We're in front.' So it proved.

I took Calum and Anna to the count for the first time. They had been too young in previous elections. I wanted them to feel the atmosphere, which is always exciting, even if you know the result (as candidates usually do, some hours before the returning officer announces it). I spent an hour and a half after my declaration doing a full media round. As Catherine said, if we were going, we were going with our heads held high.

Back home a few hours later, on the Friday morning, it was clear that we had lost. But it was equally clear that the Tories had not won. They were some way short of a majority. After a couple of hours' sleep, I spoke to my own campaign team and to some of my colleagues. I was exhausted. Once defeat was confirmed, the nervous tension that had kept me going through the campaign drained away. After three years in one of the most difficult jobs I've ever done, I wanted a rest.

In Britain, in most elections, the result is clear by breakfast time. The Prime Minister takes his leave of the Queen by lunchtime. The new Prime Minister is in Downing Street by teatime. All very brutal, but efficient. The Queen's government goes on. Not this time, though. It was obvious that if the Tories were not to form a minority government, they would have to do a deal with the Liberals. The awkwardness for us was that the constitution dictated that we remain in office until such time as a new government was formed.

So, sitting in my garden on a sunny evening, glass of wine in hand, far from the burdens of office being lifted, I was still Chancellor of the Exchequer. As the Tories were the largest party, they had first option of putting together a deal with the Liberal Democrats. We had to some extent to sit on the sidelines, although on that Friday morning I think Gordon wanted to talk to the Liberals and see if we could put together some sort of deal.

For my part, I did not see how we could. On any view, we had lost the election. We did not have the moral right or the high ground needed to form a government and then embark on highly contentious and deeply unpopular measures as we set about cutting borrowing. But that, if you like, was the principled objection. The practical one was that the numbers did not add up. Even adding the Liberals to the Labour MPs, we would still be short of a majority in the House of Commons. We would be at the mercy of the minority parties from Northern Ireland and the Scottish and Welsh Nationalists, who would be able to extract what they wanted on a daily basis.

It is possibly because of my doubts that Gordon left me off the negotiating team he put in place that day. Far from being offended, I was relieved. He told me that Vince Cable was not on the Liberal team and he wanted me to speak to him when the time was right. Everything I saw on the news pointed to a deal being done between the Tories and the Liberals. There seemed to be a real chemistry there. I began to suspect that the alchemy had started at some level before the election result was known. That belief was to become much firmer in my mind the following week when I eventually sat down with Vince Cable for what was to prove a very short meeting.

In the meantime, any thought of a restful weekend at home was shattered when the crisis that was inevitably going to hit Greece came to a head. One of the most astute decisions we ever took was to stay out of the euro. I am not against it in principle. It is possible that conditions will one day exist in which membership will be desirable. But the fact that we had our own currency, which could depreciate at a time of stress like this, was very helpful. It has always seemed to me that if you have a single currency, you need a single economic policy – which basically ties you into a political union, one way or another. That's what happens in the US. It may comprise a strong federation of states, but it is just that: the United States of America, with a single currency and a single fiscal policy.

Trying to maintain a single interest rate for seventeen very different countries is also difficult. The seeds of destruction in Ireland were sown by the very low interest rates maintained by the ECB in the early years of the last decade. That was precisely the time when higher interest rates in Ireland might have choked off the property boom which ultimately killed off first their banks and then their government. Similarly in Spain, although not affected in the same way, low interest rates fuelled an extraordinary boom in property development. Add to that the problems of a strongly growing German economy alongside weaker smaller countries like Greece and Portugal. How do you pitch the interest rate to suit everyone?

Greece had a particular set of problems. It had joined the euro for political rather than economic reasons when it was far from ready to do so. It should never be forgotten that the euro is the culmination of five decades of political commitment towards not only economic union but an ever-closer political relationship between member states. Despite that, there is a reluctance amongst some eurozone members to accept that, just as in unitary states, the richer parts need to help the poorer parts. In a single currency area like the eurozone, countries need to help each other. Greece needed to make some big changes to its economy. Its ability to collect taxes was severely impaired, and the statistics it produced and on which assessments of its economic health were made were of a highly dubious nature.

One of the measures by which the economic health of a country can be gauged is how easy it finds raising money in the markets and how much it has to pay to do this. All governments raise money from time to time, usually in tranches, sometimes over a short number of years, sometimes over longer periods of twenty-five or thirty years. The average duration of these loans in Europe is currently around seven years. In Britain it is thirteen years. That is why we don't have to raise quite so much on a regular basis. Countries in difficulties will typically end up paying a high rate of interest and will be able to raise money only for a very short time, perhaps just a year. That is what happened to Portugal just before it had to go to the European Commission to ask for help in the spring of 2011.

It was evident at the beginning of 2010 that Greece would struggle to get through the year without international help. Tim Geithner had telephoned me in March, such was his concern that Europe wasn't focusing on the growing Greek crisis. He rightly saw it as a problem not just for Europe but for the US too. The last thing the US wanted was a loss of confidence in one of the world's major currencies, which is what a Greek collapse could precipitate. There was a reluctance, though, particularly on the part of Germany and France, to call in the IMF. Their objections were largely political. It was almost as if to call in the IMF to a eurozone member would be to admit that the euro project itself was in doubt. The Greek finance minister told me after one Ecofin meeting in February that if Europe did not help soon, he would go direct to the IMF himself.

In the middle of the general election campaign, I had to attend what was to be my last meeting of the G7 finance ministers, and an annual IMF meeting, in Washington. The G7 ministers met for dinner on the Friday night under the chairmanship of Jim Flaherty, the Canadian finance minister, at the Canadian embassy in Washington. The purpose of the meeting was to try and persuade the eurozone members present to get on with it and put in place a rescue package for Greece. It was like wading through treacle. Everyone was agreed that something had to be done. But there was no agreement as to what. Christine Lagarde was especially insistent that the Germans had to act. Unfortunately,

Wolfgang Schäuble, the German finance minister, could not be there for health reasons. His top civil servant was, but he could not agree to anything in the absence of his minister.

The Greek problem rumbled on. It became acute at the end of what was, for us, election week. That Friday evening, when I was at home absorbing the results, I was rudely reminded that I was still in office. An emergency meeting of European finance ministers had been fixed for Sunday morning in Brussels, and I had to go. I was in a difficult position. We were still in government, but we had lost the election and it was more than likely there would be a new government. However, this was an occasion when we could not possibly leave an empty chair at the table. We had to be there, not just because it will always be in Britain's interest that there is a stable euro, but because the Commission was mounting a major effort to involve us in underwriting the euro. That we could not do. Gordon and I were in agreement on that.

Although British banks do not have so much direct exposure to Greek banks or to Greece more generally, many continental banks, German and French included, were exposed. Were they to be affected, that in turn would feed back into our banking system. Gordon and I were agreed that the IMF should be involved as a matter of principle. While I could see why President Sarkozy would not want his old rival, Dominique Strauss-Kahn, portrayed as the saviour of Europe, there was a principle at stake here. The IMF was designed precisely to deal with this sort of problem. What would be the point in replicating it with another, European mechanism, which would have no experience of dealing with a country in such dire straits?

The following day, Saturday, I spoke by phone to Olli Rehn, the new European commissioner responsible for finance. He pressed me on making a contribution to the new eurozone support fund. He appeared to be taken aback when I said that there was no way that Britain could possibly underwrite the euro through the fund he was proposing to set up. I said that even if I thought it was a good idea, which I didn't, I could not agree to such a major and controversial step when it was likely that there would be a new government in power next week. I warned him that if this was what he had in mind, we would remain implacably opposed. He agreed to reflect on it.

I couldn't get to Brussels in time for the Sunday morning meeting if I flew from Edinburgh. There was no alternative but to fly to London and spend the night in Downing Street. As I sat in the lounge at Edinburgh airport, my police protection team told me that Gordon was about to fly into the city for the weekend. I had thought he was in Downing Street, conducting negotiations with the Liberal Democrats. I later learned that he had wanted a break and had decided to come home, even it was only for one night. Because of flight times we couldn't meet, and I flew back to London.

It was disappointing: a day of recuperation in the early summer sunshine seemed infinitely preferable to going to London. Also, I hadn't counted on going back to Downing Street. I had physically and mentally left it on the Wednesday morning before the election. Margaret and I didn't think we would be coming back, whatever the outcome of the election. We had largely decamped from the flat. I really didn't want to return, but I had to, arriving at the Treasury late on the Saturday evening to be fully briefed for the next day's meeting.

I knew that I needed to talk to both George Osborne and Vince Cable. There was no constitutional obligation, but it seemed a matter of courtesy and common sense. I thought there was every chance they would be in government the following week. I didn't want to get myself into a position where I had imposed an obligation on them. The trouble was that, for as long as I was Chancellor, only I could take decisions on behalf of the UK – something both of them, fortunately, recognized.

Arriving at our embassy in Brussels on Sunday morning, I spoke by telephone to both men. I explained that there was every reason to believe that the markets would be in turmoil on Monday morning if we didn't sort this out. In separate conversations with each of them, I told them there was real concern that without action over the weekend the markets would also have a real go at Portugal and Spain.

I explained that the previous night there had been a call between the G7 finance ministers in which I had participated and that there was international concern, particularly from the US. The fact that there was no consensus on what to do, or clarity on the part of the eurozone members, was making the problem worse.

The European Central Bank was also meeting. It needed to provide money and support but wouldn't do so unless the European member states put together a rescue plan. There were two proposals. The first involved a European stabilization fund amounting to about 400 billion euros, designed to stabilize the euro. In my view, that funding would have to come from eurozone members only. I made it clear to both George Osborne and Vince Cable that there was no way we could be part of this. The second proposal involved converting an existing fund, amounting to about 60 billion euros, which was available to non-euro area members to help with any balance of payment problems they might encounter on entering the European Union.

The idea was to combine these two funds, mainly in order to bring the total level of support up to over 500 billion euros. The UK had been a guarantor of the smaller fund since its inception some years earlier. When I spoke to Vince Cable, he agreed with the position that I took and offered no objection. George Osborne, though, was understandably nervous about any new obligation – as, indeed, was I. He said there could only be one Chancellor and I had to do what I thought was right. But while he agreed with me on refusing to support the stabilization fund, he wondered whether we couldn't abstain on committing to this second fund. Both of us recognized that, as the vote depended on a majority, we could not block it. We were in a minority of one and there was no veto. But in my view, an abstention would not stop the proposal going through, and we would lose bargaining power over the need to get the IMF involved in an intervention.

Our conversation was amicable and workmanlike. I had no wish to cause the incoming government problems. I did, however, want to get a deal that was in Britain's best overall interest. Subsequently, both David

Cameron and George Osborne sought to give the impression that I had done something against their wishes. That is not true. That's why I've set out our conversations more fully here than I would otherwise have done. Neither George Osborne nor I wanted to be in this position, but there was no way out of it.

There are two additional points to make. The first is that when it came to the Irish bail-out at the end of 2010, George Osborne rightly agreed not just to a bilateral loan to Ireland but also to the second European fund making a contribution. He did so because if he had abstained or even voted against it, he would have been outvoted – much the same as in May 2010. The second point, which the Eurosceptic wing of the Tory party finds difficult to accept, is that it is in Britain's interest to have a stable euro, and to ensure the stability of our trading partners in Europe.

There is something frustrating about meetings of ministers in Europe. In thirteen years I don't think I ever attended one that started on time. This one certainly didn't. On top of that, there is a very different tradition of governance in European Union affairs. In this country, ministers decide and the civil service implements the policy. In the European Union, it's the Commission that comes up with proposals, to which ministers then have to react. This has always seemed to me to be the wrong way round, but it reflects the culture of some of the continental European countries. We had to engage in a battle with the Commission that was to last several hours: a prompt start would have helped.

The Commission's opening pitch showed that they were determined to dragoon the UK into supporting the euro. Time after time, over the course of several hours, I said that we were wasting time even discussing it when it was simply not possible for us. It wasn't until nearly 8 o'clock that evening that eventually they agreed that the UK would not be part of the first European stabilization fund. Even at the last minute, they tried another draft which was so opaque that it could easily have been taken as having us in the fund.

Getting IMF involvement was easier, but still difficult. Then a new set of problems arose, this time involving not us but Germany. It appeared late in the evening that the German constitutional court might be able to strike down the deal. Just why this constitutional problem had arisen at this late stage was not clear. There was a real problem now. The Asian markets were about to open. We hadn't got an agreement, and the ECB wouldn't agree to their part of the bargain, which was vital, until the ministers had reached accord.

The tension was mounting. The G7 finance ministers and central bank governors were on a conference call and were kept on hold for nearly two hours while the wrangling went on. Elena Salgado, the Spanish finance minister, was chairing the meeting, as Spain held the European Union presidency at this time. She was in the invidious position of trying to chair a meeting at the same time as trying to negotiate the text of the final statement on behalf of Spain. Spain and Portugal were also now very much in the financial firing line. The markets were worried about their comparatively high levels of borrowing. The only way we would get an agreement was for Germany to remove its objection to the deal. The German finance minister, who was still unwell, was not there. It took a telephone call to Chancellor Merkel in Berlin to unblock the deal. The day was saved.

The European stabilization fund remained virtual, in that it had still not been agreed where the funding would come from, even among the eurozone members. But the announcement did what was needed and the Greek crisis was averted, for the time being. The medicine they had to swallow was very tough indeed, although by the time the deal was finally agreed I had left office.

I gave my last interview on the BBC *Today* programme as Chancellor from the studio in Brussels and returned to London on the Monday morning. Another day and night in Downing Street beckoned. In my absence, negotiations between the Conservatives and Liberal Democrats were taking far longer than expected. The Lib Dems were speaking to us, I always suspected, as a bargaining tool with the Tories. Gordon had called a Cabinet meeting to endorse the principle of talking with the Liberals. It was always possible, I suppose, that their deal with the Tories would unravel, and for that reason I saw no harm in us talking. I am not against coalitions in principle, although in practice one involving the Labour Party was dead in the water. There were other sceptics too: David Miliband didn't think we had the moral authority to stay in government; and Jack Straw was against it for much the same reasons as I was.

There was still some rancour in Cabinet. Bob Ainsworth, with whom I've been friends for many years, said it was disgraceful that I wasn't on the negotiating team, and got very angry. He had fallen out badly with Gordon over the last few months. Bob was so vehement in his attack that Gordon later phoned to say that I shouldn't take my exclusion from the negotiating team personally. I didn't.

After the Cabinet meeting, I agreed to go out and put our case, doing a series of interviews on the green opposite the Houses of Parliament. I met both John Reid and David Blunkett forcibly denouncing any move to form a coalition between ourselves and the Liberal Democrats. It was evident that the party was deeply split on the issue. If I had thought there was any real chance of a deal between us, of course I would have demanded to be involved, not least because the Liberal Democrats at that time were congenital spenders. I am sure my presence would have been seen as a spoiler for the negotiations.

I still had not met Vince Cable for talks, but agreed with Gordon that I would try to do so next morning, Tuesday. I telephoned him and suggested we meet in my office at the Treasury. As a measure of goodwill, I arranged for my ministerial car to collect him from his home in south-west London. An hour later Karl Burke, my driver, telephoned the office and asked to be put through to me. This was unusual. He said, 'I'm at his house but he won't come out.' I had a vision of someone refusing to leave home for fear of what might await him. Eventually I spoke to Vince and he told me that Nick Clegg had made it clear he was not to meet with me now. We did eventually meet later in the day, although Vince had to make his own way to my office. I wasn't prepared to leave the ministerial car parked in Twickenham all day.

As we sat down, Vince said that there really wasn't much point in discussing anything. The deal was done with the Tories. This was no surprise to me, but I asked him how on earth he could agree with the Tory policy on cutting the deficit when he had been so outspoken in his opposition to it? He said that they had been heavily influenced by what the Governor of the Bank of England had been saying, which had put the frighteners on them. They had been led to believe that the situation was far worse than they had thought. I told him this was not true. He also said that there wasn't much between them and the Tories this financial year. That was true. The reduction in public spending they proposed was about £6 billion. Thereafter, though, the Tories were committed to going further and faster than anything the Liberal Democrats had ever contemplated. It was the years that would follow in which there would be a massive divergence between what was then Liberal policy and the Tory policy.

There was no point in pursuing the matter, though. The deal was done and, indeed, was probably hatched before the election, at least on an informal level. As far as I can see, the Liberal Democrats had junked everything they believed in on the back of being told that the Greek crisis had changed everything. It had not. Our position remained the same. The markets were not after us in the same way. The Liberals had certainly been panicked, but they were willing to be panicked because they wanted to be part of a coalition government. They could see the chance of power for the first time in nearly a century. The Tories, moreover, rightly recognized that the public remained suspicious of them. The only way they would ever get to prove themselves would be in office. They needed each other for different reasons.

It was time for us to go. Vince Cable and I decided to make small talk for a while so that no one could say the meeting had been too short. We discussed his book and he asked me whether I would write mine. As soon as he left, I telephoned Gordon and told him what had happened.

He was understandably furious. Nick Clegg was still telling him that a deal with us was possible. Indeed, Gordon was now being put in the impossible situation of having to remain as Prime Minister until Nick Clegg and David Cameron signed off their deal.

These unexpected events, first in Europe and then at home, meant that I was back in London longer than I had anticipated. Margaret caught the train down to be with me. When she rang from King's Cross, I said she might as well use the return ticket. She came to Downing Street, through the front door, and joined me in the flat. Catherine MacLeod, Sam White, Torsten Henricson-Bell and Geoffrey Spence were there too. Connie had cleaned the flat to within an inch of its life, ready for the new tenants. I had left the Treasury shortly before. I didn't want any fuss, so I gathered my private office around me and said to them: 'That's it. We're off. The new people will be here in a few hours. Let's arrange a proper farewell in happier times.' Which we did.

We stayed upstairs in the flat while downstairs Gordon was desperately trying to get to a position where he could go to the Palace and resign. Sitting in the flat was an odd sensation. We didn't belong here any more. We were very glad to have the team there with us. We looked down on Horse Guards Parade, where we had watched the changing of the guard so many times that Margaret was sure she could spot the new recruits. We looked to see whether the kestrel that nested on top of a drainpipe opposite the window was still feeding this year's fledglings. Tradition demanded that I left a bottle of wine for my successor, which I did, with a note wishing him the best of luck. I have to report that it was a good bottle of wine – modestly priced, in keeping with the times we lived in.

Happily, Dan Rosenfield arrived carrying another bottle. We raised a glass to each other, waiting in the sitting room, with the television switched on, bizarrely looking at the house in which we were sitting through the lenses of cameras mounted in helicopters whirring overhead. We couldn't go before Gordon and Sarah left; nor could we find out when they were going. It turned out that Nick Clegg was still trying to string us along to get a better deal with the Tories. Gordon quite rightly told him that he was not prepared to hang on any longer. In the early evening we watched on television as Gordon and Sarah and their boys made a dignified exit, walking up the street together. It was time for us to go too.

I wanted to leave as quickly as possible, and certainly before the new government arrived. I thought we should leave by the back door to avoid any fuss. Margaret and Catherine thought we should go out the front. We went downstairs to say our goodbyes to the Downing Street staff, the custodians and the front of house team, all of whom had been so kind and offered whatever help we needed, and to the civil servants who now were preparing for the arrival of the new government. We stood behind the No. 11 door one last time, waiting to leave. Staff from both Nos. 10 and 11 cheered us out. It was very touching.

Outside were the banks of photographers awaiting the new Prime Minister. We gave them a final wave and drove out of Downing Street. It was the end of nearly a thousand days in office.

Epilogue

Despite the protracted handover of power, the return to opposition was abrupt. It was hardly unexpected, though, and, whatever happened, I knew I would not be returning to No. 11. I was still an MP and I had to act as Shadow Chancellor for far longer than I had hoped. Gordon resigned as leader on the day he left Downing Street. He told me he intended to do so and I agreed it was for the best. Harriet Harman did a sterling job holding the fort until Ed Miliband was elected leader at the party conference in September.

I had to shadow the new Chancellor, George Osborne, for nearly five months. I had no great appetite for it, but Jack Straw and I were both clear, even though we were ready to return to the back-benches, that we had a duty to help keep the show on the road. The Labour Party, far from allowing its head to bow or its members turn against one another, as it had done thirty years earlier, was resolute. There was absolute determination that, no matter how bad the defeat, we would pick ourselves up and carry on. We may have lost nearly ninety seats, but there was a very good intake of new MPs ready to take up the fight. I had been in Parliament for ten years before we got into government. I know what opposition is like. It is a long hard slog; I badly needed a rest and a space to take stock and rebuild my political energies. I said in my first interview in opposition that I wanted to return to the back-benches as soon as a new leader was elected and a new Shadow Cabinet was in place. I wanted this to be known before the leadership election so that my decision to stand down could not appear in any way as a snub to whoever was elected.

I returned to the back-benches in September 2010 after having spent twenty-two out of my twenty-three years as an MP on the front bench. New Labour's brand may have been of its time, but I believe that its vision is as worthy today as it was in 1997. Anchored in the centre ground of British politics, it stands not just for the traditional Labour Party value of fairness, but for aspiration too. In recent times, it has become fashionable to attack the concept of a left-of-centre party governing for the entire country. But in the centre ground is where we need to be; it is where we must stay. David Miliband articulated all of this and I was disappointed and frustrated that Labour's electoral college caused him to lose so narrowly. That college needs to change and with it there needs to be an examination of our relationship with affiliated union members. However, although I supported David during the leadership election, I was ready to give my support to his brother, Ed.

The leadership election had one very serious consequence for the party. It's inevitable that when a new government is elected it enjoys a honeymoon period. It can make mistakes in the early days and it won't be held to account as strictly as it will later in its term in office. A new government can blame the outgoing government for whatever crimes or misdemeanours it chooses. And it's easier for it to do that if the former government, now in opposition, is in the middle of a leadership contest and is talking to itself. We should have concluded things by July, thereby allowing a new leader to shape our annual conference and use it as a launch pad to reinvigorate the party. Instead, the protracted campaign, which lasted until September, gave the Conservatives a major opportunity which they seized with alacrity.

The Conservatives' main priority was to cut public spending; they wanted rapid and deep cuts to eliminate the structural deficit during the course of a parliament. From the Tory viewpoint, they were landed with an unexpected political windfall, brought about by going into coalition with the Liberal Democrats. They could cut faster and harder than they would ever have dared had they secured a majority on their own. And if growth is a lot lower for longer, that will mean even deeper cuts. Faced with criticism from within, David Cameron can blame the Liberals for stopping him from serving up the red meat his party's right wing demands. After the general election, public opprobrium was largely directed against the Liberal Democrats, who were punished as political turncoats. No wonder Cameron is so attached to Nick Clegg. As things stand, the Liberals will pay a heavy price for their support for the Tories.

Reducing the deficit was a convenient excuse that provided the Conservatives with cover to make the kind of deep public spending cuts many of them were wanting to make for ideological reasons. Their message was simple: things were worse than they thought; if we didn't cut now, we'd end up like Greece; Labour was entirely to blame. They were wrong on all three counts.

When the independent Office for Budget Responsibility produced its first report in the summer of 2010, far from confirming the Tory claim that things were worse, borrowing was shown to be decreasing and growth was returning. The medicine we had administered in 2008 was working. In the face of huge scepticism, I had often said that growth would return at the end of 2009. It did. We now know that growth was higher than we thought, but any political benefit eclipsed by our refusal to accept that equally strong medicine would be needed to cut the deficit as we moved into recovery.

The Tories' claim that we were in danger of suffering the same fate as Greece did not stand up either. Greece has a tiny economy compared with that of the UK. It has endured years of economic and political turmoil. The country has many problems and being a member of the euro means that it can't allow its currency to depreciate; instead, it is tied in to the discipline of being a member of the eurozone. It is therefore in a completely different position to the UK. It is utterly mendacious to suggest otherwise. Equally, the problems experienced by other eurozone countries, such as Ireland, Portugal or even Spain, are different from those of the UK. Greece is a convenient and emotive excuse.

Their third claim, that they had no choice but to make such deep and rapid cuts, stands even less scrutiny. A growing number of commentators have become more sceptical about whether the new government can deliver on its austerity plans and, equally importantly, express concern that the cuts to public spending will prevent economic growth. Not only has the government had to downgrade its own growth forecasts, but so too have the Bank of England, the OECD and the IMF. There is no doubt, though, that Tory claims about the deficit have gained considerable traction, which Labour must confront as it develops its own critique, not just setting out where it disagrees with the new government but offering a clear and viable alternative.

The 'investment versus cuts' argument cost us dearly. It simply wasn't credible. The better argument, the one I had tried to advance and which was subsequently adopted by the Labour Party in opposition, would at least have allowed us to maintain our credibility and authority on the economy. Our policy will have to adapt to ever changing circumstances, but whatever else, it must be grounded in reality or it will have no traction with the public.

We had borrowed, of course, but the structural deficit was only 2.3 per cent of GDP in the year before the crisis. Our national debt, which was at 42.5 per cent of GDP in 1996/7, stood at 36 per cent in the year prior to the economic crisis, after a decade of Labour government. Between 1979 and 1997, the Conservative government borrowed on average 3.4 per cent of national income; between 1997 and 2007, Labour's borrowing averaged only 1.2 per cent. Historically, this is far from high. Indeed, between 1998 and 2001 we were in surplus, an almost unheard-of situation. But we mistakenly assumed that the revenue that rolled in from the financial services sector and from stamp duty would keep on coming. Our spending was based on that assumption and, when it came to an end, borrowing rose. There had been no reason to assume that revenues would fall – after all, very few foresaw the banking crisis

– but it is a timely reminder to everyone that the good times will not last forever.

When we borrowed, it was for a good reason. By 1997 it was widely acknowledged that the country's infrastructure was crumbling. There had been no serious investment in areas such as education, health or the railways for years, and the central disagreement between British political parties at the time focused not on how much more should be spent but on how much less. David Blunkett, as Labour's first Secretary of State for Education, quickly identified the need to drive up school standards, and Jack Straw and his successors at the Home Office pushed crime levels down, something that only a very few governments have successfully achieved. The NHS benefited from investment in new hospitals and state-of-the-art equipment, and patients now have greater access to better treatment. The Tories decried the drive to cut waiting times through the imposition of targets for treatment. But they worked. The Tories announced that they would be abandoned after the election in 2010, only to reinstate them twelve months later.

We reversed what seemed an inexorable rise in child poverty. Sure Start centres became a world-class model for providing support to young families, helping to improve children's life chances. Tax credits, the minimum wage and the New Deal, through which government reduces unemployment by training job-seekers, were all measures that implemented core Labour values. Above all, unemployment fell and the number of people in work rose; and by providing tax relief for working parents, we made inroads into tackling the poverty that had cascaded down through the generations. Ours was a reforming government and, as David Cameron acknowledged in 2010, Britain was a better place than it had been thirteen years before.

A government, though, isn't just about providing competent management, though that is essential. It has to be grounded in a core belief – in our case, in fairness and an aspiration to make things better for individuals and for the country as a whole.

There were areas where we did not get it right. Areas, too, where we got it wrong. We were not clear enough in our own minds about what needed reform and about what those reforms ought to be. We could have gone further in reforming the benefits system, particularly on disability and housing benefits. Those were put in place, with the best of intentions, often many decades ago and have not been adapted to the circumstances of today. The idea that there were people 'out there' who could work but didn't and were living off benefits instead is corrosive in Britain's politics. We made significant progress but more reforms were needed. Frankly, we did not face up to all the problems. But we did make significant changes to make work pay and to help families, particularly those with children. The setting up of the Jobcentre Plus network, with its emphasis on getting people into work, contributed to the fact that unemployment did not rise as much as might have been feared during the recession that followed the banking crisis. And we made significant inroads into reducing the rate of increase in the numbers of incapacity benefit claimants.

When I became Secretary of State for Social Security, I visited many dismal benefit offices with their thick protective glass screens and row upon row of shabby seats. This was no way to treat people, let alone encourage them into work. In the face of sometimes bitter opposition from the unions, every benefit office was transformed, the screens taken down, providing an environment where the question was no longer 'What benefit am I entitled to?' but rather 'How do I get back into work?'

In the health service, where we did a great deal to improve outcomes, there are two areas in particular that remain to be resolved. We must get control of costs in a system where there is no incentive to do so; and we must figure out how to drive up standards in a system that can never operate as a free market. In education we drove up standards and built new schools to replace crumbling Victorian buildings and classrooms thrown up in the 1950s and 1960s. University education expanded and science investment doubled. Maintaining first-class education is essential for our future.

If we are to become a more successful and prosperous country, this level of investment must be maintained, and that requires the political commitment to make the investment and, crucially, to find the means to finance it. For the first ten years of our government, the economy grew for a more sustained period than it had in two centuries. We avoided the downturns experienced in other countries, including the US and Japan, and created the conditions that made us the world's main destination for foreign investment. Business start-ups increased.

Although many people have argued that we should have spent less in the decade leading up to the crisis, very few – and virtually no one in British politics – were saying so consistently at the time. The Treasury is fiscally conservative and will always advise its ministers to rein in spending. But it is there to advise, and the Chancellor's choices and judgements will prevail. By 2007, with public expenditure having doubled, I believed it was time to cut the growing rate of spending – which is exactly what we did. To assume that revenues would continue to flow uninterrupted from the sometimes volatile financial services industry was a mistake. When the crash came, there was no margin to fall back on. Our economy has become more lopsided and that is something to which we must address – though there is no easy fix.

There is a broader point about the economy that needs consideration. The political orthodoxy, from the 1980s to the present day, has been that government's role in the economy should be limited to the macro level. From the time he became Shadow Chancellor in 1992, Gordon Brown overhauled our economic approach and as we approached the end of our time in office our view of the role of government had begun to change. Our experience during the crisis showed the difference that active government can make. We could have stood back and let the markets take their course, but that would have had disastrous consequences for the country as a whole. I do not understand how the Tories can argue that they would have let that happen. Surely it's the job of government to step in when things go wrong?

Government can't decree the extent to which our economy relies on the financial services industry as opposed to manufacturing – nor, indeed, the strength of our creative industries. But I do believe that targeted government intervention and support can make a difference. For example, research and development tax credits for the film industry were a driving force behind the renaissance of British cinema. Lower corporation tax and a better business environment are critical. The role of government is an important, defining difference between Labour and the Conservatives. The state is there to do those things that we as individuals cannot do alone, and we should not be afraid to acknowledge its role in economic development, in education or providing infrastructure, but also in other ways. Public spending is not a goal in itself. What matters is the result, what you get with your money, and how we help people to meet their aspirations and ease their concerns.

In September 2009, when preparing to deliver the James Callaghan Memorial Lecture in Cardiff, I was struck by Callaghan's remark that 'there is no better test of the character of a man than where he stands on the issues raised in the Beveridge Report'. Jim Callaghan, who served as Prime Minister between 1976 and 1979, was old enough to have seen the terrible impact of the Depression of the 1930s at first hand. The Beveridge Report, drawn up during the Second World War, set out the platform for what was to become the welfare state. Callaghan saw it as a 'test of character' whether or not the generation of politicians elected after the war could transform the lives of millions of people. Times have changed since then and the barriers to progress of 1945 have mostly been broken down. But there are new barriers and new challenges which are every bit as important. How do we sustain domestic growth and employment levels in a globalized economy? How do we tackle climate change? Here at home, how do we provide for an ageing population? *Our* test of character will be in how we respond to these questions.

In 1945 Clement Attlee's government, which created the welfare state, understood the essential role of the state in addressing the big social challenges of its day. The big social challenges we face may be different but they are just as big. So too with the economic challenges we face. The economic crisis of the past three years has undoubtedly hastened the shift of power to the east and to the south. We cannot assume that the markets alone will ensure we remain able to compete and to produce goods and services that the rest of the world wants. The 1980s saw a shift in the paradigm of what a government could do – a reaction against the state planning and controls that had so dominated political thinking since the 1940s – to one of far less government intervention. Now, it seems to me, the paradigm needs to shift once more. Governments cannot ordain the exact size and shape of the economy, but they can and must influence that size and shape, in order to ensure that we capitalize and build on our strengths and recognize that targeted intervention can make a difference. As an example, the aviation industry in this country employs more than 100,000 people. Without government support for the development of Airbus, the industry wouldn't be based in the UK. At a time when we are about to procure a new generation of nuclear power stations, how do we ensure that this research and development benefits the British economy? Germany and France, who are supposedly bound by the same EU procurement rules as ourselves, have managed to ensure that their firms benefit from contracts to provide railway rolling stock. We depend upon free and fair trade, and I remain completely opposed to protectionist measures. This doesn't mean that we can't use government to promote jobs in this country. That is why we need to continue to invest heavily in education and science and to promote invention and innovation wherever we can.

That isn't to say that only government can tackle these issues; it depends, too, on the efforts of millions of people. But the two must act in partnership, and one can't exist without the other. These are the themes that the Labour Party needs to address. Between the 'old left' and the 'old right' of British politics, there is an ever-greater political middle ground, which we have to occupy if government is to make a difference. Government action is not a denial of freedom; rather, it is a way of increasing freedom, of supporting people to achieve their aspirations in a rapidly changing world.

To me, what matters is what works, whether it be in the public or the private sector. We should never forget that government is elected by men and women to act in their interests both as individuals and as members of a wider society. James Callaghan's test is for all of us. We must constantly test the limits of what government can do best and where it should stand back so that public investment and private entrepreneurship can work in harmony. That was at the heart of New Labour, and for the party to move on and take back the country, it must be so again.

If we are to rebalance our economy, we will need to work closely with industry, not simply to provide the right environment for expansion but also to see where government can help. A good start might be to ensure that as we replace our ageing fleet of nuclear reactors there is some spin-off in terms of research and engineering coming to Britain. French and German industries have benefited from indirect government support and have reaped the dividends, particularly in Germany where the manufacturing base is the foundation of a strong economy. But it would be a mistake to attempt to achieve a better balance by shrinking our financial services industry. It employs more than a million people in the UK and makes a huge contribution to our economic output. It is crucial that government's role in regulating the markets be pitched just right.

Any event as catastrophic as the banking crisis must leave behind lessons, ways that we can prevent recurrence and improve our common future. We should remember that the banks are only one part of this industry, albeit an important one. The insurance industry, fund management, accounting and legal services all provide a critical economic mass in both London and Edinburgh. London needs to remain one of the world's major financial centres; I don't think we can afford to be ambivalent about that or to give the impression that we wouldn't mind if financial services went elsewhere. At a time when the world's economic centre of gravity is moving relentlessly east and south, we must ensure that we retain our dominance in this industry, as we failed to do with our engineering expertise.

But here is the dilemma: a bank is very different from an engineering company. If an engineering company goes bust, the effects are felt by the firm and its employees and by the town or city in which it operates. If a bank fails, the ramifications will reach much further, as we witnessed in 2007 and 2008. If a series of banks goes down, the effects can be devastating. And because so many people depend on financial institutions for their savings and borrowing, the regulatory regime is critical.

It was David Hume who dismissed the idea that it is only reason that governs human behaviour, and it would be hard to find a sequence of events that better demonstrates Hume's view than the illogical behaviour that drove bankers to cause the financial crisis. They didn't understand what they were doing, the risks they were taking on, or, often, the products they were selling. At the height of the crisis, one leading banker told me with pride that his bank had just decided they would no longer take on any risk they didn't understand. I think that was supposed to reassure me. It didn't; it horrified me. The top management in banks both here and in the US failed to understand – or even to ask – what was apparently making them so much profit and what were the risks. Added to which, there was very little challenge from the regulators who were supposed to be supervising them. Sir Fred Goodwin told me, when he came to my home just before Christmas 2007, that he didn't think the FSA understood his bank. I don't think they were the only ones.

We must also ask why increasingly reckless lending was not checked by the boards of the banks. It can be very difficult to challenge the behaviour of someone you know and like, particularly when times are good and profits are soaring. But that is what boards are there to do. They failed miserably, not just in the case of RBS and HBOS but in banks across the world. I have always thought that while it's understandable to ask searching questions when you are losing money, it is of equal importance to do so when you appear to be making a lot of money.

Regulatory bodies can't stand in the shoes of directors. But they must ensure that the potential vulnerabilities of an institution are understood, and must act as the voice of reason in the face of the exuberance of directors chasing bigger profits. It is sometimes felt that regulators can never know enough about an individual bank, and that it would be better simply to require banks to hold higher capital reserves as a buffer against failure. However, I don't think that is enough. What is needed is a combination of more capital and tougher regulation. Regulators need to make sure that bank boards are competent, that there are processes in place to manage risk, and that they are being followed.

I have never used the term 'light-touch regulation' because it seems to me to send the wrong signal. Regulation should be focused on where risks lie, but a 'light touch' implies precious little supervision and a lack of searching questions. That culture of sometimes lackadaisical supervision allowed a climate to development where too often regulators and boardrooms alike were happy to look away. If the music was playing, they were happy to keep on dancing. It was no different in any other country. What is essential now is to ensure that there is thorough questioning where it's needed, and critically, international cooperation among regulators.

The regulatory system needs to be more intrusive and to focus on the key questions: what happens if a critical part of the system should fail; and if it does fail, how is that failure to be managed? In 2011, the coalition government is legislating to put in place a new structure, which will not come into force until 2013. Arrangements within the Bank are far from straightforward. In particular, it is necessary to decide who calls the shots in a crisis. That should be decided now. Even if the two principals charged with making the ultimate decisions were the Governor and the Chancellor, what happens if they disagree, as was the case in 2007, over whether to inject liquidity into the economy? The Chancellor might decide, as I did, that that is what the system needs; while the Governor might reach the conclusion that the matter is one of solvency and that more capital is required. The only way in which liquidity can be provided is through the Bank. But with recapitalization, only the Chancellor can give the go-ahead because the Bank does not have the resources to do it. The only way to ensure that a crisis can be adequately dealt with is to make explicit that the ultimate decision-making authority lies with the Chancellor.

If responsibility for supervision of the financial system, as well as responsibility for monetary policy, and for smoothing the economic cycle, lies with the Bank of England, then the governance of the Bank must change. The Bank is an autocratic institution, run by its Governor. It always has been. To invest so much power in one man or woman runs counter to any modern idea of corporate governance. The court of the Bank of England, to whom the Governor is in theory answerable, is an anachronism. I tried to reform it, but I now believe that what is needed is a proper board of directors, both executive and non-executive, who will help the Governor form his or her view. He or she should be like the Prime Minister, first amongst equals. That is the only way to broaden the Bank's decision-making base and is in keeping with modern corporate governance. All this must be put in place before the new Governor is appointed in 2013.

The risk is that the present and successive governments will lapse back into a false sense of security, believing that the mistakes of the past can never be repeated. The report of the government's Banking Commission calls for more capital and for firewalls between various bank activities. That is all very sensible, but I don't believe it will stop another crisis. We have to face up to the fact that the banking system – and here we should include insurers and other institutions – is now so interlinked that regulators cannot discharge their duties as if each institution were free-standing and self-sufficient. This was brought home to me after a cursory examination of what was happening at

Northern Rock in 2007. It is vital that we get this right. Our economy needs the industry, but we need to know at all times what the consequences might be should something go drastically wrong. Risk needs to be better managed at all levels, and regulators worldwide must work more closely together.

It is inevitable in reviewing the history of our government that the relationship between the chief architects of New Labour, Tony Blair and Gordon Brown, should be minutely examined. That is not my purpose here, but to write the history of Labour's time in office two things have to be acknowledged. We would never have won so convincingly in 1997 without their combined efforts. Tony Blair was an unusual leader of a political party. He was curiously semi-detached from the Labour Party – certainly never truly of it – and perhaps because of that he was able effectively to lead us into the centre ground and keep us there. The economic groundwork, though, the shedding of old shibboleths and dearly held prejudices, fell to Gordon Brown. He was ruthless in reshaping and rebuilding a party whose economic policy had, even in the early 1990s, been forged three decades before. He deserves immense credit for that. Unfortunately, however, and especially towards the end, their deteriorating relationship and the increasing stridency of their disagreements destabilized the government and did great harm to our reputation, which it will take some time to restore.

John Smith asked me shortly before his sudden death who I would support when he was gone. I told him I would find it hard to choose, both men had such strengths. John turned to me and said sharply: 'Well, you'll have to choose.' I did, and sadly much sooner than any of us would have wanted. I supported Tony for the leadership because it seemed to me that he was able to reach out to a generation of middle Britons with whom Labour had failed to engage for the best part of thirty years. Gordon provided an economic edge to the wider appeal; his economic thinking was the ballast.

From a ringside seat, I saw the slowly dripping poison of their relationship damage our government. I don't know the precise terms of the agreement that the two of them are supposed to have reached either in the Granita restaurant in Islington or in a friend's home. Knowing them both, I suspect that each left the table thinking that he had got what he wanted. The problem was that their respective understandings were quite different. Tony may well have indicated that he intended serving perhaps two terms, while Gordon was sure that that was an absolute commitment. What I do know is that from 2004 onwards Gordon became increasingly frustrated that Tony wouldn't step down. The tension between the two camps during the general election of 2005 was barely kept under wraps, and it exploded a year later when the Brown camp became increasingly convinced that Tony was intent on remaining in his post. By 2006, following Tony's refusal to condemn the Israeli pounding of Lebanese territory that summer, the party had lost patience with him. The insurrection by the Brownites that autumn wasn't spontaneous. It was organized and it had its desired effect. Tony stepped down in 2007. It's sad that a party that spawned two such talented individuals eventually came to be riven by their civil war.

I've never been part of either camp. Perhaps it's one of my political failings – I can see both sides of an argument. But by 2006 I didn't see how Tony Blair could stay on. His reputation had been badly damaged by Iraq and the final straw for many in the party, myself included, was his failure to call a halt to what was happening in Lebanon. I had always thought that Gordon had a plan and that he would need at least three years to see it through before the next election. The obvious time for Tony to stand down would have been in the autumn of 2006 or the spring of 2007, and though I was frustrated that he didn't want to, I understood why. He wanted to rehabilitate himself on the domestic front after Iraq.

I remember talking to Tony about Gordon during one of their more public arguments – over the euro, I think. Tony said that he wanted to discuss something with Gordon and was told the only time he could do so was at 6.30 in the morning. He told me: 'You've no idea what it's like. It's like facing the dentist's drill without an anaesthetic. He goes on and on.' I thought then that perhaps Tony was exaggerating a bit. In his memoirs Tony expresses frustration that people didn't understand what it was like working with Gordon. At one point he explains how, after much agonizing, he felt he couldn't sack his Chancellor. In my three years as Chancellor, I had many occasions on which to reflect on Tony's dilemma.

Gordon has many strengths, but he is not an easy man to work with. He doesn't always see the effect his words have on people, but, temperament aside, his strong intellectual approach would trump any countervailing empathy. He is a man capable of huge gestures of generosity, but he seemed to have no conception of the effects of his sometimes appalling behaviour on those close to him, or of the political damage his way of operating – indirectly, through a cabal – could cause.

As prime minister he seemed, often, like a man out of his time. The skills learned as a young politician, and then as a precocious actor in the Labour machine of the 1960s and 1970s, were perhaps out of date. He tried desperately to make it work; he can't be accused of not trying. But as I've said before, there is no hiding place in Downing Street. Perhaps most damaging, for Gordon in particular, but for all of us in the end, was that he surrounded himself with a cadre of people whose preoccupation was the removal of Tony Blair and the installation of Gordon Brown. They had their own reasons, some political, others personal, but blind loyalty meant that Gordon was only told that which he wanted – or could bear – to hear and that meant, ultimately, that he was ill-served. Speaking truth to power never came into it.

It would be wrong to claim that there was a plot to get rid of Tony Blair; there was no plot. A plot is secret. This was an open campaign, and as far as the Brownite cabal was concerned, you were with them or against them. It was a fairly brutal regime, and many of us fell foul of it.

After Gordon became Prime Minister, the cabal sought fresh enemies and as Chancellor I quickly found myself in the firing line. Their underhand tactics, particularly the continuous briefings and leaks to the media, were difficult to bear and were also incredibly damaging to the reputation of the party. Tony and Gordon dominated the Labour Party for more than ten years and were an overwhelming force for good, but by the end their feud allowed a cancer to grow which, I believe, contributed to our defeat in 2010. The lessons of this crisis have yet to be fully learned and the consequences of what happened are still playing out. There never was a full scale inquiry although the Treasury select committee, under the highly respected leadership of my colleague John McFall, MP, shone a light on many of the practices that led to the crash. The FSA report into the RBS debacle is yet to come. A lot of repair work is needed over the next few years if confidence is to be restored.

The three years I spent at No. 11 were an incredible experience. Within weeks of taking office, I was thrust into the limelight in a way I had never before experienced. I had to deal with a crisis the scale of which I could never have imagined. As I said at the beginning of this book, events transformed my time as Chancellor, which I suspect would have been rather briefer had the economic crisis not taken hold and had Gordon not been weakened by growing unrest within the party. Events took over, but I am proud of the extent to which my team rose to the extraordinary challenges we faced. We had to take decisions that, had they been wrong, would have had devastating consequences. I had a sense throughout of what needed to be done and I fought tooth and nail, often in the face of both overt and covert opposition from No. 10, to proceed as I saw fit.

We didn't get everything right, as I've explained in this book, but we did chart a way through. The effects could so easily have been far worse. My deepest regret is that, during the 2010 election, the government failed to capitalize on our successful handling of the financial crisis, and for that I accept my share of responsibility. We in the Labour Party had lost our collective vision and sense of purpose, and we need now to get it back again. I am never knowingly over-optimistic, but I do believe that if we can learn from what happened and be confident in ourselves and in our values, a new generation can rise to the test and the Labour Party can regroup and once again be elected to government.

Timeline

2007

27 June   Tony Blair steps down as prime minister and is replaced by Gordon Brown.

17 July   Bear Stearns announces its two troubled hedge funds are virtually worthless following bursting of the real estate bubble.

19 July   Federal Reserve chairman Ben Bernanke warns that the crisis in the US sub-prime lending market could cost up to $100 billion.

9 August   French investment bank BNP Paribas freezes three funds because of its exposure to the sub-prime mortgage market. In response to the turmoil, the European Central Bank pumps 95 billion euros into the credit markets to improve liquidity. The US Federal Reserve says it will put $12 billion of temporary reserves into the US banking system.

14 August   Financial Services Authority (FSA) discloses concerns about Northern Rock to the Treasury and Bank of England.

13 September   BBC reveals that Northern Rock has asked for, and has been granted, emergency financial support from the Bank of England in its role as lender of last resort.

14 September   Depositors queue to withdraw their savings from Northern Rock branches around the country.

17 September	Chancellor makes a statement on the situation in the financial markets and announces that the government will guarantee all existing deposits in Northern Rock.
19 September	Bank of England announces an injection of £10 billion into the money markets in an attempt to bring down three-month inter-bank interest rates.
20 September	Treasury announces extended protection for Northern Rock customers.
6 October	Gordon Brown calls off snap autumn election. Critics accuse him of 'bottling' a decision because the Conservatives are polling well.
9 October	Treasury confirms that the guarantee arrangements previously announced to protect existing depositors of Northern Rock will be extended to all new retail deposits made after 19 September.
18 October	Package containing two CDs of Child Benefit data sent from HMRC to the National Audit Office, containing details of 25 million individuals, is lost.
30 October	Merrill Lynch chief resigns after the bank unveils $7.9 billion exposure to bad debt.
4 November	Chuck Prince resigns as chief executive of Citigroup, as the bank reveals it is facing an additional $8–11 billion of losses on mortgage-related securities.
6 December	President Bush outlines plans to freeze rates on sub-prime mortgages for five years to help people hit by the US housing market crisis. Bank of England cuts interest rates by 0.25 per cent to 5.5 per cent.

2008

2 January	Price of oil hits $100 per barrel for the first time.
21 January	Global stock indexes, including the FTSE 100, record their greatest falls since 9/11 terrorist attacks.
17 February	Chancellor announces Northern Rock will be taken into a

period of temporary public ownership; in so doing, government rejects the two private sector offers.

17 February	Northern Rock is nationalized.
18 February	Northern Rock shares suspended. Banking (Special Provisions) Bill has first reading in Commons and, in a statement to the Commons, Chancellor states that 'the Government have no intention at present to use the Bill to bring any institution other than Northern Rock into temporary public ownership'.
7 March	US Federal Reserve makes $200 billion available to major banks, saying it has taken action 'to address heightened liquidity pressures'.
14 March	Bear Stearns receives emergency lending from Federal Reserve, via JPMorgan Chase.
17 March	Bear Stearns, Wall Street's fifth-largest bank, is acquired by JPMorgan Chase.
11 April	Council of Mortgage Lenders warns that mortgage funding could be cut by half in 2008.
21 April	Bank of England launches scheme allowing banks temporarily to swap high-quality mortgage-backed and other securities for UK Treasury bills under the special liquidity scheme; however, responsibility for losses on their loans would remain with the banks.
22 April	Royal Bank of Scotland announces a plan to raise money from its shareholders with a £12 billion rights issue, the biggest in UK corporate history.
8 July	British Chambers of Commerce quarterly report finds the credit crunch and rising costs have dented the most important sectors of the economy and there are serious risks of recession in the UK. FTSE 100 Index briefly dips into a 'bear market', suffering a 20 per cent fall from recent highs.
31 July	UK house prices show their biggest annual fall since the Nationwide began its housing survey in 1991, a decline of 8.1 per cent.

28 August	Nationwide reveals that UK house prices have fallen by 10.5 per cent in a year.
29 August	Chancellor warns that the economy is facing its worst crisis for sixty years in an interview with the *Guardian*, saying that the downturn will be more 'profound and long-lasting' than most had feared.
7 September	Mortgage lenders Fannie Mae (Federal National Mortgage Association) and Freddie Mac (Federal Home Loan Mortgage Corporation) are rescued by the US government in one of the largest bail-outs in US history.
10 September	Wall Street bank Lehman Brothers posts a loss of $3.9 billion for the three months to August. European Commission warns that the UK, Germany and Spain will go into recession by the end of the year.
15 September	Lehman Brothers files for Chapter 11 bankruptcy protection, becoming the first major bank to collapse since the start of the credit crisis. US bank Merrill Lynch is taken over by Bank of America for $50 billion.
17 September	Bank of England announces extension of the final date of the drawdown period for its special liquidity scheme from 21 October 2008 to 30 January 2009. Lloyds TSB agrees to buy HBOS. American International Group (AIG), one of the world's biggest insurers, saved from the brink of collapse after US Federal Reserve agrees $85 billion bail-out; the deal gives the US government a 79.9 per cent stake in the insurer.
18 September	FSA announces a ban on short-selling of financial stocks and an obligation to disclose significant 'short' positions, a move also adopted by the Irish financial regulator.
29 September	Bradford and Bingley is broken up; its retail side is taken over by Santander and the mortgage and loan books nationalized.
1 October	Bank of England begins providing covert liquidity to HBOS; this support peaks at £25.4 billion on 13 November.
7 October	Bank of England begins providing covert liquidity to Royal Bank of Scotland; this support peaks at £36.6 billion on 17 October.

13 October	Chancellor makes statement to the Commons on the recapitalization of HBOS, Lloyds TSB and RBS, with the government taking significant shareholdings in the three banks and its capital investment totalling £37 billion. Chancellor also issues a written statement on the contingencies fund and the action taken on the Icelandic banks Kaupthing and Landsbanki.
24 October	Office of National Statistics announces that UK GDP fell by 0.5 per cent in the second quarter of 2008, the first contraction since the second quarter of 1992, when the British economy was at the end of its last recession, and the biggest drop since the fourth quarter of 1990.
19 November	IMF approves a £1.4 billion loan for Iceland. British, Dutch and German governments later confirm that they will give Iceland a combined total of $6.3 billion in loans to cover the cost of compensating Icesave account holders.
14 December	Irish government announces a recapitalization programme for credit institutions in Ireland of up to 10 billion euros.
19 December	Outgoing President Bush announces $17.4 billion in short-term loans to General Motors and Chrysler, the money coming from the 'troubled asset relief programme'.
21 December	Irish government announces recapitalization investment of 2 billion euros each in Allied Irish Bank and Bank of Ireland, and 1.5 billion euros in Anglo Irish Bank.
31 December	FTSE 100 Index closes down 31.3 per cent since the beginning of the year, the biggest annual fall since the index began.

2009

15 January	Irish government nationalizes Anglo Irish Bank.
5 March	Bank of England announces that it will undertake a policy of 'quantitative easing'; the Bank will purchase £75 billion of assets using money which it will create.
9 March	FTSE 100 Index hits six-year low at 3460.
30 March	Dunfermline Building Society, which announced £26

million in losses, principally arising from its residential and commercial mortgage assets, is taken over by Nationwide building society.

2 April   Prime minister meets leaders of the world's largest economies arriving at the G20 summit in London.

4 April   Treasury select committee releases the report *The Banking Crisis: The Impact of the failure of the Icelandic Banks*.

22 April   Treasury publishes Budget 2009.

9 December   In the pre-Budget report, government announces a tax of 50 per cent will apply to discretionary bonuses above £25,000 awarded in the period from the pre-Budget report to 5 April 2010, for each individual employee.

18 December   In its six-monthly financial stability report, Bank of England reports 'The financial system has been significantly more stable over the past six months, underpinned by the authorities' sustained support for the banking system and monetary policy measures.'

2010

25 February   Royal Bank of Scotland announces a loss of £3.6 billion for 2009, but says it will pay £1.3 billion in bonuses to staff.

24 March   Chancellor sounds a note of caution in his Budget statement, saying 'There are still uncertainties. Financial markets are febrile. Oil prices have increased by over 50 per cent. Bank credit, while improved, still remains weak in many parts of the world. Confidence has not fully returned to either businesses or consumers.'

6 April   Gordon Brown calls general election for 6 May.

6 May   General election results in a hung parliament, as Labour takes 258 seats (29 per cent of the vote and a loss of 89 seats) to the Tories' 306 (36 per cent of the vote and in increase of 97 seats) and Lib Dems' 57 (23 per cent of the vote and a loss of 5 seats).

11 May   Gordon Brown resigns as Prime Minister.

Index

A Note on the Author

Alistair Darling is the Member of Parliament for Edinburgh South West. Initially appointed as Chief Secretary to the Treasury in 1997, he moved to become Secretary of State for Social Security in 1998 and then Secretary of State for Work and Pensions in 2002. He then spent four years as Secretary of State for Transport, also becoming Secretary of State for Scotland in 2003. He served as Secretary of State for Trade and Industry in 2006, before Gordon Brown promoted him to Chancellor in 2007, a post he held until the change of government in May 2010.